KT-155-401

ARCTIC OCEAN
50-51

Greenland
50-51

Alaska & Western Canada
22-23

CONTINENTAL MAP:
NORTH AMERICA
20-21

C A N A D A

Eastern Canada
24-25

Pacific
States
36-37

Central &
Mountain States
32-33

Great Lakes
30-31

Northeastern
States
26-27

UNITED STATES
OF AMERICA

Southwestern
States
34-35

Southern States
28-29

PACIFIC OCEAN
128-129

ATLANTIC
OCEAN
52- 53

Mexico
38-39

Central America &
the Caribbean
42-43

Northern
South America
44-45

CONTINENTAL MAP:
CENTRAL & SOUTH AMERICA
40-41

Brazil
46-47

CONTINENTAL MAP:
OCEANIA
130-131

New Zealand
134

Southern
South America
48-49

ANTARCTICA
50-51

THE EYEWITNESS

ATLAS
OF THE
WORLD

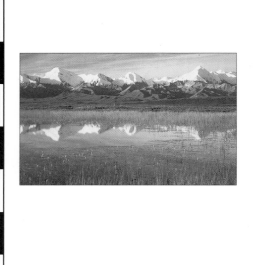  

THE EYEWITNESS
ATLAS
OF THE
WORLD

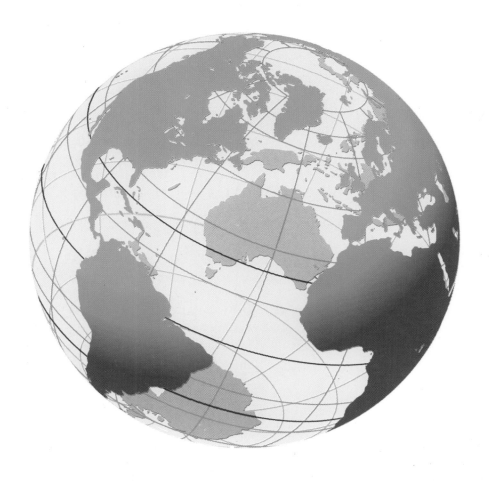

DORLING KINDERSLEY
LONDON • NEW YORK • STUTTGART • MOSCOW

CONSULTANTS

Consultant editor
Dr. David R. Green, Department of Geography, King's College

Digital mapping consultant
Professor Jan-Peter A. L. Muller, Professor of Image Understanding and Remote Sensing,
Department of Photogrammetry and Surveying, University College London

Digital base map production
Department of Photogrammetry and Surveying, University College London:
Philip Eales (Producer) • Kevin Tildsley • David Rees •
James Pearson • Peter Booth • Tim Day • Planetary Visions Ltd

Contributors
Peter Clark, Former Keeper, Royal Geographical Society, London •
Martin McCauley, Senior Lecturer in Politics,
School of Slavonic and East European Studies, University of London

Dorling Kindersley would also like to thank
Dr. Andrew Tatham, Keeper, and the Staff of the Royal Geographical Society, London,
for their help and advice in preparing this Atlas

Project art editor: Nicola Liddiard
Project editors: Elizabeth Wyse and Caroline Lucas
Project cartographer: Julia Lunn

Editorial: Jayne Parsons • Phillip Boys • Chris Whitwell • Donna Rispoli •
Margaret Hynes • Ailsa Heritage • Sue Peach • Laura Porter

Design: Lesley Betts • Rhonda Fisher • Paul Blackburn • Jay Young

Cartography: Roger Bullen • Michael Martin • James Mills-Hicks • James Anderson •
Yahya El-Droubie • Tony Chambers • Simon Lewis • Caroline Simpson

Illustrations: John Woodcock • Kathleen McDougall • Mick Gillah • David Wright

Photography: Andy Crawford • Tim Ridley • Steve Gorton

Picture research: Clive Webster • Charlotte Bush •
Sharon Southren • Frances Vargo • Caroline Brook

Editorial director: Andrew Heritage
Art director: Chez Picthall
Production: Susannah Straughan

A DORLING KINDERSLEY BOOK

First published in Great Britain in 1994
by Dorling Kindersley Limited,
9 Henrietta Street, London WC2E 8PS

Copyright © 1994 Dorling Kindersley Limited, London
Reprinted in 1994
Second Edition 1996

*All rights reserved. No part of this publication may be reproduced, stored in a retrieval system, or transmitted in any form or by any means,
electronic, mechanical, photocopying, recording or otherwise, without the prior written permission of the copyright owner.*

A CIP catalogue record for this book is available from the British Library.

ISBN 0-7513-6015-5

Reproduced by Colourscan, Singapore
Printed and bound in Milan by New Interlitho

CONTENTS

NORTH AMERICA • 20-21

CENTRAL AND SOUTH AMERICA • 40-41

EUROPE • 54-55

AFRICA • 86-87

NORTH AND WEST ASIA • 102-103

SOUTH AND EAST ASIA • 114-115

OCEANIA • 130-131

THE EARTH IN SPACE

THE EARTH IS ONE OF NINE PLANETS that orbit a large star – the Sun. Together they form the solar system. All life on Earth – plant, animal and human – depends on the Sun. Its energy warms our planet's surface, powers the wind and waves, drives the ocean currents and weather systems, and recycles water. Sunlight also gives plants the power to photo-synthesize – to make the foods and oxygen on which organisms rely. The fact that the Earth is habitable at all is due to its precise position in the solar system, its daily spin, and an annual journey round the Sun at a constant tilt. Without these, and the breathable atmosphere that cloaks and protects the Earth, it would be as barren as our near-neighbours Venus and Mars.

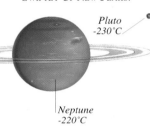

Asteroid belt

Mars 687 days

Jupiter 12 years

Uranus 84 years

Mercury 88 days

Earth 365 days (1 year)

Venus 225 days

Neptune 165 years

Saturn 29 years

Pluto 248 years

THE SOLAR SYSTEM
Although the planets move at great speeds, they do not fly off in all directions into space because the Sun's gravity holds them in place. This keeps the planets circling the Sun. A planet's "year" is the time it takes to make one complete trip round the Sun. The diagram shows the length of the planet's year in Earth-days or Earth-years.

THE SUN
The Sun is 1,392,000 km (865,000 miles) across. It has a core temperature of 14 million°C and a surface temperature of 5,500°C.

Saturn -180°C

Jupiter -150°C

Venus 465°C

Mars -23°C

Mercury Day: 430°C Night: -180°C

Earth 15°C

YOU CAN USE THIS SENTENCE TO REMEMBER THE SEQUENCE OF PLANETS: MANY VERY EAGER MOUNTAINEERS JOG SWIFTLY UP NEW PEAKS.

Pluto -230°C

Uranus -210°C

Neptune -220°C

Venus 108,200,000 km (67,200,000 miles)

Jupiter 778,330,000 km (483,000,000 miles)

Above: *The relative sizes of the Sun and planets, with their average temperature.*

Mercury 57,910,000 km (36,000,000 miles)

Earth 149,500,000 km (92,900,000 miles)

Mars 227,940,000 km (141,600,000 miles)

Saturn 1,426,980,000 km (886,700,000 miles)

Uranus 2,870,990,000 km (1,783,000,000 miles)

Neptune 4,497,070,000 km (2,800,000,000 miles)

Pluto 5,913,520,000 km (3,670,000,000 miles)

Above: The planets and their distances from the Sun.

THE LIFE ZONE: THE EARTH SEEMS TO BE THE ONLY HABITABLE PLANET IN OUR SOLAR SYSTEM. MERCURY AND VENUS, WHICH ARE CLOSER TO THE SUN, ARE HOTTER THAN AN OVEN. MARS, AND PLANETS STILL FARTHER OUT, ARE COLDER THAN A DEEP FREEZE.

Huge solar flares, up to 200,000 km (125,000 miles) long, lick out into space

THE FOUR SEASONS
The Earth always tilts in the same direction on its 950 million-km (590 million-mile) journey around the Sun. This means that each hemisphere in turn leans towards the Sun, then leans away from it. This is what causes summer and winter.

It takes 365 days 6 hours 9 minutes 9 seconds for the Earth to make one revolution around the Sun. This is the true length of an Earth "year"

MARCH 21ST (EQUINOX)
Spring in the Northern hemisphere; autumn in the Southern hemisphere. At noon, the Sun is overhead at the Equator. Everywhere on Earth has 12 hours of daylight, 12 hours of darkness.

DECEMBER 21ST (SOLSTICE)
Summer in the Southern hemisphere; winter in the Northern hemisphere. At noon, the Sun is overhead at the Tropic of Capricorn. The South Pole is in sunlight for 24 hours, and the North Pole is in darkness for 24 hours.

The Earth travels around the Sun at 107,244 km per hour (66,600 miles per hour)

To North Star

The Earth takes 23 hours 56 minutes 4 seconds to rotate once. This is the true length of an Earth "day"

Sun

JUNE 21ST (SOLSTICE)
Summer in the Northern hemisphere; winter in the Southern hemisphere. At noon, the Sun is overhead at the Tropic of Cancer. The North Pole is in sunlight for 24 hours, and the South Pole is in darkness for 24 hours.

SEPTEMBER 21ST (EQUINOX)
Autumn in the Northern hemisphere; spring in the Southern hemisphere. At noon, the Sun is overhead at the Equator. Everywhere on Earth has 12 hours of daylight, 12 hours of darkness.

South Pole

24 HOURS IN THE LIFE OF PLANET EARTH
The Earth turns a complete circle (360°) in 24 hours, or 15° in one hour. Countries on a similar line of longitude (or "meridian") usually share the same time. They set their clocks in relation to "Greenwich Mean Time" (GMT). This is the time at Greenwich (London, England), on longitude 0°. Countries east of Greenwich are ahead of GMT. Countries to the west are behind GMT.

Noon everywhere on this meridian

   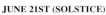

0° 15°W 30°W 45°W 60°W 75°W 90°W 105°W 120°W 135°W 150°W 165

Noon at: Greenwich / Dakar / E. Greenland / Rio de Janeiro / Caracas / New York / Mexico City / Calgary / Los Angeles / E. Alaska / Honolulu / (Pacific Ocean

Greenwich time: 1200 hrs / 1100 hrs / 1000 hrs / 0900 hrs / 0800 hrs / 0700 hrs / 0600 hrs / 0500 hrs / 0400 hrs / 0300 hrs / 0200 hrs / 0100 hrs

MOON AND EARTH

Craters made by collision with meteors

The Moon is a ball of barren rock 3,476 km (2,156 miles) across. It orbits the Earth every 27.3 days at an average distance of 384,400 km (238,700 miles). The Moon's gravity is only one-sixth that of Earth – too small to keep an atmosphere around itself, but strong enough to exert a powerful pull on the Earth. The Moon and Sun together create tides in the Earth's oceans. The period between successive high tides is 12 hours 25 minutes. The highest (or "spring") tides occur twice a month, when the Moon, Sun and Earth are in line.

The Moon's surface temperature falls from 105°C in sunlight to -155°C when it turns away from the Sun

MAGNET EARTH

The Earth acts like a gigantic bar magnet. As the Earth spins in space, swirling currents are set up within its molten core. These movements generate a powerful magnetic field.

Magnetic North Pole, close to the true North Pole

THE GEOGRAPHICAL NORTH AND SOUTH POLES ARE THE TWO ENDS OF THE EARTH'S AXIS, THE LINE AROUND WHICH THE EARTH SPINS.

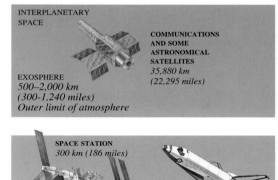

The magnetic field spreads out into space

Magnetic South Pole

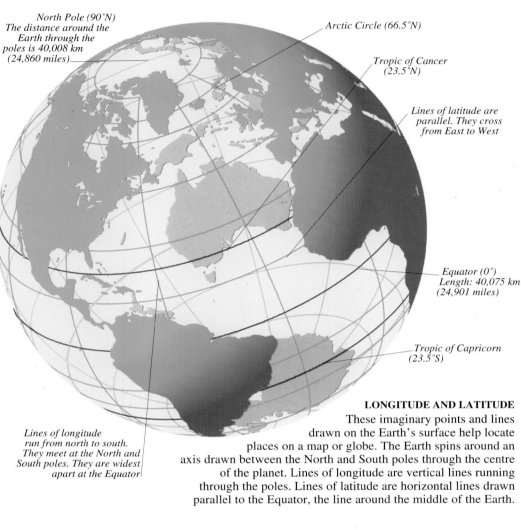

North Pole (90°N) The distance around the Earth through the poles is 40,008 km (24,860 miles)

Arctic Circle (66.5°N)

Tropic of Cancer (23.5°N)

Lines of latitude are parallel. They cross from East to West

Equator (0°) Length: 40,075 km (24,901 miles)

Tropic of Capricorn (23.5°S)

Lines of longitude run from north to south. They meet at the North and South poles. They are widest apart at the Equator

THE ATMOSPHERE

An envelope of gases such as nitrogen and oxygen surrounds our planet. It provides us with breathable air, filters the Sun's rays and retains heat at night.

Height in km (miles)

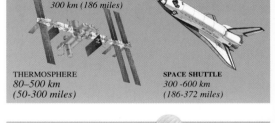

INTERPLANETARY SPACE

COMMUNICATIONS AND SOME ASTRONOMICAL SATELLITES 35,880 km (22,295 miles)

EXOSPHERE 500–2,000 km (300–1,240 miles) *Outer limit of atmosphere*

40,000 (25,000)

SPACE STATION 300 km (186 miles)

THERMOSPHERE 80–500 km (50–300 miles)

SPACE SHUTTLE 300 -600 km (186-372 miles)

500 (300)

MESOSPHERE 50–80 km (31–50 miles)

WEATHER BALLOON up to 50 km (31 miles)

80 (50)

STRATOSPHERE 15–50 km (9–31 miles)

50 (31)

OZONE LAYER 15-30 km (9-18 miles)

PASSENGER AIRCRAFT 8-16 km (5-10 miles)

CLOUDS *Usually below 10 km (6 miles)*

SKYDIVING *Typical leap: 4 km (2.5 miles)*

HELICOPTER *Usually below 2.5 km (1.5 miles)*

KITE *Usually below 0.1 km, (0.06 miles)*

TROPOSPHERE 0–15 km (0-9 miles)

Sea level

LONGITUDE AND LATITUDE

These imaginary points and lines drawn on the Earth's surface help locate places on a map or globe. The Earth spins around an axis drawn between the North and South poles through the centre of the planet. Lines of longitude are vertical lines running through the poles. Lines of latitude are horizontal lines drawn parallel to the Equator, the line around the middle of the Earth.

DIAMETER OF EARTH AT EQUATOR: 12,756 KM (7,927 MILES). DIAMETER FROM POLE TO POLE: 12,714 KM (7,900 MILES). MASS: 5,988 MILLION, MILLION MILLION TONNES (TONS).

Cold air descends from the poles towards the Equator

Warm air and water travel to the poles from the Equator

Air circulates between the poles and the Equator in stages called "cells"

Winds and currents do not move in straight lines because the Earth spins

WINDS AND CURRENTS

The world's winds and ocean currents are caused by the way the Sun heats the Earth's surface. More heat energy arrives at the Equator than at the poles because the Earth is curved and tilted. Warm air and warm water carry much of this energy towards the poles, heating up the higher latitudes. Meanwhile cool air and water moves back towards the Equator, lowering its temperature.

180°	165°E	150°E	135°E	120°E	105°E	90°E	75°E	60°E	45°E	30°E	15°E	0°
Wellington 2400 hrs	(Pacific Ocean) 2300 hrs	Sydney 2200 hrs	Tokyo 2100 hrs	Manila 2000 hrs	Jakarta 1900 hrs	Dacca 1800 hrs	Karachi 1700 hrs	Muscat 1600 hrs	Baghdad 1500 hrs	Cairo 1400 hrs	Berlin 1300 hrs	Greenwich 1200 hrs

THE EARTH'S STRUCTURE

THE EARTH IS IN SOME WAYS like an egg, with a thin shell around a soft interior. Its hard, rocky outer layer – the crust – is up to 70 km (45 miles) thick under the continents, but less than 8 km (5 miles) thick under the oceans. This crust is broken into gigantic slabs, called "plates", in which the continents are embedded. Below the hard crust is the mantle, a layer of rocks so hot that some melt and flow in huge swirling currents. The Earth's plates do not stay in the same place. Instead, they move, carried along like rafts on the currents in the mantle. This motion is very slow – usually less than 5 cm (2 in) a year – but enormously powerful. Plate movement makes the Earth quake and volcanoes erupt, causes immense mountain ranges such as the Himalayas to grow where plates collide, and explains how over millions of years whole continents have drifted across the face of the planet.

Pangaea

DRIFTING CONTINENTS
Currents of molten rock deep within the mantle slowly move the continents. Over time, they appear to "drift" across the Earth's surface.

200 MILLION YEARS AGO
All of today's continents were joined in one supercontinent, called Pangaea. It began to break up about 180 million years ago.

"Africa"
"India"
"Atlantic Ocean" opening up

120 MILLION YEARS AGO
The Atlantic Ocean splits Pangaea into two. India has broken away from Africa.

"North America" *"Asia"*
"India"

"Australia" *North America*
Europe
Asia
"Antarctica"

40 MILLION YEARS AGO
India is moving closer to Asia. Australia and Antarctica have separated.

South America
Austral[...]
Indi[...]
Africa
Antarctica

TODAY
India has collided with Asia, pushing up the Himalaya Mountains.

Great Rift Valley, now sea

50 MILLION YEARS IN THE FUTURE?
If today's plate movements continue, the Atlantic Ocean will be 1,250 km (775 miles) wider. Africa and Europe will fuse, the Americas will separate again, and Africa east of the Great Rift Valley will be an island.

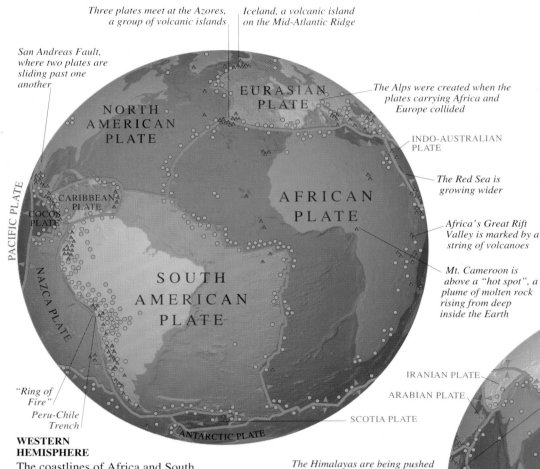

Three plates meet at the Azores, a group of volcanic islands
Iceland, a volcanic island on the Mid-Atlantic Ridge

San Andreas Fault, where two plates are sliding past one another

EURASIAN PLATE

NORTH AMERICAN PLATE

The Alps were created when the plates carrying Africa and Europe collided

INDO-AUSTRALIAN PLATE

PACIFIC PLATE

CARIBBEAN PLATE
COCOS PLATE

AFRICAN PLATE

The Red Sea is growing wider

NAZCA PLATE

SOUTH AMERICAN PLATE

Africa's Great Rift Valley is marked by a string of volcanoes

Mt. Cameroon is above a "hot spot", a plume of molten rock rising from deep inside the Earth

"Ring of Fire"
Peru-Chile Trench

ANTARCTIC PLATE

IRANIAN PLATE
ARABIAN PLATE
SCOTIA PLATE

WESTERN HEMISPHERE
The coastlines of Africa and South America "fit" one another like huge jigsaw pieces. This is because they were once joined. Then, about 180 million years ago, a crack appeared in the Earth's crust. Hot liquid rock (magma) rose through the crack and cooled, forming new oceanic crust on either side. As the ocean grew wider, the continents moved apart. The process continues today.

The "Ring of Fire" passes through Japan.

Mariana Trench, 11,033 m (6.8 miles) deep, where an ocean plate dives into the mantle

EURASIAN PLATE

PACIFIC PLATE

PHILIPPINE PLATE

The Himalayas are being pushed up by the collision of India with the rest of Asia

AFRICAN PLATE

The Java Trench, 7,450 m (4.6 miles) deep, runs parallel to a long chain of active volcanoes in Southeast Asia

INDO-AUSTRALIAN PLATE

ANTARCTIC PLATE

KEYBOX

△	*Major active volcano*
○	*Major earthquake*
	Colliding plates
	Sliding plates
	Spreading plates

THE ATLANTIC OCEAN IS GROWING WIDER BY 2.5 CM (1 IN) A YEAR – ABOUT THE SAME SPEED THAT FINGERNAILS GROW. THE NAZCA PLATE IS SLIDING THREE TIMES FASTER UNDER SOUTH AMERICA, PUSHING UP THE ANDES.

EASTERN HEMISPHERE
Most earthquakes and volcanoes occur around the edges of crustal plates (or plate margins). Australia, in the middle of the Indo-Australian plate, has no active volcanoes and is rarely troubled by earthquakes. Things are very different in neighbouring New Zealand and New Guinea, which lie on the notorious Pacific "Ring of Fire". The Ring is an area of intense volcanic activity which forms a line all the way round the Pacific rim, through the Philippines, Japan and North America, and down the coast of South America to New Zealand.

The Hawaiian islands lie over a "hot spot"

Highly volcanic New Zealand lies on the "Ring of Fire"

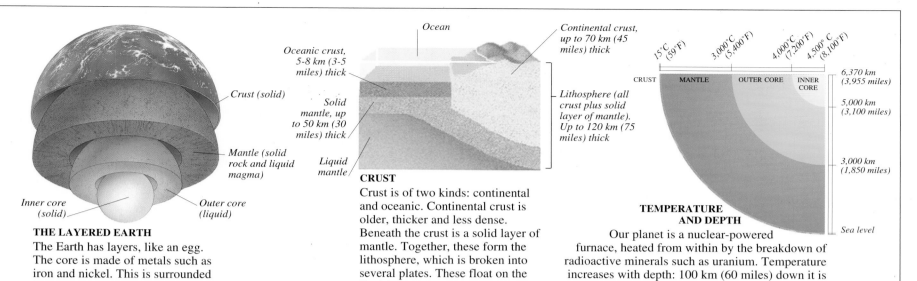

THE LAYERED EARTH
The Earth has layers, like an egg.
The core is made of metals such as
iron and nickel. This is surrounded
by a rocky mantle and a thin crust.

CRUST
Crust is of two kinds: continental
and oceanic. Continental crust is
older, thicker and less dense.
Beneath the crust is a solid layer of
mantle. Together, these form the
lithosphere, which is broken into
several plates. These float on the
liquid mantle layer.

**TEMPERATURE
AND DEPTH**
Our planet is a nuclear-powered
furnace, heated from within by the breakdown of
radioactive minerals such as uranium. Temperature
increases with depth: 100 km (60 miles) down it is
1,350°C (2,460°F), hot enough for rocks to melt.

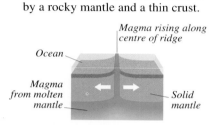

SPREADING PLATES
When two plates move apart, molten
rock (magma) rises from the mantle
and cools, forming new crust. This
is called a constructive margin. Most
are found in oceans.

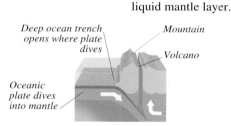

COLLIDING PLATES THAT DIVE
When two ocean plates or an ocean
plate and a continent plate collide,
the denser plate is forced under the
other, diving down into the mantle.
These are destructive margins.

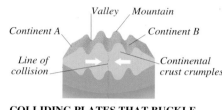

COLLIDING PLATES THAT BUCKLE
When two continents collide, their
plates fuse, crumple and push
upwards. Mountain ranges such as
the Himalayas and the Urals have
been formed in this way.

SLIDING PLATES
When two plates slide past one
another, intense friction is created
along the "fault line" between them,
causing earthquakes. These are called
conservative margins.

ICELAND, MID-ATLANTIC RIDGE
Most constructive margins are found
beneath oceans, but here in volcanic
Iceland one comes to the surface.

VOLCANO, JAVA
Diving plates often build volcanic
islands and mountain chains. Deep
ocean trenches form offshore.

FOLDING STRATA, ENGLAND
The clash of continental plates may
cause the Earth to buckle and twist
far from the collision zone.

SAN ANDREAS FAULT
A huge earthquake is expected soon
somewhere along California's San
Andreas Fault, seen here.

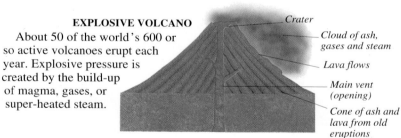

EXPLOSIVE VOLCANO
About 50 of the world's 600 or
so active volcanoes erupt each
year. Explosive pressure is
created by the build-up
of magma, gases, or
super-heated steam.

SOME MAJOR QUAKES AND ERUPTIONS
This map shows some of the worst natural disasters in recorded history.
Over one million earthquakes and about 50 volcanic eruptions are detected
every year. Most are minor or occur where there are few people, so there
is no loss of human life or great damage to property. But crowded cities
and poorly-constructed buildings are putting ever-greater numbers at risk.

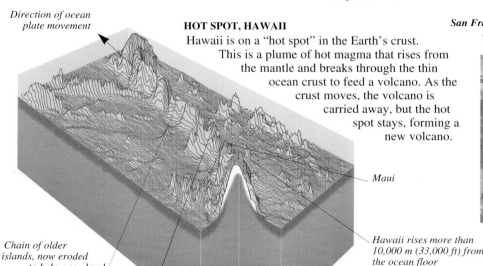

HOT SPOT, HAWAII
Hawaii is on a "hot spot" in the Earth's crust.
This is a plume of hot magma that rises from
the mantle and breaks through the thin
ocean crust to feed a volcano. As the
crust moves, the volcano is
carried away, but the hot
spot stays, forming a
new volcano.

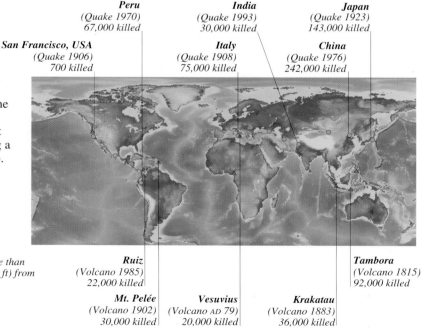

Peru
(Quake 1970)
67,000 killed

India
(Quake 1993)
30,000 killed

Japan
(Quake 1923)
143,000 killed

San Francisco, USA
(Quake 1906)
700 killed

Italy
(Quake 1908)
75,000 killed

China
(Quake 1976)
242,000 killed

Ruiz
(Volcano 1985)
22,000 killed

Tambora
(Volcano 1815)
92,000 killed

Mt. Pelée
(Volcano 1902)
30,000 killed

Vesuvius
(Volcano AD 79)
20,000 killed

Krakatau
(Volcano 1883)
36,000 killed

SHAPING THE LANDSCAPE

LANDSCAPES ARE CREATED AND CHANGED – even destroyed – in a continuous cycle. Over millions of years, constant movements of the Earth's plates have built its continents, islands and mountains. But as soon as new land is formed, it is shaped (or "eroded") by the forces of wind, water, ice and heat. Sometimes change is quick, as when a river floods and cuts a new channel, or a landslide cascades down a mountain slope. But usually change is so slow that it is invisible to the human eye. Extremes of heat and cold crack open rocks and expose them to attack by wind and water. Rivers and glaciers scour out valleys, the wind piles up sand dunes, and the sea attacks shorelines and cliffs. Eroded materials are blown away or carried along by rivers, piling up as sediments on valley floors or the sea bed. Over millions of years these may be compressed into rock and pushed up to form new land. As soon as the land is exposed to the elements, the cycle of erosion begins again.

ICE ACTION, ALASKA
Areas close to the North Pole are permanently covered in snow and ice. Glaciers are rivers of ice that flow towards the sea. Some glaciers are more than 60 km (40 miles) long.

KEYBOX

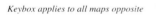

Area covered in ice today	Area drained by major river
Ice and snow 18,000 years ago	Protected coastline
Desert	Coast affected by tidal swell
Wind direction (simplified)	Coast affected by storm waves

Keybox applies to all maps opposite

THE "ROOF OF NORTH AMERICA"
Steeply-sloping Denali (also called Mt. McKinley), Alaska, is North America's highest mountain at 6,194 m (20,320 ft). It is a fairly "young" mountain, less than 70 million years old. The gently sloping Appalachians in the east of the continent are very much older. Once, they were probably higher than Denali is today. But more than 300 million years of ice, rain and wind have ground them down.

SEA ACTION, CAPE COD
Cape Cod, a sandy peninsula 105 km (65 miles) long, juts out like a beckoning finger into the Atlantic Ocean. Its strangely-curved coastline has been shaped by wave action.

THIS SECTION OF THE GLOBE SHOWS NORTH AMERICA AND THE DIFFERENT FORCES WORKING ON THE LANDSCAPE. THE LANDSCAPE IN EVERY PART OF THE WORLD IS CHANGED BY THE ACTION OF ICE, RUNNING WATER, SEA WAVES AND WIND.

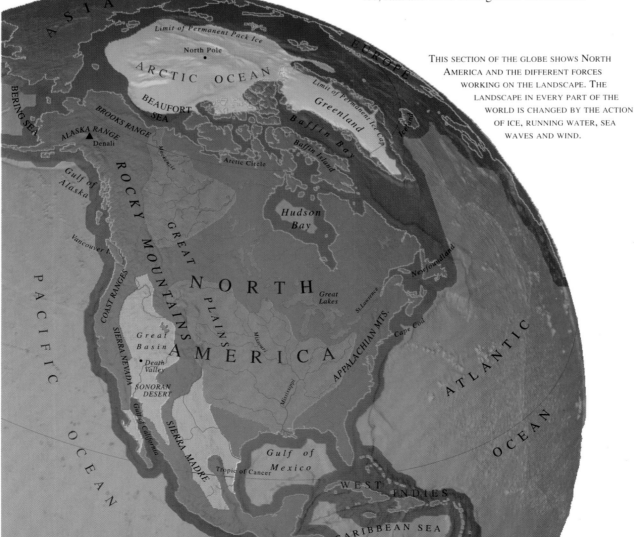

WIND ACTION, DEATH VALLEY
Death Valley is the hottest, driest place in North America. Its floor is covered in sand and salt. Winds sweeping across the valley endlessly reshape the loose surface.

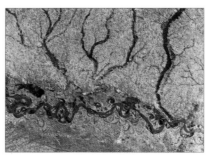
WATER ACTION, MISSISSIPPI
The Mississippi River and its many tributaries frequently change course. Where two loops are close together, the river may cut a new path between them, leaving an "ox-bow lake".

Ice floats because it is less dense than sea water   *Only one-ninth of an iceberg shows above sea level*

A GLACIER REACHES THE SEA
When a glacier enters the sea, its front edge or "snout" breaks up and forms icebergs – a process called calving. These "ice mountains" are then carried away by ocean currents.

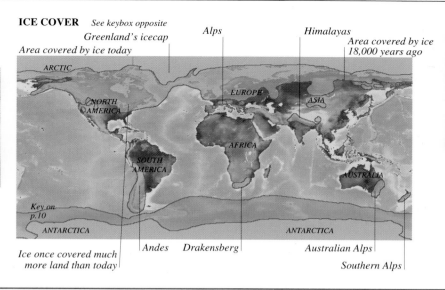

ICE COVER   *See keybox opposite*

Greenland's icecap   Alps   Himalayas

Area covered by ice today   Area covered by ice 18,000 years ago

ARCTIC

EUROPE   ASIA

NORTH AMERICA

AFRICA

SOUTH AMERICA

AUSTRALIA

Key on p.10

ANTARCTICA   ANTARCTICA

Ice once covered much more land than today   Andes   Drakensberg   Australian Alps   Southern Alps

NORDFJORD, NORWAY
One sign of glacial action on the landscape is the fjord. These long, narrow, steep-sided inlets are found along the coasts of Norway, Alaska, Chile and New Zealand. They mark the points where glaciers once entered the sea.

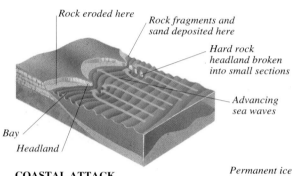

Rock eroded here   *Rock fragments and sand deposited here*

Hard rock headland broken into small sections

Advancing sea waves

Bay

Headland

COASTAL ATTACK
The ceaseless push and pull of waves on a shore can destroy even the hardest rocks. The softest rocks are eroded first, leaving headlands of hard rock that survive a little longer.

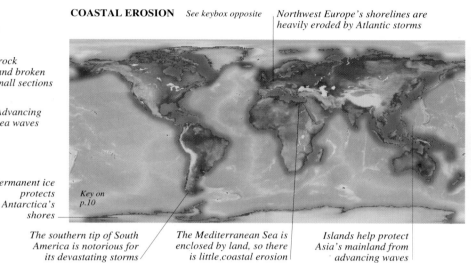

COASTAL EROSION   *See keybox opposite*   *Northwest Europe's shorelines are heavily eroded by Atlantic storms*

Permanent ice protects Antarctica's shores

Key on p.10

The southern tip of South America is notorious for its devastating storms   *The Mediterranean Sea is enclosed by land, so there is little coastal erosion*   *Islands help protect Asia's mainland from advancing waves*

WAVE POWER
The powerful action of waves on an exposed coast can erode a coastline by several metres (feet) a year.

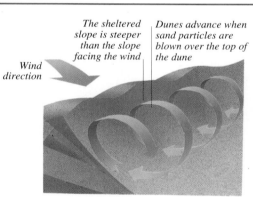

The sheltered slope is steeper than the slope facing the wind   *Dunes advance when sand particles are blown over the top of the dune*

Wind direction

DESERT DUNE
Dunes are slow-moving mounds or ridges of sand found in deserts and along some coastlines. They only form when the wind's direction and speed is fairly constant.

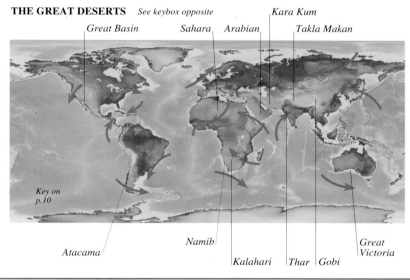

THE GREAT DESERTS   *See keybox opposite*   Kara Kum

Great Basin   Sahara   Arabian   Takla Makan

Key on p.10

Atacama   Namib   Great Victoria

Kalahari   Thar   Gobi

NAMIB DESERT, SOUTHERN AFRICA
The sand dunes seen in the centre of the picture are about 50 m (160 feet) high. Winds are driving them slowly but relentlessly towards the right. Not all deserts are sandy. Wind may blow away all the loose sand and gravel, leaving bare rock.

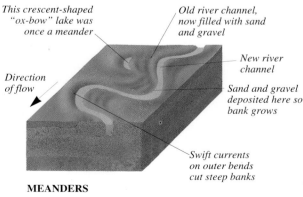

This crescent-shaped "ox-bow" lake was once a meander   *Old river channel, now filled with sand and gravel*

New river channel

Direction of flow

Sand and gravel deposited here so bank grows

Swift currents on outer bends cut steep banks

MEANDERS
River banks are worn away most on the outside of bends, where water flows fastest. Eroded sand and gravel are built up into banks on the inside of bends, in slower-moving water.

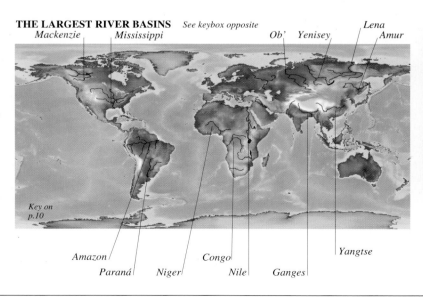

THE LARGEST RIVER BASINS   *See keybox opposite*   Lena

Mackenzie   Mississippi   Ob'   Yenisey   Amur

Key on p.10

Amazon   Congo   Yangtse

Paraná   Niger   Nile   Ganges

WINDING RIVER, ALASKA
The more a river meanders across a plain, the longer it becomes and the more slowly it flows.

CLIMATE AND VEGETATION

THE EARTH IS the only planet in our solar system which supports life. Most of our planet has a breathable atmosphere, and sufficient light, heat and water to support a wide range of plants and animals. The main influences on an area's climate are the amount of sunshine it receives (which varies with latitude and season), how close it is to the influence of ocean currents, and its height above sea level. Since there is more sunlight at the Equator than elsewhere, and rainfall is highest here too, this is where we find the habitats which have more species of plants and animals than anywhere else: rainforests, coral reefs and mangrove swamps. Where rainfall is very low, and where it is either too hot, such as in deserts, or too cold, few plants and animals can survive. Only the icy North and South Poles, and the frozen tops of high mountains, are practically without life of any sort.

WEATHER EXTREMES
Weather is a powerful influence on how we feel, the clothes we wear, the buildings we live in, the colour of our skin, the plants that grow around us, and what we eat and drink. Extreme weather events such as heatwaves, hurricanes, blizzards, tornadoes, sandstorms, droughts and floods, can be terrifyingly destructive.

TORNADO
Tornadoes are whirlwinds of cold air that develop when thunderclouds cross warm land. They are extremely violent and unpredictable. Windspeeds often exceed 300 km (180 miles) per hour.

TROPICAL STORMS
These devastating winds develop when air spirals upwards above warm seas. More air is sucked in and the storm begins to move. They bring torrential rain, thunder and lightning and destruction.

DROUGHT
Long periods without water kill plants. Stripped of its protective covering of vegetation, the soil is easily blown away.

OCEAN CURRENTS
Currents are a powerful influence on climates. They are like great rivers in the ocean that carry warm water (orange) away from the Equator and cold water (blue) towards the Equator.

Labrador current
Equatorial currents
North Pacific current
California current
E. Greenland current
Gulf Stream
Canaries current
Benguela current
Monsoon Drift
Oya Shio current

NORTH AMERICA
EUROPE
ASIA
AFRICA
SOUTH AMERICA
AUSTRALIA
ANTARCTICA

Brazil current
Peru current
Antarctic circumpolar current
Agulhas current
W. Australia current

MAIN STORM ZONES
Storms combine very high winds with heavy rainfall (tropical storms) or driving snow (blizzards). Typhoons, cyclones, hurricanes and willy-willies are regional names for tropical storms.

Tropical storms
Hurricanes, August to October
Blizzards
Blizzards, November to March
Typhoons, April to December

Areas prone to flooding
Cyclones, May to December
Willy-willies, December to April

TEMPERATURE
Average temperatures are very different around the world. Areas close to the Equator are usually hot (orange on the map); those close to the Poles usually cold (deep blue). The hottest areas move during the year from the Southern to the Northern hemispheres.

Average January temperature

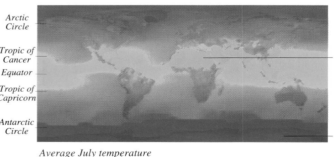
Average July temperature

Arctic Circle
Tropic of Cancer
Equator
Tropic of Capricorn
Antarctic Circle

Highest: 58°C (136°F), Saharan Libya

Lowest: -89°C (-129°F), Antarctica

RAINFALL
The wettest areas (grey) lie near the Equator. The driest are found close to the tropics, in the centre of continents, or at the poles. Elsewhere, rainfall varies with the season, but it is usually highest in summer. Asia's wet season is known as the monsoon.

Average January rainfall

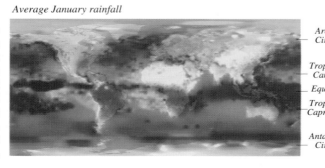

Average July rainfall

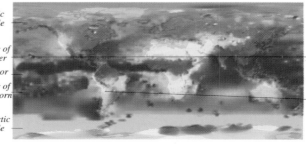

Arctic Circle
Tropic of Cancer
Equator
Tropic of Capricorn
Antarctic Circle

Highest in 1 year: 11.68 m (460 in), Hawaii

Lowest: No rain in more than 14 years, Atacama

BROADLEAF FOREST
Temperate climates have no great extremes of temperature, and drought is unusual. Forests usually contain broad-leaved trees, such as beech or oak, that shed their leaves in autumn.

TUNDRA
As long as frozen soil melts for at least two months of the year, some mosses, lichens and ground-hugging shrubs can survive. They are found around the Arctic Circle and on mountains.

NEEDLELEAF FOREST
Forests of cone-bearing, needleleaf trees such as pine and fir cover much of northern North America, Europe and Asia. They are ever-green and can survive long frozen winters. Most have tall, straight trunks and down-pointing branches. This reduces the amount of snow that can settle on them. The forest floor is dark because leaves absorb most of the incoming sunlight.

TRAVELLING SOUTHWARD FROM THE NORTH POLE, A NUMBER OF DISTINCT LIFE ZONES OR "BIOMES" CAN BE SEEN. PLANT AND ANIMAL LIFE IS CLOSELY ADAPTED TO LOCAL CLIMATE.

MEDITERRANEAN
The hot dry summers and warm wet winters typical of the Mediterranean region are also found in small areas of Southern Africa, the Americas and Australia. Mediterranean-type vegetation can vary from dense forest to thinly spread evergreen shrubs, like these.

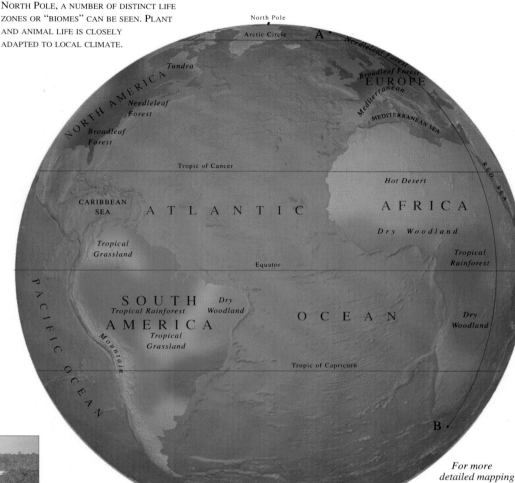

For more detailed mapping of vegetation zones, see the individual maps that introduce each continent.

MOUNTAIN
Vegetation changes with height because the temperature drops and wind increases. Even on the Equator, mountain peaks can be covered in snow. Although trees may cloak the lower slopes, at higher altitudes they give way to sparser vegetation. Near the top, only tundra-type plants can survive.

TROPICAL RAINFOREST
The lush forests found near the Equator depend on year-round high temperatures and heavy rainfall. Worldwide, they may contain 50,000 different kinds of trees and support several million other plant and animal species. Trees are often festooned with climbing plants, or covered with ferns and orchids that have rooted in pockets of water and soil on trunks and branches.

DRY WOODLAND
Plants in many parts of the tropics have to cope with high temperatures and long periods without rain. Some store water in enlarged stems or trunks, or limit water losses by having small, spiny leaves. In dry (but not desert) conditions, trees are widely spaced, with expanses of grassland between, called savannah.

HOT DESERT
Very few plants and animals can survive in hot deserts. Rainfall is low – under 10 cm (4 in) a year. Temperatures often rise above 40°C (104 °F) during the day, but drop to freezing point at night. High winds and shifting sands can be a further hazard to life. Only specially adapted plants, such as cacti, can survive.

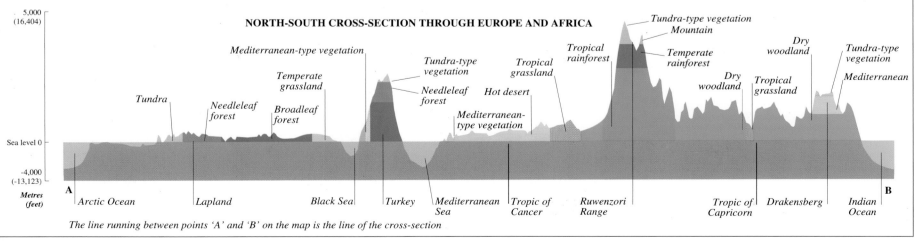

NORTH-SOUTH CROSS-SECTION THROUGH EUROPE AND AFRICA

The line running between points 'A' and 'B' on the map is the line of the cross-section

PEOPLE AND PLANET

SOON, THERE WILL BE 6,000 million people on Earth, and numbers are rising at the rate of about one million every week. People are not distributed evenly. Some areas, such as parts of Europe, India and China, are very densely populated. Other areas – particularly deserts, polar regions and mountains – can support very few people. Almost half of the world's population now lives in towns or cities. This is quite a recent development. Until 1800, most people lived in small villages in the countryside, and worked on the land. But since then more and more people have lived and worked in much larger settlements. A century ago, most of the world's largest cities were in Europe and North America, where new industries and businesses were flourishing. Today, the most rapidly-growing cities are in Asia, South America and Africa. People who move to these cities are usually young adults, so the birth rate amongst these new populations is very high.

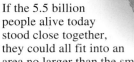

A CROWDED PLANET?
If the 5.5 billion people alive today stood close together, they could all fit into an area no larger than the small Caribbean island of Jamaica. Of course, so many people could not live in such a small place. Areas with few people are usually very cold, such as land near the poles and in mountains, or very dry, such as deserts. Areas with large populations often have fertile land and a good climate for crops. Cities support huge populations because they are wealthy enough to buy in everything they need.

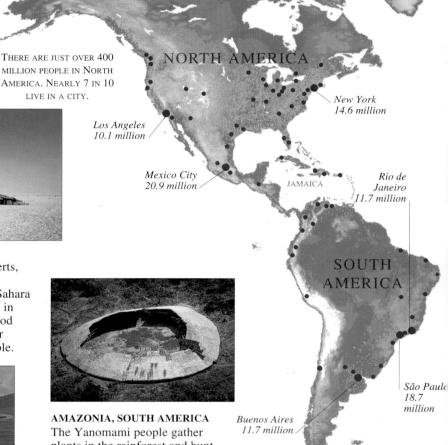

THERE ARE JUST OVER 400 MILLION PEOPLE IN NORTH AMERICA. NEARLY 7 IN 10 LIVE IN A CITY.

New York 14.6 million

Los Angeles 10.1 million

Mexico City 20.9 million

Rio de Janeiro 11.7 million

São Paulo 18.7 million

Buenos Aires 11.7 million

THERE ARE ABOUT 300 MILLION PEOPLE IN SOUTH AMERICA. MORE THAN 7 IN 10 LIVE IN A CITY.

KEYBOX

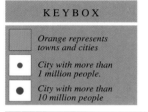

Orange represents towns and cities

● City with more than 1 million people.

● City with more than 10 million people

London

MILLIONAIRE CITIES 1900
Less than a century ago there were only 13 cities with more than one million people living in them. All the cities were in the northern hemisphere. The largest was London, with seven million people.

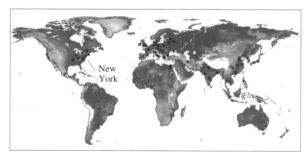
New York

MILLIONAIRE CITIES 1950
By 1950, there were nearly 70 cities with more than one million inhabitants. The largest was New York.

WORLD POPULATION GROWTH 1500–2020
Each figure on the graph represents 500 million people. Note: One billion is 1,000 million.

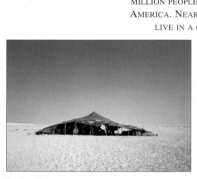

SAHARA, AFRICA
The Sahara, like all deserts, is thinly populated. The Tuareg of the northern Sahara are nomads. They travel in small groups because food sources are scarce. Their homes have to be portable.

MONGOLIA, ASIA
Traditionally, Mongolia's nomadic people lived by herding their animals across the steppe. Today, their felt tents, or *gers*, are often set up next to more permanent houses.

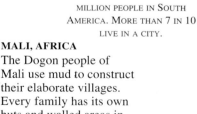

AMAZONIA, SOUTH AMERICA
The Yanomami people gather plants in the rainforest and hunt game, but they also grow crops in small forest gardens. Several families live together in a "village" under one huge roof.

MALI, AFRICA
The Dogon people of Mali use mud to construct their elaborate villages. Every family has its own huts and walled areas in which their animals are penned for the night.

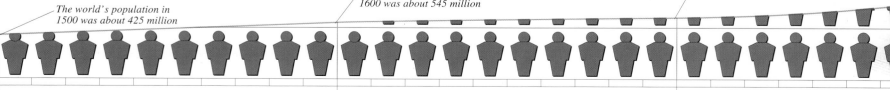

The world's population in 1500 was about 425 million

The world's population in 1600 was about 545 million

The world's population in 1700 was about 610 million.

1500   1600   1700

POOR SUBURB
Densely-populated "shanty towns" have grown on the fringes of many cities in the developing world. Houses are usually built from discarded materials.

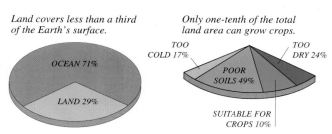

RICH SUBURB
Cities are often surrounded by areas where the richest people live. Population densities are low, and the houses may be luxurious, with large gardens or swimming pools. People in these suburbs rely on their cars for transport. This allows them to live a great distance from places of work and leisure in the city centre.

Land covers less than a third of the Earth's surface.

OCEAN 71%

LAND 29%

Only one-tenth of the total land area can grow crops.

TOO COLD 17%

TOO DRY 24%

POOR SOILS 49%

SUITABLE FOR CROPS 10%

CULTIVATION
Only a small proportion of the Earth's surface can grow crops. It may be possible to bring more land – such as deserts – into production, but yields may be low and costly.

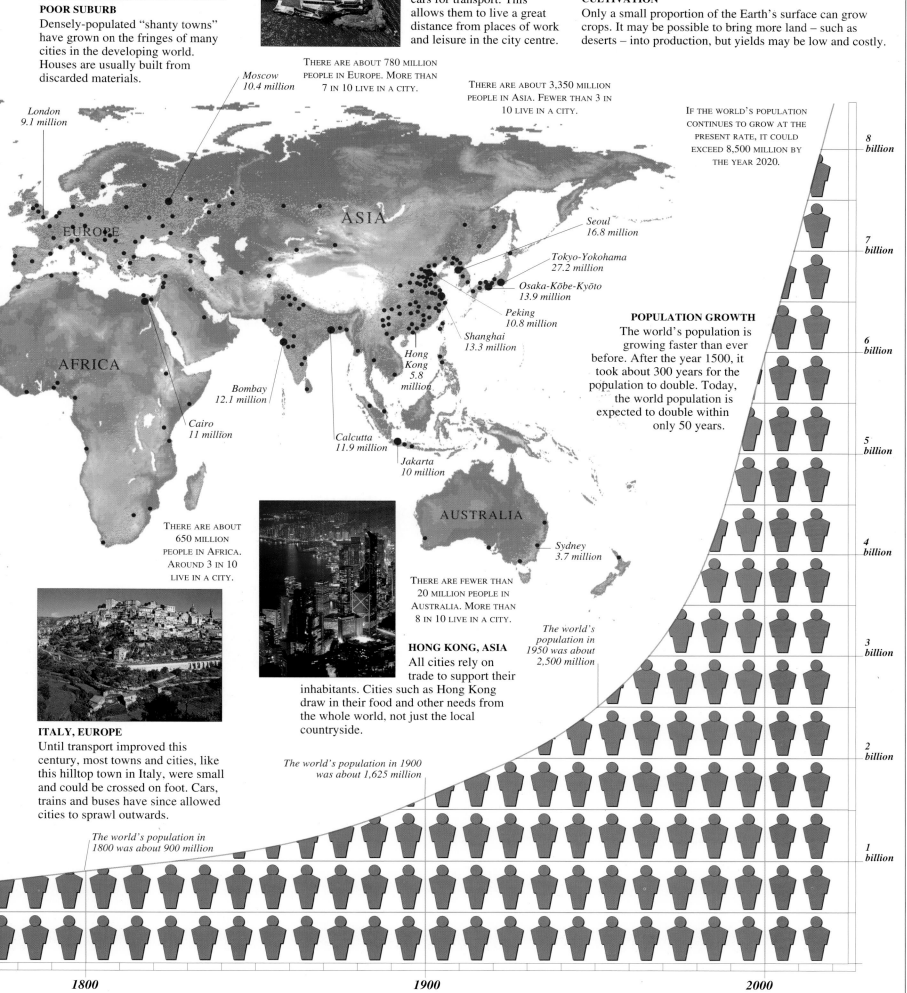

Moscow 10.4 million

THERE ARE ABOUT 780 MILLION PEOPLE IN EUROPE. MORE THAN 7 IN 10 LIVE IN A CITY.

THERE ARE ABOUT 3,350 MILLION PEOPLE IN ASIA. FEWER THAN 3 IN 10 LIVE IN A CITY.

London 9.1 million

IF THE WORLD'S POPULATION CONTINUES TO GROW AT THE PRESENT RATE, IT COULD EXCEED 8,500 MILLION BY THE YEAR 2020.

EUROPE

ASIA

Seoul 16.8 million

Tokyo-Yokohama 27.2 million

Osaka-Kōbe-Kyōto 13.9 million

Peking 10.8 million

Shanghai 13.3 million

Hong Kong 5.8 million

AFRICA

Bombay 12.1 million

POPULATION GROWTH
The world's population is growing faster than ever before. After the year 1500, it took about 300 years for the population to double. Today, the world population is expected to double within only 50 years.

Cairo 11 million

Calcutta 11.9 million

Jakarta 10 million

THERE ARE ABOUT 650 MILLION PEOPLE IN AFRICA. AROUND 3 IN 10 LIVE IN A CITY.

AUSTRALIA

Sydney 3.7 million

THERE ARE FEWER THAN 20 MILLION PEOPLE IN AUSTRALIA. MORE THAN 8 IN 10 LIVE IN A CITY.

The world's population in 1950 was about 2,500 million

HONG KONG, ASIA
All cities rely on trade to support their inhabitants. Cities such as Hong Kong draw in their food and other needs from the whole world, not just the local countryside.

ITALY, EUROPE
Until transport improved this century, most towns and cities, like this hilltop town in Italy, were small and could be crossed on foot. Cars, trains and buses have since allowed cities to sprawl outwards.

The world's population in 1900 was about 1,625 million

The world's population in 1800 was about 900 million

8 billion

7 billion

6 billion

5 billion

4 billion

3 billion

2 billion

1 billion

1800

1900

2000

15

THE WORLD TODAY

THERE ARE 192 INDEPENDENT countries in the world today. With the exception of Antarctica every land area of the Earth's surface belongs to, or is claimed by, one country or another. In 1950, there were only 82 countries; but since then many former colonies of the European countries have gained independence. The final stage in this process was the break-up of the Soviet Union after 1990. The world's nations vary enormously in size and shape. The largest country in the world is the Russian Federation; the smallest is the Vatican City.

ENCLAVES
If part of a country's territory has become separated from the rest of the country, and is surrounded by foreign territory, it is called an enclave. Kaliningrad is part of the Russian Federation, but is cut off from it by the Baltic States.

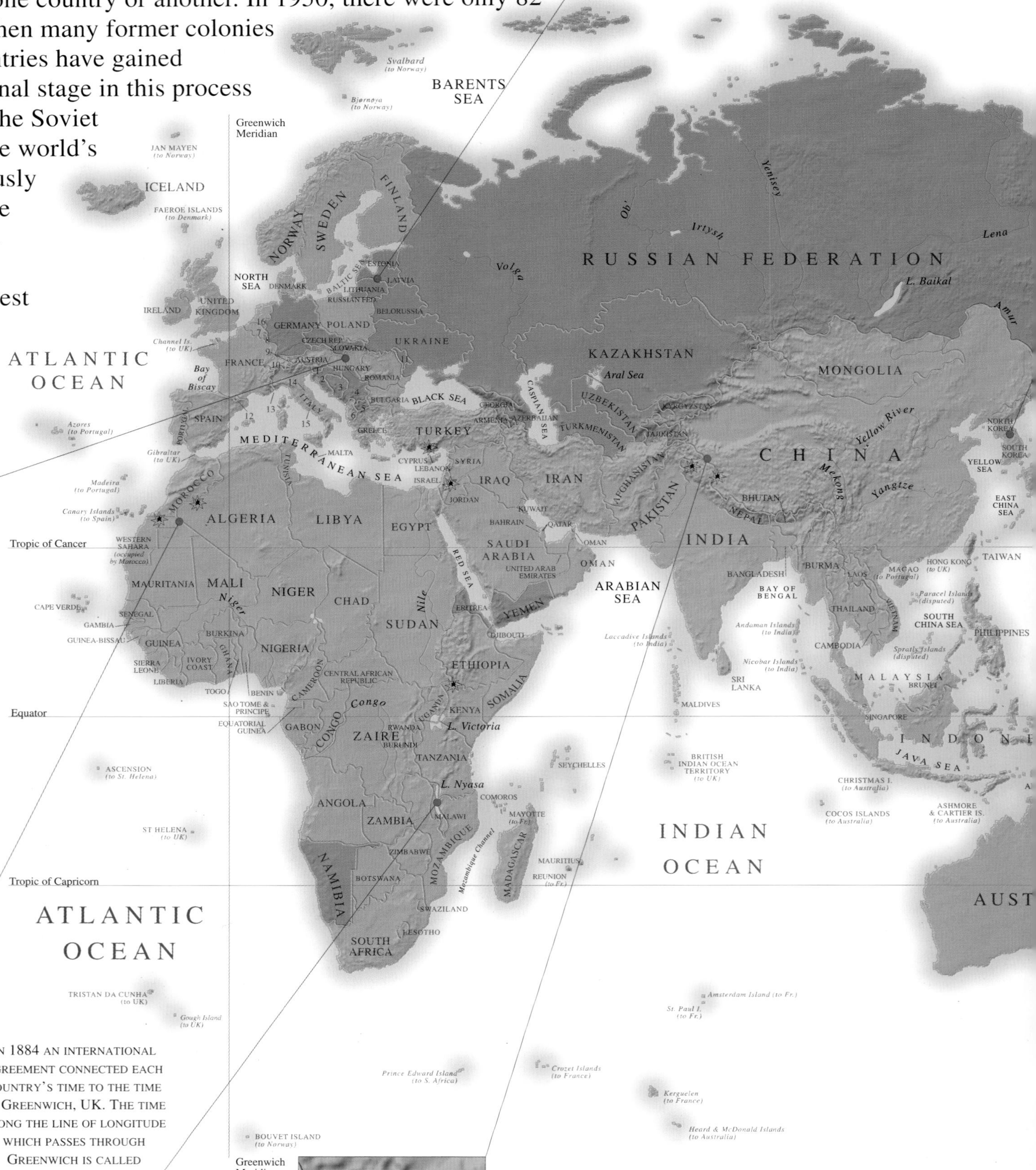

RIVER BORDERS
Over one-sixth of the world's national borders are formed by rivers. Long stretches of the Danube form borders in south-eastern Europe. It is also an important navigable waterway for over 1,600 km (1,000 miles).

KEY TO EUROPE
1 SLOVENIA
2 CROATIA
3 BOSNIA/HERZEGOVINA
4 YUGOSLAVIA
5 MACEDONIA
6 ALBANIA
7 BELGIUM
8 LUXEMBOURG
9 LIECHTENSTEIN
10 SWITZERLAND
11 MOLDAVIA
12 ANDORRA
13 MONACO
14 SAN MARINO
15 VATICAN CITY
16 NETHERLANDS

STRAIGHT LINE BORDERS
The borders of many countries in Africa and other former colonial territories are straight lines. This was the simplest solution for colonial administrators, who often knew little of the country's geography or population.

IN 1884 AN INTERNATIONAL AGREEMENT CONNECTED EACH COUNTRY'S TIME TO THE TIME AT GREENWICH, UK. THE TIME ALONG THE LINE OF LONGITUDE WHICH PASSES THROUGH GREENWICH IS CALLED GREENWICH MEAN TIME.

LAKE BOUNDARIES
Countries which lie next to lakes usually fix their borders in the middle of the lake. Complicated agreements between colonial powers led to the awkward division of Lake Nyasa.

BORDER DISPUTES
There are many disputed territories and borders in the world today. The Chinese, for example, control part of northern India. They reject the 19th-century border drawn up by the British which incorporated the region into India. Look for ✷

THE CHANGING MAP
Borders between nations can change dramatically during their history. In 1500, Poland was Europe's largest nation; between 1772 and 1795 it was absorbed into Prussia, Russia and Austria. After World War I it became an independent country, but its borders changed again in 1945 following German and Russian invasions.

In 1634, Poland was Europe's biggest nation.

K L M N O P Q R S T

1 2 3 4 5 6 7 8 9 10 11 12 13 14 15 16

MILITARY BORDERS

At the end of World War II, Korea was occupied by Soviet and American troops. In 1950, after the troops were withdrawn, the communist north attempted to invade the south. In 1953, North and South Korea were divided along the 38° line of latitude. This border has remained heavily fortified.

CHINA
NORTH KOREA
SOUTH KOREA

THE LONGEST BORDER

The border between the USA and Canada is the longest in the world. It cuts through the centre of the Great Lakes. To the west of Michigan, the border runs along the 49° line of latitude. The border slices through the American territory of Point Robert, separating it from the rest of the USA.

CANADA
Strait of Georgia
Point Robert
USA

ARCTIC OCEAN

International Date Line

BEAUFORT SEA

Greenland (to Denmark)

Baffin Bay

Alaska (to USA)
Yukon

Mackenzie

Great Slave L.

Hudson Bay

BERING SEA

Gulf of Alaska

CANADA

ATLANTIC OCEAN

PACIFIC OCEAN

Missouri

UNITED STATES OF AMERICA

St Pierre and Miquelon (to France)

KEY TO CARIBBEAN

17 *CAYMAN IS. (to UK)*
18 *NAVASSA (to USA)*
19 *ARUBA (to Neth.)*
20 *NETHERLANDS ANTILLES (to Neth.)*
21 *ST. VINCENT AND GRENADINES*
22 *MARTINIQUE (to Fr.)*
23 *TURKS AND CAICOS IS. (to UK)*
24 *ST. CHRISTOPHER AND NEVIS*
25 *MONTSERRAT (to UK)*
26 *BRITISH VIRGIN IS. (to UK)*
27 *VIRGIN IS. (to USA)*
28 *ANTIGUA AND BARBUDA*
29 *ANGUILLA (to UK)*
30 *GUADELOUPE (to Fr.)*

Mississippi

Bermuda (to UK)

MIDWAY IS. (to USA)

Hawaii (to USA)

Revillagigedo Islands (to Mexico)

MEXICO

Gulf of Mexico

BAHAMAS

CUBA

DOMINICAN REPUBLIC
HAITI

JOHNSTON ATOLL (to USA)

NORTHERN MARIANAS IS. (to USA)

WAKE I. (to USA)

MARSHALL ISLANDS

GUATEMALA
BELIZE
HONDURAS
EL SALVADOR
NICARAGUA
COSTA RICA
PANAMA

JAMAICA
PUERTO RICO
DOMINICA
SAINT LUCIA
BARBADOS
GRENADA
TRINIDAD & TOBAGO

CARIBBEAN SEA

MICRONESIA

KINGMAN REEF (to USA)
PALMYRA ATOLL (to USA)

HOWLAND I. (to USA)
BAKER I. (to USA)

Jarvis Island (to USA)

Clipperton Island (to France)

VENEZUELA
GUYANA
SURINAM
FRENCH GUYANA (to Fr.)

NAURU

KIRIBATI

Galápagos Is. (to Ecuador)

COLOMBIA

ECUADOR

Amazon

PAPUA NEW GUINEA

SOLOMON ISLANDS

TUVALU

TOKELAU (to NZ)

WALLIS & FUTUNA (to Fr.)

WESTERN SAMOA

AMERICAN SAMOA (to USA)

COOK ISLANDS (to NZ)

PERU

Purus

BRAZIL

Claimed by Argentina

CORAL SEA

CORAL SEA IS. (to Australia)

VANUATU

FIJI

TONGA

NIUE (to NZ)

FRENCH POLYNESIA (to Fr.)

BOLIVIA

CHILE ARGENTINA

Claimed by Chile

NEW CALEDONIA (to France)

PITCAIRN IS. (to UK)

Easter Island (to Chile)

San Ambrosio Island (to Chile)
San Félix I. (to Chile)

PARAGUAY

Paraná

URUGUAY

MOUNTAIN BORDERS

Mountain ranges such as the Pyrenees, Alps and Himalayas form natural borders between many countries. In the Andes, border disputes between Chile and Argentina centred on finding the highest point in the mountain range which divided them.

NORFOLK I. (to Australia)

Lord Howe Island (to Australia)

NEW ZEALAND

TASMAN SEA

PACIFIC OCEAN

Juan Fernández Islands (to Chile)

CHILE

ARGENTINA

Chatham Island (to NZ)

Bounty Island (to NZ)

Antipodes Islands (to NZ)

Auckland Islands (to NZ)

Campbell Island (to NZ)

THE WORLD IS DIVIDED INTO 24 TIME ZONES. THE 180° LINE OF LONGITUDE IS CALLED THE INTERNATIONAL DATE LINE. PLACES JUST WEST OF THIS LINE ARE 24 HOURS AHEAD OF PLACES TO THE EAST. SO, BY TRAVELLING EAST ACROSS THE DATE LINE YOU CAN GO BACK A WHOLE DAY.

FALKLAND IS. (to UK)

SOUTH GEORGIA (to UK)

SOUTH SANDWICH IS. (to UK)

MacQuarie Island (to Australia)

International Date Line

Peter the First Island (to Norway)

PRUSSIA
Warsaw
RUSSIA
Moscow
Kiev
AUSTRIA

From 1772, Poland was part of Austria, Russia and Prussia.

POLAND
Warsaw
Moscow
Kiev

After World War I, Poland became a nation again.

POLAND
Warsaw
Moscow
Kiev

After World War II, the Polish borders were again redrawn.

KEYBOX

Present-day countries established before 1990.

New countries created since 1990.

International borders

Disputed borders

Key to maps: *Certain symbols will appear on every spread, and are listed below. These symbols represent physical features, or the country's infrastructure: borders, transport, settlement.*

International border: Border between countries which is mutually recognized.

De facto border: Border used in practice, but not mutually agreed between two countries.

Claimed border: Border which is not mutually recognized – where territory belonging to one country is claimed by

Map area division: This line indicates that a country is treated on two different spreads in the Atlas. It is not an international border.

River border: International borders of any of the first three categories which run along rivers or lakes.

Wadi border: International borders of any of the first three categories which run along wadis (seasonal watercourses).

State border: Border used in some large countries to show their internal divisions.

Main road

Main railway

Main canal

Main oceanic shipping route

PARIS *Capital city*

ALBANY *State or administrative capital*

Lyons *Major town*

Tampico *Other important town*

⊕ *Major international airport*

⚓ *Major port*

River

Waterfall

Wadi (seasonal watercourse)

Lake

Seasonal lake

▲ 3,000 m *Spot height of mountains*

▼ -3,000 m *Spot depth of oceans*

Abbreviations: *The following abbreviations are used on maps:*

Arch. = Archipelago
C. = Cape
Fr. = France
L. = Lake
I. = Island
Is. = Islands
Mts. = Mountains
Neth. = Netherlands
NZ. = New Zealand

Pen. = Peninsula
R. = River
Res. = Reservoir
Fed. = Federation
W. = Wadi
UK = United Kingdom
USA = United States of America

HOW TO USE THIS ATLAS

THE MAPS IN THIS ATLAS are organized by continent: North America; Central and South America; Europe; Africa; North and West Asia; South and East Asia; Oceania. Each section of the book opens with a large double page spread introducing you to the physical geography – landscapes, climate, animals and vegetation – of the continent. On the following pages, the continent is divided by country, or group of countries. These pages deal with the human geography; each detailed map is supplemented by photographs, illustrations and landscape models. Finally, a glossary defines difficult terms used in the text, and the index provides a list of all place names in the Atlas and facts about each country.

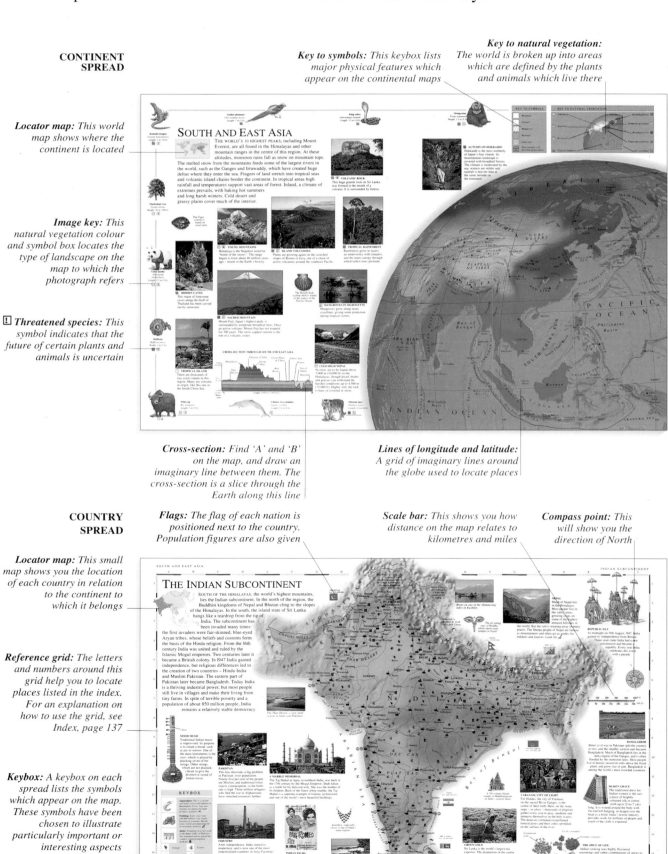

CONTINENT SPREAD

Locator map: This world map shows where the continent is located

Image key: This natural vegetation colour and symbol box locates the type of landscape on the map to which the photograph refers

⚠ *Threatened species: This symbol indicates that the future of certain plants and animals is uncertain*

Key to symbols: This keybox lists major physical features which appear on the continental maps

Key to natural vegetation: The world is broken up into areas which are defined by the plants and animals which live there

Cross-section: Find 'A' and 'B' on the map, and draw an imaginary line between them. The cross-section is a slice through the Earth along this line

Lines of longitude and latitude: A grid of imaginary lines around the globe used to locate places

COUNTRY SPREAD

Locator map: This small map shows you the location of each country in relation to the continent to which it belongs

Reference grid: The letters and numbers around this grid help you to locate places listed in the index. For an explanation of how to use the grid, see Index, page 137

Keybox: A keybox on each spread lists the symbols which appear on the map. These symbols have been chosen to illustrate particularly important or interesting aspects of the country

Flags: The flag of each nation is positioned next to the country. Population figures are also given

Scale bar: This shows you how distance on the map relates to kilometres and miles

Compass point: This will show you the direction of North

HOW THIS ATLAS WAS MADE

MAKING UP-TO-DATE and accurate maps of the world is a complicated process which draws upon the skills of geographers, researchers, cartographers (or map-makers) and designers. The maps in the *Eyewitness Atlas of the World* are completely new. They have been created using the latest computerized techniques. At the heart of this process was the development of a computerized model of the Earth. Computers store vast amounts of information. Cartographers used this technology to create precise maps, which may be regarded as the most accurate representation of the Earth's surface achieved in atlas form.

MAPS AND PROJECTIONS

Map-makers have a problem: the Earth is round, but a map is flat. In order to represent a curved surface on a flat page, the image of the Earth's surface needs to be stretched and distorted. The mathematical way of achieving this is by using a projection. There are three main types of projection used in this atlas.

CYLINDRICAL PROJECTION

This is most commonly used to make maps of the whole world. The image is rolled out to form a rectangular shape. The image becomes distorted as it moves away from the Equator towards the poles.

CONIC PROJECTION

This is useful for making regional maps and is most often used in this atlas. Distortion occurs as lines converge as they move away from the centre of the map.

ORTHOGRAPHIC PROJECTION

This kind of projection is useful for mapping polar regions. The image appears as though you were looking at the Earth from Space. Distortion increases as you move away from the centre of the map.

THE EARTH MODEL

To create a faithful representation of the Earth's relief – the shape of coastlines, mountains, valleys and plains – an enormous model of the Earth (called a "terrain model") was constructed using a computer. This was achieved by combining and processing various sets of data. Then other features, such as roads, railways, place names and coloured vegetation areas, were added to complete each map.

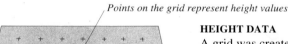

Points on the grid represent height values

HEIGHT DATA

A grid was created which covers the whole of the Earth's surface. Each point on the grid has an accurate height value. The grid was fed into the computer, and formed the basic framework for the terrain model.

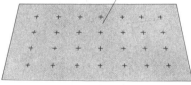

Data records the height of individual hills and mountains

LARGE SCALE MAPS

For large-scale maps, this basic framework was combined with a data set of land heights, which record the height of the summit of every hill and mountain. This produced a much more detailed framework for the terrain model.

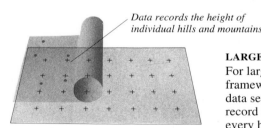

Lines join the height points to create a model

PRODUCING THE TERRAIN MODEL

The computer then transformed these elevation points into a basic terrain model known as a wire-frame model. The computer does this by joining the individual height points with lines, creating a realistic image of the Earth's surface.

Colour is added to the wire-frame model

THEMATIC MODELS

Models such as these appear on various pages throughout the Atlas. By adding various layers of extra information and annotations, they are a useful diagrammatic way of showing how the landscape of a particular region works.

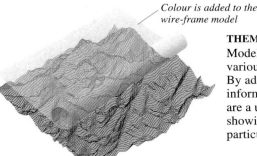

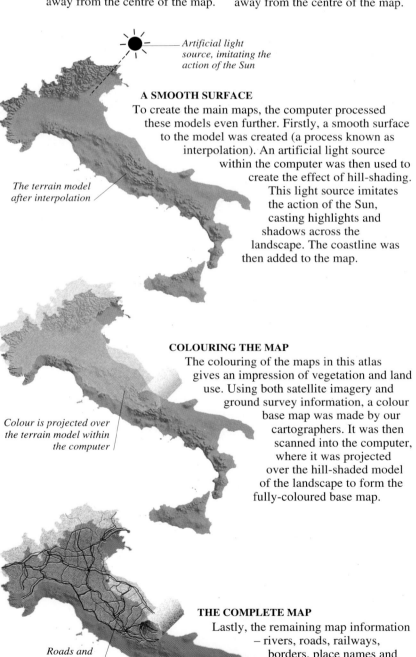

Artificial light source, imitating the action of the Sun

A SMOOTH SURFACE

To create the main maps, the computer processed these models even further. Firstly, a smooth surface to the model was created (a process known as interpolation). An artificial light source within the computer was then used to create the effect of hill-shading. This light source imitates the action of the Sun, casting highlights and shadows across the landscape. The coastline was then added to the map.

The terrain model after interpolation

COLOURING THE MAP

The colouring of the maps in this atlas gives an impression of vegetation and land use. Using both satellite imagery and ground survey information, a colour base map was made by our cartographers. It was then scanned into the computer, where it was projected over the hill-shaded model of the landscape to form the fully-coloured base map.

Colour is projected over the terrain model within the computer

THE COMPLETE MAP

Lastly, the remaining map information – rivers, roads, railways, borders, place names and other symbols – were carefully compiled from the most up-to-date sources. These were traced into the computer and combined with the coloured landscape image to create the finished map.

Roads and railways are added to the coloured terrain model

Desert swallowtail
Papilio coloro
Wingspan: 7 cm (3 in)

Collared lizard
Crotaphytus collaris
Length: 35 cm (14 in)

Raccoon
Procyon lotor
Length: 66 cm (26 in)

NORTH AMERICA

NORTH AMERICA FORMS a gigantic downward-pointing triangle, out of which two great bites have been taken – Hudson Bay and the Gulf of Mexico. Huge parallel mountain chains run down the eastern and western sides. The oldest are the Appalachians to the east, which have been worn away by wind and rain for so long that they are now considerably lower than the younger Rockies to the west. The vast landscape between the mountain chains is very flat. There are large forests in the north, while the central Great Plains are covered by grasslands on which huge herds of bison once roamed. North America is a continent of climatic extremes. In the farthest north, temperatures drop to a freezing -66°C (-87°F), and a dome of ice up to 3 km (2 miles) thick covers Greenland. In the hot deserts of the south-west, temperatures can soar to 57°C (134°F).

Triceratops, a vegetarian dinosaur that lived in western North America 70 million years ago.

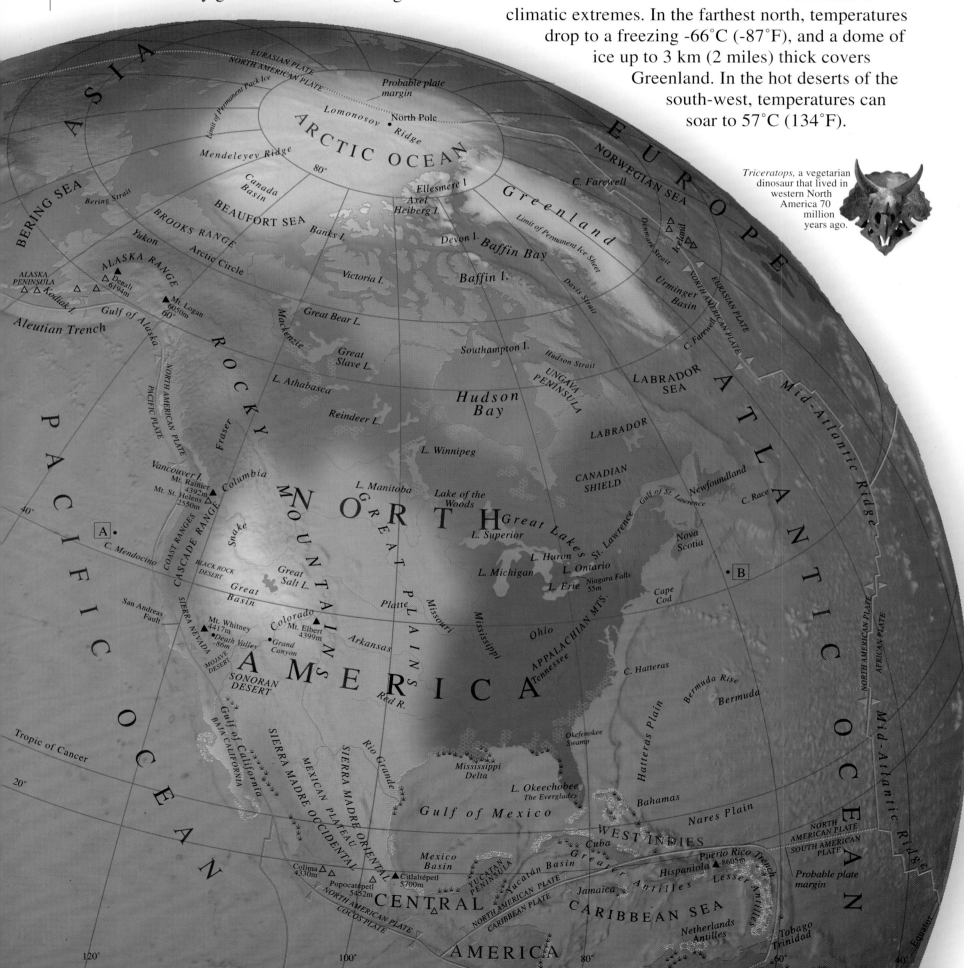

Douglas fir cone
Pseudotsuga menziesii
Length: 8 cm (3 in)

Road runner
Geococcyx californianus
Length: 60 cm (2 ft)

Loggerhead turtle
Caretta caretta
Length: 1.2 m (4 ft)

AUTUMN IN ALASKA
Only tundra – short grasses, low shrubs and small trees – can survive the northern climate. In the brief Alaskan summer plants burst into bloom, changing colour in the autumn.

THE ROOF OF AMERICA
When water-laden ocean air rises over the Alaska Range, moisture freezes and falls as snow. It is so cold that mountain slopes as low as 900 m (3,000 ft) are always snow-covered.

Eutrephoceras, which lived in North America 100 million years ago. It swam by squirting water out of its body cavity.

VOLCANIC ACTIVITY
The volcanic island of Iceland is part of the Mid-Atlantic Ridge. Intense heat generated deep underground creates bubbling hot mud pools and hot springs.

Coast redwood
Sequoia sempervirens
Height: 100 m (330 ft)

Priscacara, a perch that swam in North America's lakes and rivers 50 million years ago.

RAINFORESTS
Temperate rainforests thrive between the Pacific and the Coast Ranges. Their lush growth is made possible by heavy rainfall carried inland by moist ocean winds.

RIVERS, TREES AND GRASSLAND
For millions of years rivers flowing east from the Rockies have deposited silt on the Great Plains. This has helped to create a deep and very fertile soil which supports huge areas of grassland.

NORTHERN FORESTS
Forests grow across most of the northern region and on cold mountain slopes. These contain mostly needleleaf trees which are well suited to growing in cold conditions.

Bald eagle
Haliaeetus leucocephalus
Wingspan: 2.2 m (7 ft)

DRY WINDS AND SAND DUNES
Dry winds blowing from the centre of the continent, combined with the lack of rain, are responsible for the extensive deserts in the south-west. Because the climate is so dry, vegetation is sparse.

DESERT RIVER
The brown silt-laden waters of the Colorado River have cut a spectacular gorge through solid rock – the Grand Canyon. It is nearly 2,000 m (6,135 ft) deep.

OKEFENOKEE SWAMP
Okefenokee Swamp is part of the complex river system of the south-east. This large wetland area has a warm climate, providing a haven for reptiles such as alligators and snakes. It is also an important resting place for many migratory birds.

American beaver
Castor canadensis
Length: 1.6 m (5 ft)

DESERT TREES
With searing temperatures and low rainfall, deserts are home to plants which are adapted to conserve water, like cacti and the Joshua Trees shown here.

KEY TO SYMBOLS

▲	*Mountain*
△	*Volcano*
⚘	*Mangroves*
	Wetlands
	Coral reef
	Plate margins showing direction of movement

KEY TO NATURAL VEGETATION

Mountain

Temperate rainforest

Cold desert

Mediterranean-type

Hot desert

Dry woodland

Tundra

Needleleaf forest

Temperate grassland

Broadleaf forest

Tropical rainforest

CROSS-SECTION THROUGH NORTH AMERICA

Great Basin
Lake Michigan
Mississippi
Lake Erie
Coast Ranges
Great Plains
Appalachians Mts.
Pacific Ocean
Rocky Mts.
Cape Cod
Atlantic Ocean

3,000 (9,843)
Sea level 0
-4,500 (-14,764)
Metres (feet)

A   *Length: 5,800 km (3,600 miles)*   B

Hooded seal
Cystophora cristata
Length: 3 m (10 ft)

Moose
Alces alces
Shoulder height: 2 m (7 ft)

21

WESTERN CANADA AND ALASKA

THOUSANDS OF YEARS AGO the first people to settle in North America crossed the Bering Strait and arrived in present-day Alaska. Their descendants – peoples such as the Inuit (Eskimos) – still inhabit this region. European emigrants began to arrive in large numbers in the 19th century. Alaska was bought by the USA from Russia for $7.2 million in 1867. Many Americans thought this was a waste of money until gold was discovered there in 1896 and then oil in 1968. Canada is a huge country with a small population, most of whom live in cities within about 160 km (100 miles) of the Canada-US border. The fertile plains and dense forest in the south give way to tundra and icefields further north.

ALASKAN OIL
The USA's largest oilfield is at Prudhoe Bay in Alaska. But drilling is made difficult by temperatures as low as -79° C (-110° F), ground that is frozen for most of the year, and long periods of darkness in winter.
Look for

UNITED STATES
POP: 255,082,000
(ALASKA)
POP: 587,000

PIPELINE
When the 1,270 km (795 miles) long Trans-Alaskan pipeline from Prudhoe Bay to the ice-free port of Valdez was constructed, it was feared it would harm the environment and wildlife of this remote and beautiful region. To prevent disruption to the moose and caribou migration routes, and to stop the pipeline from freezing, it was raised on stilts above ground. The pipeline crosses plains, mountain ranges and several rivers on its southerly journey.

LOGGING
About 40 per cent of Canada is covered in forest. Until recently, there were no controls on logging, and huge areas of forest were cut down. Trees like this one are used to make lumber or plywood. Look for

KEYBOX

Oil: *Alberta is rich in oil, but new sources are being sought, such as the tar sands near Athabasca where the oil has to be separated from the sand. Look for*

Border: *The world's longest undefended border runs between Canada and the USA. People and goods can cross it with few restrictions. Look for*

Radar: *The joint Canada-US Distant Early Warning system has been a key component in the defence of the North American continent since 1957. Look for*

🐂	Cattle	⛏	Mining
🌾	Cereals	⛏	Coal
🌲	Timber	🛢	Gas
🐟	Fishing	🏭	Industrial centre

CALGARY STAMPEDE
The city of Calgary in Alberta started life as a centre of the cattle trade. Although today it is an oil centre, its cowboy traditions are continued in the Stampede, a huge rodeo held every July. For ten days spectators watch displays that include bronco-busting, bull-riding and chuck-wagon racing.

VANCOUVER
This city began as a small settlement for loggers and is now a major port. Grain from Canada's prairies and timber from its forests are shipped from Vancouver's ice-free harbour to countries across the Pacific. The city has attracted many immigrants; at first from Europe, then Asia and, most recently, from Hong Kong.

Brilliant autumn colours in British Columbia.

Map labels

ARCTIC OCEAN
Bering Strait
Kotzebue Sound
Colville
BROOKS RANGE
Barrow
BEAUFO...
Mackenzi... Bay
Tuktoyaktuk
Prudhoe Bay
Gold
Kotzebue
Nome
Norton Sound
Yukon
Porcupine
Old Crow
Inuvik
Ft. McPherson
St. Lawrence I.
St. Matthew I.
Nunivak I.
Bethel
ALASKA (USA)
Fairbanks
Gold
Yukon
Dawson
Norman W...
IN...
Attu I.
Agattu I.
Kiska I.
Adak I.
Atka I.
Amlia I.
Aleutian Islands
BERING SEA
Umnak I.
Dutch Harbor
Unalaska I.
Unimak I.
Bristol Bay
Iliamna L.
ALASKA RANGE
Dairy
Palmer
Anchorage
Kenai
Homer
Seward
Valdez
Tanana
Pelly
YUKON TERRITORY
Norman W...
Shelikof Strait
Kodiak
Kodiak I.
Gulf of Alaska
Kluane L.
Lead
Silver
Faro
Zinc
Haines Junction
WHITEHORSE
C...
Teslin L.
Skagway
Haines
Watson Lake
ROCKY MO...
JUNEAU
Sitka
Fort...
Petersburg
Wrangell
Alexander Archipelago
Ketchikan
PACIFIC OCEAN
Queen Charlotte Is.
Prince Rupert
Kitimat
Silver
Copper
Nechako
Princ... Georg...
Queen Charlotte Sound
BRITIS...
COLUM...
Port Alice
Campbell River
Kar... Squar...
Vancouver I.
Trans-Canada Highway
Vanco...
VICTOR...

Mountains are mirrored in Lake Louise, Alberta.

Caribou roam the northern parts of Canada and Alaska.

TRANSPORT

In a country as vast as Canada, transport is vital. When the Canadian Pacific Railway was completed in 1885, the country's east and west coasts were linked for the first time. Roads like the Trans-Canada Highway also helped to open up the country, especially the wilderness areas. Here, a highway crosses a spectacular part of Alberta.

SALMON FISHING

The main fish caught on Canada's west coast is the Pacific salmon. The bulk of the catch is canned. The cans are made at aluminium smelting plants like the one at Kitimat, where the plant is powered by hydro-electricity produced by the damming and reversing of the Nechako River. Look for

Pacific salmon

Edmontonia, a dinosaur once found in Alberta.

KWAKIUTL

The Kwakiutl, among the first peoples to settle along Canada's west coast, were skilled artisans. Families displayed their wealth and prestige in posts carved with animal and human figures. Other carved pieces were created for the *potlach*, a celebration of gift giving. When this was banned in 1884, many artifacts were destroyed. Since the 1950s, native artists have revived the traditional techniques.

SNOWSHOES

Snowshoes, made from wooden frames strung with animal gut or leather strips, were once essential for winter travel. They are still used in areas where vehicles, such as snowmobiles, cannot manoeuvre.

THE PRAIRIES

Grain production on the vast prairies of western Canada is highly mechanized; one farmer can harvest several hundred hectares (acres) single-handed. After the grain is cut, it is stored in huge grain elevators like these before being sent by rail to cities or ports. Railways were the key to the development of farming on the prairies. Look for

Harvesting grain on the fertile prairies of Saskatchewan.

CANADA
POP: 27,800,000
(WESTERN CANADA)
POP: 8,062,000

EASTERN CANADA

THE VIKINGS WERE THE FIRST Europeans to visit eastern Canada in about ad 986. Then, in the 15th and 16th centuries two expeditions, one from England and one from France, reached Canada and each claimed it. Traders and fur trappers from the two countries followed, setting up rival trading posts and settlements. The struggle for territory led to war between Britain and France. The French were forced to give up their Canadian territories to Britain in 1763, but the French language is still spoken in the province of Quebec today. Canada eventually achieved effective independence from Britain in 1867. Today, southern Quebec and Ontario form eastern Canada's main industrial region, containing most of its population and two of its largest cities – Montreal and Toronto. The Hudson Bay area, while rich in minerals, is a wilderness of forests, rivers and lakes. Snowbound for much of the year, it is sparsely inhabited except by Inuit in the far north.

The Toronto Sky Dome, a huge stadium which seats 50,000.

FRENCH / ENGLISH
Most Canadians speak English, but the country is officially bilingual – as can be seen from the use of both French and English on this stamp which commemorates the province of New Brunswick.

Canada 32
New Brunswick 1784-1984
Nouveau Brunswick

The sap of the sugar maple tree is made into syrup and sugar. The maple leaf is Canada's national symbol.

CANADA
POP: 27,800,000
(EASTERN CANADA)
POP: 19,738,000

Evergreen and silver birch forests in southern Quebec.

TORONTO
The CN tower – the world's tallest free-standing structure – dominates the skyline of Toronto, seen here across the waters of Lake Ontario. Toronto is Canada's biggest city, the main commercial and industrial centre, and an important port. Its wealthy, multi-cultural population includes Italians, Chinese, Greeks and Poles.

INDUSTRY
Ontario is Canada's most important industrial province, and produces about 55 per cent of the country's manufactured goods. Electronics, steel and food processing are among the major industries, but cars are Ontario's main manufacturing industry and largest export. Many of the factories are owned by US multi-national companies.
Look for ⚒

ICE HOCKEY
In winter, Canadians play or watch their favourite sport: ice hockey. The country produces some of the best players in the world.

Thousand Island salad dressing

Salad dressing, named after the islands in the St. Lawrence River.

The Canadian or Horseshoe Falls at Niagara.

KEYBOX

Potatoes: The Atlantic provinces, especially Prince Edward Island, grow some of North America's finest potatoes – seed-potatoes in particular. Look for 🌱

Mining: Canada is rich in iron ore, nickel, gold, silver and other minerals and is the world's leading uranium exporter – mainly from Ontario. Look for ⛑

High-tech industry: Ottawa has most of the electronics and computer companies in Canada, centred on an area known as Silicon Valley North. Look for 🖥

🛥 Mixed fruit		⚓ Shellfishing	
⚒ Timber		⚡ Hydro-electricity	
🦴 Fishing		🏭 Industrial centre	

THE MOUNTIES
The Royal Canadian Mounted Police – the Mounties – were established in 1873 during the opening up of the vast areas in the west to trade and industry. Today, they are one of the world's most efficient and sophisticated police forces, with their headquarters in Ottawa.

OTTAWA
These Parliament Buildings in Ottawa, Canada's capital city, were inspired by the British Houses of Parliament. Many older buildings reflect the city's British origins. Others, such as the National Gallery, are thoroughly modern.

Hudson Bay

MANITOBA

C. Henrietta Ma

Severn

Winisk

C A

Attawapiskat

Attawapiskat

Akimiski

O N T A R I O

Gold

L. Seul

Albany

Gold

Kenora

Lake of the Woods

Nakina

L. Nipigon

James

Iron

Platinum

Copper

Nickel Z

Thunder Bay

Gold

Gold

Cochr

Gold

Timmins

UNITED

Lake Superior

Wawa

Uranium

Uranium

Sault Sainte Marie

Nickel

Co

Sudbury

STATES

Copper

Platin

Lake Huron

Lake Michigan

OF

AMERICA

Ow Sou

Kitch

Sarnia

London

Windsor

L. Erie

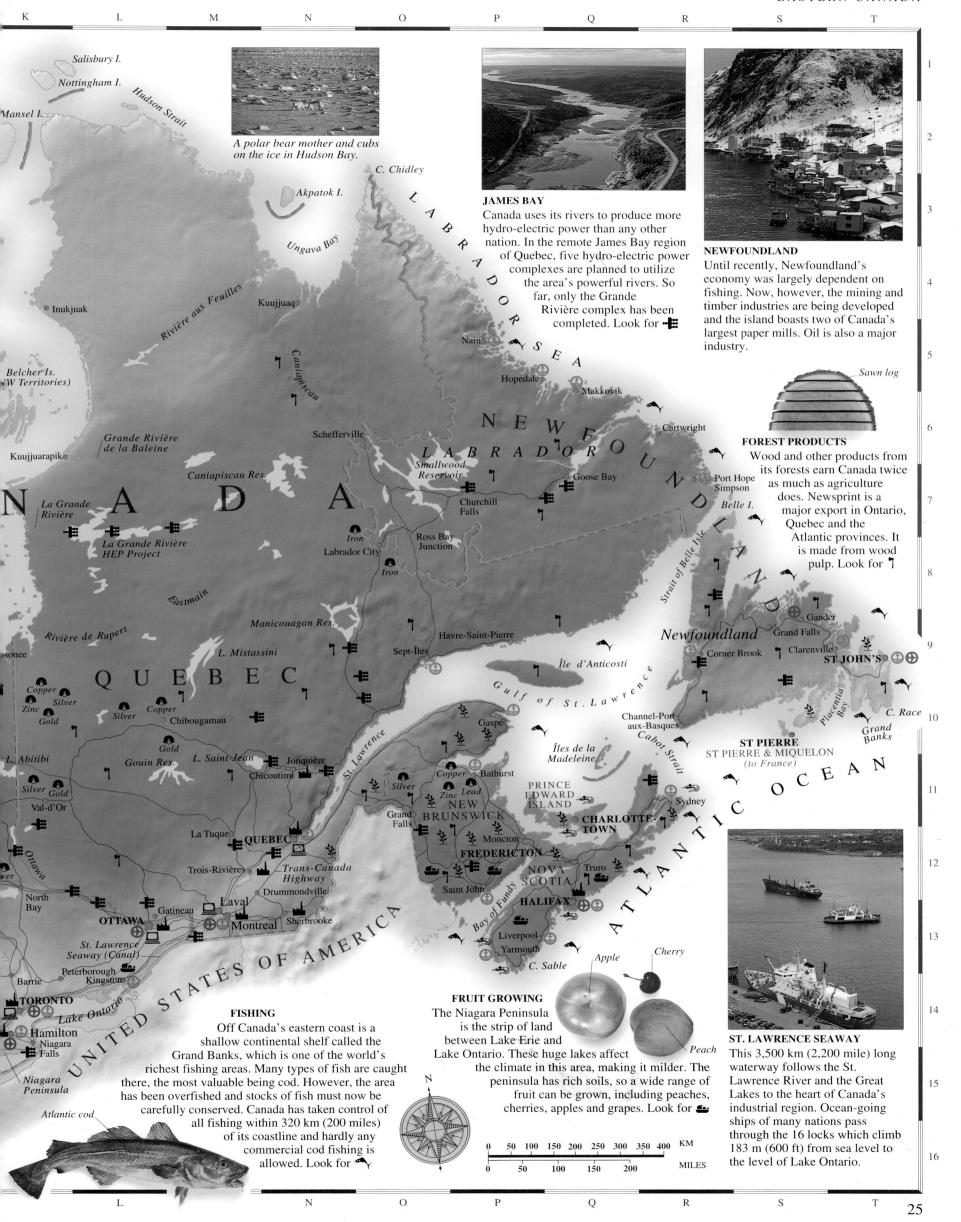

K   L   M   N   O   P   Q   R   S   T

A polar bear mother and cubs on the ice in Hudson Bay.

JAMES BAY
Canada uses its rivers to produce more hydro-electric power than any other nation. In the remote James Bay region of Quebec, five hydro-electric power complexes are planned to utilize the area's powerful rivers. So far, only the Grande Rivière complex has been completed. Look for

NEWFOUNDLAND
Until recently, Newfoundland's economy was largely dependent on fishing. Now, however, the mining and timber industries are being developed and the island boasts two of Canada's largest paper mills. Oil is also a major industry.

Sawn log

FOREST PRODUCTS
Wood and other products from its forests earn Canada twice as much as agriculture does. Newsprint is a major export in Ontario, Quebec and the Atlantic provinces. It is made from wood pulp. Look for

FISHING
Off Canada's eastern coast is a shallow continental shelf called the Grand Banks, which is one of the world's richest fishing areas. Many types of fish are caught there, the most valuable being cod. However, the area has been overfished and stocks of fish must now be carefully conserved. Canada has taken control of all fishing within 320 km (200 miles) of its coastline and hardly any commercial cod fishing is allowed. Look for

Atlantic cod

FRUIT GROWING
The Niagara Peninsula is the strip of land between Lake Erie and Lake Ontario. These huge lakes affect the climate in this area, making it milder. The peninsula has rich soils, so a wide range of fruit can be grown, including peaches, cherries, apples and grapes. Look for

Apple *Cherry* *Peach*

ST. LAWRENCE SEAWAY
This 3,500 km (2,200 mile) long waterway follows the St. Lawrence River and the Great Lakes to the heart of Canada's industrial region. Ocean-going ships of many nations pass through the 16 locks which climb 183 m (600 ft) from sea level to the level of Lake Ontario.

N

0   50   100   150   200   250   300   350   400   KM
0   50   100   150   200   MILES

Map labels:
Salisbury I., Nottingham I., Mansel I., Hudson Strait, Akpatok I., C. Chidley, Ungava Bay, LABRADOR SEA, Inukjuak, Kuujjuaq, Rivière aux Feuilles, Nain, Hopedale, Makkovik, Cartwright, Belcher Is. (NW Territories), Kuujjuarapik, Caniapiscau, Schefferville, NEWFOUNDLAND, LABRADOR, Smallwood Reservoir, Goose Bay, Port Hope Simpson, Belle I., Grande Rivière de la Baleine, Caniapiscau Res., Churchill Falls, Strait of Belle Isle, CANADA, La Grande Rivière, La Grande Rivière HEP Project, Iron, Labrador City, Iron, Ross Bay Junction, Gander, Grand Falls, Newfoundland, Corner Brook, Clarenville, ST JOHN'S, Eastmain, Manicouagan Res., Havre-Saint-Pierre, Sept-Îles, Île d'Anticosti, Rivière de Rupert, L. Mistassini, QUEBEC, Copper, Silver, Zinc, Gold, Silver, Copper, Chibougamau, Gold, Gouin Res., L. Saint-Jean, Jonquière, Chicoutimi, Gulf of St. Lawrence, Channel-Port-aux-Basques, Cabot Strait, Grand Banks, C. Race, Placentia Bay, ST PIERRE, ST PIERRE & MIQUELON (to France), Gaspé, Copper, Bathurst, Silver, Zinc, Lead, Îles de la Madeleine, PRINCE EDWARD ISLAND, Sydney, ATLANTIC OCEAN, Silver, Gold, Val-d'Or, L. Abitibi, St. Lawrence, NEW BRUNSWICK, Grand Falls, Moncton, CHARLOTTE-TOWN, La Tuque, QUEBEC, FREDERICTON, NOVA SCOTIA, Truro, Trois-Rivières, Drummondville, Saint John, HALIFAX, Ottawa, North Bay, Laval, Sherbrooke, Bay of Fundy, OTTAWA, Gatineau, Montreal, Liverpool, Yarmouth, St. Lawrence Seaway (Canal), Barrie, Peterborough, Kingston, C. Sable, TORONTO, Lake Ontario, Hamilton, Niagara Falls, Niagara Peninsula, UNITED STATES OF AMERICA

NORTHEASTERN UNITED STATES

THE FIRST INHABITANTS of Northeast America were the Native peoples, who made their living for thousands of years from fishing and farming. These peoples were among the first to encounter settlers from Europe in the 16th century, and their numbers were drastically reduced by warfare and contact with European diseases. Many of the first settlers, such as the Puritan pilgrims who sailed to Cape Cod on board the *Mayflower*, were victims of religious persecution, determined to found a brave new world in America. Most settlers were English, and they called the newly-discovered territory New England. They cleared land for farming, founded universities, built churches and established cities. Thanksgiving, celebrated throughout America, commemorates the end of the *Mayflower* pilgrims' first year and their successful harvest. Northeast America, with its rich mineral resources, good harbours and fast-flowing rivers, was the first area on the continent to become industrialized and urbanized. By the mid-19th century, immigrants from Europe were flocking to the USA, many of them settling in New York, or in other East Coast cities. Today, this region is the most densely populated and heavily industrialized area of the United States.

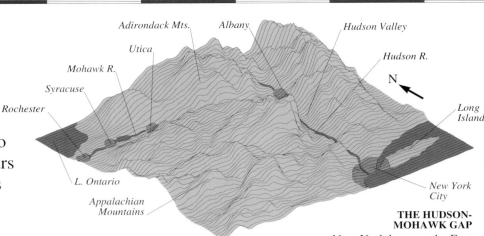

THE HUDSON-MOHAWK GAP
New York became the East Coast's leading port thanks to its fine harbour and its location at the mouth of the Hudson River. The Hudson connects with the Mohawk River, giving the city access to the continent's interior; mineral resources and industrial produce were transported along this route.

THE AMISH
This isolated Amish farmstead near Lancaster, Pennsylvania, is run without any modern technology. The Amish are a Protestant sect who came to America from Switzerland in the 18th century. They live by farming, weave all their own clothes and use horses for transport.

The spectacular Niagara Falls near Buffalo, New York State.

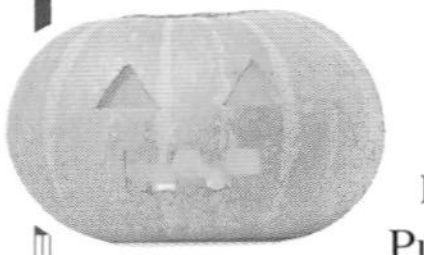

PUMPKINS
Pumpkins are grown all over New England, and pumpkin pie is a favourite American dish. Pumpkins are also hollowed out to make Jack O'Lanterns for the Hallowe'en festival.

TOMATO SOUP
Many of the fruit and vegetables for the region's big cities, especially New York, are grown in the fruit and vegetable farms, called market gardens, of New Jersey (known as "the Garden State"). Tomatoes are grown in huge quantities, and made locally into tinned tomato soup. Look for 🐂

Severe winter weather is common in New England.

KEYBOX

Sailing: Yachting is a popular pastime on New England's Atlantic coast. The Bermuda Race starts from Rhode Island. Look for ⛵

Universities: There are more centres of further education and research and development in New England than in any other part of the USA. Look for 🎓

Maple syrup: Both sugar and syrup are obtained from the sap of maple trees. Vermont is the USA's main producer. Look for ❋

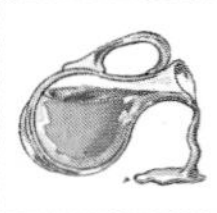

🐂	Cattle	🚢	Fishing port
🐔	Poultry	⛏	Coal
🛒	Market gardening	🏭	Industrial centre
🐟	Fishing	💻	High-tech industry

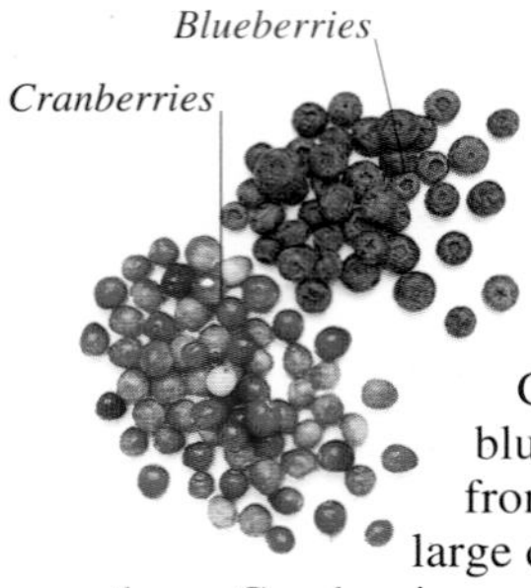

NEW ENGLAND BERRIES
Cranberries and blueberries both come from New England and large quantities are grown there. Cranberries are used in sauces, especially to go with roast turkey at Thanksgiving. Blueberries are sweeter, and are often used in pies.

Blueberries

Cranberries

UNITED STATES
POP: 255,082,000
(NORTHEASTERN STATES)
POP: 51,806,000

N

0 25 50 75 100 125 150 175 KM

0 25 50 75 100 MILES

Map labels: Adirondack Mts. · Albany · Hudson Valley · Utica · Hudson R. · Mohawk R. · Syracuse · Rochester · N · Long Island · L. Ontario · New York City · Appalachian Mountains

Map labels: CANADA · Lake Ontario · Erie Canal · Oswego · Lockport · Niagara Falls · Rochester · Batavia · Auburn · Buffalo · Geneva · NEW · Dairy · Genesee · Finger Lakes · Ithac · Dunkirk · Lake Erie · Dairy · Corning · Dai · Erie · Jamestown · Olean · Dairy · Elmira · Dairy · Meadville · Dairy · Oil City · Williamsport · Susquehanna · New Castle · PENNSYLVAN · Butler · Dairy · State College · Sunbury · Dairy · Indiana · Altoona · Lewistown · OHIO · Pittsburgh · Johnstown · Washington · APPALACHIAN MTS · HARRISBURG · Monessen · Carlisle · Dai · Uniontown · Gettysburg · York · Lancaster · WEST VIRGINIA · MARYLAND

MARITIME NEW ENGLAND

The Atlantic Ocean off New England teems with fish, and many people in this region make their living from fishing. Many towns grew wealthy as fishing and whaling ports: today, clams, mussels, lobsters, oysters and scallops are caught in large quantities. Maine lobster and clam chowder (a thick soup) are New England delicacies. Look for ⤙

VERMONT IN AUTUMN

The state of Vermont has a very small population, and much of its income comes from tourism. Visitors come to Vermont for fishing, hiking, skiing and, above all, its breathtaking mountain scenery. It is at its best in autumn, when the leaves change colour. The red leaves of the maple trees are especially striking.

Minke whales are found off the coast of Cape Cod in the summer.

Portable telephone set

HIGH-TECH

High-technology industries, such as electronics and computers, are concentrated in the Boston region and in eastern New Jersey. Universities provide expertise in research and development. There are more engineers and scientists in New Jersey than in any other state. Look for ▯

Bright yellow taxis are used in New York City.

The rugged Maine coast is popular with summer visitors.

WOODEN ARCHITECTURE

The clapboard buildings of New England copy stone and brick architecture in wood. The town of Portsmouth, New Hampshire, has outstanding examples of 18th-century wooden houses; many were built for merchants and sea captains.

RHODE ISLAND RED

Rhode Island is the smallest state in the USA. It has, however, given its name to a chicken, the Rhode Island Red, bred in the state in 1857. Used for both meat and eggs, Rhode Island Reds are now reared in Europe as well as America. Although Rhode Island is mainly industrial, poultry and dairy farming are still important. Look for ❤

Rhode Island Red cockerel

INDUSTRIAL BLIGHT

By 1900, Pennsylvania was heavily industrialized, with vast coal mines, steel mills and a heavy engineering industry. In recent years oil has replaced coal, manufacturing has declined and steel mills have closed. Today, much of Pennsylvania's industrial landscape is a desolate wasteland.

NEW YORK CITY

New York, with a population of over 7 million, is the USA's largest city. Always a major port of entry for immigrants, New York is a mix of different peoples. Manhattan is the commercial and cultural centre of the city. The Manhattan skyline and Statue of Liberty are world-famous.

The Statue of Liberty stands at the entrance to New York harbour.

THE BIG APPLE

New York City is home to many book publishers, television networks and major newspapers, dominating the national media. The stock exchange on Wall Street is the largest in the world, handling over 100 million shares a day. Nearly 100 of the largest companies in the USA are based here, and many banks have headquarters in the city.

Map labels

CANADA

MAINE

Caribou
Presque Isle
Eagle L.
Houlton
Chesuncook L.
Moosehead L.
Rockwood
West Grand L.
Calais
Eastport
Bangor
Dairy
Waterville
AUGUSTA
Lewiston
Brunswick
Portland
Biddeford
Sanford
Rochester
Dover
Portsmouth

Massena
Ogdensburg
Plattsburgh
Dairy
Burlington
Lancaster
Dairy
Rumford
Dairy
L. Champlain
MONTPELIER
WHITE MTS.
NEW HAMPSHIRE
VERMONT
NEW ENGLAND
Watertown
Dairy
Laconia
Lebanon
Rutland
Claremont
CONCORD
Manchester
Dairy
Glens Falls
Saratoga Springs
Dairy
Hudson-Mohawk Gap
Amsterdam
Schenectady
ALBANY
Bennington
Brattleboro Nashua
Greenfield
Lawrence
Lowell
Gloucester
Pittsfield
Northampton
Dairy
BOSTON
Lynn
Worcester
Springfield
MASSACHUSETTS
Cape Cod
CONNECTICUT
HARTFORD
PROVIDENCE
RHODE ISLAND
Fall River
Waterbury
Dairy
New Bedford
Danbury
Newport
New Haven
New London
Martha's Vineyard
Bridgeport
White Plains
Riverhead
Nantucket I.
Paterson
Newark
New York City
Rockville Centre
Long Island
Allentown
New Brunswick
Princeton
Long Branch
Levittown
Dairy
TRENTON
Philadelphia
Camden
Wilmington
NEW JERSEY
Newark
Vineland
Atlantic City
DOVER
Milford
DELAWARE
Georgetown
Seaford

Syracuse
Utica
Rome
Dairy
Cortland
YORK
Binghamton
CATSKILL MTS.
Kingston
Poughkeepsie
Newburgh
Middletown
Scranton
Wilkes-Barre
Hazleton
Reading
Mohawk
Delaware
Hudson
ADIRONDACK MTS.

Connecticut

Kennebec
Penobscot

ATLANTIC OCEAN

27

A B C D E F G H I J

THE SOUTHERN STATES

THIS PART OF THE USA can be divided into three broad regions. To the north, the ridges and valleys of the Appalachian Mountains form a hilly landscape, rich in coal deposits. Immediately to the south and west, the cotton-belt states, with fertile land and a warm, moist climate, are ideal for agriculture. The tropical, humid Gulf region has rich fishing resources; large cargo ports and oil terminals also line the coast. By the 19th century the South had developed an agricultural economy, based on tobacco, rice, indigo and especially cotton, cultivated by African slaves. The northern states believed that slavery in the southern states was wrong, and should be abolished. The South's defeat in the Civil War that followed devastated the region. Today, the South's economy is more varied, thanks to the discovery of oil reserves in the Gulf region and the development of industry. Florida, has experienced great population growth in recent years, becoming the fourth-largest state in the 1980s. Its population includes retired people from other states and refugees from Cuba, the Caribbean and Latin America.

Horses graze on a Kentucky farm, in the Bluegrass country.

ATLANTA
The commercial centre of the region is Atlanta, which is the hub of the South's transport network, and has one of the world's busiest airports. Raw materials flood into Atlanta and manufactured goods pour out: clothes, books, iron and steel products and Coca Cola are all made here.

DERBY DAY
Kentucky is called the "Bluegrass State" after the grasslands around the city of Lexington, which provide superb grazing for livestock. This area has the world's greatest concentration of stud farms for breeding thoroughbred horses. The Kentucky Derby, held at Louisville, is one of the world's most famous horse races.

KEYBOX

Soya beans: The main crop in the South is the soya bean. Used for oil, margarine and livestock feed, it has found both domestic and export markets. Look for

Coal: Coal, mined from the rich reserves of the Appalachian Mountains, is being overtaken by oil and gas. Look for

High-tech industry: The South, with its skilled labour force and good communications, is attracting many high-tech industries. Look for

Space centre: The Space Shuttle is launched from the Kennedy Space Center, the launch site of the US Space programme. Look for

Cereals		Fishing	
Citrus fruit		Oil	
Peanuts		Mining	
Cotton		Industrial centre	
Tobacco		Tourism	

JAZZ
Jazz developed in New Orleans in the early 1900s. Originally it was the music of the bands who marched through the streets, playing at funerals and weddings. Jazz combined many influences – "blues" and spirituals (sung by slaves) and popular songs. Wind instruments are accompanied by drums, piano and double bass.

Jazz saxophone

MISSISSIPPI
Steamboats carry tourists on scenic trips along the Mississippi, one of the world's busiest waterways. Barges transport heavy cargoes from the industrial and agricultural regions near the Great Lakes to the Gulf Coast.

Orange

Lemon

Grapefruit

Lime

Florida produces three-quarters of the USA's oranges and grapefruits.

KING COTTON
Cotton, grown on large plantations using slave labour, was once the basis of the Southern economy. Today, it is still grown on farms in some parts of the South. Look for

Okra

Prawn

Gumbo is a spicy seafood and vegetable stew from Louisiana.

BOURBON
Maize is one of Kentucky's major crops. It is used for making Bourbon whisky, which is a worldwide export.

RETIREMENT STATE
Nearly 30 per cent of Florida's inhabitants are over 55 years old. Large numbers of people retire to Florida, lured by its climate and sports facilities. Many settle in retirement developments or in the coastal cities.

Map labels

MISSOURI

OKLAHOMA

Fayetteville

BOSTON MTS.

White R. Black R.

Fort Smith

ARKANSAS

L. Ouachita

North Little Rock
LITTLE ROCK

Memph

Hot Springs

Aluminium

Arkansas

Pine Bluff

Ouachita

Mississippi

Maize

Shreveport

Greenville

TEXAS

Monroe

Yazoo

Maize

LOUISIANA

Red R.

JACKSON

Mer

Alexandria

Mississippi

MISSISSIPP

Maize

Pearl

Hattiesb

Lake Charles

Lafayette

BATON ROUGE

L. Pontchartrain
Gulfport

Marsh I.

New Orleans

Biloxi

Sulphur

Sulphur

Breton Sound

Mississippi Delta

A B C D E F G H I J

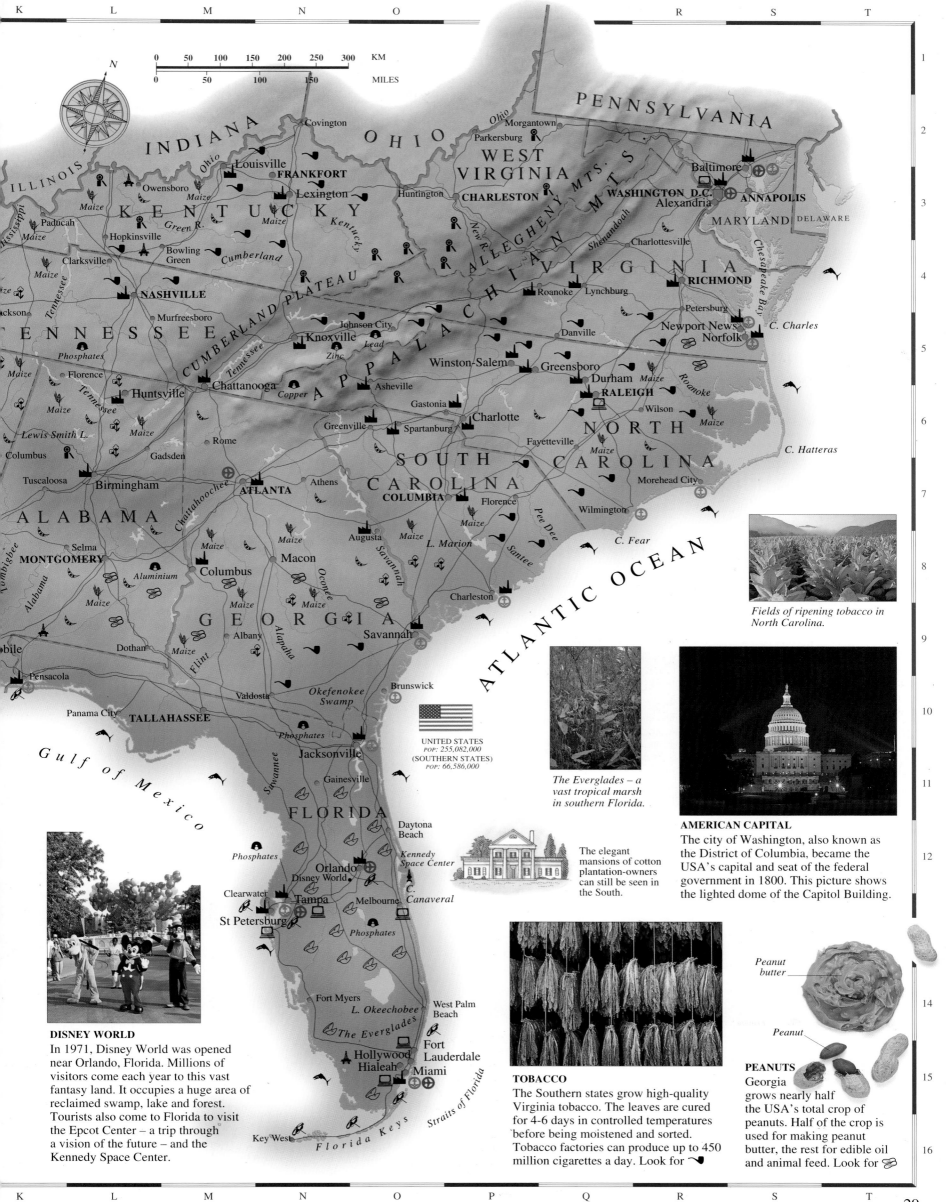

KM
0 50 100 150 200 250 300

MILES
0 50 100 150

N

ILLINOIS

INDIANA

OHIO

PENNSYLVANIA

Covington

Ohio

Morgantown

Parkersburg

WEST
VIRGINIA

Baltimore

Ohio

Louisville

FRANKFORT

Owensboro

Maize

Lexington

Huntington

CHARLESTON

WASHINGTON D.C.
Alexandria

ANNAPOLIS

Maize

KENTUCKY

Green R.

Maize

Kentucky

ALLEGHENY MTS.

MARYLAND DELAWARE

Paducah

Maize

Hopkinsville

Bowling
Green

Cumberland

Charlottesville

Shenandoah

Chesapeake Bay

Clarksville

Maize

VIRGINIA

RICHMOND

Roanoke Lynchburg

Petersburg

NASHVILLE

Murfreesboro

Johnson City

Knoxville

Lead

Danville

Newport News
Norfolk

C. Charles

TENNESSEE

Tennessee

Phosphates

Zinc

Winston-Salem

Greensboro

Durham *Maize*

RALEIGH

Maize

Florence

Chattanooga

Asheville

Copper

APPALACHIAN

Wilson

Maize

Huntsville

Maize

Gastonia

Charlotte

NORTH

C. Hatteras

Lewis Smith L.

Maize

Greenville

Spartanburg

Fayetteville

Maize

Columbus

Rome

SOUTH

CAROLINA

Gadsden

Athens

CAROLINA

Morehead City

Tuscaloosa

Birmingham

ATLANTA

COLUMBIA

Florence

Wilmington

ALABAMA

Chattahoochee

Maize

Maize

L. Marion

Pee Dee

Santee

C. Fear

MONTGOMERY

Selma

Aluminium

Columbus

Macon

Augusta

Maize

Savannah

Charleston

Maize

Oconee

Maize

Maize

GEORGIA

ATLANTIC OCEAN

bile

Dothan

Maize

Albany

Alapaha

Flint

Savannah

Pensacola

Valdosta

Okefenokee
Swamp

Brunswick

Panama City

TALLAHASSEE

Phosphates

Jacksonville

Gulf of Mexico

Suwannee

Gainesville

FLORIDA

Daytona
Beach

Kennedy
Space Center

Phosphates

Orlando
Disney World

C.
Canaveral

Clearwater

Tampa

Melbourne

St Petersburg

Phosphates

Fort Myers

L. Okeechobee

West Palm
Beach

The Everglades

Fort
Lauderdale

Hollywood
Hialeah

Miami

Key West

Florida Keys

Straits of Florida

UNITED STATES
POP: 255,082,000
(SOUTHERN STATES)
POP: 66,586,000

*Fields of ripening tobacco in
North Carolina.*

*The Everglades – a
vast tropical marsh
in southern Florida.*

AMERICAN CAPITAL
The city of Washington, also known as
the District of Columbia, became the
USA's capital and seat of the federal
government in 1800. This picture shows
the lighted dome of the Capitol Building.

The elegant
mansions of cotton
plantation-owners
can still be seen in
the South.

DISNEY WORLD
In 1971, Disney World was opened
near Orlando, Florida. Millions of
visitors come each year to this vast
fantasy land. It occupies a huge area of
reclaimed swamp, lake and forest.
Tourists also come to Florida to visit
the Epcot Center – a trip through
a vision of the future – and the
Kennedy Space Center.

TOBACCO
The Southern states grow high-quality
Virginia tobacco. The leaves are cured
for 4-6 days in controlled temperatures
before being moistened and sorted.
Tobacco factories can produce up to 450
million cigarettes a day. Look for ⌣

*Peanut
butter*

Peanut

PEANUTS
Georgia
grows nearly half
the USA's total crop of
peanuts. Half of the crop is
used for making peanut
butter, the rest for edible oil
and animal feed. Look for ⬭

THE GREAT LAKES

THE FIVE GREAT LAKES of North America – Erie, Ontario, Huron, Michigan and Superior – together form the largest area of fresh water in the world. The states of Indiana, Illinois, Michigan, Ohio, Wisconsin and Minnesota, all of which border on one or more of the lakes, are often called the industrial and agricultural heartland of the United States. This region is rich in natural resources, including coal, iron, copper and timber, and there are large areas of fertile farmland on the flat plains of the prairies. First explored by French traders, fur trappers and missionaries in the 17th century, the region began to attract large numbers of settlers in the early 1800s. Trading links were improved by the opening of the Erie Canal in 1825, which connected the region to the Atlantic Coast, while the Mississippi and other rivers gave access to the Gulf of Mexico and the rest of the continent. When railways reached the region in the 1840s, cities such as Chicago grew and prospered as freight-handling centres. Steel production and the car industry later became the main industries in the region. In recent years, a decline in these traditional industries has led to high unemployment in some areas.

Wall-eyes live in the Great Lakes, but their numbers are falling due to pollution.

HOGS
In the 19th century, huge numbers of animals from all over this region were sent to the stock-yards in Chicago for slaughter and processing. Rearing livestock is still important in Illinois. Maize and soya beans, both grown locally, are used as animal feed. Look for 🐖

HAMBURGERS
Hamburgers are America's own fast food, first produced on a massive scale in Illinois in the 1950s. It has been calculated that in every second of the day, 200 Americans are eating a hamburger. American-style hamburger take-aways can now be found all over the world.

Cherries: One-third of the world cherry crop is grown along the shores of Lake Michigan. Look for 🍒

Iron ore: Iron ore deposits are found around the shores of Lake Superior. It is mined, processed, then shipped to industrial centres in pellet form. Look for ⛑

Symbol	Label	Symbol	Label
🐂	Cattle	🌱	Soya beans
🐖	Hogs	⚜	Coal
🌾	Cereals	⛏	Oil
🥕	Sugar beet	🏭	Industrial centre
🛒	Market gardening	🚗	Vehicle manufacture

Baseball and fielder's glove. Baseball is the USA's national game.

MILWAUKEE BEER
The Great Lakes region has attracted many immigrants, especially from Germany, the Netherlands and the Scandinavian countries. Milwaukee, where many Germans settled, is home to several of the USA's largest breweries.

COLD WINTERS
The Great Lakes region has severe winters, and Minnesota, in particular, suffers from heavy snow-storms. Parts of the Great Lakes themselves can freeze over in winter, and lakeside harbours can be frozen from December to early April.

THE WINDY CITY
Chicago is situated at the southern tip of Lake Michigan. It gets its nickname – the Windy City – from the weather conditions in this area. Chicago was ideally positioned for trading with the Midwest region, and quickly became a wealthy modern city. By 1900 it had vast complexes of lumber mills, meat processing factories, railway yards and steel mills.

PRAIRIE LANDS
The fertile soil and hot, humid summers make the flat expanses of the Midwestern prairies ideal for farming. Nearly half of the world's maize crop is grown on the huge farms in this region.

An isolated farm on the open prairies of Illinois.

CORNFLAKES

Food processing is a major industry throughout this agricultural region. Wisconsin, for example, is the major producer of canned peas and sweet corn in the USA. Corn and wheat-based breakfast cereals are exported all over the world from Battle Creek, Michigan. Look for 🌱

Map labels
CANADA
MINNESOTA
NORTH DAKOTA
SOUTH DAKOTA
WISCO... (WISCONSIN)
IOWA
ILL... (ILLINOIS)
MISSOURI
Lake of the Woods
Wheat
Upper Red L.
Lower Red L.
Red Lake R.
Iron
Iron
Iron
Virginia
Bemidji
Hibbing
Leech L.
Moorhead
Mississippi
Duluth
Superior
Chequamegon Bay
Manganese
Brainerd
Mille Lacs L.
Fergus Falls
Wheat
Iron
Chippewa L.
Dairy
Dairy
St Cloud
Willmar
Beef
Maize
Dairy
Eau Claire
Minneapolis
ST PAUL
Bloomington
Stillwater
Marshfield
Maize
New Ulm
Red Wing
Iron
Wisco... Ra...
Dairy
Faribault
Mankato
Owatonna
Dairy
Wheat
Winona
Rochester
La Crosse
Fairmont
Albert Lea
Austin
Maize
Dairy
Dairy
Wisconsin
Beef
Roc... Isla...
Kew...
Galesburg
Macomb
Can...
Quincy
Jacksonvill...
Alton
East... Lo...

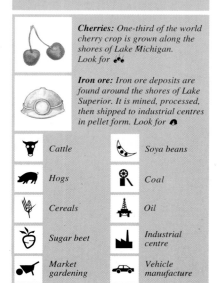

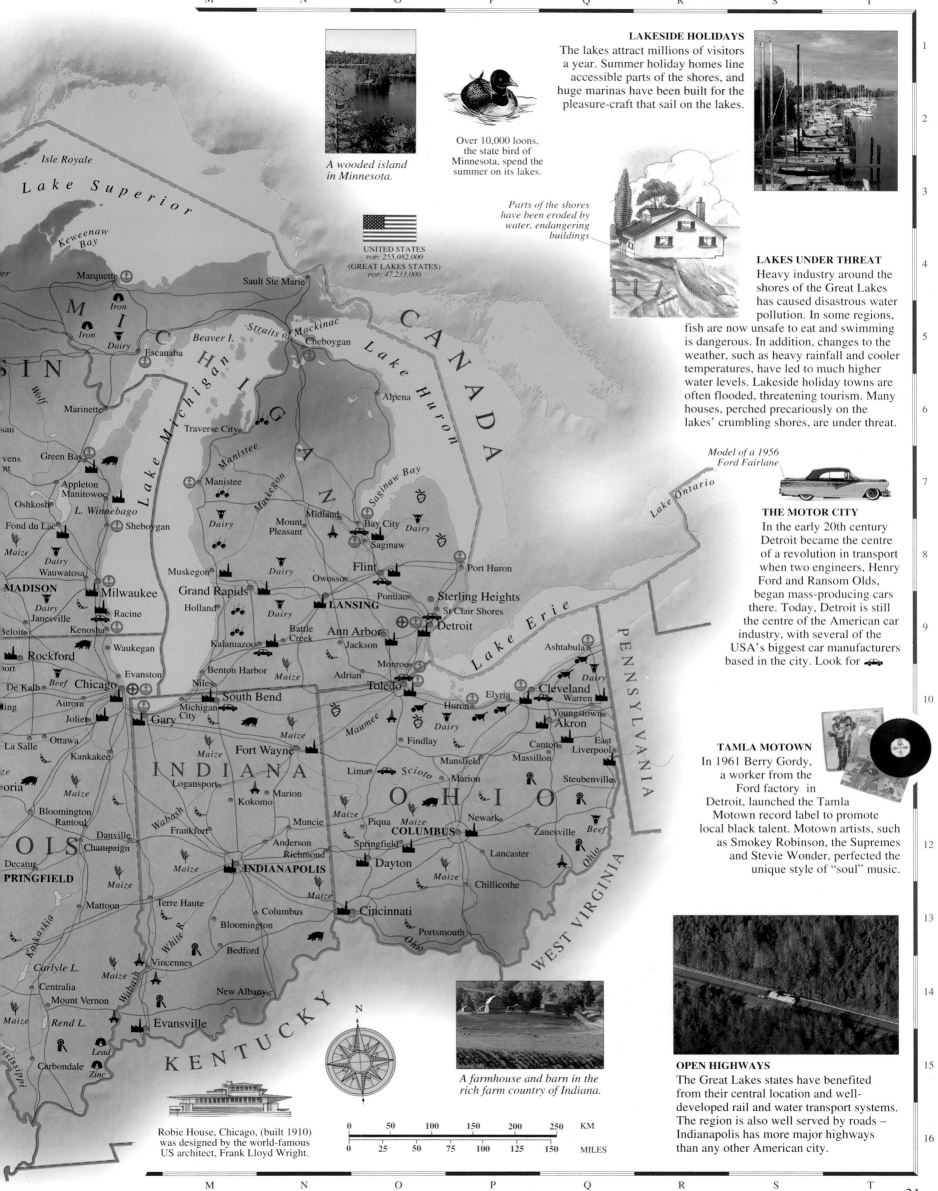

LAKESIDE HOLIDAYS

The lakes attract millions of visitors a year. Summer holiday homes line accessible parts of the shores, and huge marinas have been built for the pleasure-craft that sail on the lakes.

A wooded island in Minnesota.

Over 10,000 loons, the state bird of Minnesota, spend the summer on its lakes.

UNITED STATES
POP: 255,082,000
(GREAT LAKES STATES)
POP: 47,233,000

Parts of the shores have been eroded by water, endangering buildings

LAKES UNDER THREAT

Heavy industry around the shores of the Great Lakes has caused disastrous water pollution. In some regions, fish are now unsafe to eat and swimming is dangerous. In addition, changes to the weather, such as heavy rainfall and cooler temperatures, have led to much higher water levels. Lakeside holiday towns are often flooded, threatening tourism. Many houses, perched precariously on the lakes' crumbling shores, are under threat.

Model of a 1956 Ford Fairlane

THE MOTOR CITY

In the early 20th century Detroit became the centre of a revolution in transport when two engineers, Henry Ford and Ransom Olds, began mass-producing cars there. Today, Detroit is still the centre of the American car industry, with several of the USA's biggest car manufacturers based in the city. Look for

TAMLA MOTOWN

In 1961 Berry Gordy, a worker from the Ford factory in Detroit, launched the Tamla Motown record label to promote local black talent. Motown artists, such as Smokey Robinson, the Supremes and Stevie Wonder, perfected the unique style of "soul" music.

A farmhouse and barn in the rich farm country of Indiana.

Robie House, Chicago, (built 1910) was designed by the world-famous US architect, Frank Lloyd Wright.

OPEN HIGHWAYS

The Great Lakes states have benefited from their central location and well-developed rail and water transport systems. The region is also well served by roads – Indianapolis has more major highways than any other American city.

0 50 100 150 200 250 KM
0 25 50 75 100 125 150 MILES

CENTRAL AND MOUNTAIN STATES

THIS REGION INCLUDES the lowlands on the west bank of the Mississippi River, the vast expanses of the Great Plains, and the majestic Rocky Mountains. In climate, it is a region of extremes: hot summers alternate with cold winters, and hailstorms, blizzards and tornadoes are frequent events. Once home to large numbers of Native Americans and great herds of buffalo, the plains were settled in the 19th century; the Native Americans were pushed on to reservations and the buffalo slaughtered. Originally dismissed as a desert because of low rainfall and lack of trees, the Great Plains proved to be one of the world's great agricultural regions; today, vast amounts of cereals are grown on mechanized farms, and cattle are grazed on huge ranches. The Rockies are rich in minerals, and reserves of coal, oil and natural gas are being exploited.

The foothills of the snow-covered Rockies in Montana.

Shredded wheat

AGRICULTURAL INDUSTRIES

A great range of cereals are grown in the Midwest and transported to local cities for processing. Iowa has the largest cereal processing factory in the world, and it is in the cities of this region that many cereals are prepared for the world's breakfast tables. Cities also provide storage facilities for grain and cereals, as well as markets for grain, livestock and farm machinery.

Corn flakes   *Oats*   *Toasted rice*

COWBOYS

Cattle are raised on the Great Plains and foothills of the Rocky Mountains. Ranches often have thousands of cattle. In summer, mounted cowboys herd cattle to upland pastures and drive them back to the ranch for the winter. Cattle are then taken to markets in nearby towns for cattle auctions. Look for 🐂

WYOMING COAL

Wyoming now leads the USA in coal production. Coal from the West is in demand because it has a lower sulphur content than coal mined in the East, and causes less pollution when burnt. Shallow coal reserves are extracted from open-cast mines, like this one, which spoil the landscape. Look for ⛏

Fossils of dinosaurs, such as *Tyrannosaurus*, have been found in the foothills of the Rockies.

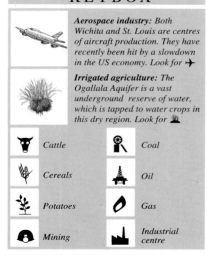

KEYBOX

✈	**Aerospace industry:** Both Wichita and St. Louis are centres of aircraft production. They have recently been hit by a slowdown in the US economy. Look for ✈
🌾	**Irrigated agriculture:** The Ogallala Aquifer is a vast underground reserve of water, which is tapped to water crops in this dry region. Look for 🌾

🐂	Cattle	⛏	Coal
🌾	Cereals	⛏	Oil
🌱	Potatoes	💧	Gas
⬤	Mining	🏭	Industrial centre

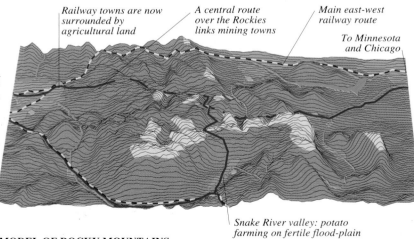

Railway towns are now surrounded by agricultural land

A central route over the Rockies links mining towns

Main east-west railway route

To Minnesota and Chicago

Snake River valley: potato farming on fertile flood-plain

N

MODEL OF ROCKY MOUNTAINS

The Rocky Mountains divide the North American continent in two; rivers to the west of the range flow towards the Pacific, while those to the east drain into the Arctic and Atlantic oceans and the Gulf of Mexico. First explored by fur trappers and traders in the 19th century, the mountain passes were used by settlers on their way west. Miners followed the settlers, and the mining towns of Montana were established. By 1869, the Transcontinental railroad had crossed the Rockies, linking the Pacific Coast with the rest of the country.

FARMING

Maize is the main crop in Iowa, while wheat is more important in the centre of this region. Nearer the Rockies, the rainfall decreases and wheat farming gives way to cattle ranching. Farming in the Midwest is large-scale and mechanized. These vast wheatfields in Nebraska stretch to the far horizon. Farmers often produce more than they can sell. Look for 🌾

Map labels:
CANADA, WASHINGTON, OREGON, NEVADA, UTAH, MONTANA, IDAHO, WYOMING
ROCKY MOUNTAINS, BITTERROOT RANGE, WIND RIVER RANGE, BIGHORN
Zinc, Lead, Coeur d'Alene, Silver, Lewiston, Salmon, Missoula, Anaconda, Butte, Copper, Dillon, Bozeman, HELENA, Canyon Ferry L., Flathead L., Kalispell, Great Falls, Shelby, Beef, Wheat, Barley, L. Elwell, Havre, Missouri, Billings, Yellowstone, Bighorn
BOISE, Nampa, Snake, Idaho Falls, Phosphate, Pocatello, Twin Falls, Beef, Wheat
Yellowstone L., Jackson L., Grand Teton Mts., Wind, Cody, Worland, Uranium, Iron, Sheridan
Rock Springs, Green R., Flaming Gorge Res., Rawlins, Pathfinder Res.

TOURISM

Huge carvings of the heads of four great American presidents – Washington, Lincoln, Jefferson and Theodore Roosevelt – can be seen at Mount Rushmore in South Dakota. Millions of people have visited the monument since its completion in 1927. The mountainous scenery and wildlife of this region attract tourists from all over the world.

Only 800 grizzly bears are left in the USA; many live in the mountains of Wyoming and Idaho.

BISON

Millions of bison (American buffalo) used to roam the Great Plains. Native Americans hunted them for food and used their hides to make clothing and shelters. Settlers and railway workers virtually wiped out the bison herds in the late 19th century, killing them for food and profit. Today, the bison population is protected and there are now about 50,000 bison living on reserves.

UNITED STATES
POP: 255,082,000
(CENTRAL & MOUNTAIN STATES)
POP: 19,050,000

The Badlands of North and South Dakota have been eroded into hills and gullies.

ON THE ROAD

An extensive road network holds this vast, sparsely-inhabited region together. Highways often run through long stretches of nearly empty land, fringed by gas stations, motels and roadside restaurants. Cars are a necessity in much of the West; in Wyoming, children of 14 can drive to school.

Popcorn, roasted and puffed-up maize, is a Midwestern export.

The Grand Teton Mountains, northern Wyoming.

GOLD RUSH

In 1874, gold was found in the Black Hills of South Dakota, a region sacred to the Sioux people. The discovery sparked a major gold rush; towns sprang up overnight, fortunes were won and lost, gambling and crime flourished. The area is still rich in minerals – South Dakota's Homestake gold mine is the biggest in the country. Look for ⛏

Broad-brimmed hats are still an essential part of the cowboy's wardrobe.

| 0 | 50 | 100 | 150 | 200 | 250 | 300 | 350 | KM |

| 0 | 50 | 100 | 150 | 200 | MILES |

Map labels

NORTH DAKOTA · SOUTH DAKOTA · MINNESOTA · WISCONSIN · IOWA · ILLINOIS · NEBRASKA · COLORADO · KANSAS · MISSOURI · OKLAHOMA · TEXAS · NEW MEXICO · ARKANSAS · KENTUCKY · TENNESSEE

Williston · Minot · Grand Forks · Glendive · Miles City · L. Sakakawea · Souris · BISMARCK · Dickinson · Jamestown · Fargo · Aberdeen · Watertown · Shadehill Res. · Moreau · Cheyenne · PIERRE · Mitchell · Belle Fourche · Black Hills · Rapid City · Mt. Rushmore · White R. · L. Francis Case · Sioux Falls · Spencer · Mason City · Dubuque · Waterloo · Cedar Rapids · Iowa City · Davenport · Yankton · Fort Dodge · Valentine · Sioux City · Ames · DES MOINES · Norfolk · Middle Loup · Torrington · Scottsbluff · Columbus · Omaha · Council Bluffs · Rathbun L. · Burlington · North Platte · Grand Island · Ogallala · LINCOLN · Maryville · Kirksville · Hastings · Harlan County L. · St Joseph · Independence · Kansas City · Columbia · St Charles · St Louis · Manhattan · TOPEKA · JEFFERSON CITY · Oakley · SMOKY HILLS · Salina · Emporia · Ottawa · L. of the Ozarks · Harry S. Truman Res. · Lead · Cape Girardeau · Smoky Hill · Hays · Great Bend · Wichita · Springfield · OZARK PLATEAU · Garden City · Hutchinson · Dodge City · Pratt · Pittsburg · Joplin · Poplar Bluff · Liberal · Arkansas City · Ponca City · OKLAHOMA CITY · Enid · Tulsa · Broken Arrow · Muskogee · Norman · Lawton · Niobrara · North Platte · Platte · Republican · Arkansas · Neosho · Chariton · Missouri · Little Missouri · Laramie · Cheyenne · Canadian R. · Red R.

A B C D I J

THE SOUTHWESTERN STATES

THE SOUTHWESTERN USA is a region of deserts and high plateaux, broken by the ridges of the southern Rocky Mountains. Many different Native American peoples lived in the Southwest. The region still has the country's largest concentration of Native Americans. The first Europeans to settle in this region were Spaniards who came north from Mexico. This mixed Spanish and Native American heritage is reflected in the region's folk art, architecture and foods. American settlers in Texas rebelled against Mexican rule in 1836, and Texas was annexed to the USA a decade later. The rest of the region became part of the USA after the Mexican War of 1846-48. Gold and silver mining and cattle-ranching attracted settlers to the region in the late 19th century, and oil became a major part of Texas's economy in the 20th century. The region's natural beauty draws tourists from all over the world.

The Saguaro cactus thrives in the deserts of Arizona.

Jordan Mormon Temple, Utah

MORMON CITY
Salt Lake City in Utah is the headquarters of the Latter-day Saints, or Mormons. They settled in Utah in the 1840s, after fleeing from the eastern states, where they had been persecuted for their beliefs. There are now more than six million Mormons worldwide.

NAVAJO RUGS
Many Navajo people live on a vast reservation in Arizona and New Mexico. They still practise weaving, pottery, silver-working and other traditional crafts. Navajo rugs are woven into geometric patterns, and coloured with natural dyes, such as juniper and blackberry.

An 11th-century pottery bowl, made by the Mogollon people.

KEYBOX

High-tech industry: The space programme has attracted high technology industries to the area. Look for 💻

Irrigated agriculture: Sprinklers fixed on central pivots create circular oases of green fields in the arid landscape. Look for 🌿

Dams: Acute water shortages are being remedied by the construction of dams on the region's rivers. Look for 🏛

Military bases: The first nuclear bombs were tested in New Mexico and Nevada. Military installations are common in the region. Look for III

Cattle		Oil
Cereals		Gas
Cotton		Industrial centre
Mining		Skiing

THE GREAT OUTDOORS
Riding, trekking, canoeing, skiing and fishing are just some of the outdoor activities which draw tourists to the Southwest. But the region's main attraction is the Grand Canyon. About 10,000 visitors each year navigate the Canyon's dangerous waters on rubber rafts, and many others explore it on foot or by donkey.

These strangely shaped rocks in Monument Valley, Arizona, have been carved by the wind.

TAOS
The *pueblo*, or village, of Taos in New Mexico is built of unbaked clay brick, called *adobe*. This style of building dates back to the Pueblo people, who lived in the region a thousand years ago, farming maize, cotton, beans and squash.

THE GRAND CANYON
Over the last million years, the Colorado River has cut its way through the rocky plateaux of northern Arizona. At the same time, the plateaux have risen. This combined action has formed the largest land gorge in the world – the Grand Canyon. It is more than 1.6 km (1 mile) deep, and 350 km (220 miles) long. Some of the oldest rocks in North America have been found at the base of the canyon.

Bright Angel Point *Colorado River* *To Lake Powell*
Grand Canyon
Eroded sediment carried down rivers creates fertile plains
To Lake Mead

N

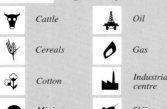

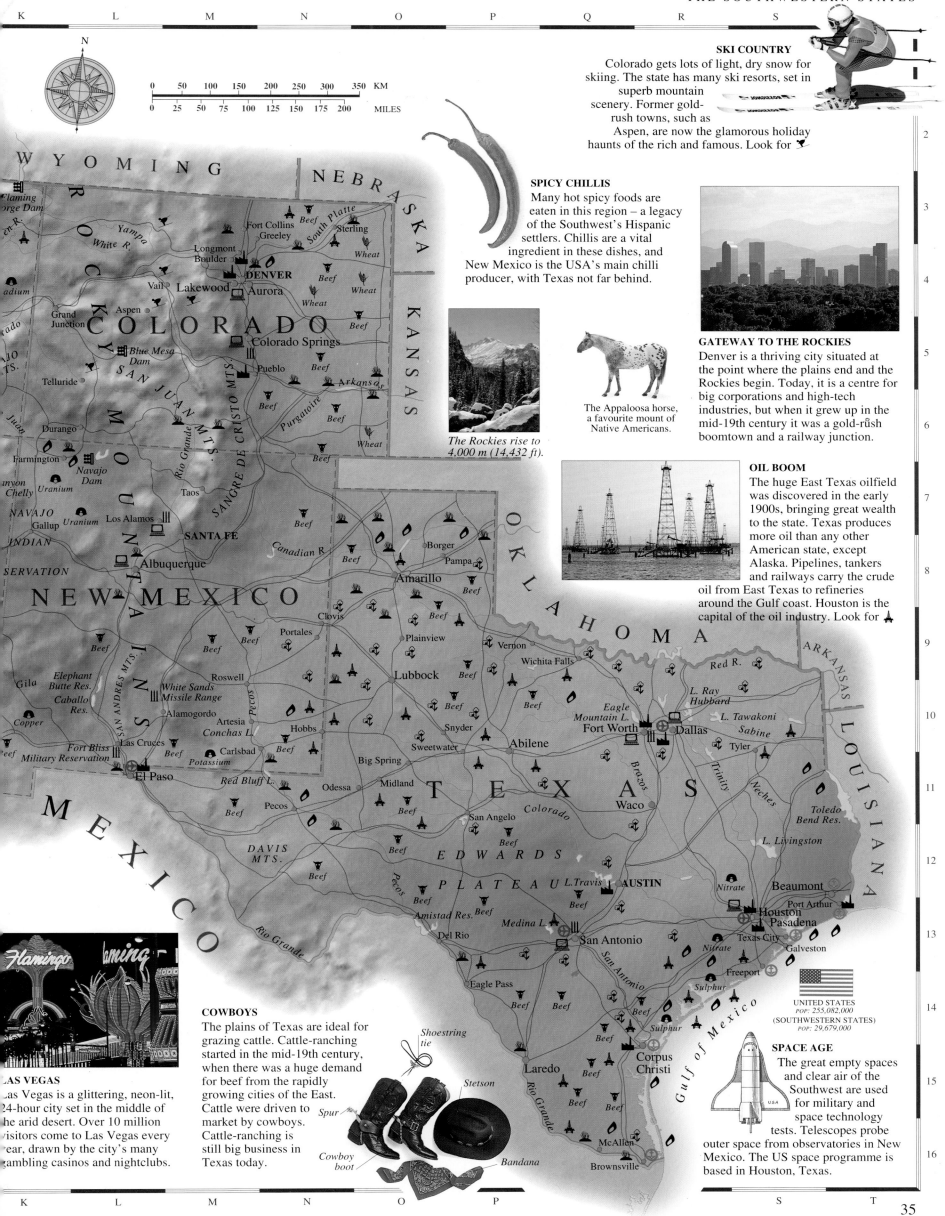

SKI COUNTRY
Colorado gets lots of light, dry snow for skiing. The state has many ski resorts, set in superb mountain scenery. Former gold-rush towns, such as Aspen, are now the glamorous holiday haunts of the rich and famous. Look for ⛷

SPICY CHILLIS
Many hot spicy foods are eaten in this region – a legacy of the Southwest's Hispanic settlers. Chillis are a vital ingredient in these dishes, and New Mexico is the USA's main chilli producer, with Texas not far behind.

GATEWAY TO THE ROCKIES
Denver is a thriving city situated at the point where the plains end and the Rockies begin. Today, it is a centre for big corporations and high-tech industries, but when it grew up in the mid-19th century it was a gold-rush boomtown and a railway junction.

The Rockies rise to 4,000 m (14,432 ft).

The Appaloosa horse, a favourite mount of Native Americans.

OIL BOOM
The huge East Texas oilfield was discovered in the early 1900s, bringing great wealth to the state. Texas produces more oil than any other American state, except Alaska. Pipelines, tankers and railways carry the crude oil from East Texas to refineries around the Gulf coast. Houston is the capital of the oil industry. Look for ⚒

LAS VEGAS
Las Vegas is a glittering, neon-lit, 24-hour city set in the middle of the arid desert. Over 10 million visitors come to Las Vegas every year, drawn by the city's many gambling casinos and nightclubs.

COWBOYS
The plains of Texas are ideal for grazing cattle. Cattle-ranching started in the mid-19th century, when there was a huge demand for beef from the rapidly growing cities of the East. Cattle were driven to market by cowboys. Cattle-ranching is still big business in Texas today.

Shoestring tie

Stetson

Spur

Cowboy boot

Bandana

UNITED STATES
POP: 255,082,000
(SOUTHWESTERN STATES)
POP: 29,679,000

SPACE AGE
The great empty spaces and clear air of the Southwest are used for military and space technology tests. Telescopes probe outer space from observatories in New Mexico. The US space programme is based in Houston, Texas.

THE PACIFIC STATES

THE PACIFIC COAST STATES boast some of the most varied scenery in the USA. California, for example, contains the snow-capped peaks of the Sierra Nevada Mountains and the lowest point in North America – Death Valley. Much of California is arid, with farming dependent on irrigation, while vast forests and well-watered fertile valleys are characteristic of Washington and Oregon. American settlers began to cross the Rockies to the Pacific coast in the 1840s. California became part of the USA as a result of the Mexican-American War (1846-48), and the discovery of gold in 1848 led to its rapid settlement. All three states are now major agricultural producers and centres of high-technology industry. In the early 1960s, California became the USA's most highly-populated state. Despite recent problems, the state's economy rivals those of many wealthy nations.

Almond

Peach

Plum

Avocado pear

AGRICULTURE
California alone produces half of the USA's fruit and vegetables. Fertile soils and a warm climate have contributed to the state's success, but dry conditions mean that much of the state's farmland has to be irrigated. California's main crops are cotton and grapes. Look for 🍇

TIMBER
Oregon and Washington are the USA's major timber producers. The region's cedar and fir forests supply one-third of the country's softwood timber. The trees are cut into logs at one of the thousands of sawmills in the forests and then floated down rivers on rafts to the large coastal cities. Some of the wood is made into paper at pulp-mills like the one pictured here. Tree-felling has reduced the region's stocks of mature trees; efforts are now being made to plant more trees. Look for 🌲

AEROSPACE
The Boeing Corporation, the world's largest aircraft manufacturer, is based in Seattle. Boeing is the city's main employer, and any decline in orders can result in unemployment. California is a major producer of military aeroplanes; cuts in US defence spending have badly affected this region. Look for ✈

Boeing 767 aircraft

Washington's Mount Rainier is permanently snow-covered.

California redwoods are evergreen trees, which can reach 100 m (330 ft).

IMMIGRATION
California attracts many immigrants from Asia and South America. Many Chinese immigrants have settled in San Francisco's Chinatown. This area of the city is a magnet for the Chinese community, and is famous for its exotic shops and restaurants. Immigrants from Latin America, especially Mexico, make up a growing part of the state's population.

Fortune-cookie, served in San Francisco's Chinese restaurants

— *Computer discs capable of storing vast amounts of information*

SILICON VALLEY
Santa Clara Valley, south of San Francisco, has one of the largest concentrations of high-technology industry in the world. Over 3,000 firms there specialize in micro-electronics and computer hardware and software. US manufacturers face increasing competition from the Far East. Look for 💾

SAN FRANCISCO
San Francisco is located on one of the world's finest natural harbours, and is the West Coast's trade and shipping centre. San Francisco is built on a hilly peninsula, with some of the steepest streets in the world. San Francisco suffers from frequent earthquakes as it is situated right on the San Andreas Fault. The city's large skyscrapers are specially designed to withstand earthquakes.

Waves batter the rugged Pacific coast of Oregon.

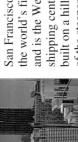

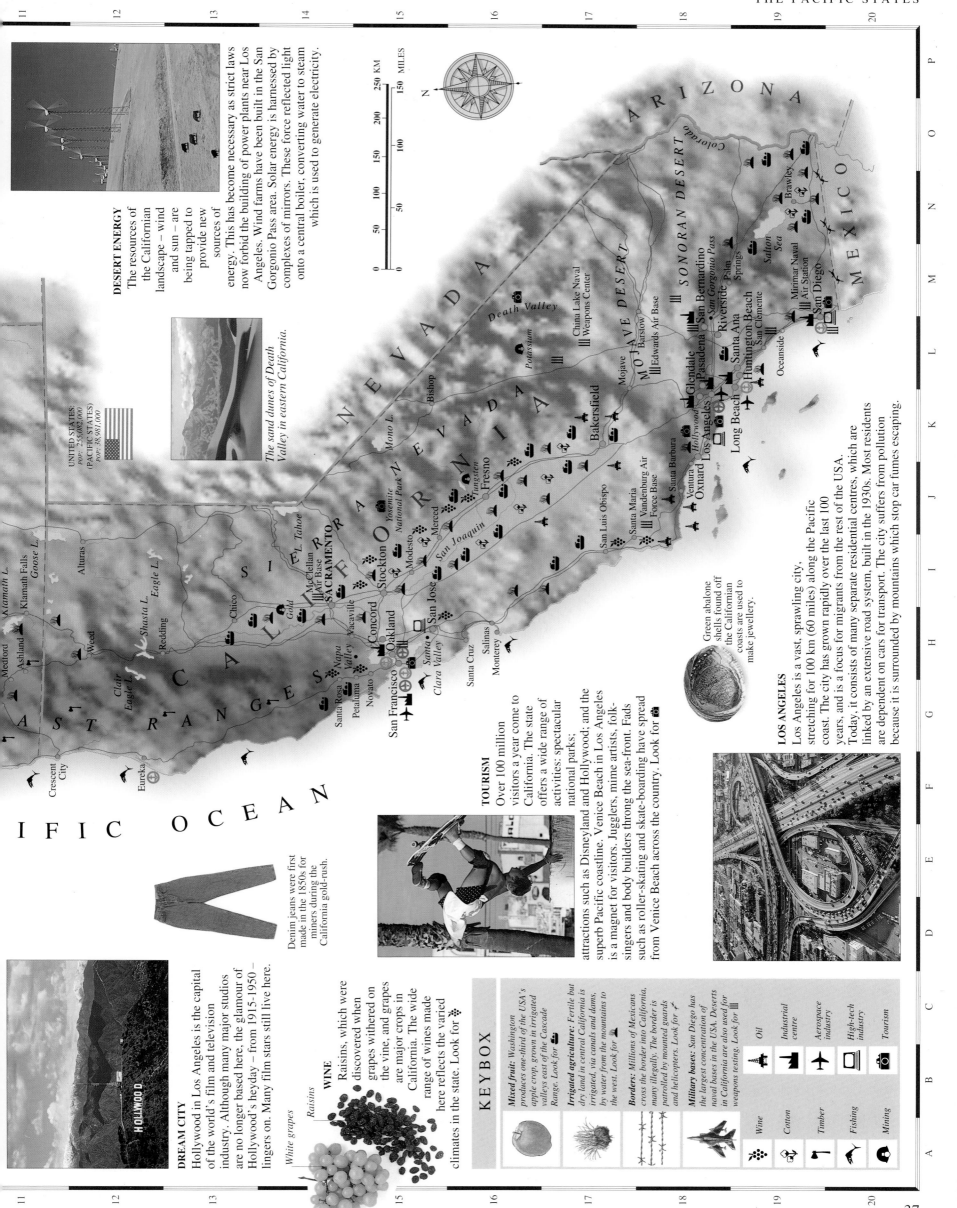

DESERT ENERGY

The resources of the Californian landscape – wind and sun – are being tapped to provide new sources of energy. This has become necessary as strict laws now forbid the building of power plants near Los Angeles. Wind farms have been built in the San Gorgonio Pass area. Solar energy is harnessed by complexes of mirrors. These force reflected light onto a central boiler, converting water to steam which is used to generate electricity.

The sand dunes of Death Valley in eastern California.

UNITED STATES
Pop: 255,082,000
(PACIFIC STATES)
Pop: 38,981,000

250 KM
150 MILES

DREAM CITY

Hollywood in Los Angeles is the capital of the world's film and television industry. Although many major studios are no longer based here, the glamour of Hollywood's heyday – from 1915–1950 – lingers on. Many film stars still live here.

HOLLYWOOD

WINE

Raisins, which were discovered when grapes withered on the vine, and grapes are major crops in California. The wide range of wines made here reflects the varied climates in the state. Look for 🍇

White grapes
Raisins

Denim jeans were first made here in the 1850s for miners during the California gold-rush.

TOURISM

Over 100 million visitors a year come to California. The state offers a wide range of activities: spectacular national parks; attractions such as Disneyland and Hollywood; and the superb Pacific coastline. Venice Beach in Los Angeles is a magnet for visitors. Jugglers, mime artists, folk-singers and body builders throng the sea-front. Fads such as roller-skating and skate-boarding have spread from Venice Beach across the country. Look for 📷

LOS ANGELES

Los Angeles is a vast, sprawling city, stretching for 100 km (60 miles) along the Pacific coast. The city has grown rapidly over the last 100 years, and is a focus for migrants from the rest of the USA. Today, it consists of many separate residential centres, which are linked by an extensive road system, built in the 1930s. Most residents are dependent on cars for transport. The city suffers from pollution because it is surrounded by mountains which stop car fumes escaping.

Green abalone shells found off the Californian coasts are used to make jewellery.

KEYBOX

Mixed fruit: Washington produces one-third of the USA's apple crop, grown in irrigated valleys east of the Cascade Range. Look for 🍎

Irrigated agriculture: Fertile but dry land in central California is irrigated, via canals and dams, by water from the mountains to the west. Look for 🌵

Borders: Millions of Mexicans cross the border into California, many illegally. The border is patrolled by mounted guards and helicopters. Look for ⚡

Military bases: San Diego has the largest concentration of naval bases in the USA. Deserts in California are also used for weapons testing. Look for ✈

Oil
Industrial centre
Aerospace industry
High-tech industry
Tourism
Wine
Cotton
Timber
Fishing
Mining

PACIFIC OCEAN

ARIZONA
MEXICO
NEVADA
CALIFORNIA
SIERRA NEVADA
COAST RANGES
MOJAVE DESERT
SONORAN DESERT
Colorado
Death Valley
Salton Sea

Crescent City
Eureka
Klamath Falls
Goose L.
Klamath L.
Alturas
Medford
Ashland
Weed
Redding
Shasta L.
Eagle L.
Clair Eagle L.
Chico
Santa Rosa
Napa Valley
Petaluma
Novato
San Francisco
Oakland
Concord
Vacaville
SACRAMENTO
McClellan Air Base
Stockton
Modesto
Santa Clara Valley
San Jose
Santa Cruz
Monterey
Salinas
Merced
Yosemite National Park
Mono L.
Bishop
Fresno
Tungsten
San Joaquin
Bakersfield
Mojave
San Luis Obispo
Santa Maria
Vandenburg Air Force Base
Santa Barbara
Ventura
Oxnard
Hollywood
Los Angeles
Glendale
Pasadena
San Bernardino
Barstow
Edwards Air Base
Potassium
China Lake Naval Weapons Center
San Gorgonio Pass
Riverside
Santa Ana
Long Beach
Huntington Beach
San Clemente
Oceanside
Palm Springs
Miramar Naval Air Station
San Diego
Brawley

37

MEXICO

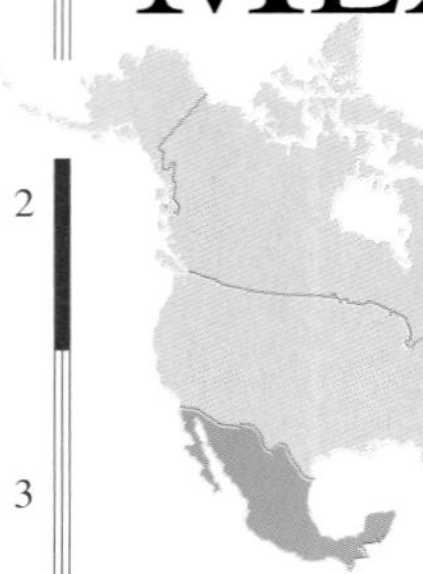

THE LAND OF MEXICO consists of a dry plateau crossed by broad valleys and enclosed to the west and east by mountains, some of which are volcanic. Baja California, the Yucatan Peninsula and along the country's coasts are the main low-lying areas. Mexico was first occupied by civilizations such as the Maya and Aztec, who built magnificent cities containing plazas, palaces and pyramids. Lured by legends of fabulous hoards of gold and silver, Spanish conquistadores invaded Mexico in 1519 and destroyed the existing civilizations. For 300 years the Spanish ruled the country, unifying it with their language and the Roman Catholic religion. Mexico succeeded in winning its independence from Spain by 1821. Today, most Mexicans are mestizo – which means they are descendants of the native peoples and the Spanish settlers. Although half the population lives in towns, many people still inhabit areas only accessible on horseback, but rail and air transport are improving. So much of the country is mountainous or dry that only 12 per cent of the land can be used for farming. Mexico has vast oil reserves and mineral riches, but suffers from over-population and huge foreign debts. Closer links with the USA promise to strengthen Mexico's economy in the future.

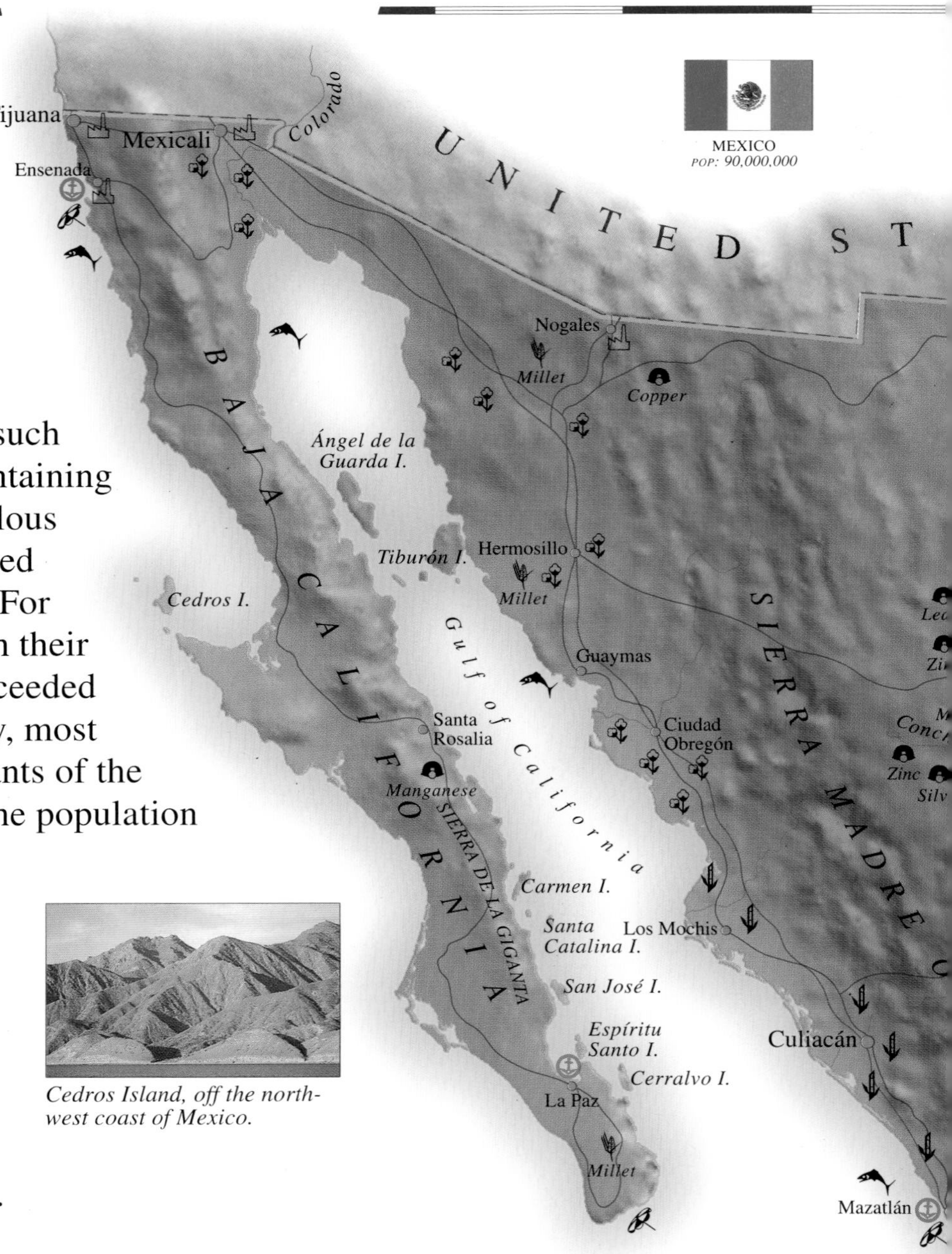
MEXICO
POP: 90,000,000
Tijuana
Mexicali
Colorado
Ensenada
UNITED ST
Nogales
Millet
Copper
BAJA CALIFORNIA
Ángel de la Guarda I.
Tiburón I.
Hermosillo
Millet
Cedros I.
Gulf of California
Guaymas
SIERRA MADRE
Santa Rosalia
Ciudad Obregón
Manganese
SIERRA DE LA GIGANTA
Carmen I.
Santa Catalina I.
Los Mochis
San José I.
Espíritu Santo I.
Culiacán
Cerralvo I.
La Paz
Millet
Mazatlán
Zinc

Cedros Island, off the north-west coast of Mexico.

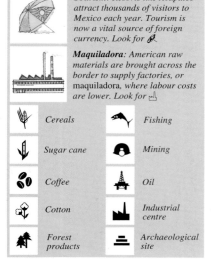

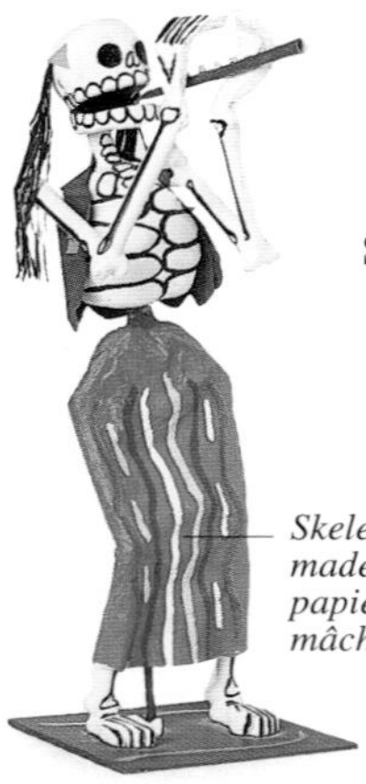
Skeleton made of papier mâché

THE DAY OF THE DEAD
Mexicans believe that life is like a flower; it slowly opens and then closes again. During the annual festival of the Day of the Dead, the streets are decorated with flowers, and ghoulish skeletons are everywhere.

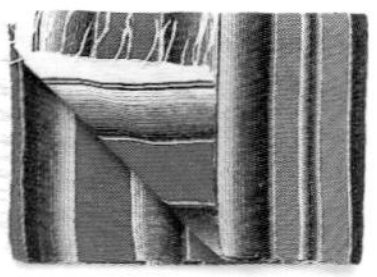

TEXTILES
Although today many fabrics are machine-made, some Mexicans still practise their traditional art of hand-weaving colourful textiles. This *sarape*, part of the traditional Mexican dress for men, is worn over the shoulder.

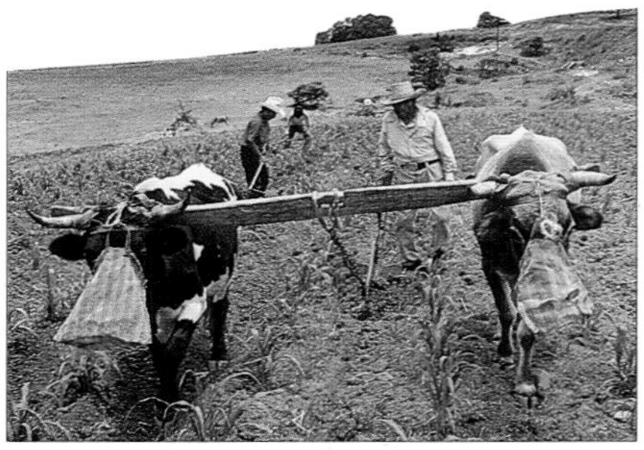

AGRICULTURE
Although Mexico is rapidly industrializing, over half the working population still makes its living from farming. They grow crops like maize, beans and vegetables, and raise cattle, sheep, pigs and chickens.

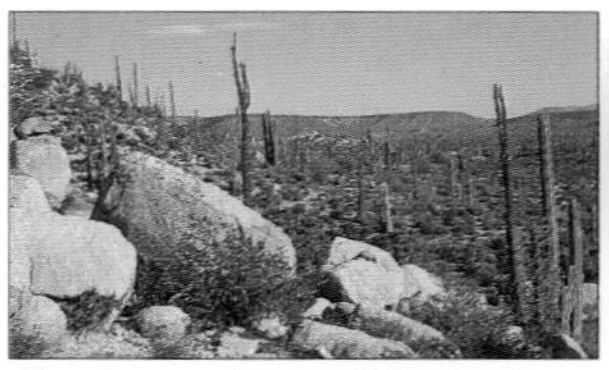
Cacti growing on Mexico's dry central plateau.

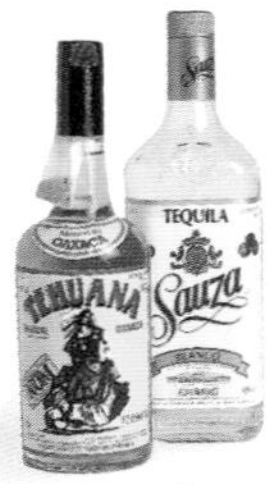
TEQUILA
Sauza

SPIKED DRINKS
The desert and dry regions of Mexico are home to many varieties of the spiny-leaved *agave* plant. Juice from two varieties is used to make the alcoholic drinks, *tequila* and *mezcal*. The *agave* plant is grown on plantations, then cooked, crushed and fermented. The drink is exported worldwide.

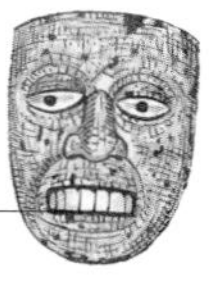
Teeth made of shell

Aztec mask, inlaid with turquoise, depicting a god.

KEYBOX

Tourism: Resorts like Acapulco attract thousands of visitors to Mexico each year. Tourism is now a vital source of foreign currency. Look for

Maquiladora: American raw materials are brought across the border to supply factories, or maquiladora, *where labour costs are lower. Look for*

Cereals	Fishing
Sugar cane	Mining
Coffee	Oil
Cotton	Industrial centre
Forest products	Archaeological site

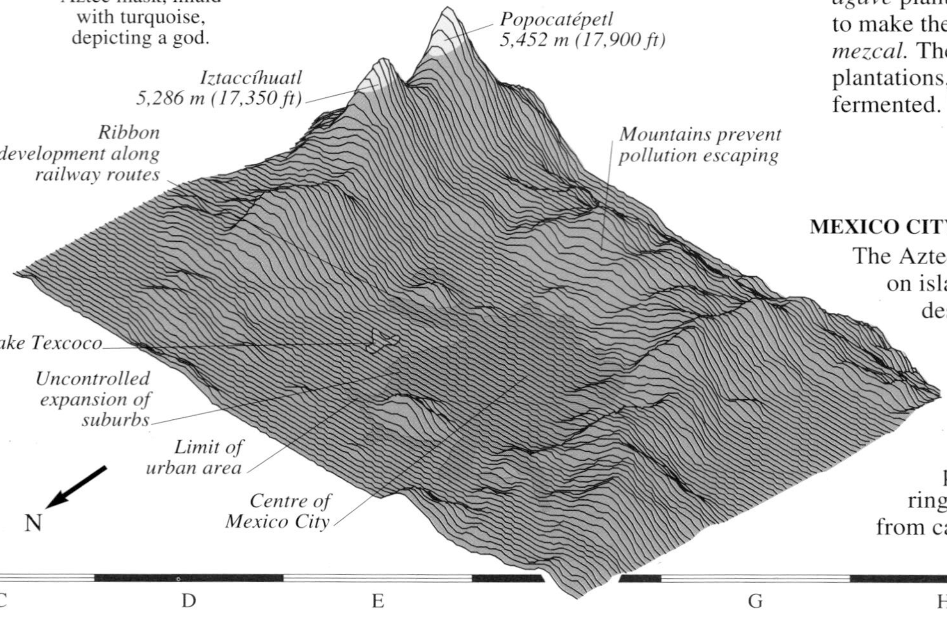
Popocatépetl
5,452 m (17,900 ft)
Iztaccíhuatl
5,286 m (17,350 ft)
Ribbon development along railway routes
Mountains prevent pollution escaping
Lake Texcoco
Uncontrolled expansion of suburbs
Limit of urban area
Centre of Mexico City
N

MEXICO CITY
The Aztec capital, Tenochtitlán, was built on islands in Lake Texcoco. The city was destroyed by the Spanish, but modern-day Mexico City is built on the ruins. By AD 2000 it is expected to be the world's largest city, containing over 20 million people. Mexico City is very polluted because it is surrounded by a ring of mountains which stop polluted air from cars and factories escaping.

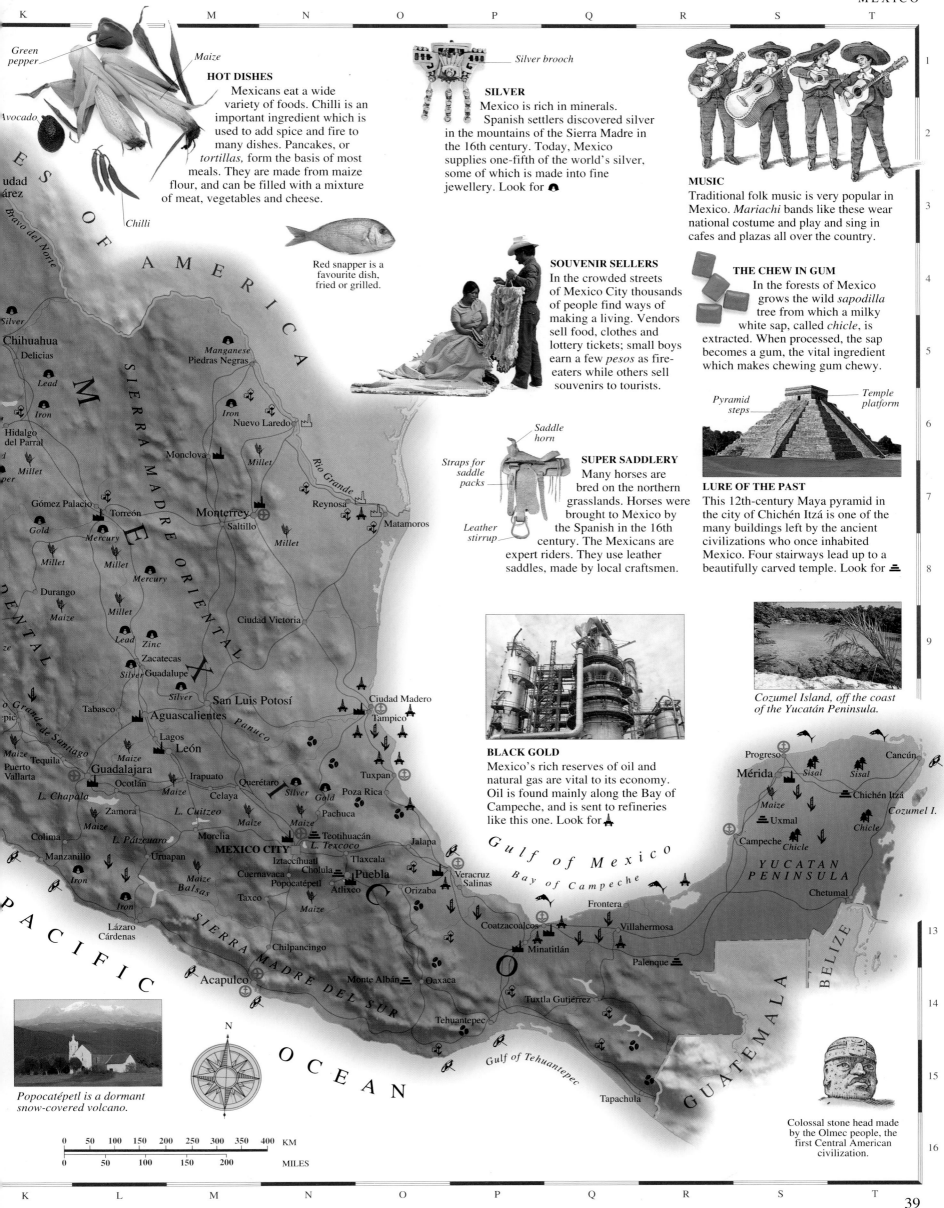

Green pepper

Maize

Avocado

HOT DISHES
Mexicans eat a wide variety of foods. Chilli is an important ingredient which is used to add spice and fire to many dishes. Pancakes, or *tortillas,* form the basis of most meals. They are made from maize flour, and can be filled with a mixture of meat, vegetables and cheese.

Chilli

Red snapper is a favourite dish, fried or grilled.

Silver brooch

SILVER
Mexico is rich in minerals. Spanish settlers discovered silver in the mountains of the Sierra Madre in the 16th century. Today, Mexico supplies one-fifth of the world's silver, some of which is made into fine jewellery. Look for

MUSIC
Traditional folk music is very popular in Mexico. *Mariachi* bands like these wear national costume and play and sing in cafes and plazas all over the country.

THE CHEW IN GUM
In the forests of Mexico grows the wild *sapodilla* tree from which a milky white sap, called *chicle,* is extracted. When processed, the sap becomes a gum, the vital ingredient which makes chewing gum chewy.

SOUVENIR SELLERS
In the crowded streets of Mexico City thousands of people find ways of making a living. Vendors sell food, clothes and lottery tickets; small boys earn a few *pesos* as fire-eaters while others sell souvenirs to tourists.

Pyramid steps

Temple platform

Saddle horn

Straps for saddle packs

SUPER SADDLERY
Many horses are bred on the northern grasslands. Horses were brought to Mexico by the Spanish in the 16th century. The Mexicans are expert riders. They use leather saddles, made by local craftsmen.

Leather stirrup

LURE OF THE PAST
This 12th-century Maya pyramid in the city of Chichén Itzá is one of the many buildings left by the ancient civilizations who once inhabited Mexico. Four stairways lead up to a beautifully carved temple. Look for

Cozumel Island, off the coast of the Yucatán Peninsula.

BLACK GOLD
Mexico's rich reserves of oil and natural gas are vital to its economy. Oil is found mainly along the Bay of Campeche, and is sent to refineries like this one. Look for

Popocatépetl is a dormant snow-covered volcano.

Colossal stone head made by the Olmec people, the first Central American civilization.

0 50 100 150 200 250 300 350 400   KM
0   50   100   150   200   MILES

Toco toucan
Ramphastos toco
Length: 60 cm (24 in)
■

Emerald tree boa
Corallus caninus
Length: 1.8 m (6 ft)
■

Geoffroy's spider monkey
Ateles geoffroyi
Length: 1.5 m (5 ft)
■ !

CENTRAL AND SOUTH AMERICA

SOUTH AMERICA is shaped like a giant triangle that tapers southward from the Equator to Cape Horn. A huge wall of mountains, the Andes, stretches for 7,250 km (4,500 miles) along the entire Pacific coast. Until three million years ago South America was not connected to North America, so life there evolved in isolation. Several extraordinary animal groups developed, including sloths and anteaters. Many unique plant species originated here too, such as the potato and tomato. South America has the world's largest area of tropical rainforest, through which the River Amazon and its many tributaries run. Central America is mountainous and forested.

■ **TROPICAL TOBAGO**
Coconut palms grow along the shores of many Caribbean islands. Palms have flexible trunks that enable them to withstand tropical storms.

Mahogany
Swietenia macrophylla
Height: 25 m (82 ft)
■ !

△ **VOLCANIC ISLANDS**
One of the extinct volcanic craters of the Galápagos Island group breaks the surface of the Pacific Ocean. Like other isolated regions of the world, many unique species have evolved here, such as the giant tortoise 1.2 m (4 ft) long.

⌄ **SEA-DWELLING TREES**
Mangroves grow along tropical coastlines. The tangled roots of Pinuelo mangroves create ideal homes for tiny aquatic species.

PAMPAS
Giant grasses up to 3 m (10 ft) high grow on Argentina's dry southern Pampas. Here, further north, more plentiful rainfall supports a few scattered trees.

Alpaca
Lama pacos
Height: 1.5 m (5 ft)
■

Archaeogeryon, a crab that lived in this region 20 million years ago.

△ **VOLCANIC ANDES**
Steam and smoke rises from Villarrica, an active volcano. Many peaks in the Andes are active or former volcanoes. Despite the intense heat within these lava-filled mountains, the highest are permanently covered in snow – even those on the Equator.

■ **THE FOREST FLOOR**
Tropical rainforest trees form such a dense canopy that little sunlight or rain can reach the ground 70 m (200 ft) below. Rainforest soils are easily washed away when the trees and plants are removed.

□ **THE BLEAK SOUTH**
Patagonia's cold desert environment contrasts starkly with the lush hot forests of Amazonia. Plants take root in the cracks of bare rock, and grow close to the ground to survive icy winds.

Passion flower
Passiflora caerulea
Across flower: 15 cm (6 in)
■

□ ▲ **BIRTH OF A RIVER**
The snow-capped peaks of the Andes are the source of the Amazon, the world's second longest river. It is 6,570 km, (4,080 miles) long.

CROSS SECTION THROUGH SOUTH AMERICA

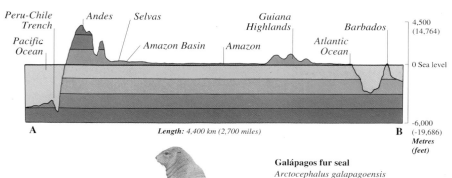

Peru-Chile Trench | Andes | Selvas | Guiana Highlands | Barbados | 4,500 (14,764)
Pacific Ocean | Amazon Basin | Amazon | Atlantic Ocean | 0 Sea level
A | *Length: 4,400 km (2,700 miles)* | B | -6,000 (-19,686) *Metres (feet)*

□ ▲ **DRY ATACAMA DESERT**
The Atacama Desert is the world's driest place outside Antarctica. Rain has not fallen in some areas for hundreds of years. Winds that pass over cold coastline currents absorb no moisture.

Giant anteater
Myrmecophaga tridactyla
Length: 2 m (7 ft)
■ !

Galápagos fur seal
Arctocephalus galapagoensis
Length: 1.8 m (6 ft)

Ocelot
Felis pardalis
Length: 1.7 m (6 ft)
■ !

NORTH
AMERICA

100°   80°   60°   Tropic of Cancer   40°   20°

Gulf of Mexico   Bahamas   *Nares*   *Plain*   ATLANTIC

SIERRA   Caicos Is.
Mexico   Turks Is.
Basin   Cuba   *Puerto Rico Trench*   NORTH AMERICAN PLATE   *Mid-Atlantic Ridge*
Yucatán Basin   Hispaniola   ▽ -8605m   SOUTH AMERICAN PLATE
YUCATÁN   *Greater*   Leeward   AFRICAN PLATE
PENINSULA   NORTH   *Jamaica*   *Antilles*   Is.   △ Mt. Pelée   B   SOUTH
AMERICAN PLATE   1397m   AMERICAN PLATE
CARIBBEAN PLATE   CARIBBEAN   SEA   Venezuelan   Barbados
▲4210m   *Basin*   *Lesser Antilles*   Trinidad   Tobago   *Demerara*
Santa Maria△   Colombian   *Plain*
3768m   *Basin*   L. Maracaibo   Orinoco Delta
CARIBBEAN PLATE   Angel Falls   ▲2810m   *Ceará*   *Plain*
Gulf of   SOUTH AMERICAN PLATE   980m
L. Nicaragua   Darien   LLANOS   GUIANA HIGHLANDS   C. de São Roque
Magdalena   *Isthmus of Panama*   Equator
COCOS RIDGE   Gulf of   Negro   *Amazon*
Panama   Probable plate   △Ruiz   Branco   *Amazon*   *Basin*   Marajó
margin   5400m   I.
Putumayo   *Amazon*   *Basin*   SOUTH   Parnaíba
COCOS PLATE   Cotopaxi   Marañón   *Tapajós*   Sobradinho
NAZCA PLATE   △5896m   *S*   *E*   *L*   *V*   *A*   *S*   Res.
Chimborazo▲   Juruá   Purus   Xingu   Araguaia   Tocantins   Brazil
Galápagos Is.   6267m   Madeira   São Francisco   *Basin*
Gallego Rise   *Peru-Chile Trench*   BRAZILIAN
Peru-Chile Trench   ▲2890m
SOUTH AMERICAN PLATE   Huascarán▲   HIGHLANDS
6768m   AMERICA
Ucayali   PLATEAU OF
NAZCA PLATE   MATO GROSSO
PACIFIC   Peru   L. Titicaca   Itaipú Res.   Santos
Basin   ALTIPLANO   AMERICA   Plateau   Tropic of Capricorn
A   Sajama▲ L. Poopó   Iguaçu Falls   Rio Grande Rise
Nazca Ridge   6520m   64m
Guallatiri△   GRAN CHACO   Paraguay
NAZCA PLATE   6060m   ATACAMA DESERT   Paraná
PACIFIC PLATE   Chile   -8064m▽   Salado   Mirim
Basin   Ojos del Salado   Lagoon
Sala y Gomez Ridge   6880m   *Peru-Chile Trench*   Uruguay   Plate
Cerro Bonete   Mirim
OCEAN   6872m   Lagoon
Roggeveen   Mercedario   PAMPAS   Argentine
Basin   6770m   Basin
Aconcagua   Colorado
6960m△   Plate
East Pacific Rise   Tupungatito
5640m
Villarrica△   Negro   Salinas Grandes   South Georgia
2840m   Salt Marsh   Falkland Escarpment   Basin
NAZCA PLATE   -40m   South   -8325m▽
ANTARCTIC PLATE   Chile Rise   Chiloé I.   PATAGONIA   Georgia   South Sandwich
Chile Rise   SOUTH AMERICAN PLATE   Trench
Falkland Is.   SCOTIA PLATE
Mornington   Strait of   SOUTH AMERICAN PLATE   SCOTIA PLATE
NAZCA PLATE   Plain   Magellan   SCOTIA PLATE   ANTARCTIC PLATE
PACIFIC PLATE   TIERRA   Cape Horn
DEL FUEGO   Antarctic Circle
Probable plate
margin   Drake Passage
Bellingshausen   ANTARCTICA   80°
Plain

The Triton shell
can be found
from Central
America to Brazil.

■ **GREAT WATERS**
The Iguaçu Falls in
Brazil are spectacular.
Water thunders over the
rim from November to
March, but at other
times slows to almost a
trickle.

Common Chilean tarantula
Grammostola spatulatus
Length: 10 cm (4 in)
□

KEY TO SYMBOLS

▲ *Mountain*

△ *Volcano*

⁂ *Mangroves*

▦ *Wetlands*

▨ *Coral reef*

▩ *Plate margins and
direction of movement*

KEY TO NATURAL VEGETATION

□ *Tropical grassland*   *Tropical rainforest* □

□ *Mountain*   *Dry woodland* □

□ *Mediterranean-type*   *Temperate rainforest* ▦

▨ *Broadleaf forest*   *Temperate grassland* □

□ *Cold desert*   *Hot desert* □

A B C D E F G H I

CENTRAL AMERICA AND THE CARIBBEAN

THE TROPICAL REGION of Central America and the Caribbean was settled by hunters and farmers many thousands of years ago. By 300 bc the Maya had established a sophisticated civilization on the mainland – ruins of their pyramids and temples can still be seen deep in the forests of Guatemala. The Maya, as well as the native peoples who lived on the Caribbean islands, were almost wiped out by European explorers who arrived in the 15th century. From this time, European nations, in particular the British, French, Spanish and Dutch, competed for control of the region and some countries did not gain independence until recently. Europeans brought slaves from Africa to work on vast sugar plantations. In the last few decades, tourism has enriched the Caribbean, but in Central America, poverty and civil wars are still major problems.

A Jamaican beach, devastated by a hurricane.

Great Bahama Bank

HAVANA (LA HABANA)
Copper Pinar del Río
Matanzas
CUBA
POP: 10,900,000

I. de la Juventud (I. of Pines)
Cienfuegos
Santa Clara

Camagüey

GREATER

Jardines de la Reina

Little Cayman
GEORGETOWN *Grand Cayman*
CAYMAN ISLANDS (to UK)
Cayman Brac

Gulf Guacanaya

JAMAICA
POP: 2,500,000

Conches from the shallow waters of the Caribbean are edible.

Savanna-la-Mar
Montego Bay
JAMAICA
Spanish Tow
Alumi
CARIBBEA

M E X I C O

GUATEMALA
POP: 10,000,000

Tikal
Altun Ha
Belize City
Flores *Belize*
San Ignacio
BELMOPAN
BELIZE
BELIZE
POP: 200,000

G U A T E M A L A
Cobán
Huehuetenango
Nickel L. Izabal
Quezaltenango
Sololá
Gulf of Honduras
Mazatenango
Zacapa
Puerto Barrios
Puerto Cortés
GUATEMALA CITY
Copán
San Pedro Sula
La Ceiba
Trujillo
Santa Rosa
Escuintla

HONDURAS
POP: 5,600,000

H O N D U R A S

EL SALVADOR
POP: 5,500,000
Santa Ana
La Esperanza
Comayagua
Patuca
La Libertad
SAN SALVADOR
TEGUCIGALPA
Coco
San Miguel
Juticalpa
Caratasca Lagoon
EL SALVADOR
San Lorenzo
Choluteca
Gold
Somoto
Copper
Puerto Cabezas
Chinandega
Corinto
Esteli
Jinotega
León
Matagalpa
Río Grande
L. Managua
Boaco
MANAGUA
Juigalpa
N I C A R A G U A
Granada
L. Nicaragua
Rivas
Bluefields
San Carlos

NICARAGUA
POP: 4,100,000

NICARAGUA
Since Nicaragua became independent in 1838 it has been devastated by civil war and foreign interference. During the 1980s, a desperate conflict took place between the socialist government and the right-wing Contras, supported by the USA. Although democracy has now been restored, little progress has been made in fighting the huge problems of poverty, ill-health and homelessness.

The ancient Maya temple of Altun Ha is hidden deep in the rainforest of Belize.

RURAL MARKETS
Many Guatemalans live in small villages, growing maize and beans and making brightly-coloured cloth, baskets, pottery and wood carvings. These goods, as well as fruit and tobacco, are sold at local markets.

P A C I F I C   O C E A N

Liberia
San Juan
C O S T A
Puntarenas
Alajuela
SAN JOSE
Puerto Limón
Cartago
Gulf of Nicoya
R I C A

COSTA RICA
POP: 3,300,000

Bocas del Toro

P A N A M A
Mosquito Gulf
Colón
Panama Canal
David
Copper Penonomé
PANAMA CITY
Gulf of Chiriquí
Santiago
Gulf of Panama
Coiba I.
Chitré
San José I.
Las Tablas
Isla del Rey
La Palma
Gulf of Darien

Hot peppe sauce, mad with spicy chillis, is used all ove the region.

PANAMA
POP: 2,600,000

C O L O M B I A

KEYBOX

Archaeological sites: Great civilizations, such as the Maya, flourished in Central America from 300 bc. They built temples, palaces and cities. Look for

Shellfishing: Shrimps and lobsters thrive in the mangrove swamps on the coasts of Central America, which provide rich feeding grounds. Look for

Shipping registry: Ships from all over the world fly Panama's flag. They register there because of low fees and limited controls on the labour force. Look for

↓	Sugar cane	🔥	Tobacco
🍌	Bananas	🌴	Timber
☕	Coffee	⛏	Mining
🌰	Cocoa	🏭	Industrial centre
⚘	Cotton	🚢	Tourism

Swamps near the Honduran coast.

N

0 50 100 150 200 250 300 350 400	KM
0 50 100 150 200	MILES

A B C D E F G

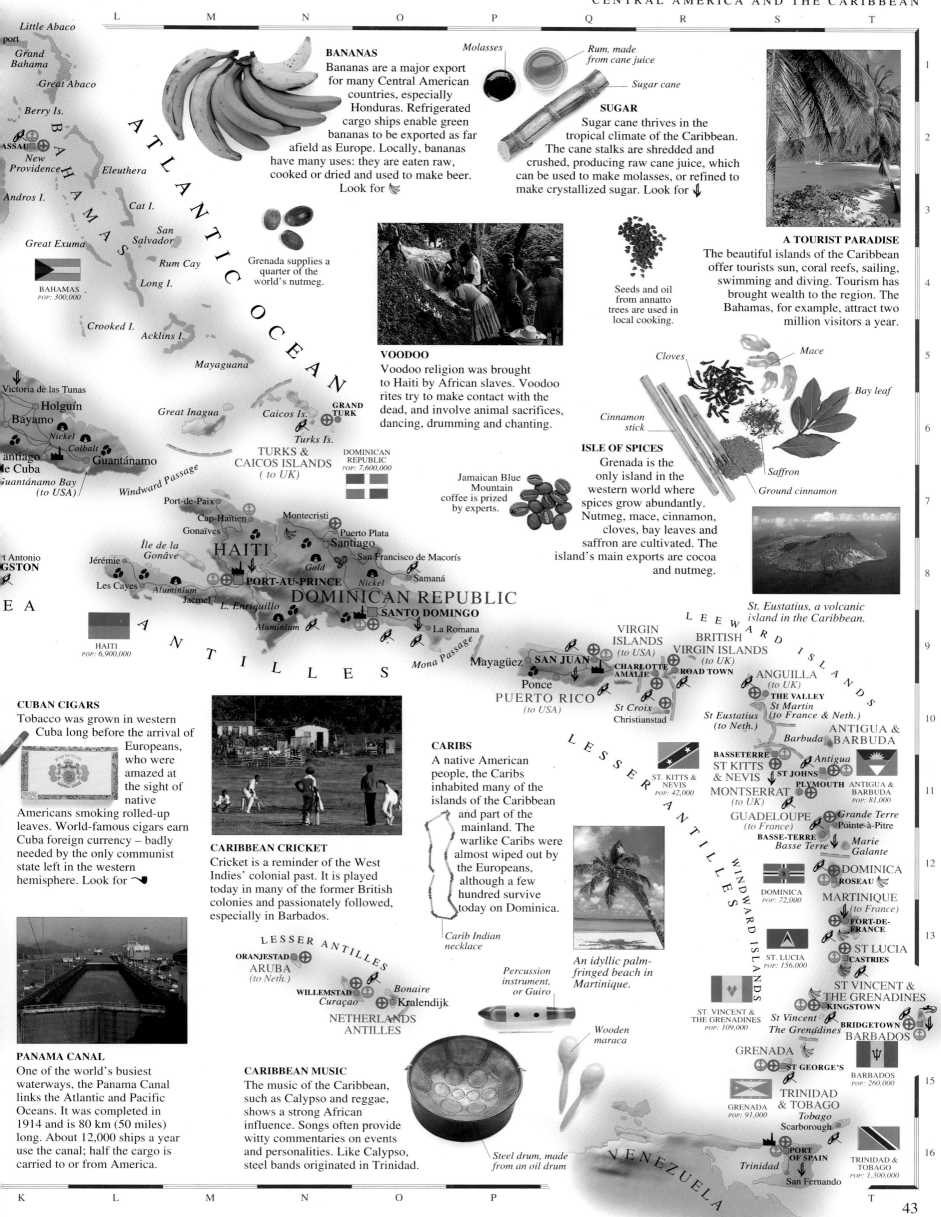

L M N O P Q R S T

Little Abaco

port

Grand Bahama

Great Abaco

Berry Is.

NASSAU
New Providence

Eleuthera

Andros I.

Cat I.

San Salvador

Rum Cay

Long I.

Great Exuma

BAHAMAS
POP: 300,000

A T L A N T I C   O C E A N

B A H A M A S

Crooked I.

Acklins I.

Mayaguana

Victoria de las Tunas

Holguín
Bayamo

Nickel

Colbalt

antiago
de Cuba   Guantánamo

uantánamo Bay
(to USA)

Windward Passage

Great Inagua

Caicos Is.

GRAND TURK

Turks Is.

TURKS & CAICOS ISLANDS
(to UK)

DOMINICAN REPUBLIC
POP: 7,600,000

BANANAS

Bananas are a major export for many Central American countries, especially Honduras. Refrigerated cargo ships enable green bananas to be exported as far afield as Europe. Locally, bananas have many uses: they are eaten raw, cooked or dried and used to make beer.
Look for

Molasses

Rum, made from cane juice

Sugar cane

SUGAR

Sugar cane thrives in the tropical climate of the Caribbean. The cane stalks are shredded and crushed, producing raw cane juice, which can be used to make molasses, or refined to make crystallized sugar. Look for

Grenada supplies a quarter of the world's nutmeg.

Seeds and oil from annatto trees are used in local cooking.

A TOURIST PARADISE

The beautiful islands of the Caribbean offer tourists sun, coral reefs, sailing, swimming and diving. Tourism has brought wealth to the region. The Bahamas, for example, attract two million visitors a year.

VOODOO

Voodoo religion was brought to Haiti by African slaves. Voodoo rites try to make contact with the dead, and involve animal sacrifices, dancing, drumming and chanting.

Cloves

Mace

Cinnamon stick

Bay leaf

Saffron

Ground cinnamon

ISLE OF SPICES

Grenada is the only island in the western world where spices grow abundantly. Nutmeg, mace, cinnamon, cloves, bay leaves and saffron are cultivated. The island's main exports are cocoa and nutmeg.

Jamaican Blue Mountain coffee is prized by experts.

Port-de-Paix

Cap-Haïtien
Gonaïves

Montecristi

Puerto Plata
Santiago

San Francisco de Macorís

Île de la Gonâve

Jérémie

HAITI

Gold

Samaná

Les Cayes

Jacmel

Aluminium

PORT-AU-PRINCE

Nickel

DOMINICAN REPUBLIC

L. Enriquillo

SANTO DOMINGO

Aluminium

La Romana

HAITI
POP: 6,900,000

A N T I L L E S

Mona Passage

Mayagüez   **SAN JUAN**

Ponce

PUERTO RICO
(to USA)

St Croix
Christiansted

VIRGIN ISLANDS
(to USA)

CHARLOTTE AMALIE   **ROAD TOWN**

BRITISH VIRGIN ISLANDS
(to UK)

St Eustatius
(to Neth.)

L E E W A R D   I S L A N D S

St. Eustatius, a volcanic island in the Caribbean.

ANGUILLA
(to UK)

THE VALLEY
St Martin
(to France & Neth.)

Barbuda   **ANTIGUA & BARBUDA**

BASSETERRE

ST KITTS & NEVIS   **ST JOHNS**   *Antigua*

ST. KITTS & NEVIS
POP: 42,000

MONTSERRAT
(to UK)

PLYMOUTH

ANTIGUA & BARBUDA
POP: 81,000

GUADELOUPE
(to France)

Grande Terre
Pointe-à-Pitre

BASSE-TERRE
Basse Terre

Marie Galante

DOMINICA
ROSEAU

DOMINICA
POP: 72,000

MARTINIQUE
(to France)

FORT-DE-FRANCE

ST. LUCIA
POP: 156,000

ST LUCIA
CASTRIES

L E S S E R   A N T I L L E S

W I N D W A R D   I S L A N D S

CARIBS

A native American people, the Caribs inhabited many of the islands of the Caribbean and part of the mainland. The warlike Caribs were almost wiped out by the Europeans, although a few hundred survive today on Dominica.

Carib Indian necklace

An idyllic palm-fringed beach in Martinique.

CUBAN CIGARS

Tobacco was grown in western Cuba long before the arrival of Europeans, who were amazed at the sight of native Americans smoking rolled-up leaves. World-famous cigars earn Cuba foreign currency – badly needed by the only communist state left in the western hemisphere. Look for

CARIBBEAN CRICKET

Cricket is a reminder of the West Indies' colonial past. It is played today in many of the former British colonies and passionately followed, especially in Barbados.

L E S S E R   A N T I L L E S

ORANJESTAD
ARUBA
(to Neth.)

WILLEMSTAD
Curaçao

Bonaire
Kralendijk

NETHERLANDS ANTILLES

Percussion instrument, or Guiro

Wooden maraca

ST VINCENT & THE GRENADINES
POP: 109,000

*St Vincent &
The Grenadines*

ST VINCENT & THE GRENADINES
KINGSTOWN

BRIDGETOWN
BARBADOS

GRENADA
ST GEORGE'S

BARBADOS
POP: 260,000

GRENADA
POP: 91,000

TRINIDAD & TOBAGO
Tobago
Scarborough

PANAMA CANAL

One of the world's busiest waterways, the Panama Canal links the Atlantic and Pacific Oceans. It was completed in 1914 and is 80 km (50 miles) long. About 12,000 ships a year use the canal; half the cargo is carried to or from America.

CARIBBEAN MUSIC

The music of the Caribbean, such as Calypso and reggae, shows a strong African influence. Songs often provide witty commentaries on events and personalities. Like Calypso, steel bands originated in Trinidad.

Steel drum, made from an oil drum

V E N E Z U E L A

Trinidad   **PORT OF SPAIN**

San Fernando

TRINIDAD & TOBAGO
POP: 1,300,000

K L M N O P T

NORTHERN SOUTH AMERICA

THIS REGION IS DOMINATED by the volcanic peaks and mountain ranges of the Andes. The powerful Incas ruled much of this area in the 15th century, and large numbers of their descendants still live in Peru, Bolivia and Ecuador today. In the 16th century, Spanish conquistadores reached South America, swept the Incas and other native peoples aside, and colonized the region from Venezuela to Bolivia.

Areas to the east were later settled by the French, Dutch and British. Although all the countries except French Guiana are now independent republics, independence has brought many problems, such as military dictatorships, high inflation, organized crime, the illegal drug trade and huge foreign debts.

Many of the cities are overcrowded, but large numbers of people still flock there from the countryside, looking for jobs.

SHRIMPS
Shrimps living in the muddy waters of Ecuador's mangrove swamps have become the country's second most important source of foreign currency, after oil. But, as the industry expands, it is destroying the mangroves – the shrimps' natural habitat. Look for ➤

MARKET DAY
Brightly dressed in their traditional Andean clothes and hats, local people display their wares in the market of the Peruvian town of Pisác. They sell fruit and vegetables, together with pottery and clothes produced for the tourist trade.

CARACAS
The discovery of oil in 1917 made Venezuela the richest country in the region. Its capital, Caracas, was built with oil money. Modern motorways and skyscrapers dominate the city, but many people live in shanty towns on the surrounding hillsides.

The lush Caribbean coastline of northern Venezuela.

Hammered gold

A figure made by ancient Colombian craftsmen.

EMERALDS
Some of the world's finest emeralds are mined near Bogotá, the capital of Colombia. Long before the Spanish invaded the country in search of gold, native peoples mined the emeralds for their gold jewellery and ceremonial objects. Look for ➤

Emerald

Quinine
Quinine from the bark of the Peruvian cinchona tree is used to treat malaria.

Cinchona leaves

The ancient Inca city of Machu Picchu in the Peruvian Andes.

SURINAM POP: 400,000

VENEZUELA POP: 20,000,000

GUYANA POP: 800,000

COLOMBIA POP: 34,000,000

ECUADOR POP: 11,300,000

KM MILES
600 350
500 300
400 250
300 200
250
200 150
100
50 100
0

Map labels

FRENCH GUIANA (to France)
CAYENNE
St Laurent-du-Maroni
Kourou
Oracoubo
Gold
Marowijne

SURINAM
PARAMARIBO
Albina
New Amsterdam
Fort Wellington
Brokopondo
Kabalebo Res.
Aluminium
Berbice
Gold
Courantyne
Suddie
Lethem
Beef

GUYANA
GEORGETOWN
Bartica
Aluminium
Gold
Diamonds
Mazaruni
Essequibo
Mabaruma
Santa Elena

VENEZUELA
CARACAS
La Guaira
Maracay
Valencia
San Juan de los Morros
San Carlos
San Felipe
Puerto Cabello
Barquisimeto
Coro
Maracaibo
Cabimas
L. Maracaibo
Mérida
San Cristóbal
Trujillo
Guanare
Barinas
Apure
San Fernando de Apure
Puerto Ayacucho
Puerto Carreño
Puerto Inírida
Mitú
Ciudad Bolívar
Ciudad Guayana
Guri Res.
Orinoco
Tucupita
Maturín
Cumaná
Barcelona
La Asunción
Margarita I.
Beef
Gold
Iron
Aluminium
Diamonds

COLOMBIA
BOGOTÁ
Medellín
Bello
Cali
Buenaventura
Palmira
Armenia
Pereira
Manizales
Ibagué
Neiva
Florencia
Villavicencio
Yopal
Tunja
Bucaramanga
Cúcuta
San Cristóbal
Arauca
Santa Marta
Barranquilla
Cartagena
Sincelejo
Montería
Quibdó
Pasto
Popayán
Mocoa
Leticia
Riohacha
Valledupar
San Andrés
Emeralds
Gold
Meta
Magdalena
Cauca
Guaviare
San José del Guaviare
Caquetá
Putumayo
Napo
Amazon
Iquitos
Beef

ECUADOR
QUITO
Guayaquil
Cuenca
Machala
Loja
Milagro
Babahoyo
Riobamba
Ambato
Latacunga
Ibarra
Esmeraldas
Santo Domingo de los Colorados
Portoviejo
Manta
Montecristi
Gulf of Guayaquil
Piura
Sullana

BRAZIL
PERU

CARIBBEAN SEA
Gulf of Venezuela
Gulf of Darién
PANAMA

PACIFIC OCEAN

COCAINE

The steep slopes of the Andes are ideally suited to growing the coca bush. The native peoples have always chewed coca leaves to protect themselves against cold and altitude sickness. But the drug cocaine, made from the leaves, is now a major world problem. Today, Colombia's economy is virtually dependent on the illegal export of cocaine.

Coca leaves

HIGHEST RAILWAY

Peru's railways are the highest in the world. The single-track railway from Lima to Huancayo in the Andes zigzags through tunnels and over wooden bridges, reaching an altitude of 4,843 m (15,885 ft) where it crosses through one of the passes.

Rug decorated with llamas, the traditional Andean pack animals

OTAVALO PEOPLE

Woollen rugs woven by the Otavalo people from Ecuador are sold all over the Americas and Europe. The Otavalo have developed new techniques, such as replacing traditional natural dyes with synthetic ones.

Strap handle

Clay body

Water jar, found at the ancient Inca city of Cusco in Peru.

BOLIVIA
POP: 7,700,000

ANDEAN CULTIVATION

On the steep hillsides of the Andes, every scrap of soil must be made to work efficiently. Like their Inca ancestors, Andean farmers suit the crop to the temperature, which gets lower higher up the mountains. This region is the original home of the potato, which can be grown successfully at high altitudes.

Permanent snow and ice

Inland river valleys: sugar, coffee

3,000 m (9,850 ft)

2,000 m (6,550 ft)

1,000 m (3,280 ft)

Altiplano: high plateaux between mountains used for grazing animals

Highland areas: barley, potatoes, wheat

Temperate zone: coffee, tobacco, corn

Coastal lowland: sugar, cacao, bananas, rice

Sea level

N

Pacific Ocean floor

Peru-Chile Trench: c.6,000 m (19,686 ft) below sea level

PERU
POP: 22,900,000

Llamas grazing on the high plains of the Andes in Bolivia.

PANAMA HATS

Panama hats are made of fibre from a palm tree that grows in the coastal forests of Ecuador. One hat can take up to three months to make.

LIMA

Pizarro, a leader of the Spanish *conquistadores*, founded Peru's capital city in the 16th century, and his bones are buried in the cathedral on the Plaza de Armas, the main square in the city's centre.

Lima Cathedral

KEYBOX

Bananas: Bananas are grown as a cash crop in Ecuador's tropical lowlands. Ecuador is now the world's main exporter.
Look for 🍌

Oil: Oil is vital to Venezuela's economy; today the country's oil revenues account for 80 per cent of its export earnings.
Look for 🗼

Archaeological sites: The remains of many magnificent ancient cities and temples can still be seen in the Andes.
Look for 🏛

Space centre: The European Space Agency launches its rocket, Ariane, from its rocket base at Kourou, French Guiana.
Look for 🚀

🐂 Cattle	🌾 Rice	🌿 Sugar cane	☕ Coffee
🌴 Timber	🦪 Shellfishing	⛏ Mining	🏭 Industrial centre

The native peoples of the Andes were the first to grow potatoes.

The Andes are the world's longest chain of mountains.

CORPUS CHRISTI

Every town commemorates its patron saint with a festival. Events, such as this colourful procession on Corpus Christi Day in Cusco, Peru, combine the religious beliefs of the native peoples with Christian ceremonies.

LAKE TITICACA

Stretching across the border between Bolivia and Peru is the world's highest lake, Lake Titicaca. 4,000 m (13,000 ft) above sea level. The Uru people sail on the lake in boats of woven reeds.

BRAZIL

BOLIVIA

PARAGUAY

ARGENTINA

CHILE

ANDES

PERU

PACIFIC OCEAN

Ucayali

Madre de Dios

Beni

Mamoré

Cajamarca
Trujillo
Chimbote
Yungay
Cerro de Pasco
Callao
LIMA
Ica
Nazca
San Juan
Mollendo
Arequipa
Tacna
Juliaca
Puno
Cusco
Machu Picchu
Ollantaytambo
Pisac
Ayacucho
Huancayo
La Oroya
Huánuco
Pucallpa

Cobija
Trinidad
Santa Cruz
San Miguel
Cochabamba
Sucre
Oruro
Potosí
Uyuni
Tarija
LA PAZ
L. Titicaca
L. Poopó

BRAZIL

OCCUPYING NEARLY HALF of South America, Brazil possesses the greatest river basin in the world. The Amazonian rainforest, which covers some two-thirds of the country, is a vast storehouse of natural riches, still largely untapped. But land is needed for agriculture, ranching and new roads, and each year vast tracts of forest are cleared. The Portuguese colonized the country in the 16th century, intermarrying with the local population. They planted sugar in the northeast, working the plantations with slaves brought from Africa. With a further influx of Europeans, Brazil is now one of the world's most populous and ethnically diverse democracies. A land of opportunity for some – like those in the industrial region round São Paulo – it is one of poverty and deprivation for many, especially in the northeast. In spite of improved industrial output, Brazil still has high unemployment and huge foreign debts.

Nuts fit into shell, like segments of an orange

Shelled nut

BRAZIL NUTS
Sometimes known as the *inferno verde*, or green hell, Brazil's vast rainforest is home to an astonishing variety of animals and plants from which products – such as chemicals, drugs and rubber – can be made. Scattered through the forest are Brazil nut trees. Their nuts can be eaten, or crushed to make an oil used in cosmetics. Look for 🌰

NATIVE PEOPLES
There were once some two million native people in Amazonia. Today only about 240,000 survive. This Xingu girl is fortunate: she was born into a tribe which lives in a protected area of the Amazon rainforest. The well-being of many peoples is threatened by the ever-shrinking rainforest and by disease, logging, farming and gold prospecting.

FOOTBALL
Football is an all-consuming passion for millions of Brazilians. It is played in every back street and on every open space, even on the beach at Rio. Sometimes the ball is only a coconut. During the World Cup, Brazil comes to a standstill.

Grandillas, one of the many exotic fruits found in Brazil.

Conga drum

DANCE MUSIC
Transported to the northeastern region of Brazil to work on the sugar plantations, African slaves brought with them the musical rhythms of their homelands. Their music has blended with other musical influences to produce the music for dances, such as the *samba* and the *lambada*. The instruments include this drum, called a *conga*.

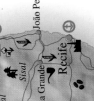
A stretch of coast near Salvador in the northeast.

A huge treetrunk in the depths of the Brazilian rainforest.

BRAZIL
POP: 156,600,000

ATLANTIC OCEAN

C. de São Roque
Natal
João Pessoa
Recife
Maceió
Fortaleza
Mossoró
Sisal
Sisal
Tungsten
Campina Grande
Parnaíba
SERRA GRANDE
Picos
São Luís
Teresina
Juazeiro
Sobradinho Res.
Aluminium
Belém
Carolina
Palmas
Macapá
SERRA PELADA
Iron
Gold
Gold
Iron
PARANAÍBA
FRENCH GUIANA (to France)
SURINAM
GUYANA
Jari
Xingu
Amazon
Santarém
Tapajós
Gold
Teles Pires
PLATEAU OF MATO GROSSO
Manganese
Balbina Res.
Manaus
Madeira
Aluminium
B R A Z I L
A M A Z O N I A
VENEZUELA
COLOMBIA
Boa Vista
Gold
Negro
Tin
Purus
Juruá
Gold
Pôrto Velho
Tin
Brazil Nuts
Rubber
Cruzeiro do Sul
Rio Branco
Rubber
Gold
Brazil Nuts
Rubber
PERU
Amazon
Beef

46

COLONIAL LEGACY

When the Portuguese arrived in Brazil in the 16th century, they brought their distinctive style of architecture. At the heart of many towns and cities in modern Brazil lie cobbled streets, squares and churches. The historic town of Ouro Prêto – centre of the 18th-century gold rush – remains today as a perfect example of a 16th century town.

CARNIVAL

Every year, just before Lent, Rio de Janeiro erupts into carnival. Often called "The Biggest Party on Earth", carnival involves five days of music and dance. The main event is the competition to find the most outrageous costumes and best decorated floats as they parade through the city to the sound of *samba* music.

The huge statue of Christ the Redeemer which towers over Rio de Janeiro.

RIO DE JANEIRO

Once the capital of Brazil, the beautiful city of Rio de Janeiro sprawls among the bays, islands and hills around Guanabara Bay. The city acts like a magnet, drawing people from poor rural areas who come in search of work. A bad lack of housing has given birth to endless shanty towns, called *favelas*, which creep up the hillsides and crowd every piece of land unfit for other development.

Guanabara Bay provides access to the sea

Suburbs have grown rapidly

Rio-Niterói Bridge

Rio de Janeiro

From Rio, good road and rail routes lead inland

Favelas lacking sanitation and other amenities

Favelas on steep slopes vulnerable to heavy rain

N

STEEL

Attracted by Brazil's steel industry, cheap labour and plentiful electricity, several multinational companies have invested money in the country. US and European car manufacturers have established successful factories around São Paulo. Look for 🚗

Brazilian-made Fiat saloon

BRASILIA

In the mid-1950s the government of Brazil decided to build a new capital city in the sparsely inhabited central plateau region. Built in the shape of an aeroplane, the futuristic city of Brasilia became the country's official capital in 1960. The wide boulevards and open spaces contain spectacular buildings, such as this cathedral.

ORANGE JUICE

Oranges are grown in the region around São Paulo, where the climate is frost-free. Over a million tonnes are picked each year. Most of it is processed into orange juice concentrates. Brazil now supplies 85 per cent of the world's orange juice, exporting it mainly to the USA and Europe. Look for 🍊

The Iguaçu River as it drops over the Iguaçu Falls.

COFFEE

Coffee originated in Africa, but Brazil is now the world's largest producer. When the trees have shed their white blossoms, the green berries ripen into red "cherries". Each cherry contains two seeds, or coffee beans, which are washed, dried and roasted. Look for ☕

The wings of the *Morpho* butterfly are often used to decorate jewellery.

GOLD MINING

Brazil has vast mineral reserves. This huge human anthill is the result of a gold rush which began in the 1980s near the Serra Pelada. Thousands of prospectors – called *garimpeiros* – burrow into the hillsides hoping to find gold. Look for ⛏

KEYBOX

Cattle: Vast areas of Brazilian rainforest have been destroyed to clear the land for cattle-ranching. Look for 🐄

Sugar cane: In the 1970s Brazil began to make an alternative to petrol out of sugar cane, but now falling oil prices have made this uneconomic. Look for 🌾

Aerospace industry: In recent years Brazil has been successful in developing an aerospace industry, designing planes that are sold worldwide. Look for ✈

Bananas

Citrus fruit

Coffee

Cocoa

Soya beans

Cotton

Tobacco

Timber

Forest products

Mining

Industrial centre

Vehicle manufacture

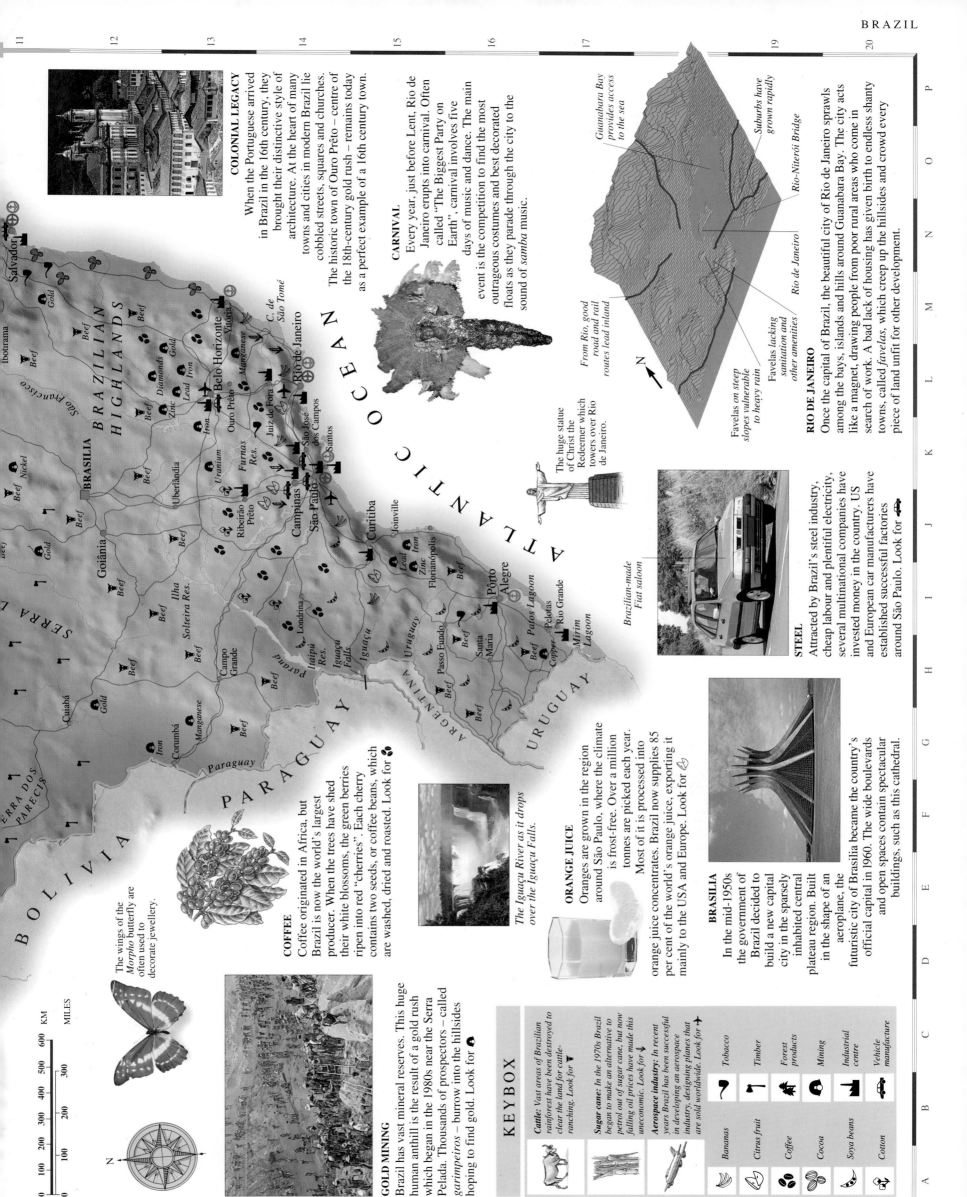

Map labels

Salvador

Gold

Ibotirama

Beef

BRAZILIAN HIGHLANDS

Beef

Beef

Vitória

Belo Horizonte

Diamonds

Gold

Manganese

Zinc

Lead

Iron

Ouro Prêto

Iron

Juiz de Fora

Rio de Janeiro

C. de São Tomé

BRASILIA

Beef

Uranium

São José dos Campos

Santos

Campinas

São Paulo

Uberlândia

Ribeirão Prêto

Curitiba

Beef

Joinville

Iron

Lead

Zinc

Florianópolis

Beef

Goiânia

Beef

Ilha Solteira Res.

Beef

Londrina

Furnas Res.

Itaipú Res.

Iguaçu Falls

Campo Grande

Beef

Iguaçu

Uruguay

Pôrto Alegre

Patos Lagoon

Rio Grande

Pelotas

Mirim Lagoon

Passo Fundo

Beef

Santa Maria

Beef

Copper

Cuiabá

Gold

Manganese

Corumbá

Iron

SERRA DOS PARECIS

BOLIVIA

Paraguay

PARAGUAY

ARGENTINA

URUGUAY

ATLANTIC OCEAN

São Francisco

Nickel

Gold

Beef

Beef

Paraná

Scale

KM

MILES

600

500

400

300

200

100

0

300

200

100

0

N

SOUTHERN SOUTH AMERICA

ALL FOUR COUNTRIES in this region were colonized in the 16th century by Spain. With the exception of Argentina, their populations are almost entirely mestizo – people of mixed Spanish and native descent. In Argentina, 98 per cent of the population is descended from European settlers, as the native peoples were killed or driven out by the immigrants. Argentina falls into three regions: the hot, damp lands of the Gran Chaco in the north, the grasslands of the Pampas in the centre and the barren plateau of Patagonia in the south. Argentina gets its wealth from the rich soil of the Pampas, where cereals are grown and vast herds of sheep and cattle graze. The Pampas spills into neighbouring Uruguay, where sheep provide the country with its main export: wool. Paraguay's economy is mainly dependent on agriculture. Chile lies coiled like a snake along the western side of the Andes, its head in the mineral-rich Atacama Desert and its tail in the icy wastes of the south. These countries all suffer from high inflation, unstable governments and poverty.

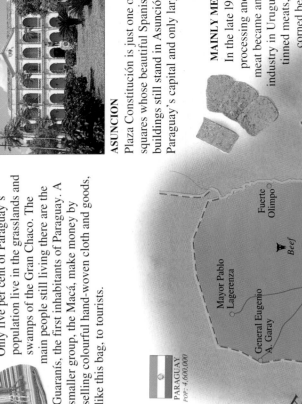

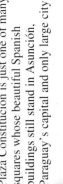

THE PEOPLES OF THE CHACO

Only five per cent of Paraguay's population live in the grasslands and swamps of the Gran Chaco. The main people still living there are the Guaraní, the first inhabitants of Paraguay. A smaller group, the Macá, make money by selling colourful hand-woven cloth and goods, like this bag, to tourists.

ASUNCION

Plaza Constitución is just one of many squares whose beautiful Spanish buildings still stand in Asunción, Paraguay's capital and only large city.

MAINLY MEAT

In the late 19th century, processing and packing meat became an important industry in Uruguay. Today, tinned meats, such as corned beef, are still a major export. Look for ⚓

Tomatoes were first grown in South America.

URUGUAY
POP: 3,100,000

ITAIPU DAM

On the mighty Paraná River is one of the world's largest hydro-electric projects, the Itaipú Dam. This joint venture between Brazil and Paraguay boosted Paraguay's economy, creating jobs for thousands of people. Look for ⚡

PARAGUAY
POP: 4,600,000

COPPER

Near Calama, Chile, shining metal is extracted from the largest open-cast copper mine in the world. Giant trucks remove thousands of tonnes (tons) of ore a day. However, the world price of copper is now falling, causing severe economic problems in Chile. Look for

The Atacama Desert in Chile is the driest place on earth.

B R A Z I L

Itaipú Dam
Ciudad del Este
Salto del Guairá

P A R A G U A Y
Pedro Juan Caballero
Concepción
Fuerte Olimpo
Mayor Pablo Lagerenza
General Eugenio A. Garay
Dr Pedro P. Peña
Filadelfia
Pozo Colorado
Pilcomayo
ASUNCION
Paraguarí
Villarica
Caazapá
San Juan Bautista
Encarnación
Posadas
San Pedro
Pilar
Formosa
Corrientes
Resistencia
Vera

G R A N   C H A C O
Bermejo
Salado

B O L I V I A
P E R Ú

A R G E N T I N A
San Salvador de Jujuy
Salta
San Miguel de Tucumán
Santiago del Estero
Catamarca
La Rioja
Córdoba
L. Mar Chiquita
Villa María
Río Cuarto
San Luis
Mercedes
San Juan
Mendoza
Godoy Cruz
San Felipe
San Rafael

A T A C A M A   D E S E R T
Arica
Iquique
Tocopilla
Calama
Chuquicamata
Antofagasta
Chañaral
Copiapó
Vallenar
Pan-American Highway
Copper
C H I L E
La Serena
Coquimbo
Ovalle
Illapel
La Ligua
Quillota
Viña del Mar

A N D E S

U R U G U A Y
Artigas
Rivera
Tacuarembó
Melo
Paysandú
Salto
Durazno
Florida
Trinta y Tres
Rocha
Fray Bentos
Mercedes
Colonia
MONTEVIDEO
River Negro Res.
Mirim Lagoon

Uruguay
Paraná
Paraná
Santa Fe
Rosario
San Nicolás
San Nicolás de los Arroyos
BUENOS AIRES
Concordia
Colón
Gualeguaychú

P A C I F I C   O C E A N

Beef
Wheat
Silver
Copper
Lead
Zinc
Iron
Lapis Lazuli

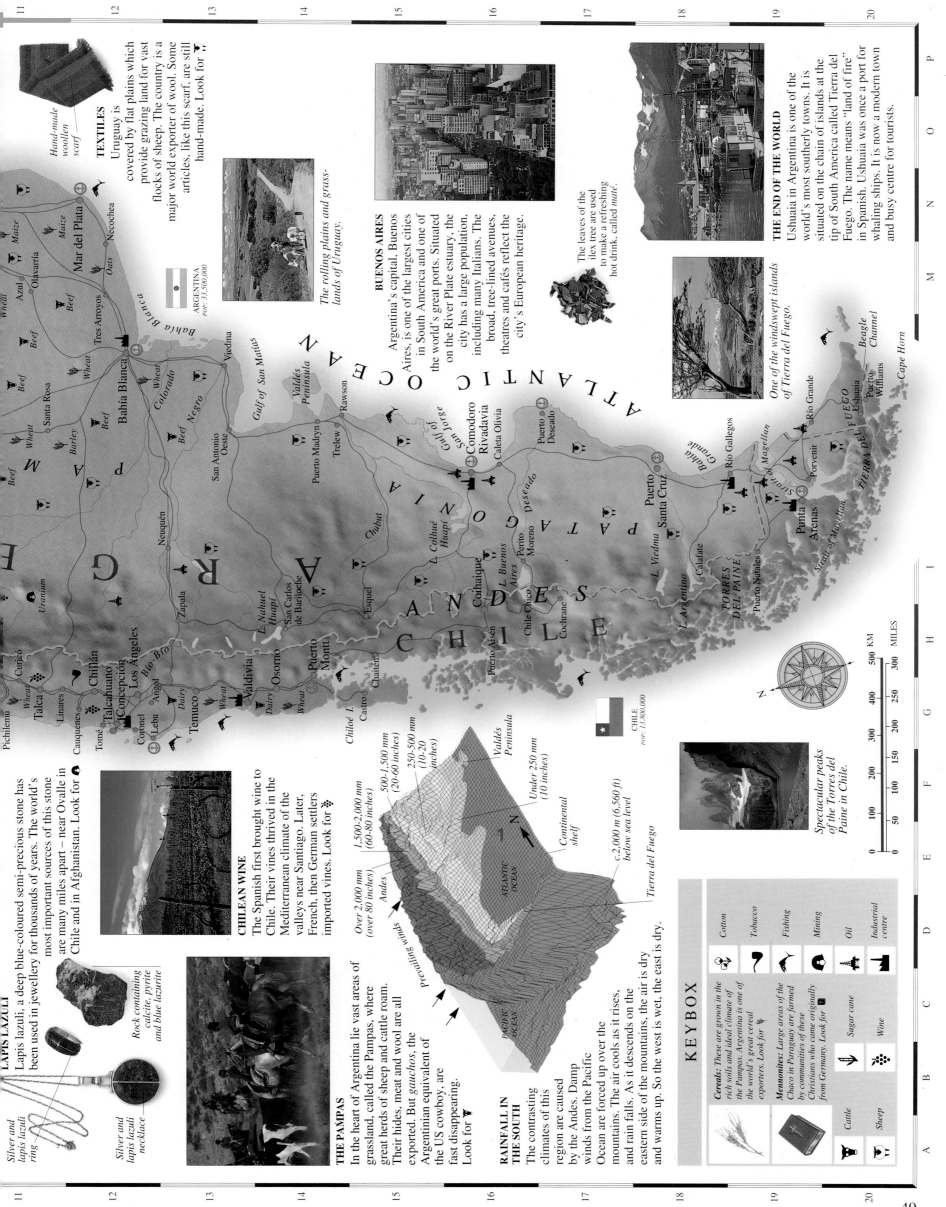

TEXTILES
Uruguay is covered by flat plains which provide grazing land for vast flocks of sheep. The country is a major world exporter of wool. Some articles, like this scarf, are still hand-made. Look for 🐑

Hand-made woollen scarf

ARGENTINA
POP: 33,500,000

The rolling plains and grass-lands of Uruguay.

BUENOS AIRES
Argentina's capital, Buenos Aires, is one of the largest cities in South America and one of the world's great ports. Situated on the River Plate estuary, the city has a large population, including many Italians. The broad, tree-lined avenues, theatres and cafés reflect the city's European heritage.

The leaves of the ilex tree are used to make a refreshing hot drink, called mate.

One of the windswept islands of Tierra del Fuego.

THE END OF THE WORLD
Ushuaia in Argentina is one of the world's most southerly towns. It is situated on the chain of islands at the tip of South America called Tierra del Fuego. The name means "land of fire" in Spanish. Ushuaia was once a port for whaling ships. It is now a modern town and busy centre for tourists.

LAPIS LAZULI
Lapis lazuli, a deep blue-coloured semi-precious stone has been used in jewellery for thousands of years. The world's most important sources of this stone are many miles apart – near Ovalle in Chile and in Afghanistan. Look for 🔷

Silver and lapis lazuli ring

Rock containing calcite, pyrite and blue lazurite

Silver and lapis lazuli necklace

CHILEAN WINE
The Spanish first brought wine to Chile. Their vines thrived in the Mediterranean climate of the valleys near Santiago. Later, French, then German settlers imported vines. Look for 🍇

THE PAMPAS
In the heart of Argentina lie vast areas of grassland, called the Pampas, where great herds of sheep and cattle roam. Their hides, meat and wool are all exported. But *gauchos*, the Argentinian equivalent of the US cowboy, are fast disappearing. Look for 🐎

RAINFALL IN THE SOUTH
The contrasting climates of this region are caused by the Andes. Damp winds from the Pacific Ocean are forced up over the mountains. The air cools as it rises, and rain falls. As it descends on the eastern side of the mountains, the air is dry and warms up. So the west is wet, the east is dry.

Spectacular peaks of the Torres del Paine in Chile.

Over 2,000 mm (over 80 inches)
1,500-2,000 mm (60-80 inches)
500-1,500 mm (20-60 inches)
250-500 mm (10-20 inches)
Under 250 mm (10 inches)

Andes
Prevailing winds
Valdés Peninsula
Continental shelf
c.2,000 m (6,560 ft) below sea level
Tierra del Fuego
ATLANTIC OCEAN
PACIFIC OCEAN
N

CHILE
POP: 13,800,000

KEYBOX

Cereals: These are grown in the rich soils and ideal climate of the Pampas. Argentina is one of the world's great cereal exporters. Look for 🌾	Cotton 🪷	Cattle 🐂
	Tobacco	Sheep 🐑
Mennonites: Large areas of the Chaco in Paraguay are farmed by communities of these Christians who came originally from Germany. Look for 📖	Fishing	
	Mining	
	Oil	
	Sugar cane →	
	Industrial centre	
	Wine 🍇	

MILES
KM
500 400 300 200 100 0
300 250 200 150 100 50 0

N

Geographic labels on map: Maize, Oats, Mar del Plata, Necochea, Olavarría, Azul, Beef, Wheat, Tres Arroyos, Santa Rosa, Bahía Blanca, Bahía Blanca, Barley, Viedma, Colorado, Río Negro, San Antonio Oeste, Neuquén, Valdés Peninsula, Rawson, Trelew, Puerto Madryn, Gulf of San Matías, Chubut, Zapala, L. Nahuel Huapí, San Carlos de Bariloche, Esquel, ANDES, PATAGONIA, Comodoro Rivadavia, Caleta Olivia, Gulf of San Jorge, Deseado, Puerto Deseado, L. Colhué Huapí, Coihaique, L. Buenos Aires, Perito Moreno, Chile Chico, Cochrane, Puerto Aisén, Chaitén, Chiloé I., Castro, Puerto Montt, Osorno, Valdivia, Temuco, Angol, Los Angeles, Concepción, Talcahuano, Coronel, Lebu, Chillán, Cauquenes, Tomé, Linares, Talca, Curicó, Pichilemu, Bío-Bío, Wheat, Dairy, L. Viedma, Calafate, L. Argentino, L. Argentino, Puerto Natales, TORRES DEL PAINE, Río Gallegos, Puerto Santa Cruz, Bahía Grande, Punta Arenas, Strait of Magellan, Porvenir, Río Grande, TIERRA DEL FUEGO, Ushuaia, Puerto Williams, Beagle Channel, Cape Horn, ARGENTINA, PAMPAS, URUGUAY, ATLANTIC OCEAN, CHILE

49

THE ANTARCTIC

THE CONTINENT OF ANTARCTICA has such a cold, harsh climate that no people live there permanently. The land is covered by a huge sheet of ice up to 2 km (1.2 miles) thick, and seas around Antarctica are frozen over. Even during the short summers, the temperature barely climbs above freezing, and the sea-ice only partly melts; in winter, temperatures can plummet to -80° C (-112° F). Few animals and plants can survive on land, but the seas around Antarctica teem with fish and mammals. The only people on the continent are scientists working in the Antarctic research stations and tourists, who come to see the dramatic landscape and the unique creatures that live here. But even these few people have brought waste and pollution to the region.

KRILL
Krill are the main food of the baleen whale. Japanese and Russian ships catch about 400,000 tonnes (tons) of krill each year, threatening the whales' food supply. Mainly used for animal feed, krill are also considered a delicacy in Japan. Krill gather in such huge numbers that they are visible from aeroplanes or even satellites.

Adélie penguins live in huge colonies on rocks or Antarctic pack ice.

Icebergs are huge blocks of ice which float in the sea.

Crozet Is. (to France)

VARIOUS NATIONS CLAIMED TERRITORY IN ANTARCTICA WHEN IT WAS FIRST DISCOVERED IN THE 19TH CENTURY. THESE CLAIMS HAVE BEEN SUSPENDED UNDER THE 1959 ANTARCTIC TREATY (SIGNED BY 39 NATIONS). STATIONS CAN BE SET UP FOR SCIENTIFIC RESEARCH, BUT MILITARY BASES ARE FORBIDDEN.

Kerguelen I. (to France)

Heard I. (to Australia)

ATLANTIC OCEAN
INDIAN OCEAN
PACIFIC OCEAN
SCOTIA SEA
WEDDELL SEA
BELLINGSHAUSEN SEA
AMUNDSEN SEA
ROSS SEA
DAVIS SEA
Drake Passage

South Orkney Is. (to UK)
Elephant I. (to UK)
South Shetland Is. (to UK)
Fimbul Ice Shelf
Riiser-Larsen Ice Shelf
Georg van Neumayer (to Germany)
Novalazarevskaya (to Russian Fed.)
QUEEN MAUD LAND
Syowa (to Japan)
Lutzow-Holm Bay
Mawson (to Australia)
C. Darnley
ENDERBY LAND
Larsen Ice Shelf
Halley (to UK)
Belgrano II (to Argentina)
Filchner Ice Shelf
Ronne Ice Shelf
Amery Ice Shelf
Lambert Glacier
Mackenzie Bay
Prydz Bay
Anvers I. (to USA)
PALMER LAND
SOUTH POLAR PLATEAU
West Ice Shelf
Peter the First I. (to Norway)
Siple (to USA)
ELLSWORTH MTS.
South Pole
Amundsen-Scott (to USA)
Vostok (to Russian Fed.)
Mirnyy (to Russian Fed.)
Shackleton Ice Shelf
TRANSANTARCTIC MTS.
MARIE BYRD LAND
Getz Ice Shelf
Ross Ice Shelf
Vincennes Bay
Cape Poinsett
Scott Base (to New Zealand)
C. Colbeck
McMurdo Sound
VICTORIA LAND
WILKES LAND
Porpoise Bay
C. Adare
Dumont d'Urville (to France)
Balleny Is.

Antarctic fishing fleets are reducing stocks of the cod icefish.

These mountains are on Anvers Island, which lies off the Antarctic peninsula.

ANTARCTIC TOURISM
Cruise liners have been bringing tourists to the Antarctic region since the 1950s. About 2-3,000 visitors a year observe the harsh beauty of the landscape and its extraordinary wildlife from the comfort of cruise ships. Look for 📷

0   250   500   750   1000 1250 1500   KM
0   250   500   750   1000 MILES

WHALES
Whales thrive in the seas around the Antarctic, which are rich in plankton and krill, their main food sources. Large-scale whale-hunting started in the 20th century, and the numbers of whales soon fell. In 1948 the International Whaling Commission was set up to regulate the numbers and species of whales killed, and to create protected areas. Look for ⤙

Blue whale

POLLUTION
The Antarctic research stations have yet to find effective ways of disposing of their waste. Although some of it is burnt, tins, bottles, machine parts and chemicals are often simply dumped near the bases, spoiling the area's natural beauty. The only solution to the problem is to take the rubbish out of Antarctica. Look for 💀

RESEARCH
The scientific base in this picture is the US Amundsen-Scott station, which is built underground at the South Pole. Scientists at the Antarctic research stations are monitoring changes to the weather and environment. Look for ⌒

KEYBOX

Oil: Much of the polar region is rich in oil, but the difficulty of drilling and moving oil, as well as environmental concerns, have slowed exploitation. Look for ⚓

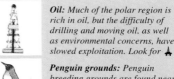
Penguin grounds: Penguin breeding grounds are found near Antarctic coasts. Some are being disturbed by tourists, airstrips and construction. Look for 🐧

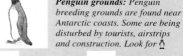

⤙ Fishing	⌒ Polar research centre
🏭 Coal	💀 Pollution
📷 Tourism	⤙ Whales

THE ARCTIC

THE ARCTIC OCEAN IS covered by drifting ice up to 30 metres (98 feet) thick, which partially melts and disperses in the summer. Much of the surrounding land is tundra – plains and moorlands that are carpeted with moss and lichens, but permanently frozen beneath the surface. People have lived around the Arctic for thousands of years, hunting the mammals and fish that live in the ocean. This region has large deposits of oil, but the harsh climate makes it difficult to extract from the ground.

FISHFINGERS
Large numbers of cod, haddock, halibut and other fish live in the Arctic Ocean. Cod and haddock are taken to fish-processing factories in Greenland. Here they are frozen, canned or – in the case of cod – made into fishfingers, and exported to the markets of the USA and Europe. Look for

ARCTIC PEOPLES
Traditionally, the people of the Arctic survived by hunting animals. They used seal skin for boats and clothing and seal fat, (blubber) for fuel. Today, tools, clothes and buildings are made from modern materials. Rifles now replace harpoons and snow-mobiles are used for transport.

The northern lights can be seen over the Arctic at night.

ICE-BREAKER
About half the Arctic Ocean is covered with ice in winter, but special ships called ice-breakers can still sail across it. In 1969, a large tanker, the *S.S. Manhattan*, penetrated the pack ice of the Northwest Passage (from eastern Canada to Alaska) for the first time.

Polar bears spend summers on the Arctic ice. They move further south in winter.

GREENLAND
The first Europeans to explore and settle Greenland were Vikings, who arrived in about 986 AD. Greenland later came under Danish rule, and is now a self-governing part of Denmark.

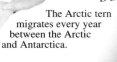
The Arctic tern migrates every year between the Arctic and Antarctica.

Mountains on Svalbard reflected in a melted ice pond.

ARCTIC COAL
The island of Spitsbergen has rich deposits of minerals, especially coal. It is part of Norway, but other countries are allowed to mine there. The Norwegian coal town of Longyearbyen is 620 miles (1,000 km) from the mainland. It can be reached by sea for only eight months a year, making it difficult and expensive to ship coal out. Coal screes and long, severe winters make this a desolate place. Look for

ARCTIC OCEAN

North Pole

ATLANTIC OCEAN

ICELAND

THE ATLANTIC OCEAN

THE WORLD'S OCEANS cover almost three-quarters of the Earth's surface. Beneath the surface of the Atlantic Ocean lie vast, featureless plains and long chains of mountains called ridges. The Mid-Atlantic Ridge is one of the world's longest mountain chains; some of its peaks are so high that they pierce the surface as volcanic islands, such as the Azores. A huge rift valley 24-48 km (15-30 miles) wide runs down the ridge's centre. The deepest part of the Atlantic is 8 km (5 miles) below the surface. On average, the Atlantic has the warmest and saltiest waters of any ocean. Before regular shipping routes were established, the Atlantic isolated America from the prosperous countries of Europe, but today it is crossed by some of the world's most important trade routes. The North Atlantic has always been one of the world's richest fishing grounds, but it has been overfished, and fish stocks are now dangerously low.

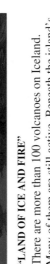

Puffins breed on rocky islands, like the Faeroes.

FISHING

Catches of cod, herring and haddock in the North Atlantic have been severely reduced by over-fishing. Fishing fleets must now travel long distances and remain at sea for months at a time. The fish are processed on the fleet's factory ship to keep them fresh. Look for ⌐

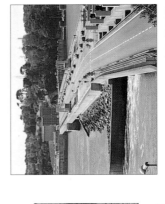

"LAND OF ICE AND FIRE"

There are more than 100 volcanoes on Iceland. Many of them are still active. Beneath the island's harsh, rocky surface lie vast natural heat reserves. This energy is used to provide hot water and central heating for much of the population. Iceland's economy is based on fishing, which accounts for about 70 per cent of its exports.

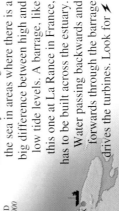

TIDAL ENERGY

Electricity can be generated from the sea in areas where there is a big difference between high and low tide levels. A barrage, like this one at La Rance in France, has to be built across the estuary. Water passing backwards and forwards through the barrage drives the turbines. Look for ⚡

WHALING

Whaling has been going on in the world's oceans for hundreds of years. But with the invention of the explosive harpoon, catches increased rapidly. Today some species of whales are threatened with extinction. Attempts are being made to ban whaling worldwide until numbers recover. Look for ⌐

British aircraft carrier

NATO

The North Atlantic Treaty Organization (NATO) is an association of North American and European countries which was established to defend its members – principally against the former Soviet Union. Look for III

An extinct volcano on an island in the West Indies.

Tomatoes and other fruit are grown in the warm climate of the Canary Islands.

CAPE VERDE
POP: 300,000

ICELAND
POP: 300,000

Map labels

ARCTIC OCEAN

Greenland

GREENLAND SEA

ICELAND
REYKJAVIK
Denmark Strait

FAEROE ISLANDS
(to Denmark)

Rockall
(to UK)

Baffin Bay

Davis Strait

LABRADOR SEA

C. Farewell

Newfoundland
St John's
Grand Bank

North-Eastern Atlantic Basin

Hudson Bay

NORTH AMERICA

Bay of Fundy
Saint John
Portland
Halifax
Gloucester
St-Lawrence
New York City
Baltimore

Bermuda
(to UK)

North American Basin

Newfoundland Basin

West Indies

New Orleans

Gulf of Mexico

Mississippi

Mid-Atlantic Ridge

SARGASSO SEA

Canary Basin

ATLANTIC

Murmansk

EUROPE

BLACK SEA

Nile
Port Said

Tallinn
Liepāja
BALTIC SEA

Kristiansund
Ålesund
Bergen
Stavanger
Haugesund
Skagen
Esbjerg
Bremerhaven
Rotterdam
Boulogne
La Rance
Lorient

NORTH SEA

Aberdeen
Grimsby

Livorno
Ancona
Naples

Marseille
MEDITERRANEAN SEA
Algiers
Sfax

A Coruña
Porto

Gibraltar
Casablanca
Safi

AFRICA

Madeira
(to Portugal)

Azores
(to Portugal)

Canary Islands
(to Spain)

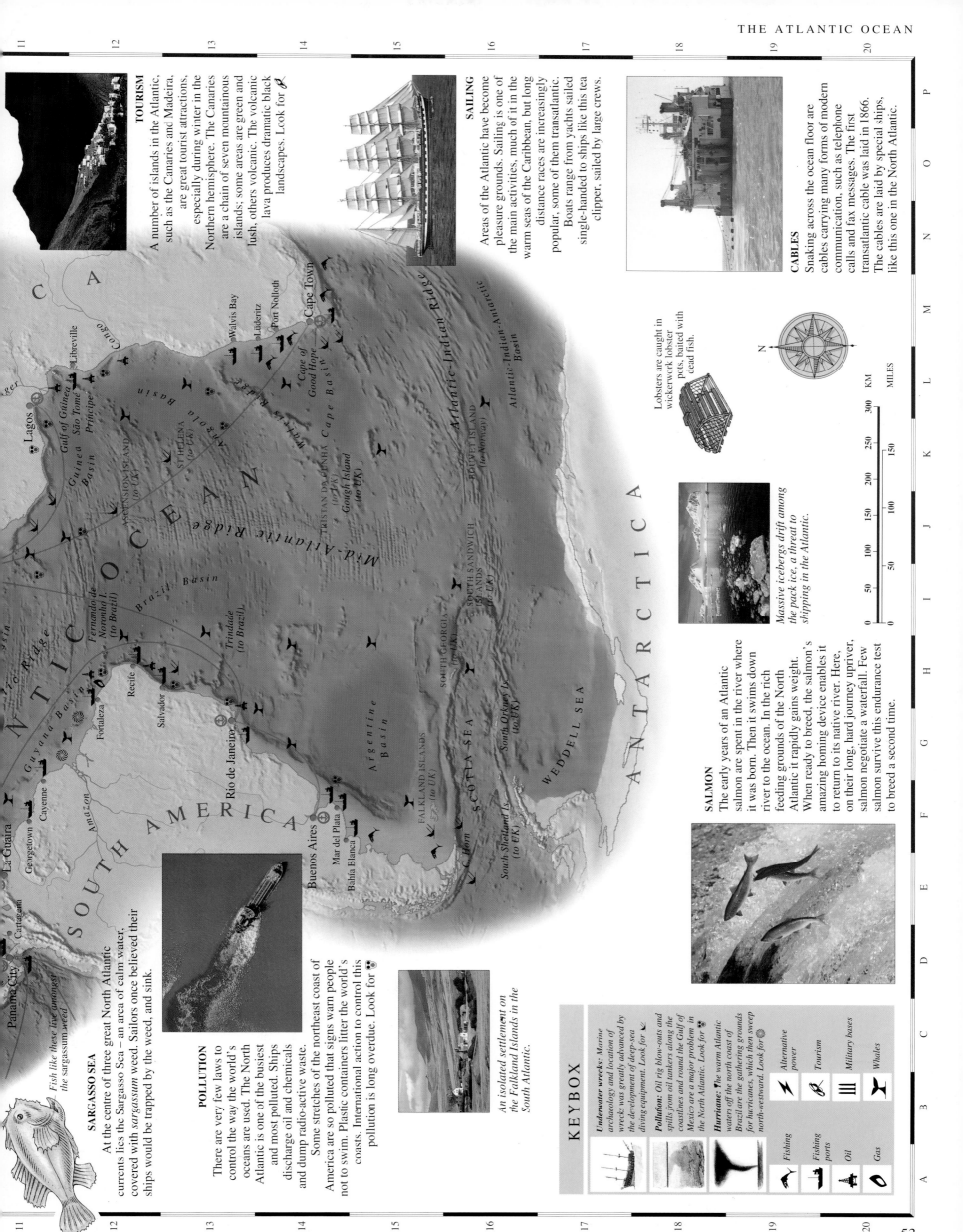

TOURISM

A number of islands in the Atlantic, such as the Canaries and Madeira, are great tourist attractions, especially during winter in the Northern hemisphere. The Canaries are a chain of seven mountainous islands; some areas are green and lush, others volcanic. The volcanic lava produces dramatic black landscapes. Look for 🏖

SAILING

Areas of the Atlantic have become pleasure grounds. Sailing is one of the main activities, much of it in the warm seas of the Caribbean, but long distance races are increasingly popular, some of them transatlantic. Boats range from yachts sailed single-handed to ships like this tea clipper, sailed by large crews.

CABLES

Snaking across the ocean floor are cables carrying many forms of modern communication, such as telephone calls and fax messages. The first transatlantic cable was laid in 1866. The cables are laid by special ships, like this one in the North Atlantic.

Lobsters are caught in wickerwork lobster pots, baited with dead fish.

Massive icebergs drift among the pack ice, a threat to shipping in the Atlantic.

SALMON

The early years of an Atlantic salmon are spent in the river where it was born. Then it swims down river to the ocean. In the rich feeding grounds of the North Atlantic it rapidly gains weight. When ready to breed, the salmon's amazing homing device enables it to return to its native river. Here, on their long, hard journey upriver, salmon negotiate a waterfall. Few salmon survive this endurance test to breed a second time.

SARGASSO SEA

At the centre of three great North Atlantic currents lies the Sargasso Sea – an area of calm water, covered with *sargassum* weed. Sailors once believed their ships would be trapped by the weed, and sink.

Fish like these live amongst the sargassum weed.

POLLUTION

There are very few laws to control the way the world's oceans are used. The North Atlantic is one of the busiest and most polluted. Ships discharge oil and chemicals and dump radio-active waste.

Some stretches of the northeast coast of America are so polluted that signs warn people not to swim. Plastic containers litter the world's coasts. International action to control this pollution is long overdue. Look for 🛢

An isolated settlement on the Falkland Islands in the South Atlantic.

KEYBOX

Underwater wrecks: Marine archaeology and location of wrecks was greatly advanced by the development of deep-sea diving equipment. Look for ⚓

Pollution: Oil rig blow-outs and spills from oil tankers along the coastlines and round the Gulf of Mexico are a major problem in the North Atlantic. Look for 🛢

Hurricane: The warm Atlantic waters off the north coast of Brazil are the gathering grounds for hurricanes, which then sweep north-westward. Look for 🌀

⚡ Alternative power	⚓ Fishing
🏖 Tourism	🚢 Fishing ports
≡ Military bases	🛢 Oil
🐋 Whales	◖ Gas

KM
0   50   100   150   200   250   300
MILES
0   50   100   150

N

SOUTH AMERICA

ANTARCTICA

ATLANTIC OCEAN

Mid-Atlantic Ridge

Atlantic-Indian Ridge

Walvis Ridge

Cape Basin

Angola Basin

Guinea Basin

Brazil Basin

Argentine Basin

Guyana Basin

Atlantic-Indian-Antarctic Basin

Cape of Good Hope

Cape Town
Port Nolloth
Lüderitz
Walvis Bay
Libreville
Gulf of Guinea
São Tomé
Príncipe
Lagos
Niger
Congo

WEDDELL SEA

SCOTIA SEA

BOUVET ISLAND (to Norway)

SOUTH SANDWICH ISLANDS (to UK)

SOUTH GEORGIA (to UK)

SOUTH ORKNEY Is. (to UK)

SOUTH SHETLAND Is. (to UK)

FALKLAND ISLANDS (to UK)

ST HELENA (to UK)
ASCENSION ISLAND (to UK)
TRISTAN DA CUNHA (to UK)
Gough Island (to UK)

Fernando de Noronha I. (to Brazil)
Trindade (to Brazil)

Recife
Salvador
Fortaleza
Cayenne
Georgetown
La Guaira
Panama City
Cartagena
Amazon

Rio de Janeiro
Buenos Aires
Mar del Plata
Bahía Blanca
Horn

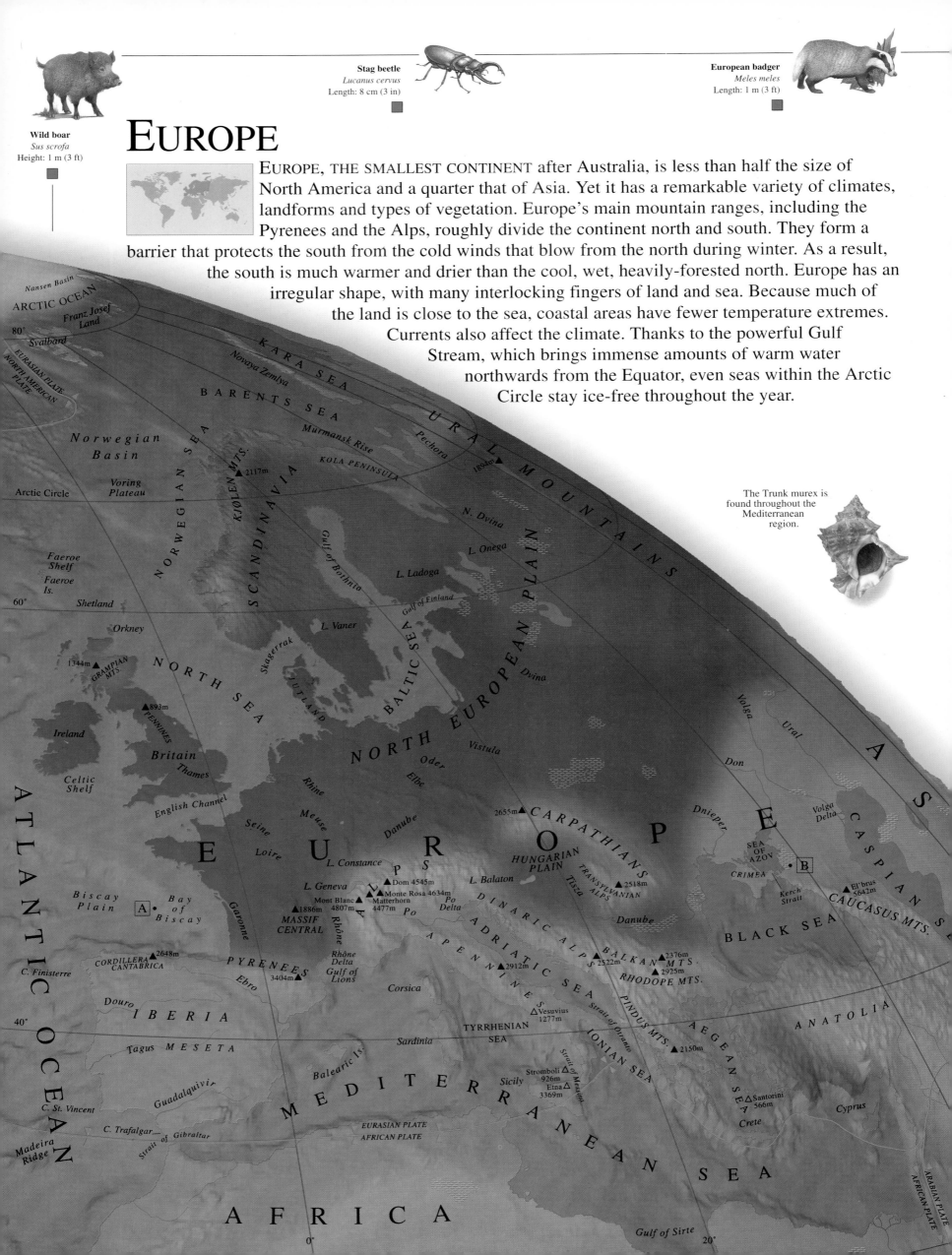

Wild boar
Sus scrofa
Height: 1 m (3 ft)

Stag beetle
Lucanus cervus
Length: 8 cm (3 in)

European badger
Meles meles
Length: 1 m (3 ft)

EUROPE

EUROPE, THE SMALLEST CONTINENT after Australia, is less than half the size of North America and a quarter that of Asia. Yet it has a remarkable variety of climates, landforms and types of vegetation. Europe's main mountain ranges, including the Pyrenees and the Alps, roughly divide the continent north and south. They form a barrier that protects the south from the cold winds that blow from the north during winter. As a result, the south is much warmer and drier than the cool, wet, heavily-forested north. Europe has an irregular shape, with many interlocking fingers of land and sea. Because much of the land is close to the sea, coastal areas have fewer temperature extremes. Currents also affect the climate. Thanks to the powerful Gulf Stream, which brings immense amounts of warm water northwards from the Equator, even seas within the Arctic Circle stay ice-free throughout the year.

The Trunk murex is found throughout the Mediterranean region.

Siberian tit
Parus cinctus
Length: 13 cm (5 in)

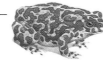

Green toad
Bufo viridis
Length: 10 cm (4 in)

Osprey
Pandion haliaetus
Wingspan: 1.6 m (5 ft)

BOGLANDS
Bogs cover many of northern Europe's wettest areas. Mosses and reeds are among the few plants that grow in waterlogged soils. Wetlands take thousands of years to develop because plants grow so slowly there.

WAVE POWER
Waves can wear away the shore, creating odd landforms. This seastack off the Orkneys in the British Isles is 135 m (450 ft) high.

Ammonites, fossil relatives of today's octopus, were once found in Europe. They died out 65 million years ago.

PIONEERING BIRCH
Light-loving silver birches are often the first trees to appear on open land. Although quick-growing, they are short-lived. After a few years birches are replaced by trees that can survive shade, such as oaks.

BARE MOUNTAIN
Ice, rain, wind and gravity strip steep slopes of all soil. Rocks pile up at the foot of peaks, where plants can take root.

FJORDS
Glaciers have cut hundreds of narrow inlets, or fjords, into Scandinavia's Atlantic coastline. The water in the inlet is calmer than in the open sea.

NEEDLELEAF FOREST
Cone-bearing trees such as pine, larch and fir cover Scandinavia. Most are evergreen: they keep their needle-like leaves even when covered in snow for many months of the year.

TREELESS TUNDRA
Arctic summers are so cool that only the topmost layer of frozen soil thaws. Only shallow-rooted plants can survive in the tundra.

English oak
Quercus robur
Height: 40 m (130 ft)

ANCIENT WOODLANDS
Relics of Europe's ancient forests, such as these oaks stunted by the rain and wind, are found only in a few valleys in southwest Britain.

This fossil of *Stauranderaster*, a starfish once found in this region, dates from around 70 million years ago.

Pine marten
Martes martes
Length: 52 cm (20 in)

DRY SOUTH
Crete is a mountainous Mediterranean island with hot dry summers. Many plants survive the summer as underground bulbs, blooming briefly in the wet spring.

YOUNG MOUNTAINS
The Alps are some of western Europe's highest mountains. They are part of an almost continuous belt that stretches from the Pyrenees in the west to the Himalayas in Asia. The Alps are still rising because of plate movements in the Mediterranean region.

Sweet briar
Rosa rubiginosa
Height: 3 m (10 ft)

CROSS-SECTION THROUGH EUROPE

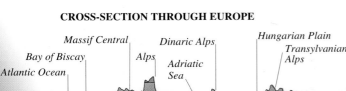

Massif Central
Dinaric Alps
Hungarian Plain
Transylvanian Alps
Bay of Biscay
Alps
Kerch Strait
Adriatic Sea
Black Sea
Atlantic Ocean
Crimea

3,000 (9,843)
0 Sea level
-4,500 (14,764)

A
Length: 4,500 km (2,800 miles)
B
Metres (feet)

KEY TO SYMBOLS

▲ *Mountain*
△ *Volcano*
⁂ *Mangroves*
▦ *Wetlands*
▨ *Coral reef*
■ *Plate margins showing direction of movement*

KEY TO NATURAL VEGETATION

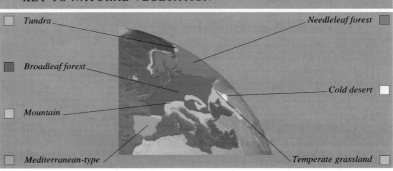

☐ *Tundra*
☐ *Broadleaf forest*
☐ *Mountain*
☐ *Mediterranean-type*
Needleleaf forest ☐
Cold desert ☐
Temperate grassland ☐

Spanish lynx
Felis lynx
Length: 1.3 m (4 ft)

55

SCANDINAVIA AND FINLAND

THE SCANDINAVIAN COUNTRIES of Norway, Sweden and Denmark and neighbouring Finland are situated around the Baltic Sea in northern Europe. During past ice ages, glaciers gouged and scoured the land, leaving deep fjords, lakes and valleys in their wake. Much of Norway and Sweden, and nearly two-thirds of Finland, is covered by dense forests of pine, spruce and birch trees. In the far north, winters are long and dark, and snow falls for about eight months of the year. Most Swedish people live in the central lowlands. Norway's economy depends on its shipbuilding, fishing and merchant fleets. Denmark is flat and low-lying, with abundant rainfall and excellent farmland. The Finnish people originally came from the east, via Russia, and consequently differ from the Scandinavians both in language and culture. All four countries have small populations, are highly industrialized and enjoy some of the highest standards of living in the world.

Deep water enables ships to reach far inland

Fish farming of salmon in sheltered waters

Rough upland grazing for sheep and goats

Coastal fishing communities are declining

Meadow crops grown for livestock

Cultivation limited to warm, south-facing slopes

Coastal islands form natural breakwaters

A NORWEGIAN FJORD
Norway is so mountainous that only three per cent of the land can be cultivated. Long inlets of sea, called fjords, cut into Norway's west coast. The best farmland is found around the head of the fjords and in the lowland areas around them. Over 70 per cent of Norway's population lives in cities, many of them in towns situated along the sheltered fjords.

NORWAY
POP: 4,300,000

The still waters of a Norwegian fjord.

FISHING
As Norway has so little farmland, fishing has always been a vital source of food. Today, about 95 per cent of the total catch is processed, about half made into fishmeal and oil. Fish-farming is on the increase, especially of salmon in the fjords. Look for ➤

Vast shoals of herring gather in the seas around Scandinavia

Fantoft Church, Bergen

LAPLAND
Lapland is a land of tundra, forests and lakes. Here the *Samer*, or Lapps, still herd reindeer for their meat and milk. Development in the north now threatens their way of life.

STAVE CHURCHES
The wooden stave churches of Norway were built between AD 1000 and 1300. There were once 600 of them, but today only 25 are still standing. A stave church has a stone foundation with a wooden frame on top. The four wooden corner posts are called staves. Further wooden extensions can be added to the basic framework.

Lego building bricks were invented in Denmark.

SKIING
For thousands of years skiing has been the most efficient way of crossing deep snow on foot. This region is often thought to be the original home of skiing – in fact "ski" is the Norwegian word for a strip of wood. Long-distance cross-country skiing, or *langlaufen*, is a popular sport in Norway, Finland and Sweden.

Scrambled egg

Prawn

Caviar

Asparagus

Smoked salmon

SMÖRGÅSBORD
Smörgåsbord means "sandwich table" in Swedish. Other countries in this region have their own versions, but the idea is the same: a great spread of local delicacies, served cold on bread, which can include ingredients such as reindeer, fish, cheese and salad.

KEYBOX

Hydro-electric power The region's mountainous terrain enables the majority of its electricity to be supplied by HEP. Look for ⊞

Bridges: Tunnels and bridges now link the Danish islands of Fyn and Sjaelland. Linking Denmark and Sweden is under discussion. Look for ⌒

🐂	Cattle	🐟	Fishing
🐖	Pigs	⛴	Fishing port
🌾	Cereals	⚓	Mining
🌲	Timber	🏭	Industrial centre

COPENHAGEN
Copenhagen's fine natural harbour and its position at the main entrance to the Baltic Sea, helped it to become a major port and Denmark's capital city. The city's tiny shops, cobbled streets, museums and cafés attract over a million tourists each year.

Danish bacon for export

DANISH AGRICULTURE
Two-thirds of the total area of Denmark is used for farming. Denmark exports agricultural products all over the world. The main products are bacon, dairy products, cereals and beef. Cereals are widely grown, but mainly as fodder for pigs. Look for 🐖

Steink

Hitra
Smøla
Vanadium
Trondheim
Molde
Iron
Ålesund
Nordfjord
Rørc
L. Fem
Sogne Fjord
Hermansverk
Gjøvik
Lillehan
L. Mjøsa
Bergen
Hardanger Fjord
Oats
Honefoss
Haugesund
Bokna Fjord
Drammen
Kongsberg
Oslo
Stavanger
Porsgrunn
Dairy
Moss
Fredrikstad
Sandnes
Arendal
Hälden
Titanium
Orra
Dairy
Dairy
Iron
Kristiansand
Oslo Fjord

S k a g e r r a k

Uddevalla
Trollhättan

DENMARK

DENMARK
POP: 5,200,000

Hjørring
Frederikshavn
Göte
Borå

Ålborg
Varber

Holstebro
Dairy
Rye
Randers
Halmstad
Ringkøbing
JUTLAND

Århus
Hälsingborg
Barley
Horsens
Helsingør
Esbjerg
Vejle
COPENHAGEN
Hässle
Ribe
Odense
Slagelse
Abenrå
Fyn
Sønderborg
Naestved
Sjaelland
Y
Nakskov
Barley
Nykøbing

GERMANY

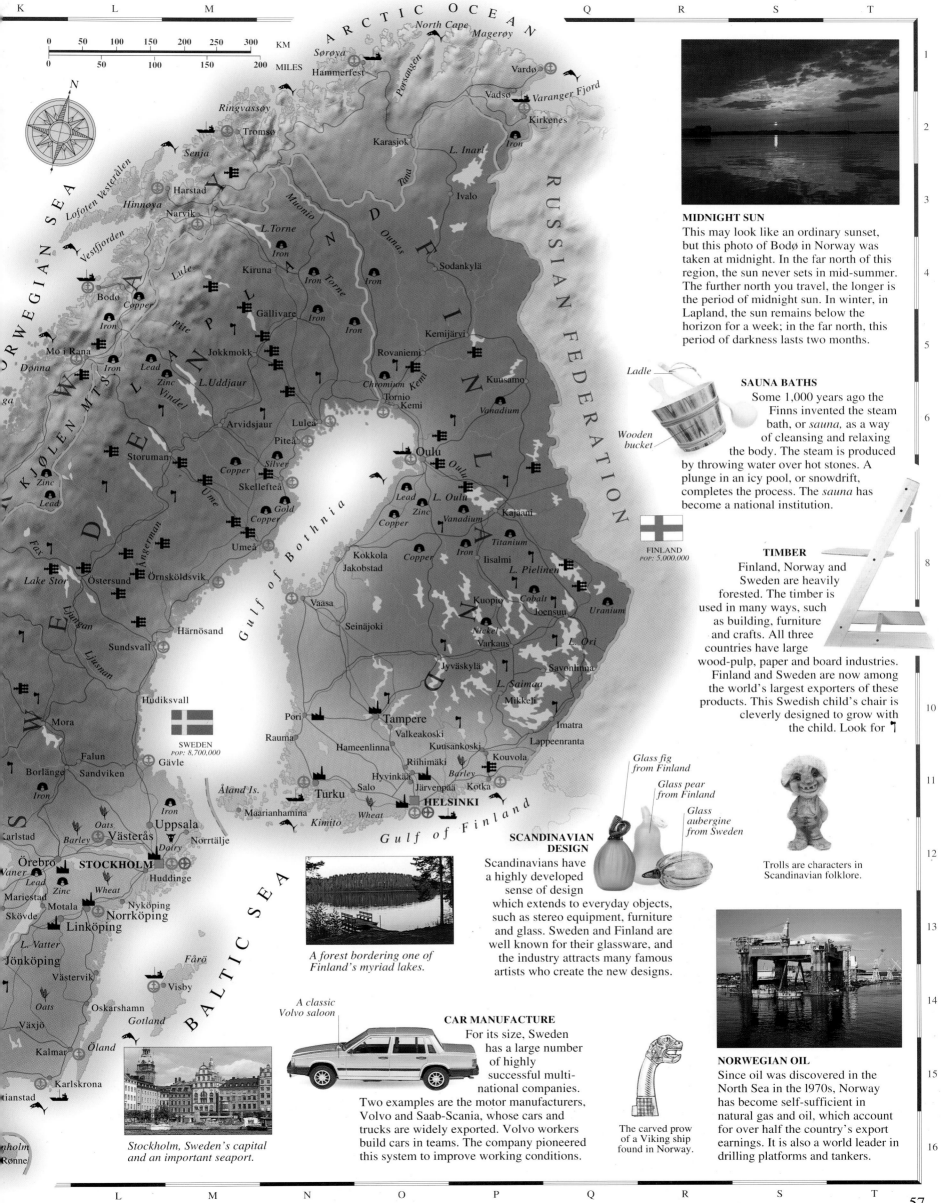

Map labels

ARCTIC OCEAN

North Cape
Magerøy
Søroya
Hammerfest
Vardø
Vadsø
Varanger Fjord
Kirkenes
Ringvassøy
Tromsø
Senja
Karasjok
L. Inari
Iron
Ivalo
Harstad
Hinnøya
Narvik
Lofoten Vesterålen
L. Torne
Muonio
Ounas
Vestfjorden
Kiruna
Iron
Torne
Iron
Sodankylä
Bodø
Copper
Lule
Gällivare
Iron
Kemijärvi
Iron
Mo i Rana
Iron
Piite
Jokkmokk
Rovaniemi
Kuusamo
Dønna
Lead
Chromium Kemi
Zinc
L. Uddjaur
Vindel
Tornio
Kemi
Vanadium
Arvidsjaur
Luleå
Zinc
Lead
Pitea
Oulu
Oulu
Storuman
Copper
Silver
Skellefteå
L. Oulu
Lead
Zinc
Kajaani
Copper
Gold
Vanadium
Copper
Titanium
Umeå
Iron
Iisalmi
Kokkola
Copper
L. Pielinen
Jakobstad
Ostersund
Örnsköldsvik
Kuopio
Cobalt
Vaasa
Joensuu
Uranium
Lake Stor
Angerman
Seinäjoki
Nickel
Fax
Ljungan
Härnösand
Varkaus
L. Ori
Sundsvall
Jyväskylä
Savonlinna
Ljusnan
L. Saimaa
Mora
Hudiksvall
Mikkeli
Falun
Borlänge
Sandviken
Imatra
Iron
Gävle
Pori
Tampere
Lappeenranta
Rauma
Valkeakoski
Kuusankoski
Karlstad
Oats
Hameenlinna
Kouvola
Barley
Åland Is.
Iron
Riihimäki
Barley
Uppsala
Salo
Kotka
Väster\u00e5s
Dairy
Hyvinkää
Järvenpää
Örebro
Norrtälje
Maarianhamina
Turku
HELSINKI
STOCKHOLM
Kimito
Wheat
Vaner
Huddinge
Lead
Zinc
Wheat
Mariestad
Nyköping
Motala
Norrköping
Skövde
Linköping
L. Vatter
Jönköping
Fårö
Västervik
Visby
Oats
Gotland
Växjö
Öland
Kalmar
Oland
Karlskrona
stianstad
holm
Rønne

NORWEGIAN SEA
RUSSIAN FEDERATION
KJØLEN MTS
LAPLAND
FINLAND
SWEDEN
Gulf of Bothnia
BALTIC SEA
Gulf of Finland

FINLAND
POP: 5,000,000

SWEDEN
POP: 8,700,000

MIDNIGHT SUN

This may look like an ordinary sunset, but this photo of Bodø in Norway was taken at midnight. In the far north of this region, the sun never sets in mid-summer. The further north you travel, the longer is the period of midnight sun. In winter, in Lapland, the sun remains below the horizon for a week; in the far north, this period of darkness lasts two months.

SAUNA BATHS

Ladle
Wooden bucket

Some 1,000 years ago the Finns invented the steam bath, or *sauna*, as a way of cleansing and relaxing the body. The steam is produced by throwing water over hot stones. A plunge in an icy pool, or snowdrift, completes the process. The *sauna* has become a national institution.

TIMBER

Finland, Norway and Sweden are heavily forested. The timber is used in many ways, such as building, furniture and crafts. All three countries have large wood-pulp, paper and board industries. Finland and Sweden are now among the world's largest exporters of these products. This Swedish child's chair is cleverly designed to grow with the child. Look for ⌐

SCANDINAVIAN DESIGN

Glass fig from Finland
Glass pear from Finland
Glass aubergine from Sweden

Scandinavians have a highly developed sense of design which extends to everyday objects, such as stereo equipment, furniture and glass. Sweden and Finland are well known for their glassware, and the industry attracts many famous artists who create the new designs.

Trolls are characters in Scandinavian folklore.

A forest bordering one of Finland's myriad lakes.

CAR MANUFACTURE

A classic Volvo saloon

For its size, Sweden has a large number of highly successful multi-national companies. Two examples are the motor manufacturers, Volvo and Saab-Scania, whose cars and trucks are widely exported. Volvo workers build cars in teams. The company pioneered this system to improve working conditions.

Stockholm, Sweden's capital and an important seaport.

The carved prow of a Viking ship found in Norway.

NORWEGIAN OIL

Since oil was discovered in the North Sea in the 1970s, Norway has become self-sufficient in natural gas and oil, which account for over half the country's export earnings. It is also a world leader in drilling platforms and tankers.

THE BRITISH ISLES

THE BRITISH ISLES CONSIST OF TWO large islands – Great Britain and Ireland – surrounded by many smaller ones. They are divided into two countries: the United Kingdom (UK), often known as Britain, and Ireland. At the end of the 18th century, the UK became the first country in the world to undergo an industrial revolution. It became the world's leading manufacturing and trading nation, and built up an empire that covered more than a quarter of the world. The UK's traditional industries, such as coal mining, textiles and car manufacturing, have declined in recent years, but service industries such as banking and insurance have been extremely successful. Ireland, which became independent from the UK in 1921, is still a mainly rural country and many Irish people make their living from farming. However, tourism and high-tech industries, such as computers and pharmaceuticals, are increasingly important. The UK and Ireland still have close trading links and many Irish people go to the UK to find work.

"THE TROUBLES"

When British Protestants settled in Ireland in the 17th century, they came into conflict with Irish Catholics, whose land they had seized. In 1921 the Protestant North refused to join the independent South. Catholics were discriminated against, in jobs and housing and violence erupted in the 1960s. British troops were sent to police the province.

AGRICULTURE AND INDUSTRY

Farming has always been Ireland's principal source of income. Dairy products, beef and potatoes are still important, but recently, the number of high-tech industries has increased.

Irish butter

OIL

Rich reserves of both oil and natural gas were found under the North Sea in the 1960s. By the late 1970s, natural gas was being piped to most homes, factories and businesses in the UK. Massive oil rigs were moored in the North Sea, and wells were dug by drilling into the ocean bed below the platforms. Oil rigs and onshore refineries brought employment to many areas, especially in eastern Scotland. But oil reserves are being steadily used up, and oil production is now in decline. Look for

Bright red letter boxes are a common sight on British streets.

FISHING

The waters of the north-east Atlantic are amongst the world's richest fishing grounds, well-stocked with mackerel, herring, cod, haddock and shellfish. The British Isles has many fishing ports, like this one in the north-east of England. But EU regulations designed to reduce catches and conserve fish stocks, are causing widespread discontent amongst fishermen. Look for

AEROSPACE

UK firms design and build a wide range of civil and military aircraft. Perhaps the most famous is Concorde, a supersonic jet created in partnership with the French. Recently, the aerospace industry has been badly hit by world recession, and UK companies have had to develop products in other areas, such as electronics and telecommunications. Look for

The supersonic jet, Concorde

INDUSTRY

Many Japanese companies, car and electronics manufacturers in particular, are now based in the UK, attracted by a skilled labour force and access to European markets. Britain's traditional industries, such as textiles, steel and pottery have been joined by newer, high-tech industries. Look for

TARTAN TOURISM

Tourism is an important source of income for Scotland. People come to enjoy the beautiful highland scenery, and visit the ancient castles. For centuries, Scotland was dominated by struggles between rival families, known as clans. Today one of the most popular tourist souvenirs is tartan – textiles woven in the colours of the clans.

Scottish shortbread

Tartan scarf

A deep inlet of water – or loch – in the north of Scotland.

Map labels

Shetland
Lerwick
Orkney
Kirkwall
Stromness
Thurso
C. Wrath
Beef
Moray Firth
Elgin
Inverness
Loch Ness
Loch Shin
Ullapool
North Minch
Little Minch
Lewis
Stornoway
Beef
Harris
Skye
North Uist
South Uist
Barra
Tiree
Coll
Canna
Rum
Eigg
Muck
Mallaig
Fort William
Mull
Oban
Colonsay
Jura
Islay
Kintyre
Arran
Beef
Outer Hebrides
ATLANTIC OCEAN
Barley
Beef
Oats
Dee
Aberdeen
Fraserburgh
Peterhead
NORTH SE[A]
GRAMPIAN MTS.
SCOTLAND
Oats
Dundee
Perth
Stirling
Firth of Forth
Edinburgh
Tweed
Loch Lomond
Clyde
Glasgow
Greenock
Firth of Clyde
Ayr
Dairy
Grangemouth
Loch Forth
Lough Foyle
NORTHERN

LONDON

The Romans founded the town they called Londinium on the River Thames in AD 43. The UK's capital is now a huge, sprawling city with seven million inhabitants. London is the country's centre of finance, politics, law, and culture, and contains many famous historical buildings, shops, museums and theatres.

Big Ben

The Houses of Parliament, London

MULTICULTURAL BRITAIN

Since the 1960s, the UK has become an increasingly multicultural society. Large numbers of immigrants have come to the UK from former colonies in Africa, the Caribbean and Asia and have greatly enriched British culture with their own traditions.

Tea, served with milk, is Britain's national drink.

HIGH FINANCE

The skyscrapers and office blocks that surround St. Paul's Cathedral in the City of London are home to one of the world's biggest financial centres. City companies specialize in banking and insurance, and lead the world in foreign currency deals. The City covers only a small area, but every day it is filled with more than half a million office workers.

FARMING

About three-quarters of the land in the UK is used for farming. The crops vary from region to region and reflect the country's varied climate and soils. Barley, wheat, vegetables and sugar beet are the main crops in the east of the country, while beef and dairy farming is a speciality in the west.

SPORT

Many sports which are now played all over the world originated in the UK. Rugby, cricket and golf were all British inventions, while the rules of modern soccer were established on the sports fields of English schools.

Soccer ball

Cricket ball

Rugby ball

The rocky coast of Cornwall in southwest England.

Dublin's fine O'Connell bridge over the R. Liffey.

English beers are made from barley, malt and hops.

NORTH SEA

UNITED KINGDOM
POP: 57,800,000

IRELAND
POP: 3,500,000

ENGLISH CHANNEL

IRISH SEA

N

KM MILES
150
75
100
50
50
25
0 0

KEYBOX

High-tech industry: Companies making scientific instruments, electronics and computers are based in southern England, Scotland and Ireland. Look for ☐

Tourism: Millions of visitors a year come to the UK to see palaces, castles, ancient monuments, cathedrals and museums. Look for 🏛

Tunnel: The Channel Tunnel, linking England and France, is 50 km (31 miles) long. Passenger and freight trains use the tunnel. Look for ◪

Airport: Heathrow, 20 km (12 miles) from London, is the world's busiest international airport. It handles 38 million passengers a year. Look for ⊕

Coal	Industrial centre	Oil refining
Aerospace industry	Vehicle manufacture	
Cattle	Sheep	Cereals
Market gardening	Fishing port	

Place names and features visible on the map include:

Donegal Bay, Sligo, Lough Erne, Dumfries, Stranraer, Bangor, Belfast, Newry, Dundalk, Lough Neagh, IRELAND, Lough Corrib, Galway Bay, Galway, Shannon, Limerick, Tralee, Killarney, Dingle Bay, Bantry Bay, Cork, Waterford, Wexford, DUBLIN, Dun Laoghaire, Lough Ree, Lough Derg, Athlone, Blackwater, Barrow, WICKLOW MTS, St George's Channel, ISLE OF MAN (to UK), DOUGLAS, Holyhead, Holy I., Anglesey, Caernarfon, Cardigan Bay, Aberystwyth, CAMBRIAN MTS, Fishguard, Milford Haven, Swansea, Cardiff, Merthyr Tydfil, BRECON BEACONS, Newport, Bristol Channel, WALES, Newcastle upon Tyne, Sunderland, Middlesbrough, Carlisle, LAKE DISTRICT, Whitehaven, Solway Firth, Tyne, Tees, PENNINES, Lancaster, Morecambe Bay, Blackpool, Preston, Bolton, Liverpool, Birkenhead, Chester, Manchester, Huddersfield, Bradford, Leeds, York, Sheffield, Hull, Kingston upon Hull, Grimsby, Humber, Lincoln, Stoke-on-Trent, Derby, Nottingham, Shrewsbury, Wolverhampton, Birmingham, Coventry, MIDLANDS, Leicester, Peterborough, The Fens, The Wash, King's Lynn, Norwich, Great Yarmouth, EAST ANGLIA, Cambridge, Ipswich, Felixstowe, Colchester, Ouse, Stratford-upon-Avon, Worcester, Gloucester, Severn, Northampton, Luton, Watford, LONDON, Heathrow, HOME COUNTIES, Reading, Oxford, Swindon, Bath, Bristol, Stonehenge, Salisbury, Crawley, Southampton, Portsmouth, Isle of Wight, Newport, Bournemouth, Brighton, Hastings, Southend-on-Sea, Canterbury, Dover, Strait of Dover, Channel Tunnel, EXMOOR, Taunton, Yeovil, Barnstaple, Bideford, DARTMOOR, Exeter, Lyme Bay, Plymouth, Falmouth, Penzance, Land's End, Isles of Scilly, CORNWALL, Lundy, Channel Is., ST. PETER PORT, GUERNSEY (to UK), JERSEY (to UK), ST. HELIER, ENGLAND

SPAIN AND PORTUGAL

SPAIN AND PORTUGAL are located on the Iberian Peninsula, which is cut off from the rest of Europe by the Pyrenees. This isolation, combined with the region's closeness to Africa and the Atlantic Ocean, has shaped the history of the two countries. The Moors, an Islamic people from North Africa, occupied the peninsula in the 8th century AD, leaving an Islamic legacy that is still evident today. In 1492 the Moors were finally expelled from Catholic Spain. The oceangoing Spanish and Portuguese took the lead in exploring and colonizing the New World, and both nations acquired substantial overseas empires. During this era, Portugal was ruled by Spain from about 1580 to 1640. Eventually, both nations lost most of their colonies, and their once-great wealth and power declined. Spain was torn apart by a vicious civil war from 1936-39, and right-wing dictators ruled both Spain and Portugal for much of the 20th century. In the 1970s, both countries emerged as modern democracies, and have since experienced rapid economic growth, benefiting from their membership of the European Union. Today, their economies are dominated by tourism and agriculture, although Spanish industry is expanding rapidly.

FISHING
Portuguese sardine

The Portuguese have fished for cod off the eastern coast of Canada for over 500 years. Dried salt cod is still a common food today. Sardines from Portugal are considered the best in the world, and are exported from fish processing factories on the coast. Look for 🏭

GROWING CORKS
Spain and Portugal produce two-thirds of the world's cork. It is made from the outer bark of these evergreen oak trees. The bark is stripped off, seasoned, flattened, then laid out in sheets.

FORTIFIED WINES
Sherry   Port

This region is famous for its fortified wines. They are made by adding extra alcohol to the wine during the fermentation process. Sherry is named after Jerez de la Frontera, while port comes from Porto. Look for 🍇

KEYBOX

Forest products: Spain and Portugal are Europe's only source of eucalyptus, which is grown for its gum, resin, oil and wood. Look for	
Fishing: Spanish fishing fleets are amongst the largest in Europe, concentrated around the northwest Atlantic coast. Look for	
Vehicle manufacture: Spain ranks sixth in world car exports, specializing in small cars. Look for	

🐑	Sheep	🚢	Fishing ports
	Citrus fruit	⛏	Mining
🍇	Wine	🏭	Industrial centre
	Vegetable oil	🤿	Tourism

LISBON
Portugal's great navigators and explorers set sail from Lisbon, on the mouth of the River Tagus. The city, which grew rich on global trade, was completely rebuilt after an earthquake destroyed two thirds of it in 1755.

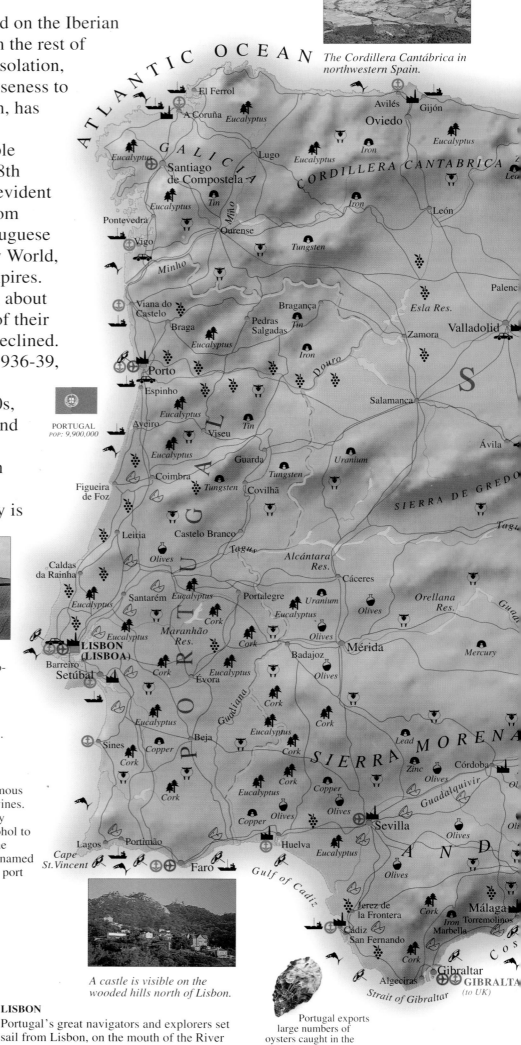

The Cordillera Cantábrica in northwestern Spain.

PORTUGAL
POP: 9,900,000

A castle is visible on the wooded hills north of Lisbon.

Portugal exports large numbers of oysters caught in the Atlantic.

Map labels:

ATLANTIC OCEAN

El Ferrol, A Coruña, Avilés, Gijón, Oviedo, GALICIA, Lugo, Iron, Santiago de Compostela, CORDILLERA CANTABRICA, Pontevedra, León, Ourense, Vigo, Tungsten, Minho, Esla Res., Viana do Castelo, Bragança, Pedras Salgadas, Zamora, Valladolid, Braga, Iron, Douro, Porto, Salamanca, Espinho, PORTUGAL, Aveiro, Viseu, Tin, Ávila, Eucalyptus, Guarda, Uranium, Coimbra, Tungsten, Covilhã, SIERRA DE GREDOS, Figueira de Foz, Tagus, Leiria, Castelo Branco, Alcántara Res., Caldas da Rainha, Cáceres, Olives, Santarém, Portalegre, Uranium, Orellana Res., Maranhão Res., Cork, Olives, LISBON (LISBOA), Badajoz, Mérida, Mercury, Barreiro, Setúbal, Évora, Olives, Guadiana, Cork, Sines, Beja, Copper, Cork, SIERRA MORENA, Lead, Zinc, Córdoba, Cork, Copper, Olives, Copper, Guadalquivir, Olives, Sevilla, Lagos, Portimão, Huelva, Eucalyptus, Cape St. Vincent, Faro, Gulf of Cadiz, Jerez de la Frontera, Cork, Málaga, Cádiz, San Fernando, Iron, Torremolinos, Marbella, Algeciras, Gibraltar, GIBRALTAR (to UK), Strait of Gibraltar

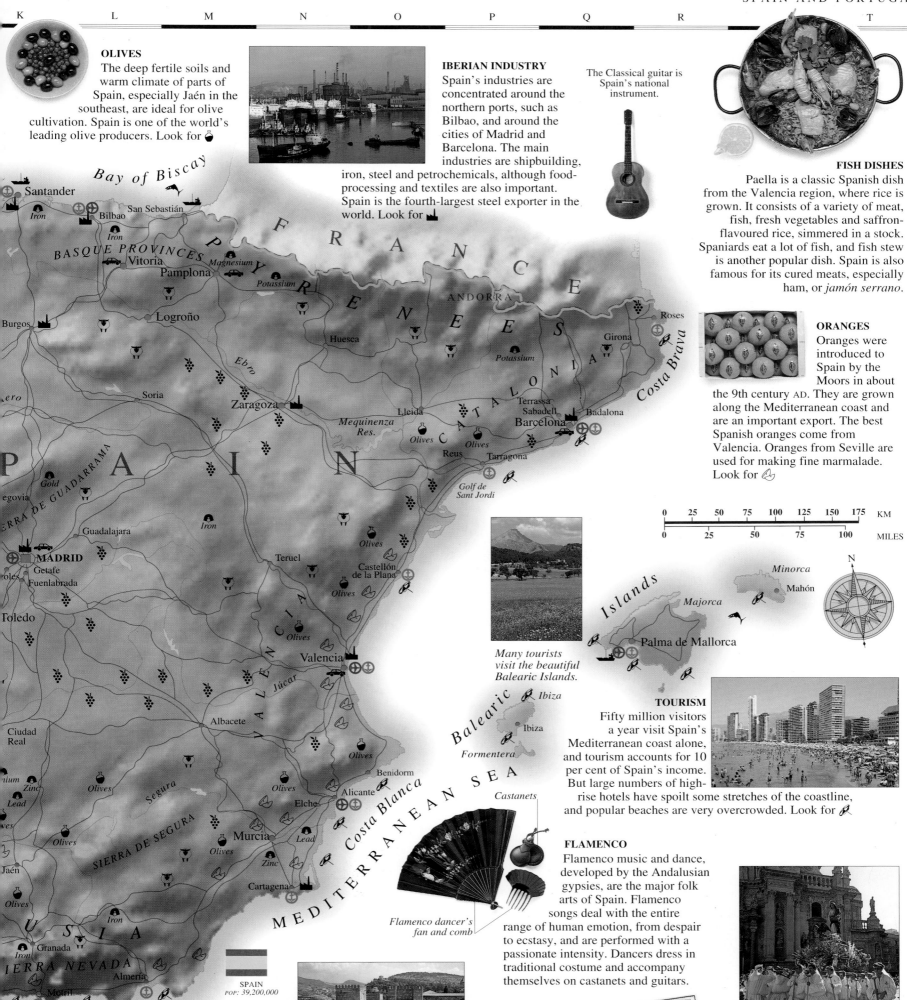

OLIVES
The deep fertile soils and warm climate of parts of Spain, especially Jaén in the southeast, are ideal for olive cultivation. Spain is one of the world's leading olive producers. Look for 🫒

IBERIAN INDUSTRY
Spain's industries are concentrated around the northern ports, such as Bilbao, and around the cities of Madrid and Barcelona. The main industries are shipbuilding, iron, steel and petrochemicals, although food-processing and textiles are also important. Spain is the fourth-largest steel exporter in the world. Look for ⚒

The Classical guitar is Spain's national instrument.

FISH DISHES
Paella is a classic Spanish dish from the Valencia region, where rice is grown. It consists of a variety of meat, fish, fresh vegetables and saffron-flavoured rice, simmered in a stock. Spaniards eat a lot of fish, and fish stew is another popular dish. Spain is also famous for its cured meats, especially ham, or *jamón serrano*.

ORANGES
Oranges were introduced to Spain by the Moors in about the 9th century AD. They are grown along the Mediterranean coast and are an important export. The best Spanish oranges come from Valencia. Oranges from Seville are used for making fine marmalade. Look for 🍊

Many tourists visit the beautiful Balearic Islands.

TOURISM
Fifty million visitors a year visit Spain's Mediterranean coast alone, and tourism accounts for 10 per cent of Spain's income. But large numbers of high-rise hotels have spoilt some stretches of the coastline, and popular beaches are very overcrowded. Look for 🏖

FLAMENCO
Flamenco music and dance, developed by the Andalusian gypsies, are the major folk arts of Spain. Flamenco songs deal with the entire range of human emotion, from despair to ecstasy, and are performed with a passionate intensity. Dancers dress in traditional costume and accompany themselves on castanets and guitars.

Castanets

Flamenco dancer's fan and comb

SPAIN
POP: 39,200,000

Gibraltar has been a British colony since the 18th century.

THE ALHAMBRA
The Alhambra, at Granada in southern Spain, is a Moorish palace and fortress built during the 13th-14th centuries. It was the Moors' last stronghold in Spain. It is a beautiful example of Moorish architecture, famous for its delicately carved stone, brilliantly patterned mosaics and tiles, and alabaster fountains.

BULLFIGHTING
In Spain, bullfighting is a national sport. During a bullfight, brightly coloured capes are fluttered to tempt the bull to charge. When it charges, the matador sticks long, pointed barbs into the bull's shoulders. Once it is exhausted, the matador uses his sword to kill the bull, exposing himself to mortal danger.

CATHOLICISM
Like the Portuguese, the Spanish blend Roman Catholicism with customs and superstitions dating back to pre-Christian times. Their *fiestas* combine religious ceremonies with wine and dancing.

| 0 | 25 | 50 | 75 | 100 | 125 | 150 | 175 | KM |
| 0 | 25 | | 50 | | 75 | | 100 | MILES |

FRANCE

FOR CENTURIES FRANCE has played a central role in European civilization. Reminders of its long history can be found throughout the land; prehistoric cave-dwellings, Roman amphitheatres, medieval cathedrals, castles, and the 17th- and 18th-century palaces of the powerful French monarchs. The French Revolution of 1789 swept away the monarchy and changed the face of France forever. The country survived the Napoleonic wars and occupation during World Wars I and II, and now has a thriving economy based on farming and industry. It is a land of varied scenery and strong regional traditions, the only country which belongs to both northern and southern Europe. Farming is still important, but many people have moved from the country to the cities. France still administers a number of overseas territories, all that remain of its once widespread empire. Today, France's population includes immigrants from its former colonies, especially Muslims from North Africa. France is one of the most enthusiastic members of the European Union.

PARIS

Paris, the capital of France, is the largest and most important city in the country. It lies on both banks of the River Seine. One of the world's great cities, Paris contains magnificent buildings, art treasures and elegant shops. The wrought-iron Eiffel Tower looms above the city, the symbol of Paris.

A cyclist in the *Tour de France*, the world's most famous cycle race.

FRANCE
POP: 57,400,000

AGRICULTURE

France is a mainly rural country producing a wide range of farm products. Some farms still use traditional methods but modern technology has transformed regions like the Paris Basin, where cereals are grown on a large scale. Look for 🌾

THE AIRBUS

Developing new aircraft is so costly that sometimes several countries form a company together to share the costs. One example is Airbus Industrie: the main factory is at Toulouse, but costs are shared by France, Germany, the UK and Spain. With successful aircraft already flying, Airbus Industrie is planning a jumbo jet. Look for ✈

KEYBOX

Market gardening: In the northwest the mild climate and sheltered conditions are ideal for growing early vegetables, called primeurs. Look for 🛒

Nuclear power: Lacking its own energy sources, France has developed its nuclear power industry. It now produces 70% of its electricity. Look for 🏭

Tourism: In the underdeveloped Mediterranean region tourism has been encouraged by the construction of attractive holiday resorts. Look for ⛱

Rail routes: France has Europe's largest rail network. Inter-city trains (TGVs), travel at speeds of up to 300 km (186 miles) per hour. Look for 🚄

🧀	Cheese	⛏	Coal
🌾	Cereals	🏭	Industrial centre
🌱	Sugar beet	✈	Aerospace industry
🍇	Wine	🚗	Vehicle manufacturing
⚫	Mining	🎿	Skiing

CHATEAUS

France has many beautiful historic buildings. Along the banks of the River Loire and its tributaries are royal palaces, or chateaus, built by the royalty of France from the 15th-17th centuries. Chambord, originally a hunting lodge, has 440 rooms and 85 staircases. Fairytale palaces like these attract thousands of visitors each year.

Fields of sunflowers can be seen in many areas of France.

Head of garlic   *Snail*

Clove of garlic

Snails, served with butter and garlic, are a great French delicacy.

Camembert

Brie

CHEESE

France is famous for its cheese. Over 300 different varieties are made. Many, like Camembert, Roquefort and Brie, are world-famous and copied in many other countries. Each region has its traditional way of making and packaging its cheeses. Goat and sheep's milk is used as well as cow's. Look for 🧀

The principality of Andorra is situated in the Pyrenees.

Map labels

Cherbourg, Le Havre, Channel Islands (to UK), St. Lô, Caen, Wheat, NORMANDY, Camembert, Iron, Île d'Ouessant, Brest, Wheat, St.Brieuc, St. Malo, TGV, Barley, Oats, Wheat, Rennes, Laval, Le Ma, Quimper, Barley, Lorient, Vannes, Barley, Iron, Angers, Belle Île, St. Nazaire, Nantes, Loire, BRITTANY, ENGLISH CHANNEL, ATLANTIC OCEAN, La Roche-sur-Yon, Wheat, Poitiers, Les Sables d'Olonne, Wheat, TGV, La Rochelle, Charente, Wheat, Saintes, Angoulême, Barley, Bordeaux, Dordogne, Arcachon, Garonne, Mont-de-Marsan, Maize, Bayonne, Maize, Pau, Tarb, PYRENEES, F R

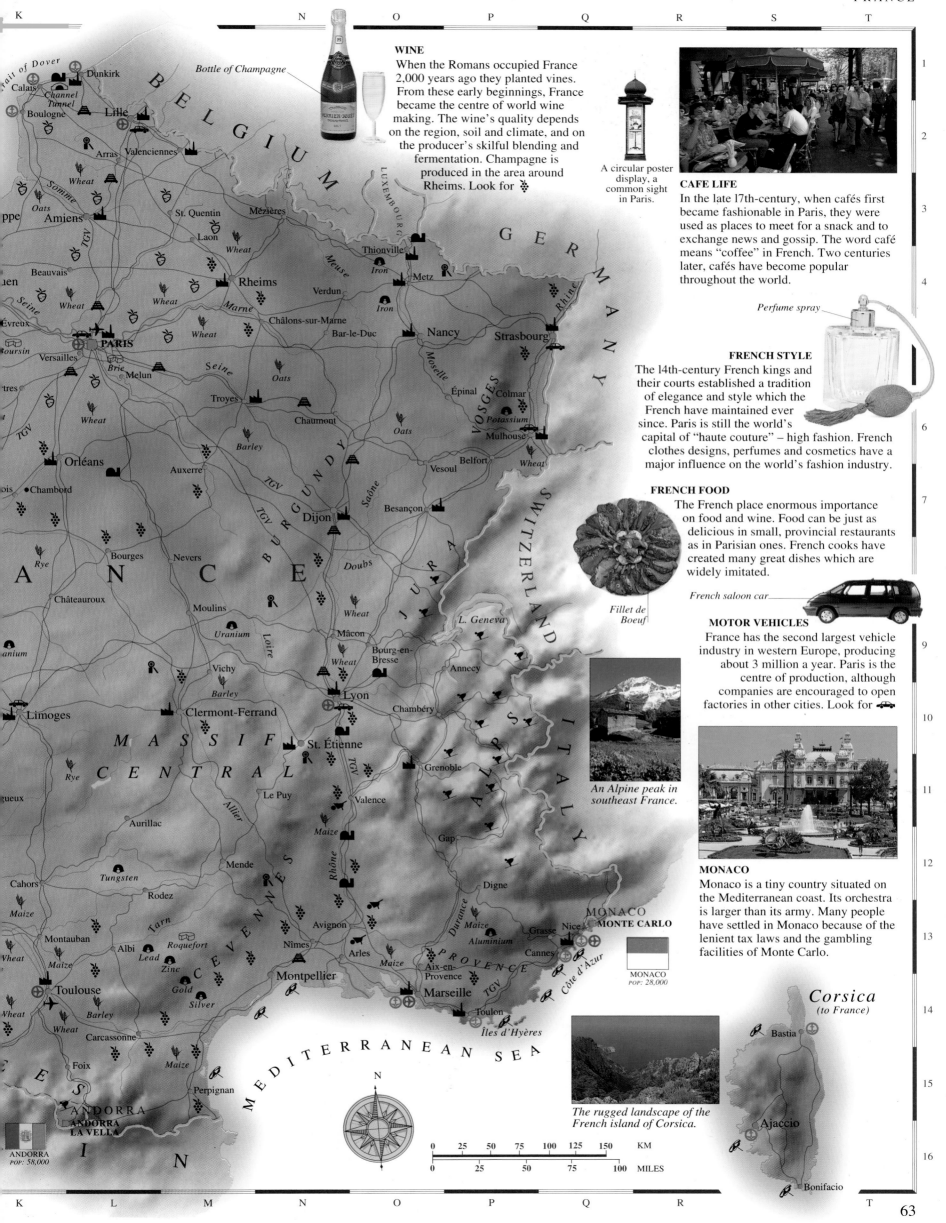

WINE

Bottle of Champagne

When the Romans occupied France 2,000 years ago they planted vines. From these early beginnings, France became the centre of world wine making. The wine's quality depends on the region, soil and climate, and on the producer's skilful blending and fermentation. Champagne is produced in the area around Rheims. Look for

A circular poster display, a common sight in Paris.

CAFE LIFE

In the late 17th-century, when cafés first became fashionable in Paris, they were used as places to meet for a snack and to exchange news and gossip. The word café means "coffee" in French. Two centuries later, cafés have become popular throughout the world.

Perfume spray

FRENCH STYLE

The 14th-century French kings and their courts established a tradition of elegance and style which the French have maintained ever since. Paris is still the world's capital of "haute couture" – high fashion. French clothes designs, perfumes and cosmetics have a major influence on the world's fashion industry.

FRENCH FOOD

The French place enormous importance on food and wine. Food can be just as delicious in small, provincial restaurants as in Parisian ones. French cooks have created many great dishes which are widely imitated.

Fillet de Boeuf

French saloon car

MOTOR VEHICLES

France has the second largest vehicle industry in western Europe, producing about 3 million a year. Paris is the centre of production, although companies are encouraged to open factories in other cities. Look for

An Alpine peak in southeast France.

MONACO

Monaco is a tiny country situated on the Mediterranean coast. Its orchestra is larger than its army. Many people have settled in Monaco because of the lenient tax laws and the gambling facilities of Monte Carlo.

MONACO
POP: 28,000

Corsica
(to France)

The rugged landscape of the French island of Corsica.

MEDITERRANEAN SEA

ANDORRA
POP: 58,000

| 0 | 25 | 50 | 75 | 100 | 125 | 150 | KM |
| 0 | 25 | 50 | 75 | 100 | MILES |

THE LOW COUNTRIES

BELGIUM, THE NETHERLANDS and Luxembourg are the most densely populated countries in Europe. They are known as the "Low Countries" because much of the land is flat and low-lying. In the Netherlands, much of the land lies below sea level, and has been reclaimed from the sea over the centuries by ingenious technology. The marshy, drained soils are extremely fertile. All three countries enjoy high living standards, with well-developed industries and excellent rail, road and waterway communications with the rest of Europe. During the course of their history, the Low Countries have often been the battleground between warring nations, and both Belgium and Luxembourg only achieved independence in the 19th century. Belgium is still divided by language – Dutch is spoken in the north, while the Walloons in the south speak French. The northern Netherlands are mainly Protestant; the rest of the region is basically Roman Catholic. Today, the Low Countries are unswerving supporters of the European Union. The cities of Brussels, The Hague and Luxembourg are all headquarters of important European institutions.

FLOWERS

The Netherlands are Europe's largest producers of flowers, and spectacular fields of spring flowers in full bloom are a major tourist attraction. Cut flowers are flown daily from the Netherlands to cities all over the world. Cultivation of bulbs such as crocuses, hyacinths, daffodils and tulips is a speciality. They have been grown here since about 1600, when they were introduced from Turkey and the Middle East. Look for

Tulip

FLOOD CONTROL

Much of the Netherlands lies below sea level, and is constantly at risk of flooding. Over the centuries, land has been painstakingly reclaimed from the sea. Barriers called dykes are built to keep the sea out and water is drained and pumped into canals. Originally the water was pumped out by windmills, but now electric pumps are used. Sluice-gates control the flow of excess water.

The rind of Dutch Edam cheese is coloured with anatto dye.

IMMIGRATION

Immigrants from the Netherlands' former colonies of Surinam, the Antilles and Indonesia have had a strong impact on Dutch life and culture. Indonesian restaurants are a common sight in Dutch cities, and *rijstafel* (rice surrounded by side dishes of egg, vegetables, meat and fish) is now a national dish.

Satay (barbecued meat)

Peanuts

Beef Rendang

Egg-fried rice

Prawns and garlic

Salad in peanut sauce

Pickled vegetables

NETHERLANDS
pop: 15,300,000

DELFT TILE

Delft pottery has been made in the Netherlands since the 17th century. The technique of glazing pottery with tin, used in Delft, came to the Netherlands from the Middle East via Spain and Italy. This Delft tile is decorated with a windmill, a familiar sight in the Netherlands. There are about 1,000 windmills still standing today, dating mainly from the 18th and 19th centuries.

CITY OF CANALS

The Dutch capital, Amsterdam, is a city of islands, built on swampy land. It is criss-crossed by 160 canals. Many of the city's finest gabled houses date from the 16th-18th centuries, when merchants grew rich from trade and exploration. Amsterdam is not only the country's historic centre, it is also its second-largest port.

ROTTERDAM

Rotterdam is one of the world's largest ports, lying within a massive built-up and industrialized area called Randstad Holland. Rotterdam is situated near the mouth of the Rhine, which is an important oil is refined locally; the port also handles minerals, grain, timber and coal.

Both Belgium and the Netherlands are major beer exporters.

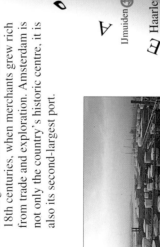

GERMANY

Delfzijl
Winschoten Wheat
Wheat Beef
Emmen
Beef
Groningen Assen
Dairy Hoogeveen
Wheat
Schiermonnikoog
Wheat
Beef Drachten Dairy Meppel
Leeuwarden Heerenveen Dairy
Zwolle
Ameland Dairy Dairy
Terschelling Wheat Wheat
Harlingen Dairy Lelystad
Flevoland Wheat
IJSSELMEER Harderwijk
Vlieland Dairy
WADDEN ZEE Hoorn Apeldoorn
Texel Purmerend Dairy
Den Helder Zaanstad AMSTERDAM
Alkmaar Amstelveen Dairy
Dairy
Wheat
Velsen
Umuiden Haarlem Wheat
Leiden

West Frisian Is.
IJssel
Deventer Almelo Wheat
Hengelo
Enschede

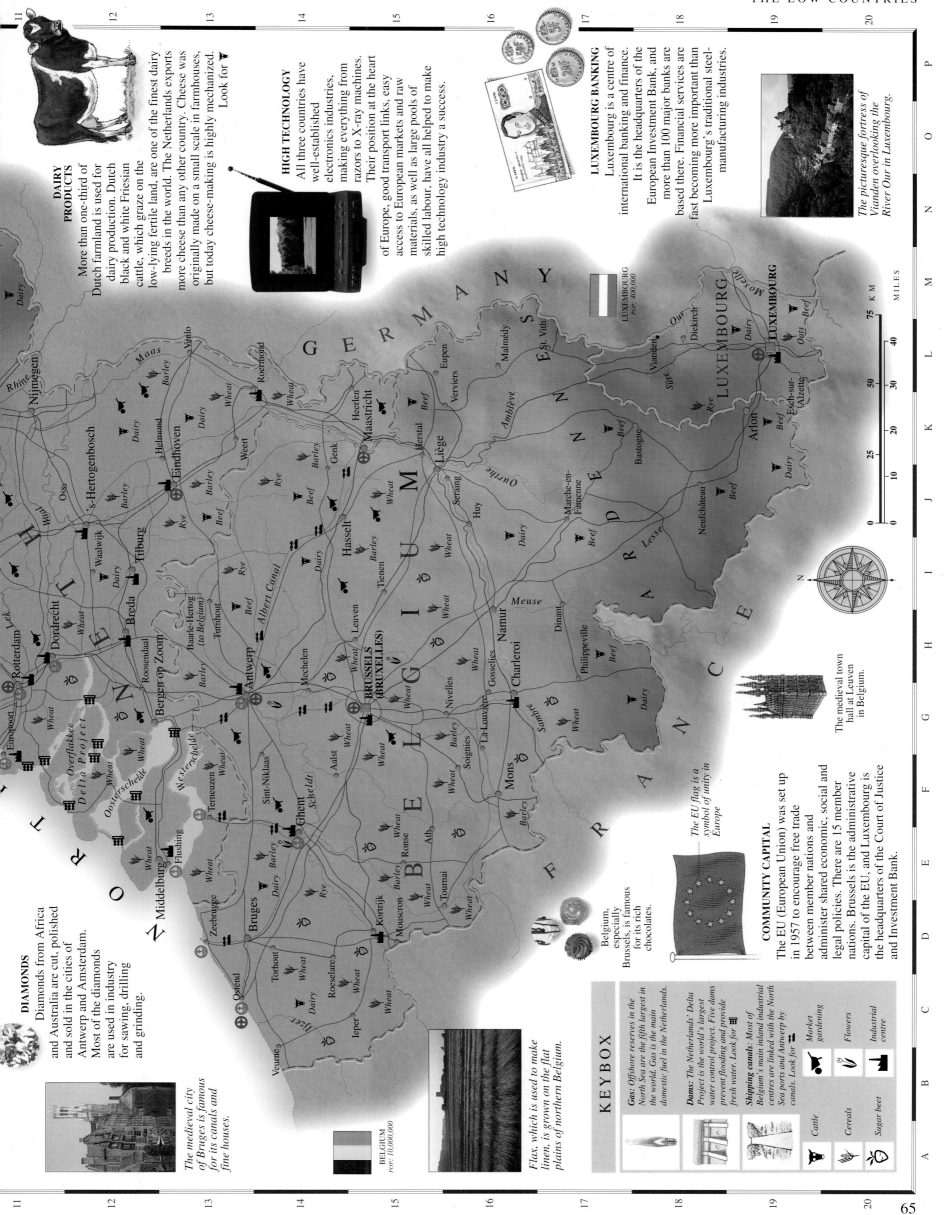

DAIRY PRODUCTS

More than one-third of Dutch farmland is used for dairy production. Dutch black and white Friesian cattle, which graze on the low-lying fertile land, are one of the finest dairy breeds in the world. The Netherlands exports more cheese than any other country. Cheese was originally made on a small scale in farmhouses, but today cheese-making is highly mechanized. Look for ▼

HIGH TECHNOLOGY

All three countries have well-established electronics industries, making everything from razors to X-ray machines. Their position at the heart of Europe, good transport links, easy access to European markets and raw materials, as well as large pools of skilled labour, have all helped to make high technology industry a success.

LUXEMBOURG BANKING

Luxembourg is a centre of international banking and finance. It is the headquarters of the European Investment Bank, and more than 100 major banks are based there. Financial services are fast becoming more important than Luxembourg's traditional steel-manufacturing industries.

The picturesque fortress of Vianden overlooking the River Our in Luxembourg.

DIAMONDS

Diamonds from Africa and Australia are cut, polished and sold in the cities of Antwerp and Amsterdam. Most of the diamonds are used in industry for sawing, drilling and grinding.

The medieval city of Bruges is famous for its canals and fine houses.

Flax, which is used to make linen, is grown on the flat plains of northern Belgium.

Belgium, especially Brussels, is famous for its rich chocolates.

COMMUNITY CAPITAL

The EU (European Union) was set up in 1957 to encourage free trade between member nations and administer shared economic, social and legal policies. There are 15 member nations. Brussels is the administrative capital of the EU, and Luxembourg is the headquarters of the Court of Justice and Investment Bank.

The EU flag is a symbol of unity in Europe

The medieval town hall at Leuven in Belgium.

KEYBOX

Gas: Offshore reserves in the North Sea are the fifth largest in the world. Gas is the main domestic fuel in the Netherlands.

Dams: The Netherlands' Delta Project is the world's largest water control project. Five dams prevent flooding and provide fresh water. Look for ⌂

Shipping canals: Most of Belgium's main inland industrial centres are linked with the North Sea ports and Antwerp by canals. Look for ⧮

Market gardening

Flowers

Industrial centre

Cattle

Cereals

Sugar beet

BELGIUM
POP: 10,000,000

LUXEMBOURG
POP: 400,000

GERMANY

NETHERLANDS

BELGIUM

FRANCE

LUXEMBOURG

ARDENNES

Rhine
Lek
Waal
Maas
Rotterdam
Nijmegen
Venlo
Dordrecht
Roermond
Europoort
Overflakkee
Delta Project
Oosterschelde
Westerschelde
's-Hertogenbosch
Eindhoven
Helmond
Heerlen
Maastricht
Waalwijk
Breda
Tilburg
Bergen op Zoom
Roosendaal
Baarle-Hertog (to Belgium)
Turnhout
Weert
Genk
Hasselt
Herstal
Liège
Seraing
Verviers
Eupen
Malmédy
St. Vith
Diekirch
Vianden
Our
Luxembourg
Moselle
Esch-sur-Alzette
Arlon
Neufchâteau
Bastogne
Marche-en-Famenne
Huy
Namur
Dinant
Philippeville
Charleroi
Gosselies
La Louvière
Nivelles
Mons
Soignies
Ath
Tournai
Mouscron
Kortrijk
Ronse
Aalst
Mechelen
Leuven
Tienen
Antwerp
Sint-Niklaas
Ghent
Terneuzen
Flushing
Middelburg
Zeebrugge
Bruges
Torhout
Roeselare
Ieper
Veurne
Ostend
Albert Canal
Scheldt
Ourthe
Amblève
Lesse
Sambre
Meuse
Sûre
BRUSSELS (BRUXELLES)

N

MILES
KM
0 10 20 25 30 40 50 75

65

GERMANY

SITUATED IN THE CENTRE OF EUROPE, Germany is now the continent's leading economic power. In the past it has been an area of great conflict; it was not until 1871 that a patchwork of independent states, who had fought bitterly for centuries, were united under Prussian leadership to form Germany. In this century Germany was defeated in two world wars. By 1945 the economy was shattered and the country divided between a Soviet-dominated communist East and a democratic West. The post-war years saw an amazing recovery in West Germany's economy. Natural advantages, such as a central position in Europe, large reserves of coal and iron, along with the construction of an efficient transport system and the determination to succeed, have all helped to create a dynamic economy. The East, on the other hand, lagged behind. In 1989, the Soviet Union began to disintegrate, and communism collapsed throughout Eastern Europe. The two halves of Germany were reunified in 1990, but problems soon became apparent. West Germans resented the huge amounts of money invested in the East to bring it up to their standards. East Germans became impatient with the slow pace of change. These resentments have led to violence against refugees, immigrants and "guest-workers", many of whom have lived in Germany for most of their lives.

CARS
Germany is Europe's largest vehicle producer, specializing in high-quality cars. American and Japanese car companies are based here, attracted by the skilled workforce. Look for 🚗

BERLIN
At the end of World War II, Germany's capital city, Berlin, was divided between the four victorious Allies. In 1961 the Berlin Wall was built to separate the Russian sector from the other three. In 1989 the wall came down: thousands of East Germans came through this Gate into the west.

Brandenburg Gate

AGRICULTURE
Germany produces all its own food, and is one of the world's main growers of sugar beet, barley and rye. Oats, rye and barley thrive in the mild, wet north, while wheat is grown in the warmer south. Look for 🌾

This decorated mug is called a stein, and is used for beer.

DRESDEN
Once Dresden was a beautiful old city, with many 18th-century buildings. But in World War II it was devastated by bombing. After extensive reconstruction, the city's historic buildings have now been restored to their former state.

Green pastures and woodland on the flat, Baltic coast.

SAUSAGES
Sausages are Germany's favourite snack. There are many regional variations; Frankfurt has even given its name to the Frankfurter sausage. Germany also has over 200 varieties of bread.

Salami

Peppered

A windmill in the fertile farmland of the northeast.

Many German towns have half-timbered buildings dating back to the Middle Ages.

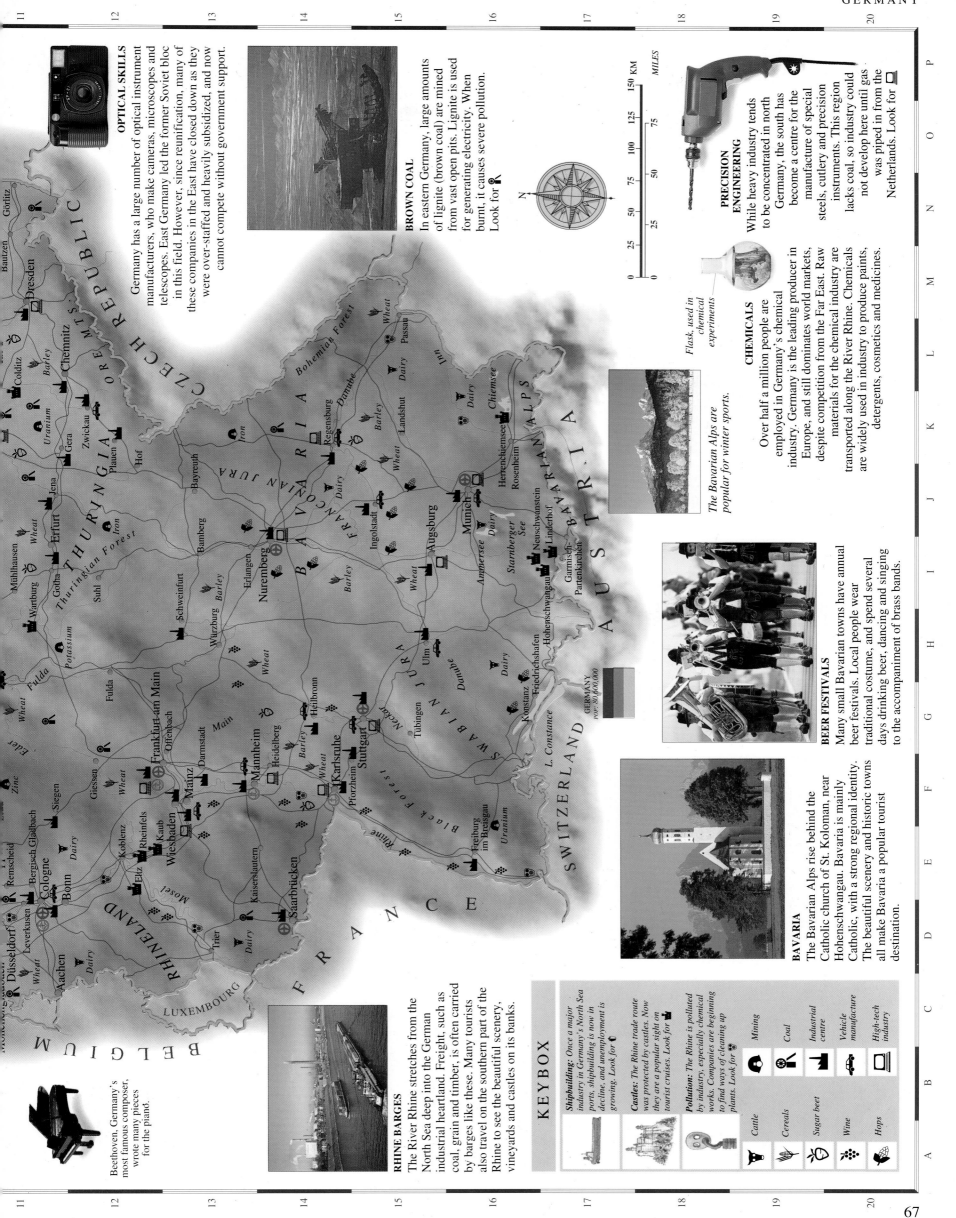

OPTICAL SKILLS
Germany has a large number of optical instrument manufacturers, who make cameras, microscopes and telescopes. East Germany led the former Soviet bloc in this field. However, since reunification, many of these companies in the East have closed down as they were over-staffed and heavily subsidized, and now cannot compete without government support.

BROWN COAL
In eastern Germany, large amounts of lignite (brown coal) are mined from vast open pits. Lignite is used for generating electricity. When burnt, it causes severe pollution. Look for 🏭

PRECISION ENGINEERING
While heavy industry tends to be concentrated in north Germany, the south has become a centre for the manufacture of special steels, cutlery and precision instruments. This region lacks coal, so industry could not develop here until gas was piped in from the Netherlands. Look for 📠

Flask, used in chemical experiments

CHEMICALS
Over half a million people are employed in Germany's chemical industry. Germany is the leading producer in Europe, and still dominates world markets, despite competition from the Far East. Raw materials for the chemical industry are transported along the River Rhine. Chemicals are widely used in industry to produce paints, detergents, cosmetics and medicines.

150 KM   MILES
125   75
100
75   50
50
25   25
0

N

The Bavarian Alps are popular for winter sports.

BEER FESTIVALS
Many small Bavarian towns have annual beer festivals. Local people wear traditional costume, and spend several days drinking beer, dancing and singing to the accompaniment of brass bands.

BAVARIA
The Bavarian Alps rise behind the Catholic church of St. Koloman, near Hohenschwangau. Bavaria is mainly Catholic, with a strong regional identity. The beautiful scenery and historic towns all make Bavaria a popular tourist destination.

Beethoven, Germany's most famous composer, wrote many pieces for the piano.

RHINE BARGES
The River Rhine stretches from the North Sea deep into the German industrial heartland. Freight, such as coal, grain and timber, is often carried by barges like these. Many tourists also travel on the southern part of the Rhine to see the beautiful scenery, vineyards and castles on its banks.

KEYBOX

Shipbuilding: Once a major industry in Germany's North Sea ports, shipbuilding is now in decline, and unemployment is growing. Look for 🚢

Castles: The Rhine trade route was protected by castles. Now they are a popular sight on tourist cruises. Look for 🏰

Pollution: The Rhine is polluted by industry, especially chemical works. Companies are beginning to find ways of cleaning up plants. Look for ⚙

🐄 Cattle	⛏ Mining
🌾 Cereals	❄ Coal
🍬 Sugar beet	🏭 Industrial centre
🍇 Wine	🚗 Vehicle manufacture
🌾 Hops	💻 High-tech industry

GERMANY
Pop: 80,600,000

Map labels: Görlitz, Bautzen, Dresden, Chemnitz, Colditz, Barley, Zwickau, Gera, Uranium, Plauen, Jena, Erfurt, Wheat, Mühlhausen, Gotha, Wartburg, Suhl, THURINGIA, THURINGIAN FOREST, Iron, Fulda, Edler, Wheat, Zinc, Siegen, Giessen, Bergisch Gladbach, Remscheid, Dairy, Cologne, Bonn, Mosel, Koblenz, Rheinfels, Eltz, Kaub, Wiesbaden, Kaiserslautern, Saarbrücken, Trier, Dairy, LUXEMBOURG, BELGIUM, Aachen, Dairy, RHINELAND, FRANCE, Black Forest, Freiburg im Breisgau, Uranium, Pforzheim, Karlsruhe, Stuttgart, Heidelberg, Heilbronn, Mannheim, Barley, Wheat, Neckar, Tübingen, Ulm, SWABIAN JURA, Danube, Friedrichshafen, L. Constance, Konstanz, SWITZERLAND, AUSTRIA, BAVARIAN ALPS, Garmisch-Partenkirchen, Linderhof, Neuschwanstein, Hohenschwangau, Rosenheim, Herrenchiemsee, Chiemsee, Dairy, Munich, Starnberger See, Ammersee, Augsburg, Ingolstadt, Wheat, Nuremberg, Erlangen, Barley, Schweinfurt, Würzburg, Bamberg, Bayreuth, FRANCONIAN JURA, BAVARIA, Regensburg, Landshut, Barley, Dairy, Passau, Inn, Wheat, BOHEMIAN FOREST, CZECH REPUBLIC, ORE MTS, Hof, Iron, Potassium, Darmstadt, Offenbach, Mainz, Frankfurt-am-Main, Main, Düsseldorf, Leverkusen

67

AUSTRIA AND SWITZERLAND

RUNNING THROUGH the middle of Austria and Switzerland are the Alps, the highest mountains in Europe. Both countries lie on Europe's main north-south trading routes, with access to the heart of Europe via the great Danube and Rhine waterways.

Switzerland was formed in the Middle Ages, when a number of Alpine communities united in defensive leagues against their more powerful neighbours. Modern Switzerland is a confederation of 23 separate provinces, called cantons. The country has three main languages – German, French and Italian. In contrast, Austria was once the centre of the Habsburg Empire, which had vast territories in Central Europe. When the Empire collapsed in 1918, Austria became an independent country. Austria has mineral resources, especially iron, and thriving industries. With few natural resources, Switzerland has concentrated instead on skilled, high-technology manufacturing.

Gold bar

BANKING
Switzerland is one of the world's main financial centres. People from all over the world put their money into Swiss bank accounts as the country is well-known for its political stability. Liechtenstein is also a major banking centre. Look for 🪙

DAIRY FARMING
Swiss dairy cattle spend winter in the Alpine valleys, and in summer are taken up to the Alpine pastures for grazing. The milk is used to make many varieties of cheese, such as Gruyère. Look for ⛥

Porcelain teeth

FALSE TEETH
Liechtenstein is the headquarters of world dental manufacture. False teeth, filling materials and plastic for crown and bridge dental work are exported to more than 100 countries.

Liechtenstein is famous for its beautiful stamps.

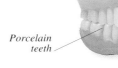
The castle at Vaduz, the capital of Liechtenstein.

GENEVA
Switzerland has not been at war for 150 years and is therefore seen as a neutral meeting place. Many international organizations have their headquarters in the city of Geneva.

KEYBOX

🏭	**Hydro-electric power:** *The Swiss pioneered hydro-electricity. Today, Austria is an important producer, tapping the potential of the Danube. Look for* ⊞
⛏	**Climbing:** *Mountaineers first started climbing the Alps in the 19th century. Some of the peaks are still thought to be the world's toughest climbs. Look for* ⛰
🚇	**Tunnels:** *There are only a few road passes through the Alps, but railway routes through tunnels are helping to ease the traffic. Look for* ⌒
☠	**Pollution:** *Tourism in the Alps, especially the heavy use of roads, is causing environmental problems. Look for* ☠

🌾	Cereals	🕐	Watchmaking
🐂	Cattle	💉	Pharmaceuticals
🍇	Wine	💰	Financial centre
🏭	Industrial centre	⛷	Skiing

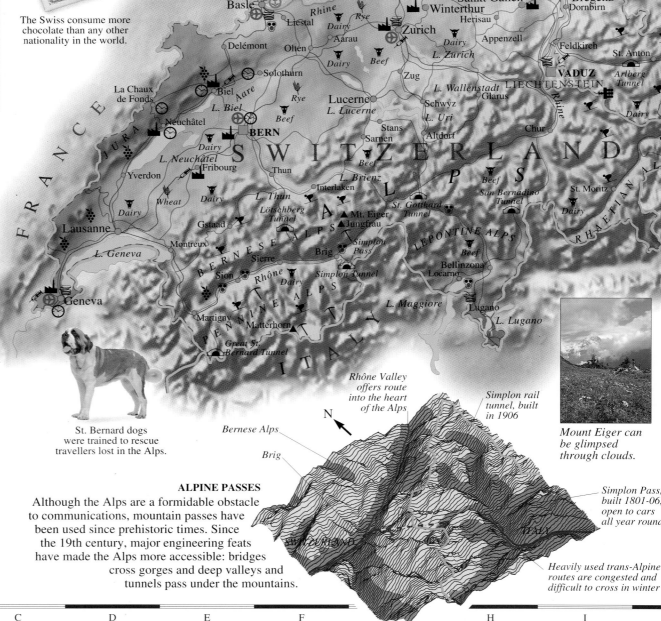

SWITZERLAND
POP: 6,900,000

LIECHTENSTEIN
POP: 29,500

GERMANY

Schaffhausen
Büsingen (to Germany)
Basle
Liestal
Rhine
Delémont
Olten
Aarau
La Chaux de Fonds
Biel
Aare
Solothurn
Neuchâtel
L. Biel
BERN
Dairy
L. Neuchâtel
Yverdon
Fribourg
Thun
Wheat
Dairy
L. Thun
Lötschberg Tunnel
Gstaad
Interlaken
L. Brienz
BERNESE ALPS
Lausanne
Montreux
Sierre
Brig
Simplon Pass
L. Geneva
Sion
Rhône
Simplon Tunnel
Geneva
Martigny
Matterhorn
PENNINE ALPS
Great St. Bernard Tunnel
ITALY

Frauenfeld
Sankt Gallen
Winterthur
Herisau
Zurich
L. Zurich
Appenzell
Zug
Lucerne
L. Lucerne
Schwyz
L. Wallenstadt
Glarus
L. Uri
Stans
Sarnen
Altdorf
Chur
St. Gotthard Tunnel
San Bernardino Tunnel
Bellinzona
Locarno
L. Maggiore
Lugano
L. Lugano

Bregenz
Dornbirn
Feldkirch
VADUZ
LIECHTENSTEIN
St. Anton
Landeck
Arlberg Tunnel
St. Moritz
RHAETIAN ALPS

SWITZERLAND
A L P S
LEPONTINE ALPS
Beef
Dairy

L. Constance

FRANCE
JURA

The Swiss consume more chocolate than any other nationality in the world.

St. Bernard dogs were trained to rescue travellers lost in the Alps.

Rhône Valley offers route into the heart of the Alps

Simplon rail tunnel, built in 1906

Mount Eiger can be glimpsed through clouds.

Bernese Alps

N

Brig

Simplon Pass, built 1801-06, open to cars all year round

Heavily used trans-Alpine routes are congested and difficult to cross in winter

ALPINE PASSES
Although the Alps are a formidable obstacle to communications, mountain passes have been used since prehistoric times. Since the 19th century, major engineering feats have made the Alps more accessible: bridges cross gorges and deep valleys and tunnels pass under the mountains.

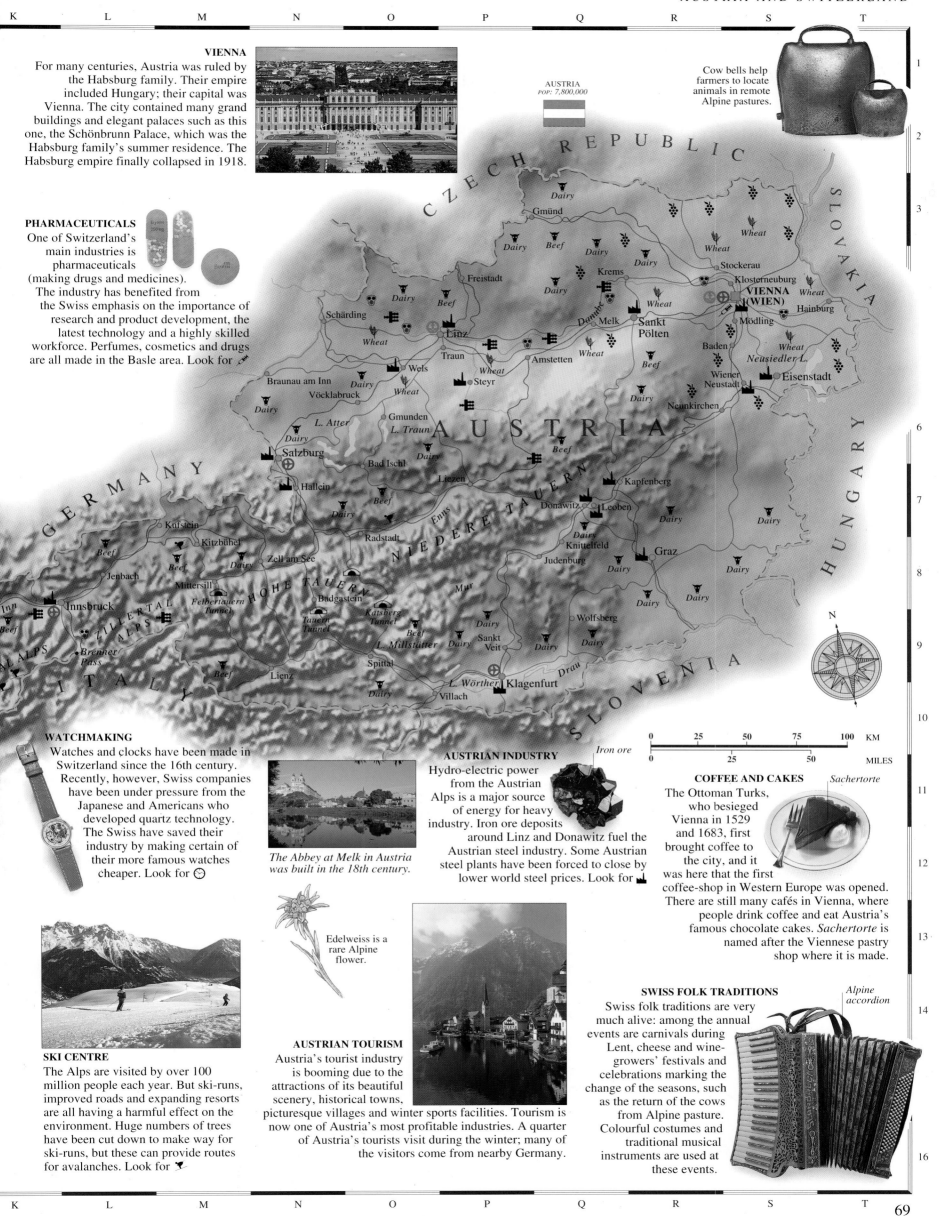

VIENNA

For many centuries, Austria was ruled by the Habsburg family. Their empire included Hungary; their capital was Vienna. The city contained many grand buildings and elegant palaces such as this one, the Schönbrunn Palace, which was the Habsburg family's summer residence. The Habsburg empire finally collapsed in 1918.

AUSTRIA
POP: 7,800,000

Cow bells help farmers to locate animals in remote Alpine pastures.

PHARMACEUTICALS

One of Switzerland's main industries is pharmaceuticals (making drugs and medicines). The industry has benefited from the Swiss emphasis on the importance of research and product development, the latest technology and a highly skilled workforce. Perfumes, cosmetics and drugs are all made in the Basle area. Look for

WATCHMAKING

Watches and clocks have been made in Switzerland since the 16th century. Recently, however, Swiss companies have been under pressure from the Japanese and Americans who developed quartz technology. The Swiss have saved their industry by making certain of their more famous watches cheaper. Look for

The Abbey at Melk in Austria was built in the 18th century.

AUSTRIAN INDUSTRY

Hydro-electric power from the Austrian Alps is a major source of energy for heavy industry. Iron ore deposits around Linz and Donawitz fuel the Austrian steel industry. Some Austrian steel plants have been forced to close by lower world steel prices. Look for

Iron ore

COFFEE AND CAKES

Sachertorte

The Ottoman Turks, who besieged Vienna in 1529 and 1683, first brought coffee to the city, and it was here that the first coffee-shop in Western Europe was opened. There are still many cafés in Vienna, where people drink coffee and eat Austria's famous chocolate cakes. *Sachertorte* is named after the Viennese pastry shop where it is made.

Edelweiss is a rare Alpine flower.

SWISS FOLK TRADITIONS

Alpine accordion

Swiss folk traditions are very much alive: among the annual events are carnivals during Lent, cheese and wine-growers' festivals and celebrations marking the change of the seasons, such as the return of the cows from Alpine pasture. Colourful costumes and traditional musical instruments are used at these events.

SKI CENTRE

The Alps are visited by over 100 million people each year. But ski-runs, improved roads and expanding resorts are all having a harmful effect on the environment. Huge numbers of trees have been cut down to make way for ski-runs, but these can provide routes for avalanches. Look for

AUSTRIAN TOURISM

Austria's tourist industry is booming due to the attractions of its beautiful scenery, historical towns, picturesque villages and winter sports facilities. Tourism is now one of Austria's most profitable industries. A quarter of Austria's tourists visit during the winter; many of the visitors come from nearby Germany.

CENTRAL EUROPE

IN 1989 THE COMMUNIST governments of Central Europe collapsed and the region entered a period of momentous change. All four countries of Central Europe only became independent states earlier this century. After World War II they were incorporated into the Soviet bloc and ruled by communist governments. These states started to industrialize rapidly, but they were heavily dependent on the former Soviet Union for their raw materials and markets. When communism collapsed in 1989, the new, democratically elected governments were faced with many problems: modernizing industry, huge foreign debts, soaring inflation, rising unemployment and terrible pollution. In 1993 the former state of Czechoslovakia was split into two countries, the Czech Republic and Slovakia.

Grudziądz, a medieval Polish town on the River Vistula.

POLLUTION
The Czech Republic is Europe's most polluted country. The pollution comes from its own industry, but also from factories in Germany. Forests are dying because of acid rain, rivers are poisoned and the scarred landscapes will take decades to recover. Look for

PUPPETS
Puppet shows are popular throughout Central Europe, but the former Czechoslovakia is acknowledged as the original home of European puppetry. Today, over a thousand Czech Republic and Slovak puppet companies perform plays.

Wooden puppet

GLASS
The Czech Republic's glass industry is centuries old. Glassware, such as this decanter and glasses, is often intricate and brightly coloured. The industry uses local supplies of sand to make the glass. Bohemian crystal is manufactured principally in the northwest around Karlovy Vary, and is also popular with the ever-increasing number of tourists.

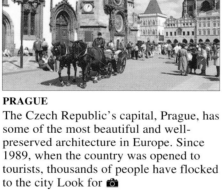

PRAGUE
The Czech Republic's capital, Prague, has some of the most beautiful and well-preserved architecture in Europe. Since 1989, when the country was opened to tourists, thousands of people have flocked to the city Look for

KEYBOX

Mining: Poland is one of the world's largest coal producers, but recently the industry has been affected by competition from abroad. Look for

Financial centre: In Hungary, the Budapest stock exchange opened in 1990, and many new banks have now opened in the city. Look for

Dam: The dam built by the Slovaks on the Danube at Gabčíkovo has caused a major dispute between Hungary and Slovakia. Look for

⚘	Cereals	🏭	Industrial centre
⚘	Sugar beet	🚢	Shipbuilding
⚓	Mixed fruit	📷	Tourism
🌱	Timber	🌿	Spas
⛑	Mining	👁	Pollution

HUNGARIAN INDUSTRY
Since the end of World War II Hungary has industrialized rapidly. It manufactures products such as aluminium, steel, electronic goods and vehicles, especially buses. But when the Soviet Union disintegrated, Hungarian manufacturers lost many of the traditional markets for their products – especially in heavy industry – and now face many problems. Look for

BEER
Some of Europe's finest beers and lagers are brewed in the Czech Republic. Pilsener lager originated in the town of Plzeň; Budweiser beer has been brewed at České Budějovice for over a century. Huge quantities of beer, the Budweiser beer in particular, are exported, principally to European countries such as Germany and the UK.

Beautifully painted eggs are sold in the Czech Republic and Slovakia at Easter.

POLAND
POP: 38,500,000

CZECH REPUBLIC
POP: 10,400,000

HUNGARY
POP: 10,500,000

N

0	50	100	150	200 KM
0	25	50	75	100 MILES

Map labels

SEA

Gulf of Danzig
Gdynia
Gdańsk
Elbląg
Wheat
Vistula
Wda
ojnice
Wheat
L. Jeziorak
Grudziądz
Rye
Barley
Bydgoszcz
Toruń
Wheat
KUJAWY
Wheat
Włocławek
L. Włocławskie
Płock Płońsk
Wheat
Kalisz
Rye
Prosna
Rye
Łódź
Wheat
Rye
Piotrków Trybunalski
Rye
Warta
Wheat
Opole
Iron
Zinc
Bytom
Gliwice
Katowice
Wheat
Rybnik
Ostrava
Bielsko-Biała
Wheat
Częstochowa
Kielce
Barley
Vistula
Sulphur
Kraków
Dunajec Tarnów
Wisłoka
Rzeszów
Wheat
WYŻYNA MAŁOPOLSKA
GALICIA
San
BESKID MTS
Ondava
L. Solińskie
CARPATHIANS
Žilina
Váh
Martin
Poprad
Prešov
Trenčín
SLOVAKIA
Banská Bystrica
Hron
Košice
Torysa
Laborec
Nitra
Mangnesite
Mangnesite
Slaná
Iron
Trnava
Nitra
Lučenec
Váh
Ipel'
Copper
Miskolc
Tisza
abčkovo
Maize
Nyíregyháza
Győr
Danube
Wheat
Debrecen
Wheat
BUDAPEST
HUNGARIAN PLAIN
Wheat
HUNGARY
Wheat
Aluminium
Maize
ékesfehérvár
Szolnok
Berettyó
Veszprém
Kecskemét
Wheat
Sárviz
Körös
L. Balaton
Maize
Maize
Wheat
Kapos
Maize
Tisza
Szekszárd
Danube
Maize
Szeged
Wheat
Maize
inium
Pécs
Baja
Maize
aluminium
Wheat
YUGOSLAVIA
CROATIA
ROMANIA

RUSSIAN FEDERATION (KALININGRAD OBLAST)
LITHUANIA
Suwałki
L. Mamry
Olsztyn
L. Śniardwy
Ełk
Rye
Rye
Rye
Narew
Białystok
Ostrołęka
Rye
Rye
POLAND
Bug
WARSAW (WARSZAWA)
Krzna
Rye
Radom
Lublin
Chełm
Barley
Barley
Wheat
Wheat
BELORUSSIA
PODLASIE
UKRAINE

SLOVAKIA
POP: 5,300,000

SOLIDARITY
Many Polish people work in heavy industries, such as coalmining and shipbuilding. In 1980 discontent over poor working conditions led to a strike at this shipyard in Gdańsk, and to the birth of Solidarity, the Soviet bloc's first independent trade union. Solidarity has significantly influenced Polish politics.

TIMBER
Beechwood toy
Apart from the lowland area around the River Danube, the landscape of the Czech Republic and Slovakia is mountainous. Both countries have relatively small populations and much of the land is still covered with forest. Both countries have large timber industries. Some timber – mainly pine – is used to make furniture. Beech is often used for the manufacture of toys. Look for ⌐

RELIGION
For a thousand years, through invasions, wars, repression – and times when the country almost ceased to exist – the Polish people have found strength in their religious faith. Even during the last 40 years of communist government – which actively discouraged religion of any kind – 90 per cent of the population remained devout Catholics.

Wild boar, shown on this Polish stamp, are still found in the region.

Morning mist rising over the western Carpathians.

PAPRIKA
The flat plains in Hungary are amongst the most fertile farming areas in Europe. Cereals, sugar beet and fruit are among the main crops. Sweet red peppers – from which paprika is made – are also grown. Paprika is a vital ingredient in many spicy Hungarian dishes.

BUDAPEST
Budapest, the Hungarian capital, was once two towns, Buda on the Danube's right bank, and Pest on the left. The town was very badly damaged during World War II, but many of its historic buildings have since been carefully restored. This vast, domed parliament building in Pest faces across the river to Buda.

Ernö Rubik, a Hungarian, invented this complex puzzle.

SPA BATHS
Hot thermal springs were used for medicinal purposes in ancient Greece and Rome. The Romans were the first to develop baths – like this one in Budapest where bathers enjoy a game of chess. Hungary now has 154 hot-spring baths, which are open to the public. The Czech Republic and Slovakia have 900 mineral springs and 58 health spas, which are reserved for medicinal purposes only. It is hoped that more foreigners will come to the region to use the thermal springs. Look for ⚘

Hungary's famous horses are bred on the Hungarian Plain.

ITALY AND MALTA

AT VARIOUS TIMES in the past 2,000 years Italy has influenced the development of European civilization. From this narrow, boot-shaped peninsula the Romans established a vast empire throughout Europe and North Africa; Christianity was first adopted as an official religion by a Roman emperor, and Rome later became the centre of the Catholic Church. In the 14th century, an extraordinary flowering of the arts and sciences, known as the Renaissance, or "rebirth", started in Italy and transformed European thought and culture. Italy at this time was divided into independent city states, and was later ruled by foreign nations, including France and Austria. But in 1870, after centuries of foreign domination, Italy became an independent and unified country. Despite a lack of natural resources, and defeat in World War II, Italy has become a major industrial power. The country has long suffered from corruption and organized crime, but recent changes show promise of more political stability in the future.

PASTA
The Italian explorer, Marco Polo, is said to have brought the recipe for pasta to Italy when he returned from his great journey to China. Pasta is a type of dough made by adding water to wheat flour. It has become one of the world's most popular foods. It can be made into different shapes, and filled with meat or vegetables.

Cappelletti (little hats)

Orecchioni (large ears)

Round tortellini (small pies)

VERONA
The ancient Romans were skilful engineers, and many of their remarkable buildings are still standing today. The foundations of much of Italy's road system was also built by the Romans. Verona is based on the Roman grid street plan. The town's ancient amphitheatre seats 22,000, and is still used.

Silk scarf

Suede shoe

DESIGN
Italians place great emphasis on design and produce beautiful looking products. This flair for design is particularly obvious in their cars and clothes. The fashion houses of Rome, Florence, Milan and Venice rival those of Paris, and Italian shoes and clothes are widely exported.

Masks like these are worn during the February carnival in Venice, which includes plays, masked balls and fireworks.

Pinnacles of the Dolomites in northeastern Italy.

VENICE
This historic city is built on a number of islands in a shallow lagoon. Many buildings stand on wooden stilts driven into the mud. Venice's future is in the balance, threatened by flooding and pollution.

THE PO VALLEY
Between the Alps and the Apennines lies a huge triangular plain, drained by Italy's greatest river, the Po. The majority of the country's agriculture, population and industry is concentrated in this region. Its major cities, such as Milan and Turin, are important industrial and commercial centres.

Turin

Milan

The Alps

Po

Farming of maize, wheat and rice

Mountain passes link Italy to the rest of Europe

Alpine rivers supply water for HEP and irrigation

Genoa: major sea port and industrial centre

N

SAN MARINO
POP: 23,000

ITALY
pop: 57,800,000

SLOVENIA

AUSTRIA

SWITZERLAND

FRANCE

ADRIATIC

LIGURIAN SEA

Gulf of Venice

SAN MARINO

TUSCANY

APENNINES

DOLOMITES

ALPS

Trieste
Udine
Belluno
Bolzano
Trento
Treviso
Mestre
Venice
Padua
Chioggia
Vicenza
Verona
L. di Garda
Bergamo
Monza
Milan
Novara
Brescia
Cremona
Mantova
Parma
Reggio nell'Emilia
Modena
Ferrara
Bologna
Piacenza
Alessandria
Asti
Turin
Cuneo
Genoa
Savona
Alassio
San Remo
La Spezia
Viareggio
Pisa
Lucca
Pistoia
Prato
Florence
Siena
Arezzo
Perugia
L. Trasimeno
Assisi
Potenza
Pesaro
Rimini
Riccione
Cérvia
Ravenna
Forlì
Ancona
Comacchio Lagoon
Aosta
L. Maggiore
L. d'Iseà
Gulf of Genoa

Piave
Adige
Arno
Po

Wheat
Maize
Olive
Iron
Marble
Manganese
Magnesium
Zinc
Pyrite

72

A distant view of the snow-capped Apennines.

MOTOR VEHICLES
Many Italian motor manufacturers are based around the cities of Milan and Turin. Italian engineers and designers have developed some of the finest cars in Europe, both high performance cars, and also cheaper, economical models. Look for

Model of Ferrari car

Sardinia, a large island in the Mediterranean.

KEYBOX
Wine: Italy is the world's largest wine producer. Recently, the wine industry has brought in rules for higher quality and better control. Look for

Oil refining: Italy is more dependent on imported fuel than any European country. Crude oil has to be imported and refined. Look for

Sightseeing: Millions of tourists visit Italy each year to see its historic towns, famous buildings and museums. Look for

Cereals		Industrial centre	
Rice		Vehicle manufacture	
Citrus fruit		Tourism	
Vegetable oil		Archaeological sites	
Mining		Pollution	

ROMAN CATHOLICS
Christianity is the world's most wide-spread religion. It is based on the life and teaching of Jesus Christ. Within Christianity there are different groups. Roman Catholicism, with its centre in Rome, is the largest group, with over a thousand million members. Catholics have a special reverence for Mary, the mother of Jesus.

VATICAN CITY
This walled city in the centre of Rome is the headquarters of the Roman Catholic Church and official residence of the Pope. It is the smallest independent state in the world, dominated by the great St. Peter's Basilica, seen here. The city has its own newspaper, coins, stamps, railway and radio stations.

Italians are passionate about football supporters.

Italian national football shirt

AGRICULTURE
Agriculture is very important to the Italian economy. The main crops are olives, citrus fruits and wine. The best farming region is the Po Valley in the north. Southern Italy has always suffered from its hilly terrain and low rainfall, but due to irrigation and more modern farming methods, agriculture has improved since the 1950s.

Bottles of Chianti are often sold in a wicker casing, called a fiasco.

MALTA
Malta's position on the Mediterranean shipping routes explains its important role in the history of the region. The Romans, Arabs, French, Turks, Spanish and British have all colonized or fought over the island. In 1964 it became independent. Today, its main income comes from tourism and its port facilities.

VATICAN CITY
POP: 1,000

MALTA
POP: 400,000

Map labels

Lecce, Otranto, Olive, Brindisi, Gallipoli, Taranto, Gulf of Taranto, Bari, Manfredonia, L. Varano, Altamura, Marble, Ofanto, Olive, Bradano, Foggia, Wheat, Campobasso, Aluminium, Tremiti Is., Benevento, Potenza, Agri, Sapri, Naples, Pompeii, Salerno, Gulf of Salerno, Sorrento, Capri, Bay of Naples, Ischia, Frosinone, Pescara, Oats, Sangro, Olive, L'Aquila, Terni, Nera, ROME (ROMA), VATICAN CITY, Ostia, Anzio, L. Bracciano, Vulci, Civitavecchia, Pontine Is.

Crotone, Catanzaro, Gulf of Squillace, Cosenza, CALABRIA, Reggio di Calabria, Strait of Messina, Stromboli, Lipari Is., Salina, Lipari, Vulcano, Filicudi, Alicudi, Messina, Taormina, Catania, Augusta, Syracuse, Enna, Caltanissetta, SICILY, Ragusa, Cefalù, Potash, Sulphur, Salso, Gulf of Gela, Palermo, Ustica, Agrigento, Belice, Trapani, Egadi Is.

IONIAN SEA, TYRRHENIAN SEA, MEDITERRANEAN SEA, ADRIATIC SEA

VALLETTA, Gozo, MALTA, Pelagie Is., Linosa, Lampedusa, Lampione, Pantelleria

Olbia, Nuoro, SARDINIA, Sassari, Copper, Tirso, Alghero, Oristano, Marina, Iglesias, Zinc, Lead, Cagliari, Gulf of Cagliari, Sarroch, C. Spartivento, San Pietro, Sant'Antioco, Strait of Bonifacio

N, KM, MILES, 150, 125, 100, 75, 50, 25, 0

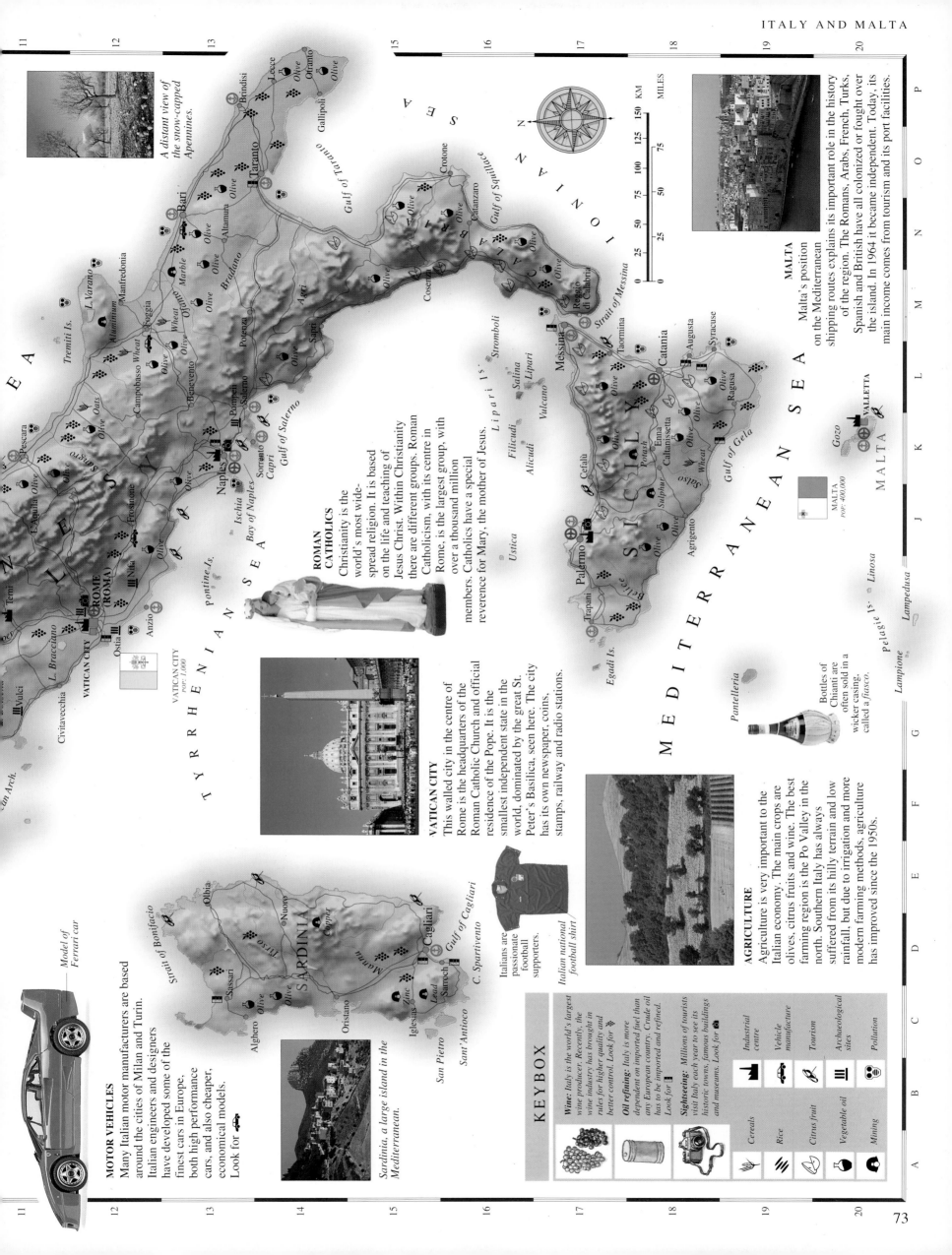

THE WESTERN BALKANS

THIS TROUBLED REGION of southeastern Europe consists of a wide variety of landscapes, religions, peoples and languages. The region was invaded many times, and from the 14th-19th centuries was occupied by the Turks. After World War II, both Albania and Yugoslavia were ruled by communist governments. When the communist leader, General Tito, died in 1980 the Yugoslav government became less centralized, and former republics now demanded their independence. Serbia, the largest and most powerful republic, resisted the break-up of Yugoslavia. In 1991, a bloody civil war broke out between Serbia and Croatia and, eventually, between Serbs and Muslims in Bosnia. Albania was isolated by its communist government from the rest of Europe and became economically backward. But the country has now shaken off its communist rulers and held democratic elections. The economy, however, is still in chaos.

SLOVENIA
POP: 2,000,000

CROATIA
POP: 4,900,000

The spectacular scenery of northern Slovenia.

Nugget of mercury ore

BOSNIA & HERZEGOVINA
POP: 4,500,000

Slovenia is a major producer of mercury, used in thermometers.

YUGO
This car, the Yugo, is manufactured in former Yugoslavia at Kragujevac. It was designed for foreign export, but the economic disruption caused by the civil war has dealt a death blow to this industry. Slovenia has had more success; French cars are made there under licence, and are sold to the domestic market.
Look for 🚗

TOURISM
Many tourists used to visit former Yugoslavia, attracted by the country's beautiful scenery, warm climate and stunning coastline. By the late 1980s, an average of nine million visitors were coming to Yugoslavia every year. However, the violent civil war has now virtually put an end to the tourist industry. Look for 🎣

UNDER FIRE
The world looked on in horror as Dubrovnik, a beautiful city with an untouched centre dating back 1,000 years, came under Serbian attack in 1991. Sarajevo, the Bosnian capital, was another casualty; many of its historic mosques and churches were hit by shells. Other historic towns in Bosnia and Croatia have also suffered irreparable damage during the war.

FOLKLORE
Variations in national costume reflect the many different traditions and peoples living in this region. In Slovenia, for example, costumes show a strong Alpine influence – leather trousers and gathered *dirndl* skirts. Further south, the costumes look more oriental. The Dubrovnik region is famous for its costume of white dresses, embroidered blouses and waistcoats. Folk-music and dancing take place at religious festivals and on market-days, and are also laid on for tourist groups.

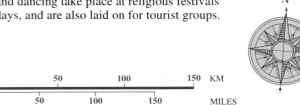

KEYBOX

Mining: Albania has some of the world's largest chromium reserves. Exports are hampered by outdated mining equipment and frequent strikes. Look for ⛏

Refugee centres: The war in former Yugoslavia has forced over a million people to leave their homes and seek asylum in nearby countries. Look for ⛺

🌾	Cereals	⛏	Coal
🐟	Mixed fruit	⚡	Hydro-electric power
🍇	Wine	🏭	Industrial centre
🚬	Tobacco	🚗	Vehicle manufacture
🐟	Fishing	🎣	Tourism

MARKETS
In peacetime, local markets in the region are packed with people and well-stocked with a wide range of produce from nearby farms. Large quantities of fruit and vegetables are grown in the mild, warm climate of the Croatian coast and in western Bosnia. Look for 🐟

N

0   50   100   150 KM
0   50   100   150 MILES

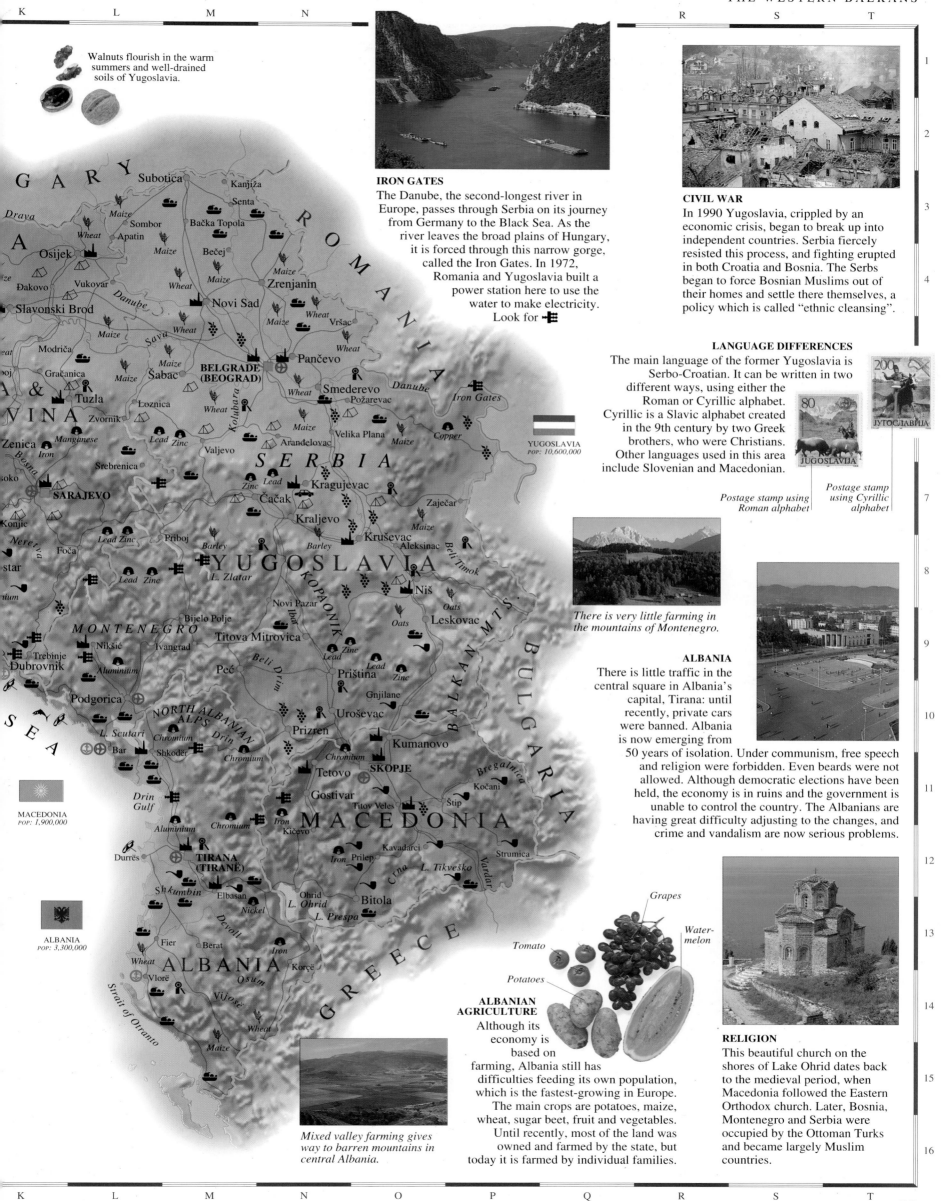

Walnuts flourish in the warm
summers and well-drained
soils of Yugoslavia.

IRON GATES

The Danube, the second-longest river in
Europe, passes through Serbia on its journey
from Germany to the Black Sea. As the
river leaves the broad plains of Hungary,
it is forced through this narrow gorge,
called the Iron Gates. In 1972,
Romania and Yugoslavia built a
power station here to use the
water to make electricity.
Look for ⊯

CIVIL WAR

In 1990 Yugoslavia, crippled by an
economic crisis, began to break up into
independent countries. Serbia fiercely
resisted this process, and fighting erupted
in both Croatia and Bosnia. The Serbs
began to force Bosnian Muslims out of
their homes and settle there themselves, a
policy which is called "ethnic cleansing".

LANGUAGE DIFFERENCES

The main language of the former Yugoslavia is
Serbo-Croatian. It can be written in two
different ways, using either the
Roman or Cyrillic alphabet.
Cyrillic is a Slavic alphabet created
in the 9th century by two Greek
brothers, who were Christians.
Other languages used in this area
include Slovenian and Macedonian.

YUGOSLAVIA
POP: 10,600,000

*Postage stamp using
Roman alphabet*

*Postage stamp
using Cyrillic
alphabet*

*There is very little farming in
the mountains of Montenegro.*

ALBANIA

There is little traffic in the
central square in Albania's
capital, Tirana: until
recently, private cars
were banned. Albania
is now emerging from
50 years of isolation. Under communism, free speech
and religion were forbidden. Even beards were not
allowed. Although democratic elections have been
held, the economy is in ruins and the government is
unable to control the country. The Albanians are
having great difficulty adjusting to the changes, and
crime and vandalism are now serious problems.

MACEDONIA
POP: 1,900,000

ALBANIA
POP: 3,300,000

Grapes

*Water-
melon*

Tomato

Potatoes

ALBANIAN
AGRICULTURE

Although its
economy is
based on
farming, Albania still has
difficulties feeding its own population,
which is the fastest-growing in Europe.
The main crops are potatoes, maize,
wheat, sugar beet, fruit and vegetables.
Until recently, most of the land was
owned and farmed by the state, but
today it is farmed by individual families.

RELIGION

This beautiful church on the
shores of Lake Ohrid dates back
to the medieval period, when
Macedonia followed the Eastern
Orthodox church. Later, Bosnia,
Montenegro and Serbia were
occupied by the Ottoman Turks
and became largely Muslim
countries.

*Mixed valley farming gives
way to barren mountains in
central Albania.*

ROMANIA AND BULGARIA

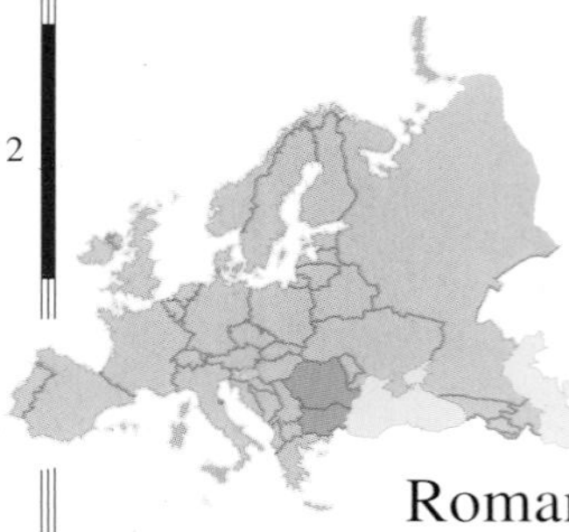

ROMANIA AND BULGARIA ARE LOCATED in the southeast of Europe, on the shores of the Black Sea. The River Danube forms the border between the two countries, and the most fertile land in the region is found in the river's vast valley and delta. Forests of oak, pine and fir trees grow on the slopes of the Carpathian and Balkan Mountains. Romania and Bulgaria were occupied by Romans, Bulgars, Hungarians and Turkish Ottomans, but this troubled history ended when they became independent countries in the late 19th and early 20th centuries. After two world wars, both countries became part of the Soviet communist bloc. Although they are no longer communist, economic reform has been slow, and unemployment, high prices and food shortages are still constant problems.

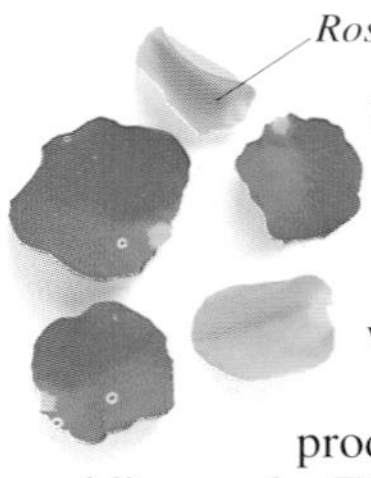

ROSE-OIL

Rose-petal

Used in perfume, rose-oil is literally worth its weight in gold. Central Bulgaria produces most of the world's supply. The world's largest rose gardens are at Kazanlŭk. Look for ✿

THE PRESIDENTIAL PALACE

Under Romania's repressive communist leader, President Ceauşescu, food and energy supplies were rationed. Despite this, the President started a series of expensive building projects, such as this presidential palace in Bucharest. In 1989, the Romanian people rose up against communism, and executed their president.

TOBACCO

Bulgaria is the world's second largest exporter of cigarettes. Tobacco is grown in the fertile valleys of the River Maritsa. This woman is sorting tobacco leaves, ready for selling. Look for 🝤

YOGHURT

Yoghurt, made from the milk of cows, sheep or goats, is an important part of the Bulgarian diet. Many Bulgarians claim that eating yoghurt helps them live to a ripe old age.

Small farms in the wooded valleys of central Romania.

The Alexander Nevsky church in Sofia celebrates liberation from Turkish rule.

Bulgaria is the world's fourth largest wine exporter.

RILA MONASTERY

The walls of Rila monastery are decorated with no less than 1,200 superb wall-paintings. The monastery became a symbol of the Bulgarians' struggle to preserve the Christian faith during centuries of Turkish rule. The monastery was originally founded in 1335, and was rebuilt after it burnt to the ground in the 19th-century.

KEYBOX

Vehicle manufacture: Romanian factories make copies of French vehicles for export to China, Russia and many Western countries. Look for 🚐

High-tech industry: Electronics earn Bulgaria foreign currency, although the computer industry is suffering from international competition. Look for 💻

Spas: Mineral springs and health treatments are provided by many spa resorts, which are a popular tourist attraction. Look for ⚘

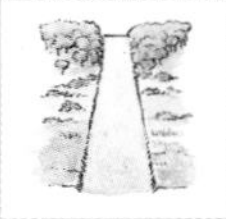

Shipping canal: The Danube-Black Sea Canal enables ships to avoid the slow journey through the Danube Delta. Look for 🛥

🐂	Cattle	⛏	Mining
🌾	Cereals	⚒	Oil
🍇	Wine	⬦	Gas
🝤	Tobacco	🏭	Industrial centre
🌹	Roses	🖋	Tourism

(Map labels: UKRAINE, HUNGARY, Satu Mare, Baia Mare, Wheat, Zinc, Lead, Copper, Gold, Oradea, Beef, Maize, Dairy, Aluminium, Cluj-Napoca, Wheat, Iron, TRANSYLVANIA, ROMANIA, Arad, Maize, Alba Iulia, Copşa Mică, Mureş, Deva, Dairy, Sibiu, Timişoara, Iron, Iron, Beef, Iron, Maize, Iron, Manganese, CARPATHIANS, Reşiţa, Râmnicu Vâlcea, Târgu Jiu, Copper, Băile Herculane, Beef, Chromium, Drobeta-Turnu-Severin, Beef, Maize, Maize, Dairy, Craiova, YUGOSLAVIA, Vidin, Wheat, Jiu, Danube, Wheat, Wheat, Iron, Maize, Maize, Beef, Mikhaylovgrad, Iskŭr, Vratsa, BULGARIA, Copper, Beef, Iron, Pravets, BALKAN, SOFIA (SOFIYA), Pernik, L. Iskŭr, Beef, Dairy, MACEDONIA, Zinc, Lead, Struma, Rila, RHODOPE MTS, Pazardz, Velingrad, Sandanski, Beef, GREECE)

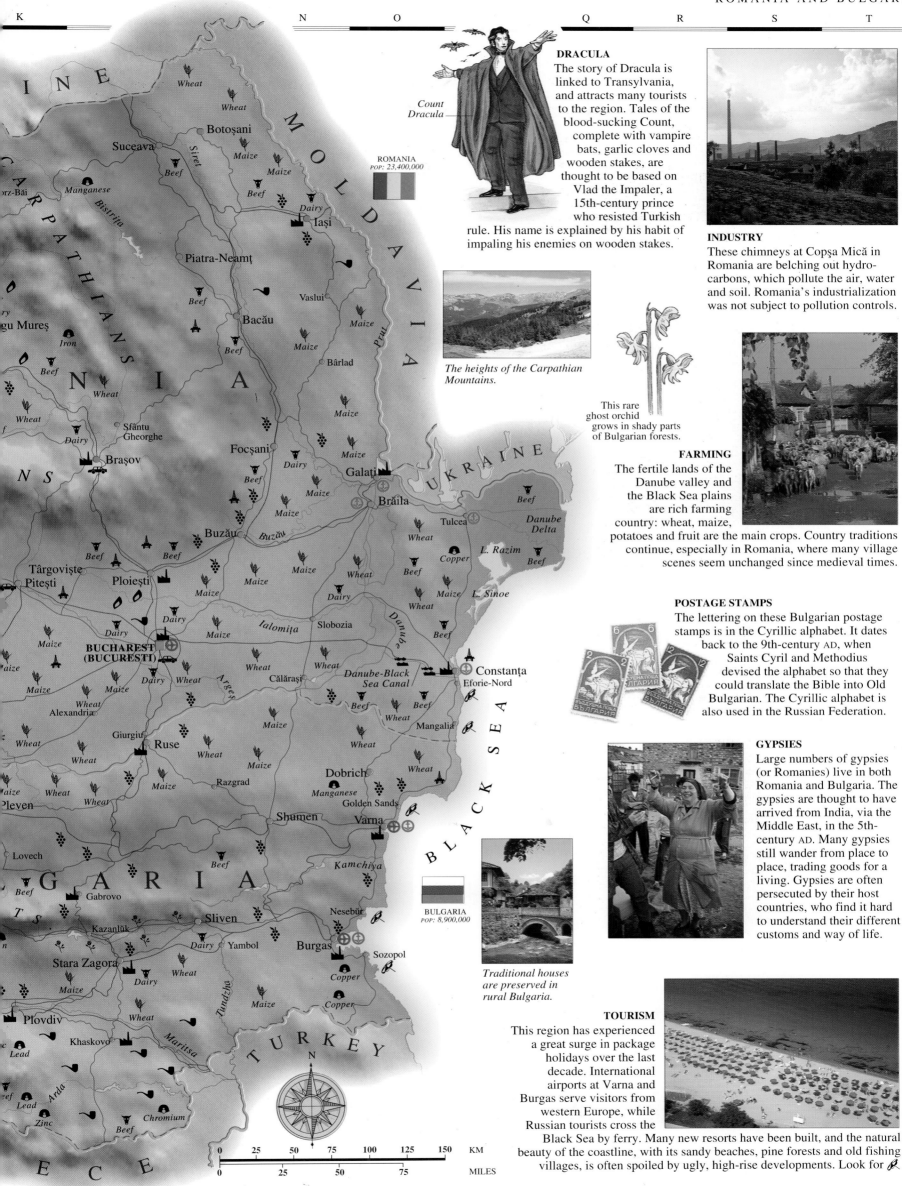

DRACULA

The story of Dracula is linked to Transylvania, and attracts many tourists to the region. Tales of the blood-sucking Count, complete with vampire bats, garlic cloves and wooden stakes, are thought to be based on Vlad the Impaler, a 15th-century prince who resisted Turkish rule. His name is explained by his habit of impaling his enemies on wooden stakes.

Count Dracula

INDUSTRY

These chimneys at Copşa Mică in Romania are belching out hydro-carbons, which pollute the air, water and soil. Romania's industrialization was not subject to pollution controls.

The heights of the Carpathian Mountains.

This rare ghost orchid grows in shady parts of Bulgarian forests.

FARMING

The fertile lands of the Danube valley and the Black Sea plains are rich farming country: wheat, maize, potatoes and fruit are the main crops. Country traditions continue, especially in Romania, where many village scenes seem unchanged since medieval times.

POSTAGE STAMPS

The lettering on these Bulgarian postage stamps is in the Cyrillic alphabet. It dates back to the 9th-century AD, when Saints Cyril and Methodius devised the alphabet so that they could translate the Bible into Old Bulgarian. The Cyrillic alphabet is also used in the Russian Federation.

GYPSIES

Large numbers of gypsies (or Romanies) live in both Romania and Bulgaria. The gypsies are thought to have arrived from India, via the Middle East, in the 5th-century AD. Many gypsies still wander from place to place, trading goods for a living. Gypsies are often persecuted by their host countries, who find it hard to understand their different customs and way of life.

Traditional houses are preserved in rural Bulgaria.

TOURISM

This region has experienced a great surge in package holidays over the last decade. International airports at Varna and Burgas serve visitors from western Europe, while Russian tourists cross the Black Sea by ferry. Many new resorts have been built, and the natural beauty of the coastline, with its sandy beaches, pine forests and old fishing villages, is often spoiled by ugly, high-rise developments. Look for

ROMANIA
POP: 23,400,000

BULGARIA
POP: 8,900,000

GREECE

FROM THE EARLIEST TIMES, the life and economy of Greece has been shaped by its geography. It is a country of rugged mountains, isolated valleys, remote peninsulas and more than 1,400 scattered islands. The difficulty of travelling by land has turned Greece into a seafaring nation, which owns the second largest fleet of merchant ships in the world. Ninety per cent of its imports and exports are carried by sea rather than by road. Most people in Greece make their living from farming, but in recent years, tourism has become an important source of income. Tourists visit Greece not only for its warm, Mediterranean climate and beautiful landscape, but also for its ancient ruins. Many of these date from the 5th-century BC, when the country was the cultural centre of the western world, the birthplace of democracy, and home of great thinkers such as Socrates, Plato and Aristotle.

Greek Orthodox bishop

THE ORTHODOX CHURCH
Most Greek Christians belong to the Orthodox Church. This was founded in Constantinople (modern Istanbul) in the 4th-century AD. The Eastern Orthodox Church established there still flourishes in Greece, Eastern Europe and Russia.

ATHENS
Athens is famous for its Acropolis ("high place"), crowned by the Parthenon temple. Smog all too often obscures the Acropolis, and cars are banned from the city on certain days to reduce pollution.

Parsley

GREEK SALAD
Many Greek farms are small, growing just enough vegetables and fruit for the farmer's family. Lettuces, cucumbers, tomatoes, olives, herbs and cheese are the most common produce.

Aubergine

Cucumber

Beef tomato

The Parthenon temple (built 432 BC) was the centre of religious life in Classical Athens.

KEYBOX

Archaeological sites: Remains from ancient Greece are found all over the country, attracting many visitors. Look for ▥

Sultanas and currants: Greece is the world's largest exporter of these fruits. Small, black currants are named after the town of Corinth. Look for ☙

The Olympic Games: The event started in Olympia in 776 BC. Sports included running, wrestling, boxing, horse racing, javelin and discus. Look for ⬤

🍋 Citrus fruit		🐬 Fishing	
🍇 Wine		⛑ Mining	
🏺 Vegetable oil		⬦ Oil	
⚓ Cotton		🏭 Industrial centre	
🚬 Tobacco		🎣 Tourism	

Tuning peg

Fretted fingerboard

Neck

String

Pegbox inlaid with mother-of-pearl

Soundhole

Body

CLASSICAL MUSIC
The bouzouki is a stringed instrument, similar to a lute or a guitar, which is used in traditional Greek music. Folk dances, national costumes and music are still very popular at religious festivals such as Easter, and on special occasions such as weddings.

Bridge

THE CORINTH CANAL
Athens is separated from the Ionian Sea by a narrow neck of land called the Isthmus of Corinth. In 1893 the Greeks cut a canal through the isthmus. It is 6.3 km (3.9 miles) long, but only just wide enough for a ship to squeeze between the cliffs on either side. Look for ⚓

Olives and cypresses grow throughout Greece.

SACRED OIL
Olives have been grown in Greece for over two thousand years. In ancient times, the olive was sacred to Athena, the goddess of war, and olive wreaths were worn as a symbol of victory. Today, olives and olive oil are major exports. Look for 🫒

Map labels

MACEDONIA

ALBANIA

GREECE

PINDUS MOUNTAINS

IONIAN SEA

Ionian Is.

PELOPONNESE

L. Prespa
L. Vegoritis
Vardar
Florina
Edessa
Kilk
Kastoria
L. Kastorias
Veroia
Thessaloniki
Chromium
Kozani
Katerini
Thermai Gulf
Grevena
Aliakmon
Larisa
Ioannina
Trikala
Corfu
Igoumenitsa
Olives
Karditsa
Olives
Arta
Chromium
Preveza
Stylis
Lefkada
Lamia
Lout Aidipso
Olives
Acheloos
Aluminum
Nickel
Olives
Astakos
L. Trichonida
Amfissa
Lefkada
Itea
Delphi
Oliv
Mesolongi
Lixouri
Kefallonia
Patrai
Gulf of Corinth
Argostoli
Gulf of Patrai
Corinth Canal
Kyllini
Andravida
Corinth
Zakynthos
Marble
Zakynthos
Katakolo
Pyrgos
Olympia
Mycenae
Epidaur
Olives
Tripoli
Nafplio
Manganese
Olives
Olives
Sparti
Leon
Kalamata
Olives
Pilos
Gulf of Messini
Gytheio
Gulf of Laconia
Neapoli
Kythira

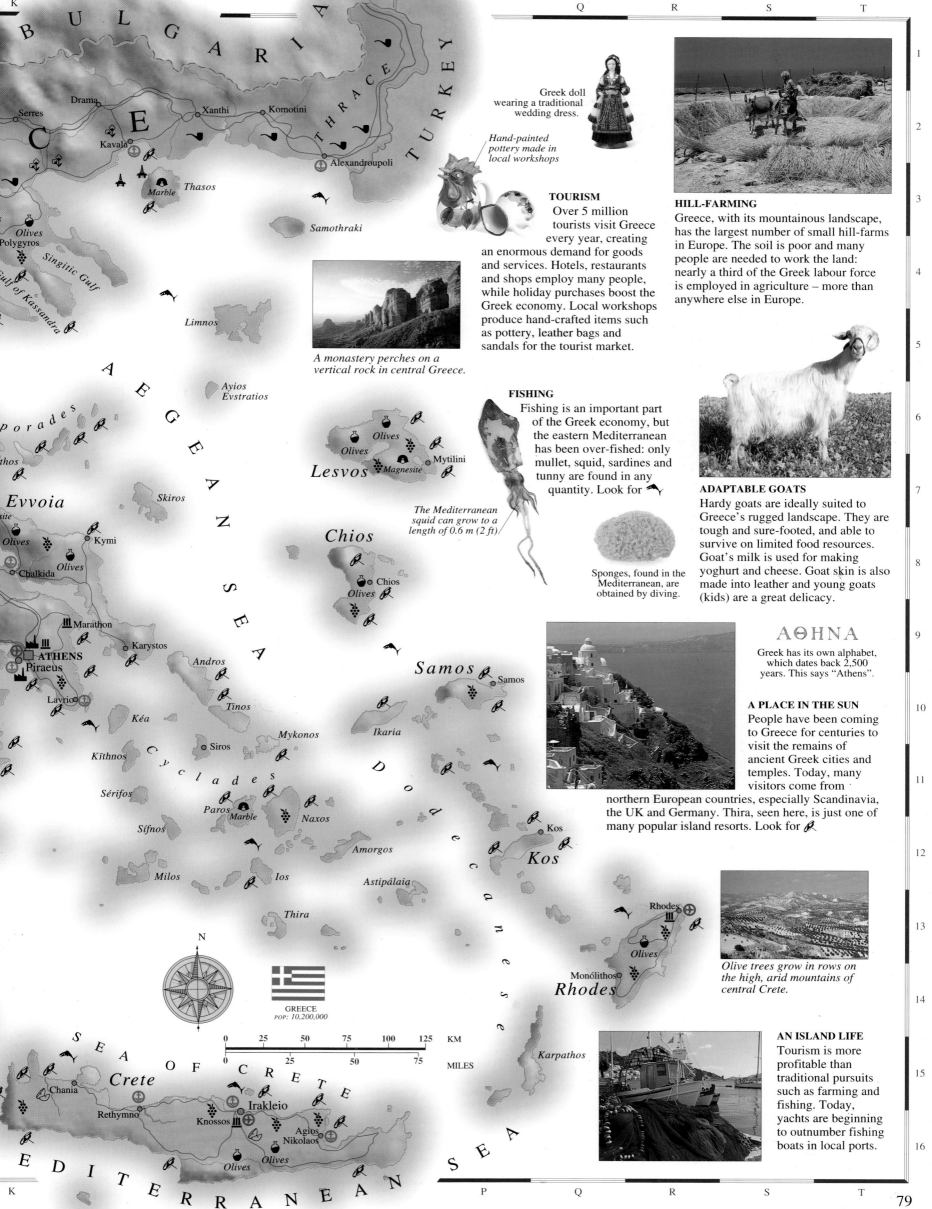

Greek doll wearing a traditional wedding dress.

Hand-painted pottery made in local workshops

TOURISM

Over 5 million tourists visit Greece every year, creating an enormous demand for goods and services. Hotels, restaurants and shops employ many people, while holiday purchases boost the Greek economy. Local workshops produce hand-crafted items such as pottery, leather bags and sandals for the tourist market.

A monastery perches on a vertical rock in central Greece.

FISHING

Fishing is an important part of the Greek economy, but the eastern Mediterranean has been over-fished: only mullet, squid, sardines and tunny are found in any quantity. Look for

The Mediterranean squid can grow to a length of 0.6 m (2 ft)

Sponges, found in the Mediterranean, are obtained by diving.

HILL-FARMING

Greece, with its mountainous landscape, has the largest number of small hill-farms in Europe. The soil is poor and many people are needed to work the land: nearly a third of the Greek labour force is employed in agriculture – more than anywhere else in Europe.

ADAPTABLE GOATS

Hardy goats are ideally suited to Greece's rugged landscape. They are tough and sure-footed, and able to survive on limited food resources. Goat's milk is used for making yoghurt and cheese. Goat skin is also made into leather and young goats (kids) are a great delicacy.

ΑΘΗΝΑ

Greek has its own alphabet, which dates back 2,500 years. This says "Athens".

A PLACE IN THE SUN

People have been coming to Greece for centuries to visit the remains of ancient Greek cities and temples. Today, many visitors come from northern European countries, especially Scandinavia, the UK and Germany. Thira, seen here, is just one of many popular island resorts. Look for

Olive trees grow in rows on the high, arid mountains of central Crete.

AN ISLAND LIFE

Tourism is more profitable than traditional pursuits such as farming and fishing. Today, yachts are beginning to outnumber fishing boats in local ports.

GREECE
POP: 10,200,000

KM
MILES
0 25 50 75 100 125

Map labels

BULGARIA
THRACE
TURKEY
Serres
Drama
Xanthi
Komotini
Kavala
Alexandroupoli
Marble
Thasos
Samothraki
Olives
Polygyros
Singitic Gulf
Gulf of Kassandra
Limnos
Ayios Evstratios
AEGEAN SEA
Sporades
thos
Evvoia
Skiros
Kymi
Olives
Chalkida
Olives
Marathon
ATHENS
Piraeus
Karystos
Lavrio
Andros
Tinos
Kéa
Kíthnos
Siros
Mykonos
Cyclades
Sérifos
Paros
Marble
Naxos
Sífnos
Milos
Ios
Amorgos
Astipálaia
Thira
Lesvos
Olives
Olives
Mytilini
Magnesite
Chios
Chios
Olives
Samos
Samos
Ikaria
Dodecanese
Kos
Kos
Rhodes
Rhodes
Monólithos
Olives
Karpathos
SEA OF CRETE
Crete
Chania
Rethymno
Knossos
Irakleio
Agios Nikolaos
Olives
Olives
MEDITERRANEAN SEA
N

THE BALTIC STATES AND BELORUSSIA

THE THREE BALTIC STATES – Latvia, Lithuania and Estonia – made history in 1990-91 when they became the first republics to declare their independence from the Soviet Union. This was the end of a long series of invasions and occupations by the Vikings, Germans, Danes, Poles and Russians. A new era had begun, but many of the old problems – food shortages, pollution, weak economies – still remained. The region's flat landscape is well-drained by lakes and rivers and is ideal for farming. The main crops are grains, sugar beet and potatoes. In Belorussia heavy industry such as machine-building and metal-working is important, while the Baltic States manufacture electronics and consumer goods. Nearly half the population of the Baltic States are Russians who have moved there to work in industry. The Baltic Sea, although much of it is frozen in the winter months, gives access to the markets of northern Europe. Industrialization has left a terrible legacy. Summer resorts along the Baltic coast have been closed to visitors because of polluted seawater, and Belorussia was badly hit by the nuclear accident at Chernobyl in the Ukraine in 1986, when 70 per cent of the radioactive fall-out landed on its territory.

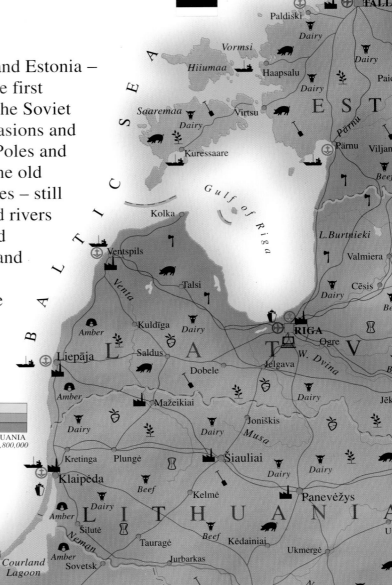

ESTONIA
POP: 1,600,000

LITHUANIA
POP: 3,800,000

NEW CURRENCY

When the three Baltic States separated from the Soviet Union, they all stopped using the rouble and introduced their own currencies. Companies which had been owned and run by the communist state came under private ownership, and the Baltic States encouraged investment in these industries from abroad.

One of the many lakes of Lithuania.

Spider, trapped in amber

BALTIC GOLD

Amber is the fossilized sap of ancient trees. The Baltic States produce two-thirds of the world's amber, most of it found along Lithuania's "amber coast". Amber has been collected and traded since prehistoric times. It is a precious stone, but is also valued for its medical properties. Even today it is used to treat rheumatism. Look for 🎧

MINSK

Although Minsk was founded over 900 years ago, it has no historic buildings. The city was virtually destroyed by bombing during World War II, when half of Minsk's population is estimated to have been killed. After the war, the city was rebuilt, and became one of the industrial centres of the former Soviet Union.

Sour cream

NATIONAL DISH

Draniki is the national dish of Belorussia. It is made of grated potatoes fried in vegetable oil and served with sour cream. Potatoes are grown everywhere, and are one of Belorussia's main products. Large numbers of dairy cattle are kept on its extensive pastureland.

Beetroot, mixed with sour cream

Draniki

KEYBOX

Cattle: The Baltic States were the centres of beef and dairy production for the former Soviet Union. Look for 🐄

Oil: The Baltic States used to obtain free oil by pipeline from the former Soviet Union. Now they depend on Estonia's oil shale deposits. Look for 🛢

Peat: This region has large supplies of peat – a fuel made from carbonized plant material found in bogs. Look for ⛏

🐖	Pigs	⛴	Fishing port
🌱	Sugar beet	⚫	Mining
🌿	Potatoes	🏭	Industrial centre
⏳	Flax	⚓	Shipbuilding
🪓	Timber	💻	High-tech industry

Map labels: Naissaar, TALLI, Paldiski, Vormsi, Dairy, Dairy, Hiiumaa, Haapsalu, Paid, Dairy, EST, Saaremaa, Virtsu, ST, Dairy, Pärnu, Viljand, Kuressaare, Pärnu, Kolka, Gulf of Riga, L. Burtnieki, Valmiera, BALTIC SEA, Ventspils, Cēsis, Venta, Talsi, Dairy, Be, Kuldīga, Dairy, Amber, RIGA, Liepāja, Saldus, Ogre, T, V, W. Dvina, Dobele, Jelgava, Be, Amber, Mažeikiai, Dairy, Jēk, Joniškis, Dairy, Dairy, Musa, Kretinga, Plungė, Šiauliai, Dairy, Klaipėda, Dairy, Beef, Kelmė, Panevėžys, Amber, LITHUANIA, Šilutė, Neman, Beef, Kėdainiai, Ute, RUSSIAN FEDERATION (KALININGRAD OBLAST), Courland Lagoon, Tauragė, Ukmergė, Amber, Sovetsk, Jurbarkas, Neris, Dairy, Amber, KALININGRAD, Kaunas, Baltiysk, Gusev, VILN, Chernyakhovsk, Marijampolė, Dairy, Dairy, Alytus, Dairy, POLAND, Druskininkai, Lida, Beef, Hrodna, Neman, BEL, Baranavich, Vawkavysk, Slonim, Pruzhany, Byaroza, Kobryn, Brest, Pi

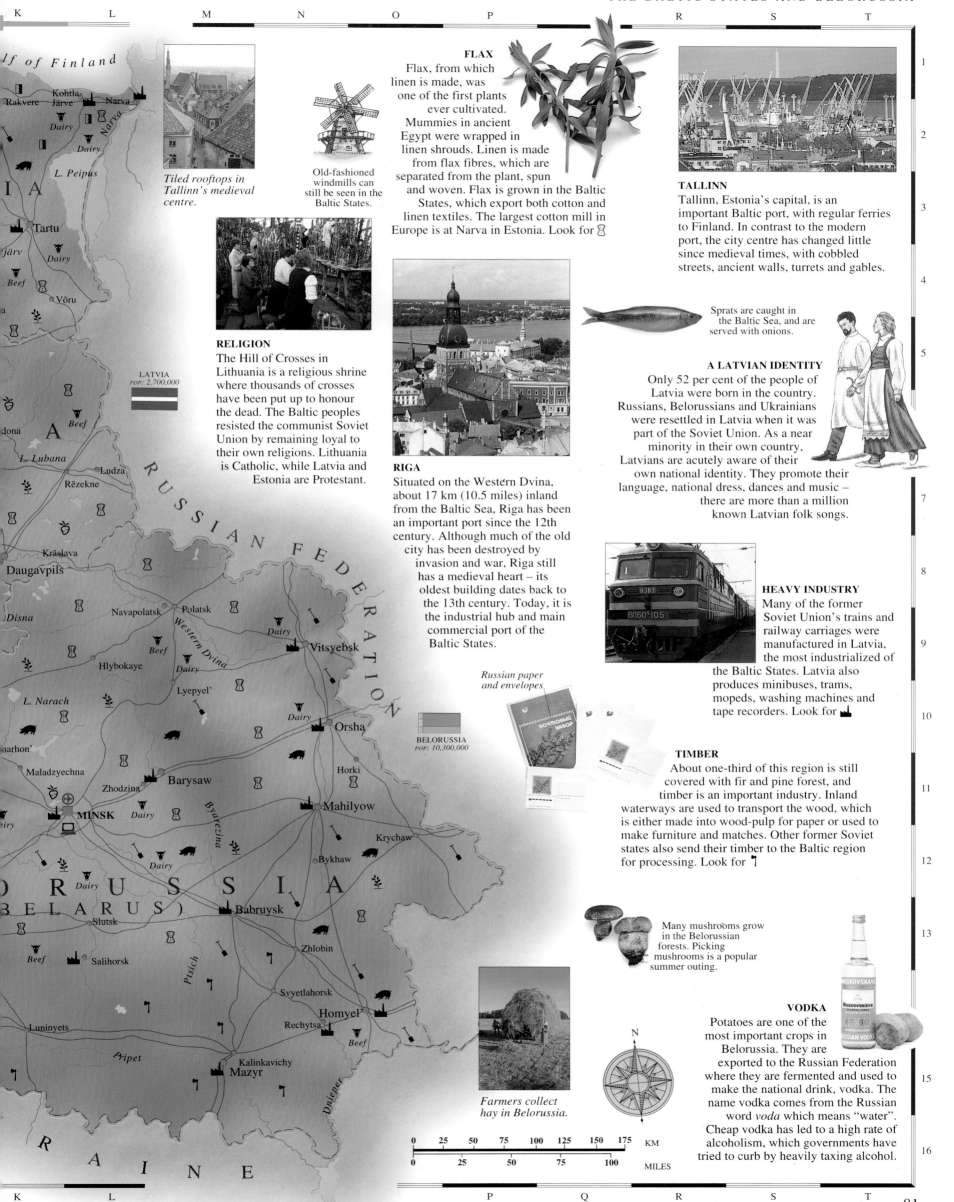

Tiled rooftops in Tallinn's medieval centre.

Old-fashioned windmills can still be seen in the Baltic States.

FLAX
Flax, from which linen is made, was one of the first plants ever cultivated. Mummies in ancient Egypt were wrapped in linen shrouds. Linen is made from flax fibres, which are separated from the plant, spun and woven. Flax is grown in the Baltic States, which export both cotton and linen textiles. The largest cotton mill in Europe is at Narva in Estonia. Look for 🜊

TALLINN
Tallinn, Estonia's capital, is an important Baltic port, with regular ferries to Finland. In contrast to the modern port, the city centre has changed little since medieval times, with cobbled streets, ancient walls, turrets and gables.

RELIGION
The Hill of Crosses in Lithuania is a religious shrine where thousands of crosses have been put up to honour the dead. The Baltic peoples resisted the communist Soviet Union by remaining loyal to their own religions. Lithuania is Catholic, while Latvia and Estonia are Protestant.

LATVIA
POP: 2,700,000

Sprats are caught in the Baltic Sea, and are served with onions.

A LATVIAN IDENTITY
Only 52 per cent of the people of Latvia were born in the country. Russians, Belorussians and Ukrainians were resettled in Latvia when it was part of the Soviet Union. As a near minority in their own country, Latvians are acutely aware of their own national identity. They promote their language, national dress, dances and music – there are more than a million known Latvian folk songs.

RIGA
Situated on the Western Dvina, about 17 km (10.5 miles) inland from the Baltic Sea, Riga has been an important port since the 12th century. Although much of the old city has been destroyed by invasion and war, Riga still has a medieval heart – its oldest building dates back to the 13th century. Today, it is the industrial hub and main commercial port of the Baltic States.

Russian paper and envelopes

BELORUSSIA
POP: 10,300,000

HEAVY INDUSTRY
Many of the former Soviet Union's trains and railway carriages were manufactured in Latvia, the most industrialized of the Baltic States. Latvia also produces minibuses, trams, mopeds, washing machines and tape recorders. Look for 🏭

TIMBER
About one-third of this region is still covered with fir and pine forest, and timber is an important industry. Inland waterways are used to transport the wood, which is either made into wood-pulp for paper or used to make furniture and matches. Other former Soviet states also send their timber to the Baltic region for processing. Look for 🜊

Many mushrooms grow in the Belorussian forests. Picking mushrooms is a popular summer outing.

Farmers collect hay in Belorussia.

VODKA
Potatoes are one of the most important crops in Belorussia. They are exported to the Russian Federation where they are fermented and used to make the national drink, vodka. The name vodka comes from the Russian word *voda* which means "water". Cheap vodka has led to a high rate of alcoholism, which governments have tried to curb by heavily taxing alcohol.

| 0 | 25 | 50 | 75 | 100 | 125 | 150 | 175 | KM |
| 0 | | 25 | | 50 | | 75 | | 100 | MILES |

EUROPEAN RUSSIA

THE RUSSIAN FEDERATION is the largest country in the world. Stretching across two continents – Europe in the west and Asia in the east – it is twice the size of the USA. The Ural Mountains form the division between the European and Asian parts of the country. The Russian Federation has fertile farmlands, vast mineral deposits and abundant timber, oil and other natural resources. Despite its size and natural wealth, Russia is currently in a state of political and economic turmoil. After centuries of rule by czars (emperors), the world's first communist government took power in Russia in 1917; five years later the country became the Union of Soviet Socialist Republics (USSR), which included many of the territories that were formerly parts of the Russian Empire. During 74 years of communist rule, the Soviet Union became an industrial and military superpower, but at an appalling cost to its people and environment. Economic problems led to liberal reforms beginning in the mid-1980s, but the reforms unleashed a whirlwind of change which led to the fall of the communist regime in December 1991. By then most of the non-Russian republics had declared independence. The new Russian Federation is now struggling to become a democracy.

RELIGION

Moscow is the spiritual centre of the Russian Orthodox church. For many decades, the Church was persecuted in Russia; today, churches are re-opening, and many Russian people are turning back to religion. Beautiful icons (religious images painted on wood), like this one, adorn the churches and people's homes.

САНКТ-ПЕТЕРБУРГ

The name "St. Petersburg", written in Russia's Cyrillic alphabet, which was devised by Christian missionaries in the 10th century.

ST. PETERSBURG

St. Petersburg, the capital of Russia from 1712-1918, was founded by Czar Peter the Great in 1703. It is built on 12 islands, linked by bridges, and has many elegant 18th-century buildings.

Northern Russia is covered with coniferous forest, called taiga.

Many wooden churches built in the 17th century still stand on small islands in Lake Onega.

MOSCOW

The city of Moscow was founded in the 12th century. At its centre is a fortified citadel called the *Kremlin*. Its stone walls enclose the grand palace of the czars, four cathedrals and a church. The *Kremlin* became the country's seat of government.

St. Basil's, Moscow, built in the 16th century

RUSSIAN FEDERATION
pop: 149,200,000
(EUROPEAN RUSSIA)
pop: 108,950,000

Map labels

KARA SEA
Novaya Zemlya
Baydarata Bay
Kara Strait
Vaygach I.
Vorkuta
MOUNTAINS
BARENTS SEA
Kolguyev I.
Pechora
Usa
Izhma
Kama
Potassium
Uranium
Chesha Bay
Mezen
Syktyvkar
KOLA PENINSULA
Murmansk
Copper
Nickel
Iron
L. Umbozero
Nickel
Iron
Phosphate
Aluminium
Pinega
Kotlas
Arkhangel'sk
WHITE SEA
Northern Dvina
Onega
Kirov
Velluga
NORWAY
FINLAND
Kem'
L. Pyaozero
L. Topozero
L. Segozero
L. Onega
Oats
Barley
Rye
Oats
Barley
Vologda
Rye
Cherepovets
Oats
Petrozavodsk
L. Ladoga
Rybinsk Res.
Kostroma
Barley
Ivanovo
Vladimir
Tver
Moscow-Volga Canal
Gzhel
MOSCOW (MOSKVA)
Aluminium
Rye
Volga
Rye
Yaroslavl'
Gulf of Finland
St. Petersburg
Rye
Novgorod
Pskov
Oats
Smolensk
Oats
Nevel'
Dnieper
Oats
Kaluga
ESTONIA
LATVIA
BELORUSSIA
RUSSIAN FEDERATION

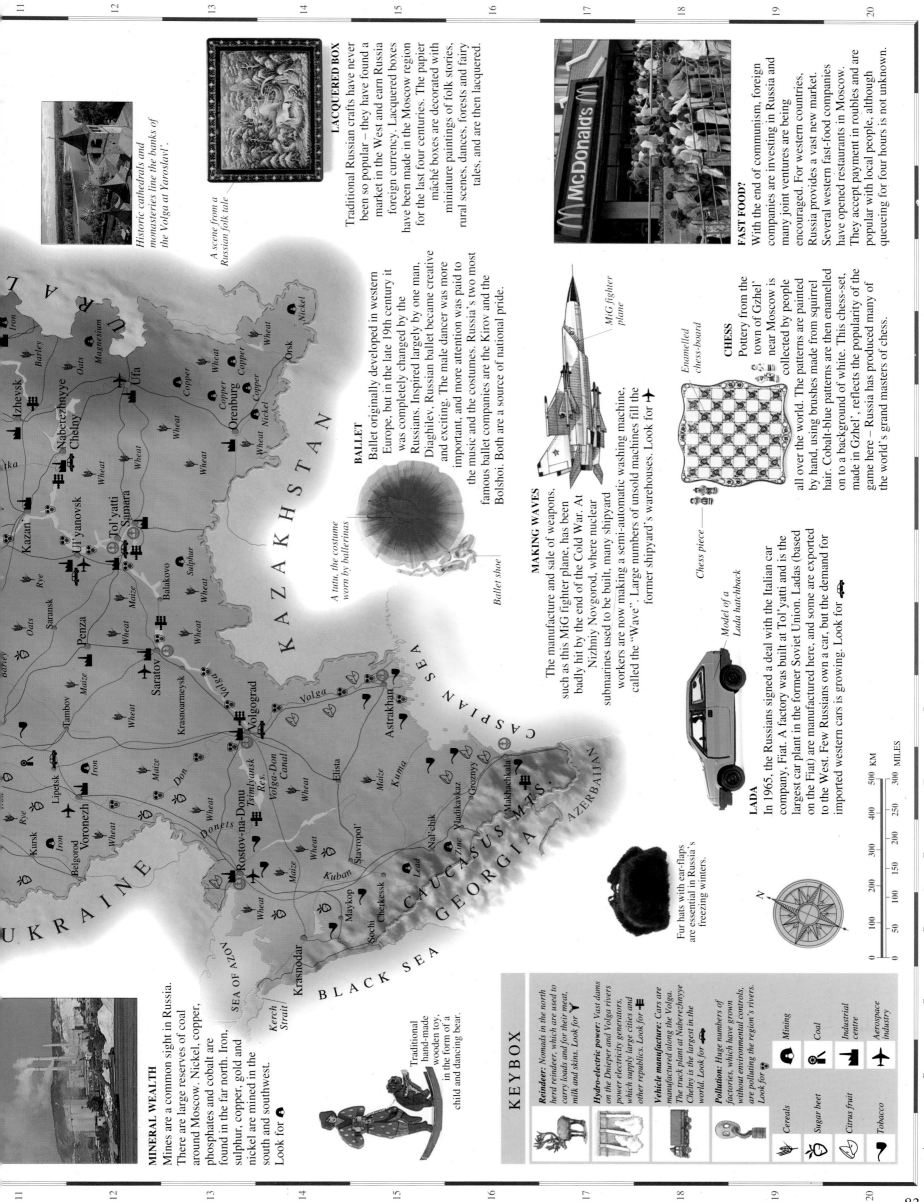

Historic cathedrals and monasteries line the banks of the Volga at Yaroslavl'.

A scene from a Russian folk tale

LACQUERED BOX

Traditional Russian crafts have never been so popular – they have found a market in the West and earn Russia foreign currency. Lacquered boxes have been made in the Moscow region for the last four centuries. The papier mâché boxes are decorated with miniature paintings of folk stories, rural scenes, dances, forests and fairy tales, and are then lacquered.

FAST FOOD?

With the end of communism, foreign companies are investing in Russia and many joint ventures are being encouraged. For western countries, Russia provides a vast new market. Several western fast-food companies have opened restaurants in Moscow. They accept payment in roubles and are popular with local people, although queueing for four hours is not unknown.

BALLET

Ballet originally developed in western Europe, but in the late 19th century it was completely changed by the Russians. Inspired largely by one man, Diaghilev, Russian ballet became creative and exciting. The male dancer was more important, and more attention was paid to the music and the costumes. Russia's two most famous ballet companies are the Kirov and the Bolshoi. Both are a source of national pride.

A tutu, the costume worn by ballerinas

Ballet shoe

MiG fighter plane

MAKING WAVES

The manufacture and sale of weapons, such as this MiG fighter plane, has been badly hit by the end of the Cold War. At Nizhniy Novgorod, where nuclear submarines used to be built, many shipyard workers are now making a semi-automatic washing machine, called the "Wave". Large numbers of unsold machines fill the former shipyard's warehouses. Look for ✈

CHESS

Pottery from the town of Gzhel' near Moscow is collected by people all over the world. The patterns are painted by hand, using brushes made from squirrel hair. Cobalt-blue patterns are then enamelled on to a background of white. This chess-set, made in Gzhel', reflects the popularity of the game here – Russia has produced many of the world's grand masters of chess.

Enamelled chess-board

Chess piece

Model of a Lada hatchback

LADA

In 1965, the Russians signed a deal with the Italian car company, Fiat. A factory was built at Tol'yatti and is the largest car plant in the former Soviet Union. Ladas (based on the Fiat) are manufactured here, and some are exported to the West. Few Russians own a car, but the demand for imported western cars is growing. Look for 🚗

MINERAL WEALTH

Mines are a common sight in Russia. There are large reserves of coal around Moscow. Nickel, copper, phosphates and cobalt are found in the far north. Iron, sulphur, copper, gold and nickel are mined in the south and southwest. Look for ⛏

Fur hats with ear-flaps are essential in Russia's freezing winters.

Traditional hand-made wooden toy, in the form of a child and dancing bear.

KEYBOX

Reindeer: Nomads in the north herd reindeer, which are used to carry loads and for their meat, milk and skins. Look for 🦌

Hydro-electric power: Vast dams on the Dnieper and Volga rivers power electricity generators, which supply large cities and other republics. Look for ⚡

Vehicle manufacture: Cars are manufactured along the Volga. The truck plant at Naberezhnyye Chelny is the largest in the world. Look for 🚗

Pollution: Huge numbers of factories, which have grown without environmental controls, are polluting the region's rivers. Look for 🏭

🌾 Cereals	⛏ Mining	
🌱 Sugar beet	⚙ Coal	
🍊 Citrus fruit	🏭 Industrial centre	
🌿 Tobacco	✈ Aerospace industry	

500 KM
300 MILES

N

UKRAINE, MOLDAVIA AND THE CAUCASIAN REPUBLICS

THE CAUCASUS MOUNTAINS run between the Black and Caspian Seas. Higher in places than the Alps, they form a natural barrier between the flat steppes of the Russian Federation to the north and the plateaux of Southwest Asia. The newly independent states to the south of the Russian Federation are rich in natural resources. Ukraine, the largest country in Europe, is dominated by a flat and fertile plain, where huge quantities of cereals are grown on large farms. Ukraine also possesses extensive coal and iron ore deposits and is heavily industrialized. Wine and fruit are produced in Moldavia and Georgia, where the climate is mild and the soil fertile. Mountainous Armenia is rich in minerals, while Azerbaijan has plentiful oil.

Cereals being harvested in the fertile fields of Ukraine.

WINE

A quarter of the former Soviet Union's wine was produced in Moldavia, which is well known for its champagne. Vines also thrive on the warm, sunny hills of eastern Georgia, where wine and brandy are produced. Look for 🍇

Georgian brandy

Moldavian wine

BORSCHT

Vegetable soups are the main food for many country people in cold regions throughout the world. Russia's famous beetroot soup, *borscht*, comes from Ukraine. There, the *borscht* also contains root vegetables, such as potatoes and carrots. *Borscht* is often served with savoury turnovers, called *piroshki*.

Borscht, beetroot soup

Sour cream

Piroshki, savoury pastries

MOLDAVIA
POP: 4,400,000

CHERNOBYL

In 1986, a radiation leak at Chernobyl nuclear power station caused panic all over Europe. More than 100,000 people were evacuated from the area around the plant, where towns now stand desolate and empty. More than two million people still live, in fear and uncertainty, in the contaminated areas.

KEYBOX

Oil: There is a large oilfield under the delta of the River Kura in Azerbaijan. Offshore wells are also being dug in the Caspian Sea. Look for ⬆	
Hydro-electric power: Dams on the River Dnieper supply water for crops and for electricity. The rivers of the Caucasus also provide electricity. Look for ⊨	
High-tech: Electrical and electronic equipment, such as TVs and computers, are made in the Caucasian republics. Look for 🖥	

🌾	Cereals	⛑	Mining
🍇	Wine	🧑	Coal
🌿	Tea	🏭	Industrial centre
🌻	Sunflowers	⛏	Tourism
🐟	Fishing	☢	Nuclear pollution

BLACK SEA TOURISM

The Crimea attracts millions of visitors who cram onto the crowded beaches to enjoy the warm sun. Many visitors come for their health, rest and a regime of healthy eating, massage and exercise. Look for ⛏

The barrier of the Caucasus Mountains blocks cold air from the north

Hardy crops, such as maize which can withstand frosts, are grown on lowlands

Mountains force humid air to rise. It falls as rain in Georgia

Grapes and fruits grown in valleys

Cotton production along lower R. Kura

THE CAUCASUS MOUNTAINS

Armenia, Azerbaijan and Georgia – the Caucasian Republics – are isolated from the Russian Federation by the Caucasus Mountains. The warm sub-tropical climate of the region allows an exotic range of crops to be grown. Georgia has a humid climate, so tea and citrus fruits are cultivated. In the drier east, the rivers running down from the mountains are used to water the fields.

BLACK BREAD

Ukraine was known as the former Soviet Union's "breadbasket". Its broad flat black earth, are intensively cultivated: wheat, buckwheat, potatoes, rye and flax are grown on vast farms. Much of Ukraine's countryside consists of endless fields of cereals, the view broken only by the occasional haystack.

Matrioshka dolls are hand-painted. Each is made from a single piece of wood.

KIEV

Kiev, founded in the 9th century, is the capital of Ukraine. St. Sophia's Cathedral, with its gilded domes, has been Kiev's most famous landmark since 1037. Kiev is situated on the banks of the River Dnieper, the republic's main waterway. It is within easy reach of the Black Sea ports, as well as being near Ukraine's industrial centre.

UKRAINE
POP: 52,200,000

The Ukraine is the world's largest producer of buckwheat. Although it is ground up to make flour, buckwheat is not a true cereal.

COAL

About a third of the former Soviet Union's coal came from the area around Donets'k in Ukraine, where there are about 40 deep mines. Miners working here are reasonably well-paid, but gas explosions and the frequent breakdown of equipment put them at risk. Death rates in these mines are 10 times higher than in mines in the USA. Look for

INDUSTRIAL HEARTLAND

Ukraine's Donbass region, with its rich reserves of coal, iron, manganese and other minerals, is a major industrial area. Heavy industry, such as iron and steel works, engineering and chemicals, still dominate the region, but today, cars, aircraft, televisions and computers are also manufactured here. Look for

CAUCASIAN CONFLICT

When the Caucasian republics were part of the Soviet Union, many different peoples were forced to live side by side. Since these countries became independent, many pent-up resentments have been unleashed. Within Muslim Azerbaijan, the Christian, mainly Armenian, region of Nagorno-Karabakh has caused great tension, and fighting has erupted.

TEA

Tea is a popular drink throughout the former Soviet Union, and over 90 per cent of the tea consumed here is grown in Georgia. Both black and green teas are grown on large tea plantations. Tea is served black and strong, with sugar or lemon. Look for

Decorated Black Sea fiddle, from Georgia.

SUNFLOWERS

Sunflowers are an important crop in southern Ukraine. The seeds, which can be eaten, contain oil and protein. Sunflower oil is used for cooking. The seeds are also used in the manufacture of margarine and soap, and are mixed with maize and peas for cattle feed. Look for

The snow-capped peaks of the Caucasus Mountains.

AZERBAIJAN
POP: 7,300,000

Caviar, served on toast

CAVIAR

The Russian sturgeon is a large fish, which can grow up to 7 m (23 ft) in length. Its eggs, called caviar, are an expensive delicacy. Sturgeon live in the Black and Caspian Seas and swim up rivers, such as the Dnieper, to breed in fresh water. Hydroelectric dams on these rivers have disrupted the sturgeons' routes, and polluted water is causing concern about falling numbers of fish. Look for

GEORGIA
POP: 5,500,000

The Swallow's Nest Castle, high on a rock near Yalta.

TEXTILES

Georgia is famous for its silk and textiles. Brightly coloured and patterned cotton fabrics are woven with gold and silver thread. Worn by women as headscarves, these fabrics are seen throughout the Caucasus.

ARMENIA
POP: 3,600,000

| 0 | 50 | 100 | 150 | 200 | 250 | 300 | KM |
| 0 | | 50 | | 100 | | 150 | MILES |

White-backed vulture
Gyps bengalensis
Wingspan: 2.2 m (7 ft)
■ ▲

Cheetah
Acinonyx jubatus
Length: 2.2 m (7 ft)
■ ■ !

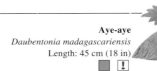

Aye-aye
Daubentonia madagascariensis
Length: 45 cm (18 in)
■ !

AFRICA

AFRICA IS THE SECOND largest continent after Asia, and the only one through which the Equator and both tropics run. It is also home to the world's longest river, the Nile. The climate and vegetation roughly mirror each other on either side of the Equator. In the extreme south, and along the Mediterranean coast in the north, hot dry summers are followed by mild wet winters. Similarly, the land around each tropic is hot and starved of rain, so great deserts have formed. Africa's immense tropical savannah grasslands are prone to drought, but around the Equator high rainfall has produced lush tropical rainforests. The volcanoes and strangely elongated lakes in the Rift Valley are evidence of cracks in the Earth's crust that threaten eventually to split Africa apart.

■ HOT SAHARA
The inhospitable Sahara desert covers one-third of Africa. Temperatures can exceed 50°C (120°F).

Burchell's zebra
Equus burchelli
Height: 1.2 m (4 ft)
■ ■

■ MISTY RAINFOREST
Tropical rainforests only grow where temperatures are always high, and rain is abundant. Here in central Africa, it rains every day – more than 2 m (7 ft) falls each year.

Malachite is a copper-rich ore found in many parts of eastern Africa.

■ THUNDERING WATERFALL
The Zambezi River winds slowly through dry woodlands before reaching the Victoria Falls. Here it plummets 108 m (354 ft), creating so much noise and spray that local people call it "the smoke that thunders".

■ GREAT RIFT VALLEY
Cracks in the Earth's crust have made a valley 6,000 km (3,750 miles) long, and up to 90 km (55 miles) wide.

Umbrella thorn acacia
Acacia tortillis
Height: 18 m (60 ft)
■

The South African Turban shell looks like a headdress made of coiled cloth.

■ SAND DUNES IN THE NAMIB
The intensely hot Namib Desert forms a narrow strip down Africa's southwest coast. Rainfall is less than 15 cm (6 in) a year, but sea mists from the cold currents along the coast provide enough moisture for some plants and animals to survive.

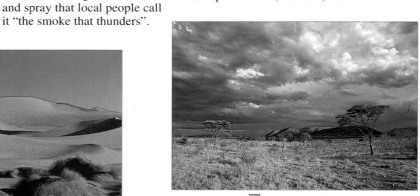

■ SERENGETI PLAIN
Savannah – grassland and open woodland – is home to huge herds of grazing animals, including wildebeest and zebra.

Gaboon viper
Bitis gabonica
Length: 2 m (7 ft)
■

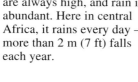

Shells like this Black Mitre can be found in shallow water along the west African coast.

■ ■ OKAVANGO DELTA
Not all rivers run to the sea. The Okavango River ends in a huge inland swamp that attracts thousands of water loving animals, such as hippopotamuses.

CROSS-SECTION THROUGH AFRICA

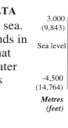

L. Victoria
Great Rift Valley (western)
Ruwenzori Mountains
Serengeti Plain
Great Rift Valley (eastern)
Atlantic Ocean
Congo Basin
Indian Ocean
3,000 (9,843)
Sea level
-4,500 (14,764)
Metres (feet)
A
Length: 4,500 km (2,800 miles)
B

■ SOUTHERN AFRICA
Rainfall is so low in southern Africa that for most of the year few plants show themselves above ground. But as soon as the rains come, a barren landscape is transformed, covered by a brilliant mass of flowers.

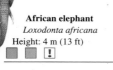

African elephant
Loxodonta africana
Height: 4 m (13 ft)
■ ■ !

Desert scorpion
Androctonus australis
Length: 8 cm (3 in)
■

Mountain gorilla
Gorilla gorilla
Height: 1.8 m (6 ft)
■ ▲ !

MEDITERRANEAN SEA

ASIA

0°   20°   40°

EURASIAN PLATE
AFRICAN PLATE   C. Bon

Madeira Ridge   Strait of
                       Gibraltar
Monaco   Madeira
Basin
                ATLAS MTS.   Nile Delta
Canary Is.   ▲ Djebal Toubkal
                  4165m   Chott El Jerid   Gulf of Sirte
                                                              Qattâra
                                                              Depression
                                                              -133m
                                                                        L. Nasser

S A H A R A   LIBYAN DESERT   Nile

                TASSILI N'AJJER
                  2158m ▲
                    ▲ 2918m
                 AHAGGAR   NUBIAN
Cape   TIBESTI   DESERT
Verde Is.   ▲ 3415m

IRANIAN PLATE
ARABIAN PLATE
                                                    Persian Gulf
                                                              Tropic of Cancer

ARABIAN
PENINSULA

RED SEA
ARABIAN PLATE
AFRICAN PLATE

S A H E L   L. Chad
C. Verde   L.
Senegal   Niger
        Massina
Black Volta   Niger   Benue
                                              Blue Nile
A F R I C A   Socotra
                                              ▲ Ras Dashen   C. Caseyr
                                                4620m   Gulf of Aden
        L. Volta   White Nile   L. Tana
Guinea   ADAMAWA   ETHIOPIAN
Basin   HIGHLANDS   HIGHLANDS   Shebeli
        Niger Delta
        Fernando Póo ▲ Mt. Cameroon   Ubangi   Sudd
Gulf of Guinea   4070m
        Príncipe I.   Congo   L. Turkana
        São Tomé I.   Basin   EAST   Somali
                                                   AFRICAN   Basin   Equator
                            A •   L. Albert   PLATEAU
                                   RUWENZORI MTS.
SOUTH   Margherita Peak L. Victoria   Kirinyaga
AMERICA   5109m ▲   5200m
Mid-Atlantic Ridge   Mt. Karisimbi ▲   SERENGETI   B • INDIAN
                                  4507m   PLAIN   ▲ Kilimanjaro
                                          Ngorongoro   5895m
                                   Congo (Zaire) Crater   Zanzibar   OCEAN

AFRICAN PLATE   Angola   L. Tanganyika   L. Rukwa
                       Basin   △ Comoro Is.
SOUTH AMERICAN PLATE   L. Mweru
                                                   L. Nyasa
                       C. Fria   Okavango   Mozambique Channel   Madagascar
Mid-Atlantic Ridge   L. Kariba   Zambezi   Tsiafajovona
                                   Victoria Falls   2643m ▲
A T L A N T I C   O C E A N   108m   Madagascar
                       Okavango   Natal   Basin
                       Delta   Limpopo   Basin   Tropic of Capricorn
        Walvis Ridge   NAMIB DESERT KALAHARI   Madagascar
                                     DESERT   Ridge

                                          ▲ 3482m
                            Orange R.   DRAKENSBERG
                       Cape   Cape of Good Hope
                       Basin   C. Agulhas
                                                              Southwest Indian Ridge
        Agulhas Ridge   Agulhas
                               Basin
AFRICAN PLATE
ANTARCTICA PLATE

BOTTLE TREES
Plants can resist drought by
reducing their leaf-size and
enlarging their stems to store
water. Here in Madagascar's
dry woodlands, huge-trunked
baobabs, or "bottle trees", grow
alongside spiny Dideria.

Black rhinoceros
Diceros bicornis
Length: 3.6 m (12 ft)
■ ■ ！

KEY TO SYMBOLS

▲ Mountain
△ Volcano
🌿 Mangroves
▒ Wetlands
░ Coral reef
▬ Plate margins with
   direction of movement

KEY TO NATURAL VEGETATION

□ Mediterranean-type   Temperate grassland □

□ Hot desert   Mountain □

□ Tropical grassland

□ Tropical rainforest   Dry woodland □

A B C D E F G H I J

NORTHWEST AFRICA

OVER THE CENTURIES, Northwest Africa has been invaded by many peoples. The entire north coast from the Red Sea to the Atlantic was once part of the Roman Empire. Later colonization by Italy, Great Britain, Turkey, Spain and France contributed to the culture of the countries, but it was the 7th-century Arab conquest which fundamentally changed the region. The conversion of the original peoples – the Berbers – to Islam, and the use of Arabic as a common language, gave these countries a sense of unity which remains today. In fact, the region is sometimes called the Maghreb, which means "west" in Arabic. In the northwest, the Atlas Mountains form a barrier between the wetter, cooler areas along the coast and the great Saharan Desert. This desert is the biggest on Earth, and is still growing. Water shortages and lack of land for farming are problems throughout the region, especially as the population of the Maghreb is increasing rapidly. In Algeria and Libya, however, the desert has revealed hidden riches – abundant oil and natural gas.

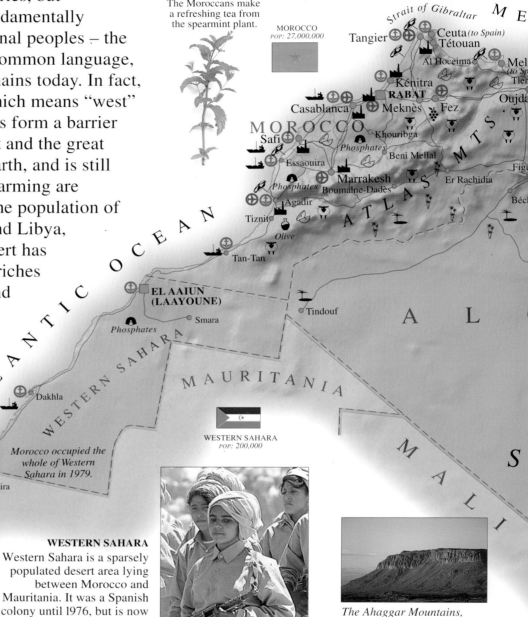

FEZ – AN ISLAMIC CITY
This view of the city of Fez in Morocco shows the flat-roofed houses that are traditional in this region. Seen from the narrow streets, the houses look blank and windowless, but this is because they are designed to face inwards on to central courtyards which are cool and private. Islamic cities may appear to be a chaotic maze of streets, but in fact they are laid out following guidelines set in the holy book of Islam, the *Koran*.

The Moroccans make a refreshing tea from the spearmint plant.

MOROCCO
POP: 27,000,000

Strait of Gibraltar

Tangier • Ceuta *(to Spain)* • Tétouan
Al Hoceima
Melilla *(to Spain)*
Kénitra • Tlemcen
RABAT
Casablanca • Meknès • Fez • Oujda
MOROCCO
Khouribga
Safi • *Phosphates* • Beni Mellal
Essaouira • Figuig
Marrakesh • Er Rachidia
Phosphates • Boumalne-Dadès • Béchar
Agadir
Tiznit • ATLAS MTS
Olive
Tan-Tan

EL AAIUN (LAAYOUNE) • Smara • Tindouf
Phosphates

WESTERN SAHARA
Dakhla
Morocco occupied the whole of Western Sahara in 1979.
Lagouira

WESTERN SAHARA
POP: 200,000

MAURITANIA

MALI

BERBERS
Berbers were the original people of Northwest Africa. When the Arabs invaded, they were driven out of the fertile coastal areas. Many Berbers still live in remote villages or towns – such as here at Boumalne-Dadès – high in the Atlas Mountains, where their lifestyle and language have remained unchanged for centuries.

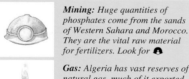
Couscous is the basic ingredient of many North African dishes. It is made of tiny pellets of flour, called semolina.

KEYBOX

Mining: Huge quantities of phosphates come from the sands of Western Sahara and Morocco. They are the vital raw material for fertilizers. Look for ⬤

Gas: Algeria has vast reserves of natural gas, much of it exported to Europe – some by pipeline to Italy across the Mediterranean Sea. Look for ⬤

Archaeological sites: Early civilizations, such as the Romans, built cities in the desert and along the coast of North Africa. Look for ⫟

🐑	Sheep	⛴	Fishing port
🍊	Citrus fruit	⛽	Oil
🌴	Dates	🏭	Industrial centre
🍇	Wine	✎	Tourism
🫗	Vegetable oil	⚓	Oases

CARPETS AND RUGS
Hand-knotted carpets and rugs, with their distinctive bold patterns and deep pile, are made throughout the region. In Morocco the most important carpet factories are in Rabat and Fez. Craftworkers often work together in cooperatives to maintain high quality and to control prices.

WESTERN SAHARA
Western Sahara is a sparsely populated desert area lying between Morocco and Mauritania. It was a Spanish colony until 1976, but is now fighting for independence from Morocco which claims two-thirds of the country, and the phosphates found there. This photo shows young members of the liberation movement.

Painted plate

Leather bag

TOURISM
Tourism is a vital source of foreign income for Morocco and Tunisia. When oil prices fell in the 1980s, tourism took the place of oil as the main source of foreign income. Modern hotels, built in traditional styles, have sprung up along the coast. Both countries produce handicrafts for tourists, such as leather and brassware. Look for ✎

The Ahaggar Mountains, Algeria, jut up in the middle of the Sahara.

THE TUAREG
The Tuareg are a nomadic tribe who inhabit a huge area of the Sahara. In the past they controlled the great camel caravans which crossed the desert to the Mediterranean, carrying slaves, ivory, gold and salt. Today, some Tuareg still follow the traditional desert way of life, but many have become settled farmers.

A B C D E F G H I J

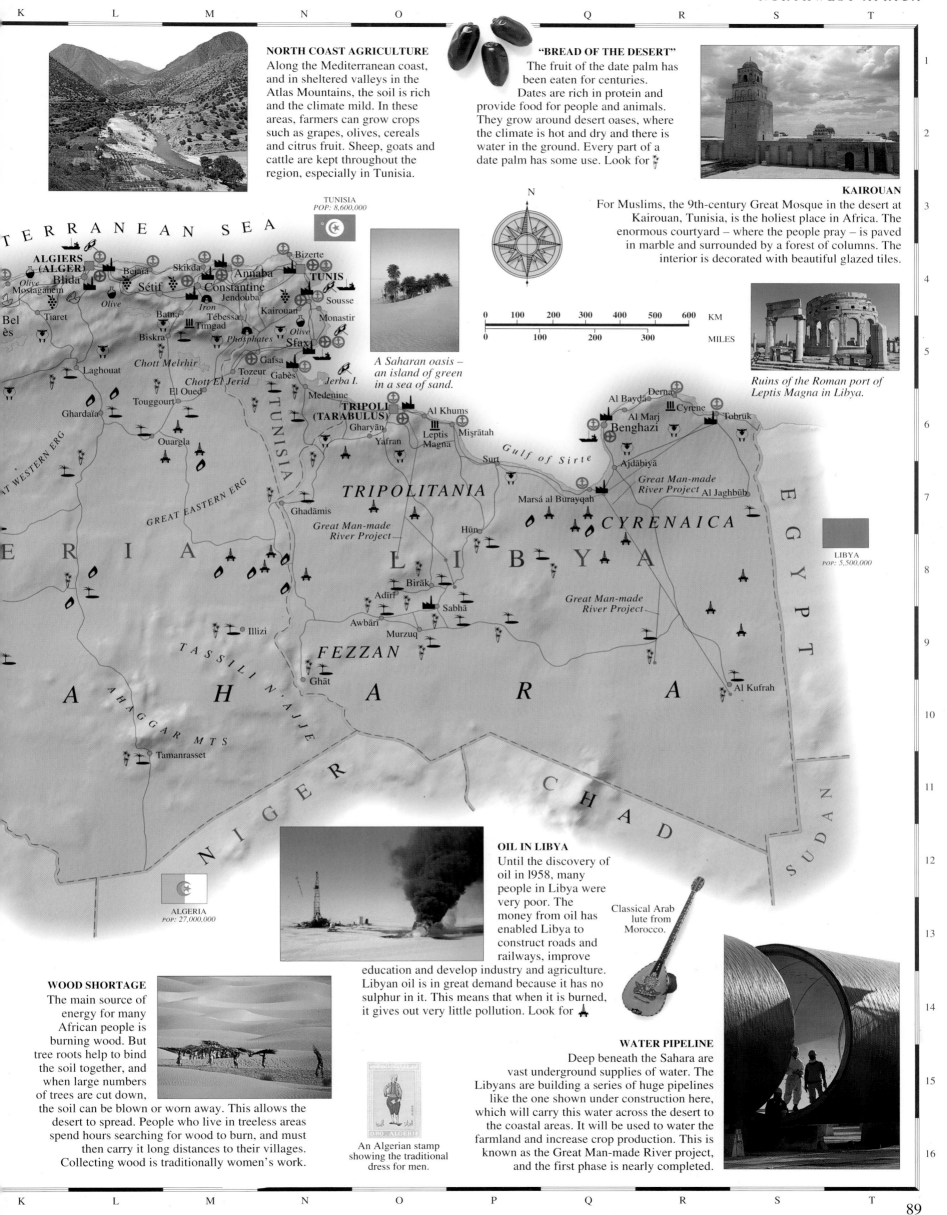

NORTH COAST AGRICULTURE
Along the Mediterranean coast, and in sheltered valleys in the Atlas Mountains, the soil is rich and the climate mild. In these areas, farmers can grow crops such as grapes, olives, cereals and citrus fruit. Sheep, goats and cattle are kept throughout the region, especially in Tunisia.

"BREAD OF THE DESERT"
The fruit of the date palm has been eaten for centuries. Dates are rich in protein and provide food for people and animals. They grow around desert oases, where the climate is hot and dry and there is water in the ground. Every part of a date palm has some use. Look for

KAIROUAN
For Muslims, the 9th-century Great Mosque in the desert at Kairouan, Tunisia, is the holiest place in Africa. The enormous courtyard – where the people pray – is paved in marble and surrounded by a forest of columns. The interior is decorated with beautiful glazed tiles.

TUNISIA
POP: 8,600,000

A Saharan oasis – an island of green in a sea of sand.

Ruins of the Roman port of Leptis Magna in Libya.

LIBYA
POP: 5,500,000

ALGERIA
POP: 27,000,000

OIL IN LIBYA
Until the discovery of oil in 1958, many people in Libya were very poor. The money from oil has enabled Libya to construct roads and railways, improve education and develop industry and agriculture. Libyan oil is in great demand because it has no sulphur in it. This means that when it is burned, it gives out very little pollution. Look for

Classical Arab lute from Morocco.

WOOD SHORTAGE
The main source of energy for many African people is burning wood. But tree roots help to bind the soil together, and when large numbers of trees are cut down, the soil can be blown or worn away. This allows the desert to spread. People who live in treeless areas spend hours searching for wood to burn, and must then carry it long distances to their villages. Collecting wood is traditionally women's work.

An Algerian stamp showing the traditional dress for men.

WATER PIPELINE
Deep beneath the Sahara are vast underground supplies of water. The Libyans are building a series of huge pipelines like the one shown under construction here, which will carry this water across the desert to the coastal areas. It will be used to water the farmland and increase crop production. This is known as the Great Man-made River project, and the first phase is nearly completed.

89

NORTHEAST AFRICA

WATERED AND FERTILIZED BY THE NILE, the longest river in the world, Egypt is a fertile strip running through the Sahara Desert. The first people settled there about 8,000 years ago and, by the time of the pharaohs, Egypt had become one of the world's first great civilizations. Today, Egypt is a relatively stable democracy, with a growing number of industries and control of the Suez Canal, one of the world's most important waterways. To the south are the highlands of Ethiopia and Eritrea. This area is fertile and well-watered in places, but recent droughts have made life precarious for the farmers and nomads who live there. The countries of Somalia, Sudan and Ethiopia have been beset by terrible problems, including drought, famine, religious conflicts and civil war. About half of Africa's 4.5 million refugees come from this area. In 1993, Eritrea gained independence from Ethiopia, after a civil war which lasted 30 years.

TOURIST SOUVENIRS
Large numbers of "ancient Egyptian" *scarabs* (beetles) and other fake antiques are made locally and sold to tourists. City streets are lined with market stalls and the small workshops where these goods are made. Tourism has stimulated this informal economy.

SUEZ CANAL
Opened in 1869, the Suez Canal is one of the world's largest artificial waterways and a vital source of income for Egypt. It connects the Red Sea with the Mediterranean, offering a short cut from Europe through the Persian Gulf to India and the Far East. On average, 21,250 ships a year use the canal.

Coptic cross

THE COPTIC CHURCH
Although most of Ethiopia is surrounded by Islamic countries, about 40 per cent of its population is Christian. The isolated Ethiopian church developed into a unique branch of Christianity, called the Coptic Church.

COTTON
Egypt produces about a third of the world's high-quality cotton. Textile industries, such as spinning, weaving and dyeing cotton are also important. Cotton is the coolest fabric to wear during hot summers. Egyptian men often wear a long-sleeved cotton garment, or *jelaba*. Look for ⚐.

Cotton jelaba

Tomb dwelling in Cairo's City of the Dead

CAIRO
Cairo is the largest city in the Islamic world and is also one of the fastest-growing. Its current population is estimated at 9.5 million, but it is said to be increasing at a rate of 1,500 people a day. New arrivals live in squalid shanty towns on the outskirts of the city. The City of the Dead, a huge ancient cemetery outside Cairo, has now been occupied by the homeless.

The gold death-mask of the Pharaoh Tutankhamun, c. 1352 BC

AGRICULTURE
Although there is fertile land in southern Ethiopia, farming methods are inefficient. The scratch plough is widely used, and – as its name implies – is only able to turn over the surface of the soil. After a few years, the goodness in the soil is used up, and crops will no longer grow.

TOURISM
Visitors from all over the world go to Egypt to see the pyramids and other ancient sites. Income from tourism helps to maintain these ancient sites. The Temple of Isis at Philae would have been flooded by the Aswân Dam, so it was moved, brick by brick, to another island. Look for 🏛.

The Giza pyramids were built as tombs for the pharaohs.

The ancient Egyptians used this reed-like plant, called papyrus, to make paper.

EGYPT
POP: 56,100,000

THE GIFT OF THE NILE
The River Nile floods in the summer, carrying rich mud from the highlands of Sudan and Ethiopia to the deserts of Egypt. This creates some of the most fertile land in the world. Nearly 99 per cent of the Egyptian population live along the banks of the Nile.

Map labels

MEDITERRANEAN SEA

Marsa Matrûh
Qattâra Depression
Alexandria
El Mansûra
Tanta
CAIRO (EL QAHIRA)
Giza
Saqqara
El Faiyûm
Helwân
Beni Suef
Asyût
Sohâg
Abydos
Valley of the Kings
El Minya
Ras Gharib
Gulf of Suez
Gulf of Aqaba
ISRAEL
SINAI
Port Said
Suez Canal
Ismâ'ilîya
Suez

E G Y P T

Nile

Qena
Thebes
Luxor
Idfu
Kom Ombo
Aswân
Philae
Aswân High Dam
L. Nasser
Abu Simbel
Wadi Halfa
Bûr Safâga

RED SEA

NUBIAN DESERT

L I B Y A
LIBYAN DESERT

Donkeys are used throughout the region for pulling carts, and as beasts of burden.

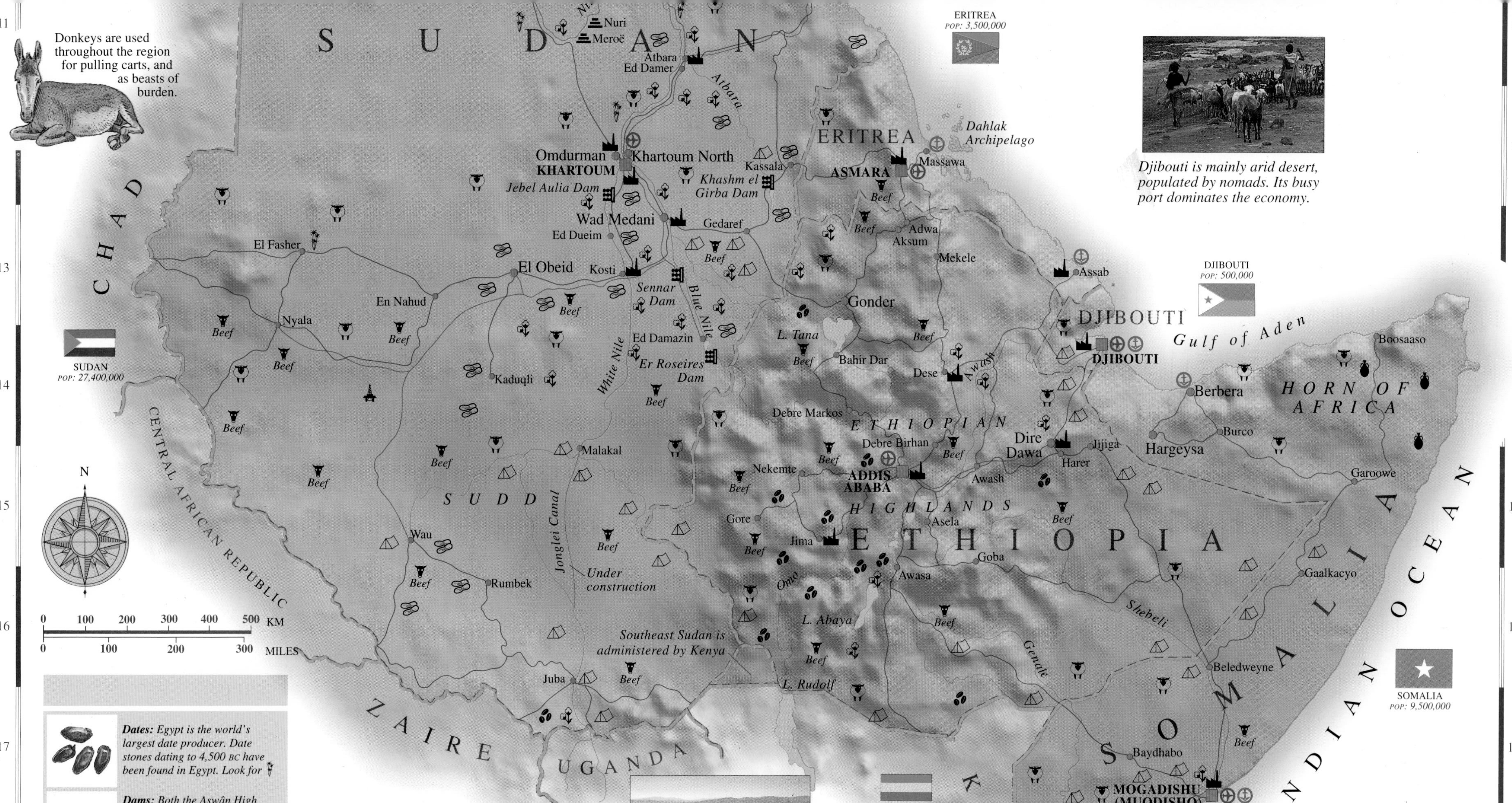

Djibouti is mainly arid desert, populated by nomads. Its busy port dominates the economy.

SOMALIA
The Somalis overthrew their brutal dictator, President Barre, in 1991. A serious drought has since turned Somalia into a disaster area. Aid efforts have been blocked by a civil war between tribes, and millions of people are starving. Many Somalis have flocked to relief camps in search of food. Look for △

INDIAN OCEAN

SOMALIA
POP: 9,500,000

DJIBOUTI
POP: 500,000

ERITREA
POP: 3,500,000

ETHIOPIA
POP: 51,300,000

Vegetables in sauce, wat

Unleavened bread, enjera

TEF
The most common food crop in Ethiopia is *tef* – a grain unique to this region. It is used to make *enjera*, a grey, unleavened bread which is eaten with meat and vegetables in a spicy sauce (*wat*). This is the Ethiopian national dish.

Coffee, grown in the Ethiopian Highlands, is a valuable crop.

NOMADISM
For centuries this region has been populated by nomads, such as the Dinka of Sudan, who live by grazing their goats and camels on any available pastureland. They move from place to place according to the seasons and the weather conditions.

Southeast Sudan is administered by Kenya

SUDAN
POP: 27,400,000

Dates: Egypt is the world's largest date producer. Date stones dating to 4,500 BC have been found in Egypt. Look for ⚬

Dams: Both the Aswân High Dam, opened in 1970, and Sudanese dam projects control the Nile, providing irrigation and electricity. Look for 🏛

Aromatic oils: Frankincense is exported by Somalia. It is taken from trees by making cuts in the bark. It is used in incense and perfume. Look for ⚱

Cattle	🐂	Oil	🛢
Sheep	🐑	Industrial centre	🏭
Coffee	☕	Archaeological sites	⛏
Groundnuts	🥜	Refugee camps	△
Cotton	🌸	Oases	🌴

KM 500 400 300 200 100 0
MILES 300 200 100 0

N

91

WEST AFRICA

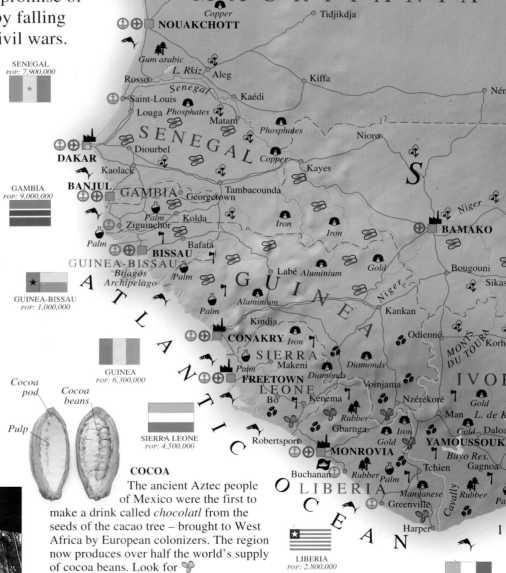

Calabash (bowl) made from a vegetable called a gourd, then decorated.

THE LANDSCAPE OF WEST AFRICA ranges from the sand dunes of the Sahara, through the dry grasslands of the Sahel region, to the tropical rainforests in the south. There is just as much variety in the peoples of the region – more than 250 different tribes live in Nigeria alone. In the north, most people are Muslim, a legacy of the Arab traders who controlled the great caravan routes across the Sahara and brought the religion with them. It was from West Africa, particularly the coastal regions, that hundreds of thousands of Africans were transported to North and South America as slaves. Today many people in West Africa make their living from farming or herding animals. Crops such as coffee and cocoa are grown on large plantations. Like the logging industry, which is also a major source of earnings, these plantations are often owned by foreign multinational companies who take most of the profits out of the region. Recent discoveries of oil and minerals offered the promise of economic prosperity, but this has been prevented by falling world prices, huge foreign debts, corruption and civil wars.

DAKAR
Dakar, the capital of Senegal, is one of the main ports in West Africa. It lies on the Atlantic coast and has a fine natural harbour, large modern docks and ship repair facilities. It is the country's main industrial centre.

KEYBOX

Vegetable oil: The oil palm is widely grown throughout West Africa. Palm oil is used by people in the region and some is exported. Look for 🌴

Research centre: At a centre in Ibadan, Nigeria, new disease-resistant varieties of maize, cassava, and other crops have been bred. Look for ⚗

Film industry: Burkina has a large film industry, subsidized by the government, with studios in Ouagadougou and an annual film festival. Look for 🎥

Shipping registry: Many of the world's shipping countries register their ships in Liberia because of low taxes and lax employment rules. Look for ⛴

🫘	Coffee	🌲	Forest products
🫘	Cocoa	🐟	Fishing
🥜	Ground nuts	⚒	Mining
🌱	Cotton	⛏	Oil
🌾	Timber	🏭	Industrial centre

Kano mosque, built to serve the largely Islamic population in northern Nigeria.

TOURISM
Tourism in this region has expanded rapidly. In the Gambia, the number of visitors has risen from 300 in 1965 to over 100,000 a year in the 1990s. Most tourists stay along the Atlantic coast, but many also go on trips into the bush.

DEFORESTATION
The population of West Africa is growing rapidly. Vast areas of forest have been cut down, either for wood or to clear farmland to feed these extra people. This problem is particularly bad in the Ivory Coast, where little forest is left. Look for 🌾

Cocoa pod
Cocoa beans
Pulp

COCOA
The ancient Aztec people of Mexico were the first to make a drink called *chocolatl* from the seeds of the cacao tree – brought to West Africa by European colonizers. The region now produces over half the world's supply of cocoa beans. Look for 🌿

AFTER INDEPENDENCE
Since independence, some African countries have been plagued by many problems, such as unstable governments and foreign debts. Ivory Coast, however, is one of West Africa's most prosperous countries. Its last president built this cathedral when he had the capital moved to his family village at Yamoussoukro.

MAURITANIA
POP: 2,200,000

SENEGAL
POP: 7,900,000

GAMBIA
POP: 9,000,000

GUINEA-BISSAU
POP: 1,000,000

GUINEA
POP: 6,300,000

SIERRA LEONE
POP: 4,500,000

LIBERIA
POP: 2,800,000

IVORY COAST
POP: 13,400,000

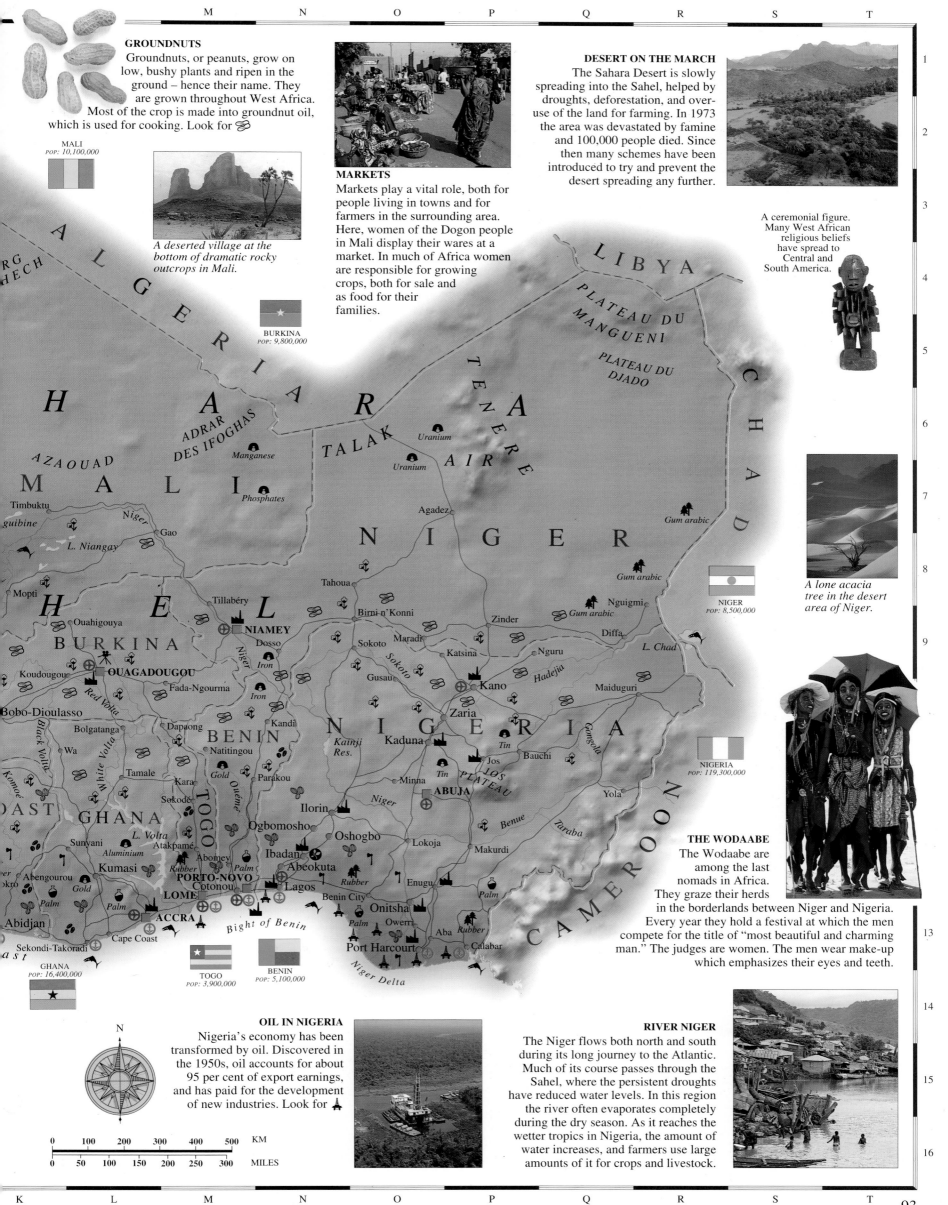

M N O P Q R S T

GROUNDNUTS
Groundnuts, or peanuts, grow on low, bushy plants and ripen in the ground – hence their name. They are grown throughout West Africa. Most of the crop is made into groundnut oil, which is used for cooking. Look for 🥜

MALI
POP: 10,100,000

A deserted village at the bottom of dramatic rocky outcrops in Mali.

MARKETS
Markets play a vital role, both for people living in towns and for farmers in the surrounding area. Here, women of the Dogon people in Mali display their wares at a market. In much of Africa women are responsible for growing crops, both for sale and as food for their families.

BURKINA
POP: 9,800,000

DESERT ON THE MARCH
The Sahara Desert is slowly spreading into the Sahel, helped by droughts, deforestation, and over-use of the land for farming. In 1973 the area was devastated by famine and 100,000 people died. Since then many schemes have been introduced to try and prevent the desert spreading any further.

A ceremonial figure. Many West African religious beliefs have spread to Central and South America.

A lone acacia tree in the desert area of Niger.

THE WODAABE
The Wodaabe are among the last nomads in Africa. They graze their herds in the borderlands between Niger and Nigeria. Every year they hold a festival at which the men compete for the title of "most beautiful and charming man." The judges are women. The men wear make-up which emphasizes their eyes and teeth.

NIGER
POP: 8,500,000

NIGERIA
POP: 119,300,000

OIL IN NIGERIA
Nigeria's economy has been transformed by oil. Discovered in the 1950s, oil accounts for about 95 per cent of export earnings, and has paid for the development of new industries. Look for ⚓

GHANA
POP: 16,400,000

TOGO
POP: 3,900,000

BENIN
POP: 5,100,000

RIVER NIGER
The Niger flows both north and south during its long journey to the Atlantic. Much of its course passes through the Sahel, where the persistent droughts have reduced water levels. In this region the river often evaporates completely during the dry season. As it reaches the wetter tropics in Nigeria, the amount of water increases, and farmers use large amounts of it for crops and livestock.

N

0 100 200 300 400 500 KM
0 50 100 150 200 250 300 MILES

Map labels:

ALGERIA
LIBYA
CHAD
CAMEROON

SAHARA
MALI
NIGER
NIGERIA
BURKINA
BENIN
GHANA
TOGO
SAHEL

PLATEAU DU MANGUENI
PLATEAU DU DJADO
TENERE
TALAK
AIR
ADRAR DES IFOGHAS
AZAOUAD
JOS PLATEAU

Timbuktu
guibine
Gao
L. Niangay
Mopti
Ouahigouya
Koudougou
OUAGADOUGOU
Bobo-Dioulasso
Bolgatanga
Wa
Tamale
Sunyani
Kumasi
Abengourou
Abidjan
Sekondi-Takoradi
Cape Coast
ACCRA
LOME
PORTO-NOVO
Cotonou
Abomey
Abeokuta
Ibadan
Ogbomosho
Oshogbo
Lagos
Benin City
Onitsha
Owerri
Aba
Port Harcourt
Calabar
Niger Delta
Bight of Benin
Enugu
Lokoja
Makurdi
Yola
ABUJA
Minna
Ilorin
Kaduna
Kainji Res.
Kandi
Parakou
Natitingou
Dapaong
Kara
Sokode
Atakpamé
L. Volta
NIAMEY
Dosso
Tillabéry
Tahoua
Birni-n'Konni
Sokoto
Maradi
Katsina
Gusau
Zaria
Kano
Nguru
Hadejia
Diffa
L. Chad
Nguigmi
Zinder
Maiduguri
Bauchi
Jos
Agadez

Niger (river)
Sokoto (river)
Benue
Taraba
Gongola
Oueme
Red Volta
Black Volta
White Volta
Komoé

Manganese
Uranium
Phosphates
Gum arabic
Iron
Tin
Gold
Rubber
Palm
Aluminium

93

CENTRAL AFRICA

MUCH OF THIS REGION IS COVERED in dense tropical rainforest, drained by the great Congo (Zaire) River and its tributaries. The climate is hot and humid. All the countries in the area have small populations – although some are increasing rapidly. French is the official language in many of the countries – a legacy from the days when they were French colonies. Zaire, the third largest country in Africa, has rich mineral deposits, but has declined economically since independence. Chad has been torn apart by civil wars, and the Central African Republic has suffered from corrupt governments. Both countries are desperately poor. Equatorial Guinea has suffered so much from bad government that some 100,000 people have emigrated. Abundant minerals and oil have made Gabon the richest country in the region. Oil is also of major importance in the Congo, and both countries have relatively large city populations. Cameroon is home to more than 200 different peoples, and is relatively prosperous.

HEALTH CLINIC

Traditional African medicine is still widely practised in this region, and western medicine has also been successfully used to cure or control many diseases. Medicines are often dispensed at village clinics like this one. But there are still major problems – many babies do not survive and there is a great shortage of doctors. In Chad, for example, over 40,000 people have to share one doctor.

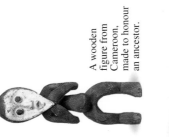

A wooden figure from Cameroon, made to honour an ancestor.

LAKE CHAD

Lake Chad lies at the point where Chad, Cameroon, Niger and Nigeria meet. Due to a series of droughts, the rivers that feed the lake have shrunk to little more than streams and reduced it to a tenth of its former size. Fish from Lake Chad – such as this *tilapia* – are a major source of food for the people who live in the surrounding areas. But each year the fishermen must haul their boats further to reach the lake's receding water.

PYGMIES

Several groups of pygmies live scattered through the rainforests of Central Africa. They still survive mainly by hunting and gathering, but also trade with their neighbours and have learnt to speak their languages. Pygmies rarely reach a height of more than 125 cms (4 ft). This pygmy hut, made of banana fronds, is in a forest clearing in the Central African Republic.

CENTRAL AFRICAN REPUBLIC
POP: 3,300,000

Forested valleys and hills around Loubomo, Congo.

CHAD
POP: 6,000,000

RELIGION

The main religion in this region is Christianity. But many Africans follow the traditional religions of their ancestors. They believe in many gods and spirits, who are often associated with natural forces or the elements, such as trees and thunder. This photo shows a ritual dance from Cameroon.

Dancer dressed as a leopard spirit

River flowing through dense rainforest in Cameroon.

CAMEROON
POP: 12,500,000

TRADITIONAL HOUSING

Traditional African houses vary from area to area, according to the building materials that are available locally. The walls of these houses in Cameroon are made of mud, and the roofs of straw. Building a house is one of the regular family tasks. As the family grows, so new houses are added to the group.

Map labels

LIBYA

SUDAN

NIGER

NIGERIA

CHAD

TIBESTI

CAMEROON

CENTRAL AFRICAN REPUBLIC

Faya

Biltine

Abéché

Am Timan

Mongo

Ati

Mao

Bol

L. Chad

N'DJAMENA

Kousseri

Maroua

Guider

Garoua

L. Lagdo

Ngaoundéré

Banyo

Bamenda

Bafoussam

Erguig

Chari

Bongor

Logone

Laï

Goré

Moundou

Salamat

Sarh

Bouar

Bossangoa

Kaga-Bandoro

Ndélé

Birao

Bria

Bambari

Sibut

Obo

Aluminium

Tin

Gold

Chromium

Copper

Diamonds

Diamonds

Uranium

Kollo

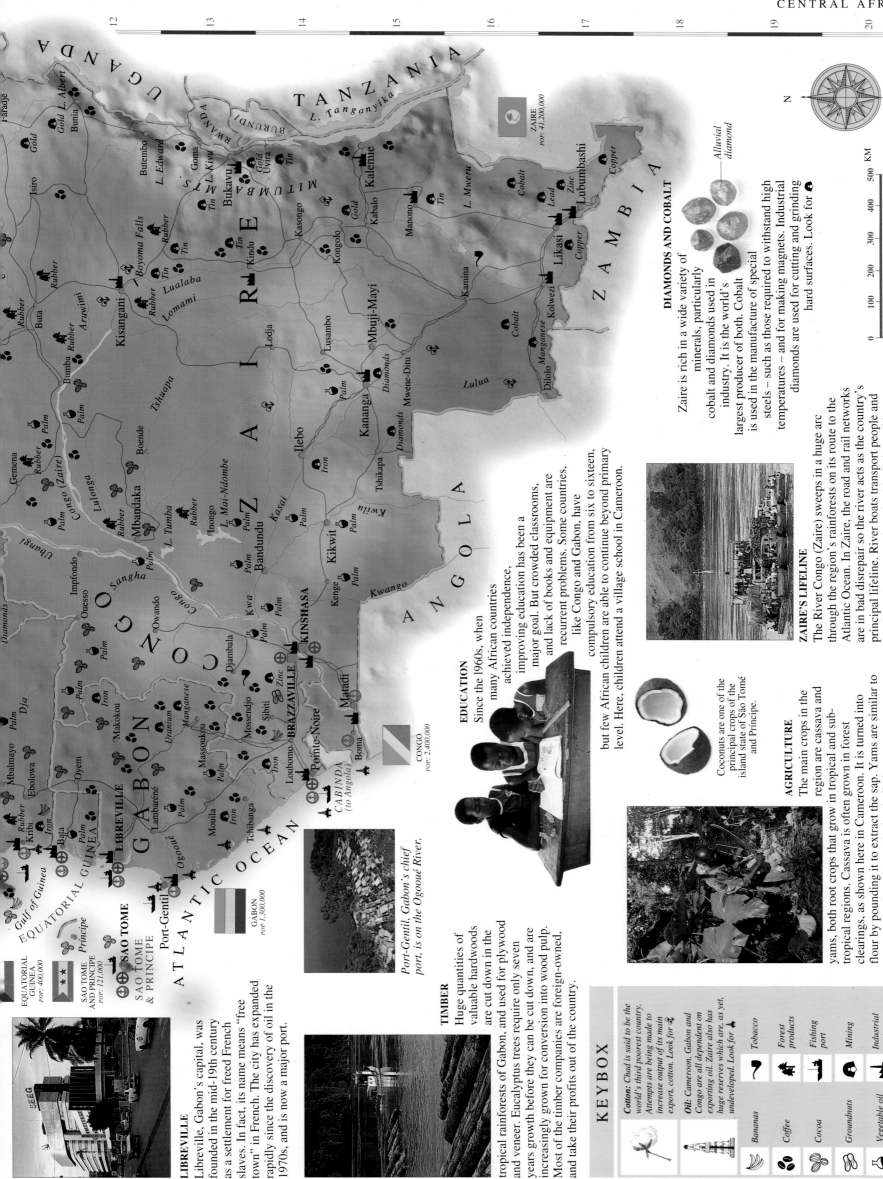

UGANDA

TANZANIA

L. Tanganyika

L. Albert

Faradje

Bunia · Gold

Gold

Isiro

Butembo

L. Edward

Goma · L. Kivu

Bukavu

Uvira · Gold

MITUMBA MTS

Boyoma Falls

Kisangani

Tin

Tin

Rubber

Tin

Kindu

Rubber

Lualaba

Lomami

Aruwimi

Rubber

Rubber

Buta

Bumba

Rubber

Gemena

Rubber

Palm

Palm

Rubber

Palm

Congo (Zaire)

Lulonga

Mbandaka

Rubber

Palm

L. Tumba

Inongo

L. Mai-Ndombe

Tshuapa

Boende

ZAIRE

POP: 41,200,000

Kasongo

Gold

Kongolo

Kabalo

L. Mweru

Manono

Tin

Kamina

Lodja

Lusambo

Mbuji-Mayi

Diamonds

Kananga

Diamonds

Mwene-Ditu

Lulua

Tshikapa

Iron

Kasai

Lodja

Kwilu

Kwilu

Palm

Kenge

Kikwit

Palm

Bandundu

L. Tumba

Kwango

ANGOLA

Impfondo

Ouesso

Sangha

Owando

Congo

Ubangi

Diamonds

GABON

Makokou

Oyem

Mbalmayo

Eboiowa

Rubber

Iron

Kribi

Bata

Iron

Palm

Dia

Palm

Manganese

Uranium

Mouila

Iron

Lambaréné

LIBREVILLE

Port-Gentil

Ogooué

Mossendjo

Sibiti

Massoukou

Loubomo

Iron

Djambala

Kwa

Palm

Palm

KINSHASA

BRAZZAVILLE

Pointe-Noire

Zinc

Matadi

Boma

CONGO

POP: 2,400,000

CABINDA
(to Angola)

GABON
POP: 1,300,000

EQUATORIAL GUINEA
POP: 400,000

SAO TOME
AND PRINCIPE
POP: 121,000

SAO TOME
& PRINCIPE

SAO TOME

Príncipe

Gulf of Guinea

EQUATORIAL GUINEA

ATLANTIC OCEAN

ZAIRE

Kalemie

Cobalt

Copper

Lubumbashi

Likasi

Copper

Lead

Zinc

Cobalt

Kolwezi

Dilolo

Manganese

ZAMBIA

Copper

Cobalt

LIBREVILLE

Libreville, Gabon's capital, was founded in the mid-19th century as a settlement for freed French slaves. In fact, its name means "free town" in French. The city has expanded rapidly since the discovery of oil in the 1970s, and is now a major port.

TIMBER

Huge quantities of valuable hardwoods are cut down in the tropical rainforests of Gabon, and used for plywood and veneer. Eucalyptus trees require only seven years growth before they can be cut down, and are increasingly grown for conversion into wood pulp. Most of the timber companies are foreign-owned, and take their profits out of the country.

Port-Gentil, Gabon's chief port, is on the Ogooué River.

EDUCATION

Since the 1960s, when many African countries achieved independence, improving education has been a major goal. But crowded classrooms, and lack of books and equipment are recurrent problems. Some countries, like Congo and Gabon, have compulsory education from six to sixteen, but few African children are able to continue beyond primary level. Here, children attend a village school in Cameroon.

Coconuts are one of the principal crops of the island state of São Tomé and Príncipe.

AGRICULTURE

The main crops in the region are cassava and yams, both root crops that grow in tropical and sub-tropical regions. Cassava is often grown in forest clearings, as shown here in Cameroon. It is turned into flour by pounding it to extract the sap. Yams are similar to potatoes, and can be mashed or boiled.

DIAMONDS AND COBALT

Zaire is rich in a wide variety of minerals, particularly cobalt and diamonds used in industry. It is the world's largest producer of both. Cobalt is used in the manufacture of special steels – such as those required to withstand high temperatures – and for making magnets. Industrial diamonds are used for cutting and grinding hard surfaces. Look for ◆

Alluvial diamond

ZAIRE'S LIFELINE

The River Congo (Zaire) sweeps in a huge arc through the region's rainforests on its route to the Atlantic Ocean. In Zaire, the road and rail networks are in bad disrepair so the river acts as the country's principal lifeline. River boats transport people and goods, and act as markets, health clinics and bars.

KEY BOX

Cotton: Chad is said to be the world's third poorest country. Attempts are being made to increase output of its main export, cotton. Look for ✿

Oil: Cameroon, Gabon and Congo are all dependent on exporting oil. Zaire also has huge reserves which are, as yet, undeveloped. Look for ⚑

🍌 Bananas	🌿 Tobacco	
☕ Coffee	🌲 Forest products	
🫘 Cocoa	⚓ Fishing port	
🥜 Groundnuts	⛏ Mining	
🛢 Vegetable oil	🏭 Industrial centre	

N

500 KM

400

300

200

100

0

300 MILES

200

100

0

CENTRAL EAST AFRICA

EAST AFRICA'S WEALTH lies in its land. Most people make their living from farming or cattle herding. Large areas covered with long grass, scrub and scattered trees, called savannah, provide grazing for domestic and wild animals alike. But some land, especially in Uganda and Zambia, cannot be used because of tsetse fly, which is dangerous to both animals and humans. Tea, coffee and tobacco are grown as cash crops throughout the area, especially in Kenya and Malawi. Uganda has great potential for farming, but for the last 20 years has been crippled by civil wars. Zambia, Rwanda, Burundi and Uganda all suffer from having no sea ports. Except in Kenya, industry everywhere is poorly developed. Only Zambia is rich in minerals. Burundi and Rwanda are densely populated, and Kenya now has the world's fastest growing population. After economic decline in the 1980s, Tanzania is slowly recovering.

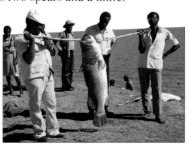

THE SAMBURU
In Kenya's northern plateau region, tribes such as the Samburu continue to follow the traditional way of life of their ancestors. They live by grazing their herds of cattle, sheep and goats on the savannah. This *moran*, or warrior, wears numerous strings of beads, distinctive ivory earrings and always carries two spears and a knife.

TRAINS
Countries with no coastline are very dependent on road and rail transport to link them to industrial centres and main ports. Although the African rail network is expanding, tracks are often poorly maintained. Here, people board a train at Kampala in Uganda.

PREDATORY FISH
Thirty years ago the Nile perch was introduced into Lake Victoria to increase fish production. Although the lake is vast, this fish now occupies every corner, and is killing off the original fish population. Look for 🐟

AIDS
AIDS is a worldwide problem, but it is particularly widespread in Africa. Many people on the continent already suffer from diseases and malnutrition, which makes them more vulnerable to the illnesses associated with AIDS.

WILDLIFE RESERVES
Africa's great plains contain some of the world's most spectacular species of wildlife. All the countries in the region have set aside huge areas as national parks where animals are protected. Wildlife safaris attract thousands of tourists and provide countries with much needed foreign income. Look for 🎫

POACHING
Africa's wildlife parks have helped preserve the animals, but poaching remains a major problem. Recently, in an attempt to save the elephants, a worldwide ban on the sale of ivory was imposed. But policing the parks is very costly; poaehers are armed and dangerous. Here, in Tanzania, wardens are burning a poacher's hut.

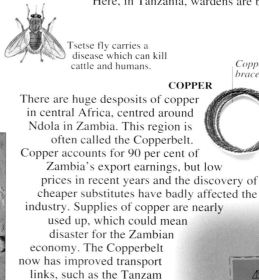

Tsetse fly carries a disease which can kill cattle and humans.

Copper bracelets

COPPER
There are huge desposits of copper in central Africa, centred around Ndola in Zambia. This region is often called the Copperbelt. Copper accounts for 90 per cent of Zambia's export earnings, but low prices in recent years and the discovery of cheaper substitutes have badly affected the industry. Supplies of copper are nearly used up, which could mean disaster for the Zambian economy. The Copperbelt now has improved transport links, such as the Tanzam Railway, which take the refined copper to various destinations. Look for ⚫

Vultures cluster in a lone tree on the Tanzanian grasslands.

KEYBOX

Coffee: *A valuable cash crop, coffee is grown in Uganda, Kenya, Tanzania and Rwanda. Kenya plans to triple production by the year 2000. Look for* 🫘

Market gardening: *Kenya has ideal conditions for growing vegetables and fruit, which are exported in large quantities, mainly to Europe. Look for* 🚜

Hydro-electric power: *The Kariba Dam on the Zambezi River, built by Zambia and Zimbabwe, supplies both nations with electricity. Look for* ⬕

Refugee camps: *Warfare in neighbouring countries has caused thousands of refugees to flee to temporary camps in the region. Look for* ⬠

🗲	Sugar cane	🌲	Forest products
🥥	Coconuts	🐟	Fishing
🌿	Tea	⚫	Mining
🏵	Cotton	🏭	Industrial centre
🪶	Tobacco	🎫	Wildlife reserves

AFRICAN VILLAGE
East African villages usually consist of a series of huts enclosed by thorn fences. This aerial photo shows a village belonging to the Masai tribe. A Masai man may have several wives. Each wife has her own huts, enclosed by a fence. The livestock is taken out to graze by day, and driven into the fenced enclosure at night.

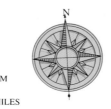

0 100 200 300 400 500	KM
0 50 100 150 200 250 300	MILES

N

ZA

Solwezi

West Lunga

Zambezi

ZAMB

Liuwa Plain

Kafue

Kafue

Mongu

KAFU FLAT

ANGOLA

Sioma

Zambezi

Victoria Falls

Choma

Livingstone

NAMIBIA BOTSWANA ZIN

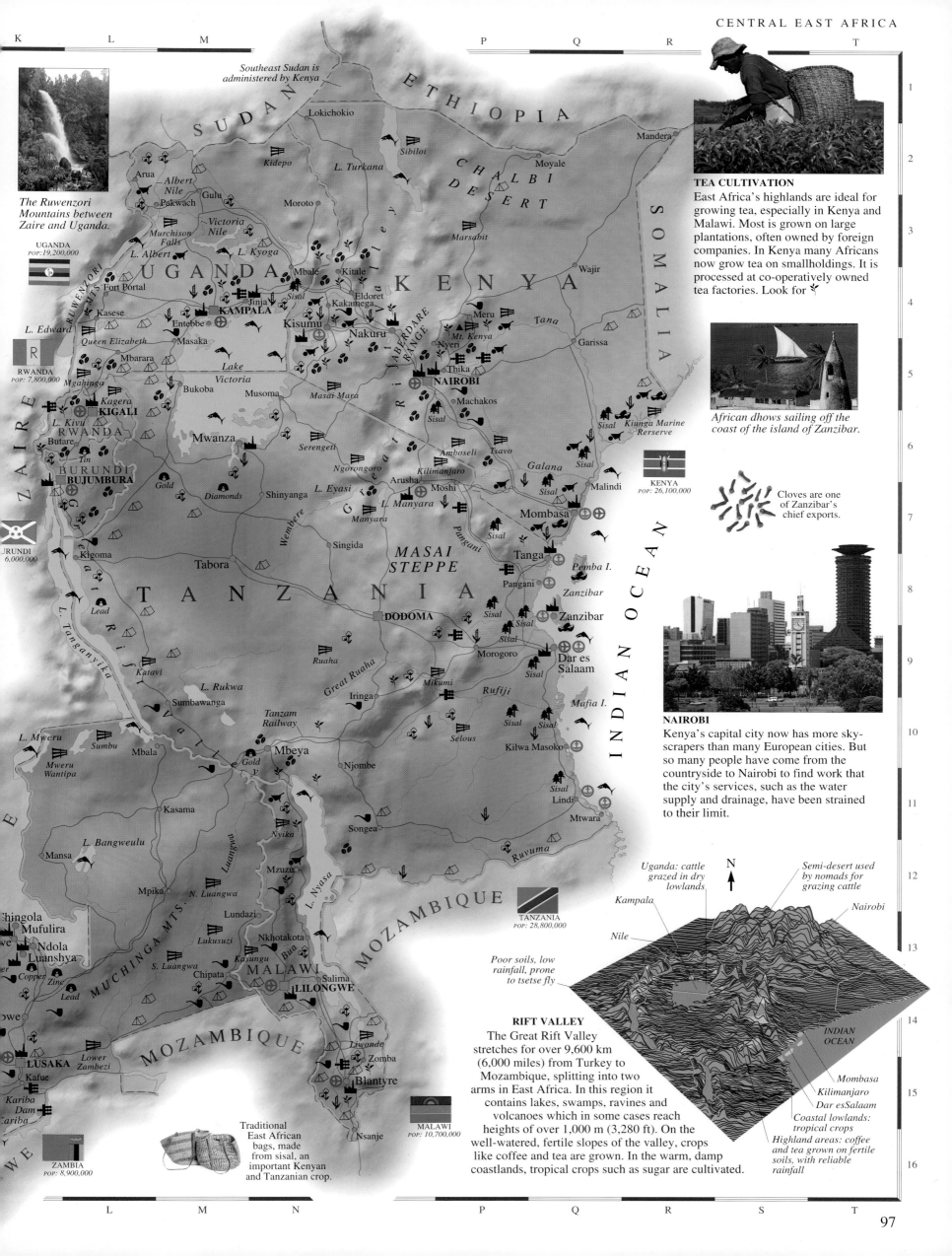

The Ruwenzori Mountains between Zaire and Uganda.

UGANDA
POP: 19,200,000

RWANDA
POP: 7,800,000

BURUNDI
POP: 6,000,000

Southeast Sudan is administered by Kenya

SUDAN

ETHIOPIA

Lokichokio

Kidepo

L. Turkana

Sibiloi

Moyale

Mandera

Arua

Albert Nile

Gulu

Moroto

Marsabit

CHALBI DESERT

Pakwach

L. Albert

Murchison Falls

Victoria Nile

Fort Portal

L. Kyoga

Mbale

Kitale

Eldoret

Wajir

KENYA

SOMALIA

Kasese

Jinja

Kakamega

Queen Elizabeth

KAMPALA

Entebbe

Kisumu

Nakuru

Meru

Mt. Kenya

Tana

Garissa

Masaka

Nyeri

Mbarara

Lake Victoria

Thika

ABERDARE RANGE

Bukoba

NAIROBI

Musoma

Masai Mara

Machakos

KIGALI

Kagera

L. Kivu

Butare

Mwanza

Serengeti

Kiunga Marine Reserve

Tin

Ngorongoro

Amboseli

Tsavo

Gold

Diamonds

Shinyanga

L. Eyasi

Kilimanjaro

Galana

Arusha

Moshi

Malindi

BUJUMBURA

L. Manyara

Manyara

Mombasa

Kigoma

Singida

Pangani

Tanga

ZAIRE

L. Tanganyika

Tabora

MASAI STEPPE

Pemba I.

Lead

DODOMA

Pangani

Zanzibar

Zanzibar

Katavi

Ruaha

Morogoro

Dar es Salaam

L. Rukwa

Great Ruaha

Mikumi

Iringa

Rufiji

Mafia I.

Sumbawanga

Tanzam Railway

Selous

L. Mweru

Sumbu

Mbala

Mbeya

Njombe

Kilwa Masoko

Mweru Wantipa

Gold

TANZANIA

Lindi

Kasama

Mtwara

L. Bangweulu

Mansa

Nyika

Songea

Ruvuma

Mzuzu

Mpika

Luangwa

L. Nyasa

Lundazi

MOZAMBIQUE

Chingola

Mufulira

N. Luangwa

Nkhotakota

Ndola

Luanshya

Lukusuzi

Kasungu

Copper

S. Luangwa

Chipata

MALAWI

Salima

Zinc

LILONGWE

Lead

MUCHINGA MTS.

Bua

MOZAMBIQUE

Liwonde

LUSAKA

Lower Zambezi

Zomba

Kafue

Blantyre

Kariba Dam

Kariba

Nsanje

INDIAN OCEAN

GREAT RIFT VALLEY

Wembere

Pangani

RWANDA

KENYA
POP: 26,100,000

TANZANIA
POP: 28,800,000

MALAWI
POP: 10,700,000

ZAMBIA
POP: 8,900,000

TEA CULTIVATION
East Africa's highlands are ideal for growing tea, especially in Kenya and Malawi. Most is grown on large plantations, often owned by foreign companies. In Kenya many Africans now grow tea on smallholdings. It is processed at co-operatively owned tea factories. Look for

African dhows sailing off the coast of the island of Zanzibar.

Cloves are one of Zanzibar's chief exports.

NAIROBI
Kenya's capital city now has more skyscrapers than many European cities. But so many people have come from the countryside to Nairobi to find work that the city's services, such as the water supply and drainage, have been strained to their limit.

Uganda: cattle grazed in dry lowlands

Kampala

Nile

N

Semi-desert used by nomads for grazing cattle

Nairobi

Poor soils, low rainfall, prone to tsetse fly

INDIAN OCEAN

Mombasa

Kilimanjaro

Dar es Salaam

Coastal lowlands: tropical crops

Highland areas: coffee and tea grown on fertile soils, with reliable rainfall

RIFT VALLEY
The Great Rift Valley stretches for over 9,600 km (6,000 miles) from Turkey to Mozambique, splitting into two arms in East Africa. In this region it contains lakes, swamps, ravines and volcanoes which in some cases reach heights of over 1,000 m (3,280 ft). On the well-watered, fertile slopes of the valley, crops like coffee and tea are grown. In the warm, damp coastlands, tropical crops such as sugar are cultivated.

Traditional East African bags, made from sisal, an important Kenyan and Tanzanian crop.

97

SOUTHERN AFRICA

THE WEALTHIEST and most dominant country in this region is South Africa. Black African lands were gradually settled in the 19th century by Dutch colonists, their descendants – the Afrikaners – and the British. When vast deposits of gold and diamonds were discovered in the late 19th century, the country became rich. In 1948 the government introduced a system of "separate development", called apartheid, which separated people according to their colour, and gave political power to whites only. This policy led to isolation and sanctions from the rest of the world's nations, which only ended after the abolition of apartheid. The first democratic elections were held in 1994. After years of conflict, South Africa has now become a more integrated society. Most of the countries around South Africa rely on its industries for trade and work. After 30 years of unrest, Namibia has now won independence from South Africa. Mozambique and Angola are both struggling for survival after years of civil war. Zimbabwe has a relatively diverse economy, based on agriculture and its rich mineral resources.

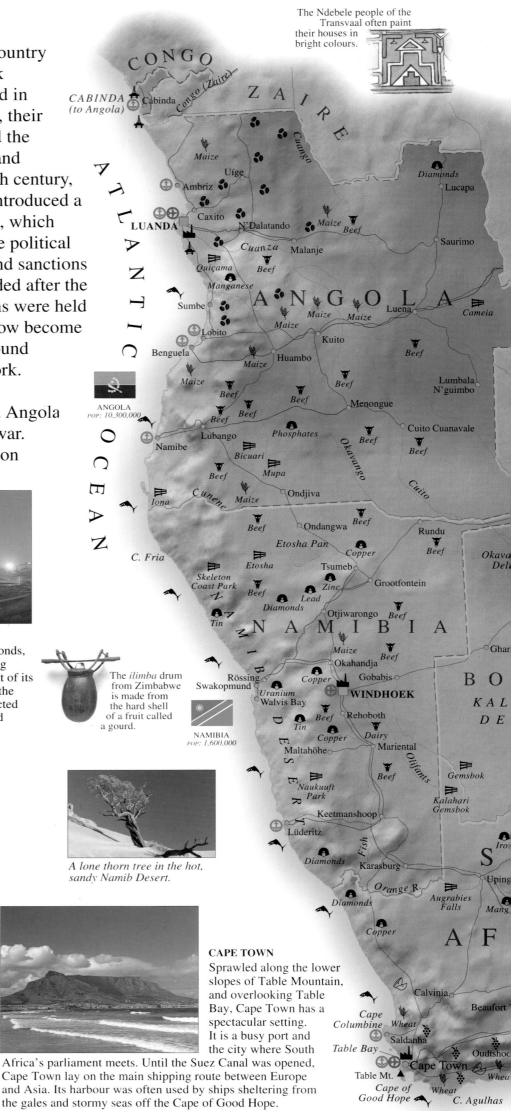

The Ndebele people of the Transvaal often paint their houses in bright colours.

ANGOLA
POP: 10,300,000

The *ilimba* drum from Zimbabwe is made from the hard shell of a fruit called a gourd.

NAMIBIA
POP: 1,600,000

INDUSTRY
South Africa is the region's industrial leader. Johannesburg, the country's largest city, is seen here behind the huge mounds of earth excavated from the gold mines. Look for 🏭

URANIUM
Namibia is rich in copper, diamonds, tin and other minerals. Its mining industry accounts for 90 per cent of its export earnings. At Rössing, in the Namib Desert, uranium is extracted from a huge open-cast mine, and exported abroad. Look for ⚛

KEYBOX

🐟	**Fishing:** Overfishing, by both foreign and local fleets, is a major threat to Namibia's once rich fishing grounds. Controls are in operation. Look for ➤
🛢	**Oil:** Civil war in Angola has disrupted industry, but its oil reserves – the only major ones in the region – so far have been little affected. Look for ⬦
🦒	**Wildlife reserves:** Most of the region's countries have set aside large areas as wildlife parks, which are popular tourist attractions. Look for ⚑

🐂	Cattle	🌱	Tea
🌾	Cereals	🟫	Tobacco
🍋	Citrus fruit	⛏	Mining
🍇	Wine	⚒	Coal
☕	Coffee	🏭	Industrial centre

BUSHMEN
Bushmen – or *San* – are one of the few groups of hunter-gatherers left in Africa. These tiny people can be traced far back into African history. Today some 1,000 bushmen still live in the harsh environment of the Kalahari Desert.

A lone thorn tree in the hot, sandy Namib Desert.

CAPE TOWN
Sprawled along the lower slopes of Table Mountain, and overlooking Table Bay, Cape Town has a spectacular setting. It is a busy port and the city where South Africa's parliament meets. Until the Suez Canal was opened, Cape Town lay on the main shipping route between Europe and Asia. Its harbour was often used by ships sheltering from the gales and stormy seas off the Cape of Good Hope.

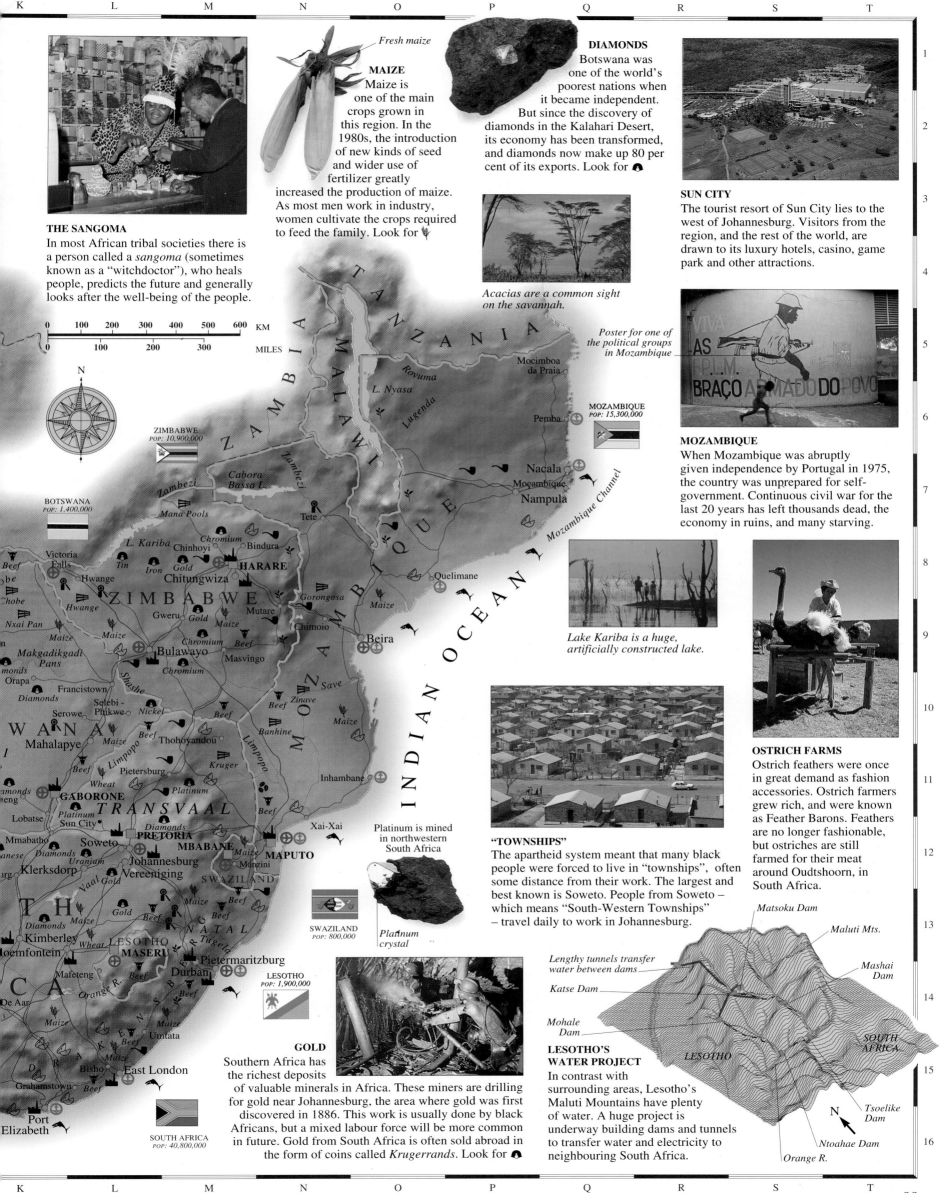

THE SANGOMA

In most African tribal societies there is a person called a *sangoma* (sometimes known as a "witchdoctor"), who heals people, predicts the future and generally looks after the well-being of the people.

Fresh maize

MAIZE

Maize is one of the main crops grown in this region. In the 1980s, the introduction of new kinds of seed and wider use of fertilizer greatly increased the production of maize. As most men work in industry, women cultivate the crops required to feed the family. Look for 🌾

DIAMONDS

Botswana was one of the world's poorest nations when it became independent. But since the discovery of diamonds in the Kalahari Desert, its economy has been transformed, and diamonds now make up 80 per cent of its exports. Look for ◆

Acacias are a common sight on the savannah.

SUN CITY

The tourist resort of Sun City lies to the west of Johannesburg. Visitors from the region, and the rest of the world, are drawn to its luxury hotels, casino, game park and other attractions.

Poster for one of the political groups in Mozambique

MOZAMBIQUE

When Mozambique was abruptly given independence by Portugal in 1975, the country was unprepared for self-government. Continuous civil war for the last 20 years has left thousands dead, the economy in ruins, and many starving.

Lake Kariba is a huge, artificially constructed lake.

OSTRICH FARMS

Ostrich feathers were once in great demand as fashion accessories. Ostrich farmers grew rich, and were known as Feather Barons. Feathers are no longer fashionable, but ostriches are still farmed for their meat around Oudtshoorn, in South Africa.

Platinum is mined in northwestern South Africa

Platinum crystal

"TOWNSHIPS"

The apartheid system meant that many black people were forced to live in "townships", often some distance from their work. The largest and best known is Soweto. People from Soweto – which means "South-Western Townships" – travel daily to work in Johannesburg.

GOLD

Southern Africa has the richest deposits of valuable minerals in Africa. These miners are drilling for gold near Johannesburg, the area where gold was first discovered in 1886. This work is usually done by black Africans, but a mixed labour force will be more common in future. Gold from South Africa is often sold abroad in the form of coins called *Krugerrands*. Look for ◆

LESOTHO'S WATER PROJECT

In contrast with surrounding areas, Lesotho's Maluti Mountains have plenty of water. A huge project is underway building dams and tunnels to transfer water and electricity to neighbouring South Africa.

Lengthy tunnels transfer water between dams

Matsoku Dam

Maluti Mts.

Katse Dam

Mashai Dam

Mohale Dam

LESOTHO

SOUTH AFRICA

Tsoelike Dam

Ntoahae Dam

Orange R.

Map labels:

ZIMBABWE POP: 10,900,000

BOTSWANA POP: 1,400,000

MOZAMBIQUE POP: 15,300,000

SWAZILAND POP: 800,000

LESOTHO POP: 1,900,000

SOUTH AFRICA POP: 40,800,000

ZAMBIA · TANZANIA · MALAWI · ZIMBABWE · MOZAMBIQUE · BOTSWANA · TRANSVAAL · NATAL · SWAZILAND · LESOTHO

INDIAN OCEAN

Mozambique Channel

L. Nyasa · Rovuma · Lugenda · Mocimboa da Praia · Pemba · Nacala · Mozambique · Nampula · Quelimane · Beira · Chimoio · Gorongosa · Tete · Cabora Bassa L. · Zambezi · Mana Pools · L. Kariba · Chinhoyi · Bindura · HARARE · Chitungwiza · Mutare · Gweru · Masvingo · Bulawayo · Hwange · Victoria Falls · Makgadikgadi Pans · Nxai Pan · Orapa · Francistown · Serowe · Selebi-Phikwe · Mahalapye · GABORONE · Lobatse · Mmabatho · Soweto · PRETORIA · Johannesburg · Vereeniging · Klerksdorp · Kimberley · Mafeteng · MASERU · Pietermaritzburg · Durban · Umtala · Bisho · East London · Grahamstown · Port Elizabeth · De Aar · MBABANE · Manzini · MAPUTO · Xai-Xai · Inhambane · Banhine · Zinave · Save · Limpopo · Kruger · Thohoyandou · Pietersburg · Shashe · Orange R. · Vaal · Tugela

Chobe · Beef · Maize · Gold · Chromium · Iron · Tin · Nickel · Diamonds · Platinum · Uranium · Wheat

KM 0 100 200 300 400 500 600

MILES 0 100 200 300

N

THE INDIAN OCEAN

THE INDIAN OCEAN is the smallest of the world's oceans, but some 5,000 islands – many of them surrounded by coral reefs – are scattered across its area. Beneath its surface three great mountain ranges converge towards the ocean's centre – an area of strong seismic and volcanic activity. The ocean reaches its greatest depth – 7,440 m (24,400 ft) – in the Java Trench. Over 1,000 million people – about a fifth of the world's population – live in the countries around the Indian Ocean, representing an immense range of cultures and religions. Heavy monsoon rain and tropical storms cause flooding along the ocean's northern coasts. The world's largest oil-fields are located around the Persian Gulf.

Sugar cane

SUGAR

Sugar was first brought to Mauritius by the Dutch in the 1600s. Ninety per cent of the island's arable farmland is covered by sugar plantations. But today sugar has been replaced in importance by textiles, which now account for nearly half the island's exports. Look for ⬇

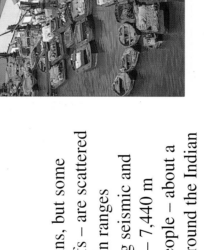

KARACHI

In the mid-19th century a railway line was built along the Indus valley to Karachi, and it developed into a large port and industrial city. When Pakistan was created an independent nation in 1947, Karachi became the country's capital. It has now been replaced by the new city of Islamabad in the north.

FISHING

Large-scale fishing is far less developed in the Indian Ocean than in either the Atlantic or Pacific. Fishing is difficult because there are relatively few areas of shallow sea. Small-scale fishing, however, provides a valuable source of food. Many fishermen, like these Sri Lankans, use basic, often inefficient methods. Tuna is the most important catch in the area. Look for ⬇

ISLANDS

The islands of the Indian Ocean include enormous ones like Madagascar, coral atolls like the Maldives, and volcanic islands like Réunion. All are threatened by rising sea levels which reduce the area of land available. Coral reefs are being eroded, leaving islands increasingly exposed to ocean tides and flooding.

MONSOON

Farmers in the lands around the Indian Ocean are wholly dependent on the coming of the monsoon rains. In May or June, the western arm of the monsoon sweeps in from the Arabian Sea, bringing torrential downpours which travel north through India. At the same time, the monsoon's eastern arm curves out of the Bay of Bengal, driving north as far as the Himalayan foothills. About 85 per cent of India's annual rainfall occurs during the monsoon periods.

Mangroves grow along many of the Indian Ocean's coasts.

COMOROS

The loggerhead turtle is one of the Indian Ocean's many endangered species.

TOURISM

The Indian Ocean islands are great tourist attractions. They welcome the money this brings, but the sheer number of visitors threatens to destroy the islands' environment. Look for ⬇

Hotel complex on an island in Mauritius

Once thought extinct, the coelacanth has been found, alive and well, off southeast Africa.

Port Said
Suez Canal
Suez
Nile
Tigris
Euphrates
Basra
Kuwait City
Manama
Persian Gulf
Chāh Bahār
Gulf of Oman
Ra's al Hadd
ARABIA
Maşīrah
Şalālah
RED SEA
Djibouti
Aden
Gulf of Aden
Socotra (to Yemen)
C. Xaafuun
Somali Basin
Mombasa
Dar es Salaam
COMOROS
MORONI
Grande Comore (to France)
MAYOTTE (to France)
Aldabra Is. (to Seychelles)
Antsiranana
C. Bobaomby
SEYCHELLES
VICTORIA
Amirante Is. (to Seychelles)
Mahé
Mascarene Plateau
Carlsberg Ridge
MALDIVES POP: 200,000
MALDIVES
MALE
Laccadive Is. (to India)
Karachi
Indus
Bombay
Madras
Cochin
C. Comorin
Dondra Head
Colombo
Sri Lanka
Trincomalee
Vishakhapatnam
Calcutta
Ganges
HIMALAYAS
A S I A
A R A B I A
ARABIAN SEA
Bay of Bengal
Andaman Is. (to India)
Nicobar Is. (to India)
ANDAMAN SEA
Rangoon
Irrawaddy
Mekong
Gulf of Thailand
SOUTH CHINA SEA
George Town
Melaka
Singapore
Strait of Malacca
Sumatra
Borneo
JAVA SEA
Java
Java Trench
CHRISTMAS I. (to Australia)
COCOS IS. (to Australia)
ASHMORE & CARTIER IS. (to Australia)
BRITISH INDIAN OCEAN TERRITORY (to UK)
Diego Garcia
Maldive Ridge
Carlsberg Ridge
INDIAN
I N D I A N
A F R I C A
Tin

STRAIT OF MALACCA

Since ancient times ships trading between the Indian and Pacific Oceans have passed through the shallow waters of the Strait of Malacca. This is the main route through the Indonesian archipelago. Ports like Melaka – seen here – have prospered from this trade.

N

KM MILES
2000 — 1000
1500 — 750
1000 — 500
500 — 250
0 — 0

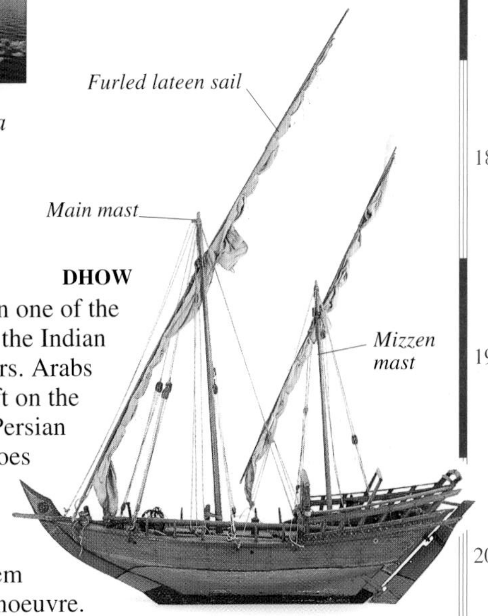

DHOW

The Arab dhow has been one of the principal sailing boats in the Indian Ocean for over 4,000 years. Arabs used these sturdy craft on the trade routes from the Persian Gulf to China. Their cargoes included spices, cowrie shells, dates and slaves. Their large lateen, or triangular, sails make them easy to manoeuvre.

Mizzen mast
Furled lateen sail
Main mast

Huge ice floes drift north from Antarctica, becoming a major hazard to shipping.

POLLUTION

The Indian Ocean is particularly at risk from oil pollution from tankers carrying oil from the Persian Gulf. The Persian Gulf itself is severely polluted by oil spills from ships, rigs and refineries. During the Gulf War of 1991, huge quantities of oil were released into the Gulf waters, causing appalling damage. Look for ⚓

AUSTRALIA
Fremantle
Cockburn Sound
North West C.
C. Leeuwin

West Australia Basin
Broken Ridge
Ninety East Ridge
Southeast Indian Ridge
South Indian Basin

OCEAN
Mid-Indian Ridge
Amsterdam I. (to France)
St Paul I. (to France)
Kerguelen Plateau
Heard I.
Macdonald Is. (to Australia)
Kerguelen (to France)
Crozet Basin
Crozet Is. (to France)
Prince Edward Is. (to South Africa)
Atlantic-Indian Basin
Southwest Indian Ridge
Madagascar Basin
Mascarene Is.
MAURITIUS
Madagascar Ridge
REUNION (to France)
Le Port
Fianarantsoa
Farafangana
Toliara
Uranium
C. Vohimena
Limpopo
Durban
Cape of Good Hope
Simon's Town
Cape Town

ANTARCTICA

MAURITIUS
POP: 1,100,000

MADAGASCAR
POP: 13,300,000

SEYCHELLES
POP: 69,000

SANCTUARY

Many species of whale breed in the Indian Ocean. In 1979 most of the Ocean was designated a whale sanctuary to protect them. The dugong – a marine mammal – is also threatened with extinction. Although it lives for up to 70 years, it matures late and produces few young in its lifetime. It is vegetarian, feeding exclusively on sea grasses.

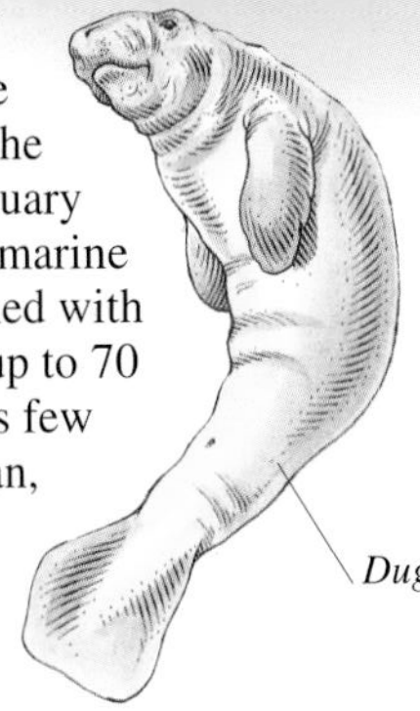

Dugong

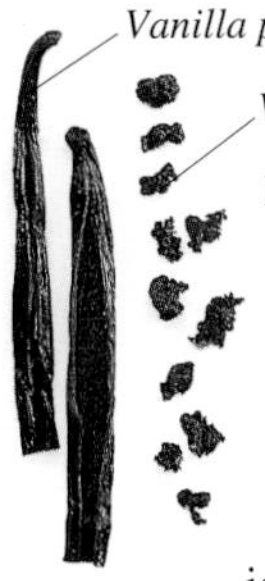

MADAGASCAR

This huge island off Africa's east coast is desperately poor. Most Madagascans make their living from farming, cattle herding or logging. In the last 25 years the population has doubled and the constant need for land and fuel has massively reduced the once extensive forests. The staple food is rice, the main exports are coffee and vanilla.

Vanilla pod
Vanilla seed

NAVAL BASES

The Indian Ocean is important to the major world powers as a link between the Atlantic and Pacific Oceans, and because it is the main route for tankers bringing oil from the Persian Gulf. The USA has a base on Diego Garcia. The French have a naval base on the island of Réunion. Look for ▥

Huge baobab trees on the island of Madagascar.

Shellfishing: An area near Karachi has been developed as a major shrimp nursery. It employs thousands of local workers. Look for 🦐

Industrial centre: Due to low labour costs and tax incentives, new industries, such as textiles, have been developed in Mauritius. Look for 🏭

Mining: Tin is dredged off the west coast of Thailand and east coast of Sumatra. Dredging can damage the seabed and mangroves. Look for

Sugar cane ⚓
Coconuts 🌴
Fishing 🎣
Fishing port ⚓
Oil 🛢

Gas
Tourism
Underwater wrecks
Whales
Military bases

101

Cedar of Lebanon
Cedrus libani
Height: 40 m (130 ft)
☐ ⚠

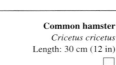

Common hamster
Cricetus cricetus
Length: 30 cm (12 in)
☐

Waxwing
Bombycilla garrulus
Length: 18 cm (8 in)
■

NORTH AND WEST ASIA

NORTH AND WEST ASIA contains some of the world's most inhospitable environments. In the south, the Arabian Peninsula is almost entirely a baking hot desert, where no plants can grow. To the north, a belt of rugged, snow-capped mountains and high plateaux cross the continent. The climate becomes drier and more extreme towards the centre of the continent. Dry hot summers contrast with bitterly cold winters. Cold deserts give way to treeless plains known as steppe, then to huge marshes, and to the world's largest needleleaf forest. In the extreme north, both land and sea are frozen for most of the year. Only in summer do the top layers of soil thaw briefly allowing plants of the tundra, such as moss and lichen, to cover the land.

■ **COLD FOREST**
Strong but flexible trunks and a tent-like shape help needleleaf trees to withstand the great weight of snow that covers them throughout the long winter.

HOT BATHS
These strange white terraces formed in the south-west of Asia in much the same way that a kettle "furs". Underground water heated by volcanic activity dissolves minerals in rocks. These are deposited when the water reaches the surface and cools.

■ **DROUGHT-TOLERANT TREES**
Plants growing near the Black Sea minimize water-loss during the long hot summers. Most have wax-covered leaves through which little water can escape.

Blue turquoise, a semi-precious stone mainly found in cold areas of north Asia.

■ **REGENERATING FOREST**
Juniper trees, unlike many plants, are able to withstand the acid soils of needleleaf forests. Here junipers cover the floor of a dense pine forest.

Arabian oryx
Oryx leucoryx
Height: 1.2 m (4 ft)
☐ ⚠

Baikal seal
Phoca sibirica
Length: 1.5 m (5 ft)
Only found in Lake Baikal

The fossilized head of *Gallimimus*, an ostrich-like dinosaur that once lived in Asia.

■ **SINAI'S ROCK "MUSHROOMS"**
In deserts, sand particles whipped along by high-speed winds create natural sculptures. Rock at the base of the "mushroom" has been more heavily eroded than rock above, leading to these unusual landforms.

■ ▲ **VOLCANO**
There are more than 30 active volcanoes on the Kamchatka peninsula, on the Pacific Ocean's "Ring of Fire". Volcanic activity is due to the deep underground movements of the Eurasian plate.

■ **FROZEN RIVER**
The River Lena rises near Lake Baikal, the world's deepest and oldest freshwater lake. Like other Siberian rivers, it flows into the Arctic Ocean and is frozen over for eight or nine months of the year.

Darkling beetle
Sternodes species
Length: 2 cm (1 in)
☐

Reindeer
Rangifer tarandus
Body length: 2.2 m (7 ft)
☐

■ **HOT DESERTS**
The Arabian desert is one of the hottest and driest places in the world. Temperatures frequently reach 45°C (120°F), and very little rain falls.

CROSS-SECTION THROUGH NORTH AND WEST ASIA

Ural Mts
Kirghiz Steppe
Iranian Plateau
Arctic Ocean
Kara Sea
Aral Sea
Kara Kum
Arabian Sea
1,500 (4,921)
0 Sea level
-3,000 (9,843)
Metres (feet)
A
Length: 6,400 km (4,000 miles)
B

☐ **COLD WINTER DESERT**
Large parts of Central Asia are covered in deserts that are hot in summer, but very cold in winter. A river has been naturally dammed to form this lake, which is unusual in this dry region.

Pallas's cat
Felis manul
Length: 65 cm (26 in)
☐

Grey wolf
Canis lupus
Length: 1.4 m (5 ft)
■ ⚠

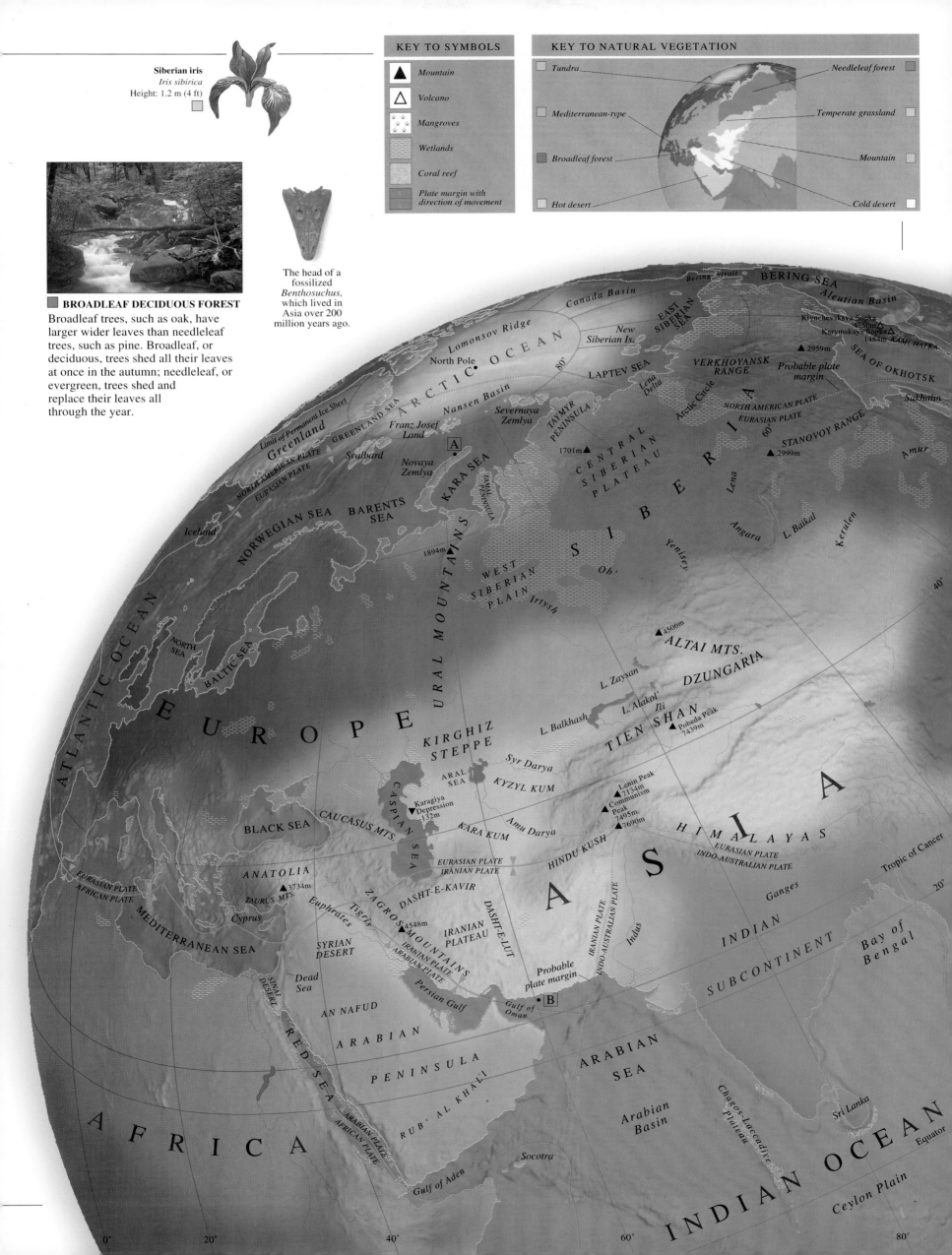

Siberian iris
Iris sibirica
Height: 1.2 m (4 ft)

KEY TO SYMBOLS

▲ Mountain
△ Volcano
🌿 Mangroves
░ Wetlands
▦ Coral reef
▨ Plate margin with direction of movement

KEY TO NATURAL VEGETATION

Tundra
Mediterranean-type
Broadleaf forest
Hot desert
Needleleaf forest
Temperate grassland
Mountain
Cold desert

The head of a fossilized *Benthosuchus,* which lived in Asia over 200 million years ago.

■ **BROADLEAF DECIDUOUS FOREST**
Broadleaf trees, such as oak, have larger wider leaves than needleleaf trees, such as pine. Broadleaf, or deciduous, trees shed all their leaves at once in the autumn; needleleaf, or evergreen, trees shed and replace their leaves all through the year.

ARCTIC OCEAN

North Pole
Lomonosov Ridge
Canada Basin
Bering Strait
BERING SEA
Aleutian Basin
New Siberian Is.
EAST SIBERIAN SEA
LAPTEV SEA
VERKHOYANSK RANGE
Klynchevskaya Sopka ▲ 4750m △
Karymskaya Sopka △ 1484m KAMCHATKA
▲ 2959m
SEA OF OKHOTSK
Nansen Basin
Greenland Sea
Limit of Permanent Ice Sheet
Greenland
Franz Josef Land
Svalbard
NORTH AMERICAN PLATE
EURASIAN PLATE
Iceland
NORWEGIAN SEA
BARENTS SEA
Severnaya Zemlya
TAYMYR PENINSULA
Lena Delta
Arctic Circle
NORTH AMERICAN PLATE
EURASIAN PLATE
60
STANOVOY RANGE ▲ 2999m
Sakhalin
Amur
Novaya Zemlya
KARA SEA
YAMAL PENINSULA
A
1701m ▲
CENTRAL SIBERIAN PLATEAU
S I B E R I A
Lena
1894m ▲
WEST SIBERIAN PLAIN
Ob
Yenisey
Angara
L. Baikal
Kerulen
Irtysh
40
NORTH SEA
BALTIC SEA
E U R O P E
URAL MOUNTAINS
ATLANTIC OCEAN
▲ 4506m
ALTAI MTS.
DZUNGARIA
L. Zaysan
L. Alakol'
Ili
KIRGHIZ STEPPE
L. Balkhash
TIEN SHAN
Pobeda Peak 7439m ▲
A S I A
Syr Darya
ARAL SEA
KYZYL KUM
Lenin Peak 7134m ▲
Communism Peak 7495m ▲
▲ 7690m
HIMALAYAS
BLACK SEA
CAUCASUS MTS.
CASPIAN SEA
Karagiya Depression 132m ▼
KARA KUM
Amu Darya
HINDU KUSH
EURASIAN PLATE
INDO-AUSTRALIAN PLATE
Tropic of Cancer
ANATOLIA
EURASIAN PLATE
AFRICAN PLATE
▲ 3734m
TAURUS MTS.
Cyprus
DASHT-E-KAVIR
ZAGROS MOUNTAINS
EURASIAN PLATE
IRANIAN PLATE
IRANIAN PLATE
INDO-AUSTRALIAN PLATE
Ganges
Indus
INDIAN
20
Euphrates
Tigris
▲ 4548m
IRANIAN PLATEAU
DASHT-E-LUT
SYRIAN DESERT
IRANIAN PLATE
ARABIAN PLATE
Probable plate margin
B
SUBCONTINENT
Bay of Bengal
MEDITERRANEAN SEA
Dead Sea
SINAI DESERT
AN NAFUD
Persian Gulf
Gulf of Oman
ARABIAN PENINSULA
ARABIAN SEA
INDIAN
RED SEA
ARABIAN PLATE
AFRICAN PLATE
RUB' AL KHALI
Chagos-Laccadive Plateau
Sri Lanka
A F R I C A
Arabian Basin
Socotra
Gulf of Aden
Ceylon Plain
INDIAN OCEAN
Equator

Probable plate margin

0°   20°   40°   60°   80°

TURKEY AND CYPRUS

SITUATED PARTLY IN EUROPE and partly in Asia, Turkey is also balanced between modern Europe and its Islamic past. For 600 years, the Ottoman Turks ruled over a great empire covering a quarter of Europe, but by the early 20th century their empire had disappeared. In the 1920s, Mustapha Kemal (Atatürk) forcibly modernized Turkish society. Today, Turkey is becoming increasingly industrialized; textile and food-processing industries dominate the economy. In the central plateau, however, farmers and herders live as they have done for centuries, adapting their lives to the harsh environment. To the north, the Black Sea is rich in fish, and the fertile areas around its shores are well-suited to farming. The beautiful western and southern coasts are strewn with the remains of ancient Greek sites, and attract 1.5 million tourists to Turkey every year.

ISTANBUL
Istanbul is divided in two by a strait of water called the Bosporus. One part of the city is in Europe, the other in Asia. Its buildings are also a mix of East and West: grand mosques, graceful minarets and exotic bazaars rub shoulders with modern shops, offices and restaurants.

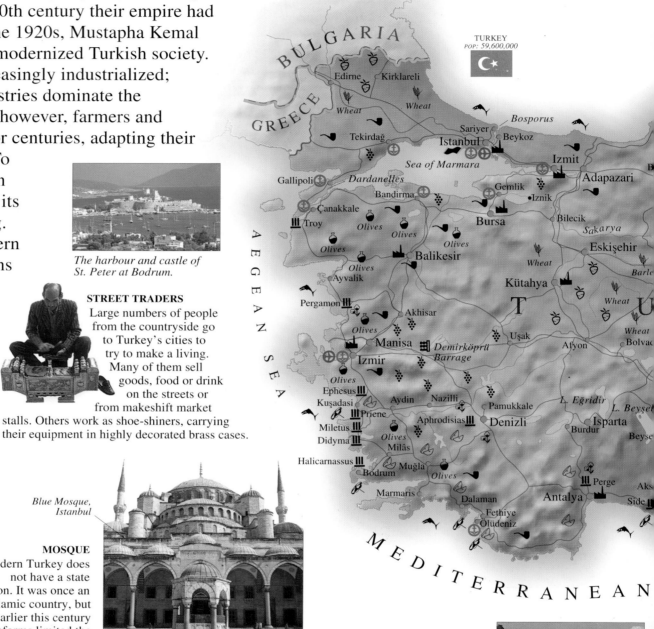

TURKEY
POP: 59,600,000

The harbour and castle of St. Peter at Bodrum.

STREET TRADERS
Large numbers of people from the countryside go to Turkey's cities to try to make a living. Many of them sell goods, food or drink on the streets or from makeshift market stalls. Others work as shoe-shiners, carrying their equipment in highly decorated brass cases.

A CLASSICAL LEGACY
The temple of Athena in Priene is one of Turkey's many ancient treasures. The Aegean coast was colonized by the ancient Greeks as early as 700 BC. Many people go to Turkey to visit the dramatic remains of Greek cities and temples. Look for ▥

Blue Mosque, Istanbul

MOSQUE
Modern Turkey does not have a state religion. It was once an Islamic country, but earlier this century reforms limited the powers of the clerics and introduced civil law. Recently, however, there has been an Islamic revival and modern Turks are going back to many customs from their rich Islamic past.

KEYBOX

 Tobacco: Turkey is a major producer. Dark, Turkish tobacco is grown around the Black Sea and Aegean coasts. Look for ↘

 Tourism: Coastal resorts are developing rapidly. Airports cater for growing numbers of visitors from northern Europe. Look for ⚐

 Dams: Ambitious dam-building programmes, especially in the south-east, are being used for hydro-electric power and for watering farmland. Look for ▦

 Cereals	 Cotton
Sugar beet	Fishing
Citrus fruit	Carpet-weaving
Wine	Industrial centre
Vegetable oil	 Archaeological site

ANKARA
Ankara has been the capital of Turkey since 1923. It is a planned, modern city with boulevards, parks and many high-rise flats. Until recently, the city suffered from terrible pollution, caused by people burning brown coal, or lignite, for heating. Now, clean natural gas is piped into the city from the Russian Federation.

Dried apricot — Almond — Hazelnut — Fig — Peach

This strange landscape is in Cappadocia, central Turkey.

AGRICULTURE
Turkey has a varied landscape and climate. This means that many different types of crop can be grown there and the Turks are able to produce all their own food. Cereals, sugar beet, grapes, nuts, cotton and tobacco are all major exports. Hazelnuts are grown along the shores of the Black Sea. Figs, peaches, olives and grapes are grown along the Mediterranean coast and in the coastal lowlands. Cereals are cultivated on the central plateau. Farms are still relatively small and only gradually being modernized, but despite this productivity is high.

TURKISH FOOD

Typical Turkish food consists of fresh fruit, vegetables, meat and fish, flavoured with spices such as cinnamon and cumin. Lamb is the most common meat. It is often grilled on a skewer to make a kebab, or minced and made into spiced meatballs, served with rice or cracked wheat (*burgul*). Goat's yoghurt is eaten everywhere, often mixed with cucumber, garlic or mint to make a refreshing side-dish.

Burgul wheat

Tomato

Olive

Bay leaf

Yoghurt with cucumber

Lamb shish kebab

Valuable Black Sea oyster beds are being destroyed by these whelks.

Veined rapa whelk

KILIMS

Knotted-pile carpets, called *kilims*, were first made many centuries ago by the Turks' nomadic ancestors. Each region of Turkey produces carpets with slightly different patterns and colours, although today chemical dyes are often used instead of the traditional vegetable colourings. Look for

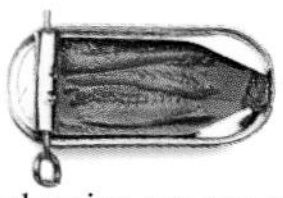

Anchovies are caught in the Black Sea.

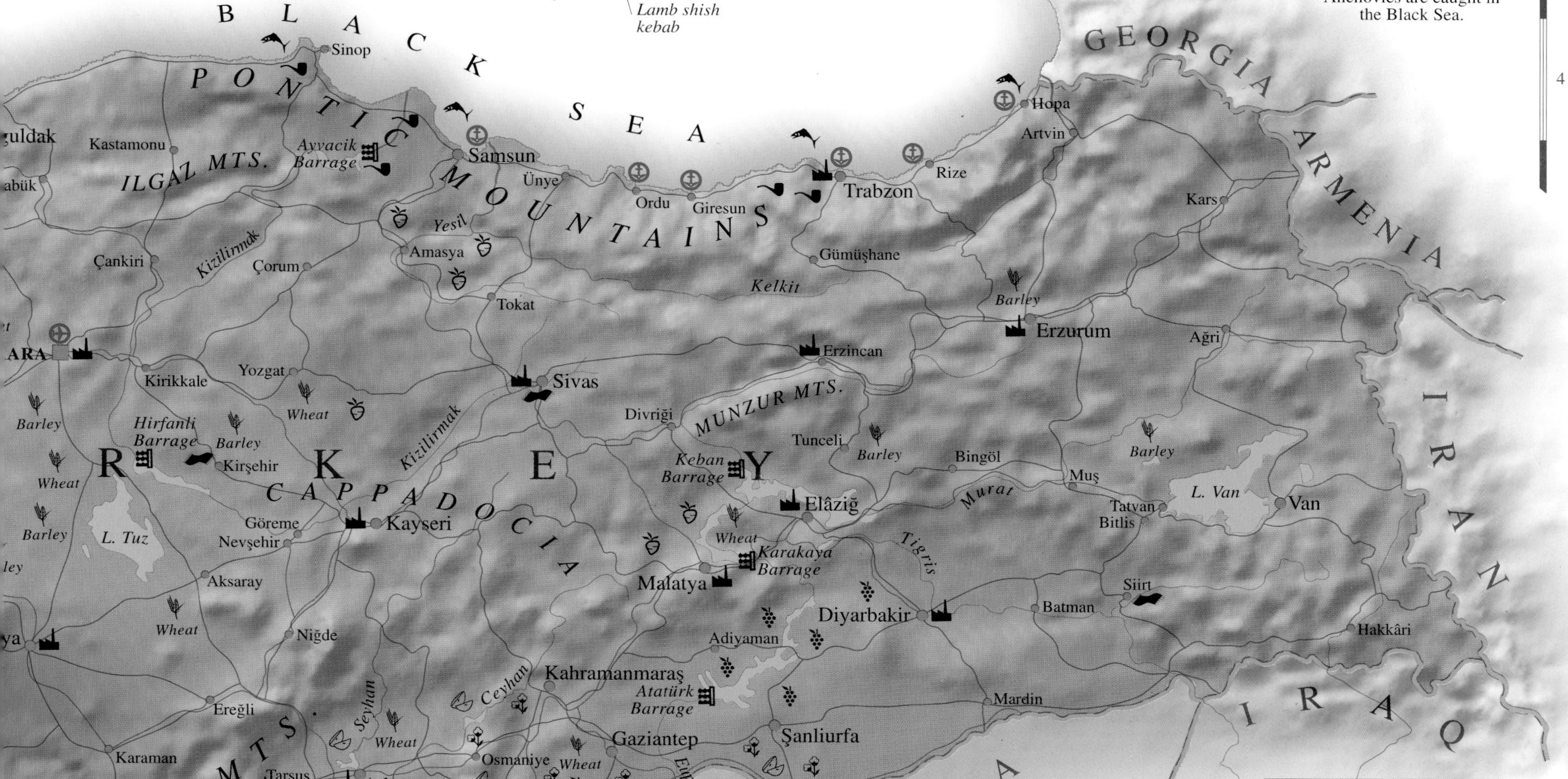

RURAL LIFE

Life in the high plateaux of central Turkey is very hard. The winters are severe, and the landscape is desolate. Most people live as nomadic herders or small-scale farmers. Many people leave these areas to live in the overcrowded cities, or go to the rich countries of northern Europe as "guest workers".

A 10th-century church on Lake Van in eastern Turkey.

N

0   50   100   150   200   250   KM

0   50   100   150   MILES

Glazed tiles made in Iznik decorate many Turkish mosques.

Turkish coffee pot

Turkish delight

COFFEE

Turkey, like other Middle Eastern countries, has a long tradition of coffee drinking. Turkish coffee is made by pounding the beans to a powder and then boiling this with sugar to make a strong, dark brew. Coffee houses are favourite meeting places, where people also smoke pipes, play cards and chat.

In 1983 the north of the island proclaimed itself the Turkish Republic of Northern Cyprus. It is only recognized by Turkey.

Mohair comes from the Angora goat, native to central Turkey.

CYPRUS
POP: 700,000

CYPRUS

Cyprus is the largest island in the east Mediterranean. Cypriots are a mixture of Greek and Turkish speakers. After independence in 1959, conflict between the two communities resulted in the United Nations sending a peace-keeping force, which still remains. Despite their presence, there was a Turkish invasion in 1974. Since then the island has been split into two parts.

WOMEN WORKERS

Although Turkish women are equal by law, traditions of male authority still persist, especially in the countryside. It is common to see old women doing back-breaking work in the fields, while their husbands look on. On the other hand, some Turkish women have succeeded in powerful jobs as politicians, judges, or bank directors.

Map labels: Sinop, Kastamonu, uldak, abük, Çankiri, Kizilirmak, ARA, Kirikkale, Yozgat, Çorum, Amasya, Yesil, Tokat, Ordu, Giresun, Ünye, Samsun, Ayvacik Barrage, ILGAL MTS., PONTIC MOUNTAINS, BLACK SEA, Trabzon, Gümüşhane, Kelkit, Hopa, Artvin, Rize, GEORGIA, ARMENIA, Kars, Ağri, Erzurum, Barley, Sivas, Divriği, Erzincan, MUNZUR MTS., Tunceli, Bingöl, Muş, Barley, IRAN, Hirfanli Barrage, Barley, Kirşehir, Wheat, R, K, Göreme, Nevşehir, Kayseri, CAPPADOCIA, Keban Barrage, Elâzığ, Murat, Tatvan Bitlis, L. Van, Van, Barley, ley, L. Tuz, Barley, Wheat, Aksaray, E, Y, Wheat, Karakaya Barrage, Malatya, Diyarbakir, Siirt, Hakkâri, ya, Wheat, Niğde, Adiyaman, Batman, Mardin, Ereğli, Seyhan, Ceyhan, Kahramanmaraş, Atatürk Barrage, Gaziantep, Şanliurfa, IRAQ, Karaman, MTS., Wheat, Osmaniye, Wheat, Euphrates, Tarsus, Adana, Kilis, AURUS, Mersin, Iskenderun, SYRIA, Silifke, Olives, Antakya, Anamur, EA, Rizokarpasso, Kyrenia, Akanthou, Salamis, NICOSIA, Famagusta, lis, Larnaca, Paphos, Limassol, CYPRUS

THE NEAR EAST

CAUGHT BETWEEN the two worlds of Europe
and Asia, the Near East is bordered on the west
by the fertile coasts of the Mediterranean Sea,
and on the east by the arid deserts of Arabia.
Some of the world's earliest civilizations were
born here, while the history of all three of the world's
great religions – Judaism, Christianity and Islam – is closely
bound up with the region. Imperial conquerors and Christian and
Muslim crusaders battled fiercely over this territory, and by the 17th century
much of the region was part of the Turkish Ottoman empire. In 1918, the Near
East came under the control of Britain and France; a dangerous mixture of
religions and passionate nationalism plunged the area into conflict. Today,
Lebanon is just beginning to emerge from a fierce civil war between Christians
and Muslims. Israel, which became a Jewish state in 1948, has been involved in
numerous wars with its neighbours and there is considerable unrest among its
Palestinian population. Many Palestinian refugees, who have left Israel, are
living in camps in Jordan and Lebanon. Despite these problems, the Near East
continues to survive economically. Israel is highly industrialized and a world
leader in advanced farming techniques. Syria has its
own reserves of oil, and is gradually becoming
more industrialized.

Carnation
Rose
Grapefruit
Orange
Lemon
Lime

FARMING
Although about half of Israel is desert,
it is self-sufficient in most food, and
actually exports agricultural
produce, especially citrus fruits and
flowers. Israeli farming uses
advanced irrigation techniques
and is highly mechanized. Many
farms are run as *kibbutzim*; the land
is owned by members, who share
work and profits. Look for

JERUSALEM THE GOLDEN
The historic city of Jerusalem is held
sacred by three major religions: Judaism,
Christianity and Islam. Throughout its
history, it has been the object of
pilgrimage and religious crusades. For
Jews, the Wailing Wall, seen here, is the
most sacred site, while the Dome of the
Rock is sacred to Muslims, reflecting
divisions within Israel.

Skull-cap, yarmulke

JUDAISM
Judaism is one of the oldest
religions in the world. Jews
believe in one God, and
the most devout
(Orthodox) follow codes
of behaviour based on
laws contained in their
holy book, the *Torah*.
This is the first part of
Old Testament and is written in
Hebrew. Modern Hebrew is the
language of Israel.

The Torah

Prayer shawl

WATER WARS
Throughout this region, water is in very
short supply. Where water resources are
shared (for example, Israel and Jordan
share the Jordan River), disputes can
occur. Israel leads the way in irrigation
techniques. Fields are watered by drip
irrigation – holes in pipes dispense
exactly the right amount of water
required, avoiding wastage.

UZI GUNS
Israel is a major
arms producer,
developing weapons for her own
army, such as this Uzi gun, as
well as medium-range missiles to
deter Arab enemies. Military service
in the Israel Defence Force (IDF) is
compulsory for all Israeli citizens.
Men must serve three years,
unmarried women two years.

*Lake Tiberias, known in the
Bible as the Sea of Galilee.*

DEAD SEA MUD
The Dead Sea, 400 m (1,300 ft) below
sea level, is an enclosed salt lake.
Salt levels are six times
higher than in other
seas, so no fish live
in these waters. The
Dead Sea is rich in
minerals, some of which
have medical properties.

*Dead Sea mud
is used as a skin
conditioner, and
cure for arthritis*

Soap made from
Dead Sea mud

KEYBOX

Cotton: Syria's most profitable
cash crop is cotton. The area of
land devoted to cotton has been
expanded in recent years.
Look for

Tourism: People come to this
region from all over the world
to visit archaeological sites,
ancient cities, and holy places.
Look for

Refugee camps: Palestinian
refugees have fled from Israel to
Jordan and Lebanon. Many fled
to Jordan from Kuwait after the
1991 Gulf War. Look for

Cereals		Mining	
Sugar beet		Oil	
Citrus fruit		Industrial centre	
Vegetable oil		Tourism	
Tobacco		Irrigated agriculture	

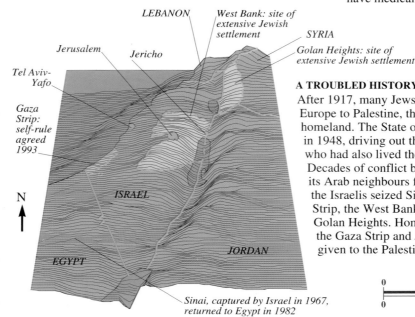

LEBANON
West Bank: site of
extensive Jewish
settlement
SYRIA
Golan Heights: site of
extensive Jewish settlement
Jerusalem
Jericho
Tel Aviv-Yafo
Gaza Strip:
self-rule
agreed
1993
N
ISRAEL
JORDAN
EGYPT

*Sinai, captured by Israel in 1967,
returned to Egypt in 1982*

A TROUBLED HISTORY
After 1917, many Jews emigrated from
Europe to Palestine, their ancient
homeland. The State of Israel was created
in 1948, driving out the Palestinian Arabs
who had also lived there for centuries.
Decades of conflict between Israel and
its Arab neighbours followed. In 1967
the Israelis seized Sinai, the Gaza
Strip, the West Bank and the
Golan Heights. Home rule of
the Gaza Strip and Jericho was
given to the Palestinians in 1994.

N

Gulf of Suez
S I

| 0 | 50 | 100 | 150 | KM |
| 0 | 25 | 50 | 75 | 100 | MILES |

Krak des Chevaliers, in Syria, is a 12th-century crusader castle.

WAR-TORN LEBANON

Lebanon became independent in 1944. Christians, about 40 per cent of the population, held most of the wealth and power. The Muslim majority felt discriminated against. This grievance exploded into a bitter civil war in 1975. Agreements have now created a fragile peace.

The pomegranate fruit is grown in Israel.

LEBANON
POP: 2,900,000

ISRAEL
POP: 5,400,000

Golan Heights: Occupied by Israel

West Bank and Gaza Strip: Occupied by Israel under Palestinian administration

SYRIA
POP: 13,800,000

Hubble bubble tobacco pipe

HUBBLE BUBBLE

Throughout the Arab world, men enjoy spending their leisure hours in cafés, drinking tea or coffee, playing cards or backgammon, and smoking. Often they smoke pipes, called hubble bubbles, which draw the smoke into the mouth through water and a long tube. Tobacco is grown in Syria, and exported to other countries in the region. Look for 🔅

The Arabian *tibia*, one of the rich variety of shells found in the Red Sea.

DAMASCUS SOUK

Damascus, the capital of Syria, is one of the oldest cities in the world – its history goes back 4,000 years. At its centre, next to the main mosque, is a typical Middle Eastern *souk* (bazaar). Small winding covered streets are lined with stalls selling a wide range of produce. Behind the stalls are the workshops where craftsmen make their wares.

The hills and plateaux of Israel's Negev Desert.

Wadi Rum in Jordan, where the desert meets sandstone hills.

JORDAN
POP: 4,400,000

ROSE-RED CITY

Petra, founded in about 400 BC, was the capital city of the Nabateans, a people from the Arabian peninsula who grew wealthy on the profits of the Arabian incense and spice trade. The city is located deep in a canyon, and its buildings are carved out of the soft pink limestone of the canyon walls. Large numbers of visitors come to Jordan to see ancient sites such as Petra and to enjoy the resorts and scuba-diving in the Red Sea.

BEDOUIN

The Bedouin are nomadic herders who live in dry regions of the Near East and Africa. They keep cattle, sheep and goats, which provide them with milk and meat and can be sold for food such as wheat, dates and coffee. The Bedouin move from place to place, following the wet and dry seasons, in search of grazing for their animals.

THE MIDDLE EAST

THE WORLD'S first cities grew up about 5,500 years ago in the area between the Tigris and Euphrates rivers. The land in this region is dry, but these early people created ingenious irrigation techniques to direct the river water on to their fields of crops. In AD 570, the Prophet Mohammed, founder of the Islamic religion, was born in Mecca, in modern-day Saudi Arabia. Islam soon spread throughout the Middle East, where it is now the dominant religion, and into Africa. In recent years, the discovery of oil has brought great wealth to the countries around the Persian Gulf, and with it, rapid industrial and social change. Both Iran and Iraq earn huge revenues from oil, but they have been troubled by dictatorship and political unrest, as well as by a ten-year war. In 1991, the region was devastated by the Gulf War, which brought UN troops to the Middle East to fight against Iraq.

Pistachio nuts
Aduki beans
Green lentils
Red lentils
Dates
Chickpeas

MIDDLE EASTERN FOOD
Farming in the Arabian peninsula has been transformed by new irrigation methods. Saudi Arabia now exports wheat; the United Arab Emirates vegetables. Pulses such as lentils and chickpeas are the main food crops elsewhere.

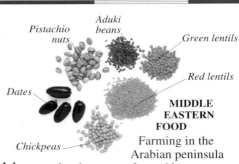

BAGHDAD
Baghdad, Iraq's capital since 1918, has grown dramatically over the last 20 years, but was badly damaged during the Gulf War. The city has been rebuilt. Massive monuments to President Hussein once again adorn its streets.

IRAQ
POP: 19,900,000

For centuries Marsh Arabs have lived in the swampy delta of the Tigris and Euphrates.

SAUDI ARABIA
POP: 16,500,000

Kufiyah, *male headdress*
Khimar, *veil worn by women*

ARAB DRESS
In summer, when temperatures in the Gulf reach 50° C (122° F), layers of loose robes and a head-dress are worn to make the heat bearable.

Hirz, *amulet charm case*

Aqaal, *used to secure headdress*

ISLAM
Mecca is Islam's holiest place and a centre of pilgrimage. Muslims believe in one God, *Allah*. They worship in mosques, and should pray five times a day, give alms, and fast for the month-long period of *Ramadan*.

Camels, known as "ships of the desert", can go for days without water, and are used to carry loads.

MAKING THE DESERT BLOOM
Water is scarce all over this region, and is carefully managed. More than 60 per cent of the world's desalination plants are in the Arabian peninsula. They are used to extract the salt from sea water to make it drinkable. Look for ◊

KEYBOX

Archaeological sites: The ancient cities of the Middle East, such as Ur, date back to 3,500 BC. They are the oldest cities in the world. Look for ▲

Dams: A series of dams and barrages have been built along the Tigris and Euphrates to provide water for the dry plains of southern Iraq. Look for ▦

Industrial centre: Saudi Arabia's economy has been dominated by oil. It is seeking to widen its range of industries. Look for ⬛

🌾 Cereals		🛢 Oil	
🌴 Dates		💧 Gas	
⋙ Rice		〰 Carpet-weaving	
🐟 Fishing		◊ Desalination plants	

YEMEN
Unlike the rest of the Arabian peninsula, Yemen has enough rainfall to water its crops. Most crops are grown on mountain terraces in the highlands. The country is self-sufficient in barley, lentils, sorghum, maize and coffee. Look for ⚘

The minaret of the Great Mosque at Sāmarrā', Iraq.

Yemen's capital, San'ā, dates back to the 7th century.

YEMEN
POP: 13,000,000

Map labels

SYRIA
JORDAN
EGYPT
SYRIAN DESERT
Gulf of Aqaba
Wādī Ḥawran
Wādī al Gh
Wādī 'Ar
'Ar 'ar
'Ann
Al Hadī
An Nabk
Tabūk
Al Jawf
Sakākah
Wheat
AN NAFUD
Ḥā'il
HEJAZ
Wheat
Wheat
Wheat
RED SEA
Yanbu 'al Bahr
Medina
NEJD
Buraydah
Wheat
Mecca
Jedda
Ṭā'if
Wheat
ASIR
SA
ARA
Al Bāḥah
Wheat
Khaybar
Barley
Abhā
Khamīs Mushayṭ
RU
Jīzān
Najrān
Sa'dah
Barley
Barley
RAMLAT
Kamarān I.
Hajjah
Al Maḥwīt
Ma'rib
SAN'A
Hodeida
Millet
Dhamār
YE
Millet
Ibb
Ḥa
Ta'izz
Al Bayḍā'
Ḥabba
Al Mukhā
Lahij
Aden
Zinjibar
Bab el Mandeb
Waḍī Banī
Ataq

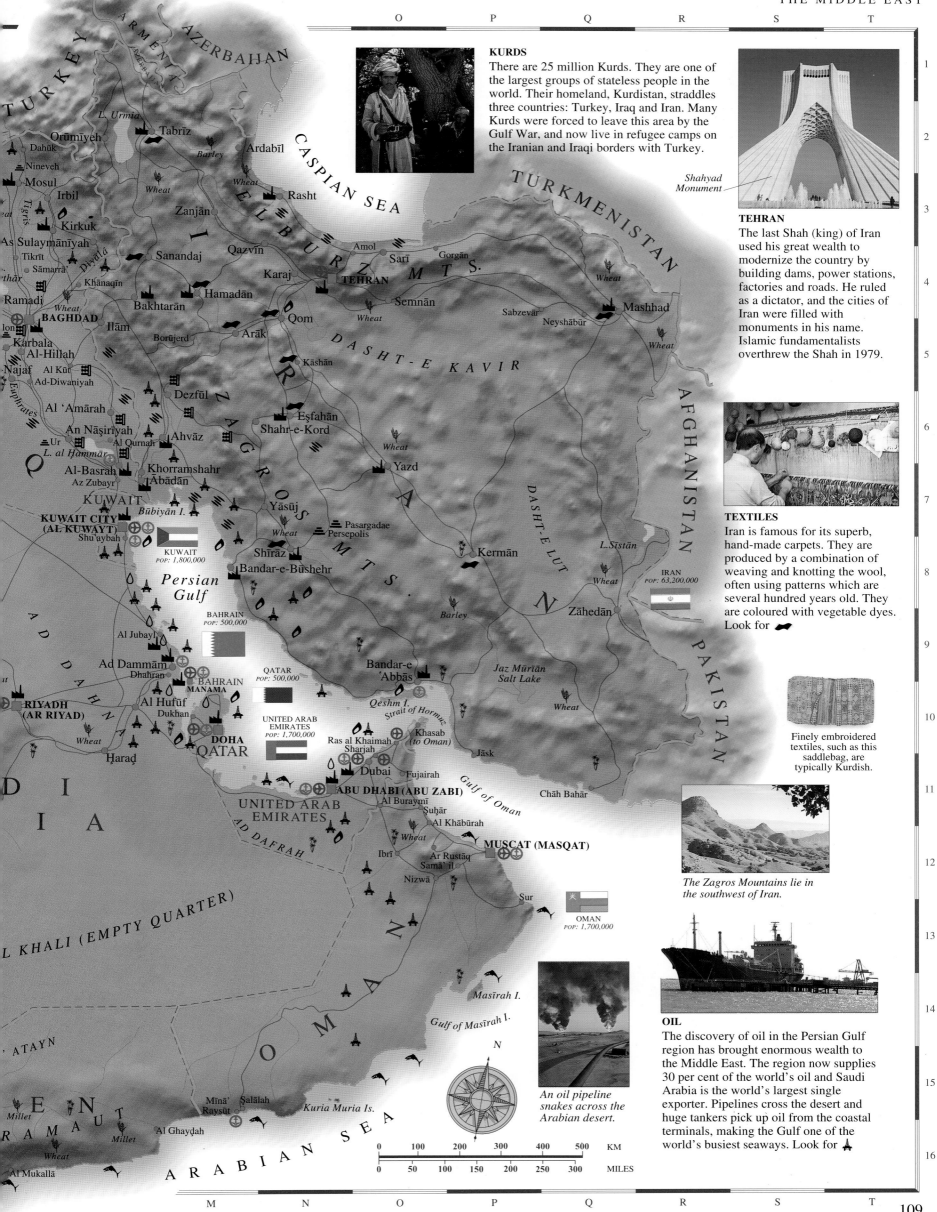

KURDS
There are 25 million Kurds. They are one of the largest groups of stateless people in the world. Their homeland, Kurdistan, straddles three countries: Turkey, Iraq and Iran. Many Kurds were forced to leave this area by the Gulf War, and now live in refugee camps on the Iranian and Iraqi borders with Turkey.

Shahyad Monument

TEHRAN
The last Shah (king) of Iran used his great wealth to modernize the country by building dams, power stations, factories and roads. He ruled as a dictator, and the cities of Iran were filled with monuments in his name. Islamic fundamentalists overthrew the Shah in 1979.

TEXTILES
Iran is famous for its superb, hand-made carpets. They are produced by a combination of weaving and knotting the wool, often using patterns which are several hundred years old. They are coloured with vegetable dyes. Look for

Finely embroidered textiles, such as this saddlebag, are typically Kurdish.

The Zagros Mountains lie in the southwest of Iran.

OIL
The discovery of oil in the Persian Gulf region has brought enormous wealth to the Middle East. The region now supplies 30 per cent of the world's oil and Saudi Arabia is the world's largest single exporter. Pipelines cross the desert and huge tankers pick up oil from the coastal terminals, making the Gulf one of the world's busiest seaways. Look for

An oil pipeline snakes across the Arabian desert.

KUWAIT
POP: 1,800,000

BAHRAIN
POP: 500,000

QATAR
POP: 500,000

UNITED ARAB EMIRATES
POP: 1,700,000

IRAN
POP: 63,200,000

OMAN
POP: 1,700,000

0 100 200 300 400 500 KM
0 50 100 150 200 250 300 MILES

109

CENTRAL ASIA

THE CENTRAL ASIAN REPUBLICS lie on the ancient Silk Road between Asia and Europe, and their historic cities grew up along this route. Afghanistan controlled the route south into Pakistan and India, through the Khyber Pass in the Hindu Kush mountains. The hot, dry deserts of Central Asia and high, rugged mountain ranges of the Pamirs and Tien Shan were not suited to agriculture. For centuries people lived as nomads, herding sheep across the empty plains, or settled as merchants and traders in the Silk Road cities. When Central Asia became part of the communist Soviet Union, everything changed: local languages and the Islamic religion (which had come to the region from the Middle East in the 8th century) were restricted; irrigation schemes made farming the arid land possible; oil, gas and other minerals were exploited; industry was developed. Today, these newly-independent republics are returning to the languages, religion and traditions of their past. Afghanistan, independent since 1750, has recently suffered terrible conflict and economic collapse.

HORSEMEN OF THE STEPPES
The nomadic peoples of the steppes travel great distances on horseback, and horse fairs and races are important events in their calendar. Ashgabat in Turkmenistan is the main breeding centre for the Akhal-Teke, a much prized racehorse, able to maintain its speed in desert conditions.

Akhal-Teke racehorse

UZBEKISTAN
POP: 21,900,000

TURKMENISTAN
POP: 4,000,000

AGRICULTURE
Farming in this dry region depends on irrigation. The Karakum Canal is 1,100 km (683 miles) long – the longest canal in the world. It carries water from the Amu Darya towards the Caspian Sea, and waters vast areas of land. Draining the river, however, has also created desert landscapes.

Opium poppies are grown all over the region. They provide illegal money for many farmers, who supply the international drug trade.

SULPHUR
Turkmenistan's sulphur deposits are amongst the largest in the world. Sulphur is used in the manufacture of gunpowder, as well as in medicine, ointment and drugs. Turkmenistan also has large reserves of oil and gas, but has been slow to make money from its resources.

MARKETS
Towns such as Samarkand have changed little since the days of the Silk Road, and are still full of merchants and traders. Bazaars and street-side stalls sell local fruit and vegetables, herbs, spices, silk and cotton.

KEYBOX

Alternative energy: Sunlight is used to generate power in Central Asia, providing a clean alternative to nuclear power. Look for ⚡

Rail route: The planned Trans-Asian Railway will connect Peking and Istanbul, via Central Asia and the Caspian Sea. Look for 🚆

🐂	Cattle	⛑	Mining
🐑	Sheep	⚒	Oil
🚢	Mixed fruit	🝆	Gas
🝐	Tobacco	◼	Carpet weaving
⚓	Cotton	🏭	Industrial centre

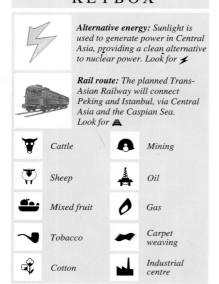

Carrots were first grown for food in Afghanistan.

CARPETS
Carpets from Uzbekistan, Turkmenistan, northern Afghanistan and other parts of this region are world-famous. They are made by hand-knotting, and are woven from fine Karakul wool. They follow distinctive geometric patterns in a range of red, brown and maroon colours. Carpets are used as saddle-cloths, tent hangings and prayer mats. Look for ◼

KARAKUL SHEEP
Karakul sheep are bred for their distinctive curly fleece. They are especially important in Afghanistan. Nomadic people have herded sheep in this region for many centuries. Each summer they take their flocks up to the lush mountain pastures, and in winter they are herded down onto the plains. Look for 🐑

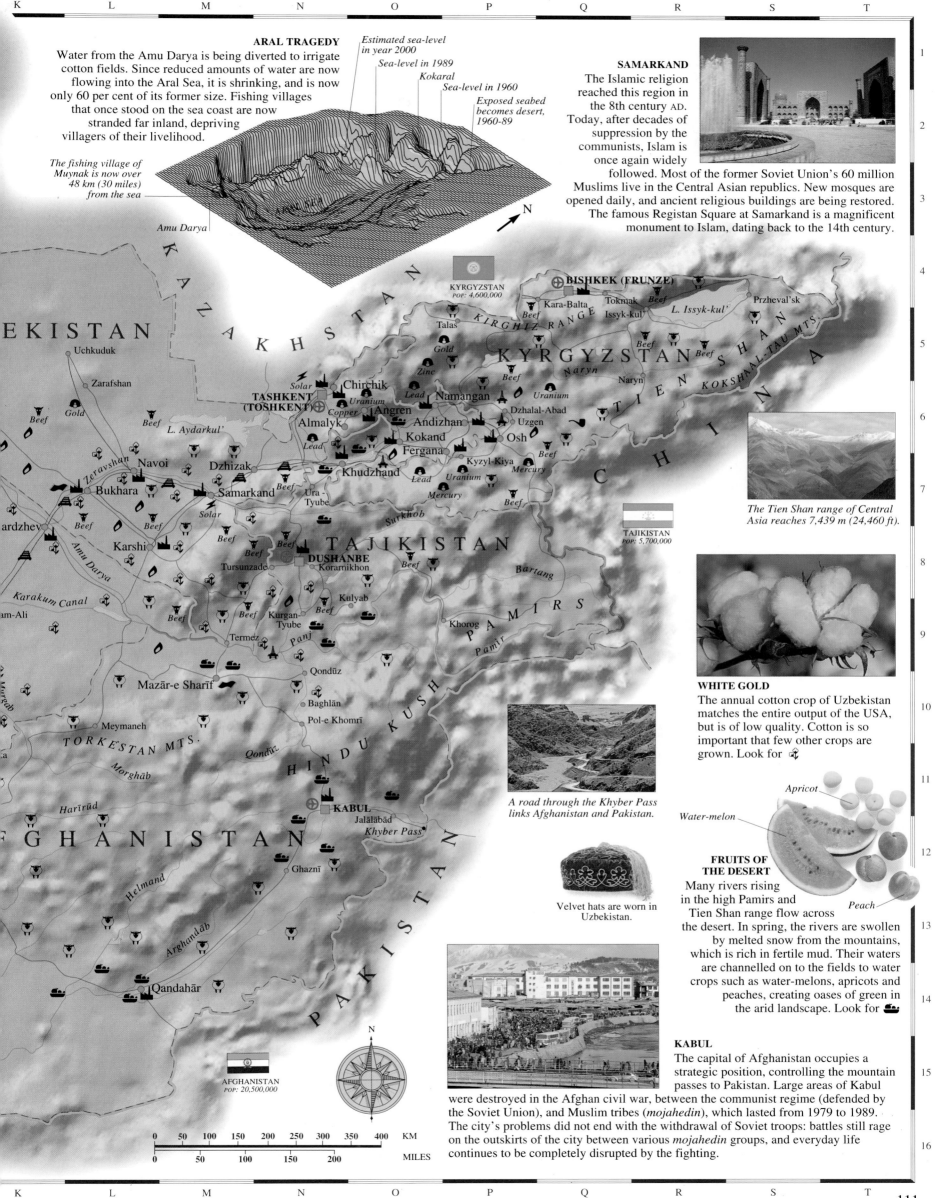

ARAL TRAGEDY

Water from the Amu Darya is being diverted to irrigate cotton fields. Since reduced amounts of water are now flowing into the Aral Sea, it is shrinking, and is now only 60 per cent of its former size. Fishing villages that once stood on the sea coast are now stranded far inland, depriving villagers of their livelihood.

The fishing village of Muynak is now over 48 km (30 miles) from the sea

Estimated sea-level in year 2000
Sea-level in 1989
Kokaral
Sea-level in 1960
Exposed seabed becomes desert, 1960-89

Amu Darya

SAMARKAND

The Islamic religion reached this region in the 8th century AD. Today, after decades of suppression by the communists, Islam is once again widely followed. Most of the former Soviet Union's 60 million Muslims live in the Central Asian republics. New mosques are opened daily, and ancient religious buildings are being restored. The famous Registan Square at Samarkand is a magnificent monument to Islam, dating back to the 14th century.

The Tien Shan range of Central Asia reaches 7,439 m (24,460 ft).

WHITE GOLD

The annual cotton crop of Uzbekistan matches the entire output of the USA, but is of low quality. Cotton is so important that few other crops are grown. Look for ⚓

A road through the Khyber Pass links Afghanistan and Pakistan.

Apricot
Water-melon
Peach

FRUITS OF THE DESERT

Many rivers rising in the high Pamirs and Tien Shan range flow across the desert. In spring, the rivers are swollen by melted snow from the mountains, which is rich in fertile mud. Their waters are channelled on to the fields to water crops such as water-melons, apricots and peaches, creating oases of green in the arid landscape. Look for ⛴

Velvet hats are worn in Uzbekistan.

KABUL

The capital of Afghanistan occupies a strategic position, controlling the mountain passes to Pakistan. Large areas of Kabul were destroyed in the Afghan civil war, between the communist regime (defended by the Soviet Union), and Muslim tribes (*mojahedin*), which lasted from 1979 to 1989. The city's problems did not end with the withdrawal of Soviet troops: battles still rage on the outskirts of the city between various *mojahedin* groups, and everyday life continues to be completely disrupted by the fighting.

KYRGYZSTAN POP: 4,600,000

TAJIKISTAN POP: 5,700,000

AFGHANISTAN POP: 20,500,000

KM / MILES

111

RUSSIA AND KAZAKHSTAN

THE URAL MOUNTAINS FORM a natural barrier between the European and the Asian parts of Russia. Although over 77 per cent of the country lies in Asia, only 27 per cent of the population live here. Siberia dominates Russia east of the Urals, stretching to the Pacific Ocean and northwards into the Arctic. The climate is severe, parts of Siberia are colder in winter than the North Pole.

Siberia has huge deposits of gold, coal, diamonds, gas and oil, but workers had to be offered high wages and housing to work there. Today, both Russia and Kazakhstan have great economic potential, but are still coping with a legacy of severe industrial pollution.

HYDRO-ELECTRIC POWER
Siberia's rivers provide 80 per cent of Russia's hydro-electric power, fuelling industry throughout eastern Russia. Massive dams, such as this one on the River Angara, provide the power for the aluminium industry. Look for ⊞

Ear of wheat

VIRGIN LANDS
In the 1950s, the Soviet Union tried to increase grain production. The empty steppes of Kazakhstan, known as the "Virgin Lands", were ploughed up to grow crops. Today, much of this farmland is reverting to steppe. Look for ⸙

KEYBOX

Industrial centre: This region produces one-third of the former USSR's iron and steel. Timber processing is also very important. Look for ◣

Pollution: Nearly 500 Soviet nuclear devices were detonated in Kazakhstan from 1949-1989. Many children in this area are malformed at birth. Look for ☢

Military bases: Russia's far East is a highly militarized area. The Russian Pacific fleet is based at Vladivostok. ICBM bases line the southeast border. Look for ⫴

⸙ Cereals	⛏ Coal
🪓 Timber	⛏ Oil
🐟 Fishing	🝆 Gas
⛏ Mining	⊞ Hydro-electric power

KAZAKH HORSEMEN
The first inhabitants of the steppe were a nomadic people who travelled on horseback, herding their sheep with them. They slept in felt tents like these, called *yurts*. Their descendants, the Kazakhs, still place great value on horses and riding skills, and horse-racing is a popular sport. The Kazakh national drink is *kumiss* – fermented mare's milk. The traditional nomadic lifestyle of the steppe has gradually been replaced by large-scale agriculture and industry.

KAZAKHSTAN
POP: 17,200,000

SPACE CENTRE
The Russian space programme is based at Baykonur in Kazakhstan, where this Buran unmanned shuttle was launched in 1988. Russia's achievements in space technology started with the launch of the Sputnik satellite in 1957. Since then, Russia has been responsible for the first man in space, the first woman cosmonaut, and the first space walk. The Mir orbital station has now been in space for over five years.

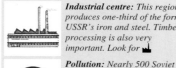

Map labels: FINLAND, ESTONIA, LATVIA, BELORUSSIA, UKRAINE, Murmansk, Iron, L. Pyaozero, KOLA PENINSULA, BARENTS SEA, Novaya Zemlya, KARA SEA, Bely, Baydarata Bay, YAMAL PENINSULA, GYD PENINS, WHITE SEA, Kolguyev I., Mezen, Pechora, Kem', Arkhangel'sk, Pskov, St. Petersburg, Petrozavodsk, Nevel', Novgorod, Rye, Aluminium, L. Onega, Onega, Kotlas, Uranum, Coal, Vorkuta, Smolensk, Cherepovets, Tver', Vologda, Oats, Chromium, Coal, Salekhard, Gulf of Ob, Nakhodka, MOSCOW, Kaluga, Yaroslavl', Syktyvkar, Ob', Pur, Bryansk, Tula, Orël, Ivanovo, Vladimir, Barley, Oats, Kama, Kirov, Cheboksary, Kazan', Platinum, Manganese, WEST SIBERIAN PLAIN, Taz, Kursk, Ryazan', Lipetsk, Nizhniy Novgorod, Saransk, Barley, Izhevsk, Perm', Serov, Platinum, Nizhniy Tagil, Irtysh, Iron, Voronezh, Tambov, Penza, Ul'yanovsk, Tol'yatti, Naberezhnyye Chelny, Oats, Yekaterinburg, Tyumen', Nizhnevartovsk, Vakh, Ket', SEA OF AZOV, Maize, Wheat, Saratov, Samara, Ufa, Gold, Copper, Iron, Chelyabinsk, Kurgan, Oats, Ob', Rostov-na-Donu, Balakovo, Sulphur, Volgograd, Ural'sk, Orenburg, Magnitogorsk, Krasnodar, BLACK SEA, Sochi, Iron, Stavropol', Cherkessk, Elista, Wheat, Ural, Wheat, Copper, Iron, Kustanai, Petropavlovsk, Kokchetay, Omsk, Itatka ICBM Base, GEORGIA, Vladikaykaz, Groznyy, Astrakhan, Atyrau, Aktyubinsk, Iron, Barley, Ishim, Wheat, Wheat, Novosibirsk, Ton, Makhachkala, Emba, Chromium, KIRGHIZ STEPPE, Akmola, Barley, Pavlodar, Wheat, Novokuznetsk, Fort Shevchenko, Aktau, Aluminium, L. Tengiz, KAZAKH UPLANDS, Irtysh, Gold, Aleysk Air Base, Biysk, CASPIAN SEA, Manganese, Copper, Karaganda, Baykonur, Arkalyk, Zhezkazgan, Semipalatinsk, Ust' Kamenogorsk, Zinc, Oats, ARAL SEA, Copper, Wheat, Balkhash, L. Zaysan, Lead, TURKMENISTAN, UZBEKISTAN, Kzyl-Orda, L. Balkhash, Ili, Syr Darya, Chu, Shymkent, Zhambyl, Kapchagay, Taldy-Kurgan, ALMA-ATA (ALMATY), KYRGYZSTAN, CHINA

Scale: 0 200 400 600 800 1000 KM / 0 100 200 300 400 500 600 MILES

N (compass)

K L M N O P Q R S T

SIBERIAN GOLD
The discovery of gold on the upper part of the River Lena in the 1840s led to a gold-rush. But conditions for 19th-century prospectors were terrible – they slept in flimsy huts in freezing temperatures, and many died. Today, the region has four major gold- fields as well as 800 diamond mines. Look for

A herd of reindeer graze on the tundra in northern Siberia.

A COLD CLIMATE
Siberian towns are built to withstand the region's harsh climate. Many houses are built on stilts, as frost damages normal foundations. Winters in the far north are extremely long – some towns do not see daylight for up to 47 days a year. Fruit and vegetables are grown locally in heated greenhouses.

Siberian huskies are used for pulling sledges and hunting.

The Kamchatka peninsula is a remote wilderness.

A child's toy wooden sledge from Siberia.

C. Dezhneva
ALASKA (USA)
Wrangel I.
Provideniya Air Base
CHUKCHI SEA
Tin
Tin
C. Navarin
Pevek
Anadyr' Air Base
Gold
Ayon I.
Ust' Chaun Air Base
Bear Is.
Ambarchik
Kolyma
OLOY RANGE
KORYAK RANGE
Cape Olyutorskiy
Pioner I.
Severnaya Zemlya
October Revolution I.
Bolshevik I.
New Siberian Islands
Indigirka
Korkodon
KOLYMA RANGE
Ossora
Karaginskiy Is.
C. Chelyuskin
LAPTEV SEA
C. Sivuchiy
TAYMYR PENINSULA
Olenëk Bay
Tiksi
Yana
Gold
Ust'-Kamchatsk
L. Taymyr
Olenëk
CENTRAL SIBERIAN PLATEAU
Gold
VERKHOYANSK RANGE
Bytantay
Gold
KAMCHATKA
Khatanga
Anabar
Copper
PUTORANA MTS.
Olenëk Air Base
Sartang
Adycha
Gold
Petropavlovsk-Kamchatskiy
Nickel
Diamonds
Lena
Magadan
Oktyabr'skiy
RUSSIAN
Vilyuy
Gold
C. Lopatka
SIBERIA
Diamonds
Yakutsk
Okhotsk
Paramushir Is.
Lower Tunguska
Suntar
Amga
Aldan
The Kurile Islands are administered by the Russian Federation, but claimed by Japan.
FEDERATION
Diamonds
Maya
DZHUGDZHUR RANGE
C. Yelizavety
Stony Tunguska
Lena
Olëkma
Gold
Vostochnyy
SEA OF OKHOTSK
Gold
Angara
Olëkma
Gold
Sakhalin
Gold
Ust'-Ilimsk
Zeya Reservoir
Poronaysk
Krasnoyarsk
Iron
Uranium
STANOVOY RANGE
Skovorodno
Komsomol'sk-na-Amure
Sovetskaya Gavan'
Kansk
Bratsk
Gold
Yuzhno-Sakhalinsk
L. Baikal
Svobodnyy ICBM Base
Gold
Molybdenum
Blagoveshchensk
Oats
Khabarovsk
Romanovka
Shilka
Gold
Amur
Oka
Angarsk
Irkutsk
Chita ICBM Base
CHINA
SEA OF JAPAN
Gold
Kyzyl
Ulan-Ude
Olovyannaya ICBM Base
Ussuri
Gold
Gold
Tin
Wheat
Tin
PACIFIC OCEAN
Tin
RUSSIAN FEDERATION
POP: 149,200,000
(SIBERIA)
POP: 40,250,000
Vladivostok
MONGOLIA
NORTH KOREA

INDUSTRIAL POLLUTION
Uncontrolled industrial growth has led to severe pollution problems in this region. The level of carbon emissions – caused by burning coal and oil – would not be acceptable in the West. Many children's illnesses in Russia are caused by contaminated air.

Lake Baikal contains 20 per cent of the world's fresh water.

Russians heat water for tea in urns called samovars.

TRIBESPEOPLE
The Chukchi people who live on the Kamchatka peninsula traditionally survive by hunting, reindeer herding and fishing. But the animals' natural habitats are slowly disappearing as forests are cut down for timber, and lakes and rivers are polluted by industrial waste. This is depriving the Chukchi hunters of their livelihood.

Fur hat

FUR
Hunters, trappers and fur-traders have been making a profitable living from Russia's animals since the 17th century. Siberia in particular has rich animal resources. The far East of the country has tigers and leopards, while the forests are home to the brown bear (often used as a symbol for Russia), sable, ermine, mink, lynx and foxes. Over-hunting has reduced the numbers of these animals in the wild, so most fur now comes from animals bred specially on fur farms.

Komodo dragon
Varanus komodoensis
Length: 3 m (10 ft)

Golden pheasant
Chrysolophus pictus
Length: 1 m (3 ft)

King cobra
Ophiophagus hannah
Length: 5.5 m (18 ft)

SOUTH AND EAST ASIA

THE WORLD'S 10 HIGHEST PEAKS, including Mount Everest, are all found in the Himalayas and other mountain ranges in the centre of this region. At these altitudes, monsoon rains fall as snow on mountain tops. The melted snow from the mountains feeds some of the largest rivers in the world, such as the Ganges and Irrawaddy, which have created huge deltas where they enter the sea. Fingers of land stretch into tropical seas and volcanic island chains border the continent. In tropical areas high rainfall and temperatures support vast areas of forest. Inland, a climate of extremes prevails, with baking hot summers and long harsh winters. Cold desert and grassy plains cover much of the interior.

■ ▲ **VOLCANIC ROCK**
This huge granite rock on Sri Lanka was formed in the mouth of a volcano. It is surrounded by forest.

Maidenhair tree
Gingko biloba
Height: 30 m (100 ft)

The Tiger cowrie is found on coral reefs.

■ ▲ **YOUNG MOUNTAINS**
Himalaya is the Nepalese word for "home of the snows". The range began to form about 40 million years ago – recent in the Earth's history.

■ △ **ISLAND VOLCANOES**
Plants are growing again on the scorched slopes of Bromo in Java, one of a chain of active volcanoes around the southeast Pacific.

■ **TROPICAL RAINFOREST**
Rainforests grow in layers: an understorey with creepers, and the main canopy through which tallest trees protrude.

Giant panda
Ailuropoda melanoleuca
Length: 1.5 m (5 ft)

■ **HIDDEN CAVES**
This maze of limestone caves along the Gulf of Thailand has been carved out by rainwater.

■ △ **SACRED MOUNTAIN**
Mount Fuji, Japan's highest peak, is surrounded by temperate broadleaf trees. Once an active volcano, Mount Fuji has not erupted for 300 years. The snow-capped summit is the rim of a volcanic crater.

The Royal cloak scallop shell is found in the waters of the Pacific Ocean.

⬇ **MANGROVES IN SILHOUETTE**
Mangroves grow along many coastlines, giving some protection during tropical storms.

Rafflesia
Rafflesia pricei
Width: 1 m (3 ft)

■ **TROPICAL ISLAND**
There are thousands of tiny coral islands in this region. Many are volcanic in origin, like this one in the South China Sea.

CROSS-SECTION THROUGH SOUTH AND EAST ASIA

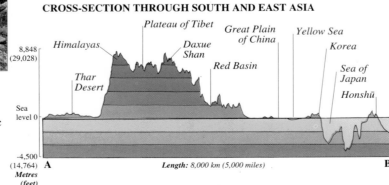

□ **COLD HIGH NEPAL**
No trees are to be found above 3,000 m (10,000 ft) in the Himalayas, though dwarf shrubs and grasses can withstand the harsher conditions up to 4,500 m (15,000 ft). Higher still, the rock is bare, or covered in snow.

Wild yak
Bos grunniens
Length: 3 m (9 ft)

Chinese river dolphin
Lipotes vexillifer
Length: 2.4 m (8 ft)

Siberian tiger
Panthera tigris
Length: 2.4 m (8 ft)

I

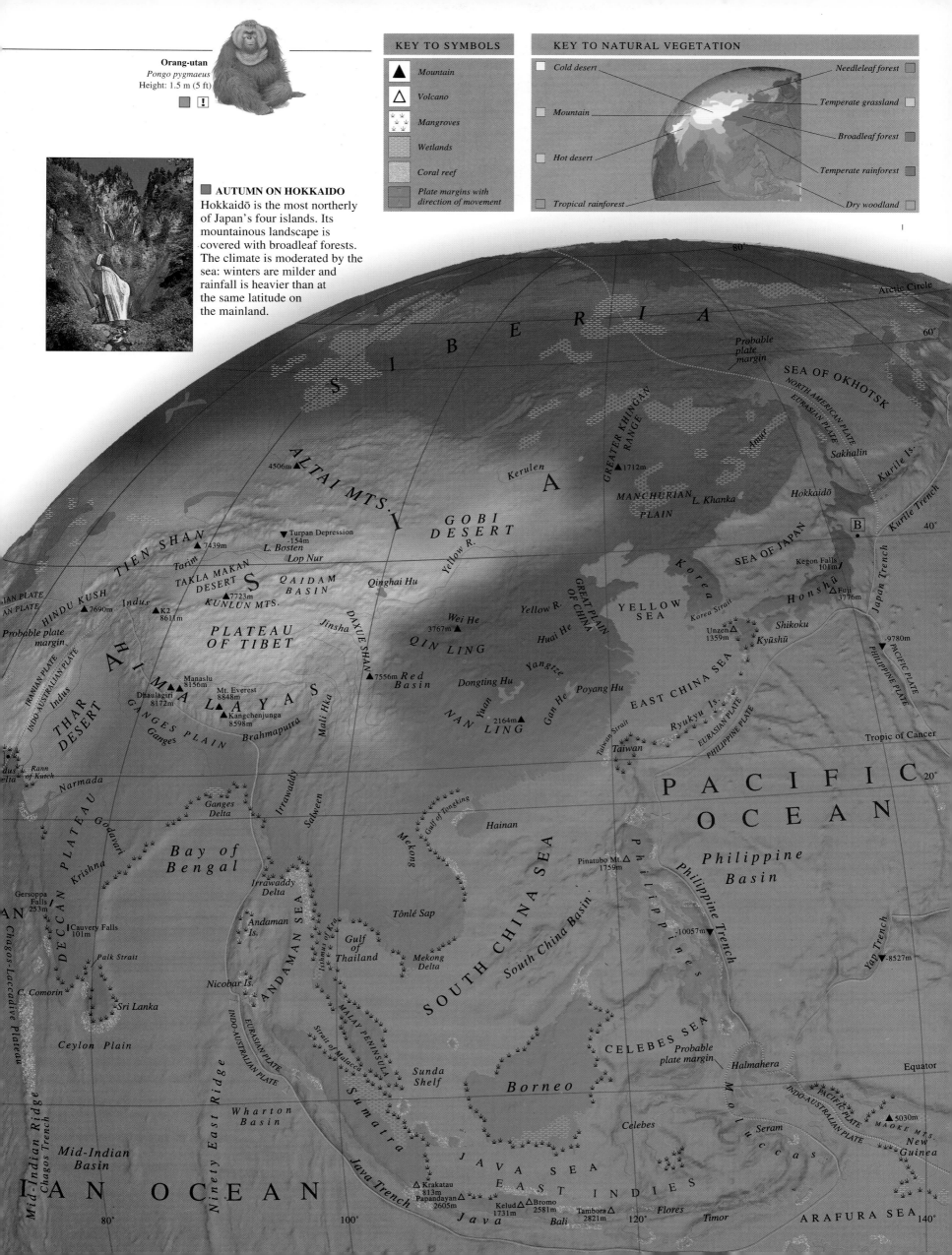

Orang-utan
Pongo pygmaeus
Height: 1.5 m (5 ft)

KEY TO SYMBOLS

▲ Mountain
△ Volcano
Mangroves
Wetlands
Coral reef
Plate margins with direction of movement

KEY TO NATURAL VEGETATION

Cold desert
Mountain
Hot desert
Tropical rainforest
Needleleaf forest
Temperate grassland
Broadleaf forest
Temperate rainforest
Dry woodland

AUTUMN ON HOKKAIDO
Hokkaidō is the most northerly of Japan's four islands. Its mountainous landscape is covered with broadleaf forests. The climate is moderated by the sea: winters are milder and rainfall is heavier than at the same latitude on the mainland.

SIBERIA

Arctic Circle

80°

60°

Probable plate margin

SEA OF OKHOTSK

NORTH AMERICAN PLATE
EURASIAN PLATE

Sakhalin

Kurile Is.

Kurile Trench

GREATER KHINGAN RANGE
▲1712m

Amur

Kerulen

MANCHURIAN PLAIN

L. Khanka

Hokkaidō

B

40°

ALTAI MTS.
4506m▲

GOBI DESERT

Korea

SEA OF JAPAN

Kegon Falls 101m

Honshū
△Fuji 3776m

TIEN SHAN
▲7439m
Tarim

Turpan Depression -154m
L. Bosten
Lop Nur

Yellow R.

YELLOW SEA

GREAT PLAIN OF CHINA

Korea Strait

Unzen△ 1359m
Kyūshū
Shikoku

-9780m

PACIFIC PLATE
PHILIPPINE PLATE

TAKLA MAKAN DESERT
QAIDAM BASIN
▲7723m
KUNLUN MTS.

Qinghai Hu

Yellow R.

Wei He
3767m▲

Huai He

EAST CHINA SEA

HINDU KUSH
Indus
▲7690m
K2 8611m

PLATEAU OF TIBET

Jinsha
DAXUE SHAN

QIN LING

Yangtze

Ryukyu Is.

EURASIAN PLATE
PHILIPPINE PLATE

IRANIAN PLATE
AN PLATE

Probable plate margin

▲7556m Red Basin

Dongting Hu

Yuan

Gan He
Poyang Hu

Taiwan Strait

Tropic of Cancer

INDO-AUSTRALIAN PLATE
Indus

H I M A L A Y A S

Manaslu 8156m
Dhaulagiri 8172m
Mt. Everest 8848m
Kangchenjunga 8598m

Brahmaputra

Mali Hka

NAN LING
2164m▲

Taiwan

PACIFIC OCEAN

20°

THAR DESERT

GANGES PLAIN
Ganges
Ganges

Rann of Kutch

Narmada

Irrawaddy

Salween

Gulf of Tongking

Hainan

Mekong

SOUTH CHINA SEA

South China Basin

Philippine Basin

Pinatubo Mt.△ 1759m

Philippines

dus Delta

DECCAN PLATEAU
Godavari
Krishna

Ganges Delta

Irrawaddy Delta

Andaman Is.

Isthmus of Kra

Gulf of Thailand

Tônlé Sap

Mekong Delta

Philippine Trench

-10057m▲

Yap Trench
▼-8527m

Gersoppa Falls 253m

Cauvery Falls 101m

Palk Strait

C. Comorin
Sri Lanka

Ceylon Plain

Nicobar Is.

ANDAMAN SEA

EURASIAN PLATE

MALAY PENINSULA
Strait of Malacca

CELEBES SEA

Probable plate margin

Halmahera

Equator

Mid-Indian Ridge
Chagos Trench
Chagos-Laccadive Plateau

Ninety East Ridge

INDO-AUSTRALIAN PLATE

Sunda Shelf

Borneo

Moluccas

INDO-AUSTRALIAN PLATE
PACIFIC PLATE

Seram

New Guinea

MAOKE MTS.
▲5030m

Mid-Indian Basin

Java Trench

Sumatra

Wharton Basin

JAVA SEA

Celebes

EAST INDIES

Flores

Timor

ARAFURA SEA

IAN OCEAN

80°

100°

△Krakatau
Papandayan△ 813m
2605m
Kelud△ 1731m
△Bromo 2581m
Java
Bali

Tambora△ 2821m
120°

140°

THE INDIAN SUBCONTINENT

SOUTH OF THE HIMALAYAS, the world's highest mountains, lies the Indian subcontinent. In the north of the region, the Buddhist kingdoms of Nepal and Bhutan cling to the slopes of the Himalayas. In the south, the island state of Sri Lanka hangs like a teardrop from the tip of India. The subcontinent has been invaded many times: the first invaders were fair-skinned, blue-eyed Aryan tribes, whose beliefs and customs form the basis of the Hindu religion. From the 16th century India was united and ruled by the Islamic Mogul emperors. Two centuries later it became a British colony. In 1947 India gained independence, but religious differences led to the creation of two countries – Hindu India and Muslim Pakistan. The eastern part of Pakistan later became Bangladesh. Today India is a thriving industrial power, but most people still live in villages and make their living from tiny farms. In spite of terrible poverty and a population of about 850 million people, India remains a relatively stable democracy.

The Thar Desert, a vast, arid region in India and Pakistan.

MOOD MUSIC
Traditional Indian music is improvised. Its purpose is to create a mood, such as joy or sorrow. One of the main instruments is the *sitar*, which is played by plucking seven of the strings. Other strings, which are not plucked, vibrate to give the distinctive sound of Indian music.

Sitar

KEYBOX

Aquaculture: This is a recent and highly successful industry in Bangladesh. Frogs' legs and shrimps are among the main products. Look for 🦐

Trekking: Every year some 250,000 trekkers visit Nepal, boosting its economy. But the extra visitors are damaging the environment. Look for 👟

Dams: Irrigation on a vast scale in the Indus Valley in Pakistan has sustained and increased the country's food production. Look for 🏛

🌾 Cereals		⚓ Cotton	
🌾 Rice		⛏ Mining	
Sugar cane		⚒ Coal	
Tea		🏭 Industrial centre	

PAKISTAN
This bus illustrates a big problem in Pakistan: over-population. Ninety-five per cent of the people are Muslim, and traditional Islam rejects contraception, so the birth-rate is high. Three million refugees, who fled the war in Afghanistan, have stretched resources further.

A MARBLE MEMORIAL
The Taj Mahal at Agra, in northern India, was built in the 17th century by the Mogul Emperor, Shah Jahan, as a tomb for his beloved wife. She was the mother of 14 children. Built of the finest white marble, the Taj Mahal is a supreme example of Islamic architecture and one of the world's most beautiful buildings.

INDUSTRY
After independence, India started to modernize, and is now one of the most industrialized countries in Asia. Factories make a wide range of goods, from cement to cars. Recently, the manufacture of goods such as machine tools and electronic equipment has increased. Local cotton is processed in mills like these in Ahmadabad. Look for 🏭

INDIAN FILMS
More films are produced in India than anywhere else in the world – including Hollywood. Bombay is the centre of the Indian film industry.

Jewellery, especially silver, is one of India's main exports.

Traditional fishing boats on the coast of Sri Lanka.

Kashmir: a "line control" w established in 19 by Simla Agreeme between Pakist and Ind

PAKISTAN
POP: 128,100,000

[Map labels: Peshawar, Mardan, Tarbela Dam, Tarbela Res., ISLAMABAD, Rawalpindi, Jinnah Barrage, Srinagar, Jhelum, Chashma Barrage, Wheat, Gujrat, Dera Ismail Khan, Sargodha, Chenab, Gujranw, Chromium, Faisalabad, Lahore, Amr, Quetta, Emerson (Trimmu) Barrage, Kasur, Okara, Dera Ghazi Khan, Multan, Islam Barrage, Panjnad Barrage, Bahawalpur, Guddu Barrage, Rahimyar Khan, Shikarpur, Wheat, Thar Desert, Larkana, Sukkur, Barl, Wheat, Jaisalmer, Ja, Ghulam Muhammad Barrage, Nawabshah, Jodhpur, Ajm, Mirpur Khas, Hyderabad, Karachi, Gandi Res., Wheat, Rann of Kutch, Kandla, Ahmadabad, Wheat, Gulf of Kutch, Jamnagar, Rajkot, Indor, Porbandar, Aluminium, Vadodara, Narmada, Bhavnagar, Tapti, Surat, Dhule, Gulf of Khambhat, Daman, Nasik, Thane, Bombay, Pune, D, Sholapur, Arabian Sea, Krishna, Aluminium, Pl, Belgaum, Dharwad, Panaji, Davange, Man, Iron, Mangalore, Chrom, Mysore, Western Ghats, Malabar Coast, Calicu, Coimbatore, Ernak, Co, Trivandrum, Nage, Iran, Afghanistan, Tobakakar Range, Chagai Hills, Makran, Indus, I N]

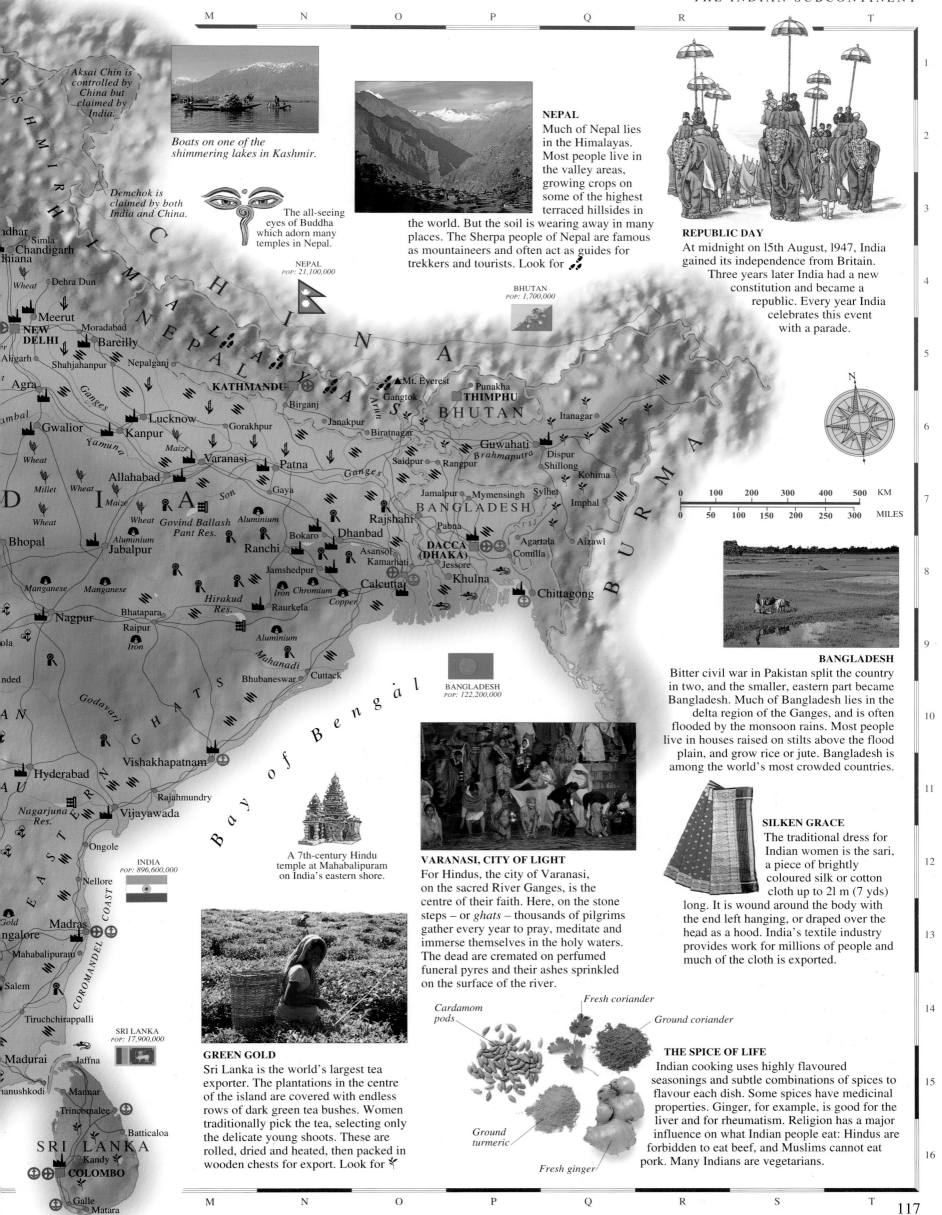

M   N   O   P   Q   R   S   T

Aksai Chin is controlled by China but claimed by India.

Boats on one of the shimmering lakes in Kashmir.

Demchok is claimed by both India and China.

The all-seeing eyes of Buddha which adorn many temples in Nepal.

NEPAL
Much of Nepal lies in the Himalayas. Most people live in the valley areas, growing crops on some of the highest terraced hillsides in the world. But the soil is wearing away in many places. The Sherpa people of Nepal are famous as mountaineers and often act as guides for trekkers and tourists. Look for

REPUBLIC DAY
At midnight on 15th August, 1947, India gained its independence from Britain. Three years later India had a new constitution and became a republic. Every year India celebrates this event with a parade.

NEPAL
POP: 21,100,000

BHUTAN
POP: 1,700,000

BANGLADESH
Bitter civil war in Pakistan split the country in two, and the smaller, eastern part became Bangladesh. Much of Bangladesh lies in the delta region of the Ganges, and is often flooded by the monsoon rains. Most people live in houses raised on stilts above the flood plain, and grow rice or jute. Bangladesh is among the world's most crowded countries.

BANGLADESH
POP: 122,200,000

A 7th-century Hindu temple at Mahabalipuram on India's eastern shore.

SILKEN GRACE
The traditional dress for Indian women is the sari, a piece of brightly coloured silk or cotton cloth up to 21 m (7 yds) long. It is wound around the body with the end left hanging, or draped over the head as a hood. India's textile industry provides work for millions of people and much of the cloth is exported.

INDIA
POP: 896,600,000

VARANASI, CITY OF LIGHT
For Hindus, the city of Varanasi, on the sacred River Ganges, is the centre of their faith. Here, on the stone steps – or *ghats* – thousands of pilgrims gather every year to pray, meditate and immerse themselves in the holy waters. The dead are cremated on perfumed funeral pyres and their ashes sprinkled on the surface of the river.

SRI LANKA
POP: 17,900,000

GREEN GOLD
Sri Lanka is the world's largest tea exporter. The plantations in the centre of the island are covered with endless rows of dark green tea bushes. Women traditionally pick the tea, selecting only the delicate young shoots. These are rolled, dried and heated, then packed in wooden chests for export. Look for

Cardamom pods

Fresh coriander

Ground coriander

Ground turmeric

Fresh ginger

THE SPICE OF LIFE
Indian cooking uses highly flavoured seasonings and subtle combinations of spices to flavour each dish. Some spices have medicinal properties. Ginger, for example, is good for the liver and for rheumatism. Religion has a major influence on what Indian people eat: Hindus are forbidden to eat beef, and Muslims cannot eat pork. Many Indians are vegetarians.

CHINA AND MONGOLIA

THE REMOTE MOUNTAINS, deserts and steppes of Mongolia and the northwestern part of China are harsh landscapes; temperatures are extreme, the terrain is rugged and distances between places are vast. Three large Autonomous Regions of China lie here – Inner Mongolia, Xinjiang and Tibet. Remote Tibet, situated on a high plateau and ringed by mountains, was invaded by China in 1950. The Chinese have systematically destroyed Tibet's traditional agricultural society and Buddhist monasteries. Most of China's ethnic minorities and Muslims (a legacy of Silk Road trade with the Middle East) are located in Inner Mongolia and Xinjiang. Roads and railways are being built to make these isolated areas accessible, and rich resources of coal are being exploited. Mongolia is a vast, isolated country. It became a communist republic in 1924, but has now re-established democracy. Most people still live by herding animals, although new industries have begun to develop.

Cylinder containing written prayer

In Tibet, written prayers are placed in prayer wheels. These small cylinders are rotated by hand.

MONGOLIAN STEPPES
About half the Mongolian population still live in the countryside, many as nomadic herders. Nomads live in *gers* – circular tents made of felt and canvas stretched over a wooden frame. They herd yak, sheep, goats, cattle and camels, and travel great distances on horseback.

KASHI MARKET
The city of Kashi is located in the far west of China. With its Muslim mosques, minarets and lively bazaar it is more like a city in the Middle East than China. Its Sunday market, the biggest in Asia, attracts up to 60,000 visitors. A vast array of goods are sold there: horses, camels, livestock, grains, spices and cloth.

KEYBOX

Timber: Forests in eastern Tibet have been cut down by the Chinese. Bare hillsides encourage soil erosion, flooding and landslides. Look for

Coal: Mongolia is a major exporter of coal to the Russian Federation. There are also open-cast mines in Xinjiang and Inner Mongolia. Look for

Pollution: Nuclear tests in Xinjiang have caused radiation fallout, pollution and many birth defects. Look for

🐂	Cattle and yaks	⛏	Mining
🐑	Sheep	🛢	Oil
🌾	Cereals	🏭	Industrial centre
🍇	Mixed fruit	🌴	Oases

The Tien Shan range in central Xinjiang.

ADAPTABLE YAKS
Herders in Mongolia and Tibet keep yaks. They thrive at high altitudes, surviving extreme cold and even burrowing under snow for grass. Yaks provide milk, butter, meat, wool and leather. In Tibet, yak's butter is served with tea. Look for

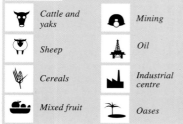

→ N

Oases: winter and spring wheat, corn, rice and cotton are grown

Passes through Tien Shan range

Takla Makan Desert

Tarim

Lop Nur: saline lake

Turpan oasis: fruit and cotton are grown on irrigated land

SILK ROAD OASES
The oases of Xinjiang lie on the edge of the Takla Makan Desert, in the foothills of the Tien Shan range. They are watered by melted snow from the mountains, and sheltered by warm winds coming down the mountain slopes. Towns grew up next to the oases, which lie along the ancient Silk Road.

The high plateau of Tibet, known as "the roof of the world".

Map labels

KAZAKHSTAN

L. Uvs
Ulaangom
Ölgiy
L. Hyarg
Altay
Irtysh
ALTAI MTS.
Hovd
Har Us L.
Beef
Karamay

XINJIANG UIGHUR
Yining
Kuytun
Shihezi
Ürümqi
Beef
AUTONOMOUS
Turpan
Maize
Hami
Iron
TIEN SHAN
Aksu
Korla
L. Bosten
Wheat
REGION
Kashi
Maize
Tarim
Maize
Tarim Basin
Shache
TAKLA MAKAN DESERT
C H
Lop Nur
Hotan
Lenghu
Da Q
Goln

KYRGYZSTAN
TAJIKISTAN
AFGHANISTAN
PAKISTAN
KARAKORUM MTS.
INDIA

Aksai Chin is controlled by China but claimed by India

Demchok is claimed by both China and India
Gar

ALTUN MTS.
KUNLUN MTS.
Beef
Yaks

TIBETAN
TANGGULA MTS.
AUTONOMOUS
Siling Co
Tangra Yumco
Nam Co
Nagqu
REGION
GANGDISE RANGE
Brahmaputra (Yarlung Zangbo)
Xigazê
Lhasa
Yaks
Nyingchi
Gyangzê
Yamzho Yumco
Nyalam
Mt. Everest
BHUTAN
NEPAL
HIMALAYAS
IND

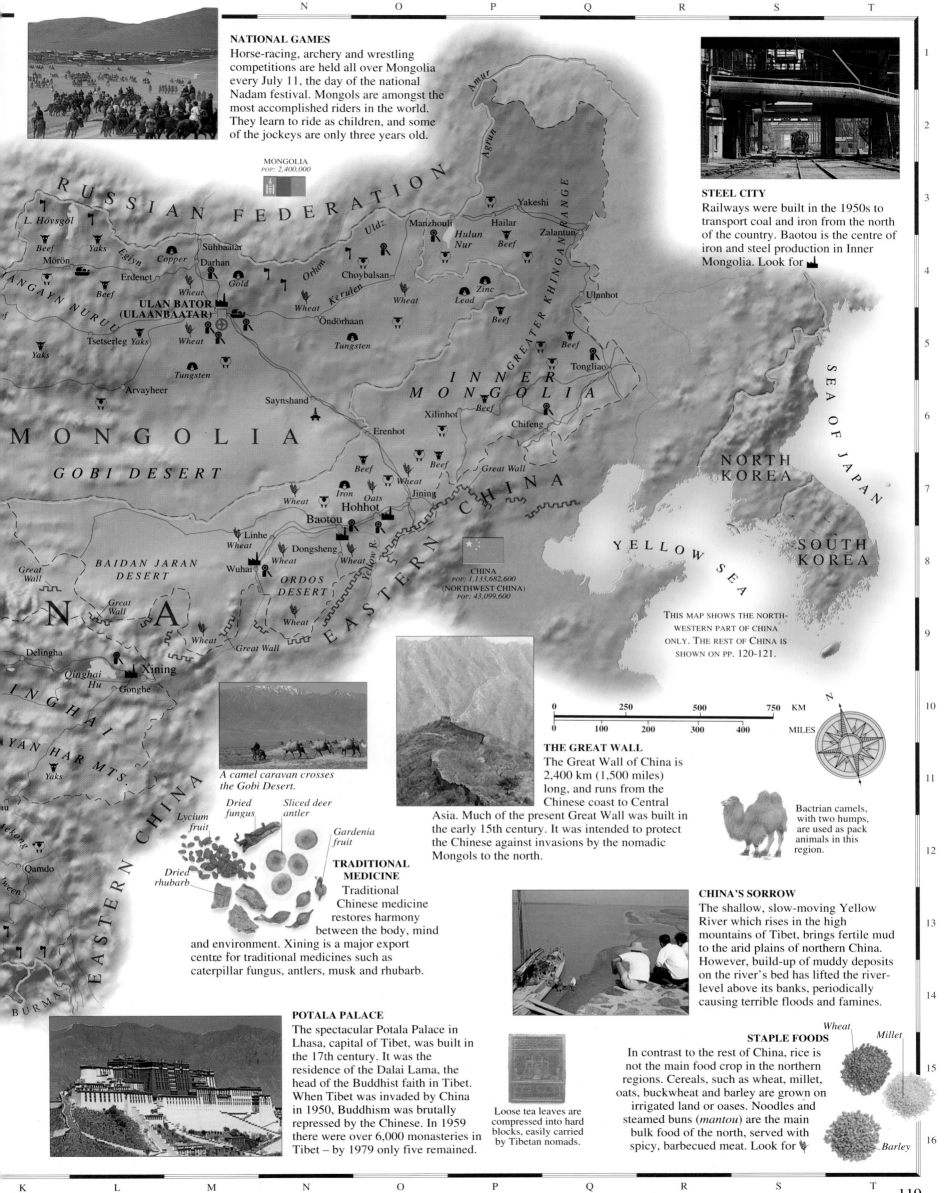

NATIONAL GAMES
Horse-racing, archery and wrestling competitions are held all over Mongolia every July 11, the day of the national Nadam festival. Mongols are amongst the most accomplished riders in the world. They learn to ride as children, and some of the jockeys are only three years old.

MONGOLIA
POP: 2,400,000

STEEL CITY
Railways were built in the 1950s to transport coal and iron from the north of the country. Baotou is the centre of iron and steel production in Inner Mongolia. Look for ⚒

CHINA
POP: 1,133,682,600
(NORTHWEST CHINA)
POP: 43,099,600

THIS MAP SHOWS THE NORTH-WESTERN PART OF CHINA ONLY. THE REST OF CHINA IS SHOWN ON PP. 120-121.

| 0 | 250 | 500 | 750 | KM |
| 0 | 100 | 200 | 300 | 400 | MILES |

A camel caravan crosses the Gobi Desert.

THE GREAT WALL
The Great Wall of China is 2,400 km (1,500 miles) long, and runs from the Chinese coast to Central Asia. Much of the present Great Wall was built in the early 15th century. It was intended to protect the Chinese against invasions by the nomadic Mongols to the north.

Bactrian camels, with two humps, are used as pack animals in this region.

Dried fungus   *Sliced deer antler*   *Lycium fruit*   *Gardenia fruit*   *Dried rhubarb*

TRADITIONAL MEDICINE
Traditional Chinese medicine restores harmony between the body, mind and environment. Xining is a major export centre for traditional medicines such as caterpillar fungus, antlers, musk and rhubarb.

CHINA'S SORROW
The shallow, slow-moving Yellow River which rises in the high mountains of Tibet, brings fertile mud to the arid plains of northern China. However, build-up of muddy deposits on the river's bed has lifted the river-level above its banks, periodically causing terrible floods and famines.

POTALA PALACE
The spectacular Potala Palace in Lhasa, capital of Tibet, was built in the 17th century. It was the residence of the Dalai Lama, the head of the Buddhist faith in Tibet. When Tibet was invaded by China in 1950, Buddhism was brutally repressed by the Chinese. In 1959 there were over 6,000 monasteries in Tibet – by 1979 only five remained.

Loose tea leaves are compressed into hard blocks, easily carried by Tibetan nomads.

STAPLE FOODS
In contrast to the rest of China, rice is not the main food crop in the northern regions. Cereals, such as wheat, millet, oats, buckwheat and barley are grown on irrigated land or oases. Noodles and steamed buns (*mantou*) are the main bulk food of the north, served with spicy, barbecued meat. Look for 🌾

Wheat   *Millet*   *Barley*

A B C D E F G H I J

CHINA AND KOREA

THE LANDSCAPE OF SOUTHEASTERN CHINA ranges from mountains and plateaux to wide river valleys and plains. One-fifth of all the people on Earth live in China – most of them in the eastern part of the country. For centuries, China was isolated from the rest of the world, ruled by powerful emperors and known to only a handful of traders. In the 19th century the European powers forced China to open its borders to trade, starting a period of rapid change. In 1949, after a long struggle between nationalists and communists, the People's Republic of China was established as a communist state. Taiwan became a separate country. The communist government has encouraged foreign investment, technological innovation and private enterprise, although calls for democracy have been suppressed. Korea has been dominated by its powerful Chinese and Japanese neighbours for many years. After World War II, Korea was divided in two. North Korea became one of the most isolated and repressive communist regimes in the world. South Korea transformed itself into a highly industrial economy.

PEKING OPERA
Traditional Chinese opera dates back 2,000 years and combines many different elements – songs, dance, mime and acrobatics. The stories are based on folktales. Make-up shows the characters' personalities – kind, loyal or wicked, for example.

Sesame oil

Dried mushroom

FOOD
Chinese food varies widely from region to region. Its most famous cuisine comes from the area around Canton, and uses a huge range of ingredients – it is said that the people from this region will "eat everything with wings except aeroplanes and everything with legs except the table". Chinese food has become popular all over the world.

Soy sauce
Dried prawn

INDUSTRY
Although China has extensive reserves of coal, iron ore and oil, its heavy industry is state-run, old-fashioned and inefficient. Seventy per cent of China's energy is provided by coal. About half China's coal comes from large, well-equipped mines; the rest is extracted from small local pits. These mines are notorious for their high accident rates. Look for 🪏

The Great Wild Goose pagoda at Xi'an was built in the 7th century AD. It formed part of a Buddhist monastery.

THIS MAP SHOWS THE SOUTH-EASTERN PART OF CHINA ONLY. THE REST OF CHINA IS SHOWN ON PP. 118-119.

KEYBOX

Hydro-electric power: China's rivers have great potential; dams lakes and canals provide flood control and irrigation as well as electricity. Look for ⬌

Economic zones: The Chinese government has set up special industrial zones, encouraging foreign investment through tax incentives. Look for 🏭

Refugees: Vietnamese refugees come to Hong Kong by boat. In 1991, there were over 61,000 Vietnamese in Hong Kong's detention camps. Look for ⌂

Borders: The most militarized border in the world divides Korea into communist North and democratic South. Look for ✈

🌾	Cereals	👷	Mining
🌿	Rice	🪏	Coal
🌱	Tea	🛢	Oil
🏴	Timber	🏭	Industrial centre
🐟	Fishing	🛳	Shipbuilding

BABY BOOM
China's population is now over a billion, stretching resources such as land, food and education to the limit. Couples with only one child receive various benefits. If a second child is born, these benefits are withdrawn.

Tea, China's national drink, is grown on terraced hillsides in the south of the country.

AGRICULTURE
China feeds its vast population from only seven per cent of the world's farm-land. In the fertile southern part of the country, the fields can yield three harvests every year – two crops of rice and a third crop of vegetables or cereals. Look for 🌿

RACIAL MINORITIES
This woman comes from the Hani people, one of the many different ethnic minorities who live in southwest China. Most minority groups live in remote, sparsely-inhabited regions. Many still follow traditional lifestyles based on herding, hunting, or growing food for their families.

MONGOLIA

WEST

WESTERN CHINA

Yumen

Great Wall

Yinch

Wuwei

NINGXIA H AUTONOMO REGION

Lanzho

Wheat

Wheat

Yalong

C

Dadu He

H

Jinsha

Mianyang

Litang

Chengdu

Maize

Leshan

Chongqing

Zigong

Xichang

Zu

Panzhihua

Aluminium

Copper

Guiyang

Dongchuan

Dali

Salween

Kunming

Maize

Hongshui He

BURMA

Gejiu

Maize

Tin

Mekong

Maize

Pingxiang

LAOS

VIETNAM

N

0	100	200	300	400	500	600	KM

0	100	200	300		MILES

A B C D E F G H I J

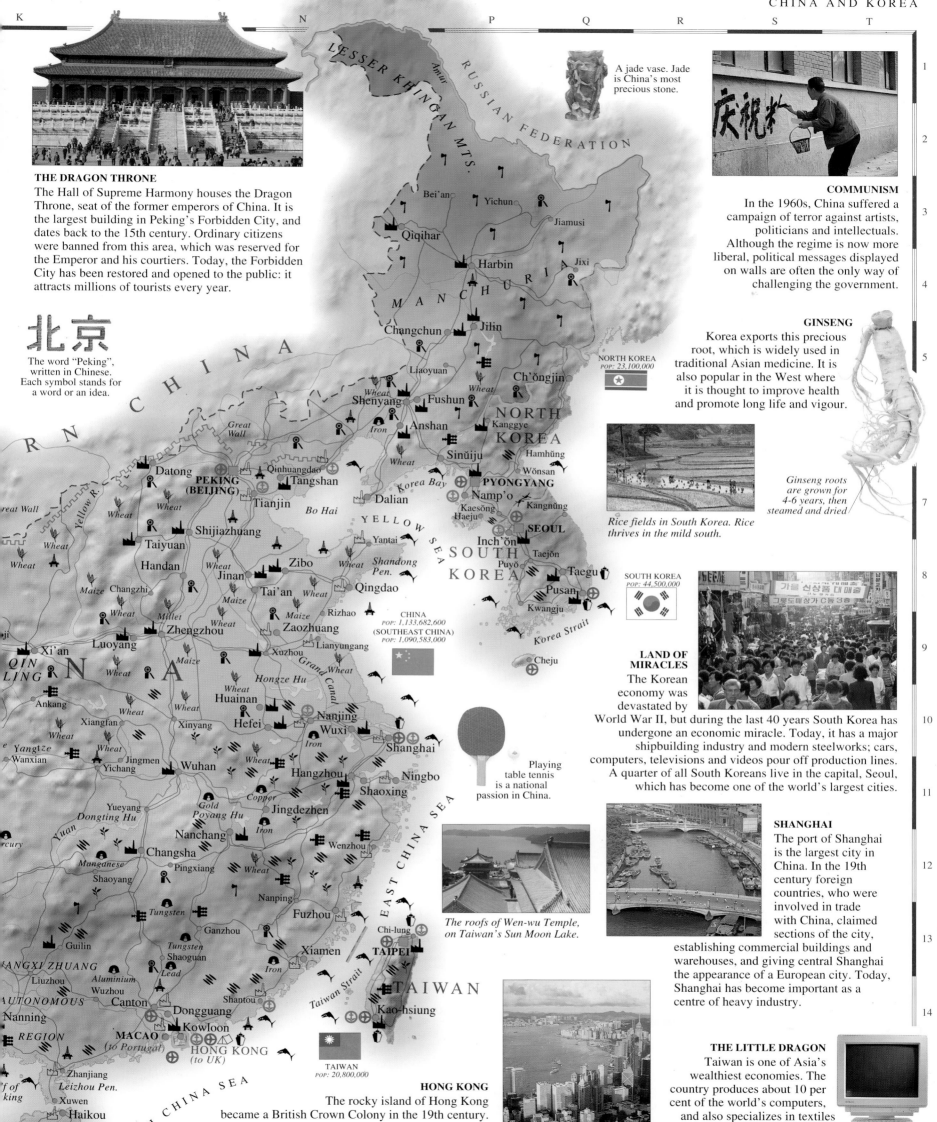

THE DRAGON THRONE
The Hall of Supreme Harmony houses the Dragon Throne, seat of the former emperors of China. It is the largest building in Peking's Forbidden City, and dates back to the 15th century. Ordinary citizens were banned from this area, which was reserved for the Emperor and his courtiers. Today, the Forbidden City has been restored and opened to the public: it attracts millions of tourists every year.

北京
The word "Peking", written in Chinese. Each symbol stands for a word or an idea.

A jade vase. Jade is China's most precious stone.

COMMUNISM
In the 1960s, China suffered a campaign of terror against artists, politicians and intellectuals. Although the regime is now more liberal, political messages displayed on walls are often the only way of challenging the government.

GINSENG
Korea exports this precious root, which is widely used in traditional Asian medicine. It is also popular in the West where it is thought to improve health and promote long life and vigour.

Ginseng roots are grown for 4-6 years, then steamed and dried

Rice fields in South Korea. Rice thrives in the mild south.

LAND OF MIRACLES
The Korean economy was devastated by World War II, but during the last 40 years South Korea has undergone an economic miracle. Today, it has a major shipbuilding industry and modern steelworks; cars, computers, televisions and videos pour off production lines. A quarter of all South Koreans live in the capital, Seoul, which has become one of the world's largest cities.

Playing table tennis is a national passion in China.

The roofs of Wen-wu Temple, on Taiwan's Sun Moon Lake.

SHANGHAI
The port of Shanghai is the largest city in China. In the 19th century foreign countries, who were involved in trade with China, claimed sections of the city, establishing commercial buildings and warehouses, and giving central Shanghai the appearance of a European city. Today, Shanghai has become important as a centre of heavy industry.

THE LITTLE DRAGON
Taiwan is one of Asia's wealthiest economies. The country produces about 10 per cent of the world's computers, and also specializes in textiles and shoe-manufacturing. The Taiwanese refer to their country as the Republic of China, but China does not recognize the country under this name.

HONG KONG
The rocky island of Hong Kong became a British Crown Colony in the 19th century. In 1997 it will be returned to China, when it will become a "special administrative region". Hong Kong has the busiest container port in the world, and is a centre of trade, finance, manufacturing and tourism.

NORTH KOREA
POP: 23,100,000

SOUTH KOREA
POP: 44,500,000

CHINA
POP: 1,133,682,600
(SOUTHEAST CHINA)
POP: 1,090,583,000

TAIWAN
POP: 20,800,000

Map labels:
RUSSIAN FEDERATION
LESSER KHINGAN MTS.
Amur
Bei'an
Yichun
Jiamusi
Qiqihar
Harbin
Jixi
MANCHURIA
Changchun
Jilin
Liaoyuan
Ch'ŏngjin
NORTH KOREA
Shenyang
Fushun
Wheat
Wheat
Anshan
Kanggye
Iron
Sinŭiju
Hamhŭng
Wŏnsan
NORTHERN CHINA
Great Wall
Datong
Qinhuangdao
Tangshan
PEKING (BEIJING)
Tianjin
Dalian
Korea Bay
PYONGYANG
Namp'o
Kangnŭng
Great Wall
Yellow R.
Wheat
Shijiazhuang
Bo Hai
Kaesŏng
Haeju
SEOUL
Inch'ŏn
Taiyuan
Yantai
YELLOW SEA
Puyŏ
Taejŏn
Handan
Wheat
Jinan
Zibo
Wheat
Shandong Pen.
SOUTH KOREA
Taegu
Maize
Changzhi
Tai'an
Wheat
Qingdao
Pusan
Millet
Wheat
Rizhao
Kwangju
Korea Strait
Zhengzhou
Zaozhuang
CHINA
Xi'an
Luoyang
Maize
Xuzhou
Lianyungang
Cheju
QIN LING
Wheat
Hongze Hu
Grand Canal
Wheat
Ankang
Wheat
Huainan
Wheat
Xiangfan
Xinyang
Hefei
Nanjing
Wuxi
Iron
Yangtze
Wanxian
Jingmen
Yichang
Wuhan
Wheat
Shanghai
Hangzhou
Ningbo
Yueyang
Gold
Copper
Shaoxing
Dongting Hu
Poyang Hu
Jingdezhen
Yuan
Nanchang
Iron
Mercury
Changsha
Wenzhou
Manganese
Pingxiang
Wheat
Shaoyang
Nanping
Tungsten
Guilin
Fuzhou
Ganzhou
Chi-lung
GUANGXI ZHUANG
Tungsten
Shaoguan
TAIPEI
Liuzhou
Aluminium
Lead
Iron
Xiamen
AUTONOMOUS
Wuzhou
TAIWAN
Nanning
Canton
Shantou
Taiwan Strait
REGION
Dongguang
MACAO (to Portugal)
Kowloon
EAST CHINA SEA
Kao-hsiung
Zhanjiang
HONG KONG (to UK)
Leizhou Pen.
Gulf of Tonking
Xuwen
Haikou
Hainan
SOUTH CHINA SEA
Sanya

JAPAN

THE LAND OF THE RISING SUN, as Japan is sometimes called, was ruled for centuries by powerful warlords called *shōguns*, who discouraged any contact with the outside world. When traders from America and Europe arrived, Japan's isolation suddenly ended, the *shōgun* was overthrown and an emperor ruled the country. Over the next century, Japan transformed itself into one of the world's richest nations, a change in fortune all the more remarkable considering the country's geography. Japan consists of four main islands and 4,000 smaller islands. The majority of its 123 million people live closely packed together around the coast, since two-thirds of the land is mountainous and thickly forested. Japan has few natural resources and has to import most of its fuel and raw materials. The Japanese have concentrated on improving and adapting technology imported from abroad. Today, Japanese companies are world leaders in many areas of research and development, a success partly due to their management techniques which ensure a well paid and loyal workforce.

The Kurile Islands are administered by the Russian Federation, but claimed by Japan.

The Japanese are skilled at *bonsai* – the art of producing miniature trees and shrubs.

The Hidaka Mountains on the large island of Hokkaidō.

FOOD
The Japanese eat a lot of fish because there is not enough farmland to keep cattle for meat or dairy produce.

Lacquer dish
Rice
Seaweed
Marinated raw fish

SHIPBUILDING
A large number of the ships sailing the world today were made in Japan. Countries such as South Korea can now build ships more cheaply, however, and Japan's industry is declining. To remain competitive, Japanese shipbuilders are building specialized ships – such as cruise liners, and developing new products like oil-drilling platforms. Look for

JAPAN
POP: 125,000,000

RICE CULTIVATION
Rice is Japan's main food. Although only about 11 per cent of the land is suitable for farming, Japan produces enough rice for its own needs. The crop is intensively cultivated on small plots of land using fertilizers and sophisticated machinery, like this rice planter. The warm, wet summers in southern Japan are ideal for growing rice. Look for

FISHING
Fish is a very popular food in Japan. Huge quantities are caught each year by the country's fishing fleet – the world's largest. One million tonnes of fish and shellfish are also bred every year in fish farms. These tuna are on sale in Tokyo's fish market. Look for

KABUKI THEATRE
There are two forms of traditional Japanese theatre: Noh and Kabuki. Noh is very old: the plays are based on myths of the gods and contain music and symbolic dancing. Kabuki theatres have plays based on stories of great heroes of the past. This photo shows a scene from a Kabuki play.

A miniature television, produced in Japan.

TRADITIONAL DRESS
Until the 19th century Japanese traditional dress varied greatly between the social classes. In the royal courts long-sleeved robes called *kimonos* were worn. Made of silk, these were wound round the body and tied with a sash. *Kimonos* are still worn on special occasions.

Silk kimono

Iturup

Kurile Islands

Yekaterina Strait
Shikotan
Kunashir
Habomai Is.

SEA OF OKHOTSK

Nemuro
Kushiro
Kitami
Abashiri
Asahikawa
Obihiro

ISHIKARI MTS.
HIDAKA MTS.

Hokkaidō

Sapporo
Ishikari
Tomakomai
Otaru
Ishikari Bay
Uchiura Bay
Hakodate
Tsugaru Strait
Fukushima
Seikan Tunnel
Okushiri-tō

La Pérouse Strait
Rebun-tō
Reshiri-tō
Wakkanai

Aomori
Hachinohe
Akita
Morioka
Hakodate

OU MTS.

Sendai
Yamagata
Kōriyama
Fukushima
Iwaki
Hitachi
Mito
Utsunomiya
Maebashi

Honshū

Niigata
Nagano
Sado
Toyama
Toyama Bay

SEA OF JAPAN

JAPAN'S CAPITAL CITY

During the 500 years of its existence, Tokyo has survived fire, flood, earthquakes and destruction by war. Each disaster has required massive rebuilding. Earthquake-resistant materials and construction techniques, which enable a building to sway rather than fall, have allowed new skyscrapers to replace older buildings. But the danger of earthquakes remains, and there are plans to move the capital to a safer site further north.

VEHICLE INDUSTRY

Japanese vehicle manufacturers became world leaders in the 1980s thanks to their stylish designs, new technology and efficient production methods. Today, motor vehicles are the country's biggest export. Japanese vehicle manufacturers have also opened a number of factories overseas – in Europe, the USA and elsewhere. Countries in areas like eastern Europe can supply cheaper labour than in Japan. Look for 🏍

Japanese motorbike

RELIGION

There are two main religions in Japan – Buddhism and Shinto. People often follow both: it is common to be married with Shinto rituals, but buried with Buddhist. There are numerous Buddhist and Shinto shrines and temples in Japan. They were usually built of wood – and therefore vulnerable to fire – and temples like Ginkakuji in Kyōto have been rebuilt several times.

Mount Fuji is Japan's sacred mountain.

KEYBOX

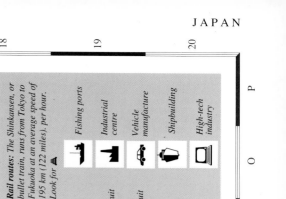

Financial centre: Japan is a leading member of the world financial community. Its stock exchange ranks second in the world. Look for 🏦

Skiing: The Japanese Alps in Honshū are excellent for skiing. In 1998, the Winter Olympics will be held near Nagano. Look for ⛷

Rail routes: The Shinkansen, or bullet train, runs from Tokyo to Fukuoka at an average speed of 195 km (122 miles), per hour. Look for 🚄

Rice	Mixed fruit	Citrus fruit	Tea	Tobacco
Fishing ports	Industrial centre	Vehicle manufacture	Shipbuilding	High-tech industry

SITE OF TOKYO

Built around Tokyo Bay, and hemmed in by mountains, Tokyo is unable to spread further inland or along the coast. The sprawling built-up region around Tokyo and Yokohama is the world's largest urban area, and is sometimes called a megalopolis. It has a population of over 27 million people, and accounts for 25 per cent of Japan's industrial production.

Rice and other crops grown in fertile volcanic soils and ideal climate

Industrial and urban areas

Tokyo Bay

Intensively cultivated lowlands due to shortage of farmland

To relieve overcrowding, developers build upwards, and into the sea on reclaimed land

Tokyo City

Mt. Fuji

SAGAMI SEA

Yokohama

COMMUTING

Most Japanese people live in the cities, but few people can afford to live in the city centres, so most people have to commute to work. Trains are fast and efficient, but so overcrowded that special guards are employed to push commuters into the carriages.

COMPUTERS

The Japanese excel at producing miniature electronic goods, such as computers and televisions. They have set such high standards that few countries can match them. A silicon "chip" able to hold 1,000 pages of newsprint in its memory is being developed.

A bottle of rice wine, or sake, Japan's national drink.

The beautiful rocky coast of the Oki Islands, which lie in the Sea of Japan.

Map labels:
OCEAN
PACIFIC
JAPAN
SEA OF JAPAN
EAST CHINA SEA
AMAKUSA SEA

Izu Is.
Sagami Sea
Kawasaki
Yokohama
Yokosuka
Mt. Fuji
Shizuoka
Hamamatsu
Okazaki
Nagoya
Gifu
L. Biwa
Mikasa Bay
Kyōto
Ōsaka
Kōbe
Wakayama
Shingū
Nakamura
Kōchi
Tokushima
Takamatsu
Okayama
Kurashiki
Tottori
Matsue
Dōzen
Dōgo
Oki Is.
CHUGOKU MTS.
Shikoku
Inland Sea
Hiroshima
Matsuyama
Uwajima
Yamaguchi
Shimonoseki
Hagi
Hamada
Kitakyūshū
Fukuoka
Saga
Tsushima
Iki
Korea Strait
Saseho
Nagasaki
Gotō Is.
Amakusa Is.
Kumamoto
Ōita
Beppu
Nobeoka
Miyazaki
Kagoshima
Ōsumi Strait
Tanega-shima
Yaku-shima
Ōsumi Is.
Kyūshū
Tokara Is.
Amami Is.
Amami-ōshima
Tokuno-shima
Okinoerabu-jima
Okinawa
Naha
Okinawa Is.
Ryukyu Is.

0 50 100 150 200 250 KM
0 50 100 150 MILES

N

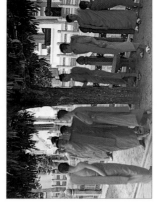

MAINLAND SOUTHEAST ASIA

MUCH OF THIS REGION is mountainous and covered with forest. Most of the people live in the great river valleys, plateaux or fertile plains. Farming is the main occupation, with rice the principal crop. Of the seven countries, only Thailand was not a British or French colony. Thais are deeply devoted to their royal family and Buddhist faith. The Federation of Malaysia includes 11 states on the mainland, joined in 1963 by Sabah and Sarawak in Borneo. This union of east and west has produced one of the world's most successful developing countries. Singapore, at first part of Malaysia, became a republic in 1965. The island controls the busy shipping routes between the Indian and Pacific Oceans. Cambodia, Laos and Vietnam have all suffered from many years of warfare. Cambodia's future is still uncertain, but the other two countries show signs of economic recovery. Burma has become increasingly isolated from the world by its repressive government.

RUBIES
Several types of precious stone are mined in the northeast of Burma. The glowing red rubies from this region are considered the finest in the world. Many people in the East believe that wearing a ruby protects you from harm. Today Burma has a virtual monopoly over the ruby trade. Look for

Ruby   Calcite

FISHING
Fish is one of the main foods in this area. Thailand has a thriving fish canning industry. Fish farming in the inland lake of Tônlé Sap, Cambodia, is also successful. Here, in Burma, fish are caught from small huts built over the water. Look for

BUDDHISM
Except for Malaysia, the main religion in this region is Buddhism. In Thailand and Burma, where almost all the people are Buddhists, every young man puts on the saffron robe, shaves his head and enters a monastery for several months.

TIMBER
Thailand was once a major producer of teak, but so much of the country's forests have been cut down that commercial logging was banned in 1989 – until forests recover. Burma is now the world's principal teak exporter. Here, huge logs float down the Irrawaddy River. Look for

Lacquer tray

Making lacquer ware is a traditional craft in Thailand.

Boats on the Irrawaddy, the great river of Burma.

BURMA (MYANMAR)
POP: 44,600,000

Poppy seeds

OPIUM
For the poor hill tribes of the "Golden Triangle" – the remote area where Burma, Laos and Thailand meet – growing opium poppies is one of the few sources of income. Useful painkillers can be made from the poppies, but so too are dangerous drugs, such as heroin and opium. The government is encouraging people in this area to grow other crops, such as flowers and tobacco.

Dried opium poppy

VIETNAM
Rice is the principal crop in this country. As Vietnam is so mountainous, most people live in the two main river deltas. Two-thirds of the farmed land is devoted to growing rice. The wet-field, or *paddy*, is planted by women. Look for

LAOS
POP: 4,600,000

Durian fruit is grown throughout the region.

Map labels:

Gulf of Tongking

Thai Nguyen, Hong Gai, Lang Son, Nam Dinh, HANOI, Hai Phong, Thanh Hoa, Vinh
Ha Giang, L. Thac Ba, L. Ba, Viet Tri, Tin, Tungsten, Iron, Chromium
Red R., Black R., Son La, Xam Nua, Xiangkhoang, Muang Pakxan
Phôngsali, Nam Ou, Louang Namtha, Louang Phrabang, VIENTIANE (VIANGCHAN), Muang Loeï
Mekong, Muang Xaignabouri, Nam Ngum Dam, Uttaradit
Myitkyina, Bhamo, Katha, Lashio, Ban Houayxay, Chiang Rai, Muang Nan, Sirikit Res.
Rubies, KUMON RANGE, Zinc, Lead, Mandalay, Amarapura, Myingyan, Chiang Mai, Iron, Muang Lampang, Tungsten, Manganese
Shwebo, Sagaing, Monywa, Pagan, Chauk, Pakokku, Pyinmana, Toungoo, Tin, Bhumiphol Res.
Chindwin, Irrawaddy, L. Inle, Taunggyi, Sittang
CHINA, BURMA, LAOS, VIETNAM, INDIA, CHIN HILLS
Minbu, Thayetmyo, Prome, Pegu, Henzada, Sandoway
Sittwe, Ramree I., Bay of Bengal, BANGLADESH
Salween, Mekong

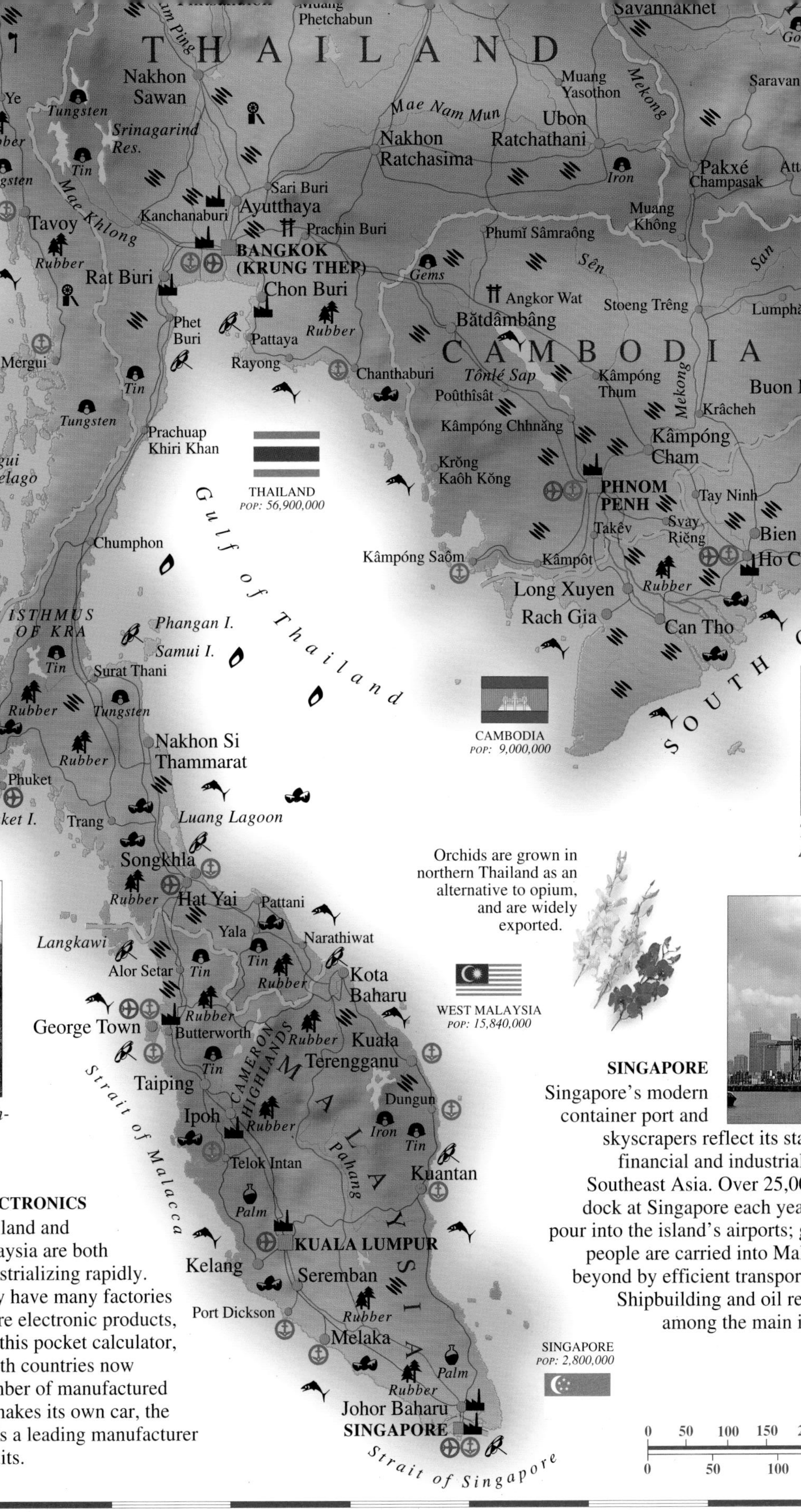

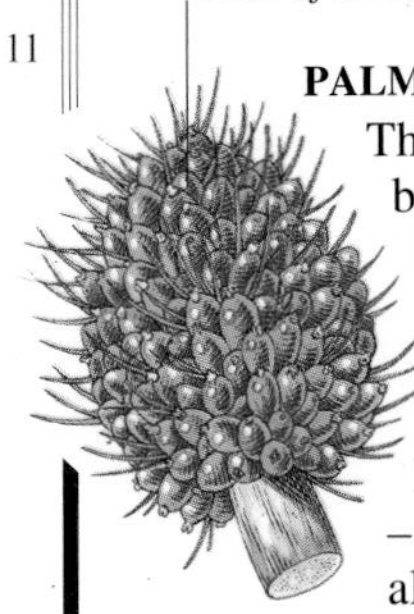

VIETNAM
POP: 70,900,000

The ancient temple (wat) of Angkor in Cambodia.

SINGAPORE

Singapore's modern container port and skyscrapers reflect its status as the financial and industrial centre of Southeast Asia. Over 25,000 vessels dock at Singapore each year; tourists pour into the island's airports; goods and people are carried into Malaysia and beyond by efficient transport systems. Shipbuilding and oil refining are among the main industries.

SINGAPORE
POP: 2,800,000

Orchids are grown in northern Thailand as an alternative to opium, and are widely exported.

CAMBODIA
POP: 9,000,000

WEST MALAYSIA
POP: 15,840,000

THAILAND
POP: 56,900,000

KM / MILES
400 / 250
350 / 200
300 / 150
250 / 100
200 / 50
150
100
50

N

The Cameron Highlands, Malaysia.

ELECTRONICS

Thailand and Malaysia are both industrializing rapidly. They have many factories where electronic products, like this pocket calculator, are assembled. Both countries now export a large number of manufactured goods. Malaysia makes its own car, the Proton; Thailand is a leading manufacturer of integrated circuits.

PALM OIL

Fruit of the oil palm

The oil palm comes from West Africa, but has been successfully introduced into Malaysia and Indonesia. Palm oil and palm kernel oil, which are used in soap and as edible oils, are made from the fruit. Malaysia started production to lessen its dependence on the rubber crop – increasingly replaced by synthetic alternatives. Look for 🖐

ELEPHANTS

Compared to a tractor, a working elephant needs little fuel, does not rust and needs no spare parts. A tractor lasts for about six years, an elephant for 30, and it is less harmful to the environment. Elephants are used to move timber and to take tourists for rides in the forest.

Siamese cats originally came from Thailand – once called Siam.

Pineapple ring

PINEAPPLES

Thailand has become the world's biggest exporter of canned pineapple, 50 per cent of the product going to the USA. The pineapples are processed in factories where the skin is removed, the stem cut out and the fruit sliced into rings or chunks. Some of the largest factories in Thailand are owned by Japanese companies.

Pineapple fruit

FLOATING MARKET

Bangkok, Thailand's capital, is a noisy, hectic city, full of Buddhist temples – *wats* – and congested with traffic. The city was built on an island in the river, and the canals – or *klongs* – were once the city's streets. The few canals that remain are still used by flat boats – called *sampans* – to transport fresh fruit and vegetables from the country-side to the floating markets where the *sampans* act as shops.

KEYBOX

Mining: *Malaysia is the world's biggest producer of tin, but its resources are becoming depleted. Look for* ⛏

Dam: *A series of dams is planned on the Mekong to provide HEP and irrigation. All six countries involved must first reach agreement. Look for* 🏛

Tourism: *Over 3 million tourists visit Thailand each year, and tourism has become a major source of foreign currency. Look for* 🦌

Fishing	
Coal	
Gas	
Industrial centre	
Archaeological site	
Rice	
Coconuts	
Vegetable oil	
Timber	
Forest products	

125

MARITIME SOUTHEAST ASIA

SCATTERED between the Indian and Pacific Oceans lies a huge crescent of mountainous tropical islands – the East Indies. The largest country in this region is Indonesia, which was ruled by the Dutch for nearly 350 years. Over half its 13,677 islands are still uninhabited. The island of Borneo is shared between Indonesia, the Malaysian enclaves of Sabah and Sarawak, and the Sultanate of Brunei. Indonesia's national motto, "Unity in diversity", ideally suits a country made up of 362 different peoples speaking over 250 dialects and languages. Indonesia's seizure of East Timor in 1975 has resulted in a long and bloody resistance by the islanders. Java, the main island, is so crowded that thousands of people have been moved to less populated islands. The Philippines, ruled for three centuries by Spain, then for 50 years by the USA, consists of over 7,000 islands. It is the only mainly Christian country in Asia. Much of the region is covered by forests, which contain some of the finest timber in the world.

COCONUTS

Indonesia and the Philippines are the world's major coconut growers. Every part of the tree has its uses, even the leaves. The kernel is dried to make copra from which a valuable oil is obtained. Look for 🥥

Kernel

STILT VILLAGES

Many of the villages in this region are built over water. The houses are made of local materials, like wood and bamboo, and built on stilts to protect them from vermin and flooding. For houses built on land, raised floors also provide shelter for the owner's animals which live underneath.

Helicopter

AIRCRAFT INDUSTRY
Indonesia has developed a thriving aircraft industry. About 12,000 workers assemble helicopters and aircraft at Bandung in Java. The factories are jointly owned by five international aircraft manufacturers. The first solely Indonesian-designed aircraft will soon be completed.

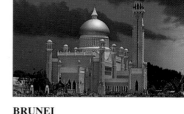

BRUNEI
The Sultanate of Brunei became rich when oil was discovered in 1929. The golden-domed mosque, built with the country's new-found wealth, towers above the capital, Bandar Seri Begawan. The small, predominantly Muslim, population pays no taxes, and enjoys free education and health care.

MALAYSIA
POP: 19,200,000
(EAST MALAYSIA: SABAH AND SARAWAK)
POP: 3,360,000

RELIGION
Although about 90 per cent of Indonesians are Muslim, many of their religious ceremonies contain elements of other religions – like Hinduism and Buddhism – which blend with local traditions and beliefs. Recently, Islam has become more dominant. More girls now wear the Islamic headdress, like these pupils at a school in Sumatra.

Borobudur, the great 8th-century Buddhist temple on Java.

BRUNEI
POP: 200,000

BANDAR SERI BEGAWAN

Dense rainforest on Sumatra is home to elephants and tigers.

KEYBOX

Vegetable oil: Indonesia is now one of the world's major producers of palm oil. It has many uses, from hydraulic brake fluids to cooking oil. Look for 🧴

Research centre: Near Manila in the Philippines the Rice Research Institute has developed many of the world's modern high-yield types of rice. Look for ⬡

Pirates: Pirate attacks on vessels in the area are increasing, especially at night and in the busy shipping lanes of the Strait of Singapore. Look for ☠

〰 Rice		🐬 Fishing	
🥥 Coconuts		⬤ Mining	
🪓 Timber		⛏ Oil	
🌲 Forest products		🏭 Industrial centre	

JAKARTA

Situated on the island of Java, Indonesia's capital Jakarta has the largest population of any city in Southeast Asia – and is still growing rapidly. It was once the centre of the region's Dutch trading empire and many typical Dutch buildings still stand in the old part of the city. At night, skyscrapers glitter above the city's modern centre.

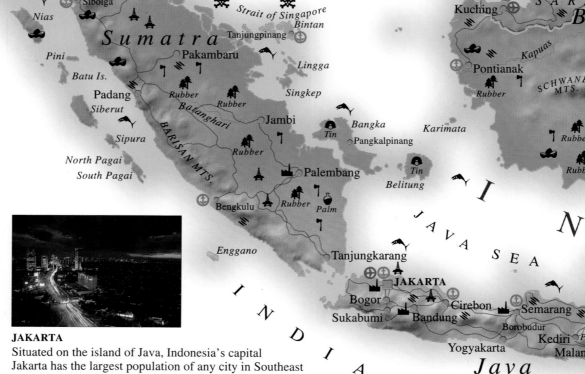

SOUTH CHINA SEA

Kota Kina

Miri
Kuala Be
BRUNE

MALAYSIA (EAST)

Sibu
Sarikei
S A R A W A K
Kuching

B o r n e o

MULLER MTS.
Kapuas
Pontianak
Rubber

SCHWANER MTS.
TAMABO RANGE
Rajang

Mendawai
Barito
Rub
Rubber

Rubber
Kualakapuas
Rubber
Banjarmasin

Banda Aceh

Rubber
Belawan
Medan
Pematangsiantar

Simeulue
L.Toba
Palm
Sibolga
Nias
Pini

S u m a t r a

Strait of Singapore
Bintan
Tanjungpinang

Natuna
Natuna Is.
Anambas Is.

Pakambaru
Lingga
Singkep

Batu Is.
Padang
Siberut
Rubber
Rubber
Jambi
Bangka
Karimata
Sipura

BARISAN MTS.
Batanghari
Rubber
Tin
Pangkalpinang

North Pagai
South Pagai
Palembang
Belitung
Tin

Bengkulu
Rubber
Palm

Enggano
JAVA SEA
Bawean

Tanjungkarang
Tanjungkarang

I N D I A N

J A V A S E A

JAKARTA
Bogor
Sukabumi
Cirebon
Bandung
Semarang
Surabaya
Borobudur
Madura
Kange

Java
Kediri
Palm
Yogyakarta
Malang
Jember
Denpasa
Ba
Banyuw

O C E A N

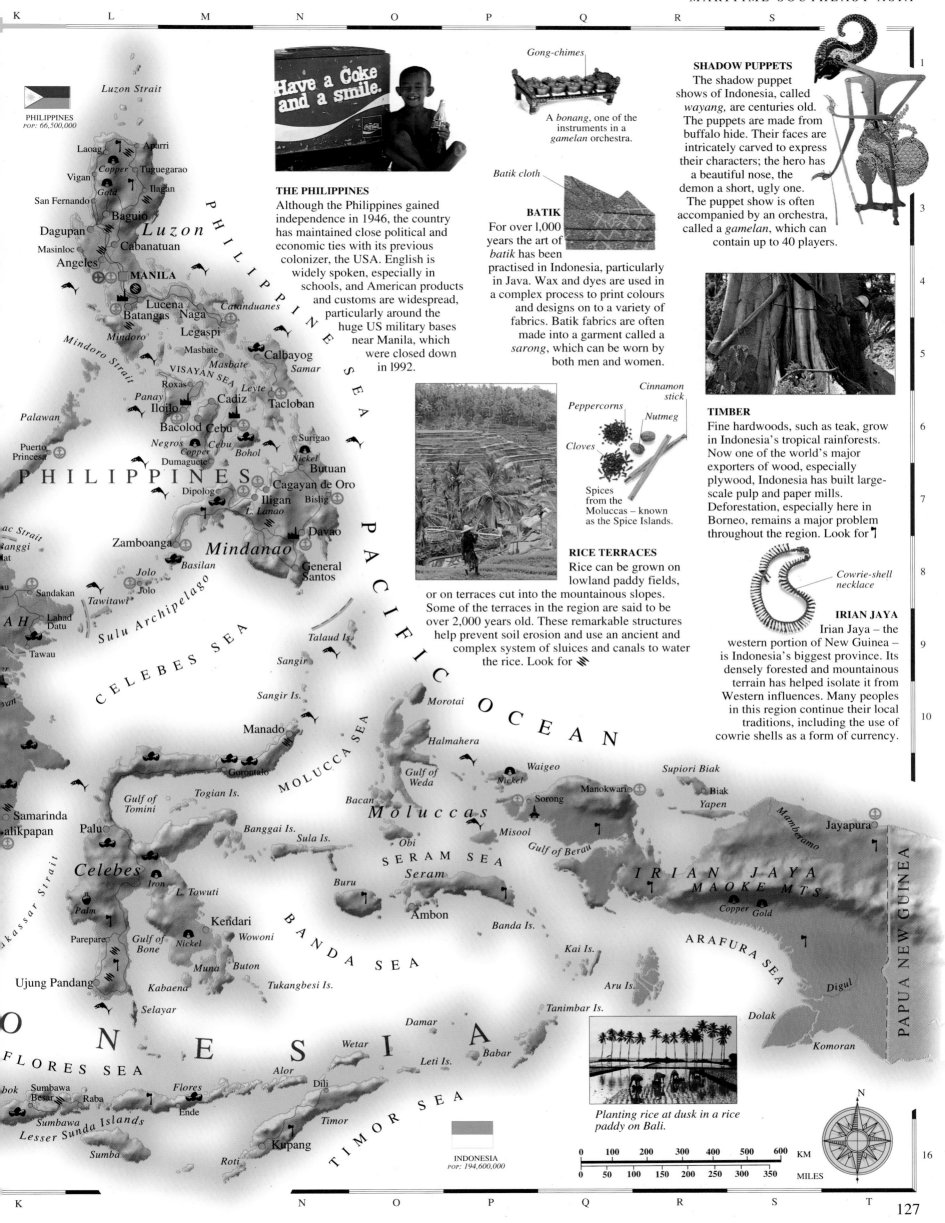

PHILIPPINES
POP: 66,500,000

Luzon Strait

Laoag Aparri
Vigan *Copper* Tuguegarao
San Fernando *Gold* Ilagan

Baguio

Dagupan *Luzon*
Masinloc Cabanatuan
Angeles
MANILA
Lucena Naga
Batangas *Catanduanes*
Mindoro Legaspi
Masbate
VISAYAN SEA *Masbate*
Roxas *Samar* Calbayog
Panay *Leyte*
Iloilo Cadiz Tacloban
Palawan
Bacolod Cebu
Puerto *Negros* *Cebu*
Princesa *Copper* *Bohol* Surigao
Dumaguete *Nickel*
Dipolog Butuan
Cagayan de Oro
Iligan Bislig
L. Lanao
Zamboanga Davao
Mindanao
Sandakan *Basilan* General
Lahad *Jolo* Santos
Datu *Jolo*
Tawau *Sulu Archipelago*

PHILIPPINE SEA

PHILIPPINES

PACIFIC OCEAN

CELEBES SEA

Talaud Is.
Sangir
Sangir Is.

Manado
Morotai
Gorontalo *Halmahera*
Gulf of
MOLUCCA SEA *Weda* Waigeo *Supiori Biak*
Nickel
Togian Is. *Bacan* Sorong Manokwari *Biak*
Gulf of Sorong *Yapen*
Palu *Tomini* *Moluccas*
Samarinda *Banggai Is.* *Misool*
alikpapan *Sula Is.* *Obi* Gulf of Berau
SERAM SEA *IRIAN JAYA*
Celebes *Seram* *MAOKE MTS.*
Iron *Buru* *Copper*
L. Towuti Ambon *Gold*
Palm *Banda Is.* *ARAFURA SEA*
Parepare Kendari *Wowoni* *Kai Is.*
Gulf of *Nickel* *Aru Is.* Digul
Bone *Muna* *Buton* *Tanimbar Is.* *Dolak*
Ujung Pandang *Kabaena* *Tukangbesi Is.*
Selayar *Komoran*

BANDA SEA

FLORES SEA *Damar*
Wetar *Babar*
lok Sumbawa *Flores* *Alor* *Leti Is.*
Besar Raba Dili
Sumbawa Ende Timor
Lesser Sunda Islands Kupang
Sumba *Roti* *TIMOR SEA*

INDONESIA
POP: 194,600,000

*Planting rice at dusk in a rice
paddy on Bali.*

PAPUA NEW GUINEA

Jayapura

THE PHILIPPINES
Although the Philippines gained independence in 1946, the country has maintained close political and economic ties with its previous colonizer, the USA. English is widely spoken, especially in schools, and American products and customs are widespread, particularly around the huge US military bases near Manila, which were closed down in 1992.

A bonang, one of the instruments in a gamelan orchestra.

Gong-chimes

Batik cloth

BATIK
For over 1,000 years the art of *batik* has been practised in Indonesia, particularly in Java. Wax and dyes are used in a complex process to print colours and designs on to a variety of fabrics. Batik fabrics are often made into a garment called a *sarong*, which can be worn by both men and women.

Cinnamon stick
Peppercorns *Nutmeg*
Cloves

Spices from the Moluccas – known as the Spice Islands.

RICE TERRACES
Rice can be grown on lowland paddy fields, or on terraces cut into the mountainous slopes. Some of the terraces in the region are said to be over 2,000 years old. These remarkable structures help prevent soil erosion and use an ancient and complex system of sluices and canals to water the rice. Look for

SHADOW PUPPETS
The shadow puppet shows of Indonesia, called *wayang*, are centuries old. The puppets are made from buffalo hide. Their faces are intricately carved to express their characters; the hero has a beautiful nose, the demon a short, ugly one. The puppet show is often accompanied by an orchestra, called a *gamelan*, which can contain up to 40 players.

TIMBER
Fine hardwoods, such as teak, grow in Indonesia's tropical rainforests. Now one of the world's major exporters of wood, especially plywood, Indonesia has built large-scale pulp and paper mills. Deforestation, especially here in Borneo, remains a major problem throughout the region. Look for

Cowrie-shell necklace

IRIAN JAYA
Irian Jaya – the western portion of New Guinea – is Indonesia's biggest province. Its densely forested and mountainous terrain has helped isolate it from Western influences. Many peoples in this region continue their local traditions, including the use of cowrie shells as a form of currency.

| 0 | 100 | 200 | 300 | 400 | 500 | 600 | KM |
| 0 | 50 | 100 | 150 | 200 | 250 | 300 | 350 | MILES |

THE PACIFIC OCEAN

THE PACIFIC IS THE LARGEST and deepest of the world's oceans. It covers a greater area of the Earth's surface than all the land areas combined. At its deepest point – 11,033 m (36,197 ft) down in the Mariana Trench – it is deep enough to cover Mount Everest. More than half the world's population lives around the shores of the Pacific. The ocean's northern and western edges, known as the outer Pacific, are fringed with chains of islands, such as the Aleutians. The inner Pacific islands fall into three main groups: Melanesia, Micronesia and Polynesia. With the development of modern communications, trade and co-operation between countries surrounding the ocean – sometimes referred to as the "Pacific Rim" – is increasing. Countries such as Japan, Australia and New Zealand want the South Pacific made into a Nuclear-Free Zone, which would prevent all testing of nuclear weapons.

MICRONESIA
POP: 101,000

The Aleutians, a chain of volcanic islands in the Pacific.

NAURU
POP: 10,000

A coral atoll in French Polynesia.

PALAU
POP: 16,000

CONTAINER PORTS
Today, fruit, meat and many other goods are moved round the world in huge metal containers. Here, a ship waits to be unloaded at Kōbe, one of Japan's main container ports.

COCONUTS
The coconut palm is called "tree of life" by Pacific Islanders because it provides so many of their daily needs, such as food and building materials. Here the white "meat" of the coconut is dried to make copra, which is edible. Look for

FISHING
Pacific Islanders fish mainly for food, although any surplus catch may be sold. Many fish are caught in the North Pacific by commercial shipping fleets operating far from their home bases. The biggest catches are made by Japan, Korea, Taiwan and the USA. The main fish caught is tuna. Look for

Skipjack tuna

KEYBOX

Fishing: Since the first salmon farms were set up in 1982 around Chiloé Island, Chile, salmon farming has become a major industry. Look for			
Mining: The South Pacific island of Nauru has become prosperous through the export of phosphates, used to make fertilizers. Look for			
Pollution: Nuclear testing carried out by the USA and France has polluted certain islands in the South Pacific. Look for			

⚓	Sugar cane	🚢	Fishing ports
	Coconuts		Tourism
	Timber		Whales
	Shellfishing	|||	Military bases

FIJI
Fiji is a group of volcanic islands surrounded by coral reefs. Although one of the few South Pacific islands to develop tourism, Fiji's economy is still dominated by the sugar cane crop – shown here being harvested. Recently, a number of tax-free factories have been set up which export a variety of products overseas; clothing, in particular, has proved very successful. Look for

Tropical growth on an island in the Tonga group.

SOLOMON ISLANDS
POP: 400,000

ISLANDS
The Pacific islands are scattered over a huge area, far from any industrial centre and from each other. Some of the islands are high and volcanic, others low coral atolls. They are home to over five million people whose one great shared resource is the sea. A huge variety of fish and shellfish are caught from small boats and by diving. In general, the soil of the islands is poor.

VANUATU
POP: 155,000

FIJI
POP: 700,000

Map labels

ASIA
SEA OF OKHOTSK
KAMCHATKA
BERING SEA
Sakhalin
Kurile Islands
Kurile Trench
Sovetskaya
Vladivostok
SEA OF JAPAN
Kushiro
Hakodate
Japan Trench
Emperor Seamounts
Tianjin
Inch'ŏn
Sendai
Yokohama
Qingdao
Pusan
Kōbe
EAST CHINA SEA
Shanghai
Nagasaki
Ningbo
Nan'ao Taiwan
Hong Kong (to UK)
Kyushu-Palau Ridge
Manila
SOUTH CHINA SEA
SOUTH EAST ASIA
Koror
PALAU
CELEBES SEA
BANDA SEA
New Guinea
ARAFURA SEA
C. York
CORAL SEA
Great Barrier Reef
NEW CALEDONIA (to France)
Nouméa
Iron Nickel
Brisbane
AUSTRALIA
Sydney
Melbourne
TASMAN SEA
PACIFIC OCEAN
MIDWAY IS. (to USA)
Mid-Pacific Seamounts
WAKE I. (to USA)
NORTHERN MARIANAS IS. (to USA)
Mariana Trench
Enewetak
GUAM (to USA)
FEDERATED STATES OF MICRONESIA
Caroline Is.
MICRONESIA
Bikini
MARSHALL ISLANDS
PALIKIR (KOLONIA)
MAJURO
HOWLA (to US)
KIRIBATI
Tarawa
BAIRIKI
BAKE (to U.)
Phosphates
YAREN NAURU
Gilbert Is. Pho
MELANESIA
TUVALU
FONGAFALE
SOLOMON IS.
HONIARA
Guadalcanal
WALLIS & FUTUNA (to France)
VANUATU
VILA
CORAL SEA IS. (to Australia)
Phosphates
SUVA FIJI
NUKU 'ALOFA
Gold
NORFOLK I. (to Australia)
Lord Howe I. (to Australia)
Kermadec Is. (to N.Z.)
Lord Howe Rise
Cook Strait
NEW ZEALAND
Wellington
Chatham (to N.Z.)
Bounty Is. (to N.Z.)
Macquarie Ridge
Auckland Is. (to N.Z.)
Antipo (to
Campbell I. (to N.Z.)
MacQuarie I. (to Australia)

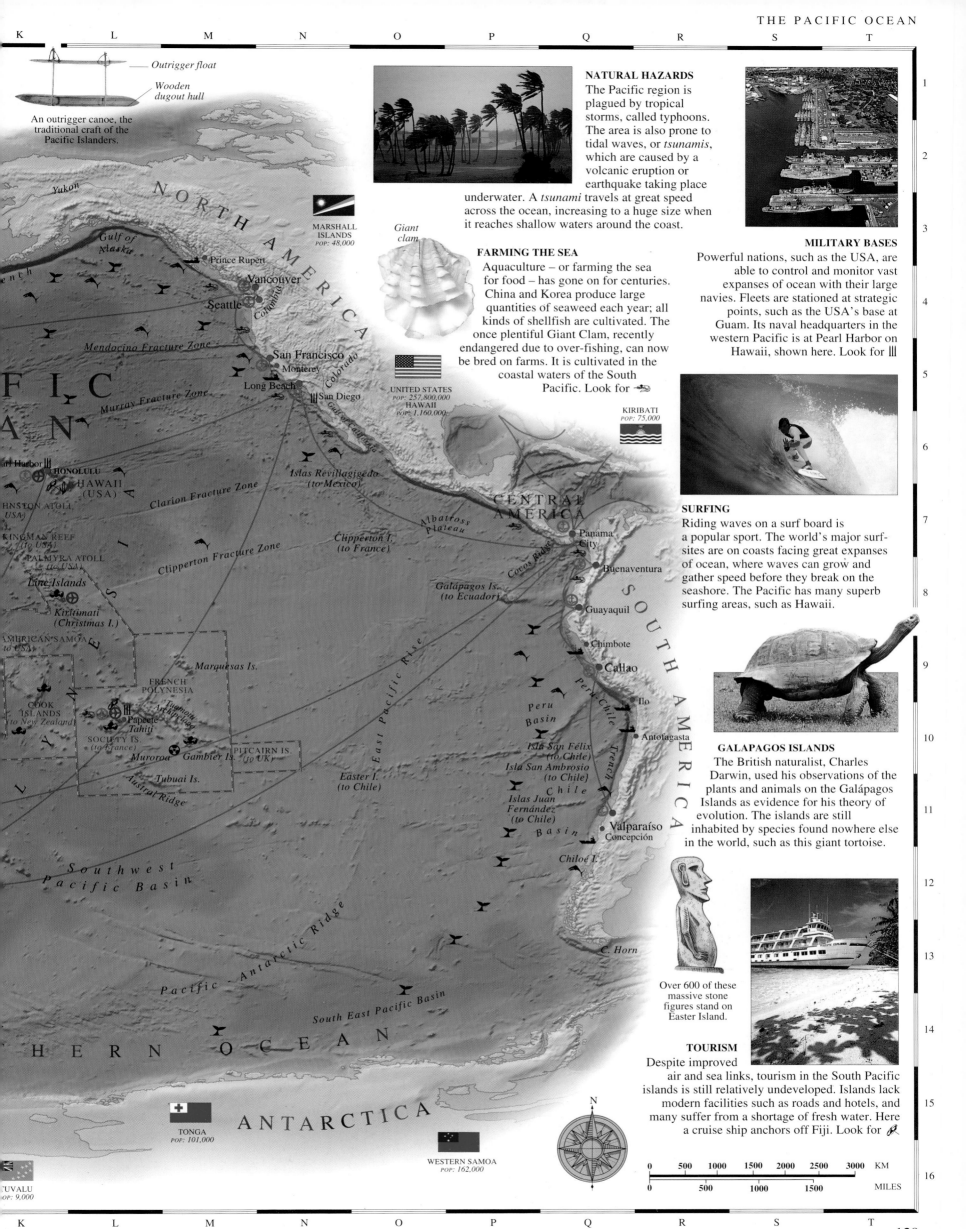

An outrigger canoe, the traditional craft of the Pacific Islanders.

—*Outrigger float*
—*Wooden dugout hull*

NATURAL HAZARDS
The Pacific region is plagued by tropical storms, called typhoons. The area is also prone to tidal waves, or *tsunamis*, which are caused by a volcanic eruption or earthquake taking place underwater. A *tsunami* travels at great speed across the ocean, increasing to a huge size when it reaches shallow waters around the coast.

MILITARY BASES
Powerful nations, such as the USA, are able to control and monitor vast expanses of ocean with their large navies. Fleets are stationed at strategic points, such as the USA's base at Guam. Its naval headquarters in the western Pacific is at Pearl Harbor on Hawaii, shown here. Look for ⫴

FARMING THE SEA
Aquaculture – or farming the sea for food – has gone on for centuries. China and Korea produce large quantities of seaweed each year; all kinds of shellfish are cultivated. The once plentiful Giant Clam, recently endangered due to over-fishing, can now be bred on farms. It is cultivated in the coastal waters of the South Pacific. Look for

SURFING
Riding waves on a surf board is a popular sport. The world's major surf-sites are on coasts facing great expanses of ocean, where waves can grow and gather speed before they break on the seashore. The Pacific has many superb surfing areas, such as Hawaii.

GALAPAGOS ISLANDS
The British naturalist, Charles Darwin, used his observations of the plants and animals on the Galápagos Islands as evidence for his theory of evolution. The islands are still inhabited by species found nowhere else in the world, such as this giant tortoise.

TOURISM
Despite improved air and sea links, tourism in the South Pacific islands is still relatively undeveloped. Islands lack modern facilities such as roads and hotels, and many suffer from a shortage of fresh water. Here a cruise ship anchors off Fiji. Look for

Over 600 of these massive stone figures stand on Easter Island.

Giant clam

MARSHALL ISLANDS
POP: 48,000

UNITED STATES
POP: 257,800,000
HAWAII
POP: 1,160,000

KIRIBATI
POP: 75,000

TONGA
POP: 101,000

WESTERN SAMOA
POP: 162,000

TUVALU
POP: 9,000

Map labels:

Yukon

NORTH AMERICA

Gulf of Alaska

Prince Rupert
Vancouver
Seattle
Columbia

Mendocino Fracture Zone

San Francisco
Monterey
Long Beach
⫴ San Diego
Colorado
Gulf of California

Murray Fracture Zone

PACIFIC OCEAN

rl Harbor ⫴
HONOLULU ⫴
HAWAII (USA)
Clarion Fracture Zone

HNSTON ATOLL (USA)

KINGMAN REEF (to USA)
PALMYRA ATOLL (to USA)
Line Islands

Kiritimati (Christmas I.)

Islas Revillagigedo (to Mexico)

Clipperton Fracture Zone

Clipperton I. (to France)

Albatross Plateau

CENTRAL AMERICA

Cocos Ridge

Panama City
Buenaventura

Galápagos Is. (to Ecuador)

Guayaquil

SOUTH AMERICA

Chimbote
Callao

Peru Basin

Peru Chile Trench

Ilo

AMERICAN SAMOA (to USA)

MICRONESIA

POLYNESIA

Marquesas Is.

COOK ISLANDS (to New Zealand)

FRENCH POLYNESIA

Tuamotu Archipelago
Papeete
Tahiti
SOCIETY IS. (to France)
Muroroa
Gambier Is.

PITCAIRN IS. (to UK)

Easter I. (to Chile)

East Pacific Rise

Isla San Félix (to Chile)
Isla San Ambrosio (to Chile)

Chile

Islas Juan Fernández (to Chile)

Basin

Antofagasta

Valparaíso
Concepción

Chiloé I.

Tubuai Is.

Austral Ridge

Southwest Pacific Basin

Pacific–Antarctic Ridge

South East Pacific Basin

THERN OCEAN

C. Horn

ANTARCTICA

N

0   500 1000 1500 2000 2500 3000   KM
0   500   1000   1500   MILES

Koala
Phascolarctos cinereus
Length: 80 cm (31 in)

Funnel-web spider
Atrax robustus
Length: 3 cm (1 in)

Raggiana's bird of paradise
Paradisaea raggiana
Length: 1.4 m (4 ft)

OCEANIA

OCEANIA INCLUDES AUSTRALIA, New Zealand and numerous island groups in the Pacific. Australia – the smallest, flattest and driest continent – has been worn down by 3,000 million years of exposure to wind and rain. Away from Australia, along the edges of the continental plates, volcanic activity is common because the plates are still moving. These plate movements greatly affect New Guinea, the Pacific Islands and New Zealand. Elsewhere in the Pacific Ocean, thousands of tiny coral islands have grown on the tops of undersea volcanic mountains. Climates vary greatly across the region, from the wet tropical climates of the islands in the outer Pacific, to the hot, dry deserts of central Australia. Tropical rainforest can be found in northern Australia and on New Guinea.

Cider gum tree
Eucalyptus gunnii
Height: 25 m (76 ft)

SURF AND SAND
Powerful waves from the Tasman Sea wash the southeast coast of Australia, creating long, sandy beaches.

AUSTRALIA'S RAINFOREST
Over 600 different types of trees grow in the tropical rainforest on the Cape York Peninsula. Mists often hang over the forest.

DESERT MOUNTAINS
For millions of years, erosion has scoured the centre of Australia. Mountains like Mount Olga have been reduced to stumps of sandstone.

Taipan
Oxyuranuus scutellatus
Length: 3.6 m (12 ft)

TROPICAL GRASSLAND
Three great deserts dominate the centre of Australia. On the desert margins, some rain falls enabling scattered trees and grasses to grow.

DRY WOODLAND
Gum trees – otherwise known as Eucalyptus – abound in Australia. Many species are adapted to dry conditions, with leaves that hang straight down to avoid the full heat of the sun.

TEMPERATE RAINFOREST
Far from other land and surrounded by ocean, much of New Zealand has high rainfall and is warm all year round. These conditions encourage the unique plants of the temperate rainforest.

HOT NEW ZEALAND
Steam rises from pools of sulphurous boiling water and mud, signs of volcanic activity along the plate margins. The heat comes from deep within the earth.

Giant white buttercup
Ranunculus lyalii
Size: 1 m (3 ft)

Black opal, a precious stone found in Australia.

THE PINNACLES
Western Australia's weird limestone pinnacles stand out in the sandy desert. Rain and plant roots have shaped the pillars over the last 25,000 years.

CROSS-SECTION THROUGH AUSTRALIA AND OCEANIA

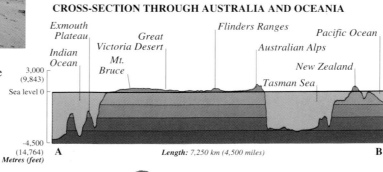

Exmouth Plateau
Indian Ocean
Victoria Desert
Mt. Bruce
Great
Flinders Ranges
Australian Alps
New Zealand
Tasman Sea
Pacific Ocean

3,000 (9,843)
Sea level 0
-4,500 (14,764)
Metres (feet)
A
Length: 7,250 km (4,500 miles)
B

NEW ZEALAND'S ALPS
Rising steeply from the coast, the Southern Alps cover 80 per cent of South Island. Glaciers moving down the mountains carved deep inlets – fjords – along the southwest coast.

130

Red kangaroo
Macropus rufus
Height: 2 m (6 ft)

Brown kiwi
Apteryx australis
Height: 35 cm (14 in)

Giant clam
Tridacna gigas
Shell: 1.5 m (5 ft)

Butterfly fish
Chaetodon auriga
Length: 20 cm (8 in)

CORAL ISLAND
Coral grows in warm shallow seas. Coral reefs surround many Pacific islands, like this one in Fiji, and form Australia's Great Barrier Reef.

The Southern triton is common in Australian waters.

Frilled lizard
Chlamydosaurus kingii
Length: 1 m (3 ft)

KEY TO SYMBOLS

▲ Mountain
△ Volcano
 Mangroves
 Wetlands
 Coral reef
 Plate margins with direction of movement

KEY TO NATURAL VEGETATION

Dry woodland
Tropical grassland
Hot desert
Temperate grassland
Tropical rainforest
Mediterranean-type
Temperate rainforest

AUSTRALIA AND PAPUA NEW GUINEA

AUSTRALIA IS A LAND OF EXTREMES. It is the world's smallest, flattest continent, with the lowest rainfall. The landscape ranges from rainforest along the north coast to arid desert – called the Outback – in the centre, to snowfields in the southeast. It is also one of the most urbanized countries; 70 per cent of the population live in towns and cities in the coastal regions, while much of the interior remains sparsely inhabited. Until two centuries ago this vast land was solely occupied by Aboriginal peoples, but in 1788 settlers from Britain established a colony on the southeast coast. Since then immigration, originally from Europe but now from Asia, has played a vital part in Australia's development. Australia is a wealthy and politically stable country with rich natural resources, steady population growth and increasingly strong trade links in the Pacific area, especially with Japan and the USA. Papua New Guinea, the eastern half of the mountainous island of New Guinea, was once an Australian colony, but became independent in 1975.

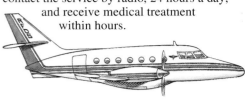

FLYING DOCTOR
In the Australian Outback, the nearest neighbour can live vast distances away. For a doctor to cover such huge areas by road would be impossible. About 60 years ago the Royal Flying Doctor Service was established. In an emergency a caller can contact the service by radio, 24 hours a day, and receive medical treatment within hours.

Quartz — Gold

MINING
Australia has large deposits of minerals such as gold, uranium, coal and diamonds. The mining of these minerals played an important part in the early development of the continent. Improved mining techniques have led to a resurgence in gold mining in Western Australia. Look for 🪖

Yam

Cassava

Cassava and yam are staple foods in Papua New Guinea.

THE GREAT OUTDOORS
Australia's climate is ideal for watersports and other outdoor activities. But Australians are increasingly aware of the danger of skin cancer due to the hole in the ozone layer above the Antarctic, and are learning to take precautions when in the sun.

KEYBOX

Cattle: Australia has about 24 million cattle and exports beef and veal to over 100 countries, especially Japan and the USA. Look for 🐂

Mining: Papua New Guinea has recently become a major producer of gold, which is mined on the mainland and on one of the outlying islands. Look for 🪖

Pearls: Large South Sea pearls are cultivated in oysters in the waters along Australia's north-west coast. These are called "cultured" pearls. Look for 🦪

🐑	Sheep	🚢	Fishing ports
🌾	Cereals	⛏	Coal
🎋	Sugar cane	🏭	Industrial centre
🌳	Timber	🚩	Major airstrips
🍇	Wine	✈	Tourism

FIRST INHABITANTS
Aboriginal peoples believe they have occupied Australia since "before time began". Early Aboriginal societies survived by hunting and gathering. They had their own traditions of story telling, distinctive ceremonies and art styles. Today, 66 per cent of Aboriginal peoples live in towns. Here, 200 years after the first European settlement, activists march through Sydney demanding land rights. The government has introduced programmes to improve Aboriginal standards of living, education and employment.

Map labels:
TIMOR SEA
INDIAN OCEAN
Melville I.
Crok
Bathurst I.
Clarence Strait
DARWIN
C. Londonderry
Joseph Bonaparte Gulf
Beef
Victoria
C. Leveque
Collier Bay
Diamonds
KIMBERLEY PLATEAU
Beef
Wyndham
Ord
KING LEOPOLD RANGES
Beef
Iron
Halls Creek
Beef
Broome
Fitzroy
Beef
NO...
Cop...
Monte Bello Is.
Barrow I.
North West C.
Dampier
Port Hedland
Iron
GREAT SANDY DESERT
TE...
HAMERSLEY RANGE
Iron
Manganese
L. Mackay
L. Macleod
Ashburton
Iron
L. Disappointment
MACDONN...
Carnarvon
Murchison
WESTERN
Gold
GIBSON DESERT
L. Carnegie
Ulu...
Shark Bay
Gold
Meekatharra
L. Wells
Dirk Hartog I.
AUSTRALIA
Gold
Gold
GREAT VICTORIA DESERT
Geraldton
Gold
Mount Magnet
Nickel
A...
Zinc
L. Barlee
Gold
Nickel
Oats
L. Moore
Kalgoorlie
Nickel
NULLARBOR PLAIN
Dairy
Wheat
Gold
Nickel
PERTH
Fremantle
Rockingham
Dairy
Gold
Great Australian Bight
C. Naturaliste
Bunbury
Dairy
Gold
Esperance
Augusta
Barley
C. Pasley
C. Leeuwin
Albany

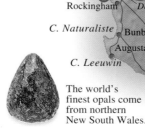

The world's finest opals come from northern New South Wales.

WINE PRODUCTION
When Europeans began to settle in Australia, they brought with them skills such as wine-making. The British first began to grow grapes in South Australia, which now produces over half the country's wines and brandies. With the continued arrival of Europeans, other grapes were added, such as the famous French and German varieties. Grapes are now grown throughout the country, but notably in Western Australia in recent years. Australia is now producing vintages of international quality. Look for 🍇

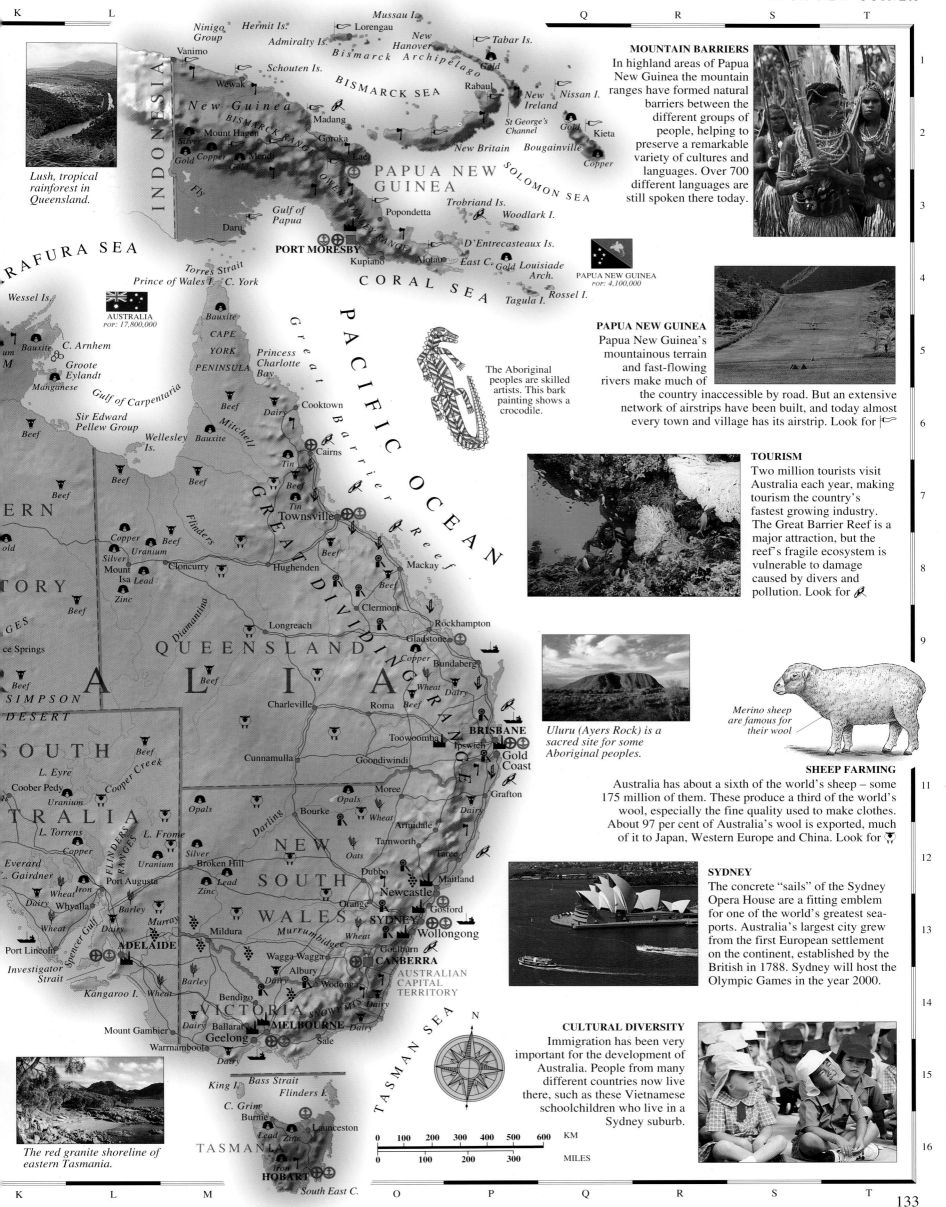

Lush, tropical rainforest in Queensland.

AUSTRALIA
POP: 17,800,000

PAPUA NEW GUINEA
POP: 4,100,000

The Aboriginal peoples are skilled artists. This bark painting shows a crocodile.

Uluru (Ayers Rock) is a sacred site for some Aboriginal peoples.

Merino sheep are famous for their wool

The red granite shoreline of eastern Tasmania.

MOUNTAIN BARRIERS
In highland areas of Papua New Guinea the mountain ranges have formed natural barriers between the different groups of people, helping to preserve a remarkable variety of cultures and languages. Over 700 different languages are still spoken there today.

PAPUA NEW GUINEA
Papua New Guinea's mountainous terrain and fast-flowing rivers make much of the country inaccessible by road. But an extensive network of airstrips have been built, and today almost every town and village has its airstrip. Look for

TOURISM
Two million tourists visit Australia each year, making tourism the country's fastest growing industry. The Great Barrier Reef is a major attraction, but the reef's fragile ecosystem is vulnerable to damage caused by divers and pollution. Look for

SHEEP FARMING
Australia has about a sixth of the world's sheep – some 175 million of them. These produce a third of the world's wool, especially the fine quality used to make clothes. About 97 per cent of Australia's wool is exported, much of it to Japan, Western Europe and China. Look for

SYDNEY
The concrete "sails" of the Sydney Opera House are a fitting emblem for one of the world's greatest sea-ports. Australia's largest city grew from the first European settlement on the continent, established by the British in 1788. Sydney will host the Olympic Games in the year 2000.

CULTURAL DIVERSITY
Immigration has been very important for the development of Australia. People from many different countries now live there, such as these Vietnamese schoolchildren who live in a Sydney suburb.

NEW ZEALAND

NEW ZEALAND LIES deep in the southern Pacific, about halfway between the Equator and the South Pole, 1,500 km (932 miles) from Australia, its nearest large neighbour. New Zealand was one of the last places on Earth to be inhabited by people. The first settlers were Maoris from the Polynesian islands in the Pacific. They were followed by Europeans, who now make up about 86 per cent of the population. From 1840 to 1907 New Zealand was a British colony. Sheep farming was the main source of wealth. But since the 1970s – when Britain joined the EU and cut its imports from New Zealand dramatically – new markets have had to be found in Southeast Asia.

RUGBY
Rugby was first played in New Zealand in 1870. Since then it has become the country's favourite sport. The national team, the "All Blacks", are world famous. They are named after their black shirts and shorts.

The volcanic peak of Mount Ngauruhoe in North Island.

AUCKLAND
Most New Zealanders live in towns. About one-third of the population lives in the city of Auckland. It is the country's main port and industrial centre, and has the world's largest Polynesian population.

Cheddar cheese

Butter

DAIRY PRODUCTS
Huge herds of dairy cattle are kept in New Zealand, mainly on North Island. Dairy produce is an important export. Large quantities of butter and cheese are sent overseas in chilled container ships. Look for ♉

GEOTHERMAL POWER
In the volcanic region of North Island, geo-thermal power stations like this one tap the vast underground supplies of hot water to generate electricity. Look for ⚡

NEW ZEALAND
POP: 3,500,000

Queen scallop

Oysters and queen scallops are bred on fish farms.

The Southern Alps in South Island.

Greenstone pendant, carved by a Maori artist.

TOURISM
Tourism is now New Zealand's largest source of foreign currency. The mild climate and spectacular scenery are ideal for trekking and the varied coastline is a sailor's paradise. National parks occupy 13 per cent of the land area. Look for 👣

FRUIT
New Zealand's mild climate is ideal for growing fruit. A lot of fruit is exported to countries in the Northern Hemisphere because the fruit season in New Zealand falls during the Northern Hemisphere's winter. Look for 🚢

Lemon

Kiwi fruit

Apple

MAORI
Maoris make up 13 per cent of the population: the majority live in urban areas. Some, like those around Gisborne, continue their traditional way of life. Here a *haka*, or war dance, is performed.

SHEEP
In New Zealand sheep have right of way on the roads and outnumber people 20-1. Sheep were first bred for their wool. But when refrigerated ships were developed, frozen lamb could be exported to Europe. Now exports go to the Middle East, Asia and the USA. Look for ♈

KEYBOX

Timber: New Zealand has recently developed its timber industry and now exports wood pulp, chipboard and veneer. Look for ❦

Fishing: Fish, especially hoki and orange roughy, have become a major export. Shellfish farming is also being developed. Look for ➤

🐂	Cattle	⚒	Hydro-electric power
🐑	Sheep	⚡	Alternative power
🚢	Mixed fruit	🏭	Industrial centre
🍇	Wine	👣	Trekking

Great Exhibition Bay
Waipapakauri
Dairy
Beef
Whangarei
Great Barrier I.
Kaipara Harbour
Coromandel
Auckland
Thames
North Island
Hamilton
Dairy
Tauranga
Bay of Plenty
Beef
Rotorua
Dairy
Beef
Gisborne
New Plymouth
Mt. Ngauruhoe
L. Taupo
Taupo
Dairy
Beef
Hawke Bay
Napier
Hastings
Wanganui
Dairy
Palmerston North
Levin
Dairy
Beef
Masterton
Cook Strait
WELLINGTON
Dairy
PACIFIC OCEAN
TASMAN SEA
Beef
Tasman Bay
Beef
Picton
Nelson
Dairy
Blenheim
Wairau
Westport
Kaikoura
Greymouth
Hurunui
SOUTHERN ALPS
Pegasus Bay
Beef
Dairy
Rakaia
Beef
Christchurch
Canterbury Bight
Beef
Timaru
Waitaki
Milford Sound
Taieri
Dairy
L. Te Anau
L. Wakatipu
Queenstown
Beef
Dunedin
TASMAN SEA
South Island
Invercargill
Dairy
Foveaux Strait
Stewart I.

N

0	50	100	150	200	250	300	KM
0		50		100		150	MILES

GLOSSARY

This list provides clear and simple meanings for certain geographical and technical terms used in this atlas.

Acid rain Rain which has been made poisonous by industrial pollution.

AIDS (Acquired Immune Deficiency Syndrome). A fatal condition spread by infected blood and certain body fluids.

Alliance A union of nations, which has been agreed by treaty for economic, political or military purposes

Alluvium Loose material, such as **silt**, sand and gravel, carried by rivers.

Alternative energy Sources of energy which can be renewed – such as solar or wind power. These forms of energy, unlike fossil fuel energy such as coal and oil, do not produce pollution.

Apartheid The policy, developed in South Africa, of separating peoples by race. Non-whites did not have the same democratic rights, and many public institutions were restricted to one race only.

Aquaculture Cultivation of fish and shellfish in lakes, **estuaries**, rivers or the sea.

Archipelago A group of islands.

Atoll A circular or horseshoe-shaped coral reef enclosing a shallow area of water.

Bilingual Speaking two languages.

Biotechnology The use of living organisms in the manufacture of food, drugs and other products. Yeast, for example, is used to make beer and bread.

Buddhism A religion that began in India in about 500 BC. It is based on the teachings of Buddha, who believed that good or evil deeds can be rewarded or punished in this life, or in other lives that will follow. Buddhists aim to achieve inner peace by living their lives according to the example set by Buddha.

Cash crop Agricultural produce grown for sale, often for foreign export, rather than to be consumed by the country or locality where it was grown.

Christianity A religion that began in the lst century BC. Christians believe in one God and follow the teachings of Jesus Christ, whom they believe was the Son of God.

Civil war A war between rival groups of people who live in the same country.

Classical Art, architecture or literature which originated in the time of the ancient Greeks and Romans.

Colony A territory which belongs to another country. Also a group of people living separately within a country.

Communism An economic and political system of the 19th and 20th centuries in which farms, factories and the goods they produce are owned by the state.

Coniferous Trees or shrubs, like pine and fir, which have needles instead of leaves. Most are evergreen.

Conquistador The word is Spanish for "conqueror", and was applied to the Spanish explorers and invaders of Mexico and parts of South America in the 16th century.

Consumer goods Objects such as food, clothing, furniture, cars and televisions which are purchased by people for their personal and private use.

Continental plates The huge, interlocking plates which make up the Earth's surface. A plate margin is an area where two plates meet and is the point at which **earthquakes** occur most frequently.

Continental shelf The edge of a landmass which forms a shallow, raised shelf in the sea.

Cosmopolitan Influenced by foreign cultures.

Cottage industry The manufacture of products – often traditional ones like textiles or pottery – by people in their own homes.

Crude oil Oil in its original state, before chemicals and other oils have been removed by various processes in a refinery.

Crusades A series of wars from the llth to 13th centuries when Christian European armies fought against non-Christian, often Islamic, armies for possession of the Holy Land, or Palestine.

Cultural heritage Anything handed down from a country's past, such as its traditions, art and architecture.

Currency The money of a particular country.

Deforestation The cutting of trees for timber or clearing of forest for farmland. The land is often left bare, leading to soil erosion and increasing the risk of flooding and landslides.

Democracy A political system in which everyone above a certain age has the right to vote for the election of his or her representative in the national and local government.

Desertification The creation of deserts either by changes in climate or by over-grazing, over-population, **deforestation** or over-cultivation.

Developing world Parts of the world which are still undergoing the process of industrialization.

Dictator A political leader who assumes absolute rule of a nation.

Earthquake A trembling or more violent movement of the ground caused by **seismic activity**. Earthquakes occur most frequently along **continental plate** margins.

Economy The organization of a country's finances, exports, imports, industry, agriculture and services.

Ecosystem A community of plants and animals dependent on each other and the habitat in which they live.

Electronics The use of electricity to produce signals that carry information and control devices, such as telephones or computers.

Emigrant A person who has moved from one country or region to settle in another country or region.

Empire A large group of countries ruled by one person – an emperor.

Equator An imaginary East-West line that circles the middle of the Earth at equal distance from the **Poles**. The Equator also marks the nearest point on the Earth's surface to the Sun, so has a consistently hot climate.

Estuary The mouth of a river, where the saltwater of the tide meets the freshwater of the river.

Ethnic diversity People of several different cultures living in the same region.

Ethnic minority A group of people who share a culture, and are outnumbered by others living in the same region.

European Union (EU) (or European Community, EC) A group of European countries linked together by treaty to promote trade, industry and agriculture within a **free-market economy.**

Exports Goods produced in a country but sold abroad.

Fauna Animals of a region.

Flora Plants of a region.

Foreign debt The money owed by one country to the government, banks or institutions of one or more other countries.

Foreign exchange Money brought into a country from abroad, usually by the sale of **exports**, by **service industries** or by tourism.

Free-market economy An economy which is regulated by the price of goods bought and sold freely in national and international markets.

Geothermal energy Electricity produced from hot rocks under the Earth's surface which heat water and produce steam which can then be used to generate electricity.

Geyser A fountain of hot water or steam that erupts periodically as a result of underground streams coming into contact with hot rocks.

Greenhouse effect A rise in the global temperature caused as heat, reflected and radiated from the Earth's surface, is trapped in the atmosphere by a build up of "greenhouse" gases, such as carbon dioxide. Also called "global warming".

Habitat A place or region where a certain animal or plant usually lives.

Heavy industry Industry that uses large amounts of energy and raw materials to produce heavy goods, such as machinery, ships or locomotives.

Hunter-gatherers People who do not grow their food, but obtain it by hunting it and gathering it from their environment. There are few hunter-gatherer groups left in the world today.

Hydro-electric power (HEP) Electricity produced by harnessing the force of falling water.

ICBM (Inter-continental Ballistic Missile) A missile, usually with a nuclear warhead, that can be fired from one continent to land in another.

Immigrant A person who has come to live in a country from another country or region.

Incentives Something that arouses or encourages people to greater efforts.

Inflation The rate at which a country's prices increase.

Informal economy An economy in which people buy and sell from each other, not through shops or markets.

Infrastructure The buildings, transport and communication links that enable goods to be produced and then moved about within a country.

Irrigation A system of watering dry areas. Water is carried or pumped to the area through pipes or channels.

Islam A religion revealed to the prophet Mohammed in the 7th century AD in the Middle East. Its followers, called Muslims (or Moslems), believe in one God, called Allah. The rules and beliefs of Islam are contained in its holy book, the Koran.

Islamic fundamentalist A person who strictly follows the rules and beliefs of Islam contained in the holy book, the Koran. See **Islam**.

Isthmus A narrow piece of land, connecting two larger bodies of land, surrounded on two sides by water.

Labour intensive An activity which requires large amounts of work or large numbers of workers to accomplish it.

Lent A period of time lasting 40 days observed by Christians during which they fast and prepare for the festival of Easter.

Lignite Woody or brown coal.

Living standards The quality of life in a country, usually measured by income, material possessions, and levels of education and health care.

Malnutrition A prolonged lack of adequate food.

Market gardening Farms and **smallholdings** growing fruit and vegetables for sale.

Megalopolis A very large or continuous urban area in which several large towns or cities have joined as their urban areas have spread.

Metropolis A major city, often the capital.

Militarized zone An area occupied by armed military forces.

Multi-national company A company which has branches, or factories, in several countries.

Nationalists Groups of people united in their wish for independence from a government or from foreign rule.

Neutral country A country which refrains from taking part in international conflicts.

Nomad A person who does not settle in one place for any length of time, but moves in search of hunting or grazing land.

Oil shale Flaky rock containing oil.

Pastoralist A person who makes a living from grazing livestock.

Peat Decomposed vegetation found in bogs. It can be dried and used as fuel.

Peninsula A strip of land surrounded on three sides by water.

Permafrost Permanently frozen ground. The surface thaws in summer but water cannot drain away through the frozen subsurface. Typical of **Subarctic** areas.

Pharmaceuticals The manufacture of medicinal drugs.

Plantation A large farm on which only one crop is usually grown.

Plate margin See **Continental plates.**

Polar regions The regions around the North and South Poles which are permanently frozen and where the temperature only rises above freezing point for a few months of the year.

Poles, the The term applied to the North and South Poles, the northernmost and southernmost points of the Earth's axis or rotation.

Prairie A Spanish/American term for a large area of grassland.

Privatization When state-owned activities and companies are taken over by private firms.

Protestant A member of one of the main Christian religions founded in the 16th century by those who did not agree with all aspects of the Roman Catholic Church. Protestantism became one of the main branches of **Christianity**.

Quota A maximum quantity imposed on the number of goods produced, imported or exported by a country.

Rainforest Dense forest found in hot and humid equatorial regions; often called tropical rainforest.

Raw materials Substances in a natural or unrefined state used in the manufacture of goods, like cotton for textiles and bauxite for aluminium.

Refugees People who flee their own country or region because of political, religious or racial persecution.

Republic The form of government in a country that has no monarch. The head of state is usually a president, like the President of the USA.

Reservation An area of land set aside for occupation by specific people, plants or animals.

Revenue Money paid to a government, like taxes.

Roman Catholic A Christian who accepts the Pope as his or her spiritual leader.

Rural In, or belonging to, the countryside.

Savannah Tropical grasslands where an annual dry season prevents the growth of most trees.

Seismic activity Tremors and shocks in the Earth's crust usually caused by the movement of plates along a fault.

Service industry An industry that supplies services, such as banking, rather than producing manufactured goods.

Shanty town An area in or around a city where people live in temporary shacks, usually without basic facilities such as running water.

Silt Small particles, finer than sand, often carried by water and deposited on river banks, at river mouths and harbours. See also **alluvium.**

Smallholding A plot of agricultural land smaller than a farm.

Socialism Political system whereby the economy is owned and controlled by the state and not by private companies or individuals.

Soviet bloc All those countries which were ruled directly or indirectly by the communist government of the former USSR.

Staple crop The main crop grown in a region.

Staple food The basic part of a diet, such as rice or bread.

Steppes An extensive, grass-covered and virtually treeless plain, such as those found in Siberia.

Stock Exchange A place where people buy and sell government bonds, **currency,** stocks and financial shares in large private companies.

Strategic Carefully planned or well placed from a military point of view.

Subarctic The climate in **polar** regions, characterized by extremely cold temperatures and long winters.

Technological The application of science through the use of machines.

Temperate The mild, variable climate found in areas between the **tropics** and cold **polar** regions.

Tropic of Cancer, Capricorn Two imaginary lines of latitude drawn on the Earth's surface above and below the Equator. The hottest parts of the world are between these two lines.

Tropics, the An area between the **Equator** and the **tropics of Cancer and Capricorn** that has heavy rainfall and high temperatures and lacks any clear seasonal variation.

Tundra Vegetation found in areas within the Arctic Circle, such as dwarf bushes, very short grasses, mosses and lichens.

United Nations (UN) An association of countries established to work together to prevent wars, and to supply aid, advice and research on an international basis.

Urban area Town, city or extensive built-up area.

West, the Those countries in Europe and North America with **free-market economies** and **democratic** governments.

Western The economic, cultural and political values shared by countries belonging to **the west**.

Dorling Kindersley would like to thank the following for their help supplying objects for photography: Catherine Lucas, Clare Carolin, Dina Adkins, Clive Webster; Russian Connections for supplying the *draniki* on p.5 and p.80; Mexicolore, London, for skeleton and *sarape* on p.38; Fiat Auto SpA for Fiat Tempra on p.47; Uruguayan Embassy for scarf on p.49; Rosenthal Studio Haus Ltd., London, for glass fruit on p.57; Heal's, London, for child's chair on p.57; Minans Restaurant, London, for *rijstafel* on p.64; Philips Consumer Electronics, London, for television on p.65; BMW (GB) Ltd., Bracknell, for car on p.66; Leica UK, London, for camera on p.67; Watches of Switzerland Ltd., London, for watch on p.69; Hannah Kodicek for puppet on p.70; Henry Marchant Ltd., London, for Bohemian glass on p.70 and ballet costume on p.83; Exico Ltd., London, for wooden duck on p.71; The Greek Shop, London, for doll on p.79; Soccer Scene, London for football shirt on p.73 and rugby shirt on p.134; Gucci, London, for shoes and scarf on p. 72; Embassy of Latvia for currency on p.80; Embassy of Lithuania for currency on p.80; The Russian Shop, London, for chess set, child's toy, lacquered box on p.83, Georgian scarf and Russian dolls on cover and p.85, *samovar* and doll on p.112 and mink hat on p.113; Liberty's, London, for rug on p.88; African Centre, London, for African sculptures on p.93, cover and p.94; Sofra Restaurant, London, for coffee pot and dish on cover and p.123; Covent Garden Oriental Carpets for carpet and saddle cloth on p.110; Ranger Arms Co. Ltd. for gun on p.106; Sandra Schneider for *yarmulke*, prayer book, shawl, etc. on p.106; Saree Emporium, London, for saris on p.117; East West Herb Shop, London, for herbal medicines on p.119; Chuntex (UK) Ltd. for computer monitor on p.121; Tourism Authority of Thailand for lacquer work on p.124.

Map symbols designed by: Kenny Laurenson

Other help supplied by: Crispian Martin St. Valery, Alastair Owens, Janet Oswald, Rosemary Cowan, Jane Lewis, Judy Chamberlain, Michael Capon and George Heritage.

Antarctic terrain supplied by Mullard Space Science Laboratory, University College London, using data from the radar altimeter aboard the European Space Agency's ERS-1 satellite

PICTURE CREDITS:

Heather Angel: 86ct. **B. and C. Alexander**: 25tl, 25tr, 51ct. **Max Alexander**: 63tcr. **P. and G. Bowater**: 69cb. **Chris Branfield**: front cover cl. **Duncan Brown**: 117bl. **J Allan Cash**: front cover bl, 31tr, 36tc, 38cr, 42cl, 42bc, 44bc, 49tcr, 56cr, 56bcl, 57bc, 57bl, 57br, 58tr, 60bl, 61c, 61bl, 61bc, 62cl, 71c, 74ct, 76c, 76bc, 78br, 92 c, 93br, 94bl, 100br, 104ct, 104cl, 105bc, 108bl, 108br, 109tr, 109bcr, 110br, 114tcr, 117cr, 120cbr, 123c, 127tc. **Cephas**: 49ctr. **Mark Chapman**: 93tcl. **J.R.Chapman**: 88cr, 88br, 96tr, 116cr, 117tl. **Oliver Crimmon**: 96ctr. **Ann Clarke**: 49bc. **John Cleare/Mountain Camera**: 40bcl. **Stephanie Colasanti**: 106cr. **Bruce Coleman**: 65br, 118br; Gene Ahrens 26cb, 27tl, 27cr; Alain Compost 126cr, 126bl; Gerald Cubitt 13bl, 98cl, 99bc, 99cb, 114ct, 114ctr, 114cbl, 126cl, Francisco J.Erize 50cl; M. P. L Fogden 35c; Jeff Foott Productions 20ct; Christer Fredriksson 86ctr; Dr. Charles Henneghien 93tc; Hans Gerd Heyer 121cbr; Udo Hirsch 129cbr; David Houston 89tl; Johnny Johnson 50cr; Herbert Kranawetter 75br; O. Langrand 95tl; Wayne Lankinen 30bcl; Thor Larsen 51bc; Leonard Lee Rue 21cbr; Luiz C. Marigo 13cbl, 40ctr; Larry Mulvehill/Black Star 120ct; John Murray 114cl, 128cbl; Orion Press 122cr; Charlie Ott 20tl; Dieter and Mary Plage 40ctl; Dr. Eckhart Pott 38c; Dr. Sandro Prato 73cl, 128cb; Fritz Prenzel 128cb, 128br; Hans Reinhard 50bl, 71bc; N.Tomalin 35tr; Konrad Wothe 101tl; Jonathan T. Wright 32c, 83tl; J. Zwanepoel 65cl. **Colorific**: Linda Bartlett 75c; Steve Benbow 75bc; Marcus Brooke 102ctl; David Burnett/Contact Press 33ctr; Paul Conklin 32cl; John Dominis 74cl; Enrico Ferorelli 33ct; Frank Hermann 94tr; Anthony Joyce 133bl; Sarah Meltzoff/Black Star 139tr; Christopher Morris/Blackstar 75tr; Peter Nacke/Picture Group 84clb; Lehtikuva Ov 14cb; Reza/Black Star 15tl; Malcolm Sanders 133tl; Michael St. Maur Sheil 99c; Peter Turnley/Blackstar 84tr. **Comstock**: 72ct. **Steven J. Cooling**: 99ct, 134cbl. **Lupe Cuhna**: 48tc. **James Davis/Worldwide**: 24bc, 46br, 52bl, 53cr, 69bl, 89ct, 107bl; WVF/Maarten Udema 112cl. **Ecoscene**: Peter Hulme back cover tr, 55tl. **Lynn Edelman**: 45bc. **Tor Eigeland**: 96cl. **Environmental Picture Library**: 92 tr, 102ctr. **Robert Estall**: 23bc. **Chris Fairclough**: 90c, 106c, 116cl, 117c; P. George 117tc. **Sydney Freelance**: 132bl. **Ronald Grant Archive**: 116bl. **Sonia Halliday**: Jane Taylor 107br. **R. Hanbury Tennison**: 77cbr. **Robert Harding**: front cover cr, 11tr, 13tr, 14cr, 15tc, 23cb, 26cr, 27bcl, 35cr, 39cb, 39bl, 45cl, 46tcr, 46tr, 49cr, 49br, 52cl, 56tcr, 56cl, 56c, 61tc, 63cbr, 65tl, 65bl, 68tr, 68cl, 68br, 76cl, 78cl, 79tr, 80cr, 89tr, 89tcr, 90br, 91bl, 93bc, 98cbl, 100tc, 111bc, 116br, 117bcr, 125tcl, 125cr, 125bcl, 125cb, 125br, 127tcr; Mohamed Amin 108cl; Bildagentur Schuster/Eckhardt 66cl, 66tr, 67cl, 78cbr; Bildagentur Schuster/Scholz 85tr; Graham Birch 126tr; C.E.Clark 99cr; C.Delu 95ctl; F.Dubes 63bc; Alan L.Durand 85cbr; Explorer/J. P. Nacivet 62c; Robert Fereck 45tc; Fournie 124cr; Robert Francis 13cl, 39c, 39bcr; Lee Frost 78c; James Green 79bcr; Ian Griffiths 94cr, 133tcr; Gavin Heller 43bl, 115tl; Michael Jenner 104cb, 107cr; Paolo Koch 126tcr; David Lomax 42cr, 43tc; Claude Martine 63cb; Photri 10tr, 10ctr, 10br, 27c; Chris Rennie 39cr, 77tr, 77ct, 110cl; Rolf Richardson 77bc; Sassoon 124tc; M. Short 79cb, 105cb, 105bl; Julia Thorne 51br; David Tokeley 116ct; Adina Tovy 29bl; Vaduz 68cr; A. C.Waltham 34c, 34bcr; Elizabeth Weiland 119tl; G. M.Wilkins 99tl; Adam Woolfitt 53cl, 64tr, 64c, 75tc, 102ct, 104br. **Paul Harris**: 24ct, 24cb, 25br, 82cl, 83br, 113tr, 113cb, 113bcr, 118tcr, 119cl, 122c. **J. Henderson**: 76cb. **John Heseltine**: 59tr. **Leila Hilland**: 133br. **Jimmy Holmes /Himalayan Images**: 118c, 118cl, 119c, 122cl, 123tl. **Pippa Hurst**: 88cl. **Hutchison Library**: 24cl, 43br, 92bl, 95cl, 107cb, 113cr; Robert Aberman 104bl; John Egan 79cr; Sarah Errington 100cr, 112bc; J.G.Fuller 129tc; John Hatt 102br; Richard House 47ctl; Victoria Ivleva 81c; Joan Klatchko 104c; R. Ian Lloyd 101tr; Michael Macintyre 121ctr, 129tr; Stephen Pern 49cr; R. Reeve 52ctr; Bernard Regent 130ctl; Kirsten Rodgers 44tc; Prue Rankin Smith 42tr; Andrei Solomonov 85ct; Tony Souter 73bl. **A. Hyman**: 110c. **ICCE**: S. M. Andrews 86ctl, 89bl. **Image Bank**: 9ccl; Peter Hendrie, 85bc; H.J.Aders 50ct; Gio Barto 88tr; Vladimir Birgos 81tcl; Ira Block 22c; David Brownell 35tcr; P. and G. Bowater 123tr; Edward W. Bower 28cl; Luis Castaneda 29bc; Gerard Champlong 34cl; Gary S. Chapman 42bcr; S. Costa 47bc; Melchior Di Giacomo 15bl, 43c; Wendy Dison 119bl; Tom Owen Edwards 51cbl, 75cr; Grant V. Faint 69tc, 122cbl; David W. Hamilton 60br; David Hiser 128ct; Don Klumpp 74c; Steve Krongard 111cr; Patti McConville 37tr; Fong Siu Nang 120bc; Nick Nicholson 129br; Albert Normandin 22bcr; Francisco Onatanon 61br; John R. Ramey 35bl; Guido Alberto Rossi front cover bcl, 43tr, 43cr, 100bcl; Steve Satushek 23tl, 36cbl, 12cb; Erik Leigh Simmons 31bc; John Lewis Stage 47tr; Peter Turner 28cb; Frank Wing 120tr; Hans Wolf 67bcr. **Images**: 61cr, 130cbl; Andris Apse 130cbr; Horizon 127br. **Impact**: B. Babanov/Vika 113tcl; A. Bradshaw/Visions 113bc; Piers Cavendish 96ct, 97ctr; Rupert Conant 71tr; Anita Corbin 126c; John Denhan 66tl; Colin Jones 28bl; Mike McQueen 114br; M. Milivojevic 70bl; Paul O'Driscoll 99tcr. **Ann Jousiffe**: 89br. **Kaleidescope**: Victor Englebert 93cbr. **Frank Lane**: D.Hoadley 12 tr; W. Wisniewski 53bl, 102cbr. **Anthony Lambert**: 77cr. **Nicki Liddiard**: 58cr. **Life File**: 48bl; Sue Davies 29c, 44tr; Juliet Highet 79br; Eddy Tan 60tr; Sergei Verein 113bl. **Catherine Lucas**: 96c. **Magnum**: Abbas 45tcr, 95bc; Eve Arnold 90bl; Bruno Barbey 92cl, 109cr, 123cl, 124bl; Rene Burri 34bl; M. Franck 91tr; S. Franklin 90ctr, 108tr; Thomas Hoepker 66cr, 67cr; David Hurn/J.Hillelson 89cb; Hiroji Kubota 119cbr; Fred Mayer 102cr; Gideon Mendel 92bc; Eli Reed 107tl; Marc Riboud 102bl, 109bc; Dennis Stock 26c, 28br; Kryn Taconis/John Hillelson 22br; Chris Steele-Perkins 91br, 98c; Dennis Stock 53tr. **Military and Research Services**/Todd Shipyards: 101tcl. **Tim Motion**: 60c, 62cr. **National Maritime Museum**: 101br. **Natural History Photographic Agency**: ANT 133ct; Anthony Bannister 86bcl; Stephen Krasemann 128tr; Dr. Ivan Polunin 114cbr; John Shaw 134cl. **Nature Photographers**: Peter Craig Cooper 98cbr; Mark Pidgeon 87bl; Roger Tidman 97tl. **New Zealand Tourist Office**: 134cr. **Nissan**: 58br. **Oxford Scientific Films**: I. Bernard 40cbr; Tony Bomford 49bcr; Lon E Lauber 11br;; Ted Mead 45c; Larry Ulrich 20tc; Konrad Wothe 40cr. **Panos**: 46cbr; Heidi Bradner 70ct; Matthew Boysons 52cr; Alain le Garsmeur 119tr. **Philips CED Publicity**: 65tcr. **Pictor**: back cover tl, 12ctr, 13cr, 14c, 22bl, 23tr, 28c, 31br, 32br, 33cbl, 47cr, 48tr, 55ctr, 59cl, 86cb, 86bcr, 90tr, 98bc, 101bc, 102cbl, 124c, 129ctr, 130bl. **John Pilkington**: 111tcr. **Pirelli Cables**: 53br. **Planet Earth Pictures**: 20tr, 20cl; Yuri Shibnev 102tr, 103tr; John Eastcott/Yva Momatiuk 13tc; William M. Smithey Jr. 21cbl. **Philip Powell**: front cover cbl. **Quadrant**: 45tr. **Donna Rispoli** 127c. **Science Photo Library**: Martin Bond 9ccr; David Parker 9 cr; Ray Ellis 13br; Simon Frazer 55cr; John Heseltine 55cbl; Michael Martin 55tcl; Novosti Press Agency 112ct. **South American Pictures**: 44cr, 45bl, 49tcr. **Spectrum**: 55ctl, 55cb; Jean Paul Nacivet 55tr. **Frank Spooner**: Tordai 88c. **John Massey Stewart**: 81tl. **Still Pictures**: 25tc; Doug Armand 100tr; Mark Edwards 38bc, 93tr, 95c, 95bl; Edward Parker 94cl; Hjalte Tin 113tl. **Tony Stone**: 10cbr 37bl, 55cbr, 58c, 67bcl, 79ct, 86tcr, 114ctl, 114cb, 123tc, 128cl, 130cb, 130br; Glen Allison 32tr; Doug Armand 69bc, 73c; John Beatty 53bc, 101bcr; Oliver Benn 40tr; Ken Biggs 12tcr; Allan Bramley 130ct; Doug Boult 24c; Michael Buselle 59bc; Julian Calder 111c, 121tl; Mike Caldwell 74bl; John Callahan 121bc; Hubert Camille 62tc; Bryn Campbell 52tc; Paul Chesley 121cr, 130ctr, 134br; Paul Damien 33tl; Nicholas De Vore 40cb; Doris De Witt 28tr; Sepp Dietrich 71cb; Richard Elliot 134cb; John Garrett 132 cl; Margaret Gowan 120bl; David Hanson 36bl, 37cbl, 71br; David Hiser 21cb, 51cl, 128bl; Ernst Hohne 67bl; Gary Irving 30bc, 30bcr; Geoff Johnson 111tr; H. Richard Johnson 11ctr; Chris Kaploka 130cr; Oldrich Karasek 70c; Mitch Kezan 96cl; Jim Kingshott 74br; Thia Konig 37ctr; Bob Krist 82tc; Hideo Kurihara 52tr, 134tc, 134ctr; Peter Lamberti 11cbr; John Lawlor 37tl; Alan Levenson 123bc; Lukasseck 34cb; Angus Mackillop 15cbl; Mike McQueen 55cl; Roger Mear 50br; Lawrence Migdale 59cr; Ian Murphy 59br, 64bl; Donald Nausbaum 41bl; Nicholas Parfitt 86cbr,96br; Tom Raymond 29cr; Mitch Reardon 2c,133cb; Steven Rothfeld 14br; David Schultz 33tr; Mark Segal 30c; Hugh Sitton 90cl, 100tcr, 104tr; Adam Smith 47cl; P. and K. Smith 36cr; Robin Smith 131bl; Bill Staley 21ctr; Alena Vikova 72tr; Charlie Waite 59bl, 73tr; Ken Wilson 133bc. **Ina Strading**: 81ct. **Survival Anglia**: 82c; Ross Bray 107bc; Andrew Park 108c. **Sygma**: Bernard Bisson 85ctr; Fabian 112tr. **Telegraph Colour Library**: 58cl, 99tr; J. C. Davies 72cbr; N. MacIntyre 122br; J. C. Meauxsoone 53tcl; P.Wadey 121tr. **Travel Photo International**: 71ct, 120cbl. **Tony Waltham**: 9cl. **Alan Watson**: 40ct. **Chris Whitwell**: 109tc, 124tr. **David Woodfall**: 81bc. **World Wildlife Fund**: 40bcr; John Newby 93cr; Mauri Rautkari 94bcl. **Zefa**: 20ctl, 29cbr, 51ctl, 66bl, 70tc, 73br, 80c, 81tr, 94br, 106ctr; P. W. Bading 22tr; Jim Brandenburg 31tl; Damm front cover br, 97cr; P. Fera 57tr, 109br; K. Goebel 27bcr, 108ct; Jens Herrman 91cb; Hunter 22cl; Janicek 105cr; Minden 96bl; Sonak 84bl; Steenmans 83tr.

INDEX

Throughout the Atlas, population figures have been taken from the latest official estimates.

HOW TO USE THE GRID

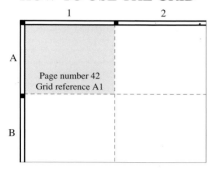

Grid references in the Index help you to find places on the map. For example, if you look up Nairobi in the Index, you will see the reference 97 O5. The first number, 97, is the page number of the map on which Nairobi appears. Find the letters and numbers which border the page, and trace a line across from the letter and down from the number. This directs you to the exact grid square in which Nairobi is located.

The numbers that appear after the names are the page numbers, followed by the grid references.

There are two sorts of factbox in the index. Countries that are more important economically or politically in their area have a larger factbox.

In the factboxes, many statistics are not yet available for the new states of the world. When we have been unable to find the correct figure, N/A is given, which stands for not available.

Population density
This is the total population divided by the land area of a country.

Average life expectancy
This is the average life expectancy at birth, barring war or natural disasters.

Literacy
This is the percentage of people over the age of 15 years who can read and write a simple sentence. Where figures for male (m) and female (f) have not been available, we have used an average (av.).

Death penalty
The countries with Yes use the death penalty regularly. Some of the states with No still have a law permitting the death penalty but do not use it.

Percentage of urban population
This is the percentage of the total population who live in towns or cities.

Calories consumed daily
The recommended daily number for a healthy life is about 2500 calories; the inhabitants of some countries consume far more than others.

The following abbreviations have been used in the index:

anc. = ancient name
Arch. = Archipelago
C. = Cape
E. = East
Ft. = Fort
I. = Island
Is. = Islands
L. = Lake
Mt. = Mountain
Mts. = Mountains
N. = North
N.P. = National Park
Pen. = Peninsula
prev. = previously
Pt. = Point
Res. = Reservoir
R. = River
S. = South
St. = Saint
var. = variant name
W. = West

A

A Coruña (var. La Coruña) Spain 52 J8, 60 G3
Aachen Germany 67 C11
Aalst Belgium 65 F14
Aarau Switzerland 68 F9
Aare *River* Switzerland 68 E9
Aba Nigeria 93 O13
Ābādān Iran 109 L7
Abajo Mountains *Mountain range* Utah, USA 35 K5
Abakan Russian Federation 112 J11
Abashiri Japan 122 M3
Abaya, L. *Lake* Ethiopia 91 J16
Abéché Chad 94 K7
Abengourou Ivory Coast 93 K12
Åbenrå Denmark 56 H16
Abeokuta Nigeria 93 N12
Aberdare Range *Mountain range* Kenya 97 O5
Aberdeen Scotland, UK 52 K7, 58 J8
Aberdeen South Dakota, USA 33 N6
Aberdeen Washington, USA 36 G7
Aberystwyth Wales, UK 59 G14
Abhā Saudi Arabia 108 H13
Abidjan Ivory Coast 93 K13
Abilene Texas, USA 35 P10
Abitibi, L. *Lake* Ontario/Quebec, Canada 25 K11
Abomey Benin 93 M12
Abu Dhabi (var. Abū Ẓabī) United Arab Emirates 109 N11
Abu Simbel *Archaeological site* Egypt 90 F9
Abū Ẓabī *see* Abu Dhabi
Abuja Nigeria 93 O11
Abydos *Archaeological site* Egypt 90 G8
Abyssinia *see* Ethiopia
Acapulco Mexico 39 M14
Accra Ghana 93 L13
Acheloos *River* Greece 78 H7
Achinsk Russian Federation 112 J10
Acklins I. *Island* Bahamas 43 M5
Aconcagua *Mountain* Argentina 41
Ad Dafrah *Desert region* United Arab Emirates 109 N12
Ad Dahna *Desert region* Saudi Arabia 109 L10
Ad Dammām Saudi Arabia 109 M9
Ad Dawḥah *see* Doha
Ad-Diwaniyah Iraq 109 K5
Adak I. *Island* Aleutian Is. Alaska, USA 22 A6
Adamawa Highlands *Physical region* Cameroon 87
Adana Turkey 105 M10
Adapazari Turkey 104 I5
Adare, C. *Cape* Victoria Land, Antarctica 50 E12
Addis Ababa Ethiopia 91 J15
Adelaide South Australia, Australia 133 L13
Aden Yemen 100 E7, 108 I16
Aden, Gulf of *Sea feature* Arabia/E Africa 87, 91 N14, 100 E7, 103, 114
Adige *River* Italy 72 I4
Adīrī Libya 89 O8
Adirondack Mts. *Mountain range* New York, USA 27 L7
Adiyaman Turkey 105 O9
Admiralty Is. *Island group* Papua New Guinea 133 N1
Adrar Algeria 88 J8
Adrar des Ifôghas *Mountain range* Mali 93 M6
Adrian Michigan, USA 31 O10
Adriatic Sea S Europe 54, 72 K10, 74 I9
Adwa Ethiopia 91 J13
Adycha *River* Russian Federation 113 N6
Aegean Sea Greece/Turkey 54, 79 M7, 104 F7
Ağri (var. Karaköse) Turkey 105 R6
Afghanistan *Country* C Asia 110-111

Afghanistan 110-111

a Dari, Pashto · **⊜** Afghani · **●** 25 · **●** 42 · **◔** £7.03 · **⚭** (m) 44% (f) 14% · **⊑** 8 · **✚** 5148 · **☻** Yes · **⌂** 18% · **¶** 2022

Africa *Continent* 8, 11, 12, 13, 15, 87, 103
African Plate *Physical feature* 8, 20, 41, 54, 87, 103, 115
'Afrīn *River* Syria/Turkey 107 N2
Afyon Turkey 104 J8
Agadez Niger 93 P7
Agadir Morocco 88 G6
Agartala India 117 P8
Agattu I. *Island* Aleutian Is. Alaska, USA 22 A4
Agen France 62 J13
Agios Nikolaos Crete, Greece 79 N16
Agra India 117 K5
Agri *River* Italy 73 M14
Agrigento Sicily 73 J18
Aguarico *River* Ecuador 44 D8
Aguascalientes Mexico 39 L10
Agulhas Basin *Sea feature* Atlantic/Indian Ocean 87
Agulhas, C. *Cape* South Africa 87, 98 J16
Agulhas current *Ocean current* Indian Ocean 12
Agulhas Ridge *Sea feature* Atlantic Ocean 87
Ahaggar *Mountain range* Algeria 87, 89 L11
Ahmadabad India 116 I8
Ahvāz Iran 109 M6
Aïr *Mountain range* Niger 93 P7
Aix-en-Provence France 63 O13
Aizawl India 117 Q8
Ajaccio Corsica 63 S16

Ajdābiyā Libya 89 Q7
Ajmer India 116 J6
Akanthou Cyprus 105 L12
Akhisar Turkey 104 H7
Akimiski I. *Island* Canada 24 J8
Akita Japan 122 K7
Akmola (var. Akmolinsk, Tselinograd) Kazakhstan 122 G11
Akmolinsk *see* Akmola
Akola India 117 K9
Akpatok I. *Island* Canada 25 N3
Akron Ohio, USA 31 O10
Aksai Chin *Disputed region* China/India 16, 117 L1, 118 F10
Aksaray Turkey 105 L8
Akseki Turkey 104 J10
Aksu China 118 F7
Aksum Ethiopia 91 J13
Aktau (var. Shevchenko) Kazakhstan 112 D10
Aktyubinsk (var. Aqtöbe) Kazakhstan 112 E10
Akyab *see* Sittwe
Al 'Amārah Iraq 109 L6
Al Azraq Jordan 107 N10
Al 'Aqabah (var. Aqaba) Jordan 107 L14
Al Bāḥah Saudi Arabia 108 H12
Al Baṣrah Iraq 109 L7
Al Baydā Syria 89 R6
Al Bayḍā' Yemen 108 I16
Al Buraymī Oman 109 O11
Al Ghaydah Yemen 109 L16
Al Hoceima Morocco 88 J4
Al Hudaydah *see* Hodeida
Al Hufūf Saudi Arabia 109 L10
Al Ḥadīthah Iraq 108 J4
Al Ḥasakah Syria 107 R2
Al Hillah Iraq 109 K5
Al Jaghbūb Libya 89 S7
Al Jawf Saudi Arabia 108 I6
Al Jubayl Saudi Arabia 109 L9
Al-Juf *see* El Djouf
Al Karak Jordan 107 M11
Al Khābūrah Oman 109 O11
Al Khums Libya 89 O6
Al Kufrah Libya 89 S10
Al Kūt Iraq 109 L5
Al Kuwayt *see* Kuwait City
Al Lādhiqīyah (var. Latakia) Syria 107 M4
Al Madīnah *see* Medina
Al Mafraq Jordan 107 M9
Al Maḥwīt Yemen 108 I15
Al Manāmah *see* Manama
Al Marj Libya 89 Q6
Al Mukallā Yemen 109 K16
Al Mukhā (var. Mocha) Yemen 108 H16
Al Qunayṭirah Syria 107 M8
Al Qurnah Iraq 109 L6
Alabama *River* Alabama, USA 29 K8
Alabama *State* USA 29
Alajuela Costa Rica 42 E13
Alakol', L. *Lake* Kazahhstan 103
Alaköl', L. *Lake* Kazahhstan 103
Alamogordo New Mexico, USA 35 M10
Åland Is. *Island group* Finland 57 M11
Alanya Turkey 105 K10
Alapaha *River* Georgia, USA 29 N9
Alaska *State* USA 22, 51
Alaska, Gulf of *Sea feature* Alaska, USA 10, 20, 22 G9, 129 L3
Alaska Peninsula *Physical feature* 20
Alaska Range *Mountain range* Alaska, USA 10, 20, 22 G7
Alassio Italy 72 C9
Alazani *River* Azerbaijan/Georgia 85 Q12
Alba Iulia Romania 76 I6
Albacete Spain 61 M10
Albania *Country* SE Europe 75

Albania 75

a Albanian · **⊜** Lek · **●** 121 · **●** 73 · **◔** £0.22 · **⚭** (av.) 15% · **⌂** 35%

Albany Georgia, USA 29 M9
Albany New York, USA 26-27
Albany Oregon, USA 36 G9
Albany Western Australia, Australia 132 G14
Albany *River* Ontario, Canada 24 J9
Albatross Plateau *Sea feature* Pacific Ocean 129 O7
Albert Canal *Waterway* Belgium 65 I14
Albert, L. *Lake* Uganda/Zaire 87, 97 L3, 95 P12
Albert Lea Minnesota, USA 30 H8
Albert Nile *River* Uganda 97 M2
Alberta *Province* Canada 23
Albertville *see* Kalemie
Albi France 63 L13
Albina Surinam 44 O6
Ålborg Denmark 56 I14
Albuquerque New Mexico, USA 35 L8
Albury New South Wales, Australia 133 N14
Alcántara Res. *Reservoir* Spain 60 H9
Aldabra Is. *Island group* Seychelles, Indian Ocean 100 F9
Aldan *River* Russian Federation 113 N9
Aleg Mauritania 92 G7
Aleksinac Serbia, Yugoslavia 75 O8
Alençon France 62 J6
Aleppo *see* Halab
Alert *Research centre* Canada 51 O11
Alessandria Italy 72 D7
Ålesund Norway 52 L7, 56 H8
Aleutian Basin *Sea feature* Bering Sea 103
Aleutian Is. *Island group* Alaska, USA 22 B6, 128 J4
Aleutian Trench *Sea feature* Pacific Ocean 20, 128 J4

Alexander Arch. *Island group* Alaska, USA 22 H11
Alexandretta *see* Iskenderun
Alexandria (var. El Iskandarîya) Egypt 90 F6
Alexandria Louisiana, USA 28 H8
Alexandria Romania 77 L10
Alexandria Virginia, USA 29 R3
Alexandroupoli Greece 79 N2
Aleysk Air Base *Military centre* Russian Federation 112 I11
Algeciras Spain 60 I15
Alger *see* Algiers
Algeria *Country* N Africa 88-89

Algeria 88-89

a Arabic · **⊜** Dinai · **●** 11 · **●** 66 · **◔** £0.64 · **⚭** (m) 70% (f) 45% · **⊑** 74 · **✚** 43 · **☻** Yes · **⌂** 52% · **¶** 2866

Alghero Sardinia 73 G13
Algiers (var. Alger; anc. Icosium) Algeria 52 K9, 89 L4
Aliakmon *River* Greece 78 I4
Alicante Spain 61 N11
Alice Springs Northern Territory, Australia 133 K9
Alicudi *Island* Lipari Is., Sicily 73 K16
Aligarh India 117 K5
Alkmaar Netherlands 64 H8
Allahabad India 117 M7
Allegheny Mts. *Mountain range* West Virginia, USA 29 Q3
Allentown Pennsylvania, USA 27 K12
Allier *River* France 63 M11
Alma-Ata (var. Almaty) Kazakhstan 112 G13
Almalyk Uzbekistan 111 N6
Almaty *see* Alma-Ata
Almelo Netherlands 64 M9
Almería Spain 61 L14
Alor *Island* Indonesia 127 N15
Alor Setar Malaysia 125 I17
Alotau Papua New Guinea 133 O4
Alpena Michigan, USA 31 O6
Alphen aan den Rijn Netherlands 64 H10
Alps *Mountain range* C Europe 8, 11, 54, 63 P11, 68 G11, 72 D6
Altai Mts. *Mountain range* Asia 103, 105, 118 I5
Altamura Italy 73 N13
Altay Mongolia 118 J5
Altdorf Switzerland 68 G10
Altiplano *Physical region* Bolivia 41
Alton Illinois, USA 31 J13
Altoona Pennsylvania, USA 26 I12
Altun Ha *Archaeological site* Belize 42 C6
Altun Mts. *Mountain range* China 118 H9
Alturas California, USA 37 I12
Alytus Lithuania 80 I10
Am Timan Chad 94 K8
Amakusa Is. *Island group* Japan 123 C15
Amakusa Sea *Sea feature* Japan 123 B15
Amami Is. *Island group* Japan 123 B19
Amami-ōshima *Island* Amami Is., Japan 123 B18
Amarapura Burma 124 G7
Amarillo Texas, USA 35 O8
Amasya Turkey 105 M5
Amazon *River* S America 41, 44 G9, 46 H7, 53 F12
Amazon Basin *Physical region* Brazil 11, 41
Amazonia *Physical region* S America 44 G8, 46 C8
Ambarchik Russian Federation 51 R5, 113 O4
Ambato Ecuador 44 C9
Amblève *River* Belgium 65 K16
Ambon Ambon, Indonesia 127 O13
Amboseli *National park* Kenya 97 P6
Ambre, Cap d' *see* Bobaomby, C.
Ambriz Angola 98 C4
Ameland *Island* West Frisian Is. Netherlands 64 K6
American Samoa *Dependent territory* Polynesia, Pacific Ocean 129 K9
Amersfoort Netherlands 64 J10
Amery Ice Shelf *Coastal feature* Indian Ocean Coast, Antarctica 50 G8
Ames Iowa, USA 33 Q9
Amfissa Greece 78 I8
Amga *River* Russian Federation 113 N9
Amherst Burma 125 G11
Amiens France 63 L3
Amirante Is. *Island group* Seychelles 100 F9
Amistad Res. *Reservoir* Mexico/Texas, USA 35 O13
Amlia I. *Island* Aleutian Is., Alaska, USA 22 B7
Amman (var. Rabbah Ammon; anc. Philadelphia) Jordan 107 M10
Ammassalik Greenland 51 N15
Ammersee Germany 67 I16
Amol Iran 109 O4
Amorgos *Island* Cyclades, Greece 79 O12
Amritsar India 116 J3
Amstelveen Netherlands 64 I10
Amsterdam Netherlands 64 H9
Amsterdam New York, USA 27 L9
Amsterdam I. *Island* Indian Ocean 101 I13
Amstetten Austria 69 P5
Amu Darya *River* C Asia 103, 111 L8
Amundsen Gulf *Sea feature* Northwest Territories, Canada 23 K6
Amundsen-Scott *Research centre* Antarctica 50 E9
Amundsen Sea Pacific Ocean, Antarctica 50 C10

a Language (official or most commonly spoken) · **⊜** Currency · **●** Population density per square kilometre · **●** Average life expectancy · **◔** Price of 1 dozen hen's eggs · **⚭** Literacy · **⊑** Number of TVs per 1,000 people · **✚** Number of people per doctor · **☻** Death penalty · **⌂** Percentage of urban-based population · **¶** Average number of calories consumed daily per person

137

Ballarat – Bologna

Ballarat Victoria, Australia 133 M14
Balleny Is. *Island group* Pacific Ocean, Antarctica 50 F12
Balsas *River* Mexico 39 M12
Baltic Sea N Europe 52 M7, 54-55, 57 M13, 70 J1, 80 G4, 103
Baltimore Maryland, USA 29 S3
Baltimore Virginia, USA 52 D9
Baltiysk Russian Federation 80 E9
Bălți Moldavia 84 G7
Bamako Mali 92 I9
Bambari Central African Republic 94 K10
Bamenda Cameroon 94 E10
Ban Houayxay Laos 124 J9
Banda Is. *Island group* Indonesia 127 P13
Banda Sea SE Asia 127 N13, 128 F9
Bandar-e Abbās Iran 109 O9
Bandar-e Būshehr Iran 109 M8
Bandar Seri Begawan (var. Brunei Town) Brunei 126 J9
Bandirma Turkey 104 H6
Bandon Oregon, USA 36 F10
Bandundu (prev. Banningville) Zaire 95 I14
Bandung Java, Indonesia 126 G15
Bangalore India 117 K13
Bangassou Central African Republic 94 L10
Banggai Is. *Island group* Indonesia 127 N12
Banggi *Island* Malaysia 127 K8
Bangka *Island* Indonesia 126 G12
Bangkok (var. Krung Thep) Thailand 125 J12
Bangladesh (prev. East Pakistan) *Country* S Asia 117

Bangladesh 117

a Bengali • ≋ Taka • ♦ 812 • ● 52 • ◒ £0.68 • ◗ (m) 47% (f) 22% • ☐ 5 • ✚ 6219 • ✿ Yes • ⌂ 16% • ¶ 2021

Bangor Maine, USA 27 Q6
Bangor Northern Ireland, UK 59 F11
Bangui Central African Republic 94 J10
Bangweulu, L. *Lake* Zambia 97 L12
Banhine N.P. *National park* Mozambique 99 N10
Bani *River* Mali 92 J9
Banja Luka Bosnia and Herzegovina 74 J5
Banjarmasin Borneo, Indonesia 126 J13
Banjul (prev. Bathurst) Gambia 92 F9
Banks I. *Island* Northwest Territories, Canada 20, 23 L5, 51 N8
Banks L. *Lake* Washington, USA 36 J6
Banningville *see* Bandundu
Banská Bystrica Slovakia 71 L11
Bantry Bay *Sea feature* Ireland 59 A14
Banyo Cameroon 94 F10
Banyuwangi Java, Indonesia 126 J15
Baoji China 121 K9
Baotou China 119 N8
Bar Montenegro, Yugoslavia 75 L10
Bar-le-Duc France 63 N5
Baranavichy (var. Baranovichi) Belorussia 80 J13
Baranovichi *see* Baranavichy
Barbados *Country* West Indies 43 T14

Barbados 43

a English • ≋ Dollar • ♦ 600 • ● 75 • ◒ £1.65 • ◗ (m) 99% (f) 99% • ⌂ 45%

Barbados *Island* West Indies 41
Barbuda *Island* Antigua & Barbuda 43 T10
Barcelona Spain 61 Q6
Barcelona Venezuela 44 J4
Bareilly India 117 L5
Barents Sea Arctic Ocean 51 R12, 54, 82 L5, 103
Bari Italy 73 N13
Barinas Venezuela 44 G5
Barisan Mts. *Mountain range* Sumatra, Indonesia 126 E12
Barito *River* Borneo, Indonesia 126 J11
Bârlad Romania 77 N5
Barlee, L. *Lake* Western Australia, Australia 132 G12
Barnaul Russian Federation 112 I11
Barnstaple England, UK 59 G16
Baroda *see* Vadodara
Barquisimeto Venezuela 44 H4
Barra *Island* Scotland, UK 58 E8
Barranquilla Colombia 44 E4
Barreiras Brazil 47 K11
Barreiro Portugal 60 F10
Barrie Ontario, Canada 25 K14
Barrow Alaska, USA 22 H4
Barrow *River* Ireland 59 D13
Barrow I. *Island* Western Australia, Australia 132 E8
Barstow California, USA 37 M18
Bartang *River* Tajikistan 111 P8
Bartica Guyana 44 M6
Barysaw (var. Borisov) Belorussia 81 M11
Basel *see* Basle
Basilan *Island* Philippines 127 M8
Basle (var. Basel) Switzerland 68 F8
Basque Provinces *Region* Spain 61 L4
Basra Iraq 100 E4
Bass Strait *Channel* Australia 131, 133 N15
Basse-Terre Guadeloupe 43 S12
Basse Terre *Island* Guadeloupe 43 S12
Bassein Burma 124 E10
Basseterre St Kitts & Nevis 43 S10
Bastia Corsica 63 S14
Bastogne Belgium 65 K18
Basutoland *see* Lesotho
Bata Equatorial Guinea 95 E11
Batangas Luzon, Philippines 127 L4
Batanghari *River* Sumatra, Indonesia 126 E12
Batavia New York, USA 26 I8
Batavia *see* Jakarta
Bătdâmbâng Cambodia 125 K13
Bath England, UK 59 I16
Bathurst I. *Island* Northern Territory, Australia 132 I5
Bathurst I. *Island* Northwest Territories, Canada 23 M4
Bathurst New Brunswick, Canada 25 P11
Bathurst *see* Banjul
Batman Turkey 105 Q8
Batna Algeria 89 M4
Baton Rouge Louisiana, USA 28 I9
Batticaloa Sri Lanka 117 L16
Battle Creek Michigan, USA 31 N9
Batu Is. *Island group* Indonesia 126 D11
Bat'umi Georgia 85 O13
Bauchi Nigeria 93 P11
Bautzen Germany 67 N11
Bavaria *Region* Germany 67 J14
Bavarian Alps *Mountain range* Austria/Germany 67 J17
Bawean *Island* Indonesia 126 I14
Bay City Michigan, USA 31 O8
Bayamo Cuba 43 K6
Bayan Har Mts. (var. Bayan Har Shan) *Mountain range* China 119 K11
Bayan Har Shan *see* Bayan Har Mts.
Baydaratа Bay *Sea feature* Russian Federation 82 O6, 112 I6
Baydhabo (var. Baidoa) Somalia 91 M17
Baykonur Kazakhstan 112 F11
Bayonne France 62 H14
Bayram-Ali Turkmenistan 111 K9
Bayreuth Germany 67 J13
Beagle Channel *Channel* Argentina 49 L20
Bear Is. *Island group* Russian Federation 113 O4
Bear L. *Lake* Idaho/Utah, USA 34 J2
Beaufort Sea Arctic Ocean 10, 20, 22 J6, 51 N7
Beaufort West South Africa 98 J15
Beaumont Texas, USA 35 T12
Beauvais France 63 L4
Beaver I. *Island* Michigan, USA 31 M5
Bečej Serbia, Yugoslavia 75 M4
Béchar Algeria 88 J6
Bedford Indiana, USA 31 M13
Be'er Sheva' *see* Beersheba
Beersheba (var. Be'er Sheva') Israel 107 L11
Bei'an China 121 P3
Beijing *see* Peking
Beira Mozambique 99 O9, 101 D11
Beirut (var. Beyrouth; anc. Berytus) Lebanon 107 M7
Beja Portugal 60 G12
Bejaïa Algeria 89 L4
Belarus *see* Belorussia
Belawan Sumatra, Indonesia 126 D9
Belaya Tserkov *see* Bila Tserkva
Belcher Islands *Island group* Canada 25 K5
Beledweyne Somalia 91 M16
Belém Brazil 46 J7
Belfast Northern Ireland UK 59 F11
Belfort France 63 P6
Belgaum India 116 I11
Belgian Congo *see* Zaire
Belgium *Country* W Europe 65

Belgium 65

a Dutch, French • ≋ Franc • ♦ 304 • ● 76 • ◒ £1.25 • ◗ (m) 99% (f) 99% • ☐ 452 • ✚ 309 • ✿ No • ⌂ 97% • ¶ 3902

Belgorod Russian Federation 83 E12
Belgorod-Dnestrovskiy *see* Bilhorod-Dnistrovs'kyy
Belgrade (var. Beograd) Serbia, Yugoslavia 75 N5
Belgrano II *Research centre* Antarctica 50 D7
Beli Drim *River* Serbia, Yugoslavia 75 N9
Beli Timok *River* Serbia, Yugoslavia 75 P8
Belice *River* Sicily 73 I18
Belitung *Island* Indonesia 126 G13
Belize *Country* C America 42

Belize 42

a English • ≋ Dollar • ♦ 8 • ● 68 • ◒ £0.92 • ◗ (m) 93% (f) 93% • ⌂ 50%

Belize *River* Belize 42 C6
Belize City Belize 42 C6
Belle Fourche *River* Wyoming, USA 33 K7
Belle Île *Island* France 62 G8
Belle Isle *Island* Newfoundland, Canada 25 R7
Belle Isle, Strait of *Channel* Newfoundland, Canada 25 R8
Bellevue Washington, USA 36 H6
Bellingham Washington, USA 36 H5
Bellingshausen Plain *Sea feature* Pacific Ocean 41
Bellingshausen Sea Pacific Ocean, Antarctica 50 B9
Bellinzona Switzerland 68 H12
Bello Colombia 44 E6
Belluno Italy 72 H6
Belmopan Belize 42 C6
Belo Horizonte Brazil 47 L13
Beloit Wisconsin, USA 31 K9
Belorussia (var. Belarus) *Country* NE Europe 80-81

Belorussia 80-81

a Belorussian • ≋ Ruble • ♦ 50 • ● 73 • ◒ £2.31 • ◗ (m) 99% (f) 99% • ☐ 268 • ✚ 246 • ✿ Yes • ⌂ 66% • ¶ N/A

Belyy Is. *Island group* Russian Federation 112 I5
Bemidji Minnesota, USA 30 G3
Benares *see* Varanasi
Bend Oregon, USA 36 I9
Bendery *see* Tighina
Bendigo Victoria, Australia 133 M14
Benevento Italy 73 L13
Bengal, Bay of *Sea feature* India/SE Asia 103, 100 J6, 115, 117 P9, 124 D9
Benghazi Libya 89 Q6
Bengkulu Sumatra, Indonesia 126 E13
Benguela Angola 98 G6
Benguela current *Ocean current* S Atlantic Ocean 12
Beni *River* Bolivia 45 H13
Beni Mellal Morocco 88 I6
Beni Suef Egypt 90 F7
Benidorm Spain 61 O11
Benin (prev. Dahomey) *Country* W Africa 93

Benin 93

a French • ≋ Franc • ♦ 44 • ● 51 • ◒ £0.86 • ◗ (m) 32% (f) 16% • ⌂ 38%

Benin, Bight of *Sea feature* W Africa 93 N13
Benin City Nigeria 93 O12
Bennington Vermont, USA 27 M9
Benton Harbor Michigan, USA 31 M10
Benue *River* Cameroon/Nigeria 87, 93 P12
Beograd *see* Belgrade
Beppu Japan 123 D14
Berat Albania 75 M13
Berau, Gulf of *Sea feature* Irian Jaya, Indonesia 126 Q12
Berberä Somalia 91 M14
Berbérati Central African Republic 95 H11
Berbice *River* Guyana 44 M7
Berdyans'k Ukraine 85 L8
Berettyő *River* Hungary/Romania 71 N14
Bereza *see* Byaroza
Bergama *see* Pergamon
Bergamo Italy 72 E6
Bergen Norway 52 K7, 56 H10
Bergen *see* Mons
Bergen op Zoom Netherlands 65 G12
Bergisch Gladbach Germany 67 E11
Bering Sea Pacific Ocean 10, 20, 22 C7, 103, 113 R5, 128 J3
Bering Strait *Channel* Arctic Ocean/Pacific Ocean 20, 22 E4, 103, 128 J2
Berlin Germany 66 L9
Bermejo *River* Argentina/Bolivia 48 K5
Bermuda *Dependent territory* Atlantic Ocean 52 F9
Bermuda *Island* Atlantic Ocean 20
Bermuda Rise *Sea feature* Atlantic Ocean 20
Bern Switzerland 68 E10
Bernese Alps *Mountain range* Switzerland 68 F12
Beroea *see* Ḥalab
Berry Is. *Island group* Bahamas 43 K2
Bertoua Cameroon 94 G10
Beruni Uzbekistan 110 J5
Berytus *see* Beirut
Besançon France 63 O7
Beskid Mts. *Mountain range* C Europe 71 L9
Bethel Alaska, USA 22 E7
Bethlehem West Bank 107 L10
Beykoz Turkey 104 I5
Beyrouth *see* Beirut
Beyşehir Turkey 104 J9
Beyşehir, L. *Lake* Turkey 104 J9
Bezmein Turkmenistan 110 H8
Bhamo Burma 124 H6
Bhatapara India 117 M9
Bhavnagar India 116 I8
Bhopal India 117 K8
Bhubaneswar India 117 N9
Bhumiphol Res. *Reservoir* Thailand 124 H10
Bhutan *Country* S Asia 117

Bhutan 117

a Dzongkha • ≋ Ngultrum • ♦ 31 • ● 49 • ◒ £0.56 • ◗ (m) 51% (f) 25% • ⌂ 5%

Biak *Island* Indonesia 127 R11
Białystok Poland 71 O4
Bicuari N.P. *National park* Angola 98 G7
Biddeford Maine, USA 27 O8
Biel Switzerland 68 E9
Biel, L. *Lake* Switzerland 68 E10
Bielefeld Germany 66 F10
Bielsko-Biała Poland 71 L9
Bien Hoa Vietnam 125 N14
Big Spring Texas, USA 35 O11
Bighorn *River* Montana/Wyoming, USA 32 J6
Bighorn Mts. *Mountain range* Wyoming, USA 32 J7
Bihać Bosnia and Herzegovina 74 I5
Bijagós Archipelago *Island group* Guinea-Bissau 92 F10
Bijelo Polje Montenegro, Yugoslavia 75 M9
Bikini *Island* Marshall Islands, Pacific Ocean 128 I7
Bila Tserkva (var. Belaya Tserkov) Ukraine 84 I5
Bilbao Spain 61 L3
Bilecik Turkey 104 I6
Bilhorod-Dnistrovs'kyy (var. Belgorod-Dnestrovskiy) Ukraine 84 I8
Billings Montana, USA 32 I6
Biloxi Mississippi, USA 28 J9
Biltine Chad 94 K7
Bindura Zimbabwe 99 M8
Binghamton New York, USA 27 K10
Bingöl Turkey 105 Q7
Bintan *Island* Indonesia 126 F11
Bío-Bío *River* Chile 49 H12
Birāk *Oasis* Libya 89 O8
Birao Central African Republic 94 L8
Biratnagar Nepal 117 O6
Birganj Nepal 117 N6
Birkenhead England, UK 59 H13
Birmingham Alabama, USA 29 L7
Birmingham England, UK 59 I14
Birni n'Konni Niger 93 O9
Biscay, Bay of *Sea feature* Spain 54, 61 L3
Biscay Plain *Sea feature* Atlantic Ocean 54
Bishkek (prev. Frunze) Kyrgyzstan 111 Q4
Bisho South Africa 99 L15
Bishop California, USA 37 K15
Biskra Algeria 89 L5
Bislig Mindanao, Philippines 127 N7
Bismarck North Dakota, USA 33 M5
Bismarck Arch. *Island group* Papua New Guinea 133 O1
Bismarck Range *Mountain range* Papua New Guinea 131, 133 N2
Bismarck Sea Papua New Guinea 131, 132 O1
Bissau Guinea-Bissau 92 F10
Bistrița Romania 76 J3
Bitlis Turkey 105 R8
Bitola Macedonia 75 O13
Bitterroot Range *Mountain range* Idaho/Montana USA 32 G6
Biysk Russian Federation 112 I11
Bizerte Tunisia 89 N4
Bjelovar Croatia 74 J3
Black Forest (var. Schwarzwald) *Physical region* Germany 67 F15
Black Hills *Mountain range* South Dakota/Wyoming, USA 33 L7
Black R. (var. Song Da) *River* China/Vietnam 124 L8
Black R. *River* Arkansas/Missouri USA 28 J4
Black Rock Desert *Desert region* Nevada, USA 20, 34 F1
Black Sea (var. Chernoye More, Kara Deniz) Asia/Europe 52 N8, 54, 77 P11, 85 M11, 103, 105 N4
Black Volta *River* West Africa 87, 93 K10
Blackpool England, UK 59 H12
Blackwater *River* Ireland 59 C14
Blagoveshchensk Russian Federation 113 O11
Blanca, Bahía *Sea feature* Argentina 49 L12
Blanca, Costa *Coastal region* Spain 61 O11
Blanco, Cape *see* Nouadhibou, Râs
Blanice *River* Czech Republic 70 H10
Blantyre Malawi 97 O15
Blenheim New Zealand 134 G9
Blida Algeria 89 L4
Bloemfontein South Africa 99 K13
Blois France 63 K7
Bloomington Illinois, USA 31 K12
Bloomington Indiana, USA 31 M13
Bloomington Minnesota, USA 30 H6
Blue Mesa Dam *Dam* Colorado, USA 35 L5
Blue Mountains *Mountain range* Oregon/Washington USA 36 K9
Blue Nile (var. Bahr el Azraq) *River* Ethiopia/Sudan 87, 91 H13
Blue Nile *River* 87
Bluefields Nicaragua 42 E11
Bo Sierra Leone 92 H12
Bo Hai *Sea feature* China 121 N7
Boa Vista Brazil 46 F6
Boaco Nicaragua 42 D10
Bobaomby, C. (var. Cap d' Ambre) *Cape* Madagascar 100 E10
Bobo-Dioulasso Burkina 93 K10
Bóbr *River* Poland 70 I6
Bobruysk *see* Babruysk
Bocas del Toro Panama 42 F14
Bochum Germany 66 E10
Bodensee *see* Constance, L.
Bodø Norway 57 L4
Bodrum Turkey 104 G9
Boende Zaire 95 K12
Bogor Java, Indonesia 126 G14
Bogotá (prev. Santa Fe) Colombia 44 E6
Bohemian Forest (var. Böhmerwald) *Physical region* Czech Republic/Germany 67 L14
Böhmerwald *see* Bohemian Forest
Bohol *Island* Philippines 127 M6
Boise Idaho, USA 32 F8
Bokaro India 117 N8
Bokna Fjord *Coastal feature* Norway 56 H11
Bol Chad 94 H7
Bolgatanga Ghana 93 L10
Bolivia *Country* S America 45

Bolivia 45

a Aymara, Quechua, Spanish • ≋ Boliviano • ♦ 7 • ● 60 • ◒ £0.52 • ◗ (m) 85% (f) 70% • ☐ 163 • ✚ 2100 • ✿ No • ⌂ 51% • ¶ 1916

Bologna Italy 72 G8

a Language (official or most commonly spoken) • ≋ Currency • ♦ Population density per square kilometre • ● Average life expectancy • ◒ Price of 1 dozen hen's eggs • ◗ Literacy • ☐ Number of TVs per 1,000 people • ✚ Number of people per doctor • ✿ Death penalty • ⌂ Percentage of urban-based population • ¶ Average number of calories consumed daily per person

a Language (official or most commonly spoken) · 🕮 Currency · ♦ Population density per square kilometre · ♥ Average life expectancy · ◔ Price of 1 dozen hen's eggs · ♥ Literacy · 🖵 Number of TVs per 1,000 people ·
✚ Number of people per doctor · ☢ Death penalty · 🏠 Percentage of urban-based population · ᑫ Average number of calories consumed daily per person

141

Corfu *Island* Ionian Is. Greece 78 E5
Corinth Greece 78 J9
Corinth Canal *Waterway* Greece 78 J9
Corinth, Gulf of *Sea feature* Greece 78 I9
Corinto Nicaragua 42 C10
Cork Ireland 59 C14
Corner Brook Newfoundland, Canada 25 R9
Corning New York, USA 26 J10
Cornwall *Region* England, UK 59 F17
Cornwallis I. *Island* Northwest Territories, Canada 23 N4
Coro Venezuela 44 H4
Coromandel New Zealand 134 H4
Coromandel Coast *Coastal region* India 117 L13
Coronel Chile 49 G12
Corpus Christi Texas, USA 35 R15
Corrib, Lough *Lake* Ireland 59 B12
Corrientes Argentina 48 M7
Corse see Corsica
Corsica (var. Corse) *Island* France 54, 63 S15
Cortellazzo Italy 72 I7
Cortland New York, USA 27 K9
Çorum Turkey 105 M6
Corumbá Brazil 47 G13
Corvallis Oregon, USA 36 G9
Cosenza Italy 73 N13
Costa Rica *Country* C America 42

Costa Rica 42

ⓐ Spanish · ⓔ Colon · ♦ 56 · ♥ 75 · ◔ £0.48 · ♨ (m) 93% (f) 93% · ⌂ 47%

Côte d'Azur *Coastal region* France 63 Q13
Côte d'Ivoire see Ivory Coast
Cotonou Benin 93 R7
Cotopaxi *Volcano* Ecuador 41
Cottbus Germany 66 M10
Council Bluffs Iowa, USA 33 P10
Courantyne *River* Guyana/Surinam 44 N7
Courland Lagoon *Coastal feature* Lithuania/Russian Federation 80 F9
Courtrai see Kortrijk
Coventry England, UK 59 J14
Covilhã Portugal 60 G8
Covington Kentucky, USA 29 N2
Cozumel I.. *Island* Mexico 39 T11
Cracow see Kraków
Craiova Romania 76 J9
Cranbook British Columbia, Canada 23 K15
Crawley England, UK 59 K16
Cree L. *Lake* Saskatchewan, Canada 23 M12
Cremona Italy 72 F7
Cres *Island* Croatia 74 G5
Crescent City California, USA 37 F11
Crete *Island* Greece 54, 79 L15
Crete, Sea of Greece 79 M15
Crimea (var. Krym) *Peninsula* Ukraine 54, 85 K9
Crna *River* Macedonia 75 O12
Croatia (var. Hrvatska) *Country* SE Europe 74-75

Croatia 74-75

ⓐ Serbo-Croat · ⓔ Dinar · ♦ 81 · ♥ 72 · ◔ £1.20 · ♨ (m) 96% (f) 84% · ⌨ N/A · ✚ 523 · ☻ No · ⌂ 51% · � N/A

Croker I. *Island* Northern Territory, Australia 132 J4
Crooked I. *Island* Bahamas 43 L5
Crotone Italy 73 O16
Crozet Basin *Sea feature* Indian Ocean 101 G13
Crozet Is. *Island group* Indian Ocean 50 I5, 101 F14
Cruzeiro do Sul Brazil 46 A9
Cuango *River* Southern Africa 98 H3
Cuanza *River* Angola 98 G4
Cuba *Country* Caribbean Sea 42-43

Cuba 42-43

ⓐ Spanish · ⓔ Peso · ♦ 97 · ♥ 76 · ◔ £1.04 · ♨ (m) 95% (f) 93% · ⌨ 207 · ✚ 333 · ☻ Yes · ⌂ 75% · �)3141

Cuba *Island* Caribbean Sea 20, 41
Cubango see Okavango *River*
Cúcuta Colombia 44 F5
Cuenca Ecuador 44 C9
Cuernavaca Mexico 39 N12
Cuiabá Brazil 47 G12
Cuito *River* Southern Africa 98 I8
Cuito Cuanavale Angola 98 I7
Cuitzeo, L. *Lake* Mexico 39 M11
Culiacán Mexico 39 J8
Cumaná Venezuela 44 M4
Cumberland *River* Kentucky/Tennessee, USA 29 M4
Cumberland Plateau *Physical feature* USA 29 M5
Cumberland Sound *Sea feature* Baffin I. Northwest Territories, Canada 23 R6
Cunene *River* Angola/Namibia 98 G8
Cuneo Italy 72 B8
Cunnamulla Queensland, Australia 133 N11
Curaçao *Island* Netherlands Antilles 43 N14
Curicó Chile 49 G11
Curitiba Brazil 47 J15
Cusco Peru 45 F13
Cuttack India 117 N9
Cuxhaven Germany 66 G7
Cyclades *Island group* Greece 79 M11

Cyprus *Country* Mediterranean Sea 105

Cyprus 105

ⓐ Greek, Turkish · ⓔ Pound and Lira · ♦ 77 · ♥ 77 · ◔ £0.61 · ♨ (m) 98% (f) 91% · ⌂ 53%

Cyprus *Island* Mediterranean Sea 54, 103
Cyrenaica *Region* Libya 89 R7
Cyrene *Archaeological site* Libya 89 R6
Czech Republic *Country* C Europe 70-71

Czech Republic 70-71

ⓐ Czech · ⓔ Koruna · ♦ 131 · ♥ 74 · ◔ £0.47 · ♨ (m) 99% (f) 99% · ⌨ 412 · ✚ 43 · ☻ No · ⌂ 77% · �, 3632

Czechoslovakia see Czech Republic and Slovakia
Częstochowa Poland 71 L8

D

Da Lat Vietnam 125 O14
Da Nang Vietnam 125 O11
Da Qaidam China 118 J9
Da Yunhe see Grand Canal
Dacca (var. Dhaka) Bangladesh 117 P8
Dadu He *River* China 120 I10
Dagupan Luzon, Philippines 127 L3
Dahlak Archipelago *Island group* Eritrea 91 K12
Dahomey see Benin
Dahūk Iraq 109 K2
Dakar Senegal 92 F8
Dakhla Western Sahara 88 E9
Đakovo Croatia 75 K4
Dalaman Turkey 104 H10
Dali China 120 H13
Dalian China 121 O7
Dallas Texas, USA 35 R10
Dalles, The Oregon, USA 36 I8
Dalmatia *Region* Croatia 74 I7
Daloa Ivory Coast 92 J12
Daman India 116 I9
Damar *Island* Indonesia 127 O14
Damascus (var. Dimashq) Syria 107 M7
Dambovitei see Bucharest
Dampier Western Australia, Australia 132 F8
Danbury Connecticut, USA 27 M11
Danmark see Denmark
Danube (var. Donau, Dunaj) *River* C Europe 16, 54, 67 L14, 69 Q4, 71 L14, 75 L4, 76 I10
Danube Delta *Delta* Romania 77 D7
Danube-Black Sea Canal *Waterway* Romania 77 O9
Danville Illinois, USA 31 L12
Danville Virginia, USA 29 Q5
Danzig see Gdańsk
Danzig, Gulf of *Sea feature* Poland/Russian Federation 71 L1
Dapaong Togo 93 M10
Dar es Salaam Tanzania 97 Q9, 100 D9
Dar'ā Syria 107 M9
Dardanelles *Channel* Turkey 104 G5
Darhan Mongolia 119 M4
Darien, Gulf of *Sea feature* Panama/Colombia 41, 42 I15, 44 D5
Darling *River* New South Wales, Australia 131, 133 N12
Darmstadt Germany 67 F13
Darnley, C. *Cape* Indian Ocean Coast, Antarctica 50 G8
Dartmoor *Physical region* England, UK 59 G17
Daru Papua New Guinea 133 M3
Darwin Northern Territory, Australia 132 J5
Dashkhovuz (prev. Tashauz) Turkmenistan 110 J5
Dasht-e Kavir (var. Great Salt Desert) *Desert region* Iran 103, 109 O5
Dasht-e Lut *Desert region* Iran 103, 109 P7
Datong China 121 L6
Daugava see Dvina, Western
Daugavpils Latvia 81 K8
Davangere India 116 J12
Davao Mindanao, Philippines 127 N7
Davenport Iowa, USA 33 S9
David Panama 42 E14
Davis Dam *Dam* Arizona, USA 34 H7
Davis Mts. *Mountain range* Texas, USA 35 N12
Davis Sea Indian Ocean, Antarctica 50 H9
Davis Strait *Channel* Greenland/Canada 20, 23 R5, 51 M13, 52 F7
Dawson Yukon Territory, Canada 22 I8
Dawson Creek British Columbia, Canada 23 K12
Daxue Shan *Mountain range* China 115
Dayr az Zawr Syria 107 Q4
Dayton Ohio, USA 31 O12
Daytona Beach Florida, USA 29 O12
De Aar South Africa 99 K14
De Kalb Illinois, USA 31 K10
Dead Sea (var. Bahrat Lut) *Salt Lake* Israel/Jordan 103, 107 M10
Death Valley *Physical feature* California, USA 10, 20, 37 M16
Debre Birhan Ethiopia 91 J14
Debre Markos Ethiopia 91 I14
Debrecen Hungary 71 N13
Decatur Illinois, USA 31 K8
Deccan Plateau *Physical region* India 115, 116 J10
Dee *River* Scotland, UK 58 J8

Dehra Dun India 117 K4
Del Rio Texas, USA 35 O13
Delaware *River* USA 27 L11
Delaware *State* USA 27
Delémont Switzerland 68 E9
Delft Netherlands 65 G11
Delfzijl Netherlands 64 N6
Delicias Mexico 39 K5
Delingha China 119 K9
Delphi *Archaeological site* Greece 78 I8
Demchok *Disputed region* China/India 117 L3, 118 F11
Demerara Plain *Sea feature* Atlantic Ocean 41
Demirköprü Barrage *Dam* Turkey 104 H8
Den Helder Netherlands 64 H7
Denali (prev. Mt. McKinley) *Mountain* Alaska, USA 10, 20
Denizli Turkey 104 H9
Denmark (var. Danmark) *Country* Scandinavia 56-57

Denmark 56-57

ⓐ Danish · ⓔ Krone · ♦ 121 · ♥ 75 · ◔ £1.81 · ♨ (m) 99% (f) 99% · ⌨ 535 · ✚ 375 · ☻ No · ⌂ 65% · ⅐ 3628

Denmark Strait *Channel* Greenland/Iceland 20, 51 O15, 52 I7
Denpasar Bali, Indonesia 126 J15
D'Entrecasteaux Is. *Island group* Papua New Guinea 133 P4
Denver Colorado, USA 35 M4
Dera Ghazi Khan Pakistan 116 H4
Dera Ismail Khan Pakistan 116 I3
Derby England, UK 59 J14
Derg, Lough *Lake* Ireland 59 C13
Derna Libya 89 R6
Des Moines Iowa, USA 33 Q9
Des Moines *River* Iowa/Minnesota, USA 33 Q9
Dese Ethiopia 91 J14
Deseado *River* Argentina 49 J16
Desna *River* Russian Federation/Ukraine 84 J3
Dessau Germany 66 K10
Detroit Michigan, USA 31 O9
Deva Romania 76 I6
Deventer Netherlands 64 L10
Devoll *River* Albania 75 M13
Devon I. *Island* Northwest Territories, Canada 20, 23 O4, 51 N11
Dezfūl Iran 109 L4
Dezhneva *Cape* Russian Federation 113 Q2
Dhahran (var. Az Zahran) Saudi Arabia 109 M9
Dhaka see Dacca
Dhamār Yemen 108 I16
Dhanbad India 117 N8
Dhanushkodi India 117 K15
Dharwad India 116 J12
Dhaulagiri *Mountain* Tibet 115
Dhule India 116 J9
Diamantina *River* Queensland/South Australia, Australia 133 M9
Dickinson North Dakota, USA 33 L5
Didim see Didyma
Didyma (var. Didim) *Archaeological site* Turkey 104 G9
Diego Garcia *Island* British Indian Ocean Territory, Indian Ocean 100 H9
Diégo-Suarez see Antsiranana
Diekirch Luxembourg 65 L18
Dieppe France 63 K3
Diffa Niger 93 Q9
Digne France 63 P12
Digul *River* Indonesia 127 T14
Dijlah see Tigris
Dijon France 63 N7
Dikson *Research centre* Russian Federation 51 T10
Dili Timor, Indonesia 127 N15
Dillon Montana, USA 32 H6
Dilolo Zaïre 95 H14
Dimashq see Damascus
Dimbokro Ivory Coast 93 K12
Dinant Belgium 65 H17
Dinaric Alps *Mountain range* Bosnia and Herzegovina/Croatia 74, 75
Dingle Bay *Sea feature* Ireland 59 A14
Diourbel Senegal 92 F8
Dipolog Mindanao, Philippines 127 M7
Dire Dawa Ethiopia 91 L14
Dirk Hartog I. *Island* Western Australia, Australia 132 E10
Disappointment, L. *Lake* Western Australia, Australia 132 H9
Disna, L. *Lake* Lithuania 81 K9
Disney World Florida, USA 29 N12
Dispur India 117 Q6
Divriği Turkey 105 Q8
Diyālā *River* Iraq 109 L4
Diyarbakir Turkey 105 Q8
Dja *River* Cameroon 95 H11
Djado, Plateau du *Physical region* Niger 93 R5
Djambala Congo 95 H13
Djebel Toubkal *Mountain* Morocco 87
Djibouti Djibouti 91 L14, 100 D7
Djibouti *Country* E Africa 91

Djibouti 91

ⓐ Arabic, French · ⓔ Franc · ♦ 19 · ♥ 49 · ◔ £1.13 · ♨ (m) 63% (f) 36% · ⌂ 81%

Dnepropetrovsk see Dnipropetrovs'k
Dnieper (var. Dnipro) *River* E Europe 54, 81 M15, 82 E10, 84 I5

Dniester *River* Ukraine 84 F5
Dnipro see Dnieper
Dnipropetrovs'k Ukraine 85 K6
Dobele Latvia 80 H6
Doboj Bosnia and Herzegovina 75 K5
Dobrich Bulgaria 77 O11
Dodecanese *Island group* Greece 79 P13
Dodge City Kansas, USA 33 N13
Dodoma Tanzania 97 O8
Dōgo *Island* Oki Is. Japan 123 E11
Doha (var. Ad Dawḥah) Qatar 109 M10
Dolak *Island* Indonesia 126 S14
Dolomites *Mountain range* Alps Italy 72 H6
Dolores Argentina 49 N11
Dom *Mountain* Switzerland 54
Dominica *Country* Caribbean Sea 43 T12

Dominica 43

ⓐ English · ⓔ Dollar · ♦ 96 · ♥ 75 · ◔ £1.45 · ♨ (av.) 94% · ⌂ 41%

Dominican Republic *Country* Caribbean Sea 43

Dominican Republic 43

ⓐ Spanish · ⓔ Peso · ♦ 149 · ♥ 67 · ◔ £0.42 · ♨ (m) 85% (f) 82% · ⌂ 60%

Don *River* Russian Federation 54, 83 F13
Donau see Danube
Donawitz Austria 69 Q7
Donbass *Physical region* Ukraine 85 M6
Dondra Head *Cape* Sri Lanka 100 I7
Donegal Bay *Sea feature* Ireland 59 C11
Donets *River* Russian Federation/Ukraine 83 E13, 85 L5
Donets'k Ukraine 85 M7
Dong Hoi Vietnam 124 N10
Dongchuan China 120 I12
Dongguang China 121 M14
Dongsheng China 119 N8
Dongting Hu *Lake* China 115, 121 L11
Dønna *Island* Norway 57 K5
Donostia see San Sebastián
Doornik see Tournai
Dordogne *River* France 62 J12
Dordrecht Netherlands 65 H11
Dornbirn Austria 68 I8
Dortmund Germany 66 E10
Dortmund-Ems Canal *Waterway* Germany 66 E9
Dosso Niger 93 N9
Dothan Alabama, USA 29 L9
Douala Cameroon 95 E11
Doubs *River* France 63 O8
Douglas Arizona, USA 34 J11
Douglas Isle of Man, UK 59 G12
Douro (var. Duero) *River* Portugal 54, 60 H6
Dover Delaware, USA 27 K14
Dover England, UK 59 L16
Dover New Hampshire, USA 27 O8
Dover, Strait of *Channel* France/UK 59 M17, 63 K1
Dōzen *Island* Oki Is. Japan 123 E11
Drachten Netherlands 64 L7
Drake Passage *Channel* Atlantic Ocean/Pacific Ocean 41, 50 A7
Drakensberg *Mountain range* Lesotho/South Africa 11, 87, 99 L14
Drama Greece 79 L2
Drammen Norway 56 I11
Drau (var. Drava) *River* SE Europe 69 Q9
Drava (var. Drau) *River* SE Europe 75 K3
Drawa *River* Poland 70 I4
Dresden Germany 67 M11
Drin *River* Albania/Macedonia 75 M10
Drin Gulf *Sea feature* Albania 75 L11
Drobeta-Turnu-Severin Romania 76 H9
Drumheller Alberta, Canada 23 M12
Drummondville Quebec, Canada 25 M12
Druskininkai Lithuania 80 I11
Dubai United Arab Emirates 109 O11
Dubăsari (var. Dubossary) Moldova 84 H7
Dubbo New South Wales, Australia 133 O12
Dublin (var. Baile Atha Cliath; anc. Eblana) Ireland 59 E13
Dubossary see Dubăsari
Dubrovnik Croatia 75 K9
Dubuque Iowa, USA 33 R8
Duero (var. Douro) *River* Spain 61 K6
Dugi Otok *Island* Croatia 74 G7
Duisburg Germany 66 D10
Dukhan Qatar 109 M10
Duluth Minnesota, USA 30 I4
Dumaguete Negros, Philippines 127 M6
Dumfries Scotland, UK 59 H11
Dumont d'Urville *Research centre* Antarctica 50 F12
Dun Laoghaire Ireland 59 E13
Dunaj see Danube
Dunajec *River* Poland/Slovakia 71 M9
Dundalk Ireland 59 E12
Dundas (var. Ummannaq) Greenland 51 N11
Dundee Scotland, UK 58 I9
Dunedin New Zealand 134 E14
Dungun Malaysia 125 K18
Dunkerque see Dunkirk, France
Dunkirk (var. Dunkerque) France 63 L1
Dunkirk New York, USA 26 H9
Durance *River* France 63 P13
Durango Colorado, USA 35 L6

Durango – Fort Smith

Durango Mexico 39 K8
Durazno Uruguay 48 N10
Durban South Africa 99 M14, 101 C12
Durham North Carolina, USA 29 Q5
Durrës Albania 75 L12
Dushanbe (prev. Stalinabad) Tajikistan 111 N8
Düsseldorf Germany 67 D11
Dutch East Indies *see* Indonesia
Dutch Guiana *see* Surinam
Dutch Harbor Unalaska I. Aleutian Is. Alaska, USA 22 C8
Dvina *see* Dvina, Northern or Dvina, Western
Dvina, Northern *River* Russian Federation 54, 82 J8
Dvina, Western (var. Daugava) *River* NE Europe 54, 80 I6, 81 M8
Dzhalal-Abad Kyrgyzstan 111 P6
Dzhambul *see* Zhambyl
Dzhezkazgan *see* Zhezkazgan
Dzhizak Uzbekistan 111 M7
Dzhugdzhur Range *Mountain range* Russian Federation 113 O9
Dzungaria *Mountain range* China/Kazakhstan 103

E

Eagle L. *Lake* California, USA 37 I12
Eagle L. *Lake* Maine, USA 27 P3
Eagle Mountain L. *Lake* Texas, USA 35 Q10
Eagle Pass Texas, USA 35 P14
East African Plateau *Physical feature* Kenya/Uganda 87
East Anglia *Region* England, UK 59 M14
East C. *Cape* Papua New Guinea 133 P4
East China Sea China 115, 121 O12, 123 B17, 128 F6
East Frisian Is. *Island group* Germany 66 E7
East Greenland current *Ocean current* Atlantic Ocean 12
East Indies (var. Indonesia) *Island group* SE Asia 115, 131
East Liverpool Ohio, USA 31 Q11
East London South Africa 99 L15
East Pacific Ridge *Sea feature* Pacific Ocean 41
East Pacific Rise *Sea feature* Pacific Ocean 129 O9
East Pakistan *see* Bangladesh
East St. Louis Illinois, USA 30 J14
East Siberian Sea Arctic Ocean 51 R6, 103, 113 O3
Easter I. *Island* Polynesia, Pacific Ocean 129 O10
Eastern Ghats *Mountain range* India 117 L11
Eastmain *River* Quebec, Canada 25 M8
Eastport Maine, USA 27 R5
Eau Claire Wisconsin, USA 30 I6
Eblana *see* Dublin
Ebolowa Cameroon 95 F11
Ebro *River* Spain 54, 61 M5
Ecuador *Country* S America 44

Ecuador 44

a Spanish • ≋ Sucre • ♦ 38 • ● 66 • ◒ £0.31 • ◆ (m) 88% (f) 84% • ⌂ 56%

Ed Damazin Sudan 91 H14
Ed Damer Sudan 91 H11
Ed Dueim Sudan 91 G13
Ede Netherlands 64 K10
Edéa Cameroon 95 F11
Eder *River* Germany 67 G11
Edessa Greece 78 I3
Edinburgh Scotland, UK 58 I10
Edirne Turkey 104 G4
Edmonds Washington, USA 36 H6
Edmonton Alberta, Canada 23 L13
Edward, L. *Lake* Uganda/Zaire 95 O12, 97 K4
Edwards Air Base *Military centre* California, USA 37 L18
Edwards Plateau *Physical region* Texas, USA 35 P12
Eforie-Nord Romania 77 P9
Egadi Is. *Island Group* Sicily 73 H17
Egiyn *River* Mongolia/Russian Federation 119 L4
Eğridir, L. *Lake* Turkey 104 J8
Egypt *Country* NE Africa 90

Egypt 90

a Arabic • ≋ Pound • ♦ 53 • ● 61 • ◒ £0.52 • ◆ (m) 63% (f) 34% • ▭ 109 • ✚ 5092 • ☠ Yes • ⌂ 47% • ‖ 3336

Eiger, Mt. *Mountain* Switzerland 68 F11
Eigg *Island* Scotland, UK 58 F8
Eindhoven Netherlands 65 J13
Eire *see* Ireland
Eisenstadt Austria 69 S5
El Aaiún (var. Laâyoune) Western Sahara 88 F7
El Faiyûm Egypt 90 F7
El Fasher Sudan 91 D13
El Ferrol Spain 60 G3
El Iskandarîya *see* Alexandria
El Jerid, Chott *Salt lake* Tunisia 89 M5
El Juf *see* El Djouf
El Khartûm *see* Khartoum
El Mansûra Egypt 90 F6
El Minya Egypt 90 F7
El Obeid Sudan 91 F13
El Oued Algeria 89 M6
El Paso Texas, USA 35 L11
El Qâhira *see* Cairo
El Salvador *Country* C America 42

El Salvador 42

a Spanish • ≋ Colon • ♦ 256 • ● 64 • ◒ £0.59 • ◆ (m) 76% (f) 70% • ⌂ 44%

El Suweis *see* Suez
Elat Israel 107 L14
Elâziğ Turkey 105 P8
Elba *Island* Italy 72 F10
Elbasan Albania 75 M12
Elbe *River* Germany 54, 66 I8
Elbe *see* Laba
Elbert, Mt. *Mountain* Colorado, USA 20
Elbląg Poland 71 L2
El'brus *Mountain* Russian Federation 54
Elburz Mts. *Mountain range* Iran 109 N4
Elche Spain 61 N11
Eldoret Kenya 97 O4
Elephant Butte Res. *Reservoir* New Mexico, USA 35 L10
Elephant I. *Island* South Shetland Is. Antarctica 50 B6
Eleuthera *Island* Bahamas 43 L2
Elgin Scotland, UK 58 I7
Elisabethville *see* Lubumbashi
Elista Russian Federation 83 F14
Ełk Poland 71 N3
Elko Nevada, USA 34 H2
Ellensburg Washington, USA 36 I7
Ellesmere I. *Island* Northwest Territories, Canada 20, 23 N1, 51 O11
Ellsworth Mountains *Mountain range* Antarctica 50 C9
Elmira New York, USA 26 J10
Eltz *Castle* Germany 67 E12
Elwell, L. *Lake* Montana, USA 32 I4
Ely Nevada, USA 34 H4
Elyria Ohio, USA 31 P10
Emba *River* Kazakhstan 112 E10
Emden Germany 66 E7
Emerson (Trimmu) Barrage *Dam* Pakistan 116 I3
Emmen Netherlands 64 N8
Emona *see* Ljubljana
Emperor Seamounts *Sea feature* Pacific Ocean 128 I5
Emporia Kansas, USA 33 P12
Empty Quarter *see* Rub 'al Khali
Ems *River* Germany 66 E9
En Nahud Sudan 91 E13
Encarnación Paraguay 48 N7
Ende Flores, Indonesia 127 M15
Enderby Land *Region* Antarctica 50 G7
Enewetak *Island* Marshall Islands, Pacific Ocean 128 H7
Enggano *Island* Indonesia 126 E14
England *Country* UK 59
English Channel France/UK 54, 59 J17, 62 I3
Enguri *River* Azerbaijan/Georgia 85 O11
Enid Oklahoma, USA 33 O14
Enna Sicily 73 K18
Enns *River* Austria 69 P7
Enriquillo, L. *Lake* Dominican Republic 43 N8
Enschede Netherlands 64 N10
Ensenada Mexico 38 F2
Entebbe Uganda 97 M4
Enugu Nigeria 93 O12
Ephesus *Archaeological site* Turkey 104 G8
Epidaurus *Archaeological site* Greece 78 J10
Épinal France 63 P6
Equatorial Current *Ocean current* Pacific Ocean 12
Equatorial Guinea *Country* C Africa 95

Equatorial Guinea 95

a Spanish • ≋ Franc • ♦ 15 • ● 47 • ◒ £2.15 • ◆ (m) 64% (f) 37% • ⌂ 27%

Er Rachidia Morocco 88 I6
Er Roseires Dam *Dam* Sudan 91 H14
Erdenet Mongolia 119 L4
Ereğli Turkey 105 L9
Erenhot China 119 O6
Erfurt Germany 67 I11
Erg Chech *Desert region* Algeria/Mali 93 K4
Erguig *River* Chad 94 I8
Erie Pennsylvania, USA 26 G10
Erie, L. *Lake* Canada/USA 20, 24 J15, 26 G9, 31 P9
Erie Canal *Waterway* New York, USA 26 I8
Eritrea *Country* E Africa 91

Eritrea 91

a Amharic • ≋ Birr • ♦ 37 • ● 48 • ◒ N/A • ◆ (av.) 71% • ⌂ N/A

Erivan *see* Yerevan
Erlangen Germany 67 I13
Ernakulam India 116 J14
Erne, Lough *Lake* Northern Ireland, UK 59 D11
Ertix He *see* Irtysh
Erzincan Turkey 105 P6
Erzurum Turkey 105 Q6
Es Semara *see* Smara
Esbjerg Denmark 52 L7, 56 H15
Escanaba Michigan, USA 31 L5
Esch-sur-Alzette Luxembourg 65 L19
Escuintla Guatemala 42 A8
Eşfahān Iran 109 N6
Eskimo Pt. Northwest Territories, Canada 23 O10
Eskişehir Turkey 104 J6
Esla Res. *Reservoir* Spain 60 I6
Esmeraldas Ecuador 44 C8
Esperance Western Australia, Australia 132 H13
Espinho Portugal 60 F7
Espíritu Santo I. *Island* Mexico 38 H8
Esquel Argentina 49 H15
Essaouira Morocco 88 G6
Essen Germany 66 E10
Essequibo *River* Guyana 44 M7
Estelí Nicaragua 42 D10
Estevan Saskatchewan, Canada 23 N15
Estonia (var. Estonskaya SSR) *Country* NE Europe 80-81

Estonia 80-81

a Estonian • ≋ Kroon • ♦ 35 • ● 48 • ◒ £0.38 • ◆ (m) 99% (f) 99% • ⌂ 71%

Estonskaya SSR *see* Estonia
Ethiopia (var. Abyssinia) *Country* E Africa 91

Ethiopia 91

a Amharic • ≋ Birr • ♦ 48 • ● 48 • ◒ £0.50 • ◆ (av.) 29% • ▭ 2 • ✚ 38359 • ☠ Yes • ⌂ 13% • ‖ 1667

Ethiopian Highlands *Mountain range* Ethiopia 87, 91 J15
Etna *Volcano* Sicily
Etosha N.P. *National park* Namibia 98 H9
Etosha Pan *Salt basin* Namibia 98 H8
Euboea *see* Evvoia
Eugene Oregon, USA 36 G9
Eupen Belgium 65 L15
Euphrates *River* SW Asia 100 E4, 103, 105 O10, 107 R5, 109 K6
Eurasian Plate *Physical feature* 8, 20, 54, 87, 103, 115, 131
Eureka California, USA 37 F12
Europe *Continent* 8, 10, 11, 12, 13, 15, 20, 103
Europoort Netherlands 65 G11
Evanston Illinois, USA 31 L10
Evansville Indiana, USA 31 L14
Everard, L. *Lake* South Australia, Australia 133 K12
Everest, Mt. (var. Qomolangma Feng) *Mountain* China/Nepal 115, 117 O5
Everett Washington, USA 35 H6
Everglades, The *Swamp region* Florida, USA 20, 29 O14
Évora Portugal 60 G11
Évreux France 63 K5
Evvoia (var. Euboea) *Island* Greece 79 K7
Exeter England, UK 59 G16
Exmoor *Physical region* England, UK 59 G16
Exmouth Plateau *Sea feature* Indian Ocean 131
Eyasi, L. *Lake* Tanzania 97 N7
Eyre, L. *Lake* South Australia, Australia 131, 133 L11

F

Fada-Ngourma Burkina 93 M10
Faeroe Islands *Dependent territory* Atlantic Ocean 52 J7
Faeroe Islands *Island group* Atlantic Ocean 54
Faeroe Shelf *Sea feature* Atlantic Ocean 54
Faguibine, L. *Lake* Mali 93 K7
Fairbanks Alaska, USA 22 H7
Fairmont Minnesota, USA 30 G8
Faisalabad Pakistan 116 I3
Falkland Escarpment *Sea feature* Atlantic Ocean 53 F15
Falkland Is. *Dependent territory* Atlantic Ocean 53 F15
Falkland Is. *Island group* Atlantic Ocean 41
Fall River Massachusetts, USA 27 O11
Falmouth England, UK 59 E17
Falun Sweden 57 L11
Famagusta Cyprus 105 L12
Faradje Zaire 95 O11
Farafangana Madagascar 101 E11
Farewell, Cape Greenland 52 H7
Fargo North Dakota, USA 33 O5
Faribault Minnesota, USA 30 H7
Farmington New Mexico, USA 35 K6
Faro Portugal 60 G13
Faro Yukon Territory, Canada 22 I9
Fårö *Island* Sweden 57 M13
Farvel, Cape (var. Kap Farvel) *Cape* Greenland 51 M16
Fax *River* Sweden 57 K8
Faya (var. Faya Largeau) Chad 94 J5
Faya Largeau *see* Faya
Fayetteville Arkansas, USA 28 H3
Fayetteville North Carolina, USA 29 Q6
Fdérik Mauritania 92 H4
Fear, Cape *Cape* North Carolina, USA 29 Q8
Federal Capital Territory *see* Australian Capital Territory
Fehmarn *Island* Germany 66 J6
Feira de Santana Brazil 47 N11
Felbertauern Tunnel *Tunnel* Austria 69 M8
Feldkirch Austria 68 I9
Felixstowe England, UK 59 M15
Femund, L. *Lake* Norway 56 J9
Fens, The *Physical region* England, UK 59 K14
Feodosiya Ukraine 85 K10
Fergana Uzbekistan 111 P6
Fergus Falls Minnesota, USA 30 F5
Fernando de Noronha I. *Island* Atlantic Ocean 53 I12
Fernando Póo *Island* Equatorial Guinea 87
Ferrara Italy 72 H8
Fethiye Turkey 105 H10
Feuilles, Rivère aux *River* Quebec, Canada 25 M4
Fez Morocco 88 I5
Fezzan *Physical region* Libya 89 O9
Fianarantsoa Madagascar 101 E11
Fier Albania 75 L13
Figueira de Foz Portugal 60 F8
Figuig Morocco 88 J6
Fiji *Country* Melanesia, Pacific Ocean 128 J10

Fiji 128

a English • ≋ Dollar • ♦ 41 • ● 65 • ◒ £1.17 • ◆ (m) 90% (f) 84% • ⌂ 39%

Fiji *Island group* Melanesia, Pacific Ocean 131
Filadelphia Paraguay 48 L4
Filchner Ice Shelf *Coastal feature* Atlantic Ocean Coast, Antarctica 50 D8
Filicudi *Island* Lipari Is. Sicily 73 K16
Fimbul Ice Shelf *Coastal feature* Atlantic Ocean Coast, Antarctica 50 E6
Findlay Ohio, USA 31 O11
Finger Lakes *Physical region* New York, USA 26 J9
Finisterre, C. *Coastal feature* Spain 54
Finland *Country* N Europe 57

Finland 57

a Finnish, Swedish • ≋ Markka • ♦ 16 • ● 76 • ◒ £1.54 • ◆ (m) 99% (f) 99% • ▭ 497 • ✚ 515 • ☠ No • ⌂ 60% • ‖ 3253

Finland, Gulf of *Sea feature* Baltic Sea 54, 57 O12, 81 K1, 82 E7
Firenze *see* Florence, Italy
Firth of Clyde *Sea feature* Scotland, UK 58 G10
Firth of Forth *Sea feature* Scotland, UK 58 I9
Fish *River* Namibia 98 I13
Fishguard Wales, UK 59 F15
Fitzroy *River* Western Australia, Australia 132 H7
Flagstaff Arizona, USA 34 I7
Flaming Gorge Dam *Dam* Utah, USA 35 K3
Flaming Gorge Res. *Reservoir* Utah/Wyoming, USA 32 I10
Flathead L. *Lake* Montana, USA 32 G4
Flin Flon Manitoba, Canada 23 N13
Flinders *River* Queensland, Australia 131, 133 M7
Flinders I. *Island* Tasmania, Australia 133 N15
Flinders Ranges *Mountain range* South Australia, Australia 131, 133 L12
Flint Michigan, USA 31 O8
Flint *River* Florida/Georgia 29 M9
Florence (var. Firenze) Italy 72 G9
Florence Alabama, USA 29 K5
Florence South Carolina, USA 29 P7
Florencia Colombia 44 E8
Flores Guatemala 42 B6
Flores *Island* Indonesia 115, 131, 127 M15
Flores Sea Indonesia 127 K15
Florianópolis Brazil 47 J15
Florida Uruguay 48 N10
Florida *State* USA 29 N11
Florida Keys *Island group* Florida, USA 29 O16
Florida, Straits of *Channel* Cuba/USA 29 P15
Florina Greece 78 H3
Flushing (var. Vlissingen) Netherlands 65 E13
Fly *River* Papua New Guinea 133 M3
Foča Bosnia and Herzegovina 75 L8
Focşani Romania 77 N6
Foggia Italy 73 M12
Föhr *Island* North Frisian Is. Germany 66 G5
Foix France 63 L15
Fond du Lac Wisconsin, USA 31 K8
Fongafale Tuvalu, Pacific Ocean 128 J9
Forlì Italy 72 H8
Formentera *Island* Balearic Islands 61 P11
Formosa Argentina 48 M6
Fort Bliss Military Reservation *Military centre* New Mexico, USA 35 L11
Fort Collins Colorado, USA 35 M3
Fort-de-France Martinique 43 T13
Fort Dodge Iowa, USA 33 Q8
Fort-Foureau *see* Kousseri
Fort Lamy *see* N'Djamena
Fort Lauderdale Florida, USA 29 O15
Fort McMurray Alberta, Canada 23 L12
Fort McPherson Northwest Territories, Canada 22 J7
Fort Myers Florida, USA 29 N14
Fort Nelson British Columbia, Canada 23 J11
Fort Peck L. *Lake* Montana, USA 32 J4
Fort Portal Uganda 97 L4
Fort Resolution Northwest Territories, Canada 23 L10
Fort Shevchenko Kazakhstan 112 D10
Fort Simpson Northwest Territories, Canada 23 K10
Fort Smith Arkansas, USA 28 H4
Fort Smith Northwest Territories, Canada 23 L11

a Language (official or most commonly spoken) • ≋ Currency • ♦ Population density per square kilometre • ● Average life expectancy • ◒ Price of 1 dozen hen's eggs • ◆ Literacy • ▭ Number of TVs per 1,000 people • ✚ Number of people per doctor • ☠ Death penalty • ⌂ Percentage of urban-based population • ‖ Average number of calories consumed daily per person

Fort Smith – Greensboro

Fort Smith *Region* Northwest Territories, Canada 23 L9
Fort St John British Columbia, Canada 23 K12
Fort Vermilion Alberta, Canada 23 L11
Fort Victoria *see* Masvingo
Fort Wayne Indiana, USA 31 N11
Fort Wellington Guyana 44 M6
Fort William Scotland, UK 58 G8
Fort Worth Texas, USA 35 R10
Fortaleza Brazil 46 N8, 53 H12
Forth *River* Scotland, UK 58 H9
Foveaux Strait *Channel* New Zealand 134 C14
Foxe Basin *Sea feature* Northwest Territories, Canada 23 P7
Foyle, Lough *Lake* Northern Ireland/Ireland 58 E10
France *Country* W Europe 62-63

France 62-63

a French • Franc • 103 • 77 • £1.61 • (m) 99% (f) 99% • 406 • 381 • No • 74% • 3465

Franceville *see* Massoukou
Francis Case, L. *Lake* South Dakota, USA 33 N8
Francistown Botswana 99 L10
Franconian Jura *Mountain range* Germany 67 J14
Frankfort Indiana, USA 31 M12
Frankfort Kentucky, USA 29 N3
Frankfurt am Main Germany 67 F12
Frankfurt an der Oder Germany 66 N9
Franz Josef Land *Island group* Russian Federation 51 R11, 54, 103
Fraser *River* British Columbia, Canada 20, 22 J13
Fraserburgh Scotland, UK 58 J7
Frauenfeld Switzerland 68 H8
Fray Bentos Uruguay 48 N9
Fredericton New Brunswick, Canada 25 P12
Frederikshåb (var. Paamiut) Greenland 51 M15
Frederikshavn Denmark 56 I13
Fredrikstad Norway 56 J12
Freeport Bahamas 43 K1
Freeport Illinois, USA 31 K9
Freeport Texas, USA 35 S13
Freetown Sierra Leone 92 G11
Freiburg im Breisgau Germany 67 E16
Freistadt Austria 69 P4
Fremantle Western Australia, Australia 101 M12, 132 F12
French Guiana *Dependent territory* S America 44
French Polynesia *Dependent territory* Polynesia, Pacific Ocean 129 M9
French Sudan *see* Mali
French Togo *see* Togo
Fresno California, USA 37 J16
Fria, C. *Cape* Namibia 87, 98 F9
Fribourg Switzerland 68 E10
Friedrichshafen Germany 67 G16
Frobisher Bay Baffin I. Northwest Territories, Canada 23 S7
Frobisher Bay *see* Iqaluit
Frobisher L. *Lake* Saskatchewan, Canada 23 M12
Frome, L. *Lake* South Australia, Australia 133 L12
Frontera Mexico 39 Q13
Frosinone Italy 73 J12
Frunze *see* Bishkek
Fuenlabrada Spain 61 K8
Fuerte Olimpo Paraguay 48 M4
Fujairah United Arab Emirates 109 O11
Fuji, Mt. *Mountain* Japan 115, 123 J11
Fukui Japan 123 H11
Fukuoka Japan 123 C13
Fukushima Japan 122 K5
Fukushima Japan 122 K9
Fulda Germany 67 H12
Fulda *River* Germany 67 H11
Fundy, Bay of *Sea feature* Canada 25 P13, 52 F8
Funen *see* Fyn
Furnas Res. *Reservoir* Brazil 47 K13
Fushun China 121 O6
Fuzhou China 121 N13
Fyn (var. Funen) *Island* Denmark 56 I16

G

Gaalkacyo Somalia 91 N16
Gabčíkovo Slovakia 71 K12
Gabès Tunisia 89 N5
Gabon *Country* C Africa 95

Gabon 95

a French • Franc • 5 • 54 • £2.57 • (m) 74% (f) 49% • 46%

Gaborone Botswana 99 K11
Gabrovo Bulgaria 77 L12
Gadsden Alabama, USA 29 L6
Gafsa Tunisia 89 N5
Gagnoa Ivory Coast 92 J13
Gagra Georgia 85 N11
Gainesville Florida, USA 29 N11
Gairdner, L.144 *Lake* South Australia, Australia 133 K12
Galana *River* Kenya 97 Q6
Galapagos Is. *Island group* Pacific Ocean 41, 129 P8
Galați Romania 77 O7
Galesburg Illinois, USA 30 J11
Galicia *Region* Poland 71 N9
Galicia *Region* Spain 60 G3
Galilee, Sea of *see* Tiberias, L.
Galle Sri Lanka 117 L16
Gallego Rise *Sea feature* Pacific Ocean 41
Gallia *see* Paris
Gallipoli Italy 73 P14
Gallipoli (var. Gelibolu; anc. Callipolis) Turkey 104 G5
Gällivare Sweden 57 N5
Gallup New Mexico, USA 35 K7
Galveston Texas, USA 35 S13
Galway Ireland 59 B12
Galway Bay *Sea feature* Ireland 59 B12
Gambia *Country* W Africa 92

Gambia 92

a English • Dalasi • 90 • 45 • £1.81 • (m) 39% (f) 16% • 23%

Gambier Is. *Island group* French Polynesia, Pacific Ocean 129 M10
Gan He *River* 115
Gäncä (var. Gyandzha; prev. Kirovabad) Azerbaijan 85 R13
Gander Newfoundland, Canada 25 S9
Gandi Res. *Reservoir* India 116 J7
Ganga *see* Ganges
Gangdise Range *Mountain range* China 118 G12
Ganges (var. Ganga) *River* India 100 J5, 115, 117 O7
Ganges *River basin* India 11
Ganges Delta *Delta* Bangladesh 115
Ganges Plain *Physical region* India 115
Gangtok India 117 O6
Ganzhou China 121 M13
Gao Mali 93 L8
Gap France 63 P12
Gar China 118 F11
Garda, L. *Lake* Italy 72 F6
Garden City Kansas, USA 33 M13
Garissa Kenya 97 Q5
Garmisch-Partenkirchen Germany 67 I17
Garonne *River* France 54, 62 J12
Garoowe Somalia 91 O15
Garoua Cameroon 94 G9
Garry L. *Lake* Northwest Territories, Canada 23 N8
Gary Indiana, USA 31 L10
Gaspé Quebec, Canada 25 P10
Gastonia North Carolina, USA 29 P6
Gatineau Quebec, Canada 25 L13
Gävle Sweden 57 L11
Gaya India 117 N7
Gaza Gaza Strip 107 K10
Gaza Strip *Occupied by Israel* SW Asia 107 K10
Gaziantep Turkey 105 O9
Gbarnga Liberia 92 H12
Gdańsk (prev. Danzig) Poland 71 L2
Gdynia Poland 71 K2
Gedaref Sudan 91 H13
Geelong Victoria, Australia 133 M14
Gejiu China 120 I14
Gela, Gulf of *Sea feature* Sicily 73 K19
Gelibolu *see* Gallipoli
Gelsenkirchen Germany 66 E10
Gemena Zaire 95 J11
Gemlik Turkey 104 I6
Gemsbok N.P. *National park* Botswana 98 J11
Genale *River* Ethiopia 91 K16
General Eugenio A. Garay Paraguay 41 K4
General Santos Mindanao, Philippines 127 N8
Genesee *River* New York/Pennsylvania, USA 26 I9
Geneva (var. Genève) Switzerland 68 C12
Geneva New York, USA 26 J9
Geneva, L. *Lake* France/Switzerland 54, 63 P9, 68 D12
Genève *see* Geneva, Switzerland
Genk Belgium 65 J14
Genoa (var. Genova) Italy 72 D8
Genoa, Gulf of *Sea feature* Italy 72 D8
Genova *see* Genoa
Gent *see* Ghent
Georg van Neumayer *Research centre* Antarctica 50 D6
Georgetown Delaware, USA 27 K15
Georgetown Gambia 92 G9
Georgetown Grand Cayman, Cayman Islands 42 H6
Georgetown Guyana 44 M6, 53 F11
George Town (var. Pinang)Malaysia 100 L7, 125 I17
Georgia *Country* SW Asia 85

Georgia 85

a Georgian • Ruble • 79 • 73 • N/A • N/A • 56%

Georgia *State* USA 29
Gera Germany 67 K11
Geraldton Western Australia, Australia 132 E11
Germany *Country* C Europe 66-67

Germany 66-67

a German • Mark • 228 • 77 • £1.33 • (m) 99% (f) 99% • 570 • 345 • No • 86% • 3665

Gerona *see* Girona
Gersoppa Falls *Waterfall* India 115
Getafe Spain 61 K8
Gettysburg Pennsylvania, USA 26 I13
Getz Ice Shelf *Coastal feature* Pacific Ocean Coast, Antarctica 50 C10
Ghadaf, Wādī al *Seasonal watercourse* Iraq 108 J5
Ghadāmis Libya 89 N7
Ghana (prev. Gold Coast) *Country* W Africa 93

Ghana 93

a English • Cedi • 67 • 55 • £0.76 • (m) 70% (f) 51% • 33%

Ghanzi Botswana 98 J10
Ghardaïa Algeria 89 L6
Gharyān Libya 89 O6
Ghāt *Oasis* Libya 89 N10
Ghaznī Afghanistan 111 N12
Ghent (var. Gent) Belgium 65 E14
Ghulam Muhammad Barrage *Dam* Pakistan 116 G6
Gibraltar Gibraltar 60 I15
Gibraltar *Dependent territory* Mediterranean Sea 52 K9, 60 I15
Gibraltar, Strait of *Channel* Morocco/Spain 54, 87, 88 I4, 60 I15
Gibson Desert *Desert region* Western Australia, Australia 131, 132 H10
Giessen Germany 67 F12
Gifu Japan 123 I11
Giganta, Sierra de la *Mountain range* Mexico 39 H7
Gijón Spain 60 I3
Gila *River* Arizona/New Mexico, USA 35 K10
Gilbert Is. *Island group* Kiribati, Pacific Ocean 128 J9
Gilbert Ridge *Sea feature* Pacific Ocean 131
Gillette Wyoming, USA 33 K7
Giresun Turkey 105 O5
Girona (var. Gerona) Spain 61 Q5
Gisborne New Zealand 134 I6
Giurgiu Romania 77 L10
Giza Egypt 90 F6
Gjøvik Norway 56 J10
Gladstone Queensland, Australia 133 O9
Glåma *River* Norway 56 J9
Glarus Switzerland 68 H9
Glasgow Montana, USA 33 K4
Glasgow Scotland, UK 58 H10
Glen Canyon Dam *Dam* Utah, USA 34 J6
Glendale Arizona, USA 34 I9
Glendale California, USA 37 K18
Glendive Montana, USA 33 K5
Glens Falls New York, USA 27 M8
Gliwice Poland 71 L8
Gloucester England, UK 59 I15
Gloucester Massachusetts, USA 27 O9, 52 E8
Glubokoye *see* Hlybokaye
Gmünd Austria 69 P3
Gmunden Austria 69 O6
Gnjilane Serbia, Yugoslavia 75 O10
Goba Ethiopia 91 K15
Gobabis Namibia 98 I10
Gobi Desert *Desert region* C Asia 11, 115, 119 L7
Godavari *River* India 115, 117 L10
Godhavn Greenland 51 N13
Godoy Cruz Argentina 48 H10
Godthåb (var. Nuuk) Greenland 51 M14
Goiânia Brazil 47 J12
Golan Heights *Physical region occupied by Israel* Syria 107 M8
Gold Coast Queensland, Australia 133 P11
Gold Coast *see* Ghana
Golden Sands Bulgaria 77 O11
Golmud China 118 J10
Goma Zaire 95 O13
Gomel' *see* Homyel'
Gómez Palacio Mexico 39 L7
Gonaïves Haiti 43 M7
Gonâve, Île de la *Island* Haiti 43 M8
Gonder Ethiopia 91 I13
Gonghe China 119 L10
Gongola *River* Nigeria 93 Q10
Good Hope, Cape of *Cape* South Africa 53 M14, 87, 98 I16, 101 B12
Goondiwindi Queensland, Australia 133 O11
Goose Bay Newfoundland, Canada 25 Q7
Goose L. *Lake* California/Oregon, USA 37 I11
Gorakhpur India 117 M6
Goré Chad 94 I9
Gore Ethiopia 91 H15
Göreme Turkey 105 M8
Gorgān Iran 109 O4
Gorki *see* Horki
Görlitz Germany 67 N11
Gorlovka *see* Horlivka
Gorodets Russian Federation 82 H10
Goroka Papua New Guinea 133 N2
Gorongosa N.P. *National park* Mozambique 99 N8
Gorontalo Celebes, Indonesia 127 M11
Gorzów Wielkopolski Poland 70 I4
Gosford New South Wales, Australia 133 O13
Gospić Croatia 74 H5
Gosselies Belgium 65 G16
Gostivar Macedonia 75 N11
Göteborg Sweden 56 J13
Gotha Germany 67 I11
Gotland *Island* Sweden 57 L14
Gotō Is. *Island group* Japan 123 B14
Göttingen Germany 66 H10
Gouda Netherlands 65 H11
Gough Island *Island* Atlantic Ocean 53 K14
Gouin Res. *Reservoir* Quebec, Canada 25 L11
Goulburn New South Wales, Australia 133 O13
Govind Ballash Pant Res. *Reservoir* India 117 M7
Gowd-e-Zereh *Salt pan* Afghanistan 110 J15
Gozo *Island* Malta 73 K20
Gračanica Bosnia and Herzegovina 75 K5
Grafton New South Wales, Australia 133 P11
Grahamstown South Africa 99 L15
Grampian Mts. *Mountain range* Scotland, UK 54, 58 M8
Gran Chaco *Physical region* Argentina 41, 48 K6
Granada Nicaragua 42 D11
Granada Spain 61 K13
Grand Bahama *Island* Bahamas 43 K1
Grand Banks *Sea feature* Newfoundland, Canada 25 T10, 52 G8
Grand Canal (var. Da Yunhe) *Waterway* China 121 N9
Grand Canyon *Physical feature* Arizona, USA 20, 34 I6
Grand Cayman *Island* Cayman Islands 42 H6
Grand Falls New Brunswick, Canada 25 O11
Grand Falls Newfoundland, Canada 25 S9
Grand Forks North Dakota, USA 33 O4
Grand Island Nebraska, USA 33 O10
Grand Junction Colorado, USA 35 K4
Grand Rapids Michigan, USA 31 M8
Grand Teton Mts. *Mountain range* Wyoming, USA 32 I8
Grand Turk Turks & Caicos Islands 43 N6
Grande, Bahía *Sea feature* Argentina 49 K18
Grande, Serra *Mountain range* Brazil 46 M8
Grande Comore *Island* Comoros 100 E10
Grande Prairie Alberta, Canada 23 K13
Grande Rivière de la Baleine *River* Quebec, Canada 25 L6
Grande-Terre *Island* Guadeloupe 43 T11
Grangemouth Scotland, UK 58 H9
Grants Pass Oregon, USA 37 G11
Grasse France 63 Q13
Graz Austria 69 R8
Great Abaco *Island* Bahamas 43 K1
Great Artesian Basin *Physical feature* Australia 131
Great Australian Bight *Sea feature* Australia 131, 132 J13
Great Bahama Bank *Sea feature* West Indies 42 J2
Great Barrier I. *Island* New Zealand 134 H3
Great Barrier Reef *Coral reef* Queensland, Australia 128 H10, 131, 133 O7
Great Basin *Physical region* SW USA 10, 11, 20, 34 G2
Great Bear L. *Lake* Northwest Territories, Canada 20, 23 K8
Great Bend Kansas, USA 33 O12
Great Dividing Range *Mountain range* Queensland, Austalia 131, 133 O9
Great Exhibition Bay *Sea feature* New Zealand 134 F2
Great Exuma *Island* Bahamas 43 L4
Great Falls Montana, USA 32 H5
Great Inagua *Island* Bahamas 43 M6
Great Plain of China *Physical region* China 115
Great Plains *Physical region* USA 20, 33 L7
Great Rift Valley *Physical feature* SE Africa/SW Asia 8, 87, 97 O6
Great Ruaha *River* Tanzania 97 O9
Great St. Bernard Tunnel *Tunnel* Switzerland 68 E13
Great Salt Desert *see* Dasht-e-Kavir
Great Salt L. *Salt lake* Utah, USA 20, 34 I2
Great Salt Lake Desert *Desert region* Utah, USA 34 I3
Great Sandy Desert *Desert region* Western Australia, Australia 131, 132 H8
Great Slave L. *Lake* Northwest Territories, Canada 20, 23 L10
Great Victoria Desert *Desert region* Western Australia, Australia 131, 132 I11
Great Yarmouth England, UK 59 M14
Greater Antilles *Island group* Caribbean Sea 20, 41, 43 N9
Greater Khingan Range *Mountain range* China 115, 119 Q4
Gredos, Sierra de *Mountain range* Spain 60 J8
Greece *Country* S Europe 78-79

Greece 78-79

a Greek • Drachma • 77 • 77 • £1.11 • (m) 98% (f) 89% • 196 • 300 • No • 62% • 3825

Greeley Colorado, USA 35 N3
Green Bay Wisconsin, USA 31 L7
Green R. *River* Kentucky, USA 29 M3
Green R. *River* W USA 32 I9, 35 K3
Greenfield Massachusetts, USA 27 N9
Greenland *Dependent territory* Arctic Ocean 10, 51, 52 H6
Greenland *Island* Arctic Ocean 20, 103
Greenland Sea Arctic Ocean 51 P14, 52 J6, 103
Greenock Scotland, UK 58 G9
Greensboro North Carolina, USA 29 P5

Greenville Liberia 92 I13
Greenville Mississippi, USA 28 I6
Greenville South Carolina, USA 29 O6
Greifswald Germany 66 L6
Grenada *Country* Caribbean Sea 43 S15

Grenada 43

a English • 💰 Dollar • 👤 268 • ♥ 70 • ◒ £3.10 • 📖 (av.) 90% • 🏛 34%

Grenadines, The *Island group* St Vincent & The Grenadines 43 S14
Grenoble France 63 O11
Grevena Greece 78 H4
Greymouth New Zealand 134 E10
Grim, C. *Cape* Tasmania, Australia 133 M15
Grimsby England, UK 52 K8, 59 K13
Grodno *see* Hrodna
Groningen Netherlands 64 M6
Groote Eylandt *Island* Northern Territory, Australia 133 L5
Grootfontein Namibia 98 I9
Grosseto Italy 72 G10
Groznyy Russian Federation 83 F16
Grudziądz Poland 71 L3
Gstaad Switzerland 68 E11
Guacanayabo, Gulf of *Sea feature* Cuba 42 J6
Guadalajara Mexico 39 L11
Guadalajara Spain 61 L8
Guadalcanal *Island* Solomon Islands, Pacific Ocean 128 I9
Guadalquivir *River* Spain 54, 60 I12
Guadalupe Mexico 39 L9
Guadarrama, Sierra de *Mountain range* Spain 61 K7
Guadeloupe *Dependent territory* Caribbean Sea 43 S11
Guadiana *River* Portugal/Spain 60 G11
Gualeguaychu Argentina 48 M9
Guallatiri *Volcano* Chile 41
Guam *Dependent territory* Micronesia, Pacific Ocean 128 G7
Guanare Venezuela 44 H5
Guangxi Zhuang Autonomous Region China 121 K14
Guangzhou *see* Canton
Guantánamo Cuba 43 L6
Guantánamo Bay *Sea feature* Cuba 43 L7
Guarda Portugal 60 H8
Guatemala *Country* C America 42

Guatemala 42

a Spanish • 💰 Quetzal • 👤 87 • ♥ 64 • ◒ £0.51 • 📖 (m) 63% (f) 47% • 🏛 39%

Guatemala Basin *Sea feature* Pacific Ocean 41
Guatemala City Guatemala 42 B8
Guaviare *River* Colombia/Venezuela 44 F7
Guayaquil Ecuador 44 C9, 129 Q8
Guayaquil, Gulf of *Sea feature* Ecuador/Peru 44 B9
Guaymas Mexico 38 H5
Guddu Barrage *Dam* Pakistan 116 H4
Guernsey *Dependent territory* W Europe 59 H18
Guiana Highlands *Mountain range* South America 41
Guider Cameroon 94 G8
Guilin China 121 K13
Guinea *Country* W Africa 92

Guinea 92

a French • 💰 Franc • 👤 24 • ♥ 44 • ◒ £1.21 • 📖 (m) 35% (f) 13% • 📺 7 • ✚ 10300 • ☠ Yes • 🏛 26% • 🍴 2132

Guinea, Gulf of *Sea feature* C Africa 53 L11, 87, 95 E11
Guinea Basin *Sea feature* Gulf of Guinea, Atlantic Ocean 53 K12, 87
Guinea-Bissau (prev. Portuguese Guinea) *Country* W Africa 92

Guinea-Bissau 92

a Portuguese • 💰 Peso • 👤 36 • ♥ 41 • ◒ £1.53 • 📖 (m) 50% (f) 24% • 🏛 20%

Guiyang China 120 J12
Gujranwala Pakistan 116 J3
Gujrat Pakistan 116 J3
Gulf Stream current *Ocean current* Atlantic Ocean 12
Gulf, The *see* Persian Gulf
Gulfport Mississippi, USA 28 J9
Gulja *see* Yining
Gulu Uganda 97 M2
Gümüşhane Turkey 105 P5
Gur'yev *see* Atyrau
Gusau Nigeria 93 O10
Gusev Russian Federation 80 G10
Guwahati India 117 P6
Guyana (prev. British Guiana) *Country* S America 44

Guyana 44

a English • 💰 Dollar • 👤 4 • ♥ 65 • ◒ £2.11 • 📖 (m) 97% (f) 95% • 🏛 35%

Guyana Basin *Sea feature* Atlantic Ocean 53 G11
Gwalior India 117 K6
Gwelo *see* Gweru
Gweru (prev. Gwelo) Zimbabwe 99 M9
Gyandzha *see* Gäncä
Gyangzê China 118 I13
Gyda Peninsula *Physical feature* Russian Federation 112 I6
Győr Hungary 71 K13
Gytheio Greece 78 I12
Gyumri (var. Kumayri; var. Leninakan) Armenia 85 P13
Gzhel' Russian Federation 82 G10

H

Ha Giang Vietnam 124 M7
Haapsalu Estonia 80 I2
Haarlem Netherlands 64 H9
Ḩabbān Yemen 108 J16
Habomai Is. *Island group* Japan 122 O2
Hachinohe Japan 122 L6
Hachiōji Japan 123 K11
Hadejia *River* Nigeria 93 Q9
Hadhramaut *Region* Yemen 109 K16
Haeju North Korea 121 P7
Hagen Germany 67 E11
Hagi Japan 123 D13
Hague, The Netherlands 64 G10
Hai Phong Vietnam 124 N8
Haifa (var. Ḩefa) Israel 107 L8
Haikou China 121 K15
Hā'il Saudi Arabia 108 I8
Hailar China 119 P3
Hainan *Island* China 115, 121 K16
Hainburg Austria 69 T4
Haines Alaska, USA 22 I10
Haines Junction Yukon Territory, Canada 22 H9
Haiti *Country* Caribbean Sea 43

Haiti 43

a French, Creole • 💰 Gourde • 👤 240 • ♥ 54 • ◒ £0.55 • 📖 (m) 59% (f) 47% • 🏛 28%

Ḩajjah Yemen 108 H15
Hakkâri Turkey 105 S8
Hakodate Japan 122 K5, 128 G5
Ḩalab (var. Aleppo; anc. Beroea) Syria 107 N3
Halden Norway 56 J12
Halicarnassus Turkey 104 G9
Halifax Nova Scotia, Canada 25 Q13, 52 F8
Halle Germany 66 K10
Hallein Austria 69 N7
Halley *Research centre* Antarctica 50 D7
Halls Creek Western Australia, Australia 132 I7
Halmahera *Island* Indonesia 115, 131, 127 P10
Halmstad Sweden 56 J14
Hälsingborg Sweden 56 J15
Hamada Japan 123 D12
Hamadān Iran 109 M4
Ḩamāh Syria 107 N5
Hamamatsu Japan 123 J12
Hamar Norway 56 J10
Hamburg Germany 66 H7
Hameenlinna Finland 57 O10
Hamersley Range *Mountain range* Western Australia, Australia 132 F9
Hamhŭng North Korea 121 P6
Hami (var. Kumul) China 118 J7
Hamilton New Zealand 134 G5
Hamilton Ontario, Canada 25 K14
Hamm Germany 66 F10
Ḩammār, L. al *Lake* Iraq 109 L6
Hammerfest Norway 57 O1
Hāmūn-e-Şāberī *Salt pan* Afghanistan/Iran 110 J14
Handan China 121 M8
Hangayn Nuruu *Mountain range* Mongolia 119 K4
Hangzhou China 121 O11
Hannover *see* Hanover
Hanoi Vietnam 124 M8
Hanover (var. Hannover) Germany 66 H9
Har Us L. *Lake* Mongolia 118 J5
Ḩaraḑ Saudi Arabia 109 L10
Harare (prev. Salisbury) Zimbabwe 99 M8
Harbin China 121 P4
Hardanger Fjord *Sea feature* Norway 56 H10
Harderwijk Netherlands 64 J10
Harer Ethiopia 91 L15
Hargeysa Somalia 91 M14
Harīrūd *River* C Asia 111 L11
Harlan County L. *Lake* Nebraska, USA 33 N11
Harlingen Netherlands 64 J7
Harney L. *Lake* Oregon, USA 36 K10
Härnösand Sweden 57 M9
Harper Liberia 92 I13
Harris *Island* Scotland, UK 58 F7
Harrisburg Pennsylvania, USA 26 J13
Harry S. Truman Res. *Reservoir* Missouri, USA 33 Q12
Harstad Norway 57 M3
Hartford Connecticut, USA 27 M11
Hasselt Belgium 65 J14
Hässleholm Sweden 56 J15
Hastings England, UK 59 L17
Hastings Nebraska, USA 33 O10
Hastings New Zealand 134 H7
Hat Yai Thailand 125 I16
Hatteras, Cape *Cape* North Carolina, USA 20, 29 S6
Hatteras Plain *Sea feature* Atlantic Ocean 20
Hattiesburg Mississippi, USA 28 J8
Haugesund Norway 52 K7, 56 H11
Havana (var. La Habana) Cuba 42 H3
Havre Montana, USA 32 I4
Havre-Saint-Pierre Quebec, Canada 25 P9
Hawaii *Island* Pacific Ocean 12
Hawaii *State* USA, Pacific Ocean 129 L6
Hawaiian Is. *Island group* Polynesia, Pacific Ocean 8, 129 K7
Hawke Bay *Sea feature* New Zealand 134 I7
Ḩawran, Wādī *Seasonal watercourse* Iraq 108 J4
Hay River Northwest Territories, Canada 23 L10
Hayes *River* Manitoba, Canada 23 P12
Hays Kansas, USA 33 N13
Hazleton Pennsylvania, USA 27 K12
Heads, The *Cape* Oregon, USA 36 F10
Heard and MacDonald Islands *Dependent territory see* Heard I, MacDonald Is
Heard I. *Island* Indian Ocean 50 I7, 101 H15
Heathrow *Airport* England, UK 59 K16
Heerenveen Netherlands 64 K7
Heerlen Netherlands 65 K15
Ḩefa *see* Haifa
Hefei China 121 N10
Heidelberg Germany 67 F14
Heilbronn Germany 67 G14
Heilong Jiang *see* Amur
Hejaz *Region* Saudi Arabia 108 H9
Helena Montana, USA 32 H5
Helgoland Bay (var. Helgoländer Bucht) *Sea feature* Germany 66 G6
Helgoländer Bucht *see* Helgoland Bay
Helmand *River* Afghanistan/Iran 111 L12
Helmond Netherlands 65 K12
Helsingør Denmark 56 J15
Helsinki Finland 57 O11
Helwân Egypt 90 F7
Henderson Nevada, USA 34 H7
Hengelo Netherlands 64 N10
Henrietta Maria, C. *Cape* Canada 24 J6
Henzada Burma 124 F10
Herāt Afghanistan 110 J12
Herisau Switzerland 68 H8
Herlen Gol *see* Kerulen
Hermansverk Norway 56 I9
Hermit Is. *Island group* Papua New Guinea 133 N1
Hermosillo Mexico 38 H4
Herrenchiemsee *Castle* Germany 67 K16
Herstal Belgium 65 K15
Hialeah Florida, USA 29 O15
Hibbing Minnesota, USA 30 H3
Hidaka Mts. *Mountain range* Japan 122 L4
Hidalgo del Parral Mexico 39 K6
Hierosolyma *see* Jerusalem
Hiiumaa *Island* Estonia 80 H2
Hildesheim Germany 66 H9
Hillsboro Oregon, USA 36 H8
Hilversum Netherlands 64 I10
Himalayas *Mountain range* S Asia **8**, 11, 103, 115, 117 M5, 118 H14
Ḩimş Syria 107 N5
Hindu Kush *Mountain range* 103, 111 O10, 115
Hinnøya *Island* Norway 57 L3
Hirakud Res. *Reservoir* India 117 M9
Hirfanli Barrage *Dam* Turkey 105 L7
Hiroshima Japan 123 E13
Hispania *see* Spain
Hispaniola *Island* Caribbean Sea 20, 41
Hīt Iraq 108 J4
Hitachi Japan 122 L10
Hitra *Island* Norway 56 I7
Hjørring Denmark 56 I13
Hjort Trench *Sea feature* 131
Hlybokaye (var. Glubokoye) Belorussia 81 L9
Ho Chi Minh City (prev. Saigon) Vietnam 125 N14
Hobart Tasmania, Australia 133 N16
Hobbs New Mexico, USA 35 N10
Hodeida (var. Al Hudaydah) Yemen 108 H15
Hoek van Holland Netherlands 65 G11
Hof Germany 67 J12
Hohe Tauern *Mountain range* Austria 69 N8
Hohenschwangau *Castle* Germany 67 I17
Hohhot China 119 O7
Hokkaidō *Island* Japan 115, 122 L3
Holguín Cuba 43 K6
Holland Michigan, USA 31 M9
Hollywood California, USA 37 K18
Hollywood Florida, USA 29 O15
Ḩolon Israel 107 L10
Holstebro Denmark 56 H14
Holy I. *Island* Wales, UK 59 G13
Holyhead Wales, UK 59 G13
Home Counties *Region* England, UK 59 K16
Homer Alaska, USA 22 F8
Homyel' (var. Gomel') Belorussia 81 O14
Honduras *Country* C America 42

Honduras 42

a Spanish • 💰 Lempira • 👤 47 • ♥ 65 • ◒ £0.56 • 📖 (m) 75% (f) 70% • 🏛 44%

Honduras, Gulf of *Sea feature* C America 42 C7
Hønefoss Norway 56 I11
Hong Gai Vietnam 124 N8
Hong Kong *Dependent territory* SE China 121 M14 128 E7
Hongshui He *River* China 120 J13
Hongze Hu *Lake* China 121 N9
Honiara Guadalcanal Solomon Islands, Pacific Ocean 128 I9
Honolulu Oahu Hawaiian Islands, Pacific Ocean 129 K6
Honshū *Island* Japan 115, 122 J9
Hoogeveen Netherlands 64 M8
Hoorn Netherlands 64 I8
Hoover Dam *Dam* Arizona/Nevada, USA 34 H7
Hopa Turkey 105 Q4
Hopedale Newfoundland, Canada 25 P5
Hopkinsville Kentucky, USA 29 L3
Horki (var. Gorki) Belorussia 81 O11
Horlivka (var. Gorlovka) Ukraine 85 M6
Hormuz, Strait of *Channel* Iran/Oman 109 O10
Horn of Africa *Physical region* Somalia 91 O14
Horn, Cape *Cape* Chile 49 L20, 56 F16, 129 Q14
Horsens Denmark 56 I15
Hot Springs Arkansas, USA 28 H5
Hotan China 118 F9
Houlton Maine, USA 27 Q3
Houston Texas, USA 35 S13
Hovd Mongolia 118 I5
Hövsgöl, L. *Lake* Mongolia 119 L3
Howland I. *Dependent territory* Polynesia, Pacific Ocean 128 J8
Hradec Králové Czech Republic 70 I8
Hrodna (var. Grodno) Belorussia 80 I12
Hron *River* Slovakia 71 L11
Hrvatska *see* Croatia
Huai He *River* China 115
Huainan China 121 N10
Huambo (var. Nova Lisboa) Angola 98 H6
Huancayo Peru 45 E13
Huang He *see* Yellow R.
Huánuco Peru 45 D12
Huascarán *Mountain* Peru 41
Huddersfield England, UK 59 J13
Huddinge Sweden 57 L12
Hudiksvall Sweden 57 L10
Hudson *River* New York, USA 27 M10
Hudson Bay *Sea feature* Canada 10, 20, 23 P10, 24 I5, 52 D7
Hudson-Mohawk Gap *Physical feature* New York/Vermont, USA 27 M9
Hudson Strait *Channel* Canada 20, 23 R8, 25 M2
Hue Vietnam 125 N11
Huehuetenango Guatemala 42 A7
Huelva Spain 60 H13
Huesca Spain 61 N5
Hughenden Queensland, Australia 133 N8
Hulun Nur *Lake* China 119 P4
Humber *River* England, UK 59 K13
Humboldt *River* Nevada, USA 34 H2
Hūn Libya 89 P7
Hungarian Plain *Physical region* Hungary 54, 71 L14
Hungary *Country* C Europe 70-71

Hungary 70-71

a Hungarian • 💰 Forint • 👤 114 • ♥ 71 • ◒ £0.44 • 📖 (m) 99% (f) 99% • 📺 410 • ✚ 330 • ☠ No • 🏛 61% • 🍴 3644

Huntington West Virginia, USA 29 O3
Huntington Beach California, USA 37 L19
Huntsville Alabama, USA 29 L6
Huron Ohio, USA 31 P10
Huron, Lake *Lake* Canada/USA 20, 24 J13, 31 O6
Hurunui *River* New Zealand 134 F10
Husum Germany 66 G6
Hutchinson Kansas, USA 33 O12
Huy Belgium 65 J16
Hvar *Island* Croatia 74 I8
Hwange (prev. Wankie) Zimbabwe 99 L8
Hwange N.P. *National park* Zimbabwe 99 L9
Hyargas, L. *Lake* Mongolia 118 J4
Hyderabad India 117 K11
Hyderabad Pakistan 116 H6
Hyères, Îles d' *Island* France 63 P14
Hyparis *see* Southern Bug
Hyvinkää Finland 57 O11

I

Ialomiţa *River* Romania 77 N9
Iaşi Romania 77 N3
Ibadan Nigeria 93 N12
Ibagué Colombia 44 E7
Ibar *River* Serbia, Yugoslavia 75 N9
Ibarra Ecuador 44 C8
Ibb Yemen 108 I16
Iberian Pen. *Physical region* SW Europe 54
Ibiza Ibiza, Balearic Islands, Spain 61 P10
Ibiza *Island* Balearic Islands, Spain 61 P10
Ibotirama Brazil 47 L11
Ibrī Oman 109 O12
Ica Peru 45 E14
Iceland *Country* Atlantic Ocean 51, 52 J7

Iceland 52

a Icelandic • 💰 Krona • 👤 3 • ♥ 78 • ◒ £2.72 • 📖 (m) 100% (f) 100% • 📺 320 • ✚ 376 • ☠ No • 🏛 91% • 🍴 3611

Iceland *Island* Atlantic Ocean 8, 10, 20, 103
Icosium *see* Algiers
Idaho *State* USA 32
Idaho Falls Idaho, USA 32 H8
Idfu Egypt 90 G8
Ieper Belgium 65 C15
Iglesias Sardinia 73 C15
Igoumenitsa Greece 78 F5

a Language (official or most commonly spoken) • 💰 Currency • 👤 Population density per square kilometre • ♥ Average life expectancy • ◒ Price of 1 dozen hen's eggs • 📖 Literacy • 📺 Number of TVs per 1,000 people • ✚ Number of people per doctor • ☠ Death penalty • 🏛 Percentage of urban-based population • 🍴 Average number of calories consumed daily per person

Iguaçu *River* Argentina/Brazil 47 H15
Iguaçu Falls *Waterfall* Brazil 41, 47 H14
Iisalmi Finland 57 P8
IJmuiden Netherlands 64 H9
IJssel *River* Netherlands 64 K9
IJsselmeer *Man-made lake* Netherlands 64 J8
Ijzer *River* Belgium/France 65 C14
Ikaria *Island* Greece 79 O10
Iki *Island* Japan 123 B13
Ilagan Luzon, Philippines 127 L3
Ilām Iran 109 L5
Ilebo Zaire 95 K14
Ilgaz Mts. *Mountain range* Turkey 104 L5
Ilha Solteira Res. *Reservoir* Brazil 47 I13
Ili *River* Kazakhstan 103, 112 G13
Iliamna L. *Lake* Alaska, USA 22 F8
Iligan Mindanao, Philippines 127 N7
Ilium *see* Troy
Illapel Chile 48 G10
Illinois *River* Illinois, USA 31 J13
Illinois *State* USA 30-31
Illizi Algeria 89 M9
Ilo Peru 129 Q9
Iloilo Panay, Philippines 127 M6
Ilorin Nigeria 93 N11
Imatra Finland 57 Q10
Imperial Dam *Dam* Arizona/California USA 34 H9
Impfondo Congo 95 I12
Imphal India 117 Q7
Inari, L. *Lake* Finland 57 P2
Inch'ŏn South Korea 121 P7, 128 F5
Independence Missouri, USA 33 Q11
India *Country* S Asia 116-117

India 116-117

Hindi, English • Rupee • 291 • 59 • £0.39 • (m) 64% (f) 39% • 32 • 2400 • Yes • 27% • 2229

India *Subcontinent* 8, 9, 103
Indian Desert *see* Thar Desert
Indian Ocean 87, 91, 100-101, 103, 114-115, 130-131
Indiana Pennsylvania, USA 26 H12
Indiana *State* USA 31
Indianapolis Indiana, USA 31 N12
Indigirka *River* Russian Federation 113 O5
Indo-Australian Plate *Physical feature* 8, 103, 115, 131
Indonesia (prev. Dutch East Indies) *Country* SE Asia 126-127

Indonesia 126-127

Bahasa Indonesia • Rupiah • 100 • 62 • £0.41 • (m) 84% (f) 68% • 60 • 7372 • Yes • 31% • 2750

Indore India 116 J8
Indus *River* Asia 100 H5, 103, 115, 116 G7
Indus Delta *Delta* Pakistan 115
Ingolstadt Germany 67 J15
Inhambane Mozambique 99 O11
Inland Sea Japan 123 F13
Inle, L. *Lake* Burma 124 G8
Inn *River* Austria/Germany/Switzerland 67 L15, 69 K8
Inner Mongolia (var. Nei Mongol) *Region* China 119 P6
Innsbruck Austria 69 L8
Inongo Zaire 95 J13
Insein Burma 124 F10
Interlaken Switzerland 68 F11
Inukjuak Quebec, Canada 25 K4
Inuvik Northwest Territories, Canada 22 J7
Inuvik *Region* Northwest Territories, Canada 22 J8
Invercargill New Zealand 134 C14
Inverness Scotland, UK 58 H8
Investigator Strait *Channel* South Australia, Australia 133 K14
Ioannina Greece 78 G5
Iona N.P. *National park* Angola 98 F8
Ionian Is. *Island group* Greece 78 F8
Ionian Sea Greece/Italy 54, 73 O17, 78 F8
Ios *Island* Cyclades, Greece 79 N12
Iowa *State* USA 33
Iowa City Iowa, USA 33 R9
Ipel' *River* Hungary/Slovakia 71 L12
Ipoh Malaysia 125 I18
Ipswich England, UK 59 L15
Ipswich Queensland, Australia 133 P10
Iqaluit (var. Frobisher Bay) Baffin I. Northwest Territories, Canada 23 R7
Iquique Chile 49 F4
Iquitos Peru 44 F9
Iracoubo French Guiana 44 O6
Irakleio Crete, Greece 79 M16
Iran (prev. Persia) *Country* SW Asia 109

Iran 109

Farsi • Rial • 35 • 63 • £6.09 • (m) 65% (f) 44% • 247 • 2821 • Yes • 57% • 3181

Iranian Plate *Physical feature* 8, 54, 87, 103, 115
Iranian Plateau *Physical feature* Iran 103
Irapuato Mexico 39 M11
Iraq (anc. Mesopotamia) *Country* SW Asia 108-109

Iraq 108-109

Arabic • Dinar • 45 • 63 • N/A • (m) 70% (f) 49% • 69 • 1732 • Yes • 71% • 2887

Irbid Jordan 107 M9
Irbil Iraq 109 K3
Ireland (var. Eire) *Country* W Europe 58-59

Ireland 58-59

Irish, English • Punt • 51 • 75 • £1.27 • (m) 98% (f) 98% • 276 • 633 • No • 57% • 3778

Ireland *Island* W Europe 54
Irian Jaya *Region* Indonesia 127 S12
Iringa Tanzania 97 O10
Irish Sea Ireland/UK 59 F13
Irkutsk Russian Federation 113 L12
Iron Gates *HEP station* Serbia, Yugoslavia 75 P6
Irrawaddy *River* Burma 100 K5, 115, 124 G7
Irrawaddy Delta *Delta* Burma 115
Irtysh (var. Ertix He) *River* N Asia 103, 112 H9, 118 H5
Ischia *Island* Italy 72 J13
Isea, L. d' *Lake* Italy 72 F6
Ishikari *River* Japan 122 K4
Ishikari Bay *Sea feature* Japan 122 K4
Ishikari Mts. *Mountain range* Japan 122 L3
Ishim *River* Kazakhstan/Russian Federation 112 G10
Isiro Zaire 95 N11
Iskenderun (anc. Alexandretta) Turkey 105 N10
Iskŭr *River* Bulgaria 76 J11
Iskŭr, L. *Lake* Bulgaria 76 I13
Islam Barrage *Dam* Pakistan 116 I4
Islamabad Pakistan 116 J2
Islay *Island* Scotland, UK 58 F10
Isle Royale *Island* Michigan, USA 31 K3
Ismâ 'ilîya Egypt 90 G6
Isparta Turkey 104 J9
Israel *Country* SW Asia 107

Israel 107

Hebrew, Arabic • Shekel • 240 • 76 • £0.98 • (m) 98% (f) 96% • 266 • 339 • No • 92% • 3174

Issyk-kul' (prev. Rybach'ye) Kyrgyzstan 111 R5
Issyk-kul', L. *Lake* Kyrgyzstan 111 R5
Istanbul (prev. Constantinople; anc. Byzantium) Turkey 104 H5
Itaipú Res. *Reservoir* Brazil 41, 47 H14
Itaipú Dam *Dam* Brazil/Paraguay 48 O6
Italy *Country* S Europe 9, 72-73

Italy 72-73

Italian • Lira • 196 • 78 • £1.32 • (m) 98% (f) 96% • 424 • 233 • No • 69% • 3504

Itanagar India 117 Q6
Itatka ICBM Base *Military centre* Russian Federation 112 J10
Itea Greece 78 I8
Ithaca New York, USA 26 J9
Iturup *Island* Japan 122 P1
Ivalo Finland 57 P3
Ivangrad Montenegro, Yugoslavia 75 M9
Ivano-Frankivs'k Ukraine 84 F5
Ivanovo Russian Federation 82 H10
Ivory Coast (var. Côte d'Ivoire) *Country* W Africa 92-93

Ivory Coast 92-93

French • Franc • 39 • 55 • £1.42 • (m) 67% (f) 40% • 40%

Ivory Coast *Physical region* W Africa 92 J13
Iwaki Japan 122 L9
Izabal, L. *Lake* Guatemala 42 B7
Izhevsk Russian Federation 83 K11
Izhma *River* Russian Federation 82 L8
Izmir Turkey 104 G8
Izmit Turkey 104 I5
Iznik Turkey 104 I6
Iztaccíhuatl *Mountain* Mexico 39 N12
Izu Is. *Island group* Japan 123 K12

J

Jabalpur India 116 L8
Jackson Michigan, USA 31 N9
Jackson Mississippi, USA 28 J7
Jackson Tennessee, USA 29 K5
Jackson L. *Lake* Wyoming, USA 32 I7
Jacksonville Florida, USA 29 O10
Jacksonville Illinois, USA 30 J12
Jacmel Haiti 43 M8
Jadotville *see* Likasi
Jaén Spain 61 K12
Jaffna Sri Lanka 117 L15
Jaipur India 116 J6
Jaisalmer India 116 I5
Jajce Bosnia and Herzegovina 74 J6
Jakarta (var. Batavia) Indonesia 15, 126 G14
Jakobstad Finland 57 N8
Jalālābād Afghanistan 111 O12
Jalandhar India 117 K3
Jalapa Mexico 39 O12
Jamaica *Country* Caribbean Sea 14, 42-43

Jamaica 42-43

English • Dollar • 225 • 73 • £0.54 • (m) 98% (f) 99% • 52%

Jamaica *Island* Caribbean Sea 20, 41
Jamalpur Bangladesh 117 P7
Jambi Sumatra, Indonesia 126 F12
James *River* South Dakota/North Dakota, USA 33 O7
James Bay *Sea feature* Canada 24 J7
Jamestown New York, USA 26 H10
Jamestown North Dakota, USA 33 N5
Jamnagar India 116 H8
Jamshedpur India 116 N8
Jan Mayen *Dependent territory* Arctic Ocean 51 P15
Janakpur Nepal 117 N6
Janesville Wisconsin, USA 31 K9
Japan (var. Nippon, Nihon) *Country* E Asia 122-123

Japan 122-123

Japanese • Yen • 329 • 79 • £1.38 • (m) 99% (f) 99% • 620 • 608 • Yes • 77% • 2956

Japan, Sea of E Asia 100 M9, 113 Q12, 115, 122 H9, 128 G5
Japan Trench *Sea feature* Pacific Ocean 9, 115, 128 G5
Japanese Alps *Mountain range* Japan 123 I11
Jardines de la Reina *Island group* Cuba 42 I5
Jari *River* Brazil/Surinam 46 H6
Järvenpää Finland 57 O11
Jāsk Iran 109 P10
Jasper Alberta, Canada 23 K13
Java *Island* Indonesia 100 M9, 115, 127 H15, 130-131
Java Sea Indonesia 100 M9, 115, 126 H14, 131
Java Trench *Sea feature* Indian Ocean 8, 100 L9, 115, 130
Jayapura Irian Jaya, Indonesia 127 T11
Jaz Mūrīān Salt Lake *Salt lake* Iran 109 P9
Jazīrah, Al *Region* Syria 107 R3
Jebel Aulia Dam *Dam* Sudan 91 G12
Jedda (var. Jiddah) Saudi Arabia 108 G11
Jefferson City Missouri, USA 33 R12
Jēkabpils Latvia 80 J7
Jelgava Latvia 80 I6
Jember Java, Indonesia 126 J15
Jena Germany 67 J11
Jenbach Austria 69 L8
Jendouba Tunisia 89 N4
Jerba I. *Island* Tunisia 89 N5
Jérémie Haiti 43 L8
Jerez de la Frontera Spain 60 H14
Jericho West Bank 107 M10
Jersey *Dependent territory* W Europe 59 H19
Jerusalem (var. Yerushalayim; anc. Hierosolyma) Israel 107 L10
Jesenice Slovenia 74 G2
Jessore Bangladesh 117 O8
Jeziorak, L. *Lake* Poland 71 L3
Jhelum Pakistan 116 J2
Jiamusi China 121 Q3
Jiddah *see* Jedda
Jihlava Czech Republic 70 I10
Jihlava *River* Czech Republic 70 I10
Jijiga Ethiopia 91 L14
Jilib Somalia 91 L18
Jilin China 121 P5
Jima Ethiopia 91 I15
Jinan China 121 M8
Jingdezhen China 121 N11
Jingmen China 121 L11
Jining China 119 O7
Jinja Uganda 97 M4
Jinnah Barrage *Dam* Pakistan 116 I2
Jinotega Nicaragua 42 D10
Jinsha *River* China 115, 120 H11
Jiu *River* Romania 76 J10
Jixi China 121 Q4
Jīzān Saudi Arabia 108 H14
Jizera *River* Czech Republic 70 H8
João Pessoa Brazil 46 P9
Jodhpur India 116 I6
Joensuu Finland 57 Q9
Johannesburg South Africa 99 L12
John Day *River* Oregon/Washington USA 36 J9
Johnson City Tennessee, USA 29 O5
Johnston Atoll *Dependent territory* Polynesia, Pacific Ocean 129 K7
Johnstown Pennsylvania, USA 26 H12
Johor Baharu Malaysia 125 K20
Joinville Brazil 47 J15
Jokkmokk Sweden 57 M5
Joliba *see* Niger *River*
Joliet Illinois, USA 31 L10
Jolo *Island* Philippines 127 L8
Jolo Jolo, Philippines 127 L8
Jonglei Canal *Waterway* Sudan 91 F15
Joniškis Lithuania 80 I7
Jönköping Sweden 57 K13
Jonquière Quebec, Canada 25 N11
Joplin Missouri, USA 33 Q13
Jordan (prev. Transjordan) *Country* SWAsia 107

Jordan 107

Arabic • Dinar • 38 • 68 • £0.47 • (m) 89% (f) 70% • 68%

Jordan *River* SW Asia 107 M9
Jorge, Golfo de *Sea feature* Spain 61 P7
Jos Nigeria 93 P11
Jos Plateau *Physical feature* Nigeria 93 P11
Joseph Bonaparte Gulf *Sea feature* Northern Territory/Western Australia, Australia 132 I5
Juan de Fuca, Strait of *Channel* Canada/USA 36 G6
Juan Fernández, Islas *Island group* Pacific Ocean 129 P11
Juàzeiro Brazil 46 M10
Juba *River* Somalia 91 L18
Juba Sudan 91 F16
Júcar *River* Spain 61 N10
Judenburg Austria 69 Q8
Juigalpa Nicaragua 42 D11
Juiz de Fora Brazil 47 L14
Juliaca Peru 45 G14
Julianehåb Greenland 51 M15
Juneau Alaska, USA 22 I10
Jungfrau *Mountain* Switzerland 68 F11
Junín Argentina 48 L10
Jura *Island* Scotland, UK 58 F9
Jura *Mountain range* France/Switzerland 63 O8, 68 D10
Jurbarkas Lithuania 80 H9
Juruá *River* Brazil/Peru 41, 46 B9
Juticalpa Honduras 42 D9
Jutland *Peninsula* Denmark 54, 56 H14
Juventud, I. de la (var. I. of Pines) *Island* Cuba 42 G4
Jwaneng Botswana 99 K11
Jyväskylä Finland 57 O9

K

K2 *Mountain* Tibet 115
Kabaena *Island* Indonesia 127 M14
Kabaledo Res. *Reservoir* Surinam 44 N7
Kabalo Zaire 95 N15
Kabul Afghanistan 111 N11
Kabwe Zambia 97 K14
Kaduna Nigeria 93 O10
Kaduqli Sudan 91 F14
Kaédi Mauritania 92 G7
Kaesŏng North Korea 121 P7
Kafue Zambia 97 K15
Kafue *National park* Zambia 96 J14
Kafue *River* Zambia 96 J14
Kafue Flats *Physical region* Zambia 96 J15
Kaga-Bandoro Central African Republic 94 J10
Kagera *National park* Rwanda 97 L5
Kagoshima Japan 123 C15
Kahramanmaraş Turkey 105 N9
Kai Is. *Island group* Indonesia 127 Q13
Kaikoura New Zealand 134 F10
Kainji Res. *Reservoir* Nigeria 93 N10
Kaipara Harbour *Coastal feature* New Zealand 134 G4
Kairouan Tunisia 89 N4
Kaiserslautern Germany 67 E14
Kajaani Finland 57 P7
Kakamega Kenya 97 N4
Kakhovka Res. *Reservoir* Ukraine 85 K7
Kalahari Desert *Desert region* Botswana 11, 87, 98 J11
Kalahari Gemsbok *National park* Botswana/South Africa 98 J12
Kalamata Greece 78 I12
Kalamazoo Michigan, USA 31 N9
Kalamit Gulf *Sea feature* Ukraine 84 J10
Kalemie (prev. Albertville) Zaire 95 O15
Kalgoorlie Western Australia, Australia 132 H12
Kaliningrad (prev. Königsberg) Russian Federation 80 F9
Kaliningrad Oblast *Region* Russian Federation 80
Kalinkavichy Belorussia 81 M15
Kalispell Montana, USA 32 G4
Kalisz Poland 71 K6
Kalmar Sweden 57 K15
Kaluga Russian Federation 82 F10
Kama *River* Russian Federation 82 L10
Kama Res. *Reservoir* Russian Federation 82 L10
Kamarān I. *Island* Yemen 108 H15
Kamarhati India 117 O8
Kamchatka *Peninsula* Russian Federation 103, 113 Q7, 128 I3
Kamchiya *River* Bulgaria 77 O12
Kamenets-Podol"skiy *see* Kam'yanets'-Podil's'kyy
Kamenjak, C. *Cape* Croatia 74 F5
Kamina Zaire 95 M16
Kamloops British Columbia, Canada 22 J14
Kampala Uganda 97 M4
Kâmpóng Cham Cambodia 125 M14
Kâmpóng Chhnăng Cambodia 125 L14
Kâmpóng Saôm Cambodia 125 L14
Kâmpóng Thum Cambodia 125 M13
Kâmpôt Cambodia 125 L14

Kampuchea – Kuito

Kampuchea *see* Cambodia
Kam'yanets'-Podil's'kyy (var. Kamenets-Podol"skiy) Ukraine 84 G6
Kananga (prev. Luluabourg) Zaire 95 K15
Kanazawa Japan 122 H10
Kanchanaburi Thailand 125 I12
Kandahar *see* Qandahār
Kandi Benin 93 N10
Kandla India 116 H7
Kandy Sri Lanka 117 L16
Kangaroo I. *Island* South Australia, Australia 133 L14
Kangchenjunga *Mountain* China 115
Kangean *Island* Indonesia 126 J14
Kanggye North Korea 121 P6
Kangnŭng South Korea 121 Q7
Kanjiža Serbia, Yugoslavia 75 M3
Kankakee Illinois, USA 31 L11
Kankan Guinea 92 I10
Kano Nigeria 93 P10
Kanpur India 117 L6
Kansas *State* USA 33
Kansas City Kansas, USA 33 Q11
Kansas City Missouri, USA 33 Q11
Kansk Russian Federation 113 K10
Kao-hsiung Taiwan 121 O14
Kaolack Senegal 92 F8
Kap Farvel *see* Farvel, Cape
Kapchagay Kazakhstan 112 H13
Kapfenberg Austria 69 Q7
Kapos *River* Hungary 71 K15
Kapuas *River* Borneo, Indonesia 126 I11
Kara Togo 93 M11
Kara-Balta Kyrgyzstan 111 Q4
Kara-Bogaz-Gol, Zaliv *Bay* Turkmenistan 110 F5
Kara Deniz *see* Black Sea
Kara Kum *Desert region* Turkmenistan 11, 103
Kara Sea Russian Federation 51 S11, 54, 82 O5, 103, 112 I5
Kara Strait *Channel* Russian Federation 82 N6
Karabük Turkey 105 K5
Karachi Pakistan 100 H5, 116 G6
Karaganda (var. Qaraghandy) Kazakhstan 112 G11
Karaginskiy Is. *Island Group* Russian Federation 113 Q5
Karagiya Depression *Physical region* Asia 103
Karaj Iran 109 N4
Karakaya Barrage *Dam* Turkey 105 P8
Karakinit Gulf *Sea feature* Ukraine 84 J9
Karakorum Mts. *Mountain range* C Asia 118 E9
Karaköse *see* Ağri
Karakum Canal *Waterway* Turkmenistan 111 K9
Karaman Turkey 105 K9
Karamay China 118 H5
Karasburg Namibia 98 I13
Karasjok Norway 57 O2
Karbala Iraq 109 K5
Karditsa Greece 78 I6
Kariba Dam *Dam* Zambia/Zimbabwe 97 K15
Kariba, L. *Reservoir* Zambia/Zimbabwe 87, 97 K15, 99 L8
Karimata *Island* Indonesia 126 H12
Karisimbi, Mt. *Volcano* Zaire 87
Karlovac Croatia 74 H4
Karlovy Vary Czech Republic 70 G8
Karlskrona Sweden 57 K15
Karlsruhe Germany 67 F14
Karlstad Sweden 57 K12
Karpathos *Island* Dodecanese, Greece 79 Q15
Kars Turkey 105 R5
Karshi Uzbekistan 111 L8
Karymskaya Sopka *Volcano* Siberia 103
Karystos Greece 79 L9
Kasai *River* Angola/Zaire 95 J14
Kasama Zambia 97 M11
Kasese Uganda 97 L4
Kāshān Iran 109 N5
Kashgar *see* Kashi
Kashi (var. Kashgar) China 118 E8
Kashmir *Region* S Asia 117 K2
Kaskaskia *River* Illinois, USA 31 K13
Kasongo Zaire 95 N14
Kassala Sudan 91 I12
Kassandra, Gulf of *Sea feature* Greece 79 K4
Kassel Germany 67 H11
Kastamonu Turkey 105 L5
Kastoria Greece 78 H3
Kastorias, L. *Lake* Greece 78 H3
Kasumi Lagoon *Coastal feature* Japan 122 L10
Kasungu *National park* Malawi 97 M13
Kasur Pakistan 116 J3
Katakolo Greece 78 H10
Katar *see* Qatar
Katavi *National park* Tanzania 97 M9
Katerini Greece 78 I4
Katha Burma 124 G6
Kathmandu Nepal 117 N5
Katowice Poland 71 L9
Katsberg Tunnel *Tunnel* Austria 69 O9
Katsina Nigeria 93 P9
Kattegat *Channel* Denmark/Sweden 56 I14
Kaub *Castle* Germany 67 E12
Kaufmann Peak *see* Lenin Peak
Kaunas Lithuania 80 I9
Kavadarci Macedonia 75 O12
Kavala Greece 79 L2
Kawa *Archaeological site* Sudan 91 F11
Kawasaki Japan 123 K11
Kayan *River* Borneo, Indonesia 127 K10
Kayes Mali 92 H8
Kayseri Turkey 105 M8
Kazakh Uplands *Physical region* Kazakhstan 112 G11
Kazakhstan *Country* C Asia 112

Kazakhstan 112

a Kazakh • ≋ Afghani • ♦ 6 • ● 69 • ◒ N/A • ◗ N/A • ⌂ 58%

Kazan' Russian Federation 83 J11
Kazanlŭk Bulgaria 77 L13
Kéa *Island* Cyclades, Greece 79 L10
Keban Barrage *Dam* Turkey 105 O7
Kecskemét Hungary 71 M14
Kėdainiai Lithuania 80 I9
Kediri Java, Indonesia 126 I15
Keetmanshoop Namibia 98 I12
Keewatin *Region* Northwest Territories, Canada 23 N9
Kefallonia *Island* Ionian Is. Greece 78 G8
Kegon Falls *Waterfall* Japan 115
Kelang Malaysia 125 J19
Kelkit *River* Turkey 105 P6
Kellett, Cape *Cape* Canada 51 N8
Kelmė Lithuania 80 H8
Kelud *Volcano* Java, Indonesia 115
Kem' Russian Federation 82 I6
Kemerovo Russian Federation 112 I10
Kemi Finland 57 O6
Kemi *River* Finland 57 O5
Kemijärvi Finland 57 P5
Kenai Alaska, USA 22 G8
Kendari Celebes, Indonesia 127 M13
Kenema Sierra Leone 92 H12
Kenge Zaire 95 I14
Kénitra Morocco 88 I5
Kennebec *River* Maine, USA 27 P5
Kennedy Space Center Florida, USA 29 O12
Kennewick Washington, USA 36 K8
Kenora Ontario, Canada 24 F9
Kenosha Wisconsin, USA 31 L9
Kentucky *River* Kentucky, USA 29 N3
Kentucky *State* USA 29
Kenya *Country* E Africa 97

Kenya 97

a Swahili • ≋ Shilling • ♦ 44 • ● 59 • ◒ £0.46 • ◗ (m) 80% (f) 59% • ▭ 9 • ✚ 6552 • ✪ Yes • ⌂ 24% • ⫶ 2163

Kenya, Mt. *National park* Kenya 97 P5
Kerch Ukraine 85 L9
Kerch Strait (var. Kerchens'ka Protoka) *Channel* Russian Federation/Ukraine 54, 83 C14, 85 L9
Kerchens'ka Protoka *see* Kerch Strait
Kerguelen *Island group* Indian Ocean 101 H14
Kerguelen I. *Island* Indian Ocean, Antarctica 50 I7
Kerguelen Plateau *Sea feature* Indian Ocean 101 H14
Kermadec Is. *Island group* Polynesia, Pacific Ocean 128 J11
Kermadec Trench *Sea feature* Pacific Ocean 128 J11
Kermān Iran 109 P8
Kermanshah *see* Bakhtarān
Kerulen (var. Herlen Gol) *River* Mongolia/China 103, 114, 119 N4
Ket' *River* Russian Federation 112 I10
Ketchikan Alaska, USA 22 I12
Kewanee Illinois, USA 30 J11
Keweenaw Bay *Physical feature* Michigan, USA 31 L4
Key West Florida, USA 29 N16
Khabarovsk Russian Federation 113 P11
Khambhat, Gulf of *Sea feature* India 116 I9
Khamīs Mushayṭ Saudi Arabia 108 I13
Khān Yūnis Gaza Strip 107 K11
Khānaqīn Iraq 109 L4
Khanka, Lake *Lake* 115
Khankendy *see* Xankändi
Kharkiv (var. Kharkov) Ukraine 85 L5
Kharkov *see* Kharkiv
Khartoum (var. El Khartûm) Sudan 91 G12
Khartoum North Sudan 91 G12
Khasab Oman 109 O10
Khashm el Girba Dam Sudan 91 I12
Khaskovo Bulgaria 77 L14
Khatanga *River* Russian Federation 113 K6
Khaybar Saudi Arabia 108 I13
Kherson Ukraine 84 J8
Khmel'nyts'kyy Ukraine 84 G5
Khodzheyli Uzbekistan 110 I5
Khon Kaen Thailand 125 K11
Khorog Tajikistan 111 P9
Khorramshahr Iran 109 L7
Khouribga Morocco 88 H5
Khudzhand (prev. Leninabad) Tajikistan 111 O7
Khulna Bangladesh 117 P8
Khyber Pass *Physical feature* Afghanistan/Pakistan 111 O12
Kičevo Macedonia 75 N12
Kidepo *National park* Uganda 97 N2
Kiel Germany 66 H6
Kiel Canal *Waterway* Germany 66 G6
Kielce Poland 71 M7
Kieta Bougainville, Papua New Guinea 133 Q2
Kiev (var. Kyiv) Ukraine 84 I4
Kiev Res. *Reservoir* Ukraine 84 I4
Kiffa Mauritania 92 H7
Kigali Rwanda 97 L6
Kigoma Tanzania 97 L8
Kikwit Zaire 95 J14
Kilimanjaro *National park* Kenya/Tanzania 97 P6
Kilimanjaro *Volcano* Tanzania 87
Kilis Turkey 105 N10
Kilkis Greece 78 J2
Killarney Ireland 59 B14
Kilwa Masoko Tanzania 97 Q10
Kimberley South Africa 99 K13
Kimberley Plateau *Physical region* Western Australia, Australia 131, 132 I6
Kimito *Island* Finland 57 N11
Kindu Zaire 95 M13
King I. *Island* Tasmania, Australia 133 M15
King Leopold Ranges *Mountain range* Western Australia, Australia 132 H7
King William I. *Island* Northwest Territories, Canada 23 N7
King's Lynn England, UK 59 L14
Kingman Reef *Dependent territory* Polynesia, Pacific Ocean 129 K7
Kingston Jamaica 42 J8
Kingston New York, USA 27 L10
Kingston Ontario, Canada 25 L14
Kingston-upon-Hull England, UK 59 K13
Kingstown St Vincent & The Grenadines 43 T14
Kinshasa (prev. Léopoldville) Zaire 95 H14
Kintyre *Peninsula* Scotland, UK 58 F10
Kirghiz Range *Mountain range* Kazakhstan/Kyrgyzstan 111 P5
Kirghiz Steppe *Physical Region* Kazakhstan 103, 112 F10
Kiribati *Country* Micronesia/Polynesia, Pacific Ocean 128 J8

Kiribati 128

a English, I Kiribati • ≋ Dollar • ♦ 100 • ● 56 • ◒ £2.45 • ◗ (av.) 10% • ⌂ 36%

Kirikkale Turkey 105 L6
Kirinyaga *Volcano* Kenya 87
Kiritimati (var. Christmas Island) *Dependent territory* Pacific Ocean 128 L8
Kirkenes Norway 57 P2
Kirklareli Turkey 104 G4
Kirksville Missouri, USA 33 R10
Kirkuk Iraq 109 K3
Kirkwall Orkney Scotland, UK 58 J6
Kirov Russian Federation 82 J10
Kirovabad *see* Gäncä
Kirovakan *see* Vanadzor
Kirovohrad (var. Yelyzavethrad) Ukraine 84 J6
Kiruna Sweden 57 N4
Kirşehir Turkey 105 L7
Kisangani (prev. Stanleyville) Zaire 95 M12
Kishinev *see* Chişinău
Kiska I. *Island* Aleutian Is. Alaska, USA 22 A5
Kismaayo Somalia 91 L18
Kisumu Kenya 97 N4
Kitakyūshū Japan 123 C13
Kitale Kenya 97 N4
Kitami Japan 122 M3
Kitchener Ontario, Canada 25 K14
Kíthnos *Island* Cyclades, Greece 79 L11
Kitikmeot *Region* Northwest Territories, Canada 23 M7
Kitimat British Columbia, Canada 23 I12
Kitwe Zambia 97 K13
Kitzbühel Austria 69 M8
Kiunga Marine Reserve *Nature reserve* Kenya 97 R6
Kivu, L. *Lake* Rwanda/Zaire 95 O13, 97 L6
Kiyiv *see* Kiev
Kizilirmak *River* Turkey 105 M7
Kizyl-Arbat Turkmenistan 110 H7
Kizyl-Atrek Turkmenistan 110 G8
Kjølen Mts. *Mountain range* Norway/Sweden 54, 57 K6
Klagenfurt Austria 69 P9
Klaipėda Lithuania 80 G8
Klamath Falls Oregon, USA 37 H11
Klerksdorp South Africa 99 K12
Ključ Bosnia and Herzegovina 74 I6
Klosterneuburg Austria 69 S4
Kluane L. *Lake* Yukon Territory, Canada 22 H9
Klyuchevskaya Sopka *Volcano* Siberia 103
Knin Croatia 74 I6
Knittelfeld Austria 69 Q8
Knossos *Archaeological site* Crete, Greece 79 M16
Knoxville Tennessee, USA 29 N5
Knud Rasmussen Land *Physical region* Greenland 51 O12
Ko Phangan *see* Phangan I.
Ko Phuket *see* Phuket I.
Ko Samui *see* Samui I.
Kōbe Japan 15, 123 G12, 128 G5
Koblenz Germany 67 E12
Kobryn Belorussia 80 I14
Kočani Macedonia 75 P11
Kōchi Japan 123 F13
Kodiak Kodiak I. Alaska, USA 22 F9
Kodiak I. *Island* Alaska, USA 20, 22 F9
Kohima India 117 Q7
Kohtla-Järve Estonia 81 L2
Kokand Uzbekistan 111 O6
Kokchetav (var. Kökshetaū) Kazakhstan 112 G10
Kokkola Finland 57 N8
Kokomo Indiana, USA 31 M11
Kokshaal-Tau Mts. *Mountain range* China/Kyrgyzsta 111 S5
Kökshetaū *see* Kokchetav
Kola Peninsula *Physical feature* Russian Federation 54, 82 J6
Kolda Senegal 92 G9
Kolguyev I. *Island* Russian Federation 82 M6
Kolka Latvia 80 H4
Köln *see* Cologne
Kolonia *see* Palikir
Kolubara *River* Serbia, Yugoslavia 75 M6
Kolwezi Zaire 95 M17
Kolyma *River* Russian Federation 113 O5
Kolyma Range *Mountain range* Russian Federation 113 P6
Kom Ombo *Archaeological site* Egypt 90 G9
Kommunizma, Pik *see* Communism Peak
Komoé *River* Ivory Coast 93 K11
Komoran *Island* Indonesia 127 T15
Komotini Greece 79 N2
Komsomol'sk-na-Amure Russian Federation 113 P10
Kongolo Zaire 95 N14
Kongsberg Norway 56 I11
Königsberg *see* Kaliningrad
Konjic Bosnia and Herzegovina 75 K7
Konstanz Germany 67 G16
Konya Turkey 105 K9
Kopaonik *Mountain range* Serbia, Yugoslavia 75 N8
Koper Slovenia 74 F3
Koprivnica Croatia 74 J2
Korarnikhon Tajikistan 111 N8
Korčula *Island* Croatia 74 I9
Korçë Albania 75 N13
Korčulanski Kanal *Channel* Croatia 74 I8
Korea *Region* E Asia 115
Korea Bay *Sea feature* Korea/China 121 O7
Korea Strait *Channel* Korea/Japan 115, 121 Q9, 123 B13
Korhogo Ivory Coast 92 J11
Kōriyama Japan 122 K9
Korkodon *River* Russian Federation 113 P5
Korla China 118 H7
Kornat *Island* Croatia 74 H7
Koror Palau, Pacific Ocean 128 G8
Körös *River* Hungary 71 M14
Korosten' Ukraine 84 H4
Kortrijk (var. Courtrai) Belgium 65 D15
Koryak Range *Mountain range* Russian Federation 113 Q4
Kos Kos, Greece 79 Q12
Kos *Island* Dodecanese, Greece 79 Q12
Kosciusko, Mt. *Mountain* Australia 131
Košice Slovakia 71 N11
Kossou, L. de *Lake* Ivory Coast 92 J12
Kosti Sudan 91 G13
Kostroma Russian Federation 82 H9
Koszalin Poland 70 J2
Kota India 116 J6
Kota Baharu Malaysia 125 J17
Kota Kinabalu Borneo, Malaysia 126 J8
Kotka Finland 57 P11
Kotlas Russian Federation 82 J9
Kotto *River* Central African Republic/Zaire 94 L9
Kotzebue Alaska, USA 22 G5
Kotzebue Sound *Sea feature* Alaska, USA 22 F4
Koudougou Burkina 93 L9
Kourou French Guiana 44 P6
Kousseri (prev. Fort-Foureau) Cameroon 94 H7
Kouvola Finland 57 P11
Kowl-e-Namaksār *Salt pan* Afghanistan/Iran 110 J12
Kowloon Hong Kong 121 M14
Kozani Greece 78 H4
Kra, Isthmus of *Physical region* Thailand 115, 125 H15
Krâcheh Cambodia 125 M13
Kragujevac Serbia, Yugoslavia 75 N7
Krak des Chevaliers Syria 107 M5
Krakatau *Volcano* Indonesia 9, 114
Kraków (var. Cracow) Poland 71 M9
Kralendijk Netherlands Antilles 43 O14
Kraljevo Serbia, Yugoslavia 75 N7
Kramators'k Ukraine 85 L6
Kranj Slovenia 74 G2
Krāslava Latvia 81 K8
Krasnoarmeysk Russian Federation 82 H13
Krasnodar Russian Federation 83 D14
Krasnovodsk Turkmenistan 110 F6
Krasnoyarsk Russian Federation 112 J10
Krefeld Germany 67 D11
Kremenchuk Ukraine 84 J6
Kremenchuk Res. *Reservoir* Ukraine 84 J5
Krems Austria 69 Q4
Kretinga Lithuania 80 G7
Kribi Cameroon 95 E11
Krichev *see* Krychaw
Krishna *River* India 115, 116 J11
Kristiansand Norway 56 H12
Kristianstad Sweden 57 K15
Kristiansund Norway 52 L7
Krivoy Rog *see* Kryvyy Rih
Krk *Island* Croatia 74 G4
Krka *River* Croatia 74 H7
Krŏng Kaôh Kŏng Cambodia 125 K14
Kruger N.P. *National park* South Africa 99 M11
Krung Thep *see* Bangkok
Kruševac Serbia, Yugoslavia 75 O8
Krychaw (var. Krichev) Belorussia 81 O12
Krym *see* Crimea
Kryvyy Rih (var. Krivoy Rog) Ukraine 84 J7
Krzna *River* Belorussia/Poland 71 O5
Kuala Belait Brunei 126 J9
Kuala Lumpur Malaysia 125 J19
Kuala Terengganu Malaysia 125 K18
Kualakapuas Borneo, Indonesia 126 J13
Kuantan Malaysia 125 K18
Kuba *see* Quba
Kuban *River* Russian Federation 83 E14
Kuching Borneo, Malaysia 126 H10
Kudat Borneo, Malaysia 127 K8
Kufstein Austria 69 M7
Kuito Angola 98 H6

a Language (official or most commonly spoken) • ≋ Currency • ♦ Population density per square kilometre • ● Average life expectancy • ◒ Price of 1 dozen hen's eggs • ◗ Literacy • ▭ Number of TVs per 1,000 people • ✚ Number of people per doctor • ✪ Death penalty • ⌂ Percentage of urban-based population • ⫶ Average number of calories consumed daily per person

147

Londinium – Mashhad

Londinium *see* London
London (anc. Londinium) England, UK 14, 59 K16
London Ontario, Canada 24 J15
Londonderry Northern Ireland, UK 58 E10
Londonderry, C. *Cape* Western Australia, Australia 132 H5
Londrina Brazil 47 I14
Long Beach California, USA 37 K19, 129 N5
Long Branch New Jersey, USA 27 L13
Long I. *Island* Bahamas 43 L4
Long I. *Island* New York, USA 27 N12
Long Xuyen Vietnam 125 M15
Longmont Colorado, USA 35 M4
Longreach Queensland, Australia 133 N9
Longview Washington, USA 36 H8
Longyearbyen Svalbard, Arctic Ocean 51 Q13
Lop Nur *Lake* China 115, 118 I8
Lopatka, C. *Cape* Russian Federation 113 R8
Lord Howe I. *Island* Australia, Pacific Ocean 128 I11
Lord Howe Rise *Sea feature* Pacific Ocean 128 I12, 131
Lord Howe Seamounts *Sea feature* Pacific Ocean 131
Lorengau Admiralty Is. Papua New Guinea 133 O1
Lorient France 52 K8, 62 G7
Los Alamos New Mexico, USA 35 L7
Los Angeles California, USA 14, 37 K18
Los Angeles Chile 49 G12
Los Mochis Mexico 38 I7
Lošinj *Island* Croatia 74 G5
Lot *River* France 63 K12
Lötschberg Tunnel *Tunnel* Switzerland 68 F11
Louang Namtha Laos 124 J8
Louang Phrabang Laos 124 K9
Loubomo Congo 95 G14
Louga Senegal 92 F8
Louise, L. *Lake* Alberta, Canada 23 L14
Louisiade Archipelago *Island group* Papua New Guinea 133 P4
Louisiana *State* USA 28
Louisville Kentucky, USA 29M3
Lourenço Marques *see* Maputo
Loutra Aidipsou Greece 78 J7
Louvain *see* Leuven
Lovech Bulgaria 77 K12
Lowell Massachusetts, USA 27 O9
Lower Red L. *Lake* Minnesota, USA 30 G3
Lower Tunguska *River* Russian Federation 113 L9
Lower Zambezi *National park* Zambia 97 L14
Loznica Serbia, Yugoslavia 75 L6
Lualaba *River* Zaire 95 M13
Luanda (prev. Loanda) Angola 98 G4
Luang Lagoon *Coastal feature* Thailand 125 I16
Luangwa *River* Zambia 97 M12
Luangwa, N. *National park* Zambia 97 M12
Luangwa, S. *National park* Zambia 97 M13
Luanshya Zambia 97 K13
Lubana, L. *Lake* Latvia 81 K6
Lubango Angola 98 G7
Lubbock Texas, USA 35 O9
Lübeck Germany 66 I7
Lublin Poland 71 O7
Lubumbashi (prev. Elisabethville) Zaire 95 N17
Lucapa Angola 98 I4
Lucca Italy 72 F9
Lucena Luzon, Philippines 127 L4
Lučenec Slovakia 71 L12
Lucerne (var. Luzern) Switzerland 68 G10
Lucerne, L. of *Lake* Switzerland 68 G10
Lucknow India 117 L6
Lüderitz Namibia 53 M14, 98 H12
Ludhiana India 117 K4
Ludza Latvia 81 L7
Luena Angola 98 I5
Lugano Switzerland 68 H12
Lugano, L. *Lake* Italy/Switzerland 68 H12
Lugansk *see* Luhans'k
Lugenda *River* Mozambique 99 O6
Lugo Spain 60 G3
Luhans'k (var. Lugansk; prev. Voroshilovgrad) Ukraine 85 M6
Luik *see* Liège
Luke Air Force Range *Military centre* Arizona, USA 34 H10
Lukusuzi *National park* Zambia 97 M13
Lule *River* Sweden 57 M4
Luleå Sweden 57 N6
Lulonga *River* Zaire 95 J12
Lulua *River* Angola/Zaire 95 L16
Luluabourg *see* Kananga
Lumbala N'guimbo Angola 98 J6
Lumphat Cambodia 125 N13
Lundazi Zambia 97 N13
Lundy *Island* England, UK 59 F16
Lüneburg Germany 66 I8
Luninyets Belorussia 81 K14
Luoyang China 121 L9
Lusaka Zambia 97 K15
Lusambo Zaire 95 L14
Luton England, UK 59 K15
Luts'k Ukraine 84 F4
Lutzow-Holm Bay *Sea feature* Indian Ocean Coast, Antarctica 50 G6
Luxembourg *Country* W Europe 65

Luxembourg 65

French, German, Litzebuergish • Franc • 146 • 75 • £1.67 • (m) 100% (f) 100% • 255 • 529 • No • 84% • 3902

Luxembourg Luxembourg 65 L19
Luxor Egypt 90 G8
Luzern *see* Lucerne
Luzon *Island* Philippines 127 M3
Luzon Strait *Channel* Philippines 127 L1
Lužnice *River* Czech Republic 70 H10
L'viv (var. L'vov) Ukraine 84 F5
L'vov *see* L'viv
Lyepyel' (var. Lepel') Belorussia 81 M10
Lyme Bay *Sea feature* England, UK 59 H17
Lynchburg Virginia, USA 29 Q4
Lynn Massachusetts, USA 27 O9
Lynn Lake Manitoba, Canada 23 N12
Lyon France 63 N10

M

Ma'ān Jordan 107 M12
Maarianhamina Finland 57 M11
Maas *River* Germany/Netherlands 65 L12
Maastricht Netherlands 65 K15
Mabaruma Guyana 44 L5
Macao *Dependent territory* SE China 121 M14
Macao Macao, SE China 121 M14
Macapá Brazil 46 I7
Macdonald Is. *Island group* Indian Ocean 101 H15
Macdonnell Ranges *Mountain range* Northern Territory, Australia 131, 132 J9
Macedonia (var. Makedonija) *Country* SE Europe 75

Macedonia 75

Macedonian • Denar • 79 • 72 • N/A • (av.) 93% • 54%

Maceió Brazil 46 O10
Machakos Kenya 97 P5
Machala Ecuador 44 B9
Machu Picchu *Archaeological site* Peru 45 F13
Mackay Queensland, Australia 133 O8
Mackay, L. *Lake* Northern Territory/Western Australia, Australia 131, 132 I9
Mackenzie *River* Northwest Territories, Canada 10, 20, 23 K9
Mackenzie *River basin* N America 11
Mackenzie Bay *Sea feature* Indian Ocean Coast, Antarctica 50 G8
Mackenzie Bay *Sea feature* Northwest territories/Yukon Territory, Canada 22 J6
Mackenzie King I. *Island* Northwest Territories, Canada 23 L4
Mackenzie Mts. *Mountain range* Northwest Territories, Canada 22 J9
Mackinac, Strait of *Channel* Michigan, USA 31 N5
Macleod, L. *Lake* Western Australia, Australia 132 E9
Macomb Illinois, USA 30 J12
Mâcon France 63 N9
Macon Georgia, USA 29 N8
Macoraba *see* Mecca
Macquarie I *Island* Pacific Ocean 128 I13
Macquarie Ridge *Sea feature* Pacific Ocean 128 I13, 131
Madagascar *Country* Indian Ocean 100

Madagascar 100

French, Malagasy • Franc • 21 • 51 • £1.09 • (m) 88% (f) 73% • 24%

Madagascar *Island* Indian Ocean 87
Madagascar Basin *Sea feature* Indian Ocean 87, 101 F11
Madagascar Ridge *Sea feature* Indian Ocean 87, 101 E12
Madang Papua New Guinea 133 N2
Madeira *Island* Atlantic Ocean 52 J9
Madeira *Island group* Atlantic Ocean 87
Madeira *River* Bolivia/Brazil 41, 46 F8
Madeira Ridge *Sea feature* Atlantic Ocean 54, 87
Madeleine, Îles de la (var. Magdalen Is.) *Island group* Quebec, Canada 26 Q10
Madison Wisconsin, USA 31 K8
Madona Latvia 81 K6
Madras India 100 I7, 117 L13
Madre de Dios *River* Bolivia/Peru 45 H13
Madrid Spain 61 K8
Madura *Island* Indonesia 126 I14
Madurai India 117 K15
Mae Khlong (var. Meklong) *River* Thailand 125 H12
Maebashi Japan 122 J10
Mafeteng Lesotho 99 L14
Mafia I. *Island* Tanzania 97 Q10
Magadan Russian Federation 113 P7
Magdalen Is. *see* Madeleine, Îles de la
Magdalena *River* Colombia 41, 44 E5
Magdeburg Germany 66 J9
Magellan, Strait of *Channel* Chile 41, 49 I20
Magerøy *Island* Norway 57 P1
Maggiore, L. *Lake* Italy/Switzerland 68 G12, 72 D6
Magnitogorsk Russian Federation 112 F9
Mahabalipuram India 117 L13
Mahajanga Madagascar 100 E10
Mahalapye Botswana 99 L10
Mahanadi *River* India 117 N9
Mahé *Island* Seychelles 100 F9
Mahilyow (var. Mogilev) Belorussia 81 N11
Mahón Minorca, Spain 61 S8
Mai-Ndombe, L *Lake* Zaire 95 J13
Maiduguri Nigeria 93 R10
Main *River* Germany 67 G13
Maine *State* USA 27 P4
Mainz Germany 67 F13
Maitland New South Wales, Australia 133 P12
Majorca (var. Mallorca) *Island* Balearic Islands, Spain 61 R8
Majuro Marshall Islands, Pacific Ocean 128 I8
Makarikari *see* Makgadikgadi Pans
Makassar *see* Ujung Pandang
Makassar Strait *Channel* Borneo/Celebes, Indonesia 127 K13
Makedonija *see* Macedonia
Makeni Sierra Leone 92 H11
Makeyevka *see* Makiyivka
Makgadikgadi Pans (var. Makarikari, Soa Salt Pan) *Salt basin* Botswana 99 K9
Makhachkala Russian Federation 83 F16
Makiyivka (var. Makeyevka) Ukraine 85 M7
Makkah *see* Mecca
Makkovik Newfoundland, Canada 25 Q6
Makokou Gabon 95 G12
Makran *Physical region* Pakistan 116 F5
Makurdi Nigeria 93 P12
Malabar Coast *Coastal region* India 116 I14
Malabo Equatorial Guinea 95 E11
Malacca *see* Melaka
Malacca, Strait of *Channel* SE Asia 100 L8, 115, 130
Maladzyechna (var. Molodechno) Belorussia 81 K11
Málaga Spain 60 J14
Malakal Sudan 91 G15
Malang Java, Indonesia 126 I15
Malanje Angola 98 H4
Malatya Turkey 105 O8
Malawi *Country* C Africa 97

Malawi 97

English • Kwacha • 93 • 46 • £0.68 • (m) 34% (f) 12% • 12%

Malay Pen. *Peninsula* SE Asia 115
Malaya *see* Malaysia
Malaysia (prev. Malaya) *Country* SE Asia 125

Malaysia 125

Malay • Ringgit • 56 • 70 • £0.65 • (m) 87% (f) 70% • 148 • 2708 • Yes • 43% • 2774

Malaysia (East) Borneo, SE Asia 126
Maldive Ridge *Sea feature* Indian Ocean 100 H9
Maldives *Country* Indian Ocean 100 I8

Maldives 100

Divehi • Rufiyya • 737 • 62 • £1.33 • (m) 91% (f) 92% • 30%

Male Maldives 100 I8
Malheur L. *Lake* Oregon, USA 36 K10
Mali (prev. French Sudan) *Country* W Africa 92-93

Mali 92-93

French • Franc • 7 • 48 • £1.41 • (m) 41% (f) 24% • 19%

Mali Hka *River* Burma 115
Malindi Kenya 97 Q7
Malines *see* Mechelen
Mallaig Scotland, UK 58 G8
Mallorca *see* Majorca
Malmédy Belgium 65 L16
Malmö Sweden 56 J15
Malta (var. Melita) *Country* Europe 73

Malta 73

Maltese, English • Lira • 1113 • 74 • £0.78 • (m) 96% (f) 96% • 87%

Maltahöhe Namibia 98 H11
Maluku *see* Moluccas
Mamberamo *River* Indonesia 127 S12
Mamoré *River* Bolivia 45 J14
Mamry, L. *Lake* Poland 71 N3
Man Ivory Coast 92 I12
Man, Isle of *Dependent territory* W Europe 59 G12
Manado Celebes, Indonesia 127 N10
Managua Nicaragua 42 D11
Managua, L. *Lake* Nicaragua 42 D10
Manam *Volcano* New Guinea 131
Manama (var. Al Manamah) Bahrain 100 F5, 109 M9
Manaslu *Mountain* China 115
Manaus Brazil 46 F8
Manchester England, UK 59 I13
Manchester New Hampshire, USA 27 N9
Manchuria *Region* China 121 P4
Manchurian Plain *Physical region* China 115
Mandalay Burma 124 G7
Mandera Kenya 97 R2
Mangalia Romania 77 P10
Mangalore India 116 J13
Mangla Res. *Reservoir* India/Pakistan 116 J2
Manguéni, Plateau du *Physical region* Niger 93 R5
Manhattan Kansas, USA 33 P11
Manicouagan Res. *Reservoir* Quebec, Canada 25 N9
Manila Philippines 15, 127 L4, 128 F7
Manisa Turkey 104 G8
Manistee Michigan, USA 31 M7
Manistee *River* Michigan, USA 31 M7
Manitoba *Province* Canada 23
Manitoba, L. *Lake* Manitoba, Canada 20
Manitowoc Wisconsin, USA 31 L7
Manizales Colombia 44 E6
Mankato Minnesota, USA 30 H7
Mannar Sri Lanka 117 K15
Mannheim Germany 67 F13
Mannu *River* Sardinia 73 D15
Manokwari Irian Jaya, Indonesia 127 Q11
Manono Zaire 95 N15
Mansa Zambia 97 K12
Mansel I. *Island* Canada 25 K2
Mansfield Ohio, USA 31 P11
Manta Ecuador 44 B9
Mantova (var. Mantua) Italy 72 F7
Mantua *see* Mantova
Manyara *National park* Tanzania 97 O7
Manyara, L. *Lake* Tanzania 97 O7
Manzanillo Mexico 39 K12
Manzhouli China 119 P3
Manzini Swaziland 99 M12
Mao Chad 94 H7
Maoke Mts. New Guinea 115
Maputo (prev. Lourenço Marques) Mozambique 99 N12
Mar Chiquita, L. *Salt lake* Argentina 48 K8
Mar del Plata Argentina 49 N12, 53 F14
Maracaibo Venezuela 44 G4
Maracaibo, L. *Sea feature* Venezuela 41, 44 G5
Maracay Venezuela 44 I4
Maradi Niger 93 O9
Marajó I. *Island* Brazil 41
Maramba *see* Livingstone
Maranhão Res. *Reservoir* Portugal 60 G10
Marañón *River* Peru 41, 44 D10
Marathon *Archaeological site* Greece 79 L9
Marbella Spain 60 J14
Marche-en-Famenne Belgium 65 J17
Mardan Pakistan 116 I2
Mardin Turkey 105 Q9
Margarita Island *Island* Venezuela 44 J4
Margherita Peak *Volcano* Uganda 87
Mariana Trench *Sea feature* Pacific Ocean 8, 128 G6
Marías Is. *Island group* Mexico 38 J10
Ma'rib *Archaeological site* Yemen 109 I15
Maribor Slovenia 74 H2
Marie Byrd Land *Region* Antarctica 50 C10
Marie Galante *Island* Guadeloupe 43 T12
Mariental Namibia 98 I11
Mariestad Sweden 57 K12
Marijampolė Lithuania 80 H10
Marinette Wisconsin, USA 31 L6
Marion Indiana, USA 31 N11
Marion Ohio, USA 31 P11
Marion, L. *Lake* South Carolina, USA 29 P8
Maritsa *River* SE Europe 77 M14
Mariupol' Ukraine 85 L8
Marka Somalia 91 M18
Marmara, Sea of Turkey 104 H5
Marmaris Turkey 104 H10
Marne *River* France 63 M4
Maroua Cameroon 94 H8
Marowijne *River* French Guiana/Surinam 44 O7
Marquesas Is. *Island group* French Polynesia, Pacific Ocean 129 M9
Marquette Michigan, USA 31 L4
Marrakesh Morocco 88 H6
Marsá al Burayqah Libya 89 Q7
Marsa Matrûh Egypt 90 E6
Marsabit *National park* Kenya 97 P3
Marseille France 52 L8, 63 O14
Marsh I. *Island* Louisiana, USA 28 H10
Marshall Islands *Country* Micronesia, Pacific Ocean 128 I7

Marshall Islands 128

English, Marshallese • Dollar • 265 • 65 • £1.28 • (av.) 7% • N/A

Marshfield Wisconsin, USA 30 J7
Martaban, Gulf of *Sea feature* Burma 125 G11
Martha's Vineyard *Island* Massachusetts, USA 27 O11
Martigny Switzerland 68 E12
Martin Slovakia 71 L10
Martinique *Dependent territory* Caribbean Sea 43 T13
Martre, Lac la *Lake* Northwest Territories, Canada 23 K9
Mary (prev. Merv) Turkmenistan 110 J9
Maryland *State* USA 29
Maryville Missouri, USA 33 Q10
Masada Israel 107 L11
Masai Mara *Nature reserve* Kenya 97 N5
Masai Steppe *Physical region* Tanzania 97 O8
Masaka Uganda 97 M5
Masbate Masbate, Philippines 127 M5
Masbate *Island* Philippines 127 M5
Mascarene Is. *Island group* Indian Ocean 101 G11
Mascarene Plateau *Sea feature* Indian Ocean 100 G10
Maseru Lesotho 99 L13
Mashhad Iran 109 Q4

Language (official or most commonly spoken) • Currency • Population density per square kilometre • Average life expectancy • Price of 1 dozen hen's eggs • Literacy • Number of TVs per 1,000 people • Number of people per doctor • Death penalty • Percentage of urban-based population • Average number of calories consumed daily per person

Mozyr' *see* Mazyr
Mpika Zambia 97 M12
Mtwara Tanzania 97 Q11
Muang Khammouan (var. Thakhek) Laos 124 M10
Muang Không Laos 125 M12
Muang Lampang Thailand 124 I10
Muang Loei Thailand 124 K10
Muang Nan Thailand 124 J9
Muang Pakxan Laos 124 L10
Muang Phetchabun Thailand 125 J11
Muang Phitsanulok Thailand 125 I11
Muang Xaignabouri Laos 124 K9
Muang Yasothon Thailand 125 L11
Muchinga Mts. *Mountain range* Zambia 97 L13
Muck *Island* Scotland, UK 58 F8
Mufulira Zambia 97 K13
Muğla Turkey 104 H9
Mühlhausen Germany 67 I11
Mulhouse France 63 P6
Mull *Island* Scotland, UK 58 F9
Muller Mts. *Mountain range* Indonesia 126 I11
Multan Pakistan 116 I4
Mun, Mae Nam *River* Thailand 125 K12
Muna *Island* Indonesia 127 M13
München *see* Munich
Muncie Indiana, USA 31 N12
Munich (var. München) Germany 67 J16
Münster Germany 66 E10
Munzur Mts. *Mountain range* Turkey 105 P7
Muonio *River* Sweden 57 N3
Mupa N.P. *National park* Angola 98 H7
Muqdisho *see* Mogadishu
Mur (var. Mura) *River* Austria 69 P8
Mura (var. Mur) *River* Slovenia 74 I1
Murat *River* Turkey 105 Q7
Murchison *River* Western Australia, Australia 132 F10
Murchison Falls *National park* Uganda 97 M3
Murcia Spain 61 M12
Mureş *River* Romania 76 H6
Murfreesboro Tennessee, USA 29 L5
Murgab *River* Turkmenistan 111 K10
Müritz, L. *Lake* Germany 66 L7
Murmansk Russian Federation 52 M7, 82 J5
Murmansk Rise *Sea feature* Barents Sea 54
Muroroa *Island* French Polynesia, Pacific Ocean 129 L10
Murray *River* New South Wales/South Australia, Australia 131, 133 L13
Murray Fracture Zone *Sea feature* Pacific Ocean 129 L5
Murrumbidgee *River* New South Wales, Australia 133 N13
Murzuq Libya 89 O9
Muş Turkey 105 R7
Muscat (var. Masqat) Oman 109 P12
Muscat and Oman *see* Oman
Muskegon Michigan, USA 31 M8
Muskegon *River* Michigan, USA 31 N7
Muskogee Oklahoma, USA 33 Q14
Musoma Tanzania 97 N5
Mussau I. *Island* Papua New Guinea 133 O1
Mutare (prev. Umtali) Zimbabwe 99 N9
Muynak Uzbekistan 110 I3
Mwanza Tanzania 97 M6
Mweru, L. *Lake* Zaire/Zambia 87, 95 O16, 97 K10
Mwene-Ditu Zaire 95 L15
Mweru Wantipa *National park* Zambia 97 K11
Myanmar *see* Burma
Mycenae *Archaeological site* Greece 78 J10
Myingyan Burma 124 F8
Myitkyina Burma 124 H5
Mykolayiv (var. Nikolayev) Ukraine 84 J8
Mykonos *Island* Cyclades, Greece 79 N10
Mymensingh Bangladesh 117 P7
Mysore India J13
Mytilini Lesvos, Greece 79 O7
Mzuzu Malawi 97 N12

N

Naberezhnyye Chelny Russian Federation 83 K11
Nacala Mozambique 99 Q7
Naestved Denmark 56 I16
Nafplio Greece 78 J10
Naga Cebu, Philippines 127 M4
Nagano Japan 122 J10
Nagarjuna Res. *Reservoir* India 117 K11
Nagasaki Japan 123 B14, 128 F6
Nagercoil India 116 J16
Nagorno-Karabakh *Region* Azerbaijan 85 R14
Nagoya Japan 123 I11
Nagpur India 117 K9
Nagqu China 118 I12
Nagykanizsa Hungary 70 J15
Naha Okinawa, Japan 123 A20
Nahuel Huapí, L *Lake* Argentina 49 H14
Nain Newfoundland, Canada 25 P5
Nairobi Kenya 97 O5
Naissaar *Island* Estonia 80 I1
Najrān Saudi Arabia 108 I14
Nakamura Japan 123 E14
Nakhichevan' *see* Naxçivan
Nakhodka Russian Federation 112 I7
Nakhon Ratchasima Thailand 125 K12
Nakhon Sawan Thailand 125 I11
Nakhon Si Thammarat Thailand 125 I16
Nakina Ontario, Canada 24 H10
Nakskov Denmark 56 I16
Nakuru Kenya 97 O4
Nal'chik Russian Federation 83 E15
Nam Co *Lake* China 118 I12
Nam Dinh Vietnam 124 N9

Nam Ngum Dam Laos 124 K10
Nam Theun *River* Laos 124 M10
Namangan Uzbekistan 111 O6
Namen *see* Namur
Namib Desert *Desert region* SW Africa 11, 87, 98 H11
Namibe Angola 98 F7
Namibia (prev. South-West Africa) *Country* Southern Africa 98

Namibia 98

a English · 💷 Rand · ♦ 2 · ♥ 58 · ◎ £2.44 · 💶 (m) 74% (f) 71% · 🏠 28%

Nampa Idaho, USA 32 F8
Namp'o North Korea 121 P7
Nampula Mozambique 99 P7
Namur (var. Namen) Belgium 65 H16
Nan Ling *Mountain range* 115
Nan'ao China 128 E6
Nanchang China 121 M12
Nancy France 63 O5
Nanded India 117 K10
Nanjing China 121 N10
Nanning China 121 K14
Nanping China 121 N12
Nansen Basin *Sea feature* Arctic Ocean 54, 103
Nantes France 62 H8
Nantucket I. *Island* Massachusetts, USA 27 P11
Napa Valley *Physical feature* California, USA 37 H14
Napier New Zealand 134 H7
Naples (var. Napoli) Italy 52 L9 73 K13
Naples, Bay of *Sea feature* Italy 73 K13
Napo *River* Ecuador/Peru 44 E9
Napoli *see* Naples
Narach, L. *Lake* Belorussia 81 K10
Narathiwat Thailand 125 J17
Nares Plain *Sea feature* Atlantic Ocean 20
Nares Strait *Channel* Northwest Territories, Canada 23 O1
Narew *River* Poland/Belorussia 71 N4
Narmada *River* India 115, 116 J8
Narsarsuaq Greenland 51 M15
Narva Estonia 81 L2
Narva *River* Estonia/Russian Federation 81 L2
Narvik Norway 57 M3
Naryn Kyrgyzstan 111 R5
Naryn *River* Kyrgyzstan 111 Q5
Nashua New Hampshire, USA 27 N9
Nashville Tennessee, USA 29 L4
Nasik India 116 I9
Nassau Bahamas 43 K2
Nasser, L. *Reservoir* Egypt/Sudan 87, 90 G9
Natal Brazil 46 O9
Natal *Region* South Africa 99 M13
Natal Basin *Sea feature* Indian Ocean 87
Natitingou Benin 93 M11
Natuna *Island* Natuna Is. Indonesia 126 H9
Natuna Is. *Island group* Indonesia 126 G10
Naturaliste, C. *Cape* Western Australia, Australia 132 F13
Naukuuft Park *National park* Namibia 98 H12
Nauru *Country* Micronesia, Pacific Ocean 128 I9

Nauru 128

a Nauruan · 💷 Dollar · ♦ 433 · ♥ 67 · ◎ £1.68 · 💶 (m) 99% (f) 99% · 🏠 100%

Navajo Dam *Dam* New Mexico, USA 35 L7
Navajo Indian Reservation *Reservation* USA 35 K8
Navapolatsk (var. Novopolotsk) Belorussia 81 M8
Navarin, C. *Cape* Russian Federation 113 Q3, 128 J3
Navoi Uzbekistan 111 L7
Nawabshah Pakistan 116 H6
Naxçivan (var. Nakhichevan') Azerbaijan 85 Q15
Naxos *Island* Cyclades, Greece 79 N12
Nazareth Israel 107 L8
Nazca *Archaeological site* Peru 45 E14
Nazca Plate *Physical feature* 41
Nazilli Turkey 104 H9
N'Dalatando Angola 98 G4
Ndélé Central African Republic 94 K9
N'Djamena (prev. Fort Lamy) Chad 94 H7
Ndola Zambia 97 K13
Neagh, Lough *Lake* Northern Ireland, UK 59 E11
Neapoli Greece 78 J13
Nebitdag Turkmenistan 110 G7
Nebraska *State* USA 33
Nechako *River* Alberta/British Columbia, Canada 22 J13
Neches *River* Texas, USA 35 S11
Neckar *River* Germany 67 G15
Necochea Argentina 49 M12
Negev Desert *Desert region* Israel 107 L12
Negrais, Cape *Cape* Burma 125 E11
Negro *River* Argentina 49 K13
Negro *River* Brazil/Uruguay 48 O9
Negro, Rio *River* S America 41, 46 D7
Negros *Island* Philippines 127 M6
Nei Mongol *see* Inner Mongolia
Neiva Colombia 44 E7
Nejd *Region* Saudi Arabia 108 I9
Nekemte Ethiopia 91 I15
Nellis Air Force Range *Military centre* Nevada, USA 34 G5
Nellore India 117 L12
Nelson New Zealand 134 F9

Nelson *River* Manitoba, Canada 23 O12
Néma Mauritania 92 J7
Neman (var. Nemunas) *River* Belorussia/Lithuania 80 G9
Nemunas *see* Neman
Nemuro Japan 122 O3
Neosho *River* Kansas/Oklahoma, USA 33 P12
Nepal *Country* S Asia 117

Nepal 117

a Nepali · 💷 Rupee · ♦ 142 · ♥ 52 · ◎ £0.38 · 💶 (m) 38% (f) 13% · 🏠 10%

Nepalganj Nepal 117 M5
Neretva *River* Bosnia and Herzegovina 75 K8
Neris *River* Belorussia/Lithuania 80 I9
Nesebŭr Bulgaria 77 O13
Ness, Loch *Lake* Scotland, UK 58 H8
Netherlands *Country* Europe 64-65

Netherlands 64-65

a Dutch · 💷 Guilder · ♦ 443 · ♥ 77 · ◎ £1.08 · 💶 (m) 99% (f) 99% · 🖥 495 · ✚ 414 · 💀 No · 🏠 89% · 🍴 3151

Netherlands Antilles *Dependent territory* Caribbean Sea 20, 43 O14
Neubrandenburg Germany 66 L7
Neuchâtel Switzerland 68 D10
Neuchâtel, L. of *Lake* Switzerland 68 D10
Neufchâteau Belgium 65 J18
Neumünster Germany 66 H6
Neunkirchen Austria 69 R6
Neuquén Argentina 49 I13
Neuschwanstein *Castle* Germany 67 I16
Neusiedler L. *Lake* Austria/Hungary 69 S5
Nevada *State* USA 34
Nevada, Sierra *Mountain range* Spain 61 K13
Nevada Test Site *Military centre* Nevada, USA 34 G6
Nevel' Russian Federation 82 E9
Nevers France 63 M8
Nevşehir Turkey 105 M8
New Albany Indiana, USA 31 N14
New Amsterdam Guyana 44 N6
New Amsterdam *see* New York City
New Bedford Massachusetts, USA 27 O11
New Britain *Island* Papua New Guinea 131, 133 P2
New Britain Trench *Sea feature* Pacific Ocean 131
New Brunswick New Jersey, USA 27 L12
New Brunswick *Province* Canada 25
New Caledonia *Dependent territory* Melanesia, Pacific Ocean 128 H10
New Caledonia *Island* Melanesia, Pacific Ocean 131
New Caledonia Basin *Sea feature* Pacific Ocean 131
New Castle Pennsylvania, USA 26 G11
New Delhi India 117 K5
New England *Physical region* USA 27 O6
New Guinea *Island* Indonesia/Papua New Guinea 115, 128 G9, 131, 133 M2
New Hampshire *State* USA 27
New Hanover *Island* Papua New Guinea 133 O1
New Haven Connecticut, USA 27 M11
New Hebrides Trench *Sea feature* Pacific Ocean 131
New Ireland *Island* Papua New Guinea 131, 133 P1
New Jersey *State* USA 27
New London Connecticut, USA 27 N11
New Mexico *State* USA 35
New Orleans Louisiana, USA 28 I9, 52 C9
New Plymouth New Zealand 134 G6
New Providence *Island* Bahamas 43 K2
New R. *River* Virginia/West Virginia, USA 29 P3
New Siberian Is. (var. Novosibirskiye Ostrova) *Island group* Russian Federation 51 R7, 103, 113 N4
New South Wales *State* Australia 133
New Ulm Minnesota, USA 30 G7
New York *State* NE USA 27 K9
New York City (prev. New Amsterdam) New York, USA 14, 52 E9, 27 L12
New Zealand *Country* Polynesia, Pacific Ocean 8, 131, 134

New Zealand 134

a English, Maori · 💷 Dollar · ♦ 13 · ♥ 76 · ◎ £0.88 · 💶 (m) 99% (f) 99% · 🖥 442 · ✚ 373 · 💀 No · 🏠 84% · 🍴 3362

Newark Delaware, USA 27 K14
Newark New Jersey, USA 27 L12
Newark Ohio, USA 31 P12
Newburgh New York, USA 27 L11
Newcastle New South Wales, Australia 133 O12
Newcastle upon Tyne England, UK 59 J11
Newfoundland *Island* Newfoundland, Canada 10, 20, 25 R9, 52 F8
Newfoundland *Province* Canada 25
Newfoundland Basin *Sea feature* Atlantic Ocean 52 G8
Newport Isle of Wight England, UK 59 J17
Newport Oregon, USA 36 G9
Newport Rhode Island, USA 27 N11
Newport Wales, UK 59 H15
Newport News Virginia, USA 29 S5
Newry Northern Ireland, UK 59 E12

Neyshābūr Iran 109 Q4
Ngaoundéré Cameroon 94 G9
Ngauruhoe, Mt. *Volcano* North Island, New Zealand 134 H6
Ngorongoro *Conservation area* Tanzania 97 O6
Ngorongoro Crater *Physical feature* Tanzania 87
Nguigmi Niger 93 R8
Nguru Nigeria 93 P9
Nha Trang Vietnam 125 P14
Niagara Falls New York, USA 26 H8
Niagara Falls Ontario, Canada 25 K14
Niagara Falls *Waterfall* Canada/USA 20
Niagara Peninsula *Physical feature* Canada 25 K15
Niamey Niger 93 M9
Niangay, L. *Lake* Mali 92 L8
Nias *Island* Indonesia 126 C11
Nicaragua *Country* C America 42

Nicaragua 42

a Spanish · 💷 Cordoba · ♦ 33 · ♥ 65 · ◎ £0.64 · 💶 (av.) 66% · 🏠 60%

Nicaragua, L. *Lake* Nicaragua 41, 42 D11
Nice France 63 Q13
Nicobar Is. *Island group* India, Indian Ocean 100 K7, 115
Nicosia (var. Lefkosa; prev. Levkosia) Cyprus 105 L12
Nicoya, Gulf of *Sea feature* Costa Rica 42 D13
Niedere Tauern *Mountain range* Austria 69 P7
Nifa *Archaeological site* Italy 73 I12
Niğde Turkey 105 M9
Niger *Country* W Africa 93

Niger 93

a French · 💷 Franc · ♦ 6 · ♥ 46 · ◎ £1.72 · 💶 (m) 40% (f) 17% · 🏠 20%

Niger (var. Joliba, Kworra) *River* W Africa 53 F11, 87, 93 M9
Niger Delta *Delta* Nigeria 87, 93 O14
Nigeria *Country* W Africa 93

Nigeria 93

a English · 💷 Naira · ♦ 97 · ♥ 52 · ◎ £0.39 · 💶 (m) 62% (f) 40% · 🖥 32 · ✚ 6134 · 💀 Yes · 🏠 35% · 🍴 2312

Nihon *see* Japan
Niigata Japan 122 J9
Nijmegen Netherlands 65 K11
Nikolayev *see* Mykolayiv
Nikopol' Ukraine 85 K7
Nikšić Montenegro, Yugoslavia 75 L9
Nile *River* Africa 52 N10, 87, 91 G11, 100 C5
Nile *River basin* Africa 11
Nile Delta *Delta* Egypt 87
Niles Michigan, USA 31 M10
Nîmes France 63 N13
Ninety East Ridge *Sea feature* Indian Ocean 100 J10, 115, 130
Nineveh *Archaeological site* Iraq 109 K2
Ningbo China 121 O11, 128 F6
Ningxia Hui Autonomous Region China 120 J8
Ninigo Group *Island Group* Papua New Guinea 133 M1
Niobrara *River* Nebraska, USA 33 M9
Nioro Mali 92 I8
Nipigon, L. *Lake* Ontario, Canada 24 H10
Nippon *see* Japan
Niš Serbia, Yugoslavia 75 O8
Nissan I. *Island* Papua New Guinea 133 Q1
Nitra Slovakia 71 K12
Nitra *River* Slovakia 71 K11
Niue *Dependent territory* Polynesia, Pacific Ocean 129 K10
Nivelles Belgium 65 G16
Nizhnevartovsk Russian Federation 112 I9
Nizhniy Novgorod Russian Federation 82 H10
Nizhniy Tagil Russian Federation 112 G8
Nizwā Oman 109 O12
Njombe Tanzania 97 N10
Nkhotakota Malawi 97 N13
Nkongsamba Cameroon 94 E10
Nobeoka Japan 123 D14
Nogales Mexico 38 H3
Nome Alaska, USA 22 F5
Nonacho L. *Lake* Northwest Territories, Canada 23 M10
Nordfjord *Coastal feature* Norway 56 H9
Nordhausen Germany 66 I10
Nordstrand *Island* North Frisian Is. Germany 66 G6
Nordvik *Research centre* Russian Federation 51 T9
Norfolk Nebraska, USA 33 O9
Norfolk Virginia, USA 29 S5
Norfolk I. *Dependent territory* Pacific Ocean 128 I11
Norge *see* Norway
Noril'sk Russian Federation 112 J7
Norman Oklahoma, USA 33 O15
Normandy *Region* France 62 J5
Norman Wells Northwest Territories, Canada 22 J8
Norrköping Sweden 57 L13
Norrtälje Sweden 56 M12
North Albanian Alps *Mountain range* Albania/Yugoslavia 75 M10

---

a Language (official or most commonly spoken) · 💷 Currency · ♦ Population density per square kilometre · ♥ Average life expectancy · ◎ Price of 1 dozen hen's eggs · 💶 Literacy · 🖥 Number of TVs per 1,000 people · ✚ Number of people per doctor · 💀 Death penalty · 🏠 Percentage of urban-based population · 🍴 Average number of calories consumed daily per person

151

Panama, Gulf of *Sea feature* Panama 41, 42 G15
Panama, Isthmus of *Physical feature* Panama 41
Panay *Island* Philippines 127 L6
Pančevo Serbia, Yugoslavia 75 N5
Panevėžys Lithuania 80 I8
Pangaea *Ancient Continent* 8
Pangani Tanzania 97 Q8
Pangani *River* Tanzania 97 P7
Pangkalpinang Bangka, Indonesia 126 G12
Pangnirtung Baffin I. Northwest Territories, Canada 23 R6, 51 M13
Panj (var. Pyandzh) *River* Afghanistan/Tajikistan 111 N9
Panjnad Barrage *Dam* Pakistan 116 H4
Pantelleria *Island* Italy 73 H19
Panuco *River* Mexico 39 M10
Panzhihua China 120 I12
Papandayan *Volcano* Java, Indonesia 115
Papeete Tahiti French Polynesia, Pacific Ocean 129 L10
Paphos Cyprus 105 K12
Papua, Gulf of *Sea feature* Papua New Guinea 133 N3
Papua New Guinea *Country* Australasia 133

Papua New Guinea (P.N.G.) 133

English • Kina • 9 • 55 • £2.23 • (m) 65% (f) 38% • 16%

Paraguarí Paraguay 48 N6
Paraguay *Country* S America 48

Paraguay 48

Spanish • Kina • 11 • 67 • £0.37 • (m) 92% (f) 88% • 48%

Paraguay *River* S America 41, 47 G13, 48 N5
Parakou Benin 93 N11
Paramaribo Surinam 44 O6
Paramushir Is. *Island Group* Russian Federation 113 R8
Paraná Argentina 48 L9
Paraná *River* Argentina/Paraguay 41, 47 H14, 48 M10
Paraná *River basin* S America 11
Paranaíba *River* Brazil 46 K10
Pardubice Czech Republic 70 I9
Parecis, Serra dos *Mountain range* Brazil 47 F11
Parepare Celebes, Indonesia 127 L13
Paris (anc. Gallia) France 63 L5
Parker Dam *Dam* Arizona, USA 34 H8
Parkersburg West Virginia, USA 29 P2
Parma Italy 72 F8
Parnaíba Brazil 46 M8
Parnaíba *River* Brazil 41
Pärnu Estonia 80 J3
Pärnu *River* Estonia 80 J3
Paros *Island* Cyclades, Greece 79 M11
Parry Is. *Island group* Northwest Territories, Canada 23 M4
Pas, The Manitoba, Canada 23 N13
Pasadena California, USA 37 L18
Pasadena Texas, USA 35 S13
Pasargadae *Archaeological site* Iran 109 N7
Pasley, C. *Cape* Western Australia, Australia 132 H13
Passau Germany 67 M15
Passo Fundo Brazil 47 I16
Pasto Colombia 44 D8
Patagonia *Physical region* Argentina 41, 49 J16
Paterson New Jersey, USA 27 L12
Pathfinder Res. *Reservoir* Wyoming, USA 32 J9
Patna India 117 N7
Patos Lagoon *Lake* Brazil 47 I16
Patrai Greece 78 H9
Patrai, Gulf of *Sea feature* Greece 78 G9
Pattani Thailand 125 J17
Pattaya Thailand 125 J13
Patuca *River* Honduras 42 E9
Pátzcuaro, L. *Lake* Mexico 39 L12
Pau France 62 J14
Pavlodar Kazakhstan 112 H11
Paysandú Uruguay 48 N9
Pazardzhik Bulgaria 76 J14
Peć Serbia, Yugoslavia 75 M9
Pearl *River* Louisiana/Mississippi, USA 28 J8
Pearl Harbor Oahu Hawaiian Is. Pacific Ocean 129 K6
Peary Land *Physical region* Greenland 51 P12
Pechora *River* Russian Federation 54, 82 L7
Pecos Texas, USA 35 N11
Pecos *River* New Mexico/Texas, USA 35 O12
Pécs Hungary 71 K15
Pedras Salgadas Portugal 60 G6
Pedro Juan Caballero Paraguay 48 N4
Pee Dee *River* North Carolina/South Carolina, USA 29 Q8
Pegasus Bay *Sea feature* New Zealand 134 F11
Pegu Burma 124 G10
Peipus, L. *Lake* Estonia/Russian Federation 81 L3
Peking (var. Beijing) China 15, 121 M7
Pelada, Serra *Mountain range* Brazil 46 J8
Pelagie Is. *Island group* Italy 73 H20
Pelée, Mt. *Volcano* Martinique, Caribbean Sea 9, 41
Pelješac *Peninsula* Croatia 74 J9
Pelly *River* Yukon Territory, Canada 22 I8
Peloponnese *Region* Greece 78 I10
Pelotas Brazil 47 I17
Pematangsiantar Sumatra, Indonesia 126 D10
Pemba Mozambique 99 Q6
Pemba I. *Island* Tanzania 97 Q8
Pendleton Oregon, USA 36 K8
Pennine Alps *Mountain range* Switzerland 68 F12
Pennines *Mountain range* England, UK 54, 59 I12
Pennsylvania *State* USA 26
Penobscot *River* Maine, USA 27 Q5
Penonomé Panama 42 G15
Pensacola Florida, USA 29 K10
Penticton British Columbia, Canada 23 K15
Penza Russian Federation 83 H12
Penzance England, UK 59 E17
Peoria Illinois, USA 31 K11
Pereira Colombia 44 E6
Pergamon (var. Bergama) *Archaeological site* Turkey 104 G7
Perge *Archaeological site* Turkey 104 J10
Périgueux France 63 K11
Perito Moreno Argentina 49 I16
Perm' Russian Federation 83 L11
Pernik Bulgaria 76 I13
Perpignan France 63 M15
Persepolis *Archaeological site* Iran 109 N7
Persia *see* Iran
Persian Gulf (var. The Gulf) *Sea feature* Arabia/Iran 87, 100 F5, 103, 109 M8
Perth Scotland, UK 58 I9
Perth Western Australia, Australia 132 F12
Perth Basin *Sea feature* Indian Ocean 131
Peru *Country* S America 9, 45-46

Peru 45-46

Spanish, Quechua • Sol • 17 • 63 • £0.25 • (m) 92% (f) 79% • 97 • 966 • No • 70% • 2186

Peru Basin *Sea feature* Pacific Ocean 129 P10
Peru-Chile Trench *Sea feature* Pacific Ocean 8, 129 Q11
Peru Current *Ocean current* Pacific Ocean 12
Peruć, L. *Lake* Croatia 74 I7
Perugia Italy 72 H10
Pesaro Italy 72 I9
Pescara Italy 73 K11
Peshawar Pakistan 116 I2
Petaḥ Tiqwa Israel 107 L9
Petaluma California, USA 37 G15
Peter the First I. *Dependent territory* Pacific Ocean, Antarctica 50 B9
Peterborough England, UK 59 K14
Peterborough Ontario, Canada 25 K14
Peterhead Scotland, UK 58 J8
Petersburg Alaska, USA 22 I11
Petersburg Virginia, USA 29 R4
Petra Jordan 107 M12
Petropavl *see* Petropavlovsk
Petropavlovsk (var. Petropavl) Kazakhstan 112 G10
Petropavlovsk-Kamchatskiy Russian Federation 113 R7
Petrozavodsk Russian Federation 82 H7
Pevek Russian Federation 51 Q5, 113 P3
Pforzheim Germany 67 F15
Phangan I. (var. Ko Phangan) *Island* Thailand 125 I15
Phet Buri Thailand 125 I13
Philadelphia, Jordan *see* Amman
Philadelphia Pennsylvania, USA 27 K13
Philae *Archaeological site* Egypt 90 G9
Philippeville Belgium 65 H17
Philippine Basin *Sea feature* Pacific Ocean 115, 131
Philippine Plate *Physical feature* 8, 115, 131
Philippine Sea Philippines 127 N4
Philippine Trench *Sea feature* Pacific Ocean 115, 131
Philippines *Country* SE Asia 127

Philippines 127

English, Filipino • Peso • 210 • 65 • £0.79 • (m) 90% (f) 90% • 48 • 6413 • No • 43% • 2375

Philippines *Island group* SE Asia 115, 131
Phnom Penh Cambodia 125 M14
Phoenix Arizona, USA 34 I9
Phoenix Is. *Island group* Kiribati, Pacific Ocean 128 J9
Phôngsali Laos 124 K8
Phuket Thailand 125 H16
Phuket I. (var. Ko Phuket) *Island* Thailand 125 H16
Phumĭ Sâmraông Cambodia 125 L12
Piacenza Italy 72 E7
Piatra-Neamț Romania 77 M4
Piave *River* Italy 72 H6
Pichilemu Chile 49 G11
Picos Brazil 46 M9
Picton New Zealand 134 G9
Piedras Negras Mexico 39 M5
Pielinen, L. *Lake* Finland 57 P8
Pierre South Dakota, USA 33 N7
Pietermaritzburg South Africa 99 M13
Pietersburg South Africa 99 M11
Piła Poland 70 J4
Pilar Paraguay 48 M6
Pilcomayo *River* Bolivia/Paraguay 48 M5
Pilos Greece 78 H12
Pilsen *see* Plzeň
Pinang *see* Georgetown
Pinar del Río Cuba 42 G3
Pinatubo Mt. *Volcano* Philippines 115
Pindus Mountains *Mountain range* Greece 54, 78 H6
Pine Bluff Arkansas, USA 28 I5
Pinega *River* Russian Federation 82 K8
Pineios *River* Greece 78 I5
Pines, I. of *see* Juventud, Isla de la
Ping, Mae Nam *River* Thailand 125 I11
Pingxiang China 120 J14, 121 M12
Pini *Island* Indonesia 126 C11
Pinnacles Desert *Desert region* Australia 131
Pinsk Belorussia 80 J15
Pioner I. *Island* Severnaya Zemlya, Russian Federation 113 K3
Piotrków Trybunalski Poland 71 L7
Piqua Ohio, USA 31 O12
Piraeus Greece 79 K9
Pisa Italy 72 F9
Pisác *Archaeological site* Peru 45 G13
Pistoia Italy 72 G9
Pitcairn Is. *Dependent territory* Polynesia, Pacific Ocean 129 M10
Pite *River* Sweden 57 M5
Piteå Sweden 57 N6
Pitești Romania 77 K8
Pittsburg Kansas, USA 33 Q13
Pittsburgh Pennsylvania, USA 26 G12
Pittsfield Massachusetts, USA 27 M9
Piura Peru 44 B10
Placentia Bay *Sea feature* Newfoundland, Canada 25 T10
Plainview Texas, USA 35 O9
Plate *River* Argentina/Uruguay 41, 48 N10
Platte *River* Nebraska, USA 20, 33 N10
Platte, North *River* Nebraska, USA 33 L10
Plattsburgh New York, USA 27 M6
Plauen German 67 K12
Plenty, Bay of *Sea feature* New Zealand 134 I5
Pleven Bulgaria 77 K11
Ploča, C. *Cape* Croatia 74 H8
Płock Poland 71 L5
Ploiești Romania 77 L8
Płońsk Poland 71 M5
Plovdiv Bulgaria 77 K14
Plungė Lithuania 80 G7
Plymouth England, UK 59 G17
Plymouth Montserrat 43 S11
Plzeň (var. Pilsen) Czech Republic 70 G9
Po *River* Italy 54, 72 C7
Po Delta *Delta* Italy 54
Pobeda Peak (var. Pik Pobedy) *Peak* China/Kyrgyzstan 103
Pobedy, Pik *see* Pobeda Peak
Pocatello Idaho, USA 32 H8
Podgorica (prev. Titograd) Montenegro, Yugoslavia 75 L10
Podlasie *Region* Poland 71 O5
Poinsett, C. *Cape* Wilkes Land, Antarctica 50 G10
Pointe-à-Pitre Guadeloupe 43 T11
Pointe-Noire Congo 95 F14
Poitiers France 62 J9
Pol-e Khomrī Afghanistan 111 N10
Poland *Country* C Europe 70-71

Poland 70-71

Polish • Zloty • 126 • 71 • £0.42 • (av.) 99% • 293 • 479 • Yes • 62% • 3505

Polatsk (var. Polotsk) Belorussia 81 M8
Polis Cyprus 105 K12
Polotsk *see* Polatsk
Poltava Ukraine 85 K5
Polygyros Greece 79 K4
Polynesia *Region* Pacific Ocean 129 K10
Pomerania *Region* Germany/Poland 70 I3
Pomeranian Bay *Sea feature* Germany/Poland 70 H2
Pompeii *Archaeological site* Italy 73 K13
Ponca City Oklahoma, USA 33 P13
Ponce Puerto Rico 43 Q9
Pontchartrain, L. *Lake* Louisiana, USA 28 I9
Pontevedra Spain 60 F4
Pontiac Michigan, USA 31 O9
Pontianak Borneo, Indonesia 126 H11
Pontic Mountains *Mountain range* Turkey 105 N5
Pontine Is. *Island group* Italy 73 I13
Poona *see* Pune
Poopó, L. *Lake* Bolivia 41, 45 H15
Popayán Colombia 44 D7
Poplar Bluff Missouri, USA 33 S13
Popocatépetl *Volcano* Mexico 20, 39 N12
Popondetta Papua New Guinea 133 O3
Poprad Slovakia 71 M10
Porbandar India 116 H8
Porcupine *River* Canada/Alaska, USA 22 H6
Pori Finland 57 N10
Poronaysk Russian Federation 113 Q10
Porpoise Bay *Sea feature* Wilkes Land, Antarctica 50 G11
Porsangen *Coastal feature* Norway 57 O1
Porsgrunn Norway 56 I12
Port Alice Vancouver I. British Columbia, Canada 22 I14
Port Angeles Washington, USA 36 G6
Port Antonio Jamaica 43 K8
Port Arthur Texas, USA 35 T13
Port-au-Prince Haiti 43 M8
Port Augusta South Australia, Australia 133 L12
Port-de-Paix Haiti 43 M7
Port Dickson Malaysia 125 J19
Port Elizabeth South Africa 99 K16
Port-Gentil Gabon 95 E13
Port Harcourt Nigeria 93 O13
Port Hedland Western Australia, Australia 132 F8
Port Hope Simpson Newfoundland, Canada 25 R7
Port Huron Michigan, USA 31 P8
Port Lincoln South Australia, Australia 133 K13
Port Louis Mauritius 101 G11
Port Moresby Papua New Guinea 133 N4
Port Nolloth South Africa 53 M14
Port of Spain Trinidad & Tobago 43 S16
Port Said (var. Bûr Sa'îd) Egypt 52 N9, 90 G6, 100 D4
Port Sudan Sudan 91 I11
Portalegre Portugal 60 G10
Portales New Mexico, USA 35 N9
Portimão Portugal 60 F13
Portland Maine, USA 27 O8, 52 E8
Portland Oregon, USA 36 H8
Porto (var. Oporto) Portugal 52 J9, 60 F6
Pôrto Alegre Brazil 47 I16
Porto-Novo Benin 93 M12
Pôrto Velho Brazil 46 D9
Portoviejo Ecuador 44 B9
Portsmouth England, UK 59 J17
Portsmouth New Hampshire, USA 27 O8
Portsmouth Ohio, USA 31 P13
Portugal *Country* SW Europe 60

Portugal 60

Portuguese • Escudo • 113 • 75 • £0.95 • (m) 89% (f) 82% • 177 • 381 • No • 34% • 3495

Portuguese Guinea *see* Guinea-Bissau
Porvenir Chile 49 J19
Posadas Argentina 48 N7
Posonium *see* Bratislava
Potash Italy 73 K18
Potenza Italy 73 M13
Potenza *River* Italy 72 J10
P'ot'i Georgia 85 O12
Potosí Bolivia 45 I16
Potsdam Germany 66 L9
Poughkeepsie New York, USA 27 L11
Poŭthĭsăt Cambodia 125 L13
Powder *River* Montana/Wyoming, USA 33 K6
Powell, L. *Lake* Utah, USA 34 J5
Poyang Hu *Lake* China 115, 121 M11
Poza Rica Mexico 39 O11
Požarevac Serbia, Yugoslavia 75 O6
Poznań Poland 70 J5
Pozo Colorado Paraguay 48 M5
Prachin Buri *Archaeological site* Thailand 125 J12
Prachin Buri Thailand 125 J12
Prachuap Khiri Khan Thailand 125 I14
Prague (var. Praha) Czech Republic 70 H9
Praha *see* Prague
Praia Cape Verde, Atlantic Ocean 52 I10
Prato Italy 72 G9
Pratt Kansas, USA 33 O13
Pravats (var. Pravets) Bulgaria 76 J12
Pravets *see* Pravats
Prešov Slovakia 71 N11
Prescott Arizona, USA 34 I8
Prespa, L. *Lake* SE Europe 75 N13, 78 G2
Presque Isle Maine, USA 27 Q2
Preston England, UK 59 I13
Pretoria South Africa 99 L12
Preveza Greece 78 G7
Priene *Archaeological site* Turkey 104 G9
Prijedor Bosnia and Herzegovina 75 I5
Prilep Macedonia 75 O12
Prince Albert Saskatchewan, Canada 23 M13
Prince Charles I. *Island* Northwest Territories, Canada 23 Q6
Prince Edward Island *Province* Canada 25
Prince Edward Is. *Island group* South Africa, Indian Ocean 101 E14
Prince George British Columbia, Canada 22 J13
Prince of Wales I. *Island* Northwest Territories, Canada 23 N5
Prince of Wales I. *Island* Queensland, Australia 133 M4
Prince Patrick I. *Island* Canada 51 N8
Prince Rupert British Columbia, Canada 22 I12, 129 M3
Princess Charlotte Bay *Sea feature* Queensland, Australia 133 N5
Princeton New Jersey, USA 27 L13
Príncipe *Island* Sao Tome & Principe 87, 95 D12
Pripet *River* E Europe 81 L15
Priština Serbia, Yugoslavia 75 N9
Prizren Serbia, Yugoslavia 75 N10
Progreso Mexico 39 S11
Prome Burma 124 F9
Prosna *River* Poland 71 K6
Provence *Region* France 63 P13
Providence Rhode Island, USA 27 O10
Provideniya Air Base *Military centre* Russian Federation 113 Q2
Provo Utah, USA 34 J3
Prudhoe Bay Alaska, USA 51 O6
Prudhoe Bay *Sea feature* Alaska, USA 22 I5
Prut *River* E Europe 77 O5
Pruzhany Belorussia 80 I14
Prydz Bay *Sea feature* Indian Ocean Coast, Antarctica 50 G8
Przheval'sk Kyrgyzstan 111 S4
Pskov Russian Federation 82 E8
Ptsich *River* Belorussia 81 M13
Ptuj Slovenia 74 I2

Language (official or most commonly spoken) • Currency • Population density per square kilometre • Average life expectancy • Price of 1 dozen hen's eggs • Literacy • Number of TVs per 1,000 people • Number of people per doctor • Death penalty • Percentage of urban-based population • Average number of calories consumed daily per person

153

St Laurent-du-Maroni – Shenandoah

St Laurent-du-Maroni French Guiana 44 O6
St Lawrence *River* Canada 10, 20, 25 O11, 52 E8
St. Lawrence, Gulf of *Sea feature* Canada 20, 25 Q10
St Lawrence I. *Island* Alaska, USA 22 E5
St. Lawrence Seaway *Waterway* Ontario, Canada 25 L13
St. Lô France 62 I4
St. Louis Missouri, USA 33 S11
St-Louis Senegal 92 F7
St Lucia *Country* Caribbean Sea 43 T13

St. Lucia 43

a English • Dollar • 249 • 72 • £1.47 • (m) 81% (f) 82% • 46%

St. Malo France 62 H5
Ste Marie, Cap *see* Vohimena, C.
St Martin *Island* Guadeloupe 43 S10
St Matthew I. *Island* Alaska, USA 22 D5
St. Moritz Switzerland 68 I11
St. Nazaire France 62 H8
St Paul Minnesota, USA 30 H6
St Paul I. *Island* Indian Ocean 101 I13
St. Peter Port Guernsey, UK 59 H18
St Petersburg Florida, USA 29 N13
St. Petersburg (prev. Leningrad) Russian Federation 82 F7
St Pierre St Pierre & Miquelon 25 S10
St Pierre & Miquelon *Dependent territory* SE Canada 25 S10
St. Quentin France 63 M3
St Vincent *Island* St Vincent & The Grenadines 43 S14
St Vincent and the Grenadines *Country* Caribbean Sea 43 T14

St Vincent and the Grenadines 43

a English • Dollar • 318 • 71 • £1.47 • (m) 96% (f) 96% • 27%

St. Vincent, Cape *Coastal feature* Portugal 54, 60 E13
St Vith Belgium 65 L17
Saintes France 62 I10
Sajama *Mountain* Bolivia 41
Sakākah Saudi Arabia 108 I6
Sakakawea, L. *Lake* North Dakota, USA 33 M4
Sakarya *River* Turkey 104 J6
Sakhalin *Island* Russian Federation 113 Q9, 28 H4
Sala y Gomez Ridge *Sea feature* Pacific Ocean 41
Salado *River* Argentina 41, 48 K8
Şalālah Oman 100 F6, 109 M15
Salamanca Spain 60 I7
Salamat *River* Chad/Sudan 94 J8
Salamis *Archaeological site* Cyprus 105 L12
Saldanha South Africa 98 I15
Saldus Latvia 80 H6
Sale Victoria, Australia 133 N14
Salekhard Russian Federation 112 H7
Salem India 117 K14
Salem Oregon, USA 36
Salerno Italy 73 L13
Salerno, Gulf of *Sea feature* Italy 73 K14
Salihorsk (var. Soligorsk) Belorussia 81 L13
Salima Malawi 97 N13
Salina Kansas, USA 33 O12
Salina Utah, USA 34 J4
Salina *Island* Lipari Is. Italy 73 L16
Salinas California, USA 37 H16
Salinas Mexico 39 P12
Salinas Grandes Salt Marsh *Physical feature* Argentina 41
Salisbury England, UK 59 I16
Salisbury *see* Harare
Salisbury I. *Island* Northwest Territories, Canada 25 K1
Salmon *River* Idaho.Washington, USA 32 F6
Salo Finland 57 O11
Salonika *see* Thessaloniki
Salso *River* Italy 73 K18
Salt *River* Arizona, USA 34 J9
Salt Lake City Utah, USA 34 J3
Salta Argentina 48 I6
Saltillo Mexico 39 M7
Salto Uruguay 48 N9
Salto del Guairá Paraguay 48 O5
Salton Sea *Lake* California, USA 20, 37 N19
Salvador Brazil 47 N11, 53 H12
Salween (var. Nu Jiang) *River* China 119 K12, 120 H13, 124 H9
Salzburg Austria 69 N6
Salzgitter Germany 66 I9
Samā'il Oman 109 P12
Samaná Dominican Republic 43 O8
Samar *Island* Philippines 127 N5
Samara Russian Federation 83 J12
Samarinda Borneo, Indonesia 127 K11
Samarkand (var. Samarqand) Uzbekistan 111 M7
Samarqand *see* Samarkand
Sāmarrā' Iraq 109 K4
Sambre *River* Belgium/France 65 G16
Samobor Croatia 74 H3
Samos Samos, Greece 79 P10
Samos *Island* Greece 79 P10
Samothraki *Island* Greece 79 N3
Samsun Turkey 105 N5
Samui I. (var. Ko Samui) *Island* Thailand 125 I15
San Ambrosio, Isla *Island* Chile 129 Q11
San Andreas Fault *Physical feature* USA 8
San Andrés Colombia 44 F6
San Andres Mts. *Mountain range* New Mexico, USA 35 L10
San Angelo Texas, USA 35 P11
San Antonio Chile 48 G10
San Antonio Texas, USA 35 Q13
San Antonio *River* Texas, USA 35 Q13
San Antonio Oeste Argentina 49 K13
San Benedetto del Tronto Italy 72 J10
San Bernadino Tunnel *Tunnel* Switzerland 68 H11
San Bernardino California, USA 37 L18
San Bernardo Chile 48 H10
San Carlos Nicaragua 42 E12
San Carlos Venezuela 44 H5
San Carlos de Bariloche Argentina 49 H14
San Clemente California, USA 37 L19
San Cristóbal Venezuela 44 F5
San Diego California, USA 37 L19, 129 N5
San Felipe Chile 48 G10
San Felipe Venezuela 44 H4
San Félix, Isla *Island* Chile 129 Q11
San Fernando Chile 49 H11
San Fernando Luzon, Philippines 127 L3
San Fernando Spain 60 H14
San Fernando Trinidad & Tobago 43 S16
San Fernando de Apure Venezuela 44 I5
San Francisco California, USA 9, 37 H15, 129 N5
San Francisco de Macorís Dominican Republic 43 O8
San Gorgonia Pass *Mountain pass* California, USA 37 L18
San Ignacio Belize 42 C6
San Joaquin *River* California, USA 37 I16
San Jorge, Gulf of *Sea feature* Argentina 49 K16
San Jose California, USA 37 H15
San José Costa Rica 42 E13
San José del Guaviare Colombia 44 F7
San José I. *Island* Mexico 38 H7
San José I. *Island* Panama 42 G15
San Juan Argentina 48 H9
San Juan Peru 45 E14
San Juan Puerto Rico 43 Q9
San Juan *River* Nicaragua 42 E12
San Juan *River* New Mexico/Utah, USA 35 K6
San Juan Bautista Paraguay 48 N6
San Juan de los Morros Venezuela 44 I5
San Juan Is. *Island group* Washington, USA 36 H5
San Juan Mts. *Mountain range* Colorado, USA 35 M6
San Lorenzo Honduras 42 C9
San Luis Argentina 48 J10
San Luis Obispo California, USA 37 I17
San Luis Potosí Mexico 39 M10
San Marino San Marino 72 I9
San Marino *Country* S Europe 72 I9

San Marino 72

a Italian • Lira • 328 • 76 • £1.02 • (m) 98% (f) 98% • 90%

San Matías, Gulf of *Sea feature* Argentina 49 K14
San Miguel El Salvador 42 C9
San Miguel *River* Bolivia 45 K14
San Miguel de Tucumán Argentina 48 I7
San Nicolás de los Arroyos Argentina 48 L10
San Pedro Paraguay 48 N5
San Pedro Sula Honduras 42 C8
San Pietro *Island* Italy 73 C15
San Rafael Argentina 48 I11
San Remo Italy 72 C9
San *River* Cambodia/Vietnam 125 N12
San *River* Poland/Ukraine 71 O8
San Salvador El Salvador 42 B9
San Salvador *Island* Bahamas 43 M3
San Salvador de Jujuy Argentina 49 I6
San Sebastián (var. Donostia) Spain 61 M3
San'ā Yemen 108 I15
Sanaga *River* Cameroon 94 F10
Sanandaj Iran 109 L4
Sandakan Borneo, Malaysia 127 K8
Sandanski Bulgaria 76 I15
Sandnes Norway 56 H12
Sandoway Burma 124 E9
Sandviken Sweden 57 L11
Sanford Maine, USA 27 O8
Sângeorz-Băi *Spa* Romania 77 K3
Sangha *River* Congo 95 I12
Sangir *Island* Indonesia 127 N9
Sangir Is. *Island group* Indonesia 127 N10
Sangre de Cristo Mts. *Mountain range* Colorado/New Mexico, USA 35 M6
Sangro *River* Italy 73 K12
Sankt Gallen Switzerland 68 H8
Sankt Pölten Austria 69 R5
Sankt Veit Austria 69 P9
Şanliurfa Turkey 105 P9
Sant' Antioco Sardinia 73 C16
Santa Ana California, USA 37 L19
Santa Ana El Salvador 42 B9
Santa Barbara California, USA 37 J18
Santa Catalina I. *Island* Mexico 38 H7
Santa Clara Cuba 42 I4
Santa Clara Valley *Physical feature* California, USA 37 H15
Santa Cruz Bolivia 44 J15
Santa Cruz California, USA 37 H16
Santa Cruz *River* Arizona, USA 34 I11
Santa Elena Venezuela 44 L7
Santa Fe Argentina 48 L9
Santa Fe New Mexico, USA 35 M8
Santa Fe *see* Bogotá
Santa Maria Brazil 47 H16
Santa Maria California, USA 37 I17
Santa Maria *Volcano* Guatemala 41
Santa Marta Colombia 44 F4
Santa Rosa Argentina 49 K11
Santa Rosa California, USA 37 H14
Santa Rosa Honduras 42 C8
Santa Rosalia Mexico 38 G5
Santander Spain 61 K3
Santarém Brazil 46 H8
Santarém Portugal 60 F10
Santee *River* South Carolina, USA 29 P8
Santiago Chile 48 H10
Santiago Dominican Republic 43 N8
Santiago Panama 42 F15
Santiago de Compostela Spain 60 F4
Santiago de Cuba Cuba 43 K6
Santiago del Estero Argentina 48 J7
Sant Jordi, Golf de *Sea feature* Spain 61 O7
Santo Domingo Dominican Republic 43 O9
Santo Domingo de los Colorados Ecuador 44 C8
Santorini *Volcano* Greece 54
Santos Brazil 47 K14
Santos Plateau *Sea feature* Atlantic Ocean 41
Sanya China 121 K16
São Francisco *River* Brazil 41, 47 L11
São José dos Campos Brazil 47 K14
São Luís Brazil 46 L8
São Paulo Brazil 14, 47 K14
São Roque, Cabo de *Cape* Brazil 46 P8
São Tomé Sao Tome & Principe 95 D12
Sao Tome and Principe *Country* C Africa 52 L12, 95

Sao Tome and Principe 95

a Portuguese • Dobra • 124 • 67 • £0.63 • (m) 73% (f) 42% • 33%

São Tomé, Cabo de *Cape* Brazil 47 M14
São Tomé I. *Island* 87
Saône *River* France 63 O7
Sapporo Japan 122 K4
Sapri Italy 73 M14
Saqqara *Archaeological site* Egypt 90 F7
Sara Buri Thailand 125 J12
Saragossa *see* Zaragoza
Sarajevo Bosnia and Herzegovina 75 K7
Saransk Russian Federation 83 H11
Saratoga Springs New York, USA 27 M9
Saratov Russian Federation 83 H12
Saravan Laos 125 N11
Sarawak *Region* Borneo, Malaysia 126 I10
Sardinia *Island* Italy 54, 73
Sargasso Sea Atlantic Ocean 52 G10
Sargodha Pakistan 116 I3
Sarh Chad 94 J9
Sarī Iran 109 O4
Sarikei Borneo, Malaysia 126 I10
Sariyer Turkey 104 I5
Sarnen Switzerland 68 G10
Sarnia Ontario, Canada 24 J14
Sarroch Sardinia 72 D16
Sartang *River* Russian Federation 113 N7
Sárvíz *River* Hungary 71 K14
Sarykamysh, L. *Lake* Turkmenistan/Uzbekistan 110 H5
Saskatchewan *Province* Canada 23
Saskatchewan *River* Canada 23 N13
Saskatoon Saskatchewan, Canada 23 M14
Satu Mare Romania 76 I2
Saudi Arabia *Country* SW Asia 108-109

Saudi Arabia 108-109

a Arabic • Riyal • 7 • 65 • £0.62 • (m) 73% (f) 48% • 283 • 633 • Yes • 77% • 2874

Sault Sainte Marie Ontario, Canada 24 I12
Sault Ste. Marie Michigan, USA 31 N4
Saurimo Angola 98 I4
Sava *River* SE Europe 74 J4
Savanna-la-Mar Jamaica 42 J7
Savannah Georgia, USA 29 O9
Savannah *River* Georgia, USA 29 O8
Savannakhét Laos 125 M11
Save *River* Mozambique/Zimbabwe 99 N10
Savona Italy 72 D8
Savonlinna Finland 57 Q9
Saxony *Region* Germany 66 H8
Saynshand Mongolia 119 N6
Scandinavia *Region* N Europe 54, 56-57
Scarborough Trinidad & Tobago 43 T16
Schaffhausen Switzerland 68 G8
Schärding Austria 69 N5
Schefferville Quebec, Canada 25 O6
Scheldt *River* W Europe 65 F14
Schenectady New York, USA 27 L9
Schiermonnikoog *Island* West Frisian Is. Netherlands 64 L5
Schleswig Germany 66 H6
Schouten Is. *Island group* Papua New Guinea 133 N1
Schwaner Mts. *Mountain range* Indonesia 126 I12
Schwarzwald *see* Black Forest
Schweinfurt Germany 67 H13
Schwerin Germany 66 J7
Schwerin, L. *Lake* Germany 66 J7
Schwyz Switzerland 68 G10
Scilly, Isles of *Island group* England, UK 59 D17
Scioto *River* Ohio, USA 31 O11
Scoresbysund Greenland 51 O15
Scotia Plate *Physical feature* 89, 41
Scotia Sea Atlantic Ocean 50 C6, 53 G16
Scotland *Country* UK 58
Scott Base *Research centre* Antarctica 50 E11
Scottsbluff Nebraska, USA 33 L9
Scottsdale Arizona, USA 34 I9
Scranton Pennsylvania, USA 27 K11
Scupi *see* Skopje
Scutari, L. *Lake* Albania/Yugoslavia 75 L10
Sea of Galilee *see* L. Tiberias
Seaford Delaware, USA 27 K16
Seal *River* Manitoba, Canada 23 O11
Seattle Washington, USA 36 H6, 129 N4
Segovia Spain 61 K7
Segozero, L. *Lake* Russian Federation 82 H7
Segura *River* Spain 61 L11
Segura, Sierra de *Mountain range* Spain 61 L12
Seikan Tunnel *Tunnel* Japan 122 K6
Seinäjoki Finland 57 N9
Seine *River* France 54, 63 M5
Sekondi-Takoradi Ghana 93 L13
Selayar *Island* Indonesia 127 L14
Selebi-Phikwe Botswana 99 L10
Selkirk Manitoba, Canada 23 O14
Selma Alabama, USA 29 L8
Selous *Game reserve* Tanzania 97 P10
Selvas *Physical region* Brazil 41
Semarang Java, Indonesia 126 H15
Semey *see* Semipalatinsk
Semipalatinsk (var. Semey) Kazakhstan 112 H12
Semnān Iran 109 O4
Sên *River* Cambodia 125 M12
Sendai Japan 122 L8, 128 G5
Senegal *Country* W Africa 92

Senegal 92

a French • Franc • 40 • 48 • £2.00 • (m) 52% (f) 25% • 38%

Senegal *River* W Africa 87, 92 G7
Senja *Island* Norway 57 M2
Sennar Dam *Dam* Sudan 91 H13
Senta Serbia, Yugoslavia 75 M3
Seoul South Korea 15, 121 P7
Sept-Îles Quebec, Canada 25 O9
Seraing Belgium 65 J16
Seram *Island* Indonesia 127 O12, 131
Seram Sea Indonesia 127 O12
Serbia *Republic* Yugoslavia 75 N6
Seremban Malaysia 125 J19
Serengeti *National park* Tanzania 97 N6
Serengeti Plain *Physical region* Tanzania 87
Sérifos *Island* Cyclades, Greece 79 L11
Serov Russian Federation 112 G8
Serowe Botswana 99 L10
Serres Greece 79 K2
Sétif Algeria 89 L4
Setúbal Portugal 60 F11
Seul, L. *Lake* Ontario, Canada 24 G9
Sevan, L. (var. Ozero Sevan) *Lake* Armenia 85 Q14
Sevan-Hrazdan *HEP scheme* Armenia 85 Q13
Sevastopol' Ukraine 84 J10
Severn *River* England, UK 59 I15
Severn *River* Ontario, Canada 24 H7
Severnaya Zemlya (var. North Land) *Island group* Russian Federation 51 S10, 103, 113 K4
Sevier L. *Lake* Utah, USA 34 I4
Sevilla (var. Seville) Spain 60 I13
Seville *see* Sevilla
Seward Alaska, USA 22 G8
Seychelles *Country* Indian Ocean 100 F9

Seychelles 100

a Seselwa • Rupee • 256 • 71 • £1.91 • (m) 55% (f) 60% • 52%

Seyhan *River* Turkey 105 M9
Sfântu Gheorghe Romania 77 L6
Sfax Tunisia 52 L9, 89 N5
Shache (var. Yarkand) China 118 E8
Shackleton Ice Shelf *Coastal feature* Indian Ocean Coast, Antarctica 50 H10
Shadehill Res. *Reservoir* South Dakota, USA 33 M6
Shahjahanpur India 117 L5
Shahr-e-Kord Iran 109 N6
Shāmīyah Desert *Desert region* Syria 107 P6
Shandong Pen. *Physical feature* China 121 O8
Shanghai China 15, 121 O10, 128 F6
Shannon Ireland 59 B13
Shannon *River* Ireland 59 C13
Shantou China 121 N14
Shaoguan China 121 M13
Shaoxing China 121 O11
Shaoyang China 121 L12
Sharjah United Arab Emirates 109 O10
Shark Bay *Sea feature* Western Australia, Australia 132 E10
Shashe *River* Botswana/Zimbabwe 99 L10
Shasta L. *Lake* California, USA 37 H12
Shebeli *River* Ethiopia/Somalia 87, 91 M16
Sheboygan Wisconsin, USA 31 L8
Sheffield England, UK 59 J13
Shelby Montana, USA 32 H4
Shelikof Strait *Channel* Alaska, USA 22 F8
Shenandoah *River* Maryland/Virginia, USA 29 Q3

a Language (official or most commonly spoken) • Currency • Population density per square kilometre • Average life expectancy • Price of 1 dozen hen's eggs • Literacy • Number of TVs per 1,000 people • Number of people per doctor • Death penalty • Percentage of urban-based population • Average number of calories consumed daily per person

Sumbu – Tongking, Gulf of

Sumbu *National park* Zambia 97 L10
Sumgait *see* Sumqayıt
Summer L. *Lake* Oregon, USA 36 I10
Sumqayıt (var. Sumgait) Azerbaijan 85 T13
Sumy Ukraine 85 K4
Sun City South Africa 99 L12
Sunbury Pennsylvania, USA 26 J12
Sunda Shelf *Sea feature* South China Sea 115, 130
Sunderland England, UK 59 J11
Sundsvall Sweden 57 L9
Suntar Russian Federation 113 M8
Sunyani Ghana 93 L12
Superior Wisconsin, USA 30 I4
Superior, L. *Lake* Canada/USA 20, 24 H11, 31 L3
Supiori *Island* Indonesia 127 R11
Sur Oman 109 P13
Surabaya Java, Indonesia 126 I15
Surat India 116 I9
Surat Thani Thailand 125 H15
Sûre *River* Belgium/Luxembourg 65 L18
Surigao Mindanao, Philippines 127 N6
Surinam (prev. Dutch Guiana) *Country* S America 44

Surinam 44

a Dutch • Gulden • 3 • 68 • £3.77 • (m) 5% (f) 5% • 47%

Surkhob *River* Tajikistan 111 O7
Surt Libya 89 P7
Susquehanna *River* USA 26 J11
Sutherland Falls *Waterfall* New Zealand 131
Suva Fiji 128 J10
Suwałki Poland 71 O2
Suwannee *River* Florida, USA 29 N11
Svalbard *Island group* Arctic Ocean 51 Q12, 54, 103
Svay Riĕng Cambodia 125 M14
Sverdlovsk *see* Yekaterinburg
Sverige *see* Sweden
Svetlogorsk *see* Svyetlahorsk
Svobodnyy ICBM Base *Military centre* Russian Federation 113 O11
Svyetlahorsk (var. Svetlogorsk) Belorussia 81 N14
Swabian Jura *Mountain range* Germany 67 G16
Swakopmund Namibia 98 G10
Swansea Wales, UK 59 G15
Swaziland *Country* Southern Africa 99

Swaziland 99

a English, Swazi • Lilangeni • 48 • 57 • £0.84 • (m) 70% (f) 66% • 33%

Sweden (var. Sverige) *Country* Scandinavia 56-57

Sweden 56-57

a Swedish • Krona • 21 • 78 • £1.98 • (m) 99% (f) 99% • 474 • 355 • No • 84% • 2960

Sweetwater Texas, USA 35 P10
Swift Current Saskatchewan, Canada 23 M15
Swindon England, UK 59 I16
Switzerland *Country* C Europe 68

Switzerland 68

a French, German, Italian • Franc • 169 • 78 • £3.03 • (m) 99% (f) 99% • 407 • 584 • No • 60% • 3562

Sydney New South Wales, Australia 15, 128 H11, 133 O13
Sydney Nova Scotia, Canada 25 R11
Syktyvkar Russian Federation 82 K9
Sylhet Bangladesh 117 P7
Sylt *Island* North Frisian Is. Germany 66 G5
Syowa *Research centre* Antarctica 50 F7
Syr Darya *River* C Asia 103, 112 F13
Syracuse New York, USA 27 K8
Syracuse *see* Siracusa
Syria (var. Aram) *Country* SW Asia 107

Syria 107

a Arabic • Pound • 70 • 66 • £0.97 • (m) 78% (f) 51% • 59 • 1347 • Yes • 50% • 3003

Syrian Desert (var. Bādiyat ash Shām) *Desert region* SW Asia 103, 107 P9, 108 I5
Szczecin Poland 70 H3
Szeged Hungary 71 M15
Székesfehérvár Hungary 71 K13
Szekszárd Hungary 71 L15
Szolnok Hungary 71 M14
Szombathely Hungary 70 J13

T

Tabar Is. *Island group* Papua New Guinea 133 P1
Tabasco Mexico 39 L10
Table Bay *Sea feature* South Africa 98 I15
Table Mt. *Mountain* South Africa 98 I16
Tábor Czech Republic 70 H10
Tabora Tanzania 97 M8
Tabríz Iran 109 L2
Tabúk Saudi Arabia 108 G6
Tacloban Leyte, Philippines 127 N6
Tacna Peru 45 G15
Tacoma Washington, USA 36 H7
Tacuarembó Uruguay 48 O9
Taegu South Korea 121 Q8
Taejôn South Korea 121 P8
Tagula I. *Island* Papua New Guinea 133 P4
Tagus (var. Tajo, Tejo) *River* Portugal/Spain 54, 60 G9
Tahiti *Island* French Polynesia, Pacific Ocean 129 L10
Tahoe, L. *Lake* California/Nevada, USA 34 E3, 37 J14
Tahoua Niger 93 O8
Tai'an China 121 N8
Taieri *River* New Zealand 134 D13
Ţá'if Saudi Arabia 108 H11
Taipei Taiwan 121 O13
Taiping Malaysia 125 I18
Taiwan *Country* E Asia 115, 121, 128 F6

Taiwan 121

a Mandarin • Dollar • 645 • 74 • £0.62 • (m) 96% (f) 87% • 387 • 913 • Yes • N/A • 2875

Taiwan Strait *Channel* China/Taiwan 115, 121 N14
Taiyuan China 121 L8
Ta'izz Yemen 108 I16
Tajikistan *Country* C Asia 111

Tajikistan 111

a Tajik • Ruble • 38 • 69 • N/A • N/A • 31%

Tajo *see* Tagus
Tak Thailand 124 I10
Takamatsu Japan 123 F12
Takêv Cambodia 125 M14
Takla Makan Desert *Desert region* China 11, 118 F9
Talak *Desert region* Niger 93 O6
Talas Kyrgyzstan 111 P5
Talaud Is. *Island group* Indonesia 127 N9
Talca Chile 49 G11
Talcahuano Chile 49 G12
Taldy-Kurgan (var. Taldyqorghan) Kazakhstan 112 H13
Taldyqorghan *see* Taldy-Kurgan
Tallahassee Florida, USA 29 M10
Tallinn (prev. Revel) Estonia 52 M7, 80 J1
Talsi Latvia 80 H5
Tamabo Range *Mountain range* Borneo, Malaysia 126 J10
Tamale Ghana 93 L11
Tamanrasset Algeria 89 L11
Tambacounda Senegal 92 G9
Tambora *Volcano* Sumbawa, Indonesia 9, 115
Tambov Russian Federation 83 G11
Tampa Florida, USA 29 N13
Tampere Finland 57 O10
Tampico Mexico 39 O10
Tamworth New South Wales, Australia 133 O12
Tan-Tan Morocco 88 G7
Tana *River* Kenya 97 Q4
Tana *River* Norway 57 O3
Tana, L. *Lake* Ethiopia 87, 91 I14
Tanami Desert *Desert region* Australia 131
Tanana *River* Alaska, USA 22 H8
Tanega-shima *Island* Japan 123 D16
Tanga Tanzania 97 Q8
Tanganyika, L. *Lake* C Africa 87, 95 O15, 97 L9
Tanggula Mountains *Mountain range* China 118 I11
Tangier Morocco 88 I4
Tangra Yumco *Lake* China 118 H12
Tangshan China 121 N7
Tanimbar Is. *Island group* Indonesia 127 Q14
Tanjungkarang Sumatra, Indonesia 126 F14
Tanjungpinang Bitan, Indonesia 126 F11
Tanta Egypt 90 F6
Tanzam Railway *Railway* Tanzania 97 N10
Tanzania *Country* E Africa 97

Tanzania 97

a English, Swahili • Shilling • 29 • 47 • £0.60 • (m) 62% (f) 31% • 33%

Taormina Italy 73 L17
Taos New Mexico, USA 35 M7
Tapachula Mexico 39 R15
Tapajós *River* Brazil 41, 46 G8
Tapti *River* India 116 J8
Taraba *River* Nigeria 93 Q12
Ţarábulus *see* Tripoli
Taranto Italy 73 O14
Taranto, Gulf of *Sea feature* Italy 73 O14
Tarawa *Island* Kiribati, Pacific Ocean 128 J8
Tarbela Dam *Dam* Pakistan 116 J2
Tarbela Res. *Reservoir* Pakistan 116 J1
Tarbes France 62 J14
Taree New South Wales, Australia 133 P12
Târgovişte Romania 77 L8
Târgu Jiu Romania 76 I8
Târgu Mureş Romania 77 K5
Tarija Bolivia 45 J17
Tarim *River* China 115, 118 G8
Tarim Basin *Physical region* China 118 G8
Tarn *River* France 63 L13
Tarnów Poland 71 N9
Tarragona Spain 61 P7
Tarsus Turkey 105 M10
Tartu Estonia 81 K3
Tarţūs Syria 107 M5
Tashauz *see* Dashkhovuz
Tashkent (var. Toshkent) Uzbekistan 111 N6
Tasman Bay *Sea feature* New Zealand 134 F8
Tasman Sea Australia/New Zealand 128 I12, 131, 133 O15, 134 D11
Tasmania *Island* Australia 131
Tasmania *State* Australia 133
Tassili n'Ajjer *Mountain range* Algeria 87, 89 M9
Tatvan Turkey 105 R7
Tauern Tunnel *Tunnel* Austria 69 N9
Taunggyi Burma 124 G8
Taunton England, UK 59 H16
Taupo New Zealand 134 H6
Taupo, L. *Lake* New Zealand 131, 134 H6
Tauragė Lithuania 80 G9
Tauranga New Zealand 134 H5
Taurus Mts. *Mountain range* Turkey 103, 105 L10
Tavoy Burma 125 H12
Tawakoni, L. *Lake* Texas, USA 35 R10
Tawau Borneo, Malaysia 127 K9
Tawitawi *Island* Philippines 127 L8
Taxco Mexico 39 N13
Tay Ninh Vietnam 125 M1
Taymyr, L. *Lake* Russian Federation 113 K5
Taymyr Peninsula *Physical feature* Russian Federation 51 T9, 103, 113 K5
Taz *River* Russian Federation 112 I8
Tbilisi (var. T'bilisi) Georgia 85 Q12
T'bilisi *see* Tbilisi
Tchibanga Gabon 95 F13
Tchien (var. Zwedru) Liberia 92 I13
Te Anau, L. *Lake* New Zealand 134 C13
Tébessa Algeria 89 M5
Tedzhen Turkmenistan 110 J9
Tedzhen *River* Iran/Turkmenistan 110 J9
Tegucigalpa Honduras 42 D9
Tehran Iran 109 N4
Tehuantepec Mexico 39 P14
Tehuantepec, Gulf of *Sea feature* Mexico 39 P15
Tejo *see* Tagus
Tekirdağ Turkey 104 G5
Tel Aviv-Yafo Israel 107 L9
Teles Pires *River* Brazil 46 G9
Telluride Colorado, USA 35 L5
Telok Intan Malaysia 125 I18
Temuco Chile 49 G13
Tengiz, L. *Lake* Kazakhstan 112 G11
Tennessee *River* SE USA 20, 29 K4
Tennessee *State* USA 28-29
Teotihuacán *Archaeological site* Mexico 39 N12
Tepic Mexico 39 K10
Tequila Mexico 39 K11
Teresina Brazil 46 M8
Termez Uzbekistan 111 M9
Terneuzen Netherlands 65 F13
Terni Italy 73 I11
Ternopil' (var. Ternopol') Ukraine 84 F5
Ternopol' *see* Ternopil'
Terrassa Spain 61 Q6
Terre Haute Indiana, USA 31 L13
Terschelling *Island* West Frisian Is. Netherlands 64 J6
Teruel Spain 61 N8
Teslin L. *Lake* Yukon Territory, Canada 22 I10
Tete Mozambique 99 N7
Tétouan Morocco 88 I4
Tetovo Macedonia 75 N11
Tevere *see* Tiber
Texas *State* USA 35
Texas City Texas, USA 35 S13
Texcoco, L. *Lake* Mexico 39 N12
Texel *Island* West Frisian Is. Netherlands 64 H7
Thac Ba, L. *Lake* Vietnam 124 M8
Thai Nguyen Vietnam 124 N8
Thailand *Country* SE Asia 124-125

Thailand 124-125

a Thai • Baht • 111 • 66 • £0.54 • (m) 96% (f) 90% • 112 • 4843 • Yes • 23% • 2316

Thailand, Gulf of *Sea feature* Thailand 100 L7, 115, 125 J15
Thakhek *see* Muang Khammouan
Thames New Zealand 134 H4
Thames *River* England, UK 54, 59 I15
Thane India 116 I9
Thanh Hoa Vietnam 124 M9
Thar Desert (var. Indian Desert) *Desert region* India/Pakistan 11, 115, 116 I5
Tharthár, L. *Lake* Iraq 109 K4
Thasos *Island* Greece 79 M3
Thaton Burma 124 G10
Thayetmyo Burma 124 F9
Thebes *Archaeological site* Egypt 90 G8
Theodore Roosevelt L. *Lake* Arizona, USA 34 I9
Thermaic Gulf *Sea feature* Greece 78 J4
Thessaloniki (var. Salonika) Greece 78 J3
Thika Kenya 97 P5
Thimphu Bhutan 117 P6
Thionville France 63 O4
Thira *Island* Cyclades, Greece 79 N13
Thiruvananthapuram *see* Trivandrum
Thohoyandou South Africa 99 M10
Thompson Manitoba, Canada 23 O12
Thrace *Region* Greece 79 N2
Thule (var. Qaanaaq) Greenland 51 O11
Thun Switzerland 68 F11
Thun, L. of *Lake* Switzerland 68 F11
Thunder Bay Ontario, Canada 24 G11
Thüringer Wald *see* Thuringian Forest
Thuringia *Region* Germany 67 J12
Thuringian Forest (var. Thüringer Wald) *Physical region* Germany 67 I12
Thurso Scotland, UK 58 I6
Tianjin China 121 N7, 128 F5
Tiaret Algeria 89 K5
Tiber (var. Tevere) *River* Italy 73 H11
Tiberias, L. (var. Sea of Galilee) *Lake* Israel 107 M8
Tibesti *Mountain range* Chad/Libya 87, 94 I4
Tibet, Plateau of *Physical feature* China 15
Tibetan Autonomous Region *Region* China 118 H12
Tiburón I. *Island* Mexico 38 G4
Tidjikdja Mauritania 92 H6
Tien Shan *Mountain range* Kyrgyzstan/China 103, 111 R6, 115, 118 G7
Tienen Belgium 65 I15
Tierra del Fuego *Island* Argentina/Chile 41, 49 K20
Tighina (var. Bendery) Moldavia 84 H8
Tigris (var. Dijlah) *River* SW Asia 100 E4, 103, 105 Q8, 107 T1, 109 K3
Tijuana Mexico 38 F1
Tikal *Archaeological site* Guatemala 42 C6
Tikrít Iraq 109 K4
Tiksi Russian Federation 51 T7, 113 M6
Tikveško, L. *Lake* Macedonia 75 O12
Tilburg Netherlands 65 I12
Tillabéry Niger 93 M8
Timaru New Zealand 134 E12
Timbuktu (var. Tombouctou) Mali 93 K7
Timgad *Archaeological site* Morocco 89 M5
Timirist, Râs *Cape* Mauritania 92 F6
Timiş *River* Romania/Serbia 76 H7
Timişoara Romania 77 G6
Timmins Ontario, Canada 24 J11
Timor *Island* Indonesia 115, 127 N16, 131
Timor Sea Australia/Indonesia 127 O16, 131, 133 I4
Tindouf Algeria 88 H8
Tinos *Island* Cyclades, Greece 79 M10
Tirana (var. Tiranë) Albania 75 M12
Tiranë *see* Tirana
Tiraspol Moldavia 84 H8
Tiree *Island* Scotland, UK 58 E8
Tirso *River* Sardinia 73 D14
Tiruchchirappalli India 117 K14
Tisza *River* Hungary 54, 71 M14
Titicaca, L. *Lake* Peru/Bolivia 41, 45 H14
Titograd *see* Podgorica
Titov Veles Macedonia 75 O11
Titova Mitrovica Serbia, Yugoslavia 75 N9
Tiznit Morocco 88 G6
Tlaxcala Mexico 39 N12
Tlemcen Algeria 88 J5
Toamasina Madagascar 100 E10
Toba, L. *Lake* Sumatra, Indonesia 126 C10
Tobago *Island* Trinidad & Tobago 20, 41, 43 T16
Tobakakar Range *Mountain range* Pakistan/Afghanistan 116 H3
Tobruk Libya 89 R6
Tocantins *River* Brazil 41, 46 J10
Tocopilla Chile 48 F5
Togian Is. *Island group* Indonesia 127 M11
Togo (prev. French Togo) *Country* W Africa 93

Togo 93

a French • Franc • 69 • 54 • £1.43 • (m) 56% (f) 31% • 26%

Tokara Is. *Island group* Japan 123 C17
Tokat Turkey 105 N6
Tokelau *Dependent territory* Polynesia, Pacific Ocean 128 J9
Tokmak Kyrgyzstan 111 Q4
Tokuno-shima *Island* Amami Is. Japan 123 B19
Tokushima Japan 123 G13
Tokyo Japan 15, 123 K11
Tol'yatti Russian Federation 83 I12
Toledo Ohio, USA 31 O10
Toledo Spain 61 K9
Toledo Bend Res. *Reservoir* Louisiana/Texas, USA 35 T11
Toliara Madagascar 101 E11
Tomakomai Japan 122 K4
Tombigbee *River* Alabama 29 K8
Tombouctou *see* Timbuktu
Tomé Chile 48 G12
Tomini, Gulf of *Sea feature* Celebes, Indonesia 127 L11
Tomsk Russian Federation 112 I10
Tonga *Country* Polynesia, Pacific Ocean 128 J10

Tonga 128

a English, Tongan • Pa'anga • 139 • 67 • £1.83 • (m) 93% (f) 93% • 31%

Tongking, Gulf of (var. Tonkin, Gulf of) *Sea feature* China/Vietnam 115, 121 K15, 124 O9

a Language (official or most commonly spoken) • Currency • Population density per square kilometre • Average life expectancy • Price of 1 dozen hen's eggs • Literacy • Number of TVs per 1,000 people • Number of people per doctor • Death penalty • Percentage of urban-based population • Average number of calories consumed daily per person

a Language (official or most commonly spoken) • Currency • Population density per square kilometre • Average life expectancy • Price of 1 dozen hen's eggs • Literacy • Number of TVs per 1,000 people • Number of people per doctor • Death penalty • Percentage of urban-based population • Average number of calories consumed daily per person

159

NORTH AMERICA

CANADA
PAGES 22-25

UNITED STATES OF AMERICA
PAGES 26-37

MEXICO
PAGES 38-39

CENTRAL AND SOUTH AMERICA

ANTIGUA & BARBUDA
PAGES 42-43

BAHAMAS
PAGES 42-43

BARBADOS
PAGES 42-43

BELIZE
PAGES 42-43

COSTA RICA

JAMAICA
PAGES 42-43

NICARAGUA
PAGES 42-43

PANAMA
PAGES 42-43

ST. CHRISTOPHER & NEVIS
PAGES 42-43

ST. LUCIA
PAGES 42-43

ST. VINCENT & THE GRENADINES
PAGES 42-43

TRINIDAD & TOBAGO
PAGES 42-43

BOLIVIA
PAGES 44-45

THE ATLANTIC OCEAN   EUROPE

CHILE
PAGES 48-49

PARAGUAY
PAGES 48-49

URUGUAY
PAGES 48-49

CAPE VERDE
PAGES 52-53

ICELAND
PAGES 52-53

DENMARK
PAGES 56-57

FINLAND
PAGES 56-57

NORWAY
PAGES 56-57

BELGIUM
PAGES 64-65

LUXEMBOURG
PAGES 64-65

THE NETHERLANDS
PAGES 64-65

GERMANY
PAGES 66-67

AUSTRIA
PAGES 68-69

LIECHTENSTEIN
PAGES 68-69

SWITZERLAND
PAGES 68-69

CZECH REPUBLIC
PAGES 70-71

BOSNIA & HERZEGOVINA
PAGES 74-75

CROATIA
PAGES 74-75

MACEDONIA
PAGES 74-75

SLOVENIA
PAGES 74-75

YUGOSLAVIA
PAGES 74-75

BULGARIA
PAGES 76-77

ROMANIA
PAGES 76-77

GREECE
PAGES 78-79

AFRICA

MOLDAVIA
PAGES 84-85

UKRAINE
PAGES 84-85

ALGERIA
PAGES 88-89

LIBYA
PAGES 88-89

MOROCCO
PAGES 88-89

TUNISIA
PAGES 88-89

WESTERN SAHARA
PAGES 88-89

DJIBOUTI
PAGES 90-91

GHANA
PAGES 92-93

GUINEA
PAGES 92-93

GUINEA-BISSAU
PAGES 92-93

IVORY COAST
PAGES 92-93

LIBERIA
PAGES 92-93

MALI
PAGES 92-93

MAURITANIA
PAGES 92-93

NIGER
PAGES 92-93

EQUATORIAL GUINEA
PAGES 94-95

GABON
PAGES 94-95

SAO TOME & PRINCIPE
PAGES 94-95

ZAIRE
PAGES 94-95

BURUNDI
PAGES 96-97

KENYA
PAGES 96-97

MALAWI
PAGES 96-97

RWANDA
PAGES 96-97

THE INDIAN OCEAN

SOUTH AFRICA
PAGES 98-99

SWAZILAND
PAGES 98-99

ZIMBABWE
PAGES 98-99

COMOROS
PAGES 100-101

MADAGASCAR
PAGES 100-101

MALDIVES
PAGES 100-101

MAURITIUS
PAGES 100-101

SEYCHELLES
PAGES 100-101

IRAN
PAGES 108-109

KUWAIT
PAGES 108-109

OMAN
PAGES 108-109

QATAR
PAGES 108-109

SAUDI ARABIA
PAGES 108-109

UNITED ARAB EMIRATES
PAGES 108-109

YEMEN
PAGES 108-109

AFGHANISTAN
PAGES 110-111

PAKISTAN
PAGES 116-117

NEPAL
PAGES 116-117

SRI LANKA
PAGES 116-117

CHINA
PAGES 118-121

MONGOLIA
PAGES 118-119

NORTH KOREA
PAGES 120-121

SOUTH KOREA
PAGES 120-121

TAIWAN
PAGES 120-121

THE PACIFIC OCEAN

BRUNEI
PAGES 126-127

INDONESIA
PAGES 126-127

PHILIPPINES
PAGES 126-127

FIJI
PAGES 128-129

KIRIBATI
PAGES 128-129

MARSHALL ISLANDS
PAGES 128-129

MICRONESIA
PAGES 128-129

NAURU
PAGES 128-129